Copyright © 2012 National Fire Protection Associa

NFPA® 400

Hazardous Materials Code

2013 Edition

This edition of NFPA 400, *Hazardous Materials Code*, was prepared by the Technical Committee on Hazardous Chemicals. It was issued by the Standards Council on May 29, 2012, with an effective date of June 18, 2012, and supersedes all previous editions.

This edition of NFPA 400 was approved as an American National Standard on June 18, 2012.

Origin and Development of NFPA 400

In 2010, for the first edition of NFPA 400, NFPA 430, NFPA 432, NFPA 434, and NFPA 490 were withdrawn as separate documents and included in their entirety in NFPA 400. This edition covered hazardous material categories found in building and fire codes such as corrosives, flammable solids, pyrophoric substances, toxic and highly toxic materials, unstable materials, and water-reactive materials. NFPA 400 also included compressed gases and cryogenic fluids by extracting NFPA 55, *Compressed Gases and Cryogenic Fuels Code*, into Chapter 21. The code established the need for additional fire protection based on quantity limits for various occupancies using the maximum allowable quantity (MAQ) concept.

In the 2013 edition, MAQ tables in Chapter 5 have been updated to be consistent with changes in fire and building codes and coordinated with requirements for industrial and medical gases based on changes to NFPA 55. The Committee has updated the table establishing MAQ values for hazardous materials stored or used in outdoor control areas. The results of the Fire Protection Research Foundation project, "Oxidizer Classification Research Project: Tests and Criteria," have been used to establish an alternative method for assigning classifications to oxidizing solids. To accomplish this the committee modified definitions for Class 1, 2, and 3 oxidizers based on the test protocol and criteria presented in the completely revised Annex G. The oxidizer table in Annex G has been updated for specific oxidizer solids based on the test results. The Committee also incorporated edits consistent with the *Manual of Style for NFPA Technical Committee Documents*.

NFPA and National Fire Protection Association are registered trademarks of the National Fire Protection Association, Quincy, Massachusetts 02169.

Technical Committee on Hazardous Chemicals

Robert J. James, *Chair*
Underwriters Laboratories Inc., FL [RT]

James C. Belke, U.S. Environmental Protection Agency, DC [E]
Elizabeth C. Buc, Fire & Materials Research Laboratory, LLC, MI [RT]
Therese Cirone, The Chlorine Institute, VA [M]
Edwin D. Cope, Cope Engineering, TX [SE]
Dirk Der Kinderen, U.S. Department of Transportation, DC [E]
Mark J. Dossett, San Diego Fire-Rescue Department, CA [E]
   Rep. California Fire Chiefs Association-Southern
Robert Fash, Las Vegas Fire & Rescue, NV [E]
   Rep. Fire Code Committee
Henry L. Febo, Jr., FM Global, MA [I]
Larry L. Fluer, Fluer, Inc., CA [M]
   Rep. Compressed Gas Association
Phillip A. Friday, Harrington Group, Inc., GA [SE]
Kent Gardner, Texas Engineering Extension Service, TX [L]
   Rep. National Volunteer Fire Council
Martin T. Gresho, FP2 Fire, Inc., CO [U]
   Rep. Sandia National Laboratories
Dennis M. Guidry, Jefferson Parish Fire Department, LA [E]
   Rep. International Fire Marshals Association
Peter Paul Howell, Mark V, Inc., WV [SE]
Noel Hsu, Orica USA Inc., CO [M]
   Rep. The Fertilizer Institute

Paul A. Iacobucci, Akzo Nobel, IL [M]
   Rep. SPI/Organic Peroxide Producers Safety Division
A. Hal Key, EYP Architecture & Engineering P.C., NY [SE]
Lynne M. Kilpatrick, Sunnyvale Department of Public Safety, CA [E]
Kevin Kreitman, City of Redding Fire Department, CA [E]
   Rep. TC on Combustible Metals and Metal Dusts
R. Kenneth Lee, PPG Industries, Inc., AR [M]
Kirk Mitchell, Kirk Mitchell & Associates, LLC, FL [M]
   Rep. Isocyanurates Industry Adhoc Committee
Eugene Y. Ngai, Chemically Speaking LLC, NJ [SE]
Anthony M. Ordile, Haines Fire & Risk Consulting, Inc., NJ [SE]
Jerald Pierrottie, Lonza Group Ltd., GA [M]
Michael J. Pokorny, Montgomery County, MD [E]
   Rep. TC on Laboratories Using Chemicals
Milton R. Shefter, Miljoy Ent. Incorporated, CA [U]
   (VL to Document: NFPA 40)
Clark D. Shepard, ExxonMobil Corporation, VA [M]
   Rep. American Chemistry Council
Frederick B. Tedford, Tedford & Pond, LLP, CT [SE]
Michael A. Viggiani, George Eastman House, NY [U]
   (VL to Document: NFPA 40)
Jerry W. Wallace, Safety Engineering Laboratories, Inc., MI [SE]

Alternates

Glen C. Argabright, Sandia National Laboratories, NM [U]
   (Alt. to M. T. Gresho)
Richard A. Craig, Compressed Gas Association, VA [M]
   (Alt. to L. L. Fluer)
A. Shane Fast, The Chlorine Institute, VA [M]
   (Alt. to T. Cirone)
Richard H. Ferguson, PPG Industries, Inc., PA [M]
   (Alt. to R. K. Lee)
Virgil W. Fowler, PotashCorp, GA [M]
   (Alt. to N. Hsu)

Kathleen A. Franklin, U.S. Environmental Protection Agency, DC [E]
   (Alt. to J. C. Belke)
Joseph M. Gravelle, Arkema Inc., PA [M]
   (Alt. to P. A. Iacobucci)
Milton L. Norsworthy, Cleveland, TN [M]
   (Alt. to J. Pierrottie)
Brian P. Sampson, Safety Engineering Laboratories, Inc., MI [SE]
   (Alt. to J. W. Wallace)

Nonvoting

Richard S. Kraus, API/Petroleum Safety Consultants, VA [M]
   Rep. TCC on Flammable and Combustible Liquids
Kathy A. Landkrohn, U.S. Department of Labor, DC [E]
Patrick A. McLaughlin, McLaughlin & Associates, RI [U]
   Rep. TC on Industrial, Storage, & Miscellaneous Occupancies

David Namyst, Intel Corporation, CA [M]
   Rep. TC on Industrial and Medical Gases
David S. Shatzer, U.S. Bureau of Alcohol, Tobacco, Firearms & Explosives, DC [E]
John E. Bugno, U.S. Department of Labor, DC [E]

Guy R. Colonna, NFPA Staff Liaison

This list represents the membership at the time the Committee was balloted on the final text of this edition. Since that time, changes in the membership may have occurred. A key to classifications is found at the back of the document.

NOTE: Membership on a committee shall not in and of itself constitute an endorsement of the Association or any document developed by the committee on which the member serves.

Committee Scope: This Committee shall have primary responsibility for documents on, and maintain current codes for, classes of hazardous chemicals and codes for specific chemicals where these are warranted by virtue of widespread distribution or special hazards.

Contents

Chapter 1	**Administration**	400–	5
1.1	Scope	400–	5
1.2	Purpose	400–	5
1.3	Application	400–	5
1.4	Retroactivity	400–	6
1.5	Equivalency	400–	6
1.6	Units and Formulas	400–	6
1.7	Enforcement	400–	7
1.8	Permits	400–	7
1.9	Facility Closure	400–	7
1.10	Emergency Planning	400–	7
1.11	Hazardous Materials Management Plan (HMMP)	400–	7
1.12	Hazardous Materials Inventory Statement (HMIS)	400–	7
1.13	Plan Review	400–	7
1.14	Technical Assistance	400–	8
Chapter 2	**Referenced Publications**	400–	8
2.1	General	400–	8
2.2	NFPA Publications	400–	8
2.3	Other Publications	400–	8
2.4	References for Extracts in Mandatory Sections	400–	9
Chapter 3	**Definitions**	400–	9
3.1	General	400–	9
3.2	NFPA Official Definitions	400–	10
3.3	General Definitions	400–	10
3.4	Special Performance-Based Definitions	400–	17
Chapter 4	**Classification of Materials, Wastes, and Hazard of Contents**	400–	18
4.1	Hazardous Material Classification	400–	18
4.2	Classification of High Hazard Contents	400–	18
4.3	Mixtures	400–	19
4.4	Multiple Hazards	400–	19
4.5	Classification of Waste	400–	19
Chapter 5	**Permissible Storage and Use Locations**	400–	19
5.1	General	400–	19
5.2	Control Areas	400–	19
5.3	Protection Levels	400–	30
5.4	Outdoor Areas	400–	32
Chapter 6	**Fundamental Requirements**	400–	32
6.1	General Requirements	400–	32
6.2	Requirements for Occupancies Storing Quantities of Hazardous Materials Exceeding the Maximum Allowable Quantities per Control Area for High Hazard Contents	400–	37
6.3	Requirements for Use, Dispensing, and Handling of Hazardous Materials in Amounts Exceeding Maximum Allowable Quantities	400–	45
Chapter 7	**Emergency Planning, Fire Risk Control, and Chemical Hazard Requirements for Industrial Processes**	400–	50
7.1	General	400–	50
7.2	Process Review and Plan Preparation	400–	50
7.3	Operating and Maintenance Procedures	400–	51
7.4	Safety Reviews	400–	51
7.5	Incident Investigation Plan	400–	51
7.6	Document Retention	400–	51
Chapter 8	**Reserved**	400–	51
Chapter 9	**Security for Hazardous Materials**	400–	51
9.1	General	400–	51
Chapter 10	**Performance-Based Option**	400–	51
10.1	General	400–	51
10.2	Performance Criteria	400–	53
10.3	Retained Prescriptive Requirements	400–	53
10.4	Design Scenarios	400–	53
10.5	Evaluation of Proposed Designs	400–	55
10.6	Safety Factors	400–	55
10.7	Documentation Requirements	400–	55
Chapter 11	**Ammonium Nitrate Solids and Liquids**	400–	56
11.1	General	400–	56
11.2	General Requirements for Storage	400–	56
11.3	Indoor Storage	400–	57
11.4	Outdoor Storage	400–	58
11.5	General Requirements for Use	400–	58
11.6	Indoor Use	400–	59
11.7	Outdoor Use	400–	59
11.8	Handling	400–	59
Chapter 12	**Corrosive Solids and Liquids**	400–	59
12.1	General	400–	59
12.2	General Requirements for Storage	400–	59
12.3	Indoor Storage	400–	60
12.4	Outdoor Storage	400–	60
12.5	General Requirements for Use	400–	60
12.6	Indoor Use	400–	60
12.7	Outdoor Use	400–	60
12.8	Handling	400–	61
Chapter 13	**Flammable Solids**	400–	61
13.1	General	400–	61
13.2	General Requirements for Storage	400–	61
13.3	Indoor Storage	400–	61
13.4	Outdoor Storage	400–	61
13.5	General Requirements for Use	400–	61

2013 Edition

13.6	Indoor Use	400– 62
13.7	Outdoor Use	400– 62
13.8	Handling	400– 62
Chapter 14	**Organic Peroxide Formulations**	**400– 62**
14.1	General	400– 62
14.2	General Requirements for Storage	400– 62
14.3	Indoor Storage	400– 63
14.4	Outdoor Storage	400– 65
14.5	General Requirements for Use	400– 65
14.6	Indoor Use	400– 66
14.7	Outdoor Use	400– 66
14.8	Handling	400– 66
Chapter 15	**Oxidizer Solids and Liquids**	**400– 66**
15.1	General	400– 66
15.2	General Requirements for Storage	400– 67
15.3	Indoor Storage	400– 68
15.4	Outdoor Storage	400– 75
15.5	General Requirements for Use	400– 75
15.6	Indoor Use	400– 76
15.7	Outdoor Use	400– 76
15.8	Handling	400– 76
Chapter 16	**Reserved**	**400– 76**
Chapter 17	**Pyrophoric Solids and Liquids**	**400– 76**
17.1	General	400– 76
17.2	General Requirements for Storage	400– 76
17.3	Indoor Storage	400– 76
17.4	Outdoor Storage	400– 77
17.5	General Requirements for Use	400– 77
17.6	Indoor Use	400– 77
17.7	Outdoor Use	400– 77
17.8	Handling	400– 78
Chapter 18	**Toxic or Highly Toxic Solids and Liquids**	**400– 78**
18.1	General	400– 78
18.2	General Requirements for Storage	400– 78
18.3	Indoor Storage	400– 78
18.4	Outdoor Storage	400– 78
18.5	General Requirements for Use	400– 78
18.6	Indoor Use	400– 79
18.7	Outdoor Use	400– 79
18.8	Handling	400– 79
Chapter 19	**Unstable (Reactive) Solids and Liquids**	**400– 79**
19.1	General	400– 79
19.2	General Requirements for Storage	400– 79
19.3	Indoor Storage	400– 80
19.4	Outdoor Storage	400– 80
19.5	General Requirements for Use	400– 80
19.6	Indoor Use	400– 81
19.7	Outdoor Use	400– 81
19.8	Handling	400– 81
Chapter 20	**Water-Reactive Solids and Liquids**	**400– 81**
20.1	General	400– 81
20.2	General Requirements for Storage	400– 81
20.3	Indoor Storage	400– 81
20.4	Outdoor Storage	400– 82
20.5	General Requirements for Use	400– 82
20.6	Indoor Use	400– 82
20.7	Outdoor Use	400– 82
20.8	Handling	400– 83
Chapter 21	**Storage, Use, and Handling of Compressed Gases and Cryogenic Fluids in Portable and Stationary Containers, Cylinders, and Tanks**	**400– 83**
21.1	General Provisions	400– 83
21.2	Building-Related Controls	400– 83
21.3	Compressed Gases	400– 87
21.4	Cryogenic Fluids	400– 99
21.5	Bulk Oxygen Systems	400–107
21.6	Bulk Hydrogen Compressed Gas Systems	400–107
21.7	Bulk Liquefied Hydrogen Systems	400–107
21.8	Gas Generation Systems	400–107
21.9	Insulated Liquid Carbon Dioxide Systems	400–107
21.10	Storage, Handling, and Use of Ethylene Oxide for Sterilization and Fumigation	400–107
21.11	Acetylene Cylinder Charging Plants	400–107
Annex A	**Explanatory Material**	**400–107**
Annex B	**Chemical Data**	**400–134**
Annex C	**Hazardous Materials Management Plans and Hazardous Materials Inventory Statements**	**400–151**
Annex D	**Security Information**	**400–160**
Annex E	**Properties and Uses of Ammonium Nitrate and Fire-Fighting Procedures**	**400–162**
Annex F	**Typical Organic Peroxide Formulations**	**400–163**
Annex G	**Oxidizers**	**400–170**
Annex H	**Compressed Gases and Cryogenic Fluids**	**400–180**
Annex I	**Emergency Response Guideline**	**400–181**
Annex J	**Sample Ordinance for Adopting NFPA 400**	**400–188**
Annex K	**Informational References**	**400–189**
Index		**400–192**

NFPA 400

Hazardous Materials Code

2013 Edition

IMPORTANT NOTE: This NFPA document is made available for use subject to important notices and legal disclaimers. These notices and disclaimers appear in all publications containing this document and may be found under the heading "Important Notices and Disclaimers Concerning NFPA Documents." They can also be obtained on request from NFPA or viewed at www.nfpa.org/disclaimers.

NOTICE: An asterisk (*) following the number or letter designating a paragraph indicates that explanatory material on the paragraph can be found in Annex A.

Changes other than editorial are indicated by a vertical rule beside the paragraph, table, or figure in which the change occurred. These rules are included as an aid to the user in identifying changes from the previous edition. Where one or more complete paragraphs have been deleted, the deletion is indicated by a bullet (•) between the paragraphs that remain.

A reference in brackets [ ] following a section or paragraph indicates material that has been extracted from another NFPA document. As an aid to the user, the complete title and edition of the source documents for extracts in mandatory sections of the document are given in Chapter 2 and those for extracts in informational sections are given in Annex K. Extracted text may be edited for consistency and style and may include the revision of internal paragraph references and other references as appropriate. Requests for interpretations or revisions of extracted text shall be sent to the technical committee responsible for the source document.

Information on referenced publications can be found in Chapter 2 and Annex K.

Chapter 1 Administration

1.1 Scope.

1.1.1* Applicability. This code shall apply to the storage, use, and handling of the following hazardous materials in all occupancies and facilities:

(1) Ammonium nitrate solids and liquids
(2) Corrosive solids and liquids
(3) Flammable solids
(4) Organic peroxide formulations
(5) Oxidizer — solids and liquids
(6) Pyrophoric solids and liquids
(7) Toxic and highly toxic solids and liquids
(8) Unstable (reactive) solids and liquids
(9) Water-reactive solids and liquids
(10)*Compressed gases and cryogenic fluids as included within the context of NFPA 55, *Compressed Gases and Cryogenic Fluids Code*

1.1.1.1 Occupancies. Unless otherwise specified in this code, all occupancy definitions and classifications shall be in accordance with the building code.

1.1.1.2 Multiple Hazards. Hazardous materials that are classified in more than one hazard category, as set forth in Section 4.1, shall conform to the code requirements for each hazard category.

1.1.2 Exemptions.

1.1.2.1 The quantity and arrangement limits in this code shall not apply to facilities that use ammonium perchlorate in the commercial manufacture of large-scale rocket motors.

1.1.2.2 This code shall not apply to the following:

(1) Storage or use of hazardous materials for individual use on the premises of one- and two-family dwellings
(2) Explosives or blasting agents, which are regulated by NFPA 495, *Explosive Materials Code*, and display fireworks, 1.3 G, which are regulated by NFPA 1124, *Code for the Manufacture, Transportation, Storage, and Retail Sales of Fireworks and Pyrotechnic Articles*
(3) Refrigerants and refrigerant oil contained within closed cycle refrigeration systems complying with the fire code and the mechanical code adopted by the jurisdiction
(4) High hazard contents stored or used in farm buildings or similar occupancies and in remote locations for on-premises agricultural use
(5) Corrosive materials in stationary batteries utilized for facility emergency power or uninterrupted power supply, or similar purposes, in accordance with NFPA 1, *Fire Code*
(6) Aerosols complying with NFPA 30B, *Code for the Manufacture and Storage of Aerosol Products*
(7) Consumer fireworks, 1.4G complying with NFPA 1124, *Code for the Manufacture, Transportation, Storage, and Retail Sales of Fireworks and Pyrotechnic Articles*
(8) Corrosive materials displayed in original packaging in mercantile occupancies and intended for personal or household use or as building materials
(9) Flammable and combustible liquids having no other physical or health hazard properties covered by this code
(10) Organic peroxide formulations that are capable of detonation as manufactured or when unpackaged or in authorized shipping containers under conditions of fire exposure, when stored, manufactured, or used in accordance with NFPA 495, *Explosive Materials Code*
(11) Combustible metals, as defined in NFPA 484, *Standard for Combustible Metals*
(12) LP-Gas complying with NFPA 58, *Liquefied Petroleum Gas Code* or NFPA 59, *Utility LP-Gas Plant Code*
(13) When approved, materials that have been satisfactorily demonstrated not to present a potential danger to public health, safety, or welfare, based upon the quantity or condition of storage
(14) The off-site transportation of hazardous materials when in accordance with Department of Transportation (DOT) regulations

1.2* Purpose. The purpose of this code shall be to provide fundamental safeguards for the storage, use, and handling of hazardous materials as listed in 1.1.1.

1.3 Application. Administrative, operational, and maintenance provisions of this code shall apply to the following:

(1) Conditions and operations arising after the adoption of the code
(2) Existing conditions and operations

1.3.1 Conflicts.

1.3.1.1 Where requirements between this code and a referenced NFPA document differ, the requirements of this code shall apply.

1.3.1.2 Where a conflict between a general requirement of this code and a specific requirement of this code exists, the specific requirement shall apply.

1.3.2 Multiple Occupancies. Where two or more classes of occupancy occur in the same building or structure and are so intermingled that separate safeguards are impracticable, means of egress facilities, construction, protection, and other safeguards shall comply with the most restrictive fire safety requirements of the occupancies involved.

1.3.3 Vehicles and Marine Vessels. Vehicles, marine vessels, or other similar conveyances, where in fixed locations and occupied as buildings, as described by Section 11.6 of NFPA *101, Life Safety Code*, shall be treated as buildings and comply with this code.

1.3.4 Buildings.

1.3.4.1 Buildings permitted for construction after the adoption of this code shall comply with the provisions stated herein for new buildings.

1.3.4.2 Repairs, renovations, alterations, reconstruction, change of occupancy, and additions to buildings shall conform with NFPA *101, Life Safety Code*, and the building code.

1.3.4.3 Newly introduced equipment, materials, and operations regulated by this code shall comply with the requirements for new construction or processes.

1.3.5 Severability. If any provision of this code or the application thereof to any person or circumstance is held invalid, the remainder of the code and the application of such provision to other persons or circumstances shall not be affected thereby.

1.4 Retroactivity. The provisions of this code reflect a consensus of what is necessary to provide an acceptable degree of protection from the hazards addressed in this code at the time the code was issued.

1.4.1 Unless otherwise specified, the provisions of this code shall not apply to facilities, equipment, structures, or installations that existed or were approved for construction or installation prior to the effective date of the code. Where specified, the provisions of this code shall be retroactive.

1.4.2 In those cases where the authority having jurisdiction (AHJ) determines that the existing condition presents an unacceptable degree of risk, the AHJ shall be permitted to apply retroactively any portions of this code deemed appropriate.

1.4.3 The retroactive requirements of this code shall be permitted to be modified if their application would be impractical in the judgment of the AHJ, and only where it is evident that a reasonable degree of safety is provided.

1.5 Equivalency. Nothing in this code is intended to prevent the use of systems, methods, or devices of equivalent or superior quality, strength, fire resistance, effectiveness, durability, and safety over those prescribed by this code.

1.5.1 Technical documentation shall be submitted to the AHJ to demonstrate equivalency.

1.5.2 The system, method, or device shall be approved for the intended purpose by the AHJ.

1.5.3 Alternatives. The specific requirements of this code shall be permitted to be altered by the AHJ to permit alternative methods that will secure equivalent fire safety, but in no case shall the alternative afford less fire safety than, in the judgment of the AHJ, that which would be provided by compliance with the provisions contained in this code.

1.5.4 Modifications. The AHJ shall be authorized to modify any of the provisions of this code upon application in writing by the owner, a lessee, or a duly authorized representative where there are practical difficulties in carrying out the provisions of the code, provided that the intent of the code is met, public safety is secured, and substantial justice is done.

1.5.5 Buildings with equivalency, alternatives, or modifications approved by the AHJ shall be considered as conforming with this code.

1.5.6 Each application for an alternative fire protection feature shall be filed with the AHJ and shall be accompanied by such evidence, letters, statements, results of tests, or other supporting information as required to justify the request.

1.5.7 The AHJ shall keep a record of the actions on the applications specified in 1.5.6, and a signed copy of the AHJ's decision shall be provided for the applicant.

1.5.8 Approval. The AHJ shall approve alternative construction systems, materials, or methods of design when it is substantiated that the proposed alternative provides an equivalent level of protection of this code.

1.5.9 Tests.

1.5.9.1 Where there is insufficient evidence of compliance with the requirements of this code, or where there is evidence that any material or method of construction does not conform to the requirements of this code, or where there is insufficient evidence to substantiate claims for alternative construction systems, materials, or methods of construction, the AHJ shall be permitted to require tests for proof of compliance at the expense of the owner or the owner's agent.

1.5.9.2 Test methods shall be as specified by this code for the material in question.

1.5.9.3 If no appropriate test methods are specified in this code, the AHJ shall be authorized to accept an applicable test procedure from another recognized source.

1.5.9.4 Copies of the results of all tests specified in 1.5.9.2 and 1.5.9.3 shall be retained in accordance with local AHJ guidance.

1.6 Units and Formulas.

1.6.1 The units of measure in this code are presented first in U.S. customary units (inch-pound units), followed by International System (SI) of Units in parentheses.

1.6.2 Either system of units shall be acceptable for satisfying the requirements in the code.

1.6.3 Users of this code shall apply one system of units consistently and shall not alternate between units.

1.6.4 The values presented for measurements in this code are expressed with a degree of precision appropriate for practical application and enforcement. It is not intended that the application or enforcement of these values be more precise than the precision expressed.

1.6.5 Where extracted text contains values expressed in only one system of units, the values in the extracted text have been retained without conversion to preserve the values established by the responsible technical committee in the source document.

1.7 Enforcement. This code shall be administered and enforced by the AHJ designated by the governing authority. See Annex J for sample wording for enabling legislation.

1.8* Permits. Permits and the permit process shall comply with the requirements of NFPA 1, *Fire Code*.

1.8.1 Plans and Specifications.

1.8.1.1 The AHJ shall have the authority to require plans and specifications to ensure compliance with applicable codes and standards.

1.8.1.2 Information that is identified by the owner as confidential shall not be made part of the public record.

1.8.2 Stop Work or Evacuation.

1.8.2.1 The AHJ shall have the authority to order an operation or use stopped and the immediate evacuation of any occupied building or area when such building or area has hazardous conditions that present imminent danger.

1.8.2.2 Whenever any work is being done contrary to provisions of this code, the AHJ is hereby authorized to order such work stopped.

1.8.2.3 The work specified in 1.8.2.2 shall immediately stop until authorized by the AHJ to proceed.

1.9 Facility Closure.

1.9.1 Where required by the AHJ, no facility storing hazardous materials listed in 1.1.1 shall close or abandon an entire storage facility without notifying the AHJ at least 30 days prior to the scheduled closing.

1.9.2 The AHJ shall be permitted to reduce the 30-day period specified in 1.9.1 when there are special circumstances requiring such reduction.

1.9.3 Facilities Out of Service.

1.9.3.1 Facilities Temporarily Out of Service. Facilities that are temporarily out of service shall continue to maintain a permit and be monitored and inspected.

1.9.3.2 Facilities Permanently Out of Service. Facilities for which a permit is not kept current or that are not monitored and inspected on a regular basis shall be deemed to be permanently out of service and shall be closed in accordance with 1.9.4.1 through 1.9.4.2.

1.9.4 Closure Plan.

1.9.4.1 Where required by the AHJ, the permit holder or applicant shall submit a closure plan to the fire department to terminate storage, dispensing, handling, or use of hazardous materials at least 30 days prior to facility closure.

1.9.4.2 The plan shall demonstrate that hazardous materials that were stored, dispensed, handled, or used in the facility have been transported, disposed of, or reused in a manner that eliminates the need for further maintenance and any threat to public health and safety.

1.10 Emergency Planning.

1.10.1 Emergency Action Plan. An emergency action plan, consistent with the available equipment and personnel, shall be established to respond to fire and other emergencies in accordance with requirements set forth in NFPA 1, *Fire Code*.

1.10.2 Activation. The facility responsible for an unauthorized release shall activate the emergency action element of the Hazardous Materials Management Plan.

1.11 Hazardous Materials Management Plan (HMMP).

1.11.1* When required by the AHJ, new or existing facilities that store, use, or handle hazardous materials covered by this code in amounts above the MAQ specified in 5.2.1.2 through 5.2.1.13 and 5.4.1.2 shall submit a hazardous materials management plan (HMMP) to the AHJ.

1.11.2 The HMMP shall be reviewed and updated as follows:

(1) Annually
(2) When the facility is modified
(3) When hazardous materials representing a new hazard category not previously addressed are stored, used, or handled in the facility

1.11.3 The HMMP shall comply with the requirements of Chapter 6.

1.12* Hazardous Materials Inventory Statement (HMIS).

1.12.1 When required by the AHJ, a hazardous materials inventory statement (HMIS) shall be completed and submitted to the AHJ.

1.12.2 The HMIS shall comply with the requirements in NFPA 1, *Fire Code*.

1.13 Plan Review.

1.13.1 Where required by the AHJ for new construction, modification, or rehabilitation, construction documents and shop drawings shall be submitted, reviewed, and approved prior to the start of such work as provided in Section 1.13.

1.13.2 The applicant shall be responsible for ensuring that the following conditions are met:

(1) The construction documents include all of the fire protection requirements.
(2) The shop drawings are correct and in compliance with the applicable codes and standards.
(3) The contractor maintains an approved set of construction documents on-site.

1.13.3 It shall be the responsibility of the AHJ to promulgate rules that cover the following:

(1) Criteria to meet the requirements of Section 1.13
(2) Review of documents and construction documents within established time frames for the purpose of acceptance or providing reasons for nonacceptance

1.13.4 Review and approval by the AHJ shall not relieve the applicant of the responsibility of compliance with this code.

1.13.5 When required by the AHJ, revised construction documents or shop drawings shall be prepared and submitted for review and approval to illustrate corrections or modifications necessitated by field conditions or other revisions to approved plans.

1.14 Technical Assistance.

1.14.1 The AHJ shall be permitted, upon prior written notification to the applicant, building owner, or owner's agent, to require a review by an independent third party with expertise in the matter to be reviewed at the submitter's expense.

1.14.2 The independent reviewer shall provide an evaluation and recommend necessary changes to the proposed design, operation, process, or new technology to the AHJ.

1.14.3 The AHJ shall be authorized to require design submittals to bear the stamp of a professional engineer.

1.14.4 The AHJ shall make the final determination as to whether the provisions of this code have been met.

Chapter 2 Referenced Publications

2.1 General. The documents or portions thereof listed in this chapter are referenced within this code and shall be considered part of the requirements of this document.

2.2 NFPA Publications. National Fire Protection Association, 1 Batterymarch Park, Quincy, MA 02169-7471.

NFPA 1, *Fire Code*, 2012 edition.
NFPA 10, *Standard for Portable Fire Extinguishers*, 2010 edition.
NFPA 13, *Standard for the Installation of Sprinkler Systems*, 2013 edition.
NFPA 14, *Standard for the Installation of Standpipe and Hose Systems*, 2010 edition.
NFPA 15, *Standard for Water Spray Fixed Systems for Fire Protection*, 2012 edition.
NFPA 30, *Flammable and Combustible Liquids Code*, 2012 edition.
NFPA 30B, *Code for the Manufacture and Storage of Aerosol Products*, 2011 edition.
NFPA 45, *Standard on Fire Protection for Laboratories Using Chemicals*, 2011 edition.
NFPA 51, *Standard for the Design and Installation of Oxygen–Fuel Gas Systems for Welding, Cutting, and Allied Processes*, 2013 edition.
NFPA 51A, *Standard for Acetylene Cylinder Charging Plants*, 2012 edition.
NFPA 51B, *Standard for Fire Prevention During Welding, Cutting, and Other Hot Work*, 2009 edition.
NFPA 52, *Vehicular Gaseous Fuel Systems Code*, 2010 edition.
NFPA 55, *Compressed Gases and Cryogenic Fluids Code*, 2013 edition.
NFPA 58, *Liquefied Petroleum Gas Code*, 2011 edition.
NFPA 59, *Utility LP-Gas Plant Code*, 2012 edition.
NFPA 59A, *Standard for the Production, Storage, and Handling of Liquefied Natural Gas (LNG)*, 2013 edition.
NFPA 68, *Standard on Explosion Protection by Deflagration Venting*, 2007 edition.
NFPA 69, *Standard on Explosion Prevention Systems*, 2008 edition.
NFPA 70®, *National Electrical Code*®, 2011 edition.
NFPA 72®, *National Fire Alarm and Signaling Code*, 2013 edition.
NFPA 99, *Health Care Facilities Code*, 2012 edition.
NFPA 101®, *Life Safety Code*®, 2012 edition.
NFPA 110, *Standard for Emergency and Standby Power Systems*, 2013 edition.
NFPA 259, *Standard Test Method for Potential Heat of Building Materials*, 2008 edition.
NFPA 318, *Standard for the Protection of Semiconductor Fabrication Facilities*, 2012 edition.
NFPA 484, *Standard for Combustible Metals*, 2012 edition.
NFPA 495, *Explosive Materials Code*, 2010 edition.
NFPA 505, *Fire Safety Standard for Powered Industrial Trucks Including Type Designations, Areas of Use, Conversions, Maintenance, and Operations*, 2011 edition.
NFPA 704, *Standard System for the Identification of the Hazards of Materials for Emergency Response*, 2012 edition.
NFPA 1124, *Code for the Manufacture, Transportation, Storage, and Retail Sales of Fireworks and Pyrotechnic Articles*, 2013 edition.
NFPA 5000®, *Building Construction and Safety Code*®, 2012 edition.

2.3 Other Publications.

2.3.1 APA Publications. American Pyrotechnics Association, P.O. Box 30438, Bethesda, MD 20824.

APA 87-1, *Standard for the Construction and Approval for Transportation of Fireworks, Novelties and Theatrical Pyrotechnics*, 2001 edition.

2.3.2 ASCE Publications. American Society of Civil Engineers, 1801 Alexander Bell Drive, Reston, VA 20191-4400.

ASCE/SEI 7, *Minimum Design Loads for Building and Other Structures*, 2010.

2.3.3 ASME Publications. American Society of Mechanical Engineers, Three Park Avenue, New York, NY 10016-5990.

ASME A13.1, *Scheme for the Identification of Piping Systems*, 2007.

ASME B31.3, *Process Piping*, 2010.

ASME International, *Boiler and Pressure Vessel Code*, "Rules for the Construction of Unfired Pressure Vessels," Section VIII, 2010.

2.3.4 ASTM Publications. ASTM International, 100 Barr Harbor Drive, P.O. Box C700, West Conshohocken, PA 19428-2959.

ASTM E 84, *Standard Test Method for Surface Burning Characteristics of Building Materials*, 2010.

ASTM E 136, *Standard Test Method for Behavior of Materials in a Vertical Tube Furnace at 750 Degrees C*, 2009.

ASTM E 681-01, *Standard Test Method for Concentration Limits of Flammability of Chemicals (Vapors and Gases)*, 2009.

ASTM E 1591, *Standard Guide for Obtaining Data for Deterministic Fire Models*, 2007.

2.3.5 CGA Publications. Compressed Gas Association, 4221 Walney Road, 5th floor, Chantilly, VA 20151-2923.

CGA C-7, *Guide to the Preparation of Precautionary Labeling and Marking of Compressed Gas Containers*, 2004.

CGA M-1, *Guide for Medical Gas Supply Systems at Consumer Sites*, 2007.

CGA P-1, *Safe Handling of Compressed Gases in Containers*, 2008.

ANSI/CGA P-18, *Standard for Bulk Inert Gas Systems at Consumer Sites*, 2006.

CGA P-20, *Standard for the Classification of Toxic Gas Mixtures*, 2009.

CGA P-23, *Standard for Categorizing Gas Mixtures Containing Flammable and Nonflammable Components*, 2008.

ANSI/CGA G13, *Storage and Handling of Silane and Silane Mixtures*, 2006.

CGA S-1.1, *Pressure Relief Device Standards – Part 1 – Cylinders for Compressed Gases*, 2007.

CGA S-1.2, *Pressure Relief Device Standards – Part 2 – Cargo and Portable Tanks for Compressed Gases*, 2009.

CGA S-1.3, *Pressure Relief Device Standards – Part 3 – Stationary Storage Containers for Compressed Gases*, 2008.

CGA V-6, *Standard Bulk Refrigerated Liquid Transfer Connections*, September 2008.

2.3.6 CTC Publications. Canadian Transport Commission, Queen's Printer, Ottawa, Ontario, Canada. (Available from the Canadian Communications Group Publication Centre, Ordering Department, Ottawa, Canada K1A 0S9.)

Transportation of Dangerous Goods Regulations.

Transport Canada, 330 Sparks Street, Ottawa, K1A 0N5, Canada.

Canadian Ministry of Transport Regulations.

2.3.7 IAPMO Publications. International Association of Plumbing and Mechanical Officials, 5001 E. Philadelphia Street, Ontario, CA 91761.

Uniform Mechanical Code, 2009 edition.

2.3.8 IME Publications. Institute of Makers of Explosives, 1120 19th Street, NW, Suite 310, Washington, DC 20036–3605.

IME Safety Library Publication No. 2, "American Table of Distances for Storage of Explosives," June 1991.

2.3.9 ISO Publications. International Organization for Standardization Publications, 1 rue de Varembé, Case Postale 56, CH-1211 Geneve 20, Switzerland.

ISO 10156, *Gases and gas mixtures – Determination of fire potential and oxidizing ability for the selection of cylinder valve outlets*, 2010.

ISO 10298, *Determination of toxicity of a gas or gas mixture*, 2010.

2.3.10 UL Publications. Underwriters Laboratories Inc., 333 Pfingsten Road, Northbrook, IL 60062-2096.

ANSI/UL 723, *Standard Test Method of Surface Burning Characteristics of Building Materials*, 2008, Revised 2010.

UL 2080, *Standard for the Fire Resistant Tanks for Flammable and Combustible Liquids*, 2000.

ANSI/UL 2085, *Standard for Protected Aboveground Tanks for Flammable and Combustible Liquids*, 1997, Revised 2010.

2.3.11 UN Publications. United Nations Publications, 2 United Nations Plaza, Room DC2-853, New York, NY 10017.

Recommendations on the Transportation of Dangerous Goods.

2.3.12 U.S. Government Publications. U.S. Government Printing Office, Washington, DC 20402.

Resource Conservation and Recovery Act (RCRA) published Oct. 21, 1976.

Title 16, Code of Federal Regulations, Part 1500, "Hazardous Substances and Articles: Administration and Enforcement."

Title 16, Code of Federal Regulations, Part 1507, "Fireworks Devices."

Title 18, Code of Federal Regulations, Part 40, "Importation, Manufacture, Distribution and Storage of Explosive Materials."

Title 21, Code of Federal Regulations, Parts 210 and 211.

Title 29, Code of Federal Regulations, Part 1910.120, "Hazardous Waste Operations and Emergency Response," Occupational Safety and Health Administration.

Title 29, Code of Federal Regulations, Part 1910.1000, "Air Contaminants."

Title 29, Code of Federal Regulations, Part 1910.1200, "Hazard Communication," Occupational Safety and Health Administration.

Title 49, Code of Federal Regulations, Parts 100 through 199 "Pipeline and Hazardous Materials," "Hazardous Materials Transportation," Safety Administration, Department of Transportation.

Title 49, Code of Federal Regulations, Part 173, DOT.

2.3.13 Other Publications.

Merriam-Webster's Collegiate Dictionary, 11th edition, Merriam-Webster Inc., Springfield, MA, 2003.

2.4 References for Extracts in Mandatory Sections.

NFPA 1, *Fire Code*, 2012 edition.
NFPA 30, *Flammable and Combustible Liquids Code*, 2012 edition.
NFPA 30B, *Code for the Manufacture and Storage of Aerosol Products*, 2011 edition.
NFPA 52, *Vehicular Gaseous Fuel Systems Code*, 2010 edition.
NFPA 55, *Compressed Gases and Cryogenic Fluids Code*, 2013 edition.
NFPA 58, *Liquefied Petroleum Gas Code*, 2011 edition.
NFPA 68, *Standard on Explosion Protection by Deflagration Venting*, 2007 edition.
NFPA 101®, *Life Safety Code*®, 2012 edition.
NFPA 318, *Standard for the Protection of Semiconductor Fabrication Facilities*, 2012 edition.
NFPA 495, *Explosive Materials Code*, 2010 edition.
NFPA 499, *Recommended Practice for the Classification of Combustible Dusts and of Hazardous (Classified) Locations for Electrical Installations in Chemical Process Areas*, 2013 edition.
NFPA 914, *Code for Fire Protection of Historic Structures*, 2010 edition.
NFPA 1124, *Code for the Manufacture, Transportation, Storage, and Retail Sales of Fireworks and Pyrotechnic Articles*, 2013 edition.
NFPA 5000®, *Building Construction and Safety Code*®, 2012 edition.

Chapter 3 Definitions

3.1* General. The definitions contained in this chapter shall apply to the terms used in this code. Where terms are not defined in this chapter or within another chapter, they shall be defined using their ordinarily accepted meanings within the context in which they are used. *Merriam-Webster's Collegiate Dictionary*, 11th edition, shall be the source for the ordinarily accepted meaning.

3.2 NFPA Official Definitions.

3.2.1* Approved. Acceptable to the authority having jurisdiction.

3.2.2* Authority Having Jurisdiction (AHJ). An organization, office, or individual responsible for enforcing the requirements of a code or standard, or for approving equipment, materials, an installation, or a procedure.

3.2.3* Code. A standard that is an extensive compilation of provisions covering broad subject matter or that is suitable for adoption into law independently of other codes and standards.

3.2.4 Labeled. Equipment or materials to which has been attached a label, symbol, or other identifying mark of an organization that is acceptable to the authority having jurisdiction and concerned with product evaluation, that maintains periodic inspection of production of labeled equipment or materials, and by whose labeling the manufacturer indicates compliance with appropriate standards or performance in a specified manner.

3.2.5* Listed. Equipment, materials, or services included in a list published by an organization that is acceptable to the authority having jurisdiction and concerned with evaluation of products or services, that maintains periodic inspection of production of listed equipment or materials or periodic evaluation of services, and whose listing states that either the equipment, material, or service meets appropriate designated standards or has been tested and found suitable for a specified purpose.

3.2.6 Shall. Indicates a mandatory requirement.

3.2.7 Should. Indicates a recommendation or that which is advised but not required.

3.3 General Definitions.

3.3.1* Absolute Pressure (Gas). Pressure based on a zero reference point, the perfect vacuum. [**55**, 2013]

3.3.2 Area.

3.3.2.1 *Control Area.* A building or portion of a building or outdoor area within which hazardous materials are allowed to be stored, dispensed, used, or handled in quantities not exceeding the MAQ.

3.3.2.2 *Indoor Area (Gas).* An area that is within a building or structure having overhead cover, other than a structure qualifying as "weather protection" in accordance with Section 6.6 of NFPA 55, *Compressed Gases and Cryogenic Fluids Code*. (See also 3.3.2.4, Outdoor Area.) [**55**, 2013]

3.3.2.3 *Organic Peroxide Storage Area.* An area used for the storage of organic peroxide formulations.

3.3.2.4 *Outdoor Area (Gas).* An area that is not an indoor area. [**55**, 2013]

3.3.2.5 *Outdoor Control Area.* An outdoor area within which hazardous materials are allowed to be stored, dispensed, used, or handled in quantities not exceeding the MAQ.

3.3.3 ASME. American Society of Mechanical Engineers. [**58**, 2011]

3.3.4 ASTM (Gas). American Society for Testing and Materials, now known as "ASTM International." [**55**, 2013]

3.3.5 Basement. A story of a building or structure having one-half or more of its height below ground level and to which access for fire-fighting purposes is unduly restricted.

3.3.6 Building. Any structure used or intended for supporting or sheltering any use or occupancy. [***101***, 2012]

3.3.7 Building Code. The building or construction code adopted by the jurisdiction.

3.3.8* Bulk Hydrogen Compressed Gas System (Gas). An assembly of equipment that consists of, but is not limited to, storage containers, pressure regulators, pressure relief devices, compressors, manifolds, and piping, with a storage capacity of more than 5000 scf (141.6 Nm^3) of compressed hydrogen gas and that terminates at the source valve. [**55**, 2013]

3.3.9* Bulk Inert Gas System (Gas). An assembly of equipment, that consists of, but is not limited to, storage containers, pressure regulators, pressure relief devices, vaporizers, manifolds, and piping, with a storage capacity of more than 20,000 ft^3 (scf) (566 m^3) of inert gas, including unconnected reserves on hand at the site, and that terminates at the source valve. [**55**, 2013]

3.3.10* Bulk Liquefied Hydrogen Gas System (Gas). An assembly of equipment that consists of, but is not limited to, storage containers, pressure regulators, pressure relief devices, vaporizers, manifolds, and piping, with a storage capacity of more than 39.7 gal (150 L) of liquefied hydrogen that terminates at the source valve. [**55**, 2013]

3.3.11* Bulk Oxygen System (Gas). An assembly of equipment, such as oxygen storage containers, pressure regulators, pressure relief devices, vaporizers, manifolds, and interconnecting piping, that has a storage capacity of more than 20,000 ft^3 (scf) (566 m^3) of oxygen and that terminates at the source valve. [**55**, 2013]

3.3.12 CFR. The Code of Federal Regulations of the United States Government. [**1**, 2012]

3.3.13 CGA (Gas). Compressed Gas Association. [**1**, 2012]

3.3.14 Combustible. A substance that will burn.

3.3.15* Combustible Dust. Any solid material, regardless of its shape, size, or chemical composition, capable of forming a cloud in air, in process specific conditions or in accidental conditions, which can propagate a self-sustaining combustion wave (deflagration or detonation) thus presenting a flash-fire or explosion hazard. [**499**, 2013]

3.3.16 Combustible Liquid. Any liquid that has a closed-cup flash point at or above 100°F (37.8°C), as determined by the test procedures and apparatus set forth in Section 4.4 [of NFPA 30, *Flammable and Combustible Liquids Code*]. Combustible liquids are classified according to Section 4.3 [of NFPA 30, *Flammable and Combustible Liquids Code*]. Combustible liquids, as defined in 3.3.30.1 and 4.2.2 [of NFPA 30, *Flammable and Combustible Liquids Code*], shall be classified in accordance with (1) Class II Liquid — Any liquid that has a flash point at or above 100°F (37.8°C) and below 140°F (60°C); (2) Class III Liquid — Any liquid that has a flash point at or above 140°F (60°C); (a) Class IIIA Liquid — Any liquid that has a flash point at or above 140°F (60°C), but below 200°F (93°C); and (b) Class IIIB Liquid — Any liquid that has a flash point at or above 200°F (93°C). [**30,** 2012]

3.3.17* Compressed Gas System. An assembly of equipment designed to contain, distribute, or transport compressed gases. [**318,** 2009]

3.3.18 Consumer Fireworks. Small fireworks devices containing restricted amounts of pyrotechnic composition, designed primarily to produce visible or audible effects by combustion, that comply with the construction, chemical composition, and labeling regulations of the U.S. Consumer Product Safety Commission (CPSC), as set forth in CPSC 16 CFR 1500 and 1507, 49 CFR 172, and APA Standard 87–1, *Standard for the Construction and Approval for Transportation of Fireworks, Novelties, and Theatrical Pyrotechnics.* [**1124,** 2013]

3.3.19 Container. A containment device including, but not limited to, cylinders, tanks, intermediate bulk containers, pressure vessels, drums, carboys, cans, bottles, boxes, bags, bins, and portable tanks that vary in shape, size, and material of construction and are used for holding, storing, and transporting hazardous materials covered by this code.

3.3.19.1* *Container (Flammable and Combustible Liquid).* Any vessel of 119 gal (450 L) or less capacity used for transporting or storing liquids. [**30,** 2012]

3.3.19.2 *Closed Container (Flammable and Combustible Liquid).* A container defined, so sealed by means of a lid or other device that neither liquid nor vapor will escape from it at ordinary temperatures. [**30,** 2012]

3.3.19.3 *ASME Container.* A container constructed in accordance with the ASME *Boiler and Pressure Vessel Code.*

3.3.19.4 *Combustible Containers.* Containers that include paper bags, fiber drums, plastic containers, and wooden or fiber boxes or barrels, as well as noncombustible containers having removable combustible liners or packing, and noncombustible containers having combustible overpacks.

3.3.19.5 *Noncombustible Containers.* Containers constructed of glass or metal that can be coated with a polymeric material no more than 1/32 in. (2 mils) in thickness.

3.3.19.6* *Nonmetallic Container (Solid, Flammable and Combustible Liquid).* A container as defined in 3.3.19 constructed of glass, plastic, fiber, or a material other than metal. [**30,** 2012]

3.3.19.7 *Ethylene Oxide Drum.* A closed container (drum) built to UN specification (1A1) and used for holding, storing, or transporting ethylene oxide.

3.3.19.8 *Intermediate Bulk Container (IBC) — (Flammable and Combustible Liquid).* Any closed vessel having a liquid capacity not exceeding 793 gal (3000 L) and intended for storing and transporting liquids as defined in Title 49 Code of Federal Regulations Parts 100–199 or in Part 6 of the United Nations *Recommendations on the Transport of Dangerous Goods.* [**30,** 2012]

3.3.19.9* *Nonmetallic Intermediate Bulk Container (Flammable and Combustible Liquid).* An intermediate bulk container as defined in 3.3.19.8 constructed of glass, plastic, fiber or a material other than metal. [**30,** 2012]

3.3.19.10 *Overpack Container.* A closed container intended to encapsulate and contain a leaking or damaged liquid or solid material container thereby preventing the release of liquids, solids, or vapors and is made of the same material or similarly protective material as the leaking or damaged container.

3.3.19.11 *Cylinder Containment Vessel (Gas).* A gastight, recovery vessel designed so that a leaking compressed gas container can be placed within its confines, thereby encapsulating the leaking container. [**55,** 2013]

3.3.19.12 *Storage Tank (Flammable and Combustible Liquid).* Any vessel having a liquid capacity that exceeds 60 gal (230 L), is intended for fixed installation, and is not used for processing. [**30,** 2012]

3.3.19.12.1* *Stationary Tank (Gas).* A packaging designed primarily for stationary installations not intended for loading, unloading, or attachment to a transport vehicle as part of its normal operation in the process of use. [**55,** 2013]

3.3.19.13 *Aboveground Tank (Flammable and Combustible Liquid).* A storage tank that is installed above grade, at grade, or below grade without backfill. [**30,** 2012]

3.3.19.13.1* *Atmospheric Tank (Flammable and Combustible Liquid).* A storage tank that has been designed to operate at pressures from atmospheric through a gauge pressure of 1.0 psi measured at the top of the tank. [**30,** 2012]

3.3.19.13.2 *Low Pressure Tank (Flammable and Combustible Liquid).* For purposes of this code, a storage tank designed to withstand an internal pressure above a gauge pressure of 1.0 psi but not more than a gauge pressure of 15 psi measured at the top of the tank. [**30,** 2012]

3.3.19.13.3 *Protected Aboveground Tank (Flammable and Combustible Liquid).* An atmospheric aboveground storage tank with integral secondary containment and thermal insulation that has been evaluated for resistance to physical damage and for limiting the heat transferred to the primary tank when exposed to hydrocarbon pool fire and is listed in accordance with ANSI/UL 2085, *Standard for Protected Aboveground Tanks for Flammable and Combustible Liquids,* or an equivalent test procedure. [**30,** 2012]

3.3.19.13.4 *Secondary Containment Tank (Flammable and Combustible Liquid).* A tank that has an inner and outer wall with an interstitial space (annulus) between the walls and which has a means of monitoring the interstitial space for a leak. [**30,** 2012]

3.3.19.13.5 *Fire Resistant Tank (Flammable and Combustible Liquid).* An atmospheric aboveground storage tank with thermal insulation that has been evaluated for resistance to physical damage and for limiting the heat transferred to the primary tank when exposed to hydrocarbon pool fire and is listed in accordance with UL 2080, *Standard for Fire Resistant Tanks for Flammable and Combustible Liquids,* or an equivalent test procedure. [**30,** 2012]

3.3.19.14* *Portable Tank (Flammable and Combustible Liquid).* Any vessel having a liquid capacity over 60 gals (230 L) intended for storing liquids and not intended for fixed installation. [**30,** 2012]

3.3.19.14.1* *Portable Tank (Gas).* Any packaging over 60 gal (227.1 L) capacity designed primarily to be loaded into or on, or temporarily attached to, a transport vehicle or ship and equipped with skids, mountings, or accessories to facilitate handling of the tank by mechanical means. [55, 2013]

3.3.19.14.2* *Nonmetallic Portable Tank (Flammable and Combustible Liquid).* A portable tank as herein defined constructed of plastic, fiber, or a material other than metal. [30, 2012]

3.3.19.15* *Pressure Vessel.* A container, process vessel, or other component designed in accordance with the ASME *Boiler and Pressure Vessel Code*, DOT, or other approved standards.

3.3.19.16* *Cylinder (Gas).* A pressure vessel designed for pressures higher than 276 kPa (40 psia) having less than 453.5 kg (1000 lb) water capacity and having a circular cross-section.

3.3.19.16.1* *Cylinder Pack (Gas)* An arrangement of cylinders into a cluster where the cylinders are confined into a grouping or arrangement with a strapping or frame system and connections are made to a common manifold. The frame system is allowed to be on skids or wheels to permit movement. [55, 2013]

3.3.19.17 *Compressed Gas Container (Gas).* A pressure vessel designed to hold compressed gas at an absolute pressure greater than 1 atmosphere at 68°F (20°C) that includes cylinders, containers, and tanks [55, 2013]

3.3.19.17.1* *Tube Trailer (Gas).* A truck or semitrailer on which a number of very long tubular compressed gas cylinders have been mounted and manifolded into a common piping system. [55, 2013]

3.3.19.18* *ISO Module.* A single unit or unit assembly of containers, IBCs, portable tanks, or cylinders permanently mounted in a frame conforming to International Organization for Standardization (ISO) requirements.

3.3.19.19* *Safety Can (Liquid).* A listed container of not more than 5.3 gal (20 L) capacity having a spring closing lid and spout cover and so designed that it will safely relieve internal pressure when subjected to fire exposure. [30, 2012]

3.3.19.20 *Aerosol Container (Liquid).* A metal can up to a maximum size of 33.8 fl oz (1000 ml) or a glass or plastic bottle up to a maximum size of 4 fl oz (118 ml) that is designed and intended to dispense an aerosol. [30B, 2011]

3.3.20 Continuous Gas Detection System (Gas). A gas detection system in which the instrument is maintained in continuous operation and the interval between sampling of any point does not exceed 30 minutes. [55, 2013]

3.3.21 Court. An open, uncovered, unoccupied space, unobstructed to the sky, bounded on three or more sides by exterior building walls. [*101*, 2012]

3.3.21.1 *Enclosed Court.* A court bounded on all sides by the exterior walls of a building or by the exterior walls and lot lines on which walls are permitted. [5000, 2012]

3.3.22 Cryogenic Fluid (Gas). A fluid with a boiling point lower than −90°C (−130°F) at an absolute pressure of 101.325 kPa (14.7 psia). [55, 2013]

3.3.23* **Cylinder (Gas).** A pressure vessel designed for pressures higher than 276 kPa (40 psia) and having a circular cross-section.

3.3.24 Cylinder Containment System (Gas). A gastight recovery system comprised of equipment or devices that can be placed over a leak in a compressed gas container, thereby stopping or controlling the escape of gas from the leaking container. [55, 2013]

3.3.25 Cylinder Containment Vessel (Gas). A gastight recovery vessel designed so that a leaking compressed gas container can be placed within its confines, thereby encapsulating the leaking container. [55, 2013]

3.3.26* **Cylinder Pack (Gas).** An arrangement of cylinders into a cluster where the cylinders are confined into a grouping or arrangement with a strapping or frame system and connections are made to a common manifold. The frame system is allowed to be on skids or wheels to permit movement. [55, 2013]

3.3.27 Deflagration. Propagation of a reaction zone at a velocity that is less than the speed of sound in the unreacted medium. [68, 2007]

3.3.28 Detached Building. A separate building that is separated from other structures or uses as required by *NFPA 5000, Building Construction and Safety Code* for a freestanding structure. [5000, 2012]

3.3.29 Detonation. Propagation of a combustion zone at a velocity that is greater than the speed of sound in the unreacted medium. [68, 2007]

3.3.30 Distributor (Gas). A business engaged in the sale or resale, or both, of compressed gases or cryogenic fluids, or both. [55, 2013]

3.3.31 DOT. U.S. Department of Transportation. [52, 2010]

3.3.32 Emergency Response. Emergency response or responding to emergencies means a response effort by employees from outside the immediate release area or by other designated responders including, but not limited to, private sector emergency responders, mutual aid groups, local fire departments, or other qualified parties to an occurrence that results, or is likely to result, in an uncontrolled release of a hazardous material.

3.3.33 Emergency Response Liaison. A person designated to act as a liaison for emergency response as defined by the emergency plan.

3.3.34 Emergency Shutoff Valve (Gas). A designated valve designed to shut off the flow of gases or liquids. [55, 2013]

3.3.34.1 *Automatic Emergency Shutoff Valve (Gas).* A designated fail-safe automatic closing valve designed to shut off the flow of gases or liquids that is initiated by a control system where the control system is activated by either manual or automatic means. [55, 2013]

3.3.34.2 *Manual Emergency Shutoff Valve (Gas).* A designated valve designed to shut off the flow of gases or liquids that is manually operated. [55, 2013]

3.3.35 Excess Flow Control (Gas). A fail-safe system or approved means designed to shut off flow due to a rupture in pressurized piping systems. [55, 2013]

3.3.36* **Exhausted Enclosure (Gas).** An appliance or piece of equipment that consists of a top, a back, and two sides that provides a means of local exhaust for capturing gases, fumes, vapors, and mists. [55, 2013]

3.3.37* Explosion Control (Gas). A means of either preventing an explosion through the use of explosion suppression, fuel reduction, or oxidant reduction systems or a means to prevent the structural collapse of a building in the event of an explosion through the use of deflagration venting, barricades, or related construction methods. [55, 2013]

3.3.38 Explosion Vent. An opening in an enclosure to relieve the developing pressure from a deflagration. [68, 2007]

3.3.39* Explosive. Any chemical compound, mixture, or device, the primary or common purpose of which is to function by explosion. [495, 2010]

3.3.40* Explosive Decomposition. Rapid chemical reaction resulting in a large, almost instantaneous, release of energy.

3.3.41* Explosive Reaction. A reaction, which includes both deflagration and detonation, producing a sudden rise in pressure with potentially destructive results.

3.3.42 Fire Prevention Code. The fire prevention code adopted by the jurisdiction.

3.3.43 Fire Protection System. Any fire alarm device or system or fire extinguishing device or system, or a combination thereof, that is designed and installed for detecting, controlling, or extinguishing a fire or otherwise alerting occupants, or the fire department, or both, that a fire has occurred. [1, 2012]

3.3.44* Flammable Liquid (Class I). Any liquid having a closed-cup flash point below 100°F (37.8°C).

3.3.45* Flammable Solid. A solid substance, other than a substance defined as a blasting agent or explosive, that is liable to cause fire resulting from friction or retained heat from manufacture, that has an ignition temperature below 212°F (100°C), or that burns so vigorously or persistently when ignited that it creates a serious hazard.

3.3.46 Gallon (Gas). A standard U.S. gallon. [55, 2013]

3.3.47 Gas.

3.3.47.1* Compressed Gas (Gas). A material, or mixture of materials, that (1) is a gas at 20°C (68°F) or less at an absolute pressure of 101.325 kPa (14.7 psia) and (2) that has a boiling point of 20°C (68°F) or less at an absolute pressure of 101.325 kPa (14.7 psia) and that is liquefied, nonliquefied, or in solution, except those gases that have no other health or physical hazard properties are not considered to be compressed gases until the pressure in the packaging exceeds an absolute pressure of 280 kPa (40.6 psia) at 20°C (68°F). [55, 2013]

3.3.47.2 Corrosive Gas (Gas). A gas that causes visible destruction of or irreversible alterations in living tissue by chemical action at the site of contact. [55, 2013]

3.3.47.3 Flammable Gas (Gas). A material that is a gas at 20°C (68°F) or less at an absolute pressure of 101.325 kPa (14.7 psia), that is ignitable at an absolute pressure of 101.325 kPa (14.7 psia) when in a mixture of 13 percent or less by volume with air, or that has a flammable range at an absolute pressure of 101.325 kPa (14.7 psia) with air of at least 12 percent, regardless of the lower limit. [55, 2013]

3.3.47.4 Flammable Liquefied Gas (Gas). A liquefied compressed gas that, when under a charged pressure, is partially liquid at a temperature of 20°C (68°F) and is flammable. [55, 2013]

3.3.47.5 Highly Toxic Gas (Gas). A chemical that has a median lethal concentration (LC_{50}) in air of 200 ppm by volume or less of gas or vapor, or 2 mg/L or less of mist, fume, or dust, when administered by continuous inhalation for 1 hour (or less if death occurs within 1 hour) to albino rats weighing between 200 g and 300 g (0.44 lb and 0.66 lb) each. [55, 2013]

3.3.47.6 Inert Gas (Gas). A nonreactive, nonflammable, noncorrosive gas such as argon, helium, krypton, neon, nitrogen, and xenon. [55, 2013]

3.3.47.7* Irritant Gas (Gas). A chemical that is not corrosive, but that causes a reversible inflammatory effect on living tissue by chemical action at the site of contact. [55, 2013]

3.3.47.8 Nonflammable Gas (Gas). A gas that does not meet the definition of a flammable gas. [55, 2013]

3.3.47.9* Other Gas (Gas). A gas that is not a corrosive gas, flammable gas, highly toxic gas, oxidizing gas, pyrophoric gas, toxic gas, or unstable reactive gas with a hazard rating of Class 2, Class 3, or Class 4 gas. [55, 2013]

3.3.47.10 Oxidizing Gas (Gas). A gas that can support and accelerate combustion of other materials. [55, 2013]

3.3.47.11 Pyrophoric Gas (Gas). A gas with an autoignition temperature in air at or below 54.4°C (130°F). [55, 2013]

3.3.47.12 Toxic Gas (Gas). A gas with a median lethal concentration (LC_{50}) in air of more than 200 ppm, but not more than 2000 ppm by volume of gas or vapor, or more than 2 mg/L, but not more than 20 mg/L of mist, fume, or dust, when administered by continuous inhalation for 1 hour (or less if death occurs within 1 hour) to albino rats weighing between 200 g and 300 g (0.44 lb and 0.66 lb) each. [55, 2013]

3.3.47.13* Unstable Reactive Gas (Gas). A gas that, in the pure state or as commercially produced, will vigorously polymerize, decompose, or condense, become self-reactive, or otherwise undergo a violent chemical change under conditions of shock, pressure, or temperature. [55, 2013]

3.3.47.13.1 Class 2 Unstable Reactive Gas (Gas). Materials that readily undergo violent chemical change at elevated temperatures and pressures. [55, 2013]

3.3.47.13.2 Class 3 Unstable Reactive Gas (Gas). Materials that in themselves are capable of detonation or explosive decomposition or explosive reaction, but that require a strong initiating source or that must be heated under confinement before initiation. [55, 2013]

3.3.47.13.3 Class 4 Unstable Reactive Gas (Gas). Materials that in themselves are readily capable of detonation or explosive decomposition or explosive reaction at normal temperatures and pressures. [55, 2013]

3.3.48* Gas Cabinet (Gas). A fully enclosed, noncombustible enclosure used to provide an isolated environment for compressed gas cylinders in storage or use. [55, 2013]

3.3.49 Gas Manufacturer/Producer (Gas). A business that produces compressed gases or cryogenic fluids, or both, or fills portable or stationary gas containers, cylinders, or tanks. [55, 2013]

3.3.50* Gas Room (Gas). A separately ventilated, fully enclosed room in which only compressed gases, cryogenic fluids, associated equipment and supplies are stored or used. [55, 2013]

3.3.51* Gaseous Hydrogen System (Gas). A system in which the hydrogen is delivered, stored, and discharged in the gaseous form to a piping system. The gaseous hydrogen system terminates at the point where hydrogen at service pressure first enters the distribution piping. [55, 2013]

3.3.52 Handling. The deliberate movement of material by any means to a point of storage or use. [1, 2012]

3.3.53* Hazard Rating (Gas). The numerical rating of the health, flammability, and self-reactivity, and other hazards of the material, including its reaction with water, specified in NFPA 704, *Standard System for the Identification of the Hazards of Materials for Emergency Response.*

3.3.54 Hazardous Materials Storage Cabinet. A metal cabinet complying with the conditions set forth in 6.1.18.

3.3.55 High Hazard Level Contents.

3.3.55.1 *High Hazard Level 1 Contents.* For definition and examples see 4.2.1.2.1

3.3.55.2 *High Hazard Level 2 Contents.* For definition and examples see 4.2.1.2.2

3.3.55.3 *High Hazard Level 3 Contents.* For definition and examples see 4.2.1.2.3

3.3.55.4 *High Hazard Level 4 Contents.* For definition and examples see 4.2.1.2.4

3.3.56* Immediately Dangerous to Life and Health (IDLH) (Gas). A concentration of airborne contaminants, normally expressed in parts per million (ppm) or milligrams per cubic meter, that represents the maximum level from which one could escape within 30 minutes without any escape-impairing symptoms or irreversible health effects. [55, 2013]

3.3.57* ISO Module (Gas). An assembly of tanks or tubular cylinders permanently mounted in a frame conforming to International Organization for Standardization (ISO) requirements. [55, 2013]

3.3.58 Limit.

3.3.58.1 *Ceiling Limit.* The maximum concentration of an airborne contaminant to which a person can be exposed.

3.3.58.2* *Permissible Exposure Limit (PEL) (Gas).* The maximum permitted 8-hour, time-weighted average concentration of an airborne contaminant. [55, 2013]

3.3.58.3* *Short-Term Exposure Limit (STEL) (Gas).* The concentration to which it is believed that workers can be exposed continuously for a short period of time without suffering from irritation, chronic or irreversible tissue damage, or narcosis of a degree sufficient to increase the likelihood of accidental injury, impairment of self-rescue, or the material reduction of work efficiency, without exceeding the daily permissible exposure limit (PEL). [55, 2013]

3.3.59* Liquefied Hydrogen System (Gas). A system into which liquefied hydrogen is delivered and stored and from which it is discharged in the liquid or gaseous form to a piping system.

3.3.60 Manufacturing Plants. Those facilities where hazardous materials are produced by chemical means or where hazardous materials are pelletized, ground, dissolved, packaged, mixed, or blended.

3.3.61 Material.

3.3.61.1 *Combustible (Material).* A material that, in the form in which it is used and under the conditions anticipated, will ignite and burn; a material that does not meet the definition of noncombustible or limited-combustible. [5000, 2012]

3.3.61.2* *Corrosive Material.* A chemical that causes visible destruction of, or irreversible alterations in, living tissue by chemical action at the site of contact.

3.3.61.3 *Hazard Material.*

3.3.61.3.1 *Health Hazard Material.* A chemical or substance classified as a toxic, highly toxic, or corrosive material in accordance with definitions set forth in this code.

3.3.61.3.2 *Physical Hazard Material.* A chemical or substance classified as a combustible liquid, explosive, flammable cryogen, flammable gas, flammable liquid, flammable solid, organic peroxide, oxidizer, oxidizing cryogen, pyrophoric, unstable (reactive), or water-reactive material.

3.3.61.4* *Hazardous Material.* A chemical or substance that is classified as a physical hazard material or a health hazard material, whether the chemical or substance is in usable or waste condition. *(See also 3.3.61.3.1, Health Hazard Material, and 3.3.61.3.2, Physical Hazard Material.)*

3.3.61.5* *Incompatible Material.* Materials that, when in contact with each other, have the potential to react in a manner that generates heat, fumes, gases, or by-products that are hazardous to life or property.

3.3.61.6* *Limited-Combustible (Material).* Refers to a building construction material not complying with the definition of noncombustible material that, in the form in which it is used, has a potential heat value not exceeding 3500 Btu/lb (8141 kJ/kg), where tested in accordance with NFPA 259, *Standard Test Method for Potential Heat of Building Materials*, and includes either of the following: (1) materials having a structural base of noncombustible material, with a surfacing not exceeding a thickness of ⅛ in. (3.2 mm) that has a flame spread index not greater than 50; or (2) materials, in the form and thickness used, having neither a flame spread index greater than 25 nor evidence of continued progressive combustion, and of such composition that surfaces that would be exposed by cutting through the material on any plane would have neither a flame spread index greater than 25 nor evidence of continued progressive combustion, when tested in accordance with ASTM E 84, *Standard Test Method of Surface Burning Characteristics of Building Materials*, or ANSI/UL 723, *Standard Test Method of Surface Burning Characteristics of Building Materials.* [5000, 2012]

3.3.61.7* *Noncombustible Material.* A material that, in the form in which it is used and under the conditions anticipated, will not ignite, burn, support combustion, or release flammable vapors, when subjected to fire or heat. Materials that are reported as passing ASTM E 136, *Standard Test Method for Behavior of Materials in a Vertical Tube Furnace at 750 Degrees C*, shall be considered noncombustible materials. [5000, 2012]

3.3.61.8 *Pyrophoric Material.* A chemical with an autoignition temperature in air at or below 130°F (54.4°C).

3.3.61.9* *Toxic Material.* A material that produces a lethal dose or a lethal concentration within any of the following categories: (1) a chemical or substance that has a median lethal dose (LD$_{50}$) of more than 50 mg/kg but not more than 500 mg/kg of body weight when administered orally to albino rats weighing between 200 g and 300 g each; (2) a chemical or substance that has a median lethal dose (LD$_{50}$) of more than 200 mg/kg but not more than 1000 mg/kg of body weight when administered by continuous contact for 24 hours, or less if death occurs within 24 hours, with the bare skin of albino rabbits weighing between 2 kg and 3 kg each; (3) a chemical or substance that has a median lethal concentration (LC$_{50}$) in air of more than 200 parts per million but not more than 2000 parts per million by volume of gas or vapor, or more than 2 mg/L but not more than 20 mg/L, of mist, fume, or dust when administered by continuous inhalation for 1 hour, or less if death occurs within 1 hour, to albino rats weighing between 200 g and 300 g each.

3.3.61.9.1* *Highly Toxic Material.* A material that produces a lethal dose or lethal concentration that falls within any of the following categories: (1) a chemical that has a median lethal dose (LD$_{50}$) of 50 mg/kg or less of body weight when administered orally to albino rats weighing between 200 g and 300 g each; (2) a chemical that has a median lethal dose (LD$_{50}$) of 200 mg/kg or less of body weight when administered by continuous contact for 24 hours, or less if death occurs within 24 hours, with the bare skin of albino rabbits weighing between 2 kg and 3 kg each or albino rats weighing 200 g and 300 g each; (3) a chemical that has a median lethal concentration (LC$_{50}$) in air of 200 parts per million by volume or less of gas or vapor, or 2 mg/L or less of mist, fume, or dust, when administered by continuous inhalation for 1 hour, or less if death occurs within 1 hour, to albino rats weighing between 200 g and 300 g each.

3.3.61.10* *Unstable (Reactive) Material.* A material that, in the pure state or as commercially produced, will vigorously polymerize, decompose or condense, become self-reactive, or otherwise undergo a violent chemical change under conditions of shock, pressure, or temperature.

3.3.61.10.1* *Class 1 Unstable (Reactive).* Materials that in themselves are normally stable, but that can become unstable at elevated temperatures and pressures.

3.3.61.10.2* *Class 2 Unstable (Reactive).* Materials that readily undergo violent chemical change at elevated temperatures and pressures.

3.3.61.10.3* *Class 3 Unstable (Reactive).* Materials that in themselves are capable of detonation or explosive decomposition or explosive reaction, but that require a strong initiating source or that must be heated under confinement before initiation.

3.3.61.10.4* *Class 4 Unstable (Reactive).* Materials that in themselves are readily capable of detonation or explosive decomposition or explosive reaction at normal temperatures and pressures.

3.3.61.11* *Water-Reactive Material.* A material that explodes, violently reacts, produces flammable, toxic, or other hazardous gases; or evolves enough heat to cause self-ignition or ignition of nearby combustibles upon exposure to water or moisture.

3.3.62 **Material Safety Data Sheet (MSDS).** The document that describes composition of a material, hazardous properties and hazard mitigation, and disposal information prepared in accordance with the Occupational Safety and Health Administration (OSHA) hazard communication standard (29 CFR, 1910.1200, "Hazard Communication").

3.3.63* **Maximum Allowable Quantity Per Control Area (MAQ).** A threshold quantity of hazardous material in a specific hazard class that once exceeded, requires the application of additional administrative procedures, construction features, or engineering controls.

3.3.64 **Mechanical Code (Gas).** The mechanical or mechanical construction code adopted by the jurisdiction. [55, 2013]

3.3.65* **Mobile Supply Unit (Gas).** Any supply source that is equipped with wheels so it is able to be moved around. [55, 2013]

3.3.66* **Nesting (Gas).** A method of securing cylinders upright in a tight mass using a contiguous three-point contact system whereby all cylinders in a group have a minimum of three contact points with other cylinders or a solid support structure (e.g., a wall or railing). [55, 2013]

3.3.67* **Normal Temperature and Pressure (NTP) (Gas).** A temperature of 21°C (70°F) at an absolute pressure of 101.325 kPa (14.7 psia). [55, 2013]

3.3.68 **Occupancy.** The purpose for which a building or other structure, or part thereof, is used or intended to be used. [ASCE/SEI 7:1.2]

3.3.68.1* *Assembly Occupancy.* An occupancy (1) used for a gathering of 50 or more persons for deliberation, worship, entertainment, eating, drinking, amusement, awaiting transportation, or similar uses: or (2) used as a special amusement building, regardless of occupant load. [101, 2012]

3.3.68.1.1 *Multipurpose Assembly Occupancy.* An assembly room designed to accommodate temporarily any of several possible assembly uses. [5000, 2012]

3.3.68.2* *Business Occupancy.* An occupancy used for the transaction of business other than mercantile. [5000, 2012]

3.3.68.3* *Day-Care Occupancy.* An occupancy in which four or more clients receive care, maintenance, and supervision, by other than their relatives or legal guardians, for less than 24 hours per day. [5000, 2012]

3.3.68.4* *Detention and Correctional Occupancy.* An occupancy used to house one or more persons under varied degrees of restraint or security where such occupants are mostly incapable of self-preservation because of security measures not under the occupants' control. [5000, 2012]

3.3.68.5* *Educational Occupancy.* An occupancy used for educational purposes through the twelfth grade by six or more persons for 4 or more hours per day or more than 12 hours per week. [5000, 2012]

3.3.68.6* *Health Care Occupancy.* An occupancy used for purposes of medical or other treatment or care of four or more persons where such occupants are mostly incapable of self-preservation due to age, physical or mental disability, or because of security measures not under the occupants' control. [5000, 2012]

3.3.68.6.1* *Ambulatory Health Care Occupancy.* An occupancy used to provide services or treatment simultaneously to four or more patients that provides, on an outpatient basis, one or more of the following: (1) treatment for patients that renders the patients incapable of taking action for self-preservation under emergency conditions without the assistance of others; (2) anesthesia that renders the patients incapable of taking action for self-preservation under emergency conditions without the assistance of others; (3) emergency or urgent care for patients who, due to the nature of their injury or illness, are incapable of taking action for self-preservation under emergency conditions without the assistance of others. [*101*, 2012]

3.3.68.7* *Industrial Occupancy.* An occupancy in which products are manufactured or in which processing, assembling, mixing, packaging, finishing, decorating, or repair operations are conducted. [5000, 2012]

3.3.68.7.1* *General Industrial Occupancy.* An industrial occupancy in which ordinary and low hazard industrial operations are conducted in buildings of conventional design suitable for various types of industrial processes. [5000, 2012]

3.3.68.7.2 *Special-Purpose Industrial Occupancy.* An industrial occupancy in which ordinary and low hazard industrial operations are conducted in buildings designed for, and suitable only for, particular types of operations, characterized by a relatively low density of employee population, with much of the area occupied by machinery or equipment. [5000, 2012]

3.3.68.8* *Mercantile Occupancy.* An occupancy used for the display and sale of merchandise. [5000, 2012]

3.3.68.9 *Mixed Occupancy.* A multiple occupancy where the occupancies are intermingled. [5000, 2012]

3.3.68.10* *Multiple Occupancy.* A building or structure in which two or more classes of occupancy exist. [5000, 2012]

3.3.68.11* *Residential Board and Care Occupancy.* An occupancy used for lodging and boarding of four or more residents, not related by blood or marriage to the owners or operators, for the purpose of providing personal care services. [5000, 2012]

3.3.68.12* *Residential Occupancy.* An occupancy that provides sleeping accommodations for purposes other than health care or detention and correctional. [5000, 2012]

3.3.68.13 *Separated Occupancy.* A multiple occupancy where the occupancies are separated by fire resistance–rated assemblies. [5000, 2012]

3.3.68.14* *Storage Occupancy.* An occupancy used primarily for the storage or sheltering of goods, merchandise, products, or vehicles. [5000, 2012]

3.3.69 Organic Peroxide. Any organic compound having a double oxygen or peroxy (-O-O-) group in its chemical structure.

3.3.70* Organic Peroxide Formulation. A pure or technically pure organic peroxide or a mixture of organic peroxides alone or in combination with one or more materials in various combinations and concentrations.

3.3.70.1 *Class I.* Class I shall describe those formulations that are more severe than a Class II but do not detonate.

3.3.70.2 *Class II.* Class II shall describe those formulations that burn very rapidly and that present a severe reactivity hazard.

3.3.70.3 *Class III.* Class III shall describe those formulations that burn rapidly and that present a moderate reactivity hazard.

3.3.70.4 *Class IV.* Class IV shall describe those formulations that burn in the same manner as ordinary combustibles and that present a minimal reactivity hazard.

3.3.70.5 *Class V.* Class V shall describe those formulations that burn with less intensity than ordinary combustibles or do not sustain combustion and that present no reactivity hazard.

3.3.71 OSHA (Gas). The Occupational Safety and Health Administration of the U.S. Department of Labor. [55, 2013]

3.3.72* Oxidizer. Any solid or liquid material that readily yields oxygen or other oxidizing gas or that readily reacts to promote or initiate combustion of combustible materials and that can, under some circumstances, undergo a vigorous self-sustained decomposition due to contamination or heat exposure.

3.3.72.1 *Class 1.* An oxidizer that does not moderately increase the burning rate of combustible materials with which it comes into contact or a solid oxidizer classified as Class 1 when tested in accordance with the test protocol set forth in G.1.

3.3.72.2 *Class 2.* An oxidizer that causes a moderate increase in the burning rate of combustible materials with which it comes into contact or a solid oxidizer classified as Class 2 when tested in accordance with the test protocol set forth in G.1.

3.3.72.3 *Class 3.* An oxidizer that causes a severe increase in the burning rate of combustible materials with which it comes into contact or a solid oxidizer classified as Class 3 when tested in accordance with the test protocol set forth in G.1.

3.3.72.4 *Class 4.* An oxidizer that can undergo an explosive reaction due to contamination or exposure to thermal or physical shock and that causes a severe increase in the burning rate of combustible materials with which it comes into contact.

3.3.73 Person. Any individual, firm, copartnership, corporation, company, association, or joint-stock association, including any trustee, receiver, assignee, or personal representative thereof. [**1124**, 2013]

3.3.74 Pile. Material in a single contiguous storage area, including any material not properly separated by appropriate distance.

3.3.75* Protection Level. A term used to describe a tier of building safety that exceeds the construction requirements for control areas to accommodate quantities of hazardous materials in excess of those permitted using the control area concept. *(See Section 5.3.)*

3.3.76 Remotely Located, Manually Activated Shutdown Control (Gas). A control system that is designed to initiate shutdown of the flow of gas or liquid that is manually activated from a point located some distance from the delivery system. [55, 2013]

3.3.77* Secondary Containment. That level of containment that is external to and separate from primary containment.

3.3.78 Spill Control. A method for the control of a hazardous materials spill.

3.3.79 Standard Cubic Foot of Gas (Gas). An amount of gas that occupies one cubic foot at an absolute pressure of 14.7 psia (101 kPa) and a temperature of 70°F (21°C). [55, 2013]

3.3.80 Storage, Compressed Gases or Cryogenic Fluids (Gas). An inventory of compressed gases or cryogenic fluids in containers that are not in the process of being examined, serviced, refilled, loaded, or unloaded.

3.3.80.1 *Bulk Solid Storage.* The storage of more than 6000 lb (2722 kg) in a single container.

3.3.80.2 *Detached Storage.* Storage in a separate building or in an outside area located away from all structures. [1, 2012]

3.3.80.2.1 *Detached Building.* A separate single-story building, without a basement or crawl space, used for the storage or use of hazardous materials and located an approved distance from all other structures.

3.3.80.2.2 *Detached Storage (Oxidizers).* Storage in either an open outside area or in a separate building containing no incompatible materials and located away from all other structures.

3.3.80.3 *Segregated Storage.* Storage in the same room or inside area but physically separated by distance, noncombustible partitions, cabinets, or enclosures from incompatible materials.

3.3.81* Storage (Hazardous Material). Hazardous material in the act of being stored as a supply reserved for future use or disposal including, but not limited to, any of the following: (1) hazardous material packaged in individual containers, without active connections, that can be handled, stacked, arranged or transported on site; (2) unconnected mobile equipment or over-the-road transport vehicles containing hazardous materials awaiting transportation; (3) mobile equipment including over-the-road transport vehicles containing hazardous materials when connected and serving as a source of supply; (4) stationary tanks containing hazardous materials, including tanks connected and serving as a source of supply.

3.3.82 Storage Height. The height from the finished floor to the top of the highest container or a pile's peak.

3.3.83* Tank.

3.3.83.1 *Container Tank.* Any vessel of 119 gal (450 L), 1000 lb (454 kg) or less water capacity used for transporting or storing hazardous chemicals.

3.3.83.2* *Portable Tank.* A container designed primarily to be loaded into or on or temporarily attached to a transport vehicle or ship and equipped with skids, mountings, or accessories to facilitate handling of the tank by mechanical means and not intended for fixed installation.

3.3.83.3* *Stationary Tank.* A vessel used for storing hazardous materials designed for stationary installations not intended for loading, unloading, or attachment to a transport vehicle or ship as part of its normal operation in the process of use.

3.3.84 Treatment System (Gas). An assembly of equipment capable of processing a hazardous gas or vapor and reducing the gas concentration to a predetermined level at the point of discharge from the system to the atmosphere.

3.3.85 TC (Gas). Transport Canada. [55, 2013]

3.3.86* Tube Trailer (Gas). A truck or semitrailer on which a number of very long compressed gas tubular cylinders have been mounted and manifolded into a common piping system. [55, 2013]

3.3.87* Use. To place a material, including solids, liquids, and gases, into action.

3.3.87.1* *Closed System Use.* Use of a solid or liquid hazardous material in a closed vessel or system that remains closed during normal operations where vapors emitted by the product are not liberated outside of the vessel or system and the product is not exposed to the atmosphere during normal operations and all uses of compressed gases.

3.3.87.2* *Open System Use.* Use of a solid or liquid hazardous material in a vessel or system that is continuously open to the atmosphere during normal operations and where vapors are liberated or the product is exposed to the atmosphere during normal operations.

3.3.88 Valve Outlet Cap or Plug (Gas). A removable device that forms a gastight seal on the outlet to the control valve that is provided on a source containing a compressed gas or cryogenic fluid. [55, 2013]

3.3.89 Valve Protection Cap (Gas). A rigid, removable cover provided for container valve protection during handling, transportation, and storage. [55, 2013]

3.3.90 Valve Protection Device (Gas). A device attached to the neck ring or body of a cylinder for the purpose of protecting the cylinder valve from being struck or from being damaged by the impact resulting from a fall or an object striking the cylinder. [1, 2012]

3.3.91 Waste. Hazardous materials that have been determined by the user to be beyond their useful life and that are awaiting disposal or processing by either public or private means.

3.4 Special Performance-Based Definitions.

3.4.1 Alternative Calculation Procedure. A calculation procedure that differs from the procedure originally employed by the design team but that provides predictions for the same variables of interest. [*101*, 2012]

3.4.2 Analysis.

3.4.2.1 *Sensitivity Analysis.* An analysis performed to determine the degree to which a predicted output will vary given a specified change in an input parameter, usually in relation to models. [5000, 2012]

3.4.2.2 *Uncertainty Analysis.* An analysis performed to determine the degree to which a predicted value will vary. [5000, 2012]

3.4.3 Data Conversion. The process of developing the input data set for the assessment method of choice. [*101*, 2012]

3.4.4 Design Fire Scenario. See 3.4.9.1.

3.4.5 Design Specification. See 3.4.19.1.

3.4.6 Design Team. A group of stakeholders including, but not limited to, representatives of the architect, client, and any pertinent engineers and other designers. [*101*, 2012]

3.4.7* Exposure Fire. A fire that starts at a location that is remote from the area being protected and grows to expose that which is being protected. [*101*, 2012]

3.4.8* Fire Model. A structured approach to predicting one or more effects of a fire. [*101*, 2012]

3.4.9* Fire Scenario. A set of conditions that defines the development of fire, the spread of combustion products throughout a building or portion of a building, the reactions of people to fire, and the effects of combustion products. [*101*, 2012]

3.4.9.1 *Design Fire Scenario.* A fire scenario selected for evaluation of a proposed design. [*914*, 2007]

3.4.10* Fuel Load. The total quantity of combustible contents of a building, space, or fire area. [*5000*, 2012]

3.4.11 Input Data Specification. See 3.4.19.2.

3.4.12 Occupant Characteristics. The abilities or behaviors of people before and during a fire. [*101*, 2012]

3.4.13* Performance Criteria. Threshold values on measurement scales that are based on quantified performance objectives. [*101*, 2012]

3.4.14* Proposed Design. A design developed by a design team and submitted to the authority having jurisdiction for approval. [*101*, 2012]

3.4.15 Safe Location. A location remote or separated from the effects of a fire so that such effects no longer pose a threat. [*101*, 2012]

3.4.16 Safety Factor. A factor applied to a predicted value to ensure that a sufficient safety margin is maintained. [*101*, 2012]

3.4.17 Safety Margin. The difference between a predicted value and the actual value where a fault condition is expected. [*101*, 2012]

3.4.18 Sensitivity Analysis. See 3.4.2.1.

3.4.19 Specification.

3.4.19.1 *Design Specification.* A building characteristic and other conditions that are under the control of the design team. [*5000*, 2012]

3.4.19.2 *Input Data Specification.* Information required by the verification method. [*101*, 2012]

3.4.20 Stakeholder. An individual, or representative of same, having an interest in the successful completion of a project. [*101*, 2012]

3.4.21 Uncertainty Analysis. See 3.4.2.2.

3.4.22 Verification Method. A procedure or process used to demonstrate or confirm that the proposed design meets the specified criteria. [*101*, 2012]

Chapter 4 Classification of Materials, Wastes, and Hazard of Contents

4.1* Hazardous Material Classification. Materials shall be classified into one or more of the following categories of hazardous materials, based on the definitions found in Chapter 3:

(1) Corrosive solids, liquids, or gases
(2) Flammable solids
(3) Flammable gases
(4) Flammable cryogenic fluids
(5) Inert cryogenic fluids
(6) Inert gases
(7) Organic peroxide formulations
(8) Oxidizer solids or liquids
(9) Oxidizing gases
(10) Oxidizing cryogenic fluids
(11) Pyrophoric solids, liquids, or gases
(12) Toxic or highly toxic solids, liquids, or gases
(13) Unstable (reactive) solids, liquids, or gases
(14) Water-reactive solids or liquids

4.2 Classification of High Hazard Contents.

4.2.1 General.

4.2.1.1 High hazard contents shall include materials defined as hazardous material in Chapter 3, whether stored, used, or handled.

4.2.1.2 High hazard contents shall include those materials defined as hazardous material solids, liquids, or gases limited to the hazard categories specified in 1.1.1 and classified in accordance with 4.2.1.2.1 through 4.2.1.2.4 whether stored, used, or handled.

4.2.1.2.1 High Hazard Level 1 Contents. High hazard Level 1 contents shall include materials that present a detonation hazard, including, but not limited to, the following hazard categories:

(1) Class 4 oxidizers
(2) Detonable pyrophoric solids or liquids
(3) Class 3 detonable and Class 4 unstable (reactive) solids, liquids, or gases
(4) Detonable organic peroxides

4.2.1.2.2 High Hazard Level 2 Contents. High hazard Level 2 contents shall include materials that present a deflagration hazard or a hazard from accelerated burning limited to the following hazard categories:

(1) Combustible dusts stored, used, or generated in a manner creating a severe fire or explosion hazard
(2) Class I organic peroxides
(3) Class 3 solid or liquid oxidizers that are used or stored in normally open containers or systems or in closed containers or systems at gauge pressures of more than 15 psi (103.4 kPa)
(4) Flammable gases
(5) Flammable cryogenic fluids
(6) Nondetonable pyrophoric solids, liquids, or gases
(7) Class 3 nondetonable unstable (reactive) solids, liquids, or gases
(8) Class 3 water-reactive solids and liquids

4.2.1.2.3 High Hazard Level 3 Contents. High hazard Level 3 contents shall include materials that readily support combustion or present a physical hazard limited to the following hazard categories:

(1) Flammable solids, other than dusts classified as high hazard Level 2, stored, used, or generated in a manner creating a high fire hazard
(2) Class II and Class III organic peroxides
(3) Class 2 solid or liquid oxidizers

(4) Class 3 solid or liquid oxidizers that are used or stored in normally closed containers or systems at gauge pressures of less than 15 psi (103.4 kPa)
(5) Class 2 unstable (reactive) materials
(6) Class 2 water-reactive solids, liquids or gases
(7) Oxidizing gases
(8) Oxidizing cryogenic fluids

4.2.1.2.4 High Hazard Level 4 Contents. High hazard Level 4 contents shall include materials that are acute health hazards limited to the following hazard categories:

(1) Corrosive solids, liquids, or gases
(2) Highly toxic solids, liquids, or gases
(3) Toxic solids, liquids, or gases

4.3 Mixtures. Mixtures shall be classified in accordance with the hazards of the mixture as a whole by an approved, qualified organization, individual, or testing laboratory.

4.4* Multiple Hazards. Hazardous materials that have multiple hazards shall conform to the code requirements for each applicable hazard category.

4.5* Classification of Waste. Waste comprised of or containing hazardous materials shall be classified in accordance with Sections 4.1 through 4.4 as applicable.

4.5.1* Waste classified in accordance with Sections 4.1 through 4.4 shall comply with the requirements of Chapters 1 through 9 and the material-specific requirements of Chapters 11 through 21 as applicable.

Chapter 5 Permissible Storage and Use Locations

5.1* General.

5.1.1 Control Areas or Special Protection Required. Hazardous materials shall be stored and used in any of the following:

(1) In control areas complying with Section 5.2
(2) In occupancies complying with requirements for protection level 1, protection level 2, protection level 3, or protection level 4 in accordance with Section 5.3
(3) In outdoor areas complying with Section 5.4

5.1.2 Weather Protection Structures. Weather protection, when provided, shall comply with 6.2.7.2.

5.1.3 High Hazard Contents. Occupancies in which high hazard contents are stored, used, or handled shall also comply with Chapter 6.

5.2 Control Areas.

5.2.1 Hazardous materials shall be permitted to be stored and used in control areas in accordance with 5.2.1 and 5.2.2.

5.2.1.1 General.

5.2.1.1.1 All occupancies shall be permitted to have one or more control areas in accordance with Section 5.2.

5.2.1.1.2 The quantity of hazardous materials in an individual control area shall not exceed the MAQ for the applicable occupancy set forth in 5.2.1.2 through 5.2.1.13, except as modified by Table 5.2.1.1.3.

5.2.1.1.3 For all occupancies not covered by 5.2.1.2 through 5.2.1.13, the MAQ of hazardous materials per control area shall be as specified in Table 5.2.1.1.3.

5.2.1.2 Assembly Occupancies. The MAQ of hazardous materials per control area in assembly occupancies shall be as specified in Table 5.2.1.2.

5.2.1.3 Educational Occupancies. The MAQ of hazardous materials per control area in educational occupancies shall be as specified in Table 5.2.1.3.

5.2.1.4 Day-Care Occupancies. The MAQ of hazardous materials per control area in day-care occupancies shall be as specified in Table 5.2.1.4.

5.2.1.5 Health Care Occupancies. The MAQ of hazardous materials per control area in health care occupancies shall be as specified in Table 5.2.1.5.

5.2.1.6 Ambulatory Health Care Occupancies. The MAQ of hazardous materials per control area in ambulatory health care occupancies shall be as specified in Table 5.2.1.6.

5.2.1.7 Detention and Correctional Occupancies. The MAQ of hazardous materials per control area in detention and correctional occupancies shall be as specified in Table 5.2.1.7.

5.2.1.8 Residential Occupancies. The MAQ of hazardous materials per control area in residential occupancies, including lodging and rooming houses, hotels, dormitories, apartments, and residential board and care facilities, shall be as specified in Table 5.2.1.8.

5.2.1.9 Mercantile Occupancies. The MAQ of hazardous materials per control area in mercantile occupancies shall be as specified in Table 5.2.1.1.3, with increased quantities permitted where storage or display areas comply with 5.2.1.13.

5.2.1.10 Business Occupancies.

5.2.1.10.1 The MAQ of hazardous materials per control area in business occupancies, other than laboratories, shall be as specified in Table 5.2.1.10.1.

5.2.1.10.2 The MAQ of hazardous materials per control area in laboratories classified as business occupancies shall be as specified in Table 5.2.1.1.3.

5.2.1.11 Industrial Occupancies. The MAQ of hazardous materials per control area in industrial occupancies shall be as specified in Table 5.2.1.1.3, with increased quantities permitted where storage areas comply with 5.2.1.13.

5.2.1.12 Storage Occupancies. The MAQ of hazardous materials per control area in storage occupancies shall be as specified in Table 5.2.1.1.3, with increased quantities permitted where storage areas comply with 5.2.1.13.

Table 5.2.1.1.3 Maximum Allowable Quantity (MAQ) of Hazardous Materials per Control Area[a]

Material	Class	High Hazard Protection Level	Storage Solid Pounds	Storage Liquid Gallons (lb)	Storage Gas[b] scf (lb)	Use — Closed Systems Solid Pounds	Use — Closed Systems Liquid Gallons (lb)	Use — Closed Systems Gas[b] scf (lb)	Use — Open Systems Solid Pounds	Use — Open Systems Liquid Gallons (lb)
Physical Hazard Materials										
Combustible liquid	See note	See note	See note	See note	See note	See note	See note	See note	See note	See note
Consumer fireworks	See note	See note	See note	See note	See note	See note	See note	See note	See note	See note
Combustible metals	See note	See note	See note	See note	See note	See note	See note	See note	See note	See note
Cryogenic fluid [55: Table 6.3.1]	Flammable	2	N/A	45[j,k]	N/A	N/A	45[j,k]	N/A	N/A	45[j,k]
	Oxidizing	3	N/A	45[c,d]	N/A	N/A	45[c,d]	N/A	N/A	45[c,d]
	Inert	N/A	N/A	NL	N/A	N/A	NL	N/A	N/A	NL
Explosives	See note	See note	See note	See note	See note	See note	See note	See note	See note	
Flammable gas[l] [55: Table 6.3.1]	Gaseous	2	N/A	N/A	1000[c,d]	N/A	N/A	1000[c,d]	N/A	N/A
	Liquefied	2	N/A	N/A	(150)[c,d]	N/A	N/A	(150)[c,d]	N/A	N/A
	Liquefied Petroleum (LP)	See note	See note	See note	See note	See note	See note	See note	See note	See note
Flammable liquid	IA	See note	See note	See note	See note	See note	See note	See note	See note	See note
	IB and IC	See note	See note	See note	See note	See note	See note	See note	See note	See note
	Combination (IA, IB, IC)	See note	See note	See note	See note	See note	See note	See note	See note	See note
Flammable solid	N/A	3	125[c,d]	N/A	N/A	125[c,d]	N/A	N/A	25[c,d]	N/A
Inert Gas	Gaseous	N/A	N/A	N/A	NL	N/A	N/A	NL	N/A	N/A
	Liquefied	N/A	N/A	N/A	NL	N/A	N/A	NL	N/A	N/A
Organic peroxide	UD	1	1[c,i]	(1)[c,i]	N/A	1/4[i]	(1/4)[i]	N/A	1/4[i]	(1/4)[i]
	I	1	5[c,d]	(5)[c,d]	N/A	1[c,d]	(1)[c,d]	N/A	1[c,d]	(1)[c,d]
	II	2	50[c,d]	(50)[c,d]	N/A	50[d]	(50)[d]	N/A	10[c,d]	(10)[c,d]
	III	3	125[c,d]	(125)[c,d]	N/A	125[d]	(125)[d]	N/A	25[c,d]	(25)[c,d]
	IV	N/A	NL	NL	N/A	NL	NL	N/A	NL	NL
	V	N/A	NL	NL	N/A	NL	NL	N/A	NL	NL
Oxidizer	4	1	1[c,i]	(1)[c,i]	N/A	1/4[i]	(1/4)[i]	N/A	1/4[i]	(1/4)[i]
	3[f]	2 or 3	10[c,d]	(10)[c,d]	N/A	2[d]	(2)[d]	N/A	2[d]	(2)[d]
	2	3	250[c,d]	(250)[c,d]	N/A	250[d]	(250)[d]	N/A	50[d]	(50)[d]
	1	N/A	4000[c,e]	(4000)[c,e]	N/A	4000[e]	(4000)[e]	N/A	1000[e]	(1000)[e]
Oxidizing gas [55: Table 6.3.1]	Gaseous	3	N/A	N/A	1500[c,d]	N/A	N/A	1500[c,d]	N/A	N/A
	Liquefied	3	N/A	N/A	(150)[c,d]	N/A	N/A	(150)[c,d]	N/A	N/A
Pyrophoric	N/A	2	4[c,i]	(4)[c,i]	N/A	1[i]	(1)[i]	N/A	NP	NP
Pyrophoric Gas [55: Table 6.3.1]	Gaseous	2	N/A	N/A	50[c,i]	N/A	N/A	50[c,i]	N/A	N/A
	Liquefied	2	N/A	N/A	(4)[c,i]	N/A	N/A	(4)[c,i]	N/A	N/A
Unstable (reactive) Gas [55: Table 6.3.1]	4	1	1[c,i]	(1)[c,i]	N/A	1/4[i]	(1/4)[i]	N/A	1/4[i]	(1/4)[i]
	3	1 or 2	5[c,d]	(5)[c,d]	N/A	1[d]	(1)[d]	N/A	1[d]	(1)[d]
	2	2	50[c,d]	(50)[c,d]	N/A	50[d]	(50)[d]	N/A	10[d]	(10)[d]
	1	N/A	NL	NL	N/A	NL	NL	N/A	NL	NL
Unstable (reactive) Gas	Liquefied 4 or 3 detonable	1	N/A	N/A	(1)[c,i]	N/A	N/A	(1)[c,i]	N/A	N/A
	3 non-detonable	2	N/A	N/A	(2)[c,d]	N/A	N/A	(2)[c,d]	N/A	N/A
	2	3	N/A	N/A	(150)[c,d]	N/A	N/A	(150)[c,d]	N/A	N/A
	1	N/A	N/A	N/A	NL	N/A	N/A	NL	N/A	N/A
Water-reactive	3	2	5[c,d]	(5)[c,d]	N/A	5[d]	(5)[d]	N/A	1[d]	(1)[d]
	2	3	50[c,d]	(50)[c,d]	N/A	50[d]	(50)[d]	N/A	10[d]	(10)[d]
	1	N/A	NL	NL	N/A	NL	NL	N/A	NL	NL

Table 5.2.1.1.3 *Continued*

Material	Class	High Hazard Protection Level	Storage Solid Pounds	Storage Liquid Gallons (lb)	Storage Gas[b] scf (lb)	Use — Closed Systems Solid Pounds	Use — Closed Systems Liquid Gallons (lb)	Use — Closed Systems Gas[b] scf (lb)	Use — Open Systems Solid Pounds	Use — Open Systems Liquid Gallons (lb)
Health Hazard Materials										
Corrosive	N/A	4	5000[c,d]	500[c,d]	N/A	5000[d]	500[d]	N/A	1000[d]	100[d]
Corrosive Gas [55: Table 6.3.1]	Gaseous	4	N/A	N/A	810[c,d,g]	N/A	N/A	810[c,d,g]	N/A	N/A
	Liquefied	4	N/A	N/A	(150)[c,d]	N/A	N/A	(150)[c,d]	N/A	N/A
Highly toxic	N/A	4	10[c,d]	(10)[c,d]	N/A	(10)[d]	(10)[d]	N/A	3[d]	(3)[d]
Highly toxic gas [55: Table 6.3.1]	Gaseous	4	N/A	N/A	20[d,g]	N/A	N/A	20[d,g]	N/A	N/A
	Liquefied	4	N/A	N/A	(5)[d,g]	N/A	N/A	(5)[d,g]	N/A	N/A
Toxic	N/A	4	500[c,d]	(500)[c,d]	N/A	500[d]	(500)[d]	N/A	125[d]	(125)[d]
Toxic gas	Gaseous	4	N/A	N/A	810[c,d]	N/A	N/A	810[c,d]	N/A	N/A
	Liquefied	4	N/A	N/A	(150)[c,d]	N/A	N/A	(150)[c,d]	N/A	N/A

UD: Unclassified detonable For SI units, 1 lb = 0.454 kg; 1 gal = 3.785 L; 1 scf = 0.0283 Nm^3.
N/A: Not applicable. NL: Not limited. NP: Not permitted.
Note: The hazardous material categories and MAQs that are shaded in this table are not regulated by NFPA 400 but are provided here for informational purposes. See Chapter 2 for the reference code or standard governing these materials and establishing the MAQs. In accordance with 1.1.1.2, materials having multiple hazards that fall within the scope of NFPA 400 shall comply with NFPA 400.
[a]Table values in parentheses correspond to the unit name in parentheses at the top of the column. The aggregate quantity in use and storage is not permitted to exceed the quantity listed for storage.
[b]Measured at NTP or 70°F (21°C) and 14.7 psia (101.3 kPa).
[c]Quantities are permitted to be increased 100 percent where stored or used in approved cabinets, gas cabinets, exhausted enclosures, gas rooms explosives magazines, or safety cans, as appropriate for the material stored, in accordance with this code. Where footnote d also applies, the increase for both footnote c and footnote d is permitted to be applied accumulatively.
[d]Maximum quantities are permitted to be increased 100 percent in buildings equipped throughout with an automatic sprinkler system in accordance with NFPA 13, *Standard for the Installation of Sprinkler Systems*. Where footnote c also applies, the increase for both footnote c and footnote d is permitted to be applied accumulatively.
[e]The permitted quantities are not limited in a building equipped throughout with an automatic sprinkler system in accordance with NFPA 13.
[f]A maximum quantity of 200 lb (91 kg) of solid or 20 gal (76 L) of liquid Class 3 oxidizer is permitted where such materials are necessary for maintenance purposes, operation, or sanitation of equipment. Storage containers and the manner of storage are required to be approved.
[g]Allowed only where stored or used in gas rooms or approved cabinets, exhausted gas cabinets or exhausted enclosures, as specified in this Code. [5000: Table 34.1.3.1]
[h]Conversion. Where quantities are indicated in pounds and when the weight per gallon of the liquid is not provided to the AHJ, a conversion factor of 10 lb/gal (1.2 kg/L) shall be used.
[i]Permitted only in buildings equipped throughout with an automatic sprinkler system in accordance with NFPA 13.
[j]None allowed in unsprinklered buildings unless stored or used in gas rooms or in approved gas cabinets or exhausted enclosures, as specified in this Code.
[k]With pressure-relief devices for stationary or portable containers vented directly outdoors or to an exhaust hood. [55: Table 6.3.1.1]
[l]Flammable gases in the fuel tanks of mobile equipment or vehicles are permitted to exceed the MAQ where the equipment is stored and operated in accordance with the fire code.

Table 5.2.1.2 Maximum Allowable Quantities (MAQ) of Hazardous Materials per Control Area in Assembly Occupancies

Material	Class	Solid Pounds	Liquid Gallons[k] (lb)	Gas[a] (at NTP) scf (lb)
Flammable and combustible liquid[b,c]	See note	See note	See note	See note
Cryogenic fluid	Flammable	N/A	10	N/A
	Oxidizing	N/A	10	N/A
Explosives[d,e,f,g]		See note	See note	See note	See note
Flammable gas[c,h]	Gaseous	N/A	N/A	NP
	Liquefied	N/A	N/A	(20)
	Liquefied Petroleum	N/A	N/A	(20)
Consumer fireworks		See note	See note	See note	See note
Flammable solid	N/A	5	N/A	N/A
Oxidizers	4	NP	NP	N/A
	3	10[i]	1 gal[i]	N/A
	2	250	25	N/A
	1	4,000	400	N/A
Oxidizing gas[h]	Gaseous	N/A	N/A	NP[h]
	Liquefied	N/A	N/A	NP[h]
Organic peroxides	I	NP	NP	N/A
	II	NP	NP	N/A
	III	25	(25)	N/A
	IV	NL	NL	N/A
	V	NL	NL	N/A
Pyrophoric materials	N/A	1	(1)	NP
Unstable reactives	4	¼	¼	NP
	3	1	1	NP
	2	10	10	NP[h]
	1	NL	NL	NP
Water-reactive	3	1	(1)	N/A
	2	10	(10)	N/A
	1	NL	NL	N/A
Corrosives	N/A	1,000	100	NP
Highly toxic	N/A	3	(3)	NP[j]
Toxic	N/A	125	(125)	NP[j]

For SI units, 1 lb = 0.454 kg; 1 gal = 3.785 L.
NTP: Normal temperature and pressure [measured at 70°F (21°C) and 14.7 psi (101 kPa)]. N/A: Not applicable. NP: Not permitted. NL: Not limited.
Note: The hazardous material categories and MAQs that are shaded in this table are not regulated by NFPA 400 but are provided here for informational purposes. See Chapter 2 for the reference code or standard governing these materials and establishing the MAQs. In accordance with 1.1.1.2, materials having multiple hazards that fall within the scope of NFPA 400 shall comply with NFPA 400.
[a] Unlimited amounts of gas are permitted to be used for personal medical or emergency medical use.
[b] Storage in excess of 10 gal (38 L) of Class I and Class II liquids combined or 60 gal (227 L) of Class IIIA liquids is permitted where stored in safety cabinets with an aggregate quantity not to exceed 180 gal (681 L).
[c] Fuel in the tank of operating mobile equipment is permitted to exceed the specified quantity where the equipment is operated in accordance with this code.
[d] The use of explosive materials required by federal, state, or municipal agencies while engaged in normal or emergency performance of duties is not required to be limited. The storage of explosive materials is required to be in accordance with the requirements of NFPA 495, *Explosive Materials Code*.
[e] The storage and use of explosive materials in medicines and medicinal agents in the forms prescribed by the official United States Pharmacopeia or the National Formulary are not required to be limited.
[f] The storage and use of propellant-actuated devices or propellant-actuated industrial tools manufactured, imported, or distributed for their intended purposes are required to be limited to 50 lb (23 kg) net explosive weight.
[g] The storage and use of small arms ammunition, and components thereof, are permitted where in accordance with NFPA 495, *Explosive Materials Code*.
[h] Containers, cylinders, or tanks not exceeding 250 scf³ (7.1 m³) content measured at 70°F (21°C) and 14.7 psi (101 kPa) and used for maintenance purposes, patient care, or operation of equipment shall be permitted.
[i] A maximum quantity of 200 lb (91 kg) of solid or 20 gal (76 L) of liquid Class 3 oxidizer is permitted where such materials are necessary for maintenance purposes, operation, or sanitation of equipment. Storage containers and the manner of storage are required to be approved.
[j] Gas cylinders not exceeding 20 scf³ (0.57 m³) measured at 70°F (21°C) and 14.7 psi (101 kPa) are permitted in gas cabinets or fume hoods. [**5000**: Table 34.1.3.2(a)]
[k] Conversion. Where quantities are indicated in pounds and when the weight per gallon of the liquid is not provided to the AHJ, a conversion factor of 10 lb/gal (1.2 kg/L) shall be used.

Table 5.2.1.3 Maximum Allowable Quantities (MAQ) of Hazardous Materials per Control Area in Educational Occupancies

Material	Class	Solid Pounds	Liquid Gallons[m] (lb)	Gas[a] (at NTP) scf (lb)
Flammable and combustible liquid[b,c]	See note	See note	See note	See note
Cryogenic fluid	Flammable	N/A	10	N/A
	Oxidizing	N/A	10	N/A
Explosives[d,e,f,g]	See note	See note	See note	See note
Flammable gas[c,h]	Gaseous	N/A	N/A	NP
	Liquefied	N/A	N/A	(20)
	Liquefied Petroleum	N/A	N/A	(20)
Consumer fireworks	See note	See note	See note	See note
Flammable solid	N/A	5	N/A	N/A
Oxidizers	4	NP	NP	N/A
	3	10[i]	1[i]	N/A
	2	250	25	N/A
	1	4,000	400	N/A
Oxidizing gas[h]	Gaseous	N/A	N/A	NP
	Liquefied	N/A	N/A	NP[h]
Organic peroxides	I	NP	NP	N/A
	II	NP	NP	N/A
	III	25	(25)	N/A
	IV	NL	NL	N/A
	V	NL	NL	N/A
Pyrophoric materials	N/A	1	(1)	NP
Unstable reactives	4	¼	¼	NP
	3	1	1	NP
	2	10	10	NP[h]
	1	NL	NL	NP
Water-reactive	3	1	(1)	N/A
	2	10	(10)	N/A
	1	NL	NL	N/A
Corrosives	N/A	1,000	100	NP
Highly toxic	N/A	3	(3)	NP[j]
Toxic	N/A	125	(125)	NP[j]

For SI units, 1 lb = 0.454 kg; 1 gal = 3.785 L; 1 ft³ = 0.0283 m³.
NTP: Normal temperature and pressure [measured at 70°F (21°C) and 14.7 psi (101 kPa)]. N/A: Not applicable. NP: Not permitted. NL: Not limited.
Note: The hazardous material categories and MAQs that are shaded in this table are not regulated by NFPA 400 but are provided here for informational purposes. See Chapter 2 for the reference code or standard governing these materials and establishing the MAQs. In accordance with 1.1.1.2, materials having multiple hazards that fall within the scope of NFPA 400 shall comply with NFPA 400.
[a]Unlimited amounts of gas are permitted to be used for personal medical or emergency medical use.
[b]Storage in excess of 10 gal (38 L) of Class I and Class II liquids combined or 60 gal (227 L) of Class IIIA liquids is permitted where stored in safety cabinets with an aggregate quantity not to exceed 180 gal (681 L).
[c]Fuel in the tank of operating mobile equipment is permitted to exceed the specified quantity where the equipment is operated in accordance with this code.
[d]The use of explosive materials required by federal, state, or municipal agencies while engaged in normal or emergency performance of duties is not required to be limited. The storage of explosive materials is required to be in accordance with the requirements of NFPA 495, *Explosive Materials Code*.
[e]The storage and use of explosive materials in medicines and medicinal agents in the forms prescribed by the official United States Pharmacopeia or the National Formulary are not required to be limited.
[f]The storage and use of propellant-actuated devices or propellant-actuated industrial tools manufactured, imported, or distributed for their intended purposes are required to be limited to 50 lb (23 kg) net explosive weight.
[g]The storage and use of small arms ammunition, and components thereof, are permitted where in accordance with NFPA 495, *Explosive Materials Code*.
[h]Containers, cylinders, or tanks not exceeding 250 scf (7.1 m³) content measured at 70°F (21°C) and 14.7 psi (101 kPa) and used for maintenance purposes, patient care, or operation of equipment shall be permitted.
[i]A maximum quantity of 200 lb (91 kg) of solid or 20 gal (76 L) of liquid Class 3 oxidizer is permitted where such materials are necessary for maintenance purposes, operation, or sanitation of equipment. Storage containers and the manner of storage are required to be approved.
[j]The permitted quantities are not limited in a building protected throughout by automatic sprinkler systems in accordance with NFPA 13, *Standard for the Installation of Sprinkler Systems*.
[k]Storage in laboratories only; additional 20 lb (9 kg) units are permitted where minimum 20 ft (6.1 m) separation is provided.
[l]Gas cylinders not exceeding 20 scf (0.57 m³) measured at 70°F (21°C) and 14.7 psi (101 kPa) are permitted in gas cabinets or fume hoods.
[m]Conversion. Where quantities are indicated in pounds and when the weight per gallon of the liquid is not provided to the AHJ, a conversion factor of 10 lb/gal (1.2 kg/L) shall be used.

Table 5.2.1.4 Maximum Allowable Quantities (MAQ) of Hazardous Materials per Control Area in Day-Care Occupancies

Material	Class	Solid Pounds	Liquid Gallons[k] (lb)	Gas[a] (at NTP) scf (lb)
Flammable and combustible liquid[b,c]	See note	See note	See note	See note
Cryogenic fluid	Flammable	N/A	10	N/A
	Oxidizing	N/A	10	N/A
Explosives[d,e,f,g]	See note	See note	See note	See note
Flammable gas[c,h]	Gaseous	N/A	N/A	N/A
	Liquefied	N/A	N/A	20
	Liquefied Petroleum	N/A	N/A	(20)
Consumer fireworks	See note	See note	See note	See note
Flammable solid	N/A	5 lb	N/A	N/A
Oxidizers	4	NP	NP	N/A
	3	10[i]	1[i]	N/A
	2	250	25	N/A
	1	4,000	400	N/A
Oxidizing gas[h]	Gaseous	N/A	N/A	NP[h]
	Liquefied	N/A	N/A	NP[h]
Organic peroxides	I	NP	NP	N/A
	II	NP	NP	N/A
	III	25	(25)	N/A
	IV	NL	NL	N/A
	V	NL	NL	N/A
Pyrophoric materials	N/A	1	(1)	NP
Unstable reactives	4	¼ lb	(¼) lb	NP
	3	1	(1)	NP
	2	10	(10)	NP[h]
	1	NL	NL	NP
Water-reactive	3	1	(1)	N/A
	2	10	(10)	N/A
	1	NL	NL	N/A
Corrosives	N/A	1,000	100	NP
Highly toxic	N/A	3	(3)	NP[j]
Toxic	N/A	125	(125)	NP[j]

For SI units, 1 lb = 0.454 kg; 1 gal = 3.785 L.
NTP: Normal temperature and pressure [measured at 70°F (21°C) and 14.7 psi (101 kPa)]. N/A: Not applicable. NP: Not permitted. NL: Not limited.
Note: The hazardous material categories and MAQs that are shaded in this table are not regulated by NFPA 400 but are provided here for informational purposes. See Chapter 2 for the reference code or standard governing these materials and establishing the MAQs. In accordance with 1.1.1.2, materials having multiple hazards that fall within the scope of NFPA 400 shall comply with NFPA 400.
[a]Unlimited amounts of gas are permitted to be used for personal medical or emergency medical use.
[b]Storage in excess of 10 gal (38 L) of Class I and Class II liquids combined or 60 gal (227 L) of Class IIIA liquids is permitted where stored in safety cabinets with an aggregate quantity not to exceed 180 gal (681 L).
[c]Fuel in the tank of operating mobile equipment is permitted to exceed the specified quantity where the equipment is operated in accordance with this code.
[d]The use of explosive materials required by federal, state, or municipal agencies while engaged in normal or emergency performance of duties is not required to be limited. The storage of explosive materials is required to be in accordance with the requirements of NFPA 495, *Explosive Materials Code*.
[e]The storage and use of explosive materials in medicines and medicinal agents in the forms prescribed by the official United States Pharmacopeia or the National Formulary are not required to be limited.
[f]The storage and use of propellant-actuated devices or propellant-actuated industrial tools manufactured, imported, or distributed for their intended purposes are required to be limited to 50 lb (23 kg) net explosive weight.
[g]Containers, cylinders, or tanks not exceeding 250 scf (7.1 m³) content measured at 70°F (21°C) and 14.7 psi (101 kPa) and used for maintenance purposes, patient care, or operation of equipment shall be permitted.
[h]The permitted quantities are not limited in a building protected throughout by automatic sprinkler systems in accordance with NFPA 13, *Standard for the Installation of Sprinkler Systems*.
[i]A maximum quantity of 200 lb (91 kg) of solid or 20 gal (76 L) of liquid Class 3 oxidizer is permitted where such materials are necessary for maintenance purposes, operation, or sanitation of equipment. Storage containers and the manner of storage are required to be approved.
[j]Gas cylinders not exceeding 20 scf (0.57 m³) measured at 70°F (21°C) and 14.7 psi (101 kPa) are permitted in gas cabinets or fume hoods.
[k]Conversion. Where quantities are indicated in pounds and when the weight per gallon of the liquid is not provided to the AHJ, a conversion factor of 10 lb/gal (1.2 kg/L) shall be used.

Table 5.2.1.5 Maximum Allowable Quantities (MAQ) of Hazardous Materials per Control Area in Health Care Occupancies

Material	Class	Solid Pounds	Liquid Gallons[k] (lb)	Gas[a] (at NTP) scf (lb)
Flammable and combustible liquid[b,c]	See note	See note	See note	
Cryogenic fluid	Flammable	N/A	10	N/A
	Oxidizing	N/A	10	N/A
Explosives[d,e,f]	See note	See note	See note	See note
Flammable gas[c,g]	Gaseous	N/A	N/A	NP
	Liquefied	N/A	N/A	(20)
	Liquefied Petroleum	N/A	N/A	(20)
Consumer fireworks	See note	See note	See note	See note
Flammable solid	N/A	5	N/A	N/A
Oxidizers	4	NP	NP	N/A
	3	10[h]	1[h]	N/A
	2	250	25	N/A
	1	4,000[i]	400[i]	N/A
Oxidizing gas[h]	Gaseous	N/A	N/A	NP[h]
	Liquefied	N/A	N/A	NP[h]
Organic peroxides	I	NP	NP	N/A
	II	NP	NP	N/A
	III	1,500	1,500	N/A
	IV	100,000	100,000	N/A
	V	NL	NL	N/A
Pyrophoric materials	N/A	NP	NP	NP
Unstable reactives	4	NP	NP	NP
	3	NP	NP	NP
	2	10	10	NP[g]
	1	NL	NL	NP
Water-reactive	3	1	1	N/A
	2	10	10	N/A
	1	NL	NL	N/A
Corrosives	N/A	1,000	100	NP
Highly toxic	N/A	3	3	NP[j]
Toxic	N/A	125	125	NP[j]

For SI units, 1 lb = 0.454 kg; 1 gal = 3.785 L.
NTP: Normal temperature and pressure [measured at 70°F (21°C) and 14.7 psi (101 kPa)]. N/A: Not applicable. NP: Not permitted. NL: Not limited.
Note: The hazardous material categories and MAQs that are shaded in this table are not regulated by NFPA 400 but are provided here for informational purposes. See Chapter 2 for the reference code or standard governing these materials and establishing the MAQs. In accordance with 1.1.1.2, materials having multiple hazards that fall within the scope of NFPA 400 shall comply with NFPA 400.
[a]Unlimited amounts of gas are permitted to be used for personal medical or emergency medical use.
[b]Storage in excess of 10 gal (38 L) of Class I and Class II liquids combined or 60 gal (227 L) of Class IIIA liquids is permitted where stored in safety cabinets with an aggregate quantity not to exceed 180 gal (681 L).
[c]Fuel in the tank of operating mobile equipment is permitted to exceed the specified quantity where the equipment is operated in accordance with this code.
[d]The use of explosive materials required by federal, state, or municipal agencies while engaged in normal or emergency performance of duties is not required to be limited. The storage of explosive materials is required to be in accordance with the requirements of NFPA 495, *Explosive Materials Code*.
[e]The storage and use of explosive materials in medicines and medicinal agents in the forms prescribed by the official United States Pharmacopeia or the National Formulary are not required to be limited.
[f]The storage and use of propellant-actuated devices or propellant-actuated industrial tools manufactured, imported, or distributed for their intended purposes are required to be limited to 50 lb (23 kg) net explosive weight.
[g]Containers, cylinders, or tanks not exceeding 250 scf (7.1 m³) content measured at 70°F (21°C) and 14.7 psi (101 kPa) and used for maintenance purposes, patient care, or operation of equipment shall be permitted.
[h]A maximum quantity of 200 lb (91 kg) of solid or 20 gal (76 L) of liquid Class 3 oxidizer is permitted where such materials are necessary for maintenance purposes, operation, or sanitation of equipment. Storage containers and the manner of storage are required to be approved.
[i]The permitted quantities are not limited in a building protected throughout by automatic sprinkler systems in accordance with NFPA 13, *Standard for the Installation of Sprinkler Systems*.
[j]Gas cylinders not exceeding 20 scf (0.57 m³) measured at 70°F (21°C) and 14.7 psi (101 kPa) are permitted in gas cabinets or fume hoods.
[k]Conversion. Where quantities are indicated in pounds and when the weight per gallon of the liquid is not provided to the AHJ, a conversion factor of 10 lb/gal (1.2 kg/L) shall be used.

Table 5.2.1.6 Maximum Allowable Quantities (MAQ) of Hazardous Materials per Control Area in Ambulatory Health Care Occupancies

Material	Class	Solid Pounds	Liquid Gallons[k] (lb)	Gas[a] (at NTP) scf (lb)
Flammable and combustible liquid[b,c]	See note	See note	See note	See note
Cryogenic fluid	Flammable	N/A	10	N/A
	Oxidizing	N/A	10	N/A
Explosives[d,e,f]	See note	See note	See note	See note
Flammable gas[c,g]	Gaseous	N/A	N/A	NP
	Liquefied	N/A	N/A	(20)
	Liquefied Petroleum	N/A	N/A	(20)
Consumer fireworks	See note	See note	See note	See note
Flammable solid	N/A	5	N/A	N/A
Oxidizers	4	NP	NP	NP
	3	10[h]	1[h]	NP
	2	250	25	NP
	1	4,000[i]	400[i]	NP
Oxidizing gas[h]	Gaseous	N/A	N/A	NP[h]
	Liquefied	N/A	N/A	NP[h]
Organic peroxides	I	NP	NP	N/A
	II	NP	NP	N/A
	III	25	(25)	N/A
	IV	NL	NL	N/A
	V	NL	NL	N/A
Pyrophoric materials	N/A	NP	NP	NP
Unstable reactives	4	NP	NP	NP
	3	NP	NP	NP
	2	10	10	NP[g]
	1	NL	NL	NP
Water-reactive	3	1	(1)	N/A
	2	10	10	N/A
	1	NL	NL	N/A
Corrosives	N/A	1,000	100	NP
Highly toxic	N/A	3	(3)	NP[j]
Toxic	N/A	125	(125)	NP[j]

For SI units, 1 lb = 0.454 kg; 1 gal = 3.785 L.
NTP: Normal temperature and pressure [70°F (21°C) and 14.7 psi (101 kPa)]. N/A: Not applicable. NP: Not permitted. NL: Not limited.
Note: The hazardous material categories and MAQs that are shaded in this table are not regulated by NFPA 400 but are provided here for informational purposes. See Chapter 2 for the reference code or standard governing these materials and establishing the MAQs. In accordance with 1.1.1.2, materials having multiple hazards that fall within the scope of NFPA 400 shall comply with NFPA 400.
[a]Unlimited amounts of gas are permitted to be used for personal medical or emergency medical use.
[b]Storage in excess of 10 gal (38 L) of Class I and Class II liquids combined or 60 gal (227 L) of Class IIIA liquids is permitted where stored in safety cabinets with an aggregate quantity not to exceed 180 gal (681 L).
[c]Fuel in the tank of operating mobile equipment is permitted to exceed the specified quantity where the equipment is operated in accordance with this code.
[d]The use of explosive materials required by federal, state, or municipal agencies while engaged in normal or emergency performance of duties is not required to be limited. The storage of explosive materials is required to be in accordance with the requirements of NFPA 495, *Explosive Materials Code*.
[e]The storage and use of explosive materials in medicines and medicinal agents in the forms prescribed by the official United States Pharmacopeia or the National Formulary are not required to be limited.
[f]The storage and use of propellant-actuated devices or propellant-actuated industrial tools manufactured, imported, or distributed for their intended purposes are required to be limited to 50 lb (23 kg) net explosive weight.
[g]Containers, cylinders, or tanks not exceeding 250 scf (7.1 m^3) content measured at 70°F (21°C) and 14.7 psi (101 kPa) and used for maintenance purposes, patient care, or operation of equipment shall be permitted.
[h]A maximum quantity of 200 lb (91 kg) of solid or 20 gal (76 L) of liquid Class 3 oxidizer is permitted where such materials are necessary for maintenance purposes, operation, or sanitation of equipment. Storage containers and the manner of storage are required to be approved.
[i]The permitted quantities are not limited in a building protected throughout by automatic sprinkler systems in accordance with NFPA 13, *Standard for the Installation of Sprinkler Systems*.
[j]Gas cylinders not exceeding 20 scf (0.57 m^3) measured at 70°F (21°C) and 14.7 psi (101 kPa) are permitted in gas cabinets or fume hoods.
[k]Conversion. Where quantities are indicated in pounds and when the weight per gallon of the liquid is not provided to the AHJ, a conversion factor of 10 lb/gal (1.2 kg/L) shall be used.

Table 5.2.1.7 Maximum Allowable Quantities (MAQ) of Hazardous Materials per Control Area in Detention and Correctional Occupancies[a]

Material	Class	Solid Pounds	Liquid Gallons[k] (lb)	Gas[a] (at NTP) scf (lb)
Flammable and combustible liquid[b,c]	See note	See note	See note	See note
Cryogenic fluid	Flammable	N/A	10	N/A
	Oxidizing	N/A	10	N/A
Explosives[d,e,f,g]	See note	See note	See note	See note
Flammable gas[c,h]	Gaseous	N/A	N/A	NP
	Liquefied	N/A	N/A	(20)
	Liquefied Petroleum	N/A	N/A	(20)
Consumer fireworks	See note	See note	See note	See note
Flammable solid	N/A	5	N/A	N/A
Oxidizers	4	NP	NP	N/A
	3	10[i]	1[i]	N/A
	2	250	25	N/A
	1	4,000	400	N/A
Oxidizing gas[h]	Gaseous	N/A	N/A	NP
	Liquefied	N/A	N/A	N/A
Organic peroxides	I	NP	NP	N/A
	II	NP	NP	N/A
	III	25	(25)	N/A
	IV	NL	NL	N/A
	V	NL	NL	N/A
Pyrophoric materials	NA	1	(1)	NP
Unstable reactives	4	1/4	(1/4)	NP
	3	1	(1)	NP
	2	10	10	NP[h]
	1	NL	NL	NP
Water-reactive	3	1	(1)	N/A
	2	10	(10)	N/A
	1	NL	NL	N/A
Corrosives	N/A	1,000	100	NP
Highly toxic	N/A	3	3	NP[j]
Toxic	N/A	125	125	NP[j]

For SI units, 1 lb = 0.454 kg; 1 gal = 3.785 L.
NTP: Normal temperature and pressure [measured at 70°F (21°C) and 14.7 psi (101 kPa)]. N/A: Not applicable. NP: Not permitted. NL: Not limited.
Note: The hazardous material categories and MAQs that are shaded in this table are not regulated by NFPA 400 but are provided here for informational purposes. See Chapter 2 for the reference code or standard governing these materials and establishing the MAQs. In accordance with 1.1.1.2, materials having multiple hazards that fall within the scope of NFPA 400 shall comply with NFPA 400.
[a]Unlimited amounts of gas are permitted to be used for personal medical or emergency medical use.
[b]Storage in excess of 10 gal (38 L) of Class I and Class II liquids combined or 60 gal (227 L) of Class IIIA liquids is permitted where stored in safety cabinets with an aggregate quantity not to exceed 180 gal (681 L).
[c]Fuel in the tank of operating mobile equipment is permitted to exceed the specified quantity where the equipment is operated in accordance with this code.
[d]The use of explosive materials required by federal, state, or municipal agencies while engaged in normal or emergency performance of duties is not required to be limited. The storage of explosive materials is required to be in accordance with the requirements of NFPA 495, *Explosive Materials Code*.
[e]The storage and use of explosive materials in medicines and medicinal agents in the forms prescribed by the official United States Pharmacopeia or the National Formulary are not required to be limited.
[f]The storage and use of propellant-actuated devices or propellant-actuated industrial tools manufactured, imported, or distributed for their intended purposes are required to be limited to 50 lb (23 kg) net explosive weight.
[g]The storage and use of small arms ammunition, and components thereof, are permitted where in accordance with NFPA 495, *Explosive Materials Code*.
[h]Containers, cylinders, or tanks not exceeding 250 scf (7.1 m³) content measured at 70°F (21°C) and 14.7 psi (101 kPa) and used for maintenance purposes, patient care, or operation of equipment shall be permitted.
[i]A maximum quantity of 200 lb (91 kg) of solid or 20 gal (76 L) of liquid Class 3 oxidizer is permitted where such materials are necessary for maintenance purposes, operation, or sanitation of equipment. Storage containers and the manner of storage are required to be approved.
[j]Gas cylinders not exceeding 20 scf (0.57 m³) measured at 70°F (21°C) and 14.7 psi (101 kPa) are permitted in gas cabinets or fume hoods.
[k]Conversion. Where quantities are indicated in pounds and when the weight per gallon of the liquid is not provided to the AHJ, a conversion factor of 10 lb/gal (1.2 kg/L) shall be used.

Table 5.2.1.8 Maximum Allowable Quantities of Hazardous Materials per Control Area in Residential Occupancies Consisting of Lodging and Rooming Houses, Hotels, Dormitories, Apartments, and Residential Board and Care Facilities

Material	Class	Solid Pounds	Liquid Gallons[1] (lb)	Gas[a] (at NTP) scf (lb)
Flammable and combustible liquid[b,c]	See note	See note	See note	See note
Cryogenic fluid	Flammable	N/A	10	N/A
	Oxidizing	N/A	10	N/A
Explosives[d,e,f,g]	See note	See note	See note	See note
Flammable gas[c,h]	Gaseous	N/A	N/A	NP
	Liquefied[j]	N/A	N/A	(20)
	Liquefied Petroleum	N/A	N/A	(20)
Consumer fireworks	See note	See note	See note	See note
Flammable solid	N/A	5	N/A	N/A
Oxidizers	4	NP	NP	N/A
	3	10[i]	1[i]	N/A
	2	250	25	N/A
	1	4,000	400	N/A
Oxidizing gas[h]	Gaseous	N/A	N/A	NP[h]
	Liquefied	N/A	NL	N/A
Organic peroxides	I	NP	NP	N/A
	II	NP	NP	N/A
	III	25	(25)	N/A
	IV	NL	NL	N/A
	V	NL	NL	N/A
Pyrophoric materials	N/A	1	(1)	NP
Unstable reactives	4	¼	(¼)	NP
	3	1	(1)	NP
	2	10	(10)	NP[h]
	1	NL	NL	NP
Water-reactive	3	1	(1)	N/A
	2	10	(10)	N/A
	1	NL	NL	N/A
Corrosives	N/A	1,000	100	NP
Highly toxic	N/A	3	(3)	NP[k]
Toxic	N/A	125	(125)	NP[k]

For SI units, 1 lb = 0.454 kg; 1 gal = 3.785 L.
NTP: Normal temperature and pressure [measured at 70°F (21°C) and 14.7 psi (101 kPa)]. N/A: Not applicable. NP: Not permitted. NL: Not limited.
Note: The hazardous material categories and MAQs that are shaded in this table are not regulated by NFPA 400 but are provided here for informational purposes. See Chapter 2 for the reference code or standard governing these materials and establishing the MAQs. In accordance with 1.1.1.2, materials having multiple hazards that fall within the scope of NFPA 400 shall comply with NFPA 400.

[a]Unlimited amounts of gas are permitted to be used for personal medical or emergency medical use.
[b]Storage in excess of 10 gal (38 L) of Class I and Class II liquids combined or 60 gal (227 L) of Class IIIA liquids are permitted where stored in safety cabinets with an aggregate quantity not to exceed 180 gal (681 L).
[c]Fuel in the tank of operating mobile equipment is permitted to exceed the specified quantity where the equipment is operated in accordance with this code.
[d]The use of explosive materials required by federal, state, or municipal agencies while engaged in normal or emergency performance of duties is not required to be limited. The storage of explosive materials is required to be in accordance with the requirements of NFPA 495, *Explosive Materials Code*.
[e]The storage and use of explosive materials in medicines and medicinal agents in the forms prescribed by the official United States Pharmacopeia or the National Formulary are not required to be limited.
[f]The storage and use of propellant-actuated devices or propellant-actuated industrial tools manufactured, imported, or distributed for their intended purposes are required to be limited to 50 lb (23 kg) net explosive weight.
[g]The storage and use of small arms ammunition, and components thereof, are permitted where in accordance with NFPA 495, *Explosive Materials Code*.
[h]Containers, cylinders, or tanks not exceeding 250 scf (7.1 m^3) content measured at 70°F (21°C) and 14.7 psi (101 kPa) and used for maintenance purposes, patient care, or operation of equipment shall be permitted.
[i]A maximum quantity of 200 lb (91 kg) of solid or 20 gal (76 L) of liquid Class 3 oxidizer is permitted where such materials are necessary for maintenance purposes, operation, or sanitation of equipment. Storage containers and the manner of storage are required to be approved.
[j]Storage containers are not permitted to exceed 0.325 ft^3 (0.0092 m^3) capacity.
[k]Gas cylinders not exceeding 20 scf (0.57 m^3) measured at 70°F (21°C) and 14.7 psi (101 kPa) are permitted in gas cabinets or fume hoods.
[l]Conversion. Where quantities are indicated in pounds and when the weight per gallon of the liquid is not provided to the AHJ, a conversion factor of 10 lb/gal (1.2 kg/L) shall be used.

Table 5.2.1.10.1 Maximum Allowable Quantities (MAQ) of Hazardous Materials per Control Area in Business Occupancies

Material	Class	Solid Pounds	Liquid Gallons[j] (lb)	Gas[a,i] (at NTP) scf (lb)
Flammable and combustible liquid[b,c]	See note	See note	See note	See note
Cryogenic fluid	Flammable	N/A	10	N/A
	Oxidizing	N/A	10	N/A
Explosives[d,e,f,g]	See note	See note	See note	See note
Flammable gas[c]	Gaseous	N/A	N/A	1000
	Liquefied	N/A	N/A	(20)
	Liquefied Petroleum	N/A	N/A	(20)
Consumer fireworks	See note	See note	See note	See note
Flammable solid	N/A	5	N/A	N/A
Oxidizers	4	NP	NP	NP
	3	10[h]	1[h]	NP
	2	250	25	NP
	1	4,000	400	NP
Oxidizing gas	Gaseous	N/A	N/A	1500
	Liquefied	NA	15	N/A
Organic peroxides	I	NP	NP	N/A
	II	NP	NP	N/A
	III	1500	1500	N/A
	IV	100,000	100,000	N/A
	V	NL	NL	N/A
Pyrophoric materials	N/A	1	(1)	10
Unstable reactives	4	¼	(¼)	2
	3	1	(1)	10
	2	10	(10)	750
	1	NL	NL	NL
Water-reactive	3	1	(1)	N/A
	2	10	(10)	N/A
	1	NL	NL	N/A
Corrosives	N/A	1000	(100)	810
Highly toxic[i]	N/A	3	(3)	20
Toxic[i]	N/A	125	(125)	810

For SI units, 1 lb = 0.454 kg; 1 gal = 3.785 L; 1 scf^3 = 0.0283 m^3.
NTP: Normal temperature and pressure [measured at 70°F (21°C) and 14.7 psi (101 kPa)]. N/A: Not applicable. NP: Not permitted. NL: Not limited.
Note: The hazardous material categories and MAQs that are shaded in this table are not regulated by NFPA 400 but are provided here for informational purposes. See Chapter 2 for the reference code or standard governing these materials and establishing the MAQs. In accordance with 1.1.1.2, materials having multiple hazards that fall within the scope of NFPA 400 shall comply with NFPA 400.
[a]Unlimited amounts of gas are permitted to be used for personal medical or emergency medical use.
[b]Storage in excess of 10 gal (38 L) of Class I and Class II liquids combined or 60 gal (227 L) of Class IIIA liquids is permitted where stored in safety cabinets with an aggregate quantity not to exceed 180 gal (681 L).
[c]Fuel in the tank of operating mobile equipment is permitted to exceed the specified quantity where the equipment is operated in accordance with this code.
[d]The use of explosive materials required by federal, state, or municipal agencies while engaged in normal or emergency performance of duties is not required to be limited. The storage of explosive materials is required to be in accordance with the requirements of NFPA 495, *Explosive Materials Code*.
[e]The storage and use of explosive materials in medicines and medicinal agents in the forms prescribed by the official United States Pharmacopeia or the National Formulary are not required to be limited.
[f]The storage and use of propellant-actuated devices or propellant-actuated industrial tools manufactured, imported, or distributed for their intended purposes are required to be limited to 50 lb (23 kg) net explosive weight.
[g]The storage and use of small arms ammunition, and components thereof, are permitted where in accordance with NFPA 495, *Explosive Materials Code*.
[h]A maximum quantity of 200 lb (91 kg) of solid or 20 gal (76 L) of liquid Class 3 oxidizer is permitted where such materials are necessary for maintenance purposes, operation, or sanitation of equipment. Storage containers and the manner of storage are required to be approved.
[i]Gas cylinders not exceeding 20 scf (0.57 m^3) measured at 70°F (21°C) and 14.7 psi (101 kPa) are permitted in gas cabinets or fume hoods.
[j]Conversion. Where quantities are indicated in pounds and when the weight per gallon of the liquid is not provided to the AHJ, a conversion factor of 10 lb/gal (1.2 kg/L) shall be used.

5.2.1.13 Special Quantity Limits for Mercantile, Industrial, and Storage Occupancies.

5.2.1.13.1 General. Where storage in mercantile, industrial, and storage occupancies is in compliance with all of the special controls set forth in 5.2.1.13.2, the MAQ of selected hazardous materials shall be permitted to be increased in accordance with 5.2.1.13.3.

5.2.1.13.2 Special Controls Required for Increased Quantities. Where quantities of hazardous materials are increased in accordance with 5.2.1.13.3, such materials shall be stored in accordance with the following limitations:

(1) Storage and display of solids shall not exceed 200 lb/ft^2 (976.4 kg/m^2) of floor area actually occupied by solid merchandise.
(2) Storage and display of liquids shall not exceed 20 gal/ft^2 (76 L/m^2) of floor area actually occupied by liquid merchandise.
(3) Storage and display height shall not exceed 6 ft (1.8 m) above the finished floor.
(4) Individual containers less than 5 gal (19 L) or less than 25 lb (11 kg) shall be stored or displayed on pallets, racks, or shelves.
(5) Racks and shelves used for storage or display shall be in accordance with 6.1.13.
(6) Containers shall be listed or approved for the intended use.
(7) Individual containers shall not exceed 100 lb (45.4 kg) capacity for solids or a 10 gal (38 L) capacity for liquids.
(8) Incompatible materials shall be separated in accordance with 6.1.12.
(9) Except for surfacing, floors shall be of noncombustible construction.
(10) Aisles 4 ft (1.2 m) in width shall be maintained on three sides of the storage or display area.
(11) Hazard identification signs shall be provided in accordance with 6.1.8.

5.2.1.13.3 Special Maximum Allowable Quantity Increases for Storage in Mercantile, Storage, and Industrial Occupancies. The aggregate quantity of nonflammable solid and nonflammable or noncombustible liquid hazardous materials permitted within a single control area of a mercantile, storage, or industrial occupancy shall be permitted to exceed the MAQ specified in Table 5.2.1.1.3, without complying with Protection Level 2, Protection Level 3, or Protection Level 4, provided that the quantities comply with Table 5.2.1.13.3(a) and Table 5.2.1.13.3(b) and that materials are displayed and stored in accordance with the special limitations in 5.2.1.13.2.

5.2.2 Construction Requirements for Control Areas.

5.2.2.1 Number of Control Areas. The maximum number of control areas within a building shall be in accordance with Table 5.2.2.1.

5.2.2.2 Where only one control area is present in a building, no special construction provisions shall be required.

5.2.2.3 Where more than one control area is present in a building, control areas shall be separated from each other by fire barriers in accordance with Table 5.2.2.1.

5.3 Protection Levels.

5.3.1 Where the quantity of hazardous materials in storage or use exceeds the MAQ for indoor control areas as set forth in Section 5.2, the occupancy shall comply with the requirements for protection level 1, protection level 2, protection level 3, or protection level 4, as required for the material in storage or use as defined in 6.2.2 through 6.2.5.

5.3.2 Protection level 5 shall apply to semiconductor fabrication facilities where required by the building code.

5.3.3 Protection Level 1.

5.3.3.1 Buildings containing quantities of hazardous materials exceeding the MAQ of high hazard level 1 contents permitted in control areas shall comply with applicable regulations for protection level 1, as set forth in the applicable sections of Chapter 6, Chapters 11 through 21, and the building code.

5.3.3.2 High hazard level 1 contents shall include materials that present a detonation hazard as defined in 4.2.1.2.1.

5.3.4 Protection Level 2.

5.3.4.1 Buildings, and portions thereof, containing quantities of hazardous materials exceeding the MAQ of high hazard level 2 contents permitted in control areas shall comply with applicable regulations for protection level 2, as set forth in the applicable sections of Chapter 6, Chapters 11 through 21, and the building code.

5.3.4.2 High hazard level 2 contents shall include materials that present a deflagration hazard or a hazard from accelerated burning as defined in 4.2.1.2.2.

5.3.5 Protection Level 3.

5.3.5.1 Buildings, and portions thereof, containing quantities of hazardous materials exceeding the MAQ of high hazard level 3 contents permitted in control areas shall comply with applicable regulations for protection level 3, as set forth in the applicable sections of Chapter 6, Chapters 11 through 21, and the building code.

Table 5.2.1.13.3(a) Maximum Allowable Quantity (MAQ) per Indoor and Outdoor Control Area for Selected Hazard Categories in Mercantile, Storage, and Industrial Occupancies

Hazard Category	Maximum Allowable Quantity[a,b] Solids lb	Solids kg	Liquids gal	Liquids L
Physical Hazard Materials: Nonflammable and Noncombustible Solids and Liquids				
Oxidizers				
Class 3	1,150	522	115	435
Class 2	2,250	1021	225	852
Class 1	18,000[c]	8165[c]	1,800[c]	6814[c]

Note: Maximum quantities for hazard categories not shown are required to be in accordance with Table 5.2.1.1.3.

[a]Maximum quantities are permitted to be increased 100 percent in buildings that are sprinklered in accordance with NFPA 13, *Standard for the Installation of Sprinkler Systems*. Where footnote b also applies, the increase for both footnotes is permitted to be applied.

[b]Maximum quantities are permitted to be increased 100 percent where stored in approved storage cabinets in accordance with NFPA 1, *Fire Code*. Where footnote (a) also applies, the increase for both footnotes is permitted to be applied.

[c]Quantities are not limited in buildings protected by an automatic sprinkler system complying with NFPA 13. [5000: Table 34.1.3.3.1(a)]

Table 5.2.1.13.3(b) Maximum Allowable Quantity (MAQ) per Indoor and Outdoor Control Area for Selected Hazard Categories in Mercantile and Storage Occupancies

Hazard Category	Maximum Allowable Quantity[a,b,c]			
	Solids		Liquids	
	lb	kg	gal	L
Physical Hazard Materials: Nonflammable and Noncombustible Solids and Liquids				
Unstable (reactive)				
Class 3	550	250	55	208
Class 2	1,150	522	115	435
Water-reactive				
Class 3	550	250	55	208
Class 2	1,150	522	115	435
Health Hazard Materials: Nonflammable and Noncombustible Solids and Liquids				
Corrosive	10,000	4536	1,000	3785
Highly toxic[d]	20	9	2	8
Toxic[d]	1,000	454	100	378

[a]Maximum quantities for hazard categories not shown are required to be in accordance with Table 5.2.1.1.3.
[b]Maximum quantities are permitted to be increased 100 percent in buildings that are sprinklered in accordance with NFPA 13, *Standard for the Installation of Sprinkler Systems*. Where footnote b also applies, the increase for both footnotes can be applied.
[c]Maximum quantities are permitted to be increased 100 percent where stored in approved storage cabinets in accordance with NFPA 1, *Fire Code*. Where footnote (a) also applies, the increase for both footnotes is permitted to be applied. [5000:Table 34.1.3.3.1(b)]
[d]Toxic or highly toxic solids or liquids displayed in original packaging in mercantile or storage occupancies and intended for maintenance, operation of equipment, or sanitation when contained in individual packaging not exceeding 100 lb (45.4 kg) shall be limited to an aggregate of 1200 lb (544.3 kg) or 220 gal (832.8 L). The increases allowed by footnotes a, b, and c shall not apply to highly toxic solids and liquids.

5.3.5.2 High hazard level 3 contents shall include materials that readily support combustion or present a physical hazard as defined in 4.2.1.2.3.

5.3.6 Protection Level 4.

5.3.6.1 Buildings, and portions thereof, containing quantities of hazardous materials exceeding the MAQ of high hazard level 4 contents permitted in control areas shall comply with applicable regulations for protection level 4, as set forth in the applicable sections of Chapter 6, Chapters 11 through 21, and the building code.

5.3.6.2 High hazard level 4 contents shall include materials that are acute health hazards as defined in 4.2.1.2.4.

5.3.7 Detached Building Required for High Hazard Level 2 and High Hazard Level 3 Materials. Buildings required to comply with protection level 2 or 3 and containing quantities of high hazard contents exceeding the quantity limits set forth in Table 5.3.7 shall be in accordance with 6.2.3.4 or 6.2.4.4, as applicable.

Table 5.2.2.1 Design and Number of Control Areas

Floor Level	Maximum Allowable Quantity per Control Area (%)*	Number of Control Areas per Floor	Fire Resistance Rating for Fire Barriers† (hr)
Above grade			
>9	5.0	1	2
7–9	5.0	2	2
4–6	12.5	2	2
3	50.0	2	1
2	75.0	3	1
1	100.0	4	1
Below grade			
1	75.0	3	1
2	50.0	2	1
Lower than 2	NP	NP	N/A

NP: Not permitted. N/A: Not applicable.
*Percentages represent the MAQ per control area shown in Table 5.2.1.1.3, with all the increases permitted in the footnotes of that table.
†Fire barriers are required to include floors and walls, as necessary, to provide a complete separation from other control areas.

Table 5.3.7 High Hazard Level 2 and High Hazard Level 3 Materials — Detached Building Required

Material	Class	Maximum Quantity Without a Detached Building	
		Solids and Liquids (tons)	Gases scf (Nm³) [m³]*
Individual bulk compressed gas systems	N/A	N/A	15,000 (425)
Oxidizers	3	1,200	N/A
	2	2,000	N/A
Organic peroxides	II	25	N/A
	III	50	N/A
Unstable (reactive) materials	3, nondetonable	1	2,000 (57)
	2	25	10,000 (283)
Water-reactive materials	3	1	N/A
	2, deflagrating	25	N/A
Pyrophoric gases	N/A	N/A	2,000 (57)

For SI units, 1 ton = 0.9 met ton.
N/A: Not applicable.
[55: Table 6.5]
*See Table 21.2.5.

5.4 Outdoor Areas.

5.4.1 Outdoor Control Areas.

5.4.1.1 General.

5.4.1.1.1 Hazardous materials shall be permitted to be stored or used in outdoor control areas in accordance with 5.4.1.2 and 5.4.1.3.

5.4.1.1.2 Where storage or use is in an outdoor control area, compliance with the outdoor storage and use requirements in Chapters 11 through 21 shall not be required.

5.4.1.2 Maximum Allowable Quantity per Outdoor Control Area. Maximum allowable quantities of hazardous materials in an outdoor control area shall be as specified in Table 5.2.1.13.3(a) and Table 5.2.1.13.3(b) or Table 5.4.1.2.

5.4.1.3 Number of Outdoor Control Areas.

5.4.1.3.1 A single outdoor control area shall be permitted on any property.

5.4.1.3.2 Where a property exceeds 10,000 ft^2 (929 m^2), a group of two outdoor control areas shall be permitted where approved and where each control area is separated by a minimum distance of 50 ft (15 m).

5.4.1.3.3 Where a property exceeds 35,000 ft^2 (3252 m^2), additional groups of outdoor control areas shall be permitted where approved, provided that each group is separated by a minimum distance of 300 ft (91 m).

5.4.2 Outdoor Storage and Use Areas. Where the quantity of hazardous materials in outdoor storage or use exceeds the MAQ for outdoor control areas as set forth in Table 5.4.1.2, the outdoor area shall comply with the applicable outdoor requirements of Chapter 6 and Chapters 11 through 21.

Chapter 6   Fundamental Requirements

6.1 General Requirements.

6.1.1 Applicability. Storage, use, and handling of hazardous materials in any quantity shall comply with Section 6.1.

6.1.1.1* Storage of hazardous materials in quantities exceeding the MAQ set forth in Chapter 5 shall comply with Section 6.2 and the applicable material specific requirements in Chapters 11 through 21.

6.1.1.2* The use, dispensing, and handling of hazardous materials in quantities exceeding the MAQ set forth in Chapter 5 shall comply with Section 6.3 and the applicable material specific requirements in Chapters 11 through 21.

6.1.2* Material Safety Data Sheets (MSDS). Material safety data sheets (MSDS) shall be available on the premises for hazardous materials regulated by this code. When approved, MSDSs shall be permitted to be retrievable by electronic access.

6.1.3 Release of Hazardous Materials.

6.1.3.1 Prohibited Releases. Hazardous materials shall not be released into a sewer, storm drain, ditch, drainage canal, lake, river, or tidal waterway; upon the ground, a sidewalk, a street, or a highway; or into the atmosphere, unless such release is permitted by the following:

(1) Federal, state, or local governing regulations
(2) Permits of the jurisdictional air quality management board
(3) National Pollutant Discharge Elimination System permit
(4) Waste discharge requirements established by the jurisdictional water quality control board
(5) Sewer pretreatment requirements for publicly or privately owned treatment works

6.1.3.2 Control and Mitigation of Unauthorized Releases. Provisions shall be made for controlling and mitigating unauthorized releases.

6.1.3.3 Records of Unauthorized Releases. Accurate records of the unauthorized release of hazardous materials shall be kept by the permittee.

6.1.3.4* Notification of Unauthorized Releases. The fire department shall be notified immediately or in accordance with approved emergency procedures when an unauthorized release becomes reportable under state, federal, or local regulations.

6.1.3.5 Container Failure. When an unauthorized release due to primary container failure is discovered, the involved primary container shall be repaired or removed from service.

6.1.3.6 Overpack Containers. Overpack containers shall be permitted to be used as a means to provide protection for primary containers to be transported for repair or removal from service.

6.1.3.7 Responsibility for Cleanup of Unauthorized Releases.

6.1.3.7.1 The person, firm, or corporation responsible for an unauthorized release shall institute and complete all actions necessary to remedy the effects of such unauthorized release, whether sudden or gradual, at no cost to the AHJ.

6.1.3.7.2 When deemed necessary by the AHJ, cleanup of an unauthorized release shall be permitted to be initiated by the fire department or by an authorized individual or firm, and costs associated with such cleanup shall be borne by the owner, operator, or other person responsible for the unauthorized release.

6.1.4* Personnel Training. Persons in areas where hazardous materials are stored, dispensed, handled, or used shall be trained in the hazards of the materials employed and actions required by the emergency plan. The level of training to be conducted shall be consistent with the responsibilities of the persons to be trained in accordance with 6.1.4.1 through 6.1.4.5.

6.1.4.1 Awareness. The training provided for persons designated in 6.1.4 shall include awareness training in accordance with 6.1.4.1.1 through 6.1.4.1.3.

6.1.4.1.1 Completion. Initial training shall be completed prior to beginning work in the work area.

6.1.4.1.2 Hazard Communications. Training shall be provided prior to beginning work in the work area to enable personnel to recognize and identify hazardous materials stored, dispensed, handled, or used on site and where to find safety information pertaining to the hazards of the materials employed.

6.1.4.1.3 Emergency Plan. Training shall be provided prior to beginning work in the work area to enable personnel to implement the emergency plan.

6.1.4.2 Operations Personnel. Persons engaged in storing, using, or handling hazardous materials shall be designated as operations personnel and shall be trained in accordance with 6.1.4.1 and 6.1.4.2.1 through 6.1.4.2.6.

Table 5.4.1.2 Maximum Allowable Quantities of Hazardous Materials per Outdoor Control Area

Material	Class	Storage Solid Pounds	Storage Liquid Gallons (lb)	Storage Gas scf (lb)	Use — Closed Systems Solid Pounds	Use — Closed Systems Liquid Gallons (lb)	Use — Closed Systems Gas scf (lb)	Use — Open Systems Solid Pounds	Use — Open Systems Liquid Gallons (lb)
Physical Hazard Materials									
Flammable gas									
Gaseous		N/A	N/A	3000	N/A	N/A	1500	N/A	N/A
Liquefied		N/A	N/A	(300)	N/A	N/A	(150)	N/A	N/A
Flammable solid		500	N/A	N/A	250	N/A	N/A	50	N/A
Organic peroxide	Detonable	1	(1)	N/A	¼	(¼)	N/A	¼	(¼)
Organic peroxide	I	20	20	N/A	10	(10)	N/A	2	2
	II	200	200	N/A	100	(100)	N/A	20	20
	III	500	500	N/A	250	(250)	N/A	50	50
	IV	NL	NL	N/A	NL	NL	N/A	NL	NL
	V	NL	NL	N/A	NL	NL	N/A	NL	NL
Oxidizer	4	2	(2)	N/A	1	(¼)	N/A	¼	(¼)
	3	40	(40)	N/A	20	(2)	N/A	2	(2)
	2	1000	(1000)	N/A	500	(250)	N/A	50	(50)
	1	NL	NL	N/A	NL	NL	N/A	NL	NL
Oxidizing gas									
Gaseous		N/A	N/A	6000	N/A	N/A	6000	N/A	N/A
Liquefied		N/A	N/A	(600)	N/A	N/A	(300)	N/A	N/A
Pyrophoric		8	(8)	100	4	(4)	10	0	0
Unstable (reactive)	4	2	(2)	20	1	(1)	2	¼	(¼)
	3	20	(20)	200	10	(10)	10	1	(1)
	2	200	(200)	1000	100	(100)	250	10	(10)
	1	NL	NL	1500	NL	NL	NL	NL	NL
Water-reactive	3	20	(20)	N/A	10	(10)	N/A	1	(1)
	2	200	(200)	N/A	100	(100)	N/A	10	(10)
	1	NL	NL	N/A	NL	NL	N/A	NL	NL
Health Hazard Materials									
Corrosive		20000	2000	N/A	10000	1000	N/A	1000	100
Corrosive gas									
Gaseous		N/A	N/A	1620	N/A	N/A	810	N/A	N/A
Liquefied		N/A	N/A	(300)	N/A	N/A	(150)	N/A	N/A
Highly toxic		20	(20)	N/A	10	(10)	N/A	3	(3)
Highly toxic gas									
Gaseous		N/A	N/A	40*	N/A	N/A	20*	N/A	N/A
Liquefied		N/A	N/A	(8)*	N/A	N/A	(4)*	N/A	N/A
Toxic		1000	(1000)	N/A	500	50	N/A	125	(125)
Toxic gas									
Gaseous		N/A	N/A	1620	N/A	N/A	810	N/A	N/A
Liquefied		N/A	N/A	(300)	N/A	N/A	(150)	N/A	N/A

For SI units, 1 lb = 0.454 kg; 1 gal = 3.785 L; 1 scf^3 = 0.0283 Nm^3.
N/A: Not applicable. NL: Not limited.
Notes:
(1) Table values in parentheses correspond to the unit name in parentheses at the top of the column.
(2) For gallons of liquids, divide the amount in pounds by 10.
(3) The aggregate quantities in storage and use shall not exceed the quantity listed for storage.
(4) The aggregate quantity of nonflammable solid and nonflammable or noncombustible liquid hazardous materials allowed in outdoor storage per single property under the same ownership or control used for retail or wholesale sales is permitted to exceed the MAQ when such storage is in accordance with 5.2.1.13.3.
*Permitted only where stored or used in approved exhausted gas cabinets, exhausted enclosures, or fume hoods.

6.1.4.2.1 Physical and Health Hazard Properties. Operations personnel shall be trained in the chemical nature of the materials, including their physical hazards and the symptoms of acute or chronic exposure as provided by the material safety data sheet (MSDS) furnished by the manufacturer or other authoritative sources.

6.1.4.2.2 Dispensing, Using, and Processing. Operations personnel shall be trained in the use of specific safeguards applicable to the dispensing, processing, or use of the materials and equipment employed.

6.1.4.2.3 Storage. Operations personnel shall be trained in the application of storage arrangements and site-specific limitations on storage for the materials employed.

6.1.4.2.4 Transport (Handling). Operations personnel involved in materials handling shall be trained in the requirements for on-site transport of the materials employed.

6.1.4.2.5 Actions in an Emergency. Operations personnel shall be trained in the necessary actions to take in the event of an emergency, including the operation and activation of emergency controls prior to evacuation.

6.1.4.2.6 Changes. Training shall be provided whenever a new hazardous material is introduced into the work area that presents a new physical or health hazard, or when new information is obtained pertaining to physical or health hazards of an existing hazardous material that has not been included in previous training, and when there are changes in any of the following:

(1) Equipment
(2) Operations
(3) Hazardous materials

6.1.4.3 Emergency Response Liaison.

6.1.4.3.1 Responsible persons shall be designated and trained to be emergency response (ER) liaison personnel.

6.1.4.3.2 Emergency response liaison personnel shall do the following:

(1) Aid emergency responders in pre-planning responses to emergencies
(2) Identify locations where hazardous materials are located
(3) Have access to material safety data sheets
(4) Be knowledgeable in the site emergency response procedures

6.1.4.4* Emergency Responders. Emergency responders shall be trained to be competent in the actions to be taken in an emergency event.

6.1.4.4.1* Emergency Response Team Leader. Persons acting as ER team leaders shall be trained under the Incident Command System concept or equivalent.

6.1.4.4.2* Response to Incipient Events. Responses to incidental releases of hazardous materials where the material can be absorbed, neutralized, or otherwise controlled at the time of release by employees in the immediate release area, or by maintenance personnel, shall not be considered emergency responses as defined within the scope of this code.

6.1.4.4.3* On-Site Emergency Response Team. When an on-site emergency response team is provided, emergency responders shall be trained in accordance with the requirements of the specific site emergency plan or as required by federal, state, or local governmental agencies.

6.1.4.5 Training Mandated by Other Agencies. Training required by federal, state, or local regulations that is required based on the quantity or type of hazardous materials stored, dispensed, handled, or used shall be conducted in accordance with the requirements of and under the jurisdiction of the governing agency.

6.1.4.6 Documentation. Training shall be documented and made available to the AHJ upon written request.

6.1.5 Ignition Source Controls.

6.1.5.1 Smoking. Smoking shall be prohibited in the following locations:

(1) Within 25 ft (7.6 m) of outdoor storage areas, dispensing areas, or open use areas
(2) In rooms or areas where hazardous materials are stored or dispensed or used in open systems in amounts requiring a permit in accordance with Section 1.8

6.1.5.2 Open Flames and High-Temperature Devices. Open flames and high-temperature devices shall not be used in a manner that creates a hazardous condition.

6.1.5.3 Energy-Consuming Equipment. Energy-consuming equipment with the potential to serve as a source of ignition shall be listed or approved for use with the hazardous materials stored or used.

6.1.5.3.1* Powered Industrial Trucks. Powered industrial trucks shall be operated and maintained in accordance with NFPA 505, *Fire Safety Standard for Powered Industrial Trucks Including Type Designations, Areas of Use, Conversions, Maintenance, and Operations.* [**1**:10.18]

6.1.6 Systems, Equipment, and Processes. Processes, methods, specifications, equipment testing and maintenance, design standards, performance, installation, equipment design and construction, and other pertinent criteria shall be in accordance with this section.

6.1.6.1 Design and Construction of Containers and Tanks. Containers, cylinders, and tanks shall be designed and constructed in accordance with approved standards. Containers, cylinders, tanks, and other means used for containment of hazardous materials shall be of an approved type.

6.1.6.2 Piping, Tubing, Valves, and Fittings. Piping, tubing, valves, fittings, and related components used for hazardous materials shall be in accordance with the following:

(1) Piping, tubing, valves, fittings, and related components shall be designed and fabricated from materials compatible with the material to be contained and shall be of a strength and durability to withstand the pressure, structural and seismic stress, and exposure to which they are subject.
(2) Piping and tubing shall be identified in accordance with ASME A13.1, *Scheme for the Identification of Piping Systems,* to indicate the material conveyed.
(3) Accessible manual valves, or fail-safe emergency shutoff valves operated by a remotely located manually or automatically activated shutdown control, shall be installed on supply piping and tubing at the following locations:
    (a) Point of use
    (b) Tank or bulk source
(4) Manual emergency shutoff valves and remotely located manually activated shutdown controls for emergency shutoff valves shall be identified, and the location shall be clearly visible, accessible, and indicated by means of a sign.

(5) Backflow prevention or check valves shall be provided when the backflow of hazardous materials could create a hazardous condition or cause the unauthorized discharge of hazardous materials.
(6) Liquids classified in accordance with NFPA 704, *Standard System for the Identification of the Hazards of Materials for Emergency Response*, shall be carried in pressurized piping above a gauge pressure of 15 psi (103 kPa) having a hazard ranking as follows:

   (a) Health hazard Class 3 or Class 4
   (b) Flammability Class 4
   (c) Instability Class 3 or Class 4

(7) The pressurized piping specified in 6.1.6.2(6) shall be provided with an approved means of leak detection and emergency shutoff or excess flow control in accordance with the following:

   (a) Where the piping originates from within a hazardous material storage room or area, the excess flow control shall be located within the storage room or area.
   (b) Where the piping originates from a bulk source, the excess flow control shall be located at the bulk source.
   (c) Piping for inlet connections designed to prevent backflow shall not be required to be equipped with excess flow control.

6.1.6.3 Additional Regulations for Supply Piping for Health Hazard Materials. Supply piping and tubing for liquids or solids having a health hazard ranking of Class 3 or Class 4 in accordance with NFPA 704, *Standard System for the Identification of the Hazards of Materials for Emergency Response*, shall be in accordance with ASME B31.3, *Process Piping*, and the following:

(1) Piping and tubing utilized for the transmission of highly toxic, toxic, or highly volatile corrosive liquids shall have welded, threaded, or flanged connections throughout, except for connections located within a ventilated enclosure, or an approved method of drainage or containment.
(2) Piping and tubing shall not be located within corridors, within any portion of a means of egress required to be enclosed in fire resistance–rated construction, or in concealed spaces in areas not classified as protection level 1 through protection level 4 occupancies.

6.1.6.4 Equipment, Machinery, and Alarms. Equipment, machinery, and required detection and alarm systems associated with the use, storage, or handling of hazardous materials shall be listed or approved.

6.1.7 Empty Containers and Tanks. Empty containers and tanks previously used for the storage of hazardous materials shall be free from residual material and vapor as defined by DOT, the Resource Conservation and Recovery Act (RCRA), or other regulating authority or shall be maintained as specified for the storage of hazardous material.

6.1.8 Signs.

6.1.8.1 General.

6.1.8.1.1 Design and Construction. Signs shall be durable, and the size, color, and lettering of signs shall be in accordance with nationally recognized standards.

6.1.8.1.2 Language. Signs shall be in English as the primary language or in symbols permitted by this code.

6.1.8.1.3 Maintenance. Signs shall meet the following criteria:

(1) They shall not be obscured.
(2) They shall be maintained in a legible condition.
(3) They shall not be removed, unless for replacement.

6.1.8.2 Hazardous Materials Identification.

6.1.8.2.1 NFPA 704 Placard. Visible hazard identification signs in accordance with NFPA 704, *Standard System for the Identification of the Hazards of Materials for Emergency Response*, shall be placed at the following locations, except where the AHJ has received a hazardous materials management plan and a hazardous materials inventory statement in accordance with Sections 1.11 and 1.12 and has determined that omission of such signs is consistent with safety:

(1) On stationary aboveground tanks
(2) On stationary aboveground containers
(3) At entrances to locations where hazardous materials are stored, dispensed, used, or handled in quantities requiring a permit
(4) At other entrances and locations designated by the AHJ

6.1.8.2.2 Identification of Containers, Cartons, and Packages. Individual containers, cartons, or packages shall be conspicuously marked or labeled in accordance with nationally recognized standards.

6.1.8.3 No Smoking Signs. Where "no smoking" is not applicable to an entire site or building, signs shall be provided as follows:

(1) In rooms or areas where hazardous materials are stored or dispensed or used in open systems in amounts requiring a permit in accordance with Section 1.8
(2) Within 25 ft (7.6 m) of outdoor storage, dispensing, or open-use areas

6.1.9 Protection from Vehicles.

6.1.9.1 Guard posts or other approved means shall be provided to protect the following where subject to vehicular damage:

(1) Storage tanks and connected piping, valves, and fittings
(2) Storage areas containing tanks or portable containers except where the exposing vehicles are powered industrial trucks used for transporting the hazardous materials
(3) Use areas

6.1.9.2 Where guard posts are installed, the posts shall meet the following criteria:

(1) They shall be constructed of steel not less than 4 in. (102 mm) in diameter and concrete filled.
(2) They shall be spaced not more than 4 ft (1.2 m) between posts on center.
(3) They shall be set not less than 3 ft (0.9 m) deep in a concrete footing of not less than a 15 in. (381 mm) diameter.
(4) They shall be set with the top of the posts not less than 3 ft (0.9 m) above ground.
(5) They shall be located not less than 5 ft (1.5 m) from the tank.

6.1.10 Electrical Wiring and Equipment.

6.1.10.1 General. Electrical wiring and equipment shall be installed in accordance with *NFPA 70, National Electrical Code.*

6.1.10.2 Static Accumulation. When processes or use conditions exist where flammable gases, dusts, or vapors can be ignited by static electricity, means shall be provided to prevent the accumulation of a static charge and to dissipate the static charge to ground.

6.1.11 Protection from Light. Materials that are sensitive to light shall be stored in containers designed to protect them from such exposure.

6.1.12 Separation of Incompatible Materials.

6.1.12.1 Incompatible materials in storage and storage of materials incompatible with materials in use shall be separated when the stored materials are in containers having a capacity of more than 5 lb (2.268 kg) or ½ gal (1.89 L).

6.1.12.2 Separation shall be accomplished by one of the following methods:

(1) Segregating incompatible materials storage by a distance of not less than 20 ft (6.1 m)
(2) Isolating incompatible materials storage by a noncombustible partition extending not less than 18 in. (457 mm) above and to the sides of the stored material or by a noncombustible partition that interrupts the line of sight between the incompatible materials
(3) Storing liquid and solid materials in hazardous materials storage cabinets complying with 6.1.18
(4) Storing compressed gases in gas cabinets or exhausted enclosures complying with Chapter 21

6.1.12.3 Materials that are incompatible shall not be stored within the same cabinet or enclosure.

6.1.13 General Storage.

6.1.13.1 Storage. The storage arrangement of materials shall be in accordance with this chapter and the material specific requirements of Chapters 11 through 21 as applicable.

6.1.13.2 Shelf Storage. Shelving shall be constructed to carry the design loads and shall be braced and anchored in accordance with the seismic design requirements of the applicable building code.

6.1.13.2.1 Shelf Construction.

6.1.13.2.1.1 Shelving shall be treated, coated, or constructed of materials that are compatible with the hazardous materials stored.

6.1.13.2.1.2 Shelves shall be provided with a lip or guard where used for the storage of individual containers, except under either of the following conditions:

(1) Where storage is located in hazardous materials storage cabinets or laboratory furniture specifically designed for such use
(2) Where amounts of hazardous materials in storage do not exceed the quantity threshold for requiring a permit in accordance with Section 1.8

6.1.13.2.2 Shelf storage of hazardous materials shall be maintained in an orderly manner.

6.1.14* Seismic Protection. Machinery and equipment utilizing hazardous materials in areas subject to seismic activity shall be seismically anchored in accordance with the building code.

6.1.14.1 Shock Padding. Materials that are shock sensitive shall be padded, suspended, or otherwise protected against accidental dislodgement and dislodgement during seismic activity.

6.1.15 Outdoor Storage and Use Areas. Outdoor storage and use areas for hazardous materials shall comply with the following:

(1) Outdoor storage and use areas shall be kept free of weeds, debris, and common combustible materials not necessary to the storage or use of hazardous materials.
(2) The area surrounding an outdoor storage and use area shall be kept clear of weeds, debris, and common combustible materials not necessary to the storage or use of hazardous materials for a minimum distance of 15 ft (4.5 m).
(3) Outdoor storage and use areas for hazardous materials shall be located not closer than 20 ft (6.1 m) from a property line that can be built upon, a street, an alley, or a public way, except that a 2-hour fire barrier wall, without openings and extending not less than 30 in. (762 mm) above and to the sides of the storage area, shall be permitted in lieu of such distance.

6.1.16 Maintenance Required.

6.1.16.1* Equipment, machinery, and required detection and alarm systems associated with hazardous materials shall be maintained in an operable condition.

6.1.16.2 Stationary tanks not used for a period of 90 days shall be safeguarded or removed in an approved manner.

6.1.16.2.1 The tanks specified in 6.1.16.2 shall have the fill line, gauge opening, and pump connection secured against tampering.

6.1.16.2.2 Vent lines shall be maintained.

6.1.16.2.3* Tanks that are to be placed back in service shall be tested in an approved manner.

6.1.16.3 The following shall apply to defective containers, cylinders, and tanks:

(1) They shall be removed from service, repaired, or disposed of in an approved manner.
(2) Overpack containers shall be permitted to be used as a means to provide protection for primary containers that are transported for repair or removal from service.

6.1.16.4 Defective equipment or machinery shall be removed from service and repaired or replaced.

6.1.16.5 Required detection and alarm systems that are defective shall be replaced or repaired.

6.1.17 Testing.

6.1.17.1 The equipment, devices, and systems listed in 6.1.17.2.1 shall be tested at one of the intervals listed in 6.1.17.2.2. Written records of the tests conducted or maintenance performed shall be maintained.

6.1.17.2 Testing shall not be required under the following conditions:

(1) Where approved written documentation is provided that testing will damage the equipment, device, or system and the equipment, device, or system is maintained as specified by the manufacturer
(2) Where equipment, devices, and systems fail in a fail-safe manner
(3) Where equipment, devices, and systems self-diagnose and report trouble, with records of the self-diagnosis and trouble reporting made available to the AHJ
(4) Where system activation occurs during the required test cycle for the components activated during the test cycle

(5) Where approved maintenance in accordance with 6.1.16.1 is performed not less than annually or in accordance with an approved schedule, in which case the testing requirements set forth in 6.1.17.2.1 and 6.1.17.2.2 are permitted to apply.

6.1.17.2.1 Equipment, Devices, and Systems Requiring Testing. The following equipment, devices, and systems shall be tested in accordance with 6.1.17 and 6.1.17.2.2:

(1) Limit control systems for liquid level, temperature, and pressure required by 6.2.1.7
(2) Monitoring and supervisory systems required by 6.2.1.1

6.1.17.2.2 Testing Frequency. The equipment, systems, and devices listed in 6.1.17.2.1 shall be tested at one of the following frequencies:

(1) Not less than annually
(2) In accordance with the approved manufacturer's requirements
(3) In accordance with approved recognized industry standards
(4) In accordance with an approved schedule

6.1.18 Hazardous Materials Storage Cabinets. When storage cabinets are used to increase MAQ per control area or to otherwise comply with a specific provision in Chapter 6, such cabinets shall be in accordance with the following:

(1) Cabinets shall be constructed of metal.
(2) The interior of cabinets shall be treated, coated, or constructed of materials that are nonreactive with the hazardous material stored, and such treatment, coating, or construction shall include the entire interior of the cabinet.
(3) Cabinets shall be either listed as suitable for the intended storage or constructed in accordance with the following:
    (a) Cabinets shall be of steel having a thickness of not less than 0.044 in. (1.12 mm) (18 gauge).
    (b) The cabinet, including the door, shall be double-walled with 1½ in. (38.1 mm) airspace between the walls.
    (c) Joints shall be riveted or welded and shall be tight-fitting.
    (d) Doors shall be well fitted, self-closing, and equipped with a self-latching device.
    (e) The bottoms of cabinets utilized for the storage of liquids shall be liquidtight to a minimum height of 2 in. (51 mm).
    (f) For requirements regarding electrical equipment and devices within cabinets used for the storage of hazardous liquids, compressed gases, or cryogenic fluids, see *NFPA 70, National Electrical Code.*
(4) Cabinets shall be marked in conspicuous lettering that reads as follows: HAZARDOUS — KEEP FIRE AWAY

6.1.19 Installation of Tanks. Installation of tanks shall be in accordance with 6.1.19.1 through 6.1.19.2.

6.1.19.1 Underground Tanks.

6.1.19.1.1 Underground tanks used for the storage of liquid hazardous materials shall be provided with secondary containment.

6.1.19.1.2 In lieu of providing secondary containment for an underground tank, an aboveground tank in an underground vault complying with NFPA 30, *Flammable and Combustible Liquids Code*, shall be permitted.

6.1.19.2 Aboveground Tanks. Aboveground stationary tanks installed outdoors and used for the storage of hazardous materials shall be located and protected in accordance with the requirements for outdoor storage of the particular material involved and in accordance with the requirements of Chapters 11 through 21.

6.1.19.2.1 Aboveground tanks that are installed in vaults complying with NFPA 30, *Flammable and Combustible Liquids Code*, shall not be required to comply with location and protection requirements for outdoor storage.

6.1.19.2.2 Aboveground tanks that are installed inside buildings and used for the storage of hazardous materials shall be located and protected in accordance with the requirements for indoor storage of the particular material involved.

6.1.19.2.3 Marking. Aboveground stationary tanks shall be marked as required by 6.1.8.2.1.

6.1.20 When required, fire alarm systems and smoke detection systems shall be installed in accordance with *NFPA 72, National Fire Alarm and Signaling Code.*

6.2 Requirements for Occupancies Storing Quantities of Hazardous Materials Exceeding the Maximum Allowable Quantities per Control Area for High Hazard Contents.

6.2.1 Indoor Storage General Requirements. The requirements set forth in 6.2.1 provide general design requirements for protection levels and shall apply to buildings, or portions thereof, that are required to comply with protection level 1 through protection level 4 where required by Section 5.3. [**5000:**34.3.2]

6.2.1.1 Fire Protection Systems. Buildings, or portions thereof, required to comply with protection level 1 through protection level 4 shall be protected by an approved automatic fire sprinkler system complying with Section 13.3 of NFPA 1, *Fire Code.* [**5000:**34.3.2.1]

6.2.1.1.1 The design of the sprinkler system shall be not less than ordinary hazard group 2 in accordance with NFPA 13, *Standard for the Installation of Sprinkler Systems*, except as follows:

(1) Where different requirements are specified in Chapters 11 through 21 of NFPA 400
(2) Where the materials or storage arrangement requires a higher level of sprinkler system protection in accordance with nationally recognized standards
(3) Where approved alternative automatic fire extinguishing systems are permitted

6.2.1.1.2 Electronic supervision of supervisory signals shall be provided in accordance with Section 13.3 of NFPA 1, *Fire Code.* [**5000:**34.3.2.1.1]

6.2.1.1.3 Waterflow alarms shall be monitored in accordance with Section 13.3 of NFPA 1, *Fire Code.* [**5000:**34.3.2.1.2]

6.2.1.1.4 Rooms or areas that are of noncombustible construction with wholly noncombustible contents shall not be required to comply with 6.2.1.1. [**5000:**34.3.2.1.3]

6.2.1.2 Building Height Exception. The height of a single-story building, or portion thereof, containing only tanks or industrial process equipment shall not be limited based on the type of construction. [**5000:**34.3.2.2]

6.2.1.3 Separation of Occupancies Having High Hazards. The separation of areas containing high hazard contents from each other and from other use areas shall be as required by Table 6.2.1.3 and shall not be permitted to be reduced with the installation of fire protection systems as required by 6.2.1.1. [**5000:**34.3.2.3]

Table 6.2.1.3 Required Separation of Occupancies Containing High Hazard Contents (hr)

Occupancy	Protection Level 1	Protection Level 2	Protection Level 3*	Protection Level 4	Protection Level 5
Apartment buildings	NP	4	3	4	4
Assembly ≤ 300	NP	4	3	2	4
Assembly > 300 and ≤ 1000	NP	4	3	2	4
Assembly > 1000	NP	4	3	2	4
Board and care, small	NP	4	3	4	4
Board and care, large	NP	4	3	4	4
Business	NP	2	1	1	1
Day-care > 12	NP	4	3	4	4
Day-care homes	NP	4	3	4	4
Detention and correctional	NP	4	3	4	4
Dwellings, one- and two-family	NP	4	3	4	4
Educational	NP	4	3	2	3
Health care, ambulatory	NP	4	4	4	4
Health care, nonambulatory	NP	4	4	4	4
Hotels and dormitories	NP	4	3	4	4
Industrial, general purpose	NP	2	1	1	1
Industrial, special purpose	NP	2	1	1	1
Lodging and rooming houses	NP	4	3	4	4
Mercantile, Class A	NP	2	1	1	1
Mercantile, Class B	NP	2	1	1	1
Mercantile, Class C	NP	2	1	1	1
Mercantile, covered mall	NP	2	1	1	1
Mercantile, bulk retail	NP	2	1	1	1
Protection Level 1	—	NP	NP	NP	NP
Protection Level 2	NP	—	1	2	2
Protection Level 3	NP	1	—	1	1
Protection Level 4	NP	2	1	—	1
Protection Level 5	NP	2	1	1	—
Storage, low and ordinary hazard	NP	2	1	1	1

NP: Not permitted.
*Rooms in excess of 150 ft² (14 m²) storing flammable liquids, combustible liquids, or Class 3 oxidizers are required to be provided with not less than a 2-hour separation.
[**5000:** Table 34.3.2.3]

6.2.1.4 Egress. Egress from areas required to comply with protection level 1, protection level 2, protection level 3, or protection level 4 shall comply with Chapter 14 of NFPA 1, *Fire Code*. [**5000:**34.3.2.4]

6.2.1.4.1 Travel Distance Limit. Travel distance to an exit from areas required to comply with protection level 1 through protection level 4 shall not exceed the distance given in Table 6.2.1.4.1, measured as required in Chapter 14 of NFPA 1, *Fire Code*. [**5000:**34.3.2.4.1]

Table 6.2.1.4.1 Travel Distance Limits

Protection Level	Distance ft	Distance m
1	75	23
2	100	30
3	150	46
4	175	53
5	200	61

[**5000:** Table 34.3.2.4.1]

6.2.1.4.2 Capacity of Means of Egress. Egress capacity for high hazard contents areas shall be based on 0.7 in. (18 mm) per person for stairs or 0.4 in. (10 mm) per person for level components and ramps in accordance with 14.8.3 of NFPA 1, *Fire Code*. [**5000:**34.3.2.4.2]

6.2.1.4.3 Number of Means of Egress. Not less than two means of egress shall be provided from each building, or portion thereof, required to comply with Section 6.2, unless rooms or spaces do not exceed 200 ft² (18.6 m²), have an occupant load not exceeding three persons, and have a travel distance to the room door not exceeding 25 ft (7.6 m). [**5000:** 34.3.2.4.3]

6.2.1.4.4 Dead Ends. Means of egress, for other than rooms or spaces that do not exceed 200 ft² (18.6 m²), have an occupant load not exceeding three persons, and have a travel distance to the room door not exceeding 25 ft (7.6 m), shall be arranged so that there are no dead ends in corridors. [**5000:**34.3.2.4.4]

6.2.1.4.5 Doors. Doors serving high hazard contents areas with occupant loads in excess of five shall be permitted to be provided with a latch or lock only if the latch or lock is panic hardware or fire exit hardware complying with 14.5.3.3 of NFPA 1, *Fire Code*. [**5000:**34.3.2.4.5]

6.2.1.5 Ventilation. Buildings, or portions thereof, in which explosive, flammable, combustible, corrosive, or highly toxic dusts, mists, fumes, vapors, or gases are, or might be, emitted shall be provided with mechanical exhaust ventilation or natural ventilation where natural ventilation can be shown to be acceptable for the materials as stored. [**5000**:34.3.2.5.1]

6.2.1.5.1 Solids and liquids stored in closed containers shall not be required to comply with 6.2.1.5. [**5000**:*34.3.2.5.1.2*]

6.2.1.5.2 Mechanical exhaust systems shall comply with the mechanical code. [**5000**:34.3.2.5.2]

6.2.1.5.3 Mechanical ventilation shall be at a rate of not less than 1 ft³/min/ft² (5.1 L/s/m²) of floor area over areas required to comply with protection level 1 through protection level 4. [**5000**:34.3.2.5.3]

6.2.1.5.4 Ventilation requirements shall be determined by calculations based on anticipated fugitive emissions or by sampling of the actual vapor concentration levels under normal operating conditions. [**5000**:34.3.2.5.5]

6.2.1.5.5 Make-up air shall be provided, and provision shall be made for locating make-up air openings to avoid short-circuiting the ventilation. [**5000**:34.3.2.5.6]

6.2.1.5.6 Ducts conveying explosives or flammable vapors, fumes, or dusts shall extend directly to the exterior of the building without entering other spaces. [**5000**:34.3.2.5.7]

6.2.1.5.6.1 Exhaust ducts shall not extend into or through ducts and plenums. [**5000**:34.3.2.5.7.1]

6.2.1.5.6.2 Ducts conveying vapor or fumes having flammable constituents less than 25 percent of their lower flammability limit shall be permitted to pass through other spaces. [**5000**:34.3.2.5.7.2]

6.2.1.5.7 Emissions generated by workstations shall be removed from the areas in which they are generated by means of local exhaust installed in accordance with the mechanical code.

6.2.1.5.8 The location of supply and exhaust openings shall be in accordance with the mechanical code. [**5000**:34.3.2.5.9]

6.2.1.5.9 Systems shall operate continuously unless alternate designs are approved. [**5000**:34.3.2.5.11]

6.2.1.5.10 A manual shutoff control for ventilation equipment required by 6.2.1.5 shall be provided outside the room adjacent to the principal access door to the room. [**5000**:34.3.2.5.12]

6.2.1.5.11 The shutoff control described in 6.2.1.5.10 shall be of the break-glass type and shall be labeled as follows:

VENTILATION SYSTEM EMERGENCY SHUTOFF

[**5000**:34.3.2.5.13]

6.2.1.5.12 Exhaust ventilation shall be arranged to consider the density of the potential fumes or vapors released. [**5000**:34.3.2.5.14]

6.2.1.5.12.1 For fumes or vapors that are lighter than air, exhaust shall be taken from a point within 12 in. (305 mm) of the high point of the room or area in which they are generated.

6.2.1.5.12.2 For fumes or vapors that are heavier than air, exhaust shall be taken from a point within 12 in. (305 mm) of the floor. [**5000**:34.3.2.5.14.1]

6.2.1.5.12.3 The location of both the exhaust and inlet air openings shall be arranged to provide air movement across all portions of the floor or room to prevent the accumulation of vapors. [**5000**:34.3.2.5.14.2]

6.2.1.5.12.4 Exhaust ventilation shall not be recirculated within the room or building if the materials stored are capable of emitting hazardous vapors. [**5000**:34.3.2.5.14.3]

6.2.1.5.12.5 Recirculation shall be permitted where it is monitored continuously using a fail-safe system that is designed to automatically sound an alarm, stop recirculation, and provide full exhaust to the outside in the event that vapor–air mixtures in concentrations over one-fourth of the lower flammable limit are detected. [**5000**:34.3.2.5.14.4]

6.2.1.5.12.6 Air contaminated with explosive or flammable vapors, fumes, or dusts, or with radioactive materials, shall not be recirculated.

6.2.1.6* Explosion Control. Buildings, or portions thereof, required to comply with protection level 1 through protection level 3 and containing materials shown in Table 6.2.1.6 shall be provided with a means of explosion control. [**5000**:34.3.2.6]

Table 6.2.1.6 Explosion Control Requirements

Hazard Category	Class	Protection Method
Combustible dust presenting an explosion hazard	NA	Explosion control*
Organic peroxides	Unclassified	Barricade†
	Class I	Barricade†
Oxidizer liquids and solids	Class 4	Barricade†
Unstable (reactive)	Class 4	Barricade†
	Class 3, detonating	Barricade†
	Class 3, deflagrating	Explosion control*
Water-reactive liquids and solids	Class 3	Explosion control*
	Class 2, deflagrating	Explosion control*

NA: Not applicable.
*Explosion control is required to be a deflagration prevention method, such as combustible concentration reduction or oxidant concentration reduction, or a deflagration control method complying with NFPA 69, *Standard on Explosion Prevention Systems*, or an approved, engineered deflagration-venting method.
†Barricades are required to comply with NFPA 495, *Explosive Materials Code*.
[**5000**: Table 34.3.2.6]

6.2.1.7 Limit Controls. Limit controls shall be provided in accordance with 6.2.1.7.1 and 6.2.1.7.2.

6.2.1.7.1 Temperature Control. Materials that must be kept at temperatures other than normal ambient temperatures to prevent a hazardous reaction shall be provided with an approved means to maintain the temperature within a safe range.

6.2.1.7.1.1 Redundant temperature control equipment that will operate on failure of the primary temperature control system shall be provided.

6.2.1.7.1.2 The use of alternative means that prevent a hazardous reaction shall be permitted subject to the approval of the AHJ.

6.2.1.7.2 Pressure Control.

6.2.1.7.2.1 Stationary tanks and equipment containing hazardous material liquids that can generate pressures exceeding design limits due to exposure fires or internal reaction shall have some form of construction or other approved means that will relieve excessive internal pressure.

6.2.1.7.2.2 The termination point for piped vent systems used for the purpose of operational or emergency venting shall be located to prevent impingement exposure on the system served and to minimize the effects of high-temperature thermal radiation or the effects of contact with the material being vented from the escaping plume on the supply system, personnel, adjacent structures, and ignition sources.

6.2.1.8 Standby and Emergency Power.

6.2.1.8.1 Where mechanical ventilation, treatment systems, temperature control, alarm, detection, or other electrically operated safety systems are required by this code or the building code, such systems shall be provided with standby power or emergency power as required by 6.2.1.8. [5000:34.3.2.7.1]

6.2.1.8.2 Standby power for mechanical ventilation, exhaust treatment, and temperature control systems shall not be required where such systems are engineered and approved as fail-safe. [5000:34.3.2.7.2]

6.2.1.8.3 The secondary source of power shall be an approved means of legally required standby power in accordance with *NFPA 70, National Electrical Code*.

6.2.1.9 Spill Control and Secondary Containment for Hazardous Materials Liquids and Solids.

6.2.1.9.1 General. Buildings, or portions thereof, required to comply with Protection Level 1 through Protection Level 4 shall be provided with spill control and secondary containment in accordance with 6.2.1.9.2 and 6.2.1.9.3, except for outdoor storage on containment pallets complying with 6.2.7.3.3.

6.2.1.9.2 Spill Control.

6.2.1.9.2.1 Buildings, or portions thereof, used for storage of hazardous materials liquids in individual containers having a capacity of more than 55 gal (208.2 L) shall be provided with spill control to prevent the flow of liquids to adjoining areas.

6.2.1.9.2.2 Where spill control is required, floors in indoor locations and similar surfaces in outdoor locations shall be constructed to contain a spill from the largest single vessel by one of the following methods:

(1) Liquidtight sloped or recessed floors in indoor locations or similar areas in outdoor locations
(2) Liquidtight floors in indoor locations or similar areas in outdoor locations provided with liquidtight raised or recessed sills or dikes
(3) Sumps and collection systems

6.2.1.9.2.3 Except for surfacing, the floors, sills, dikes, sumps, and collection systems shall be constructed of noncombustible material, and the liquidtight seal shall be compatible with the material stored.

6.2.1.9.2.4 Where liquidtight sills or dikes are provided, they shall not be required at perimeter openings that are provided with an open-grate trench across the opening that connects to an approved collection system.

6.2.1.9.3 Secondary Containment.

6.2.1.9.3.1 Buildings, or portions thereof, used for any of the following shall be provided with secondary containment:

(1) Storage of liquids where the capacity of an individual vessel exceeds 55 gal (208.2 L) or the aggregate capacity of multiple vessels exceeds 1000 gal (3785 L)
(2) Storage of solids where the capacity of an individual vessel exceeds 550 lb (248.8 kg) or the aggregate capacity of multiple vessels exceeds 10,000 lb (4524.8 kg)

6.2.1.9.3.2 Buildings, or portions thereof, containing only hazardous materials in listed secondary containment tanks or systems shall not be required to comply with 6.2.1.9.3.1.

6.2.1.9.3.3 Buildings, or portions thereof, containing only ammonium nitrate solids, organic peroxide solids, flammable solids, pyrophoric solids, or corrosive solids shall not be required to comply with 6.2.1.9.3.1.

6.2.1.9.3.4 The building, room, or area shall contain or drain the hazardous materials and fire protection water through the use of one of the following methods:

(1) Liquidtight sloped or recessed floors in indoor locations or similar areas in outdoor locations
(2) Liquidtight floors in indoor locations or similar areas in outdoor locations provided with liquidtight raised or recessed sills or dikes
(3) Sumps and collection systems
(4) Drainage systems leading to an approved location

6.2.1.9.3.5 Where incompatible materials are present in open containers or systems, such materials shall be separated from each other in the secondary containment system.

6.2.1.9.3.6 Secondary containment for indoor storage areas shall be designed to contain a spill from the largest vessel plus the design flow volume of fire protection water calculated to discharge from the fire-extinguishing system over the minimum required system design area, or area of the room or area in which the storage is located, whichever is smaller, for a period of 20 minutes.

6.2.1.9.3.7 A monitoring method shall be provided to detect hazardous materials in the secondary containment system.

6.2.1.9.3.8 The monitoring method specified in 6.2.1.9.3.7 shall be permitted to be visual inspection of the primary or secondary containment or other approved means.

6.2.1.9.3.9 Where secondary containment is subject to the intrusion of water, a monitoring method for detecting water shall be provided.

6.2.1.9.3.10 Where monitoring devices are provided, they shall be connected to distinct visual or audible alarms.

6.2.1.9.3.11 Where remote containment systems are provided, drainage systems shall be in accordance with the plumbing code, as referenced in Chapter 2, and the following provisions also shall be met:

(1) The slope of floors in indoor locations to drains or similar areas in outdoor locations shall be not less than 1 percent.
(2) Drains from indoor storage areas shall be sized to carry the volume of the fire protection water, as determined by the design density discharged from the automatic fire-extinguishing system over the minimum required system design area, or area of the room or area in which the storage is located, whichever is smaller.

(3) Materials of construction for drainage systems shall be compatible with the materials stored.
(4) Separate drainage systems shall be provided to avoid mixing incompatible materials where such materials are present in an open-use condition.
(5) Drains shall terminate in an approved location away from buildings, valves, means of egress, fire access roadways, adjoining property, and storm drains.

6.2.1.10 Floors in Storage Rooms. Floors in storage areas for ammonium nitrate, organic peroxides, oxidizers, pyrophoric materials, unstable (reactive) materials, water-reactive solids and liquids, corrosive materials, and toxic and highly toxic materials shall be of liquidtight, noncombustible construction.

6.2.1.11 Supervision of Alarm, Detection, and Automatic Fire-Extinguishing Systems. Alarm, detection, and automatic fire-extinguishing systems required by Chapter 6 or other chapters of this code regulating hazardous materials shall be supervised by an approved central, proprietary, or remote station service or shall initiate audible and visual signals at a constantly attended on-site location.

6.2.2 Protection Level 1.

6.2.2.1 General. Buildings, or portions thereof, required to comply with protection level 1 shall comply with 6.2.2 and the building code.

6.2.2.2 Detached Building Required.

6.2.2.2.1* Buildings required to comply with protection level 1 shall be used for no other purpose, shall not exceed one story in height, and shall be without basements, crawl spaces, or other under-floor spaces. [**5000**:34.3.3.2.1]

6.2.2.2.2 Roofs of buildings described in 6.2.2.2.1 shall be of lightweight construction with suitable thermal insulation to prevent sensitive material from reaching its decomposition temperature. [**5000**:34.3.3.2.2]

6.2.2.2.3 Buildings required to comply with both protection level 1 and protection level 4 shall comply with the most restrictive requirements for both protection levels. [**5000**:34.3.3.2.3]

6.2.2.3 Minimum Distance to Property Lines or Horizontal Separation. Buildings required to comply with protection level 1 shall be set back from property lines, or be provided with a horizontal separation in accordance with *NFPA 5000, Building Construction and Safety Code*, by a distance of not less than 75 ft (23 m) and of not less than that required by Table 6.2.2.3. [**5000**:34.3.3.3]

6.2.2.3.1 Explosives that are in accordance with NFPA 495, *Explosive Materials Code*, shall not be required to comply with 6.2.2.3. [**5000**:34.3.3.3.1]

6.2.2.3.2 Distances shall be measured from the perimeter wall to property lines, including those on a public way. [**5000**:34.3.3.3.2]

6.2.2.3.3 Quantities of explosives used in applying Table 6.2.2.3 shall be based on equivalent pounds (kilograms) of TNT. [**5000**:34.3.3.3.3]

6.2.2.4 Frangible Building. Frangible buildings complying with 7.4.1.3.5.3 of *NFPA 5000, Building Construction and Safety Code*, shall not be required to be protected with an automatic sprinkler system. [**5000**:34.3.3.4]

6.2.3 Protection Level 2.

6.2.3.1 General. Buildings, or portions thereof, required to comply with protection level 2 shall comply with 6.2.1 and 6.2.3.2 through 6.2.3.5.2. [**5000**:34.3.4.1]

6.2.3.2 Exterior Wall Required.

6.2.3.2.1 Buildings, or portions thereof, required to comply with protection level 2 shall be located on property such that not less than 25 percent of the perimeter wall is an exterior wall. [**5000**:34.3.4.2.1]

6.2.3.2.2 Rooms utilized for the use, dispensing, mixing, and storage of flammable and combustible liquids having a floor area of not more than 500 ft^2 (46.5 m^2) shall not be required to be located on the outer perimeter of the building where such rooms comply with NFPA 30, *Flammable and Combustible Liquids Code*. [**5000**:34.3.4.2.2]

6.2.3.3 Minimum Distance to Property Lines or Horizontal Separation.

6.2.3.3.1 Buildings, or portions thereof, required to comply with protection level 2 shall be set back from property lines, or be provided with a horizontal separation in accordance with 7.3.4.2 of *NFPA 5000, Building Construction and Safety Code*, at the following distances:

(1) Not less than 30 ft (9.1 m) where the area of the occupancy exceeds 1000 ft^2 (93 m^2) and a detached building is not required
(2) Not less than 50 ft (15 m) where a detached building is required by Table 5.3.7.
(3) Not less than the distances required by Table 6.2.2.3 for buildings containing materials with explosive characteristics

[**5000**:34.3.4.3.1]

6.2.3.3.2 Distances shall be measured from the walls enclosing the protection level 2 area to property lines, including those on a public way, or in accordance with 7.3.4.2 of *NFPA 5000, Building Construction and Safety Code*, for buildings on the same lot. [**5000**:34.3.4.3.2]

6.2.3.4 Detached Building Required.

6.2.3.4.1* Buildings required to comply with protection level 2 and containing quantities of high hazard contents exceeding the quantity limits set forth in Table 5.3.7 shall be used for no other purpose, shall not exceed one story in height, and shall be without basements, crawl spaces, or other under-floor spaces. [**5000**:34.3.4.4.1]

6.2.3.4.2 Buildings that contain high hazard level 2 contents also shall be permitted to contain high hazard level 3 or high hazard level 4 contents, provided that the materials are separated as otherwise required by the provisions of this code and NFPA 1, *Fire Code*. [**5000**:34.3.4.4.2]

6.2.3.4.3 The roofs of buildings specified in 6.2.3.4.1 shall be of lightweight construction.

6.2.3.5 Water-Reactive Materials.

6.2.3.5.1 Rooms or areas containing Class 2 or Class 3 water-reactive materials shall be resistant to water penetration. [**5000**:34.3.4.5.1]

Table 6.2.2.3 The American Table of Distances for Storage of Explosives

Quantity of Explosive Materials[1,2,3,4]		Distances in Feet							
		Inhabited Buildings[9]		Public Highways Traffic Volume of 3,000 Vehicles/Day or Less[11]		Passenger Railways — Public Highways with Traffic Volume of More Than 3,000 Vehicles/Day[10,11]		Separation of Magazines[12]	
Pounds Over	Pounds Not Over	Barricaded[6,7,8]	Un-barricaded	Barricaded[6,7,8]	Un-barricaded	Barricaded[6,7,8]	Un-barricaded	Barricaded[6,7,8]	Un-barricaded
0	5	70	140	30	60	51	102	6	12
5	10	90	180	35	70	64	128	8	16
10	20	110	220	45	90	81	162	10	20
20	30	125	250	50	100	93	186	11	22
30	40	140	280	55	110	103	206	12	24
40	50	150	300	60	120	110	220	14	28
50	75	170	340	70	140	127	254	15	30
75	100	190	380	75	150	139	278	16	32
100	125	200	400	80	160	150	300	18	36
125	150	215	430	85	170	159	318	19	38
150	200	235	470	95	190	175	350	21	42
200	250	255	510	105	210	189	378	23	46
250	300	270	540	110	220	201	402	24	48
300	400	295	590	120	240	221	442	27	54
400	500	320	640	130	260	238	476	29	58
500	600	340	680	135	270	253	506	31	62
600	700	355	710	145	290	266	532	32	64
700	800	375	750	150	300	278	556	33	66
800	900	390	780	155	310	289	578	35	70
900	1,000	400	800	160	320	300	600	36	72
1,000	1,200	425	850	165	330	318	636	39	78
1,200	1,400	450	900	170	340	336	672	41	82
1,400	1,600	470	940	175	350	351	702	43	86
1,600	1,800	490	980	180	360	366	732	44	88
1,800	2,000	505	1,010	185	370	378	756	45	90
2,000	2,500	545	1,090	190	380	408	816	49	98
2,500	3,000	580	1,160	195	390	432	864	52	104
3,000	4,000	635	1,270	210	420	474	948	58	116
4,000	5,000	685	1,370	225	450	513	1,026	61	122
5,000	6,000	730	1,460	235	470	546	1,092	65	130
6,000	7,000	770	1,540	245	490	573	1,146	68	136
7,000	8,000	800	1,600	250	500	600	1,200	72	144
8,000	9,000	835	1,670	255	510	624	1,248	75	150
9,000	10,000	865	1,730	260	520	645	1,290	78	156
10,000	12,000	875	1,750	270	540	687	1,374	82	164
12,000	14,000	885	1,770	275	550	723	1,446	87	174
14,000	16,000	900	1,800	280	560	756	1,512	90	180
16,000	18,000	940	1,880	285	570	786	1,572	94	188
18,000	20,000	975	1,950	290	580	813	1,626	98	196
20,000	25,000	1,055	2,000	315	630	876	1,752	105	210
25,000	30,000	1,130	2,000	340	680	933	1,866	112	224
30,000	35,000	1,205	2,000	360	720	981	1,962	119	238
35,000	40,000	1,275	2,000	380	760	1,026	2,000	124	248
40,000	45,000	1,340	2,000	400	800	1,068	2,000	129	258
45,000	50,000	1,400	2,000	420	840	1,104	2,000	135	270
50,000	55,000	1,460	2,000	440	880	1,140	2,000	140	280
55,000	60,000	1,515	2,000	455	910	1,173	2,000	145	290
60,000	65,000	1,565	2,000	470	940	1,206	2,000	150	300
65,000	70,000	1,610	2,000	485	970	1,236	2,000	155	310
70,000	75,000	1,655	2,000	500	1,000	1,263	2,000	160	320

Table 6.2.2.3 *Continued*

Quantity of Explosive Materials[1,2,3,4]		Distances in Feet							
		Inhabited Buildings[9]		Public Highways Traffic Volume of 3,000 Vehicles/Day or Less[11]		Passenger Railways — Public Highways with Traffic Volume of More Than 3,000 Vehicles/Day[10,11]		Separation of Magazines[12]	
Pounds Over	Pounds Not Over	Barricaded[6,7,8]	Un-barricaded	Barricaded[6,7,8]	Un-barricaded	Barricaded[6,7,8]	Un-barricaded	Barricaded[6,7,8]	Un-barricaded
75,000	80,000	1,695	2,000	510	1,020	1,293	2,000	165	330
80,000	85,000	1,730	2,000	520	1,040	1,317	2,000	170	340
85,000	90,000	1,760	2,000	530	1,060	1,344	2,000	175	350
90,000	95,000	1,790	2,000	540	1,080	1,368	2,000	180	360
95,000	100,000	1,815	2,000	545	1,090	1,392	2,000	185	370
100,000	110,000	1,835	2,000	550	1,100	1,437	2,000	195	390
110,000	120,000	1,855	2,000	555	1,110	1,479	2,000	205	410
120,000	130,000	1,875	2,000	560	1,120	1,521	2,000	215	430
130,000	140,000	1,890	2,000	565	1,130	1,557	2,000	225	450
140,000	150,000	1,900	2,000	570	1,140	1,593	2,000	235	470
150,000	160,000	1,935	2,000	580	1,160	1,629	2,000	245	490
160,000	170,000	1,965	2,000	590	1,180	1,662	2,000	255	510
170,000	180,000	1,990	2,000	600	1,200	1,695	2,000	265	530
180,000	190,000	2,010	2,010	605	1,210	1,725	2,000	275	550
190,000	200,000	2,030	2,030	610	1,220	1,755	2,000	285	570
200,000	210,000	2,055	2,055	620	1,240	1,782	2,000	295	590
210,000	230,000	2,100	2,100	635	1,270	1,836	2,000	315	630
230,000	250,000	2,155	2,155	650	1,300	1,890	2,000	335	670
250,000	275,000	2,215	2,215	670	1,340	1,950	2,000	360	720
275,000	300,000	2,275	2,275	690	1,380	2,000	2,000	385	770

Superscript numerals refer to explanatory footnotes.
Explanatory Notes Essential to the Application of the American Table of Distances for Storage of Explosives.
(1) "Explosive materials" means explosives, blasting agents, and detonators.
(2) "Explosives" means any chemical compound, mixture, or device, the primary or common purpose of which is to function by explosion. A list of explosives determined to be within the coverage of Title 18, United States Code, Chapter 40, "Importation, Manufacture, Distribution and Storage of Explosive Materials," is issued at least annually by the Director of the Bureau of Alcohol, Tobacco, and Firearms of the Department of the Treasury. For quantity and distance purposes, detonating cord of 50 grains per foot should be calculated as equivalent to 8 lb (3.7 kg) of high explosives per 1000 ft (305 m). Heavier or lighter core loads should be rated proportionately.
(3) "Blasting agents" means any material or mixture consisting of fuel and oxidizer, intended for blasting, and not otherwise defined as an explosive, provided that the finished product, as mixed for use or shipment, cannot be detonated by means of a No. 8 test blasting cap where unconfined.
(4) "Detonator" means any device containing any initiating or primary explosive that is used for initiating detonation. A detonator may not be permitted to contain more than 10 g of total explosives by weight, excluding ignition or delay charges. The term includes, but is not limited to, electric blasting caps of instantaneous and delay types, blasting caps for use with safety fuses, detonating cord delay connectors, and nonelectric instantaneous and delay blasting caps that use detonating cord, shock tube, or any other replacement for electric leg wires. All types of detonators in strengths through No. 8 cap should be rated at 1½ lb (0.7 kg) of explosives per 1000 caps.
(5) For strengths higher than No. 8 cap, the manufacturer should be consulted.
(6) "Magazine" means any building, structure, or container, other than an explosives manufacturing building, approved for the storage of explosive materials.
(7) "Natural barricade" means natural features of the ground, such as hills, or timber of sufficient density that the surrounding exposures that need protection cannot be seen from the magazine when the trees are bare of leaves.
(8) "Artificial barricade" means an artificial mound or revetted wall of earth of a minimum thickness of 3 ft (0.9 m).
(9) "Barricaded" means the effective screening of a building containing explosive materials from the magazine or another building, a railway, or a highway by a natural or an artificial barrier. A straight line from the top of any sidewall of the building containing explosive materials to the eave line of any magazine or other building or to a point 12 ft (3.7 m) above the center of a railway or highway shall pass through such barrier.
(10) "Inhabited building" means a building regularly occupied in whole or part as a habitation for human beings, or any church, schoolhouse, railroad station, store, or other structure where people are accustomed to assemble, but does not include any building or structure occupied in connection with the manufacture, transportation, storage, or use of explosive materials.
(11) "Railway" means any steam, electric, or other railroad or railway that carries passengers for hire.
(12) "Public highway" means any road, street, or way, whether on public or private property, open to public travel.
(13) Where two or more storage magazines are located on the same property, each magazine shall comply with the minimum distances specified from inhabited buildings, railways, and highways, and, in addition, they should be separated from each other by not less than the distances shown for "separation of magazines," except that the quantity of explosive materials contained in detonator magazines shall govern with regard to the spacing of said detonator magazines from magazines containing other explosive materials. If any two or more magazines are separated from each other by less than the specified "separation of magazines" distances, such magazines, as a group, shall be considered as one magazine, and the total quantity of explosive materials stored in such group shall be treated as if stored in a single magazine located on the site of any magazine of the group, and shall comply with the minimum specified distances from other magazines, inhabited buildings, railways, and highways.
(14) Storage in excess of 300,000 lb (136,200 kg) of explosive materials in one magazine generally is not necessary for commercial enterprises.
(15) This table applies only to the manufacture and permanent storage of commercial explosive materials. It is not applicable to the transportation of explosives or any handling or temporary storage necessary or incident thereto. It is not intended to apply to bombs, projectiles, or other heavily encased explosives.
(16) Where a manufacturing building on an explosive materials plant site is designed to contain explosive materials, the building shall be located at a distance from inhabited buildings, public highways, and passenger railways in accordance with the American Table of Distances based on the maximum quantity of explosive materials permitted to be in the building at one time.
Source: Reprinted from *IME Safety Library Publication No. 2*, with permission of the Institute of Makers of Explosives, revised in June of 1991.
[**495**: Table 9.4.1(b)]

6.2.3.5.2 Piping for conveying water, other than fire protection piping, shall not route over or through areas containing Class 2 or Class 3 water-reactive materials, unless isolated by approved liquidtight construction. [**5000**:34.3.4.5.2]

6.2.4 Protection Level 3.

6.2.4.1 General. Buildings, or portions thereof, required to comply with protection level 3 shall comply with 6.2.1 and 6.2.4.2 through 6.2.4.7.2. [**5000**:34.3.5.1]

6.2.4.2 Exterior Wall Required.

6.2.4.2.1 Buildings, or portions thereof, required to comply with protection level 3 shall be located on property such that not less than 25 percent of the perimeter wall is an exterior wall. [**5000**:34.3.5.2.1]

6.2.4.2.2 Rooms utilized for the use, dispensing, mixing, and storage of flammable and combustible liquids having a floor area of not more than 500 ft^2 (46.5 m^2) shall not be required to be located on the outer perimeter of the building where such rooms are in accordance with NFPA 30, *Flammable and Combustible Liquids Code*. [**5000**:34.3.5.2.2]

6.2.4.3 Minimum Distance to Property Lines or Horizontal Separation.

6.2.4.3.1 Buildings, or portions thereof, required to comply with protection level 3 shall be set back from property lines, or be provided with a horizontal separation in accordance with 7.3.4.2 of *NFPA 5000, Building Construction and Safety Code*, at the following distances:

(1) Not less than 30 ft (9.1 m) where the area of the occupancy exceeds 1000 ft^2 (93 m^2) and a detached building is not required
(2) Not less than 50 ft (15 m) where a detached building is required by Table 5.3.7
(3) Not less than the distances required by Table 34.3.3.3 of *NFPA 5000, Building Construction and Safety Code*, for buildings containing materials with explosive characteristics

[**5000**:34.3.5.3.1]

6.2.4.3.2 Distances shall be measured from the walls enclosing the protection level 3 area to property lines, including those on a public way, or in accordance with 7.3.4.2 of *NFPA 5000, Building Construction and Safety Code*, for buildings on the same lot. [**5000**:34.3.5.3.2]

6.2.4.4 Detached Building Required.

6.2.4.4.1* Buildings required to comply with protection level 3 and containing quantities of high hazard contents exceeding the quantity limits set forth in Table 5.3.7 shall be used for no other purpose, shall not exceed one story in height, and shall be without basements, crawl spaces, or other under-floor spaces. [**5000**:34.3.5.4.1]

6.2.4.4.2 Buildings that contain high hazard level 3 contents also shall be permitted to contain high hazard level 2 or high hazard level 4 contents, provided that the materials are separated as otherwise required by the provisions of this code and NFPA 1, *Fire Code*. [**5000**:34.3.5.4.2]

6.2.4.5 Detached Unprotected Building. Where acceptable to the AHJ, based on a determination that a protected building is not practical and an assessment of acceptable risk, storage buildings required to comply with protection level 3 shall be permitted without fire protection systems, provided that the following provisions are met:

(1) The building, or portions thereof, shall have a horizontal separation of at least 200 ft (61 m) from exposed business, industrial, mercantile, and storage occupancies on the same lot and from any property line that is or can be built upon. Where protection for exposures is provided in accordance with 6.2.4.5(9), the horizontal separation shall be at least 100 ft (30.5 m).
(2) The building, or portions thereof, shall have a horizontal separation of at least 1000 ft (305 m) from exposed occupancies other than business, industrial, mercantile, and storage occupancies on the same lot and from any property line that is or can be built upon. Where protection for exposures is provided in accordance with 6.2.4.5(9), the horizontal separation shall be at least 500 ft (150 m).
(3) The building shall not exceed one story in height.
(4) The building shall not have basements, crawl spaces, or other under-floor accessible spaces.
(5) Egress from the building shall not exceed 50 percent of the distances listed in Table 6.2.1.4.1, measured as required in 11.6.2 of *NFPA 5000, Building Construction and Safety Code*, and in compliance with 34.3.2.4.2 through 34.3.2.4.5 of *NFPA 5000, Building Construction and Safety Code*.
(6) The building shall comply with the requirements of the following:
 (a) 34.3.2.2 of *NFPA 5000, Building Construction and Safety Code*, for building height
 (b) 6.2.1.5 for ventilation
 (c) 6.2.1.6 for explosion control
 (d) 6.2.1.8 for standby and emergency power
 (e) 6.2.1.10 for floor construction
 (f) Table 34.3.2.10 of *NFPA 5000, Building Construction and Safety Code*, for unprotected vertical openings
(7) Spill control shall comply with 6.2.1.9.
(8) Secondary containment shall comply with 6.2.1.9.3, except that containment for fire protection water shall not be required if the building is not provided with a fire protection sprinkler system.
(9) Where credit is taken for protection for exposures in accordance with 34.3.5.5(1) and 34.3.5.5(2) of *NFPA 5000, Building Construction and Safety Code*, protection of exposures shall consist of fire protection for structures on property adjacent to the storage building that is provided by (1) a public fire department or (2) a private fire brigade maintained on the property adjacent to the storage building, either of which shall be capable of providing cooling water streams to protect the property adjacent to the storage building.

[**5000**:34.3.5.5]

6.2.4.6 Roofs. The roofs of buildings specified in 6.2.4.4.1 shall be of lightweight construction.

6.2.4.7 Water-Reactive Materials.

6.2.4.7.1 Rooms or areas containing Class 2 or Class 3 water-reactive materials shall be resistant to water penetration. [**5000**:34.3.5.7.1]

6.2.4.7.2 Piping for conveying water, other than fire protection piping, shall not route over or through areas containing Class 2 or Class 3 water-reactive materials, unless isolated by approved liquidtight construction. [**5000**:34.3.5.7.2]

6.2.5 Protection Level 4.

6.2.5.1 Buildings, or portions thereof, required to comply with protection level 4 shall comply with 6.2.1 and 6.2.5.2. [**5000**:34.3.6]

6.2.5.2 Highly Toxic Solids and Liquids. Highly toxic solids and liquids not stored in approved hazardous materials storage cabinets shall be isolated from other hazardous materials storage by a 1-hour fire barrier. [**5000**:34.3.6.2]

6.2.6 Protection Level 5. In addition to the requirements set forth elsewhere in *NFPA 5000, Building Construction and Safety Code*, buildings, and portions thereof, required to comply with protection level 5 shall comply with NFPA 1, *Fire Code*, and NFPA 318, *Standard for the Protection of Semiconductor Fabrication Facilities*. [**5000**:34.3.7.1]

6.2.7 Outdoor Storage. Outdoor storage areas shall be in accordance with the requirements of Chapters 11 through 21, as applicable.

6.2.7.1 Clearance from Combustibles. Clearance from combustibles shall comply with 6.1.15(2).

6.2.7.2 Weather Protection. Where weather protection is provided for sheltering outside hazardous material storage areas, such storage areas shall be considered outside storage areas, provided that all of the following conditions are met: [**5000**:34.2.6]

(1) The overhead structure shall be approved noncombustible construction with a maximum area of 1500 ft^2 (140 m^2) except that area increases based on location or fire protection systems under the requirements of the building code shall be allowed.
(2) Supports and walls shall not obstruct more than one side or more than 25 percent of the perimeter of the storage area.
(3) The distance from the structure and the structural supports to buildings, lot lines, or public egress to a public way shall not be less than the distance required by Chapters 11 through 21 for an outside hazardous material storage area without weather protection.
(4) Weather protection structures containing storage of explosive or detonable materials shall be considered indoor storage.

6.2.7.3 Secondary Containment.

6.2.7.3.1 General. Where secondary containment is required, it shall be in accordance with 6.2.1.9.3.

6.2.7.3.2 Where Required. Where required by Table 6.2.7.3.2, outdoor storage areas used for hazardous materials solids or liquids shall be provided with secondary containment in accordance with 6.2.1.9.3.

6.2.7.3.3 Containment Pallets. Where used as a substitute for spill control and secondary containment for outdoor storage in accordance with 6.2.1.9.1, containment pallets shall comply with the following:

(1) A liquidtight sump accessible for visual inspection shall be provided.
(2) The sump shall be designed to contain not less than 66 gal (249.8 L).
(3) Exposed surfaces shall be compatible with the material stored.
(4) Containment pallets shall be protected to prevent collection of rainwater within the sump.

6.3 Requirements for Use, Dispensing, and Handling of Hazardous Materials in Amounts Exceeding Maximum Allowable Quantities.

6.3.1* General. The following shall apply to aggregate quantities of hazardous materials used, dispensed, or handled:

(1) Where the aggregate quantity of hazardous materials used, dispensed, or handled exceeds the MAQ, the requirements set forth in Section 6.3 shall apply, except as specified in 6.3.1.1.
(2) Where the aggregate quantity of hazardous materials used, dispensed, or handled does not exceed the MAQ, Section 6.3 shall not apply.

6.3.1.1 Uses Not Required to Comply. The following use conditions shall not be required to comply with Section 6.3:

(1) Corrosives used in stationary lead–acid battery systems used for standby power, emergency power, or uninterrupted power supply complying with Chapter 52 of NFPA 1, *Fire Code*
(2) Application and release of pesticide products and materials intended for use in weed abatement, erosion control, soil amendment or similar applications, where applied in accordance with the manufacturer's instructions and label directions

6.3.1.2 Limit Controls.

6.3.1.2.1 General. Limit controls shall be provided in accordance with 6.3.1.2.1 through 6.3.1.2.4.2.

6.3.1.2.2 Temperature Control. Process tanks and equipment, which involve temperature control of the material to prevent a hazardous reaction, shall be provided with limit controls to maintain the temperature within a safe range. [**1**:60.4.4]

6.3.1.2.3 Pressure Control.

6.3.1.2.3.1 Stationary tanks and equipment containing hazardous materials liquids that can generate pressures exceeding design limits due to exposure fires or internal reaction shall have a form of construction or other approved means that relieves excessive internal pressure. [**1**:60.4.4]

6.3.1.2.3.2 The means of pressure relief shall vent to an approved location.

6.3.1.2.3.3 Where required by Chapter 21, the means of pressure relief shall vent to an exhaust scrubber or treatment system.

6.3.1.2.4 Liquid Level.

6.3.1.2.4.1 High Level. Open tanks in which hazardous materials are used shall be equipped with a liquid level limit control or other means to prevent overfilling of the tank. [**1**:60.4.4]

6.3.1.2.4.2 Low Level. Open tanks and containers in which hazardous materials are heated shall be equipped with approved automatic shutoff controls, which will sense low liquid levels and shut off the source of heat. [**1**:60.4.4]

6.3.1.3 Standby and Emergency Power. Standby or emergency power shall be provided in accordance with 6.3.1.3.1 and 6.3.1.3.2 for required mechanical ventilation, treatment systems, temperature control, alarm, detection, or other electrically operated safety systems. [**5000**:34.3.2.7.1]

6.3.1.3.1 Standby power for mechanical ventilation, exhaust treatment, and temperature control systems shall not be required where such systems are engineered and approved as fail-safe. [**5000**:34.3.2.7.2]

Table 6.2.7.3.2 Required Secondary Containment — Hazardous Materials Solids and Liquids Storage

Material	Class	Outdoor Storage Solids	Outdoor Storage Liquids
Physical Hazard Materials			
Flammable solids		NR	NA
Organic peroxide liquids	I	NR	NR
	II	NR	NR
	III	NR	NR
	IV	NR	NR
Oxidizer liquids	4	NR	NR
	3	NR	NR
	2	NR	NR
Pyrophoric liquids		NR	R
Unstable (reactive) liquids	4	R	R
	3	R	R
	2	R	R
	1	NR	NR
Water reactive liquids	3	R	R
	2	R	R
	1	NR	NR
Health Hazard Materials			
Corrosive liquids		NR	R
Highly toxic liquids		R	R
Toxic liquids		R	R

NR: Not required. NA: Not applicable. R: Required.

6.3.1.3.2 The secondary source of power shall be an approved means of legally required standby power in accordance with NFPA 70, National Electrical Code. [**5000**:34.3.2.7.3]

6.3.1.4 Spill Control and Secondary Containment for Hazardous Materials Liquids.

6.3.1.4.1 Spill Control. Where spill control is specifically required in 6.3.2 or 6.3.3, such systems shall be in accordance with 6.3.1.4.1.1 through 6.3.1.4.1.3.

6.3.1.4.1.1 General. Where spill control is required, floors in indoor locations and similar surfaces in outdoor locations shall be constructed to contain a spill from the largest single vessel by one of the following methods:

(1) Liquidtight sloped or recessed floors in indoor locations or similar areas in outdoor locations
(2) Liquidtight floors in indoor locations or similar areas in outdoor locations provided with liquidtight raised or recessed sills or dikes
(3) Sumps and collection systems

[**5000**:34.3.2.8.2.2]

6.3.1.4.1.2 Except for surfacing, the floors, sills, dikes, sumps, and collection systems shall be constructed of noncombustible material, and the liquidtight seal shall be compatible with the material stored. [**5000**:34.3.2.8.2.3]

6.3.1.4.1.3 Where liquidtight sills or dikes are provided, they shall not be required at perimeter openings that are provided with an open-grate trench across the opening that connects to an approved collection system. [**5000**:34.3.2.8.2.4]

6.3.1.4.2 Secondary Containment. Where secondary containment is specifically required in 6.3.2 or 6.3.3, such systems shall be in accordance with 6.3.1.4.2.1 through 6.3.1.4.2.10.

6.3.1.4.2.1 Buildings, or portions thereof, containing only hazardous materials in listed secondary containment tanks or systems shall not be required to comply with 6.3.1.4.2. [**5000**:34.3.2.8.3.2]

6.3.1.4.2.2 Secondary containment shall be achieved by means of drainage control where required by NFPA 30, Flammable and Combustible Liquids Code. [**5000**:34.3.2.8.3.4]

6.3.1.4.2.3 The building, room, or area shall contain or drain the hazardous materials and fire protection water through the use of one of the following methods:

(1) Liquidtight sloped or recessed floors in indoor locations or similar areas in outdoor locations

(2) Liquidtight floors in indoor locations or similar areas in outdoor locations provided with liquidtight raised or recessed sills or dikes
(3) Sumps and collection systems
(4) Drainage systems leading to an approved location

[**5000**:34.3.2.8.3.5]

6.3.1.4.2.4 Where incompatible materials are present in open containers or systems, such materials shall be separated from each other in the secondary containment system. [**5000**:34.3.2.8.3.6]

6.3.1.4.2.5 Secondary containment for indoor storage areas shall be designed to contain a spill from the largest vessel plus the design flow volume of fire protection water calculated to discharge from the fire-extinguishing system over the minimum required system design area, or area of the room or area in which the storage is located, whichever is smaller, for a period of 20 minutes. [**5000**:34.3.2.8.3.7]

6.3.1.4.2.6 A monitoring method shall be provided to detect hazardous materials in the secondary containment system. [**5000**:34.3.2.8.3.8]

6.3.1.4.2.7 The monitoring method shall be permitted to be visual inspection of the primary or secondary containment, or other approved means. [**5000**:34.3.2.8.3.9]

6.3.1.4.2.8 Where secondary containment is subject to the intrusion of water, a monitoring method for detecting water shall be provided. [**5000**:34.3.2.8.3.10]

6.3.1.4.2.9 Where monitoring devices are provided, they shall be connected to distinct visual or audible alarms. [**5000**:34.3.2.8.3.11]

6.3.1.4.2.10 Where remote containment systems are provided, drainage systems shall be in accordance with the plumbing code, as referenced in Chapter 2, and the following provisions also shall be met:

(1) The slope of floors in indoor locations to drains or similar areas in outdoor locations shall be not less than 1 percent.
(2) Drains from indoor storage areas shall be sized to carry the volume of the fire protection water, as determined by the design density discharged from the automatic fire-extinguishing system over the minimum required system design area, or area of the room or area in which the storage is located, whichever is smaller
(3) Materials of construction for drainage systems shall be compatible with the materials stored
(4) Separate drainage systems shall be provided to avoid mixing incompatible materials where such materials are present in an open-use condition
(5) Drains shall terminate in an approved location away from buildings, valves, means of egress, fire access roadways, adjoining property, and storm drains.

[**5000**:34.3.2.8.3.12]

6.3.1.5 Lighting. Lighting by natural or artificial means shall be provided, and artificial lighting, where provided, shall be in accordance with nationally recognized standards. [**1**:60.4.6]

6.3.1.6 System Design.

6.3.1.6.1 Systems shall be suitable for the use intended and shall be designed by persons competent in such design. [**1**:60.4.8]

6.3.1.6.2 Where nationally recognized good practices or standards have been established for the processes employed, they shall be followed in the design. [**1**:60.4.8]

6.3.1.6.3 Controls shall be designed to prevent materials from entering or leaving process or reaction systems at other than the intended time, rate, or path. [**1**:60.4.8]

6.3.1.6.4 Where automatic controls are provided, they shall be designed to be fail-safe. [**1**:60.4.8]

6.3.1.7 Liquid Transfer.

6.3.1.7.1 Approved containers shall be used where liquids are dispensed from containers. [**1**:60.4.9]

6.3.1.7.2 Liquids having a hazard ranking of 3 when exceeding 5.3 gal (20 L), or liquids having a hazard ranking of 4 when exceeding 1.1 gal (4 L), shall be transferred by one of the following methods:

(1) From safety cans
(2) Through an approved closed-piping system
(3) From containers or tanks by an approved pump taking suction through an opening in the top of the container or tank
(4) For other than highly toxic liquids, from containers or tanks by gravity through an approved self-closing or automatic-closing valve where the container or tank and dispensing operations are provided with spill control and secondary containment complying with 6.3.1.4.1 through 6.3.1.4.2.10
(5) By the use of approved engineered liquid transfer systems

[**1**:60.4.9]

6.3.1.8 Supervision of Alarm, Detection, and Automatic Fire-Extinguishing Systems. Alarm, detection, and automatic fire-extinguishing systems required by Section 6.3 shall be supervised by an approved central, proprietary, or remote station service or shall initiate an audible and visual signal at a constantly attended on-site location. [**1**:60.4.5]

6.3.2 Indoor Dispensing and Use.

6.3.2.1 General Indoor Requirements.

6.3.2.1.1 Fire Protection Systems.

6.3.2.1.1.1 General. Indoor dispensing and use areas shall be provided with approved fire protection systems in accordance with 6.2.1.1.

6.3.2.1.1.2 Fire-Extinguishing System for Laboratory Fume Hoods and Spray Booths. In addition to the requirements of 6.2.1.1, laboratory fume hoods and spray booths where flammable materials are dispensed or used shall be protected by an automatic fire-extinguishing system.

6.3.2.1.2 Protection Level 1 through Protection Level 4. Buildings and structures required to comply with protection level 1, protection level 2, protection level 3, or protection level 4 controls shall be constructed in accordance with the specific protection level controls of Section 6.2 and the requirements of *NFPA 5000, Building Construction and Safety Code.*

6.3.2.1.2.1 Building Height Exception. The height of a single-story building, or portion thereof, containing only tanks or industrial process equipment shall not be limited based on the type of construction. [**5000**:34.3.2.2]

6.3.2.1.2.2 Separation of Occupancies Having High Hazards. The separation of areas containing high hazard contents from each other and from other use areas shall be as required by Table 6.2.1.3 and shall not be permitted to be reduced with the installation of fire protection systems as required by 6.3.2.1.1. [**5000**:34.3.2.3]

6.3.2.1.2.3 Egress. Egress from areas required to comply with protection level 1, protection level 2, protection level 3, or protection level 4 shall comply with 6.2.1.4 and Chapter 14 of NFPA 1, *Fire Code*. [**5000:**34.3.2.4]

6.3.2.1.3 Ventilation.

6.3.2.1.3.1 General. Indoor dispensing and use areas shall be provided with exhaust ventilation in accordance with 6.2.1.5. [**5000:**34.3.2.5]

6.3.2.1.3.2 Exceptions to Ventilation Requirement. Exhaust ventilation required by 6.3.2.1.3.1 shall not be required for dispensing and use of flammable solids other than those with finely divided particles.

6.3.2.1.3.3 Standby and Emergency Power. Standby or emergency power shall be provided in accordance with 6.2.1.8.

6.3.2.1.4 Explosion Control.

6.3.2.1.4.1 General. Explosion control shall be provided in accordance with 6.2.1.6 where an explosive environment can occur because of the characteristics or nature of the hazardous materials dispensed or used, or as a result of the dispensing or use process, unless process vessels comply with 6.3.2.1.4.2. [**5000:**34.3.2.6]

6.3.2.1.4.2 Process Vessels. Additional explosion control shall not be required for materials and processes that are located in process vessels designed to fully contain or vent the worst-case explosion anticipated within the vessel under process conditions considering the most likely failure. When deflagration venting from process vessels is provided, the discharge from venting systems shall be in accordance with NFPA 68, *Standard on Explosion Protection by Deflagration Venting*, and arranged so that overpressures produced will not endanger personnel or damage the building, structure, or surrounding buildings or structures in which the process is located.

6.3.2.2 Indoor — Open Systems.

6.3.2.2.1 General. Dispensing and use of hazardous materials in open containers or systems in amounts exceeding the MAQ specified in Section 5.2 shall be in accordance with 6.3.2.2.2 through 6.3.2.2.4.2.

6.3.2.2.2 Ventilation. In addition to the requirements of 6.3.2.1.3, where liquids or solids having a health, instability, or flammability hazard ranking of Class 3 or Class 4 in accordance with NFPA 704, *Standard System for the Identification of the Hazards of Materials for Emergency Response*, are dispensed or used, mechanical exhaust ventilation shall be provided to capture fumes, mists, or vapors at the point of generation, unless such liquids or solids can be demonstrated as not creating harmful fumes, mists, or vapors.

6.3.2.2.3 Floor Construction. Except for surfacing, floors of areas where liquid or solid hazardous materials are dispensed or used in open systems shall be of noncombustible, liquidtight construction. [**5000:**34.3.2.9; **1:**60.4.7]

6.3.2.2.4 Spill Control and Secondary Containment for Hazardous Materials Liquids.

6.3.2.2.4.1 Spill Control. Buildings, or portions thereof, used for either of the following shall be provided with spill control in accordance with 6.3.1.4.1 to prevent the flow of liquids to adjoining areas:

(1) Dispensing of hazardous materials liquids into vessels exceeding a 1.1 gal (4 L) capacity

(2) Open use of hazardous materials liquids in vessels or systems exceeding a 5.3 gal (20 L) capacity

[**5000:**34.3.2.8.2.1]

6.3.2.2.4.2 Secondary Containment.

(A) Where required by Table 6.3.2.2.4.2(A), buildings, or portions thereof, used for either of the following shall be provided with secondary containment in accordance with 6.3.1.4.2.1 through 6.3.1.4.2.10:

(1) Open use of liquids where the capacity of an individual vessel or system exceeds 1.1 gal (4 L)
(2) Open use of liquids where the capacity of multiple vessels or systems exceeds 5.3 gal (20 L)

[**5000:**34.3.2.8.3.1]

Table 6.3.2.2.4.2(A) Required Secondary Containment — Hazardous Materials Liquids Use

Material	Class	Indoor Use	Outdoor Use
Physical Hazard Materials			
Organic peroxide liquids	I	R	R
	II	R	R
	III	R	R
	IV	R	R
Oxidizer liquids	4	R	R
	3	R	R
	2	R	R
Pyrophoric liquids		R	R
Unstable (reactive) liquids	4	R	R
	3	R	R
	2	R	R
	1	NR	R
Water-reactive liquids	3	R	R
	2	R	R
	1	NR	R
Health Hazard Materials			
Corrosive liquids		R	R
Highly toxic liquids		R	R
Toxic liquids		R	R

R: required. NR: Not required.

(B) Buildings, or portions thereof, containing only hazardous materials in listed secondary containment tanks or systems shall not be required to be provided with secondary containment. [**5000:**34.3.2.8.3.2]

6.3.2.3 Indoor — Closed Systems.

6.3.2.3.1 General. Dispensing and use of hazardous materials in closed containers or systems in amounts exceeding the MAQ specified in Chapter 5 shall be in accordance with 6.3.2.3.1 through 6.3.2.3.3.2.

6.3.2.3.2 Ventilation. If closed systems are designed to be opened as part of normal operations, ventilation shall be provided in accordance with 6.3.2.1.3.1.

6.3.2.3.3 Spill Control and Secondary Containment for Hazardous Materials Liquids.

6.3.2.3.3.1 Spill Control. Buildings, or portions thereof, where hazardous materials liquids are used in individual closed vessels exceeding a 55 gal (208.2 L) capacity shall be provided with spill control in accordance with 6.3.1.4.1 through 6.3.1.4.1.3 to prevent the flow of liquids to adjoining areas. [**5000:**34.3.2.8.2.1]

6.3.2.3.3.2 Secondary Containment. Where required by Table 6.3.2.2.4.2(A), buildings, or portions thereof, used for either of the following shall be provided with secondary containment in accordance with 6.3.1.4.2.1 through 6.3.1.4.2.10:

(1) Closed-use capacity of an individual vessel or system exceeds 55 gal (208 L)
(2) Closed-use aggregate capacity of multiple vessels or systems exceeds 1000 gal (3785 L)

[**5000:**34.3.2.8.3.1]

6.3.3 Outdoor Dispensing and Use.

6.3.3.1 General.

6.3.3.1.1 Location. Outdoor dispensing and use areas shall be located as required for outdoor storage of hazardous materials in quantities exceeding the MAQ. [**1:**60.4.11.1.2]

6.3.3.1.2 Clearance from Combustibles. Clearance from combustibles shall be in accordance with 6.1.15(2).

6.3.3.1.3 Weather Protection. Weather protection, when provided, shall comply with 6.2.7.2.

6.3.3.2 Outdoor — Open Systems.

6.3.3.2.1 General. In addition to the requirements set forth in 6.3.3.1 through 6.3.3.1.3, dispensing and use of hazardous materials in open containers or systems in amounts exceeding the MAQ specified in Chapter 5 shall be in accordance with 6.3.3.2.1 through 6.3.3.2.2.

6.3.3.2.2 Spill Control and Secondary Containment for Hazardous Materials Liquids.

6.3.3.2.2.1 Spill Control. Outdoor areas used for either of the following shall be provided with spill control in accordance with 6.3.1.4.1 through 6.3.1.4.1.3 to prevent the flow of liquids to adjoining areas:

(1) Dispensing of hazardous materials liquids into vessels exceeding a 1.1 gal (4 L) capacity
(2) Open use of hazardous materials liquids in vessels or systems exceeding a 5.3 gal (20 L) capacity

[**5000:**34.3.2.8.2.1]

6.3.3.2.2.2 Secondary Containment.

(A) Where Required. Where required by Table 6.3.2.2.4.2(A), outdoor areas used for either of the following shall be provided with secondary containment in accordance with 6.3.1.4.2.1 through 6.3.1.4.2.10:

(1) Open-use of liquids where the capacity of an individual vessel or system exceeds 1.1 gal (4 L)
(2) Open-use of liquids where the capacity of multiple vessels or systems exceeds 5.3 gal (20 L)

[**5000:**34.3.2.8.3.1]

(B) Incompatible Materials. Incompatible materials used in open systems shall be separated from each other in the secondary containment system.

6.3.3.3 Outdoor — Closed Systems.

6.3.3.3.1 General. In addition to the requirements set forth in 6.3.3.1 through 6.3.3.1.3, dispensing and use of hazardous materials in closed containers or systems in amounts exceeding the MAQ specified in Chapter 5 shall be in accordance with 6.3.3.3.1 through 6.3.3.3.2.2.

6.3.3.3.2 Spill Control and Secondary Containment for Hazardous Materials Liquids.

6.3.3.3.2.1 Spill Control. Outdoor areas where hazardous materials liquids are used in individual closed vessels exceeding a 55 gal (208 L) capacity shall be provided with spill control in accordance with 6.3.1.4.1 through 6.3.1.4.1.3 to prevent the flow of liquids to adjoining areas. [**5000:**34.3.2.8.2.1]

6.3.3.3.2.2 Secondary Containment. Where required by Table 6.3.2.2.4.2(A), outdoor areas used for either of the following shall be provided with secondary containment in accordance with 6.3.1.4.2.1 through 6.3.1.4.2.10:

(1) Closed-use capacity of an individual vessel or system exceeds 55 gal (208 L)
(2) Closed-use aggregate capacity of multiple vessels or systems exceeds 1000 gal (3785 L)

[**5000:**34.3.2.8.3.1]

6.3.4 Handling.

6.3.4.1 General. The handling and transportation of hazardous materials in exit access corridors or exit enclosures shall be in accordance with 6.3.4.2 through 6.3.4.4.2.

6.3.4.2 Carts and Trucks Required. Liquids in containers exceeding 5 gal (19 L) in an exit access corridor or exit enclosure shall be transported on a cart or truck.

6.3.4.2.1 Containers of hazardous materials having a hazard ranking of 3 or 4 in accordance with NFPA 704, *Standard System for the Identification of the Hazards of Materials for Emergency Response*, and transported within corridors or exit enclosures shall be on a cart or truck.

6.3.4.2.2 Where carts and trucks are required for transporting hazardous materials, they shall be in accordance with 6.3.4.3, except for the following:

(1) Two hazardous material liquid containers that are hand carried in safety carriers
(2) Not more than four drums not exceeding 55 gal (208 L) each that are transported by drum trucks
(3) Solid hazardous materials not exceeding 100 lb (45 kg) that are transported by hand trucks
(4) Single container not exceeding 50 lb (23 kg) that is hand carried

6.3.4.3 Carts and Trucks. Carts and trucks required by 6.3.4.2 to be used to transport hazardous materials shall be in accordance with 6.3.4.3.1 through 6.3.4.3.6.

6.3.4.3.1 Design. Carts and trucks used to transport hazardous materials shall be designed to provide a stable base for the commodities to be transported and shall have a means of restraining containers to prevent accidental dislodgement.

6.3.4.3.2 Speed-Control Devices. Carts and trucks shall be provided with a device that will enable the operator to control movement safely by providing stops or speed-reduction devices.

6.3.4.3.3 Construction. Construction materials for hazardous material carts or trucks shall be compatible with the material transported.

6.3.4.3.4 Spill Control. Carts and trucks transporting liquids shall be capable of containing a spill from the largest single container transported.

6.3.4.3.5 Attendance. Carts and trucks used to transport materials shall not obstruct or be left unattended within any part of a means of egress.

6.3.4.3.6 Incompatible Materials. Incompatible materials shall not be transported on the same cart or truck.

6.3.4.4 Emergency Alarm for Transportation of Hazardous Materials in Corridors or Exit Enclosures.

6.3.4.4.1 When hazardous materials having a hazard ranking of 3 or 4 in accordance with NFPA 704, *Standard System for the Identification of the Hazards of Materials for Emergency Response*, are transported through corridors or exit enclosures, there shall be an emergency telephone system, a local manual alarm station, or an approved alarm-initiating device at not more than 150 ft (46 m) intervals and at each exit throughout the transport route.

6.3.4.4.2 The signal shall be relayed to an approved central, proprietary, or remote station service or constantly attended on-site location and shall also initiate a local audible alarm. [**1**:60.4.12.2]

Chapter 7 Emergency Planning, Fire Risk Control, and Chemical Hazard Requirements for Industrial Processes

7.1* General. This chapter shall apply to emergency planning, fire risk control, and chemical hazard requirements associated with industrial processes consisting of interconnected equipment or vessels when required by 7.1.1.

7.1.1 Applicability. Except as provided in 7.1.2, the requirements of this chapter shall be applicable to facilities with the following materials, where the quantities of materials in use in an industrial process require compliance with Protection Level 1, Protection Level 2, Protection Level 3, or Protection Level 4:

(1) Unpackaged organic peroxide formulations that are capable of explosive decomposition in their unpackaged state
(2) Oxidizer Class 3 and Class 4: solids and liquids
(3) Pyrophoric solids, liquids, and gases
(4) Unstable reactive Class 3 and Class 4: solids, liquids, and gases
(5) Highly toxic solids, liquids, and gases
(6) Water-reactive liquids, Class 3

7.1.2 Analysis of Upset Conditions.

7.1.2.1 Chapter 7 shall not apply when a qualified design professional documents that the unmitigated consequences of a process upset condition will not result in the following:

(1) Explosion with blast overpressure exceeding 1 psi (6.9 kPa) at 60 ft (20 m) or at the property line, whichever is less
(2) Fire with radiant energy exceeding 1500 Btu/hr/ft^2 (4.73 kW/m^2) over 15 seconds duration at 60 ft (20 m) (flux value) or at the property line, whichever is less
(3)*Maximum airborne concentration from a release of material that, with a 1-hour exposure, would cause irreversible or other serious health effects or symptoms that could impair an individual's ability to take protective action at a distance of 60 ft (20 m) from the process or at the property line, whichever is less

7.1.2.2 Mitigation to reduce the potential risk of an unintended upset to levels below those specified in 7.1.2.1(1) through 7.1.2.1(3) shall be subject to approval by the AHJ in accordance with 7.1.3.

7.1.3 Substantiating Documentation. When required by the AHJ, a technical report substantiating a determination by the process engineer or process designer to not apply Chapter 7 shall be submitted to the AHJ for review and approval in accordance with Section 1.14.

7.2 Process Review and Plan Preparation.

7.2.1* General. Industrial processes shall be reviewed and written plans prepared by qualified personnel to ensure that fire and explosion and chemical hazards resulting from loss of containment or potential chemical interaction are prevented.

7.2.2 Fire Risk Controls.

7.2.2.1 The extent of fire risk controls provided shall be determined by means of an evaluation of the process and application of fire protection and process engineering principles.

7.2.2.2 The evaluation specified in 7.2.2.1 shall include, but shall not be limited to, an analysis of the following:

(1) Fire and chemical hazards of the process relevant to the chemicals and conditions being used
(2) Emergency relief from process vessels relevant to the properties of the materials used and the fire protection and control measures taken
(3) Effluent-handling systems for emergency relief venting
(4) Facility and equipment design, handling, and transfer requirements specified in Chapter 6 and Chapters 11 through 21, as applicable
(5) Emergency response capabilities of the local emergency services
(6) Local conditions, such as exposure to and from adjacent properties and exposure to floods, earthquakes, and severe weather conditions

7.2.3 Emergency Action Planning.

7.2.3.1 Written Emergency Action Plan. A written emergency action plan that is consistent with the personnel and equipment employed shall be developed and implemented.

7.2.3.2 Provisions Within the Emergency Action Plan. The emergency action plan shall include the following procedures in the event of a chemical emergency, fire, or explosion:

(1) Procedures for sounding the alarm
(2) Procedures for notifying and coordinating with the fire department, governmental agencies, or other emergency responders or contacts, as required
(3) Procedures for evacuating and accounting for personnel, as applicable
(4) Procedures for establishing requirements for rescue and medical duties for those requiring or performing these duties

(5) Procedures and schedules for conducting drills
(6) Procedures for shutting down and isolating equipment under emergency conditions to include the assignment of personnel responsible for maintaining critical plant functions or for shutdown of process operations
(7) Appointment and training of personnel to carry out assigned duties, including steps to be taken at the time of initial assignment, as responsibilities or response actions change, and at the time anticipated duties change
(8) Alternative measures for occupant safety, when applicable
(9) Aisles designated as necessary for movement of personnel and emergency response
(10) Maintenance of fire protection equipment
(11) Safe procedures for startup to be taken following the abatement of an emergency

7.2.3.2.1 When an on-site emergency response team is provided in accordance with 6.1.4.4.3, the emergency action plan shall include the following in addition to the requirements of 7.2.3.2:

(1) Procedures for controlling fire, explosion, or chemical hazards resulting from loss of containment
(2) Procedures for mitigating unintended chemical interactions

7.2.3.3 Plan Access. Emergency action plans shall be kept on site and accessible to affected personnel.

7.2.3.4 Plan Review. The emergency action plan shall be reviewed at least annually.

7.2.3.5 Plan Updating. The emergency action plan and related procedures shall be updated and communicated to affected personnel when conditions involving the process(es) or facilities affecting the process(es) are modified or changed in a manner that affects the plan.

7.3 Operating and Maintenance Procedures.

7.3.1 Operating Procedures.

7.3.1.1 General.

7.3.1.1.1 Operating procedures shall be developed for processes regulated by this chapter and implemented in accordance with Section 7.3.

7.3.1.1.2 Operating procedures shall be authorized and approved by personnel designated by the process owner/operator.

7.3.1.2* Contents. Operating procedures shall address the following:

(1) Each operating phase including, but not limited to, startup, operation, shutdown, and startup after unscheduled shutdown
(2) Operating limits
(3) Safety and health controls
(4) Safety systems

7.3.1.3 Review. The operating procedures shall be reviewed annually by the authorized individual per 7.3.1.1 and updated as necessary to ensure that the information is accurate and represents the manner in which the process is operated.

7.3.2 Maintenance Procedures.

7.3.2.1 General. Maintenance procedures shall be developed and implemented in accordance with Section 7.3.

7.3.2.2* Contents. Maintenance procedures shall address a schedule for inspecting and testing alarms, interlocks, and controls in accordance with one of the following frequencies:

(1) At least annually
(2) In accordance with the manufacturer's requirements
(3) In accordance with approved recognized industry standards
(4) In accordance with an approved schedule

7.4* Safety Reviews. When there are changes in chemicals, equipment, processes, or procedures, the hazards of the process shall be evaluated in accordance with the requirements of 7.2.2 prior to startup of the modified equipment or process.

7.5 Incident Investigation Plan.

7.5.1* General. An investigation of a chemical incident regulated by Chapter 7 shall be conducted when the following occurs:

(1) An incident results in a fire, explosion, or unintended release.
(2) An event does not result in a fire, explosion, or unintended release but has the potential to do so.

7.5.2 Documentation. The results of the investigation shall be documented and made available to the AHJ upon written request.

7.6 Document Retention. Documentation required by this chapter shall be retained for a period of not less than 5 years.

Chapter 8 Reserved

Chapter 9 Security for Hazardous Materials

9.1 General. The storage, dispensing, use, and handling areas shall be secured against unauthorized entry and safeguarded with such protective facilities as public safety requires.

9.1.1 Applicability. The requirements of 9.1.2 shall apply to facilities with the following materials where the quantities of materials in use in an industrial process require compliance with Protection Level 1, Protection Level 2, Protection Level 3, or Protection Level 4:

(1) Unpackaged organic peroxide formulations that are capable of explosive decomposition in their unpackaged state
(2) Oxidizer Class 3 and Class 4: solids and liquids
(3) Pyrophoric solids, liquids, and gases
(4) Unstable reactive Class 3 and Class 4: solids, liquids, and gases
(5) Highly toxic solids, liquids, and gases
(6) Water-reactive liquids, Class 3

9.1.2* Security Plan. Where required by the AHJ, a security plan to restrict unauthorized access to facilities subject to Section 9.1 shall be developed.

Chapter 10 Performance-Based Option

10.1* General.

10.1.1* Application. The requirements of this chapter shall apply to facilities designed to the performance-based option permitted by Chapter 4 of NFPA 1, *Fire Code*.

10.1.2* Goals and Objectives. The performance-based design shall meet the goals and objectives of this code in accordance with Chapter 4 of NFPA 1, *Fire Code*.

10.1.3* Approved Qualifications. The performance-based design shall be prepared by a person with qualifications acceptable to the AHJ.

10.1.4* Plan Submittal Documentation. When a performance-based design is submitted to the AHJ for review and approval, the owner shall document, in an approved format, each performance objective and applicable scenario, including any calculation methods or models used in establishing the proposed design's fire and life safety performance.

10.1.5* Independent Review. The AHJ shall be permitted to require an approved, independent third party to review the proposed design and provide an evaluation of the design to the AHJ at the expense of the owner.

10.1.6 Sources of Data. Data sources shall be identified and documented for each input data requirement that is required to be met using a source other than a required design scenario, an assumption, or a facility design specification.

10.1.6.1 The degree of conservatism reflected in such data shall be specified, and a justification for the source shall be provided.

10.1.6.2 Copies of all references relied upon by the performance-based design to support assumptions, design features, or any other part of the design shall be made available to the AHJ if requested.

10.1.7 Final Determination. The AHJ shall make the final determination as to whether the performance objectives have been met.

10.1.8* Operations and Maintenance (O&M) Manual. An approved operations and maintenance manual shall be provided by the owner to the AHJ and the fire department for review, and shall be maintained at the facility in an approved location.

10.1.9* Information Transfer to the Fire Service. Where a performance-based design is approved and used, the designer shall ensure that information regarding the operating procedures of the performance-based designed fire protection system is transferred to the owner and to the local fire service for inclusion in the prefire plan.

10.1.10* Design Feature Maintenance.

10.1.10.1 The design features required for the facility to meet the performance goals and objectives shall be maintained by the owner and be readily accessible to the AHJ for the life of the facility.

10.1.10.2 The facility shall be maintained in accordance with all documented assumptions and design specifications.

10.1.10.2.1 Any proposed changes or variations from the approved design shall be approved by the AHJ prior to the actual change.

10.1.10.2.2 Any approved changes to the original design shall be maintained in the same manner as the original design.

10.1.11* Annual Certification. Where a performance-based design is approved and used, the property owner shall annually certify that the design features and systems have been maintained in accordance with the approved original performance-based design and assumptions and any subsequent approved changes or modifications to the original performance-based design.

10.1.12 Hazardous Materials.

10.1.12.1 Performance-based designs for facilities containing high hazard contents shall identify the properties of hazardous materials to be stored, used, or handled and shall provide adequate and reliable safeguards to accomplish the following objectives, considering both normal operations and possible abnormal conditions:

(1) Minimize the potential occurrence of unwanted releases, fire, or other emergency incidents resulting from the storage, use, or handling of hazardous materials
(2) Minimize the potential failure of buildings, equipment, or processes involving hazardous materials by ensuring that such buildings, equipment, or processes are reliably designed and are suitable for the hazards present
(3) Minimize the potential exposure of people or property to unsafe conditions or events involving an unintended reaction or release of hazardous materials
(4) Minimize the potential for an unintentional reaction that results in a fire, explosion, or other dangerous condition
(5) Provide a means to contain, treat, neutralize, or otherwise handle plausible releases of hazardous materials to minimize the potential for adverse impacts to persons or property outside of the immediate area of a release
(6) Provide appropriate safeguards to minimize the risk of and limit damage and injury that might result from an explosion involving hazardous materials that present explosion hazards
(7) Detect hazardous levels of gases or vapors that are dangerous to health and alert appropriate persons or mitigate the hazard when the physiological warning properties for such gases or vapors are inadequate to warn of danger prior to personal injury
(8) Maintain power to provide for continued operation of safeguards and important systems that are relied upon to prevent or control an emergency condition involving hazardous materials
(9) Maintain ventilation where ventilation is relied upon to minimize the risk of emergency conditions involving hazardous materials
(10) Minimize the potential for exposing combustible hazardous materials to unintended sources of ignition and for exposing any hazardous material to fire or physical damage that can lead to endangerment of people or property

10.1.12.2 A process hazard analysis and off-site consequence analysis shall be conducted when required by the AHJ to ensure that people and property are satisfactorily protected from potentially dangerous conditions involving hazardous materials. The results of such analyses shall be considered when determining active and passive mitigation measures used in accomplishing the objectives of NFPA *101, Life Safety Code*, and the applicable fire prevention code.

10.1.12.3 Written procedures for pre-startup safety reviews, normal and emergency operations, management of change, emergency response, and accident investigation shall be developed prior to beginning operations at a facility. Such procedures shall be developed with the participation of employees.

10.1.13 Special Definitions. A list of special terms used in this chapter shall be as follows:

(1) Design Fire Scenario *(See 3.4.9.1.)*

(2) Design Specifications *(See 3.4.5.)*
(3) Design Team *(See 3.4.6.)*
(4) Exposure Fire *(See 3.4.7.)*
(5) Fire Model *(See 3.4.8.)*
(6) Fire Scenario *(See 3.4.9.)*
(7) Fuel Load *(See 3.4.10.)*
(8) Input Data Specification *(See 3.4.11.)*
(9) Occupant Characteristics *(See 3.4.12.)*
(10) Performance Criteria *(See 3.4.13.)*
(11) Proposed Design *(See 3.4.14.)*
(12) Safety Factor *(See 3.4.16.)*
(13) Safety Margin *(See 3.4.17.)*
(14) Sensitivity Analysis *(See 3.4.2.1.)*
(15) Stakeholder *(See 3.4.20.)*
(16) Uncertainty Analysis *(See 3.4.2.2.)*
(17) Verification Method *(See 3.4.22.)*

[1:5.1.13]

10.2 Performance Criteria.

10.2.1 General. A design shall meet the objectives specified in Section 10.1 if, for each required design scenario, assumption, and design specification, the performance criteria of 10.2.2 are met.

10.2.2* Specific Performance Criteria.

10.2.2.1* Fire Conditions. No occupant who is not intimate with ignition shall be exposed to instantaneous or cumulative untenable conditions.

10.2.2.2* Explosion Conditions. The facility design shall provide an acceptable level of safety for occupants and for individuals immediately adjacent to the property from the effects of unintentional detonation or deflagration.

10.2.2.3* Hazardous Materials Exposure. The facility design shall provide an acceptable level of safety for occupants and for individuals immediately adjacent to the property from the effects of an unauthorized release of hazardous materials or the unintentional reaction of hazardous materials.

10.2.2.4* Property Protection. The facility design shall limit the effects of all required design scenarios from causing an unacceptable level of property damage.

10.2.2.5* Public Welfare. For facilities that serve a public welfare role, the facility design shall limit the effects of all required design scenarios from causing an unacceptable interruption of the facility's mission.

10.2.2.6 Occupant Protection from Untenable Conditions. Means shall be provided to evacuate, relocate, or defend in place occupants not intimate with ignition for sufficient time so that they are not exposed to instantaneous or cumulative untenable conditions from smoke, heat, or flames.

10.2.2.7 Emergency Responder Protection. Buildings shall be designed and constructed to reasonably prevent structural failure under fire conditions for sufficient time to enable fire fighters and emergency responders to conduct search and rescue operations.

10.2.2.8 Occupant Protection from Structural Failure. Buildings shall be designed and constructed to reasonably prevent structural failure under fire conditions for sufficient time to protect the occupants.

10.3 Retained Prescriptive Requirements.

10.3.1 Systems and Features. All fire protection systems and features of the building shall comply with applicable NFPA standards or the fire prevention code for those systems and features.

10.3.2* Electrical Systems. Electrical systems shall comply with applicable NFPA standards for those systems.

10.3.3 General. The design shall comply with the following requirements in addition to the performance criteria of Section 10.2 and the methods of Sections 10.4 through 10.7 or the fire prevention code:

(1) Fundamental requirements
(2) Fire drills
(3) Smoking
(4) Open outdoor fires, incinerators, and outdoor fireplaces
(5) Fire department access
(6) Access to structures
(7) Fire protection markings
(8) Vacant buildings and premises
(9) Combustible vegetation
(10) Safeguards during building construction, alteration, and demolition operations

10.3.4* Means of Egress. The design shall comply with the following NFPA *101, Life Safety Code*, requirements in addition to the performance criteria of Section 10.2 and the methods of Sections 10.4 through 10.7:

(1) Changes in level in means of egress: 7.1.7 of NFPA *101, Life Safety Code*
(2) Guards: 7.1.8 of NFPA *101, Life Safety Code*
(3) Doors: 7.2.1 of NFPA *101, Life Safety Code*
(4) Stairs: 7.2.2 of NFPA *101, Life Safety Code*

Exception: The provisions of 7.2.2.5.1, 7.2.2.5.2, 7.2.2.6.2, 7.2.2.6.3, and 7.2.2.6.4 of NFPA 101, Life Safety Code, shall be exempted.

(5) Ramps: 7.2.5 of NFPA *101, Life Safety Code*

Exception: The provisions of 7.2.5.3.1, 7.2.5.5, and 7.2.5.6.1 of NFPA 101, Life Safety Code, shall be exempted.

(6) Fire escape ladders: 7.2.9 of NFPA *101, Life Safety Code*
(7) Alternating tread devices: 7.2.11 of NFPA *101, Life Safety Code*
(8) Capacity of means of egress: Section 7.3 of NFPA *101, Life Safety Code*

Exception: The provisions of 7.3.3 and 7.3.4 of NFPA 101, Life Safety Code, shall be exempted.

(9) Impediments to egress: 7.5.2 of NFPA *101, Life Safety Code*
(10) Illumination of means of egress: Section 7.8 of NFPA *101, Life Safety Code*
(11) Emergency lighting: Section 7.9 of NFPA *101, Life Safety Code*
(12) Marking of means of egress: Section 7.10 of NFPA *101, Life Safety Code*

10.3.5 Equivalency. Equivalent designs for the features covered in the retained prescriptive requirements mandated by 10.3.1 through 10.3.4 shall be addressed in accordance with the equivalency provisions of Section 1.5.

10.4* Design Scenarios.

10.4.1 General.

10.4.1.1 The proposed design shall be considered to meet the goals and objectives if it achieves the performance criteria for each required design scenario. The AHJ shall approve the parameters involved with required design scenarios.

10.4.1.2* Design scenarios shall be evaluated for each required scenario using a method acceptable to the AHJ and appropriate for the conditions. Each scenario shall be as challenging and realistic as any that could realistically occur in the building.

10.4.1.3* Scenarios selected as design scenarios shall include, but not be limited to, those specified in 10.4.2 through 10.4.5.

10.4.1.3.1 Design fire scenarios demonstrated by the design team to the satisfaction of the AHJ as inappropriate for the building use and conditions shall not be required to be evaluated fully.

10.4.1.3.2 Fire Design Scenario 8 *(see 10.4.2.8)* shall not be required to be applied to fire protection systems or features for which both the level of reliability and the design performance in the absence of the system or feature are acceptable to the AHJ.

10.4.1.4 Each design scenario used in the performance-based design proposal shall be translated into input data specifications, as appropriate for the calculation method or model.

10.4.1.5 Any design scenario specifications that the design analyses do not explicitly address or incorporate and that are, therefore, omitted from input data specifications shall be identified, and a sensitivity analysis of the consequences of that omission shall be performed.

10.4.1.6 Any design scenario specifications modified in input data specifications, because of limitations in test methods or other data generation procedures, shall be identified, and a sensitivity analysis of the consequences of the modification shall be performed.

10.4.2 Required Design Scenarios — Fire.

10.4.2.1* Fire Design Scenario 1. Fire Design Scenario 1 involves an occupancy-specific design scenario representative of a typical fire for the occupancy.

10.4.2.1.1 This design scenario shall explicitly account for the following:

(1) Occupant activities
(2) Number and location
(3) Room size
(4) Furnishings and contents
(5) Fuel properties and ignition sources
(6) Ventilation conditions

10.4.2.1.2 The first item ignited and its location shall be explicitly defined.

10.4.2.2* Fire Design Scenario 2. Fire Design Scenario 2 involves an ultrafast-developing fire in the primary means of egress with interior doors open at the start of the fire. This design scenario shall address the concern regarding a reduction in the number of available means of egress.

10.4.2.3* Fire Design Scenario 3. Fire Design Scenario 3 involves a fire that starts in a normally unoccupied room that can potentially endanger a large number of occupants in a large room or other area. This design scenario shall address the concern regarding a fire starting in a normally unoccupied room and migrating into the space that can, potentially, hold the greatest number of occupants in the building.

10.4.2.4* Fire Design Scenario 4. Fire Design Scenario 4 involves a fire that originates in a concealed wall- or ceiling-space adjacent to a large occupied room. This design scenario shall address the concern regarding a fire originating in a concealed space that does not have either a detection system or suppression system and then spreading into the room within the building that can, potentially, hold the greatest number of occupants.

10.4.2.5* Fire Design Scenario 5. Fire Design Scenario 5 involves a slowly developing fire, shielded from fire protection systems, in close proximity to a high occupancy area. This design scenario shall address the concern regarding a relatively small ignition source causing a significant fire.

10.4.2.6* Fire Design Scenario 6. Fire Design Scenario 6 involves the most severe fire resulting from the largest possible fuel load characteristic of the normal operation of the building. This design scenario shall address the concern regarding a rapidly developing fire with occupants present.

10.4.2.7* Fire Design Scenario 7. Fire Design Scenario 7 involves an outside exposure fire. This design scenario shall address the concern regarding a fire starting at a location remote from the area of concern and either spreading into the area, blocking escape from the area, or developing untenable conditions within the area.

10.4.2.8* Fire Design Scenario 8. Fire Design Scenario 8 involves a fire originating in ordinary combustibles in a room or area with each passive or active fire protection system or feature independently rendered ineffective. This set of design scenarios shall address concerns regarding each fire protection system or fire protection feature, considered individually, being unreliable or becoming unavailable. This scenario shall not be required to be applied to fire protection systems or features for which both the level of reliability and the design performance in the absence of the system are acceptable to the AHJ.

10.4.3 Required Design Scenarios — Explosion.

10.4.3.1* Explosion Design Scenario 1.

10.4.3.1.1 Explosion Design Scenario 1 is the detonation or deflagration of explosive materials being manufactured, stored, handled, or used in a facility.

10.4.3.1.2 Explosion Design Scenario 1 shall address the concern regarding safety of individuals not intimate with the explosion and property protection of adjacent properties and buildings.

10.4.4* Required Design Scenarios — Hazardous Materials.

10.4.4.1 Hazardous Materials Design Scenario 1. Hazardous Materials Design Scenario 1 involves an unauthorized release of hazardous materials from a single control area. This design scenario shall address the concern regarding the spread of hazardous conditions from the point of release.

10.4.4.2 Hazardous Materials Design Scenario 2. Hazardous Materials Design Scenario 2 involves an exposure fire on a location where hazardous materials are stored, used, handled, or dispensed. This design scenario shall address the concern regarding how a fire in a facility affects the safe storage, handling, or use of hazardous materials.

10.4.4.3 Hazardous Materials Design Scenario 3. Hazardous Materials Design Scenario 3 involves the application of an external factor to the hazardous material that is likely to result in a fire, explosion, toxic release, or other unsafe condition. This design scenario shall address the concern regarding the initiation of a hazardous materials event by the application of heat, shock, impact, or water onto a hazardous material being stored, used, handled, or dispensed in the facility.

10.4.4.4 Hazardous Materials Design Scenario 4.

10.4.4.4.1 Hazardous Materials Design Scenario 4 involves an unauthorized discharge with each protection system independently rendered ineffective. This set of design hazardous materials scenarios shall address concern regarding each protection system or protection feature, considered individually, being unreliable or becoming unavailable.

10.4.4.4.2* Hazardous Materials Design Scenario 4 shall not be required to be applied to protection systems or features for which both the level of reliability and the design performance in the absence of the system are acceptable to the AHJ.

10.4.5 Required Design Scenarios — Safety During Building Use.

10.4.5.1* Building Use Design Scenario 1. Building Use Design Scenario 1 involves an event in which the maximum occupant load is in the assembly building and an emergency event occurs, blocking the principal exit/entrance to the building. This design scenario shall address the concern of occupants having to take alternative exit routes under crowded conditions.

10.4.5.2 Building Use Design Scenario 2. Building Use Design Scenario 2 involves a fire in an area of a building undergoing construction or demolition while the remainder of the building is occupied. The normal fire suppression system in the area undergoing construction or demolition has been taken out of service. This design scenario shall address the concern regarding the inoperability of certain building fire safety features during construction and demolition in a partially occupied building.

10.5 Evaluation of Proposed Designs.

10.5.1 General.

10.5.1.1 A proposed design's performance shall be assessed relative to each performance objective in the fire prevention code and each applicable scenario in Section 10.4, with the assessment conducted through the use of appropriate calculation methods.

10.5.1.2 The choice of assessment methods shall require the approval of the AHJ.

10.5.2 Use. The design professional shall use the assessment methods to demonstrate that the proposed design will achieve the goals and objectives, as measured by the performance criteria in light of the safety margins and uncertainty analysis, for each scenario, given the assumptions.

10.5.3 Input Data.

10.5.3.1 Data.

10.5.3.1.1 Input data for computer fire models shall be obtained in accordance with ASTM E 1591, *Standard Guide for Obtaining Data for Deterministic Fire Models*.

10.5.3.1.2 Data for use in analytical models that are not computer-based fire models shall be obtained using appropriate measurement, recording, and storage techniques to ensure the applicability of the data to the analytical method being used.

10.5.3.2 Data Requirements. A complete listing of input data requirements for all models, engineering methods, and other calculation or verification methods required or proposed as part of the performance-based design shall be provided.

10.5.3.3 Uncertainty and Conservatism of Data. Uncertainty in input data shall be analyzed and, as determined appropriate by the AHJ, addressed through the use of conservative values.

10.5.4 Output Data. The assessment methods used shall accurately and appropriately produce the required output data from input data based on the design specifications, assumptions, and scenarios.

10.5.5 Validity. Evidence shall be provided confirming that the assessment methods are valid and appropriate for the proposed facility, use, and conditions.

10.6* Safety Factors. Approved safety factors shall be included in the design methods and calculations to reflect uncertainty in the assumptions, data, and other factors associated with the performance-based design.

10.7 Documentation Requirements.

10.7.1* General.

10.7.1.1 All aspects of the design, including those described in 10.7.2 through 10.7.14, shall be documented.

10.7.1.2 The format and content of the documentation shall be acceptable to the AHJ.

10.7.2* Technical References and Resources.

10.7.2.1 The AHJ shall be provided with sufficient documentation to support the validity, accuracy, relevance, and precision of the proposed methods.

10.7.2.2 The engineering standards, calculation methods, and other forms of scientific information provided shall be appropriate for the particular application and methodologies used.

10.7.3 Facility Design Specifications. All details of the proposed facility design that affect the ability of the facility to meet the stated goals and objectives shall be documented.

10.7.4 Performance Criteria. Performance criteria, with sources, shall be documented.

10.7.5 Occupant Characteristics. Assumptions about occupant characteristics shall be documented.

10.7.6 Design Scenarios. Descriptions of design hazards scenarios shall be documented.

10.7.7 Input Data. Input data to models and assessment methods, including sensitivity analysis, shall be documented.

10.7.8 Output Data. Output data from models and assessment methods, including sensitivity analysis, shall be documented.

10.7.9 Safety Factors. Safety factors utilized shall be documented.

10.7.10 Prescriptive Requirements. Retained prescriptive requirements shall be documented.

10.7.11* Modeling Features.

10.7.11.1 Assumptions made by the model user, and descriptions of models and methods used, including known limitations, shall be documented.

10.7.11.2 Documentation shall be provided that the assessment methods have been used validly and appropriately to address the design specifications, assumptions, and scenarios.

10.7.12 Evidence of Modeler Capability. The design team's relevant experience with the models, test methods, databases, and other assessment methods used in the performance-based design proposal shall be documented.

10.7.13 Performance Evaluation. The performance evaluation summary shall be documented.

10.7.14 Use of Performance-Based Design Option. Design proposals shall include documentation that provides anyone involved in ownership or management of the facility with all of the following notification:

(1) The facility was approved as a performance-based design with certain specified design criteria and assumptions.
(2) Any remodeling, modification, renovation, change in use, or change in the established assumptions will require a re-evaluation and re-approval.

Chapter 11 Ammonium Nitrate Solids and Liquids

11.1 General.

11.1.1* The requirements of this chapter shall apply to the storage, use, and handling of ammonium nitrate when the amount of solid or liquid ammonium nitrate exceeds the MAQ as set forth in Chapter 5.

11.1.1.1* The storage of ammonium nitrate and ammonium nitrate mixtures that are DOT Hazard Class 1 sensitive shall not be permitted by this code except on the specific approval of the authority having jurisdiction.

11.1.1.2 The agricultural application of ammonium nitrate and ammonium nitrate–based fertilizers in outdoor agricultural uses is not regulated by this code.

11.1.2 The storage, use, and handling of ammonium nitrate in any quantity shall also comply with the requirements of Chapters 1 through 4 and the applicable requirements of Chapters 5 through 10.

11.1.3 A permit shall be required from the AHJ for the storage of 1000 lb (454 kg) or more of ammonium nitrate.

11.1.4* The quantity and arrangement limits in this code shall not apply to the transient storage of ammonium nitrate in process areas at plants where ammonium nitrate is manufactured.

11.1.5 Construction Requirements. Buildings, or portions thereof, in which ammonium nitrate is stored, handled, or used shall be constructed in accordance with the building code.

11.1.5.1 The construction requirements of this code shall not apply retroactively to the storage of ammonium nitrate in existing buildings at manufacturing plants.

11.1.5.2 Storage buildings shall not have basements unless the basements are open on at least one side. Buildings over one story in height shall not be used for storage, unless approved for such use.

11.1.5.3 The exterior wall on the exposed side of a storage building within 50 ft (15.2 m) of a combustible building, forest, piles of combustible materials, and exposure hazards by ordinary combustible materials shall be of Type I construction in accordance with the building code.

11.1.5.4 In lieu of the Type I wall specified in 11.1.5.3, means of exposure protection, such as a freestanding fire barrier wall, shall be permitted to be used.

11.1.5.5 The continued use of an existing storage building or structure not in strict conformity with this code shall be approved by the AHJ in cases where such continued use will not constitute a hazard to life or adjoining property.

11.1.5.6 Buildings and structures shall be dry and free from water intrusion through the roof, walls, and floors.

11.1.5.7 Electric lamps shall be located or guarded so as to preclude contact with bags or other combustible materials.

11.2 General Requirements for Storage.

11.2.1 Spill Control. Spill control shall be provided for ammonium nitrate in accordance with 6.2.1.9.2.

11.2.1.1 If the contents of broken bags are uncontaminated, they shall be permitted to be salvaged by placing the damaged bag inside a clean, new slipover bag and closing it to prevent the discharge of contents.

11.2.1.2 Other spilled materials and discarded containers shall be gathered for disposal under the facility operating procedures for hazardous waste.

11.2.2 Drainage.

11.2.2.1 Drainage shall be provided for ammonium nitrate liquids in accordance with 6.2.1.9.3.11.

11.2.2.2 For ammonium nitrate solids the requirements of 6.2.1.9.3.11 shall not apply.

11.2.3 Secondary Containment.

11.2.3.1 Secondary containment shall be provided for ammonium nitrate in accordance with 6.2.1.9.3.

11.2.3.2 For ammonium nitrate solids, the requirements of 6.2.1.9.3 shall not apply.

11.2.4 Ventilation.

11.2.4.1 The requirements of 6.2.1.5 shall not apply.

11.2.4.2 Storage buildings shall have ventilation or be of a construction that will be self-ventilating in the event of fire.

11.2.5* Treatment Systems. (Reserved)

11.2.6 Fire Protection Systems. An automatic fire sprinkler system shall be provided in accordance with 6.2.1.1.

11.2.6.1 Automatic Sprinklers.

11.2.6.1.1 Packaged in Bags. Not more than 2500 tons (2268 metric tons) of bagged ammonium nitrate shall be stored in a building or structure not equipped with an automatic sprinkler system.

11.2.6.1.1.1* When approved by the AHJ, a quantity of bagged ammonium nitrate greater than 2500 tons (2268 metric tons) shall be permitted to be stored in a building or structure not equipped with an automatic sprinkler system.

11.2.6.1.2 Sprinkler protection shall be permitted to be required by the AHJ for the storage of less than 2500 tons (2268 metric tons) of ammonium nitrate where the location of the building or the presence of other stored materials can present a special hazard.

11.2.6.1.3 Sprinkler systems shall be of the approved type and designed and installed in accordance with NFPA 13, *Standard for the Installation of Sprinkler Systems*, and the following:

(1) Ammonium nitrate in noncombustible or combustible containers (paper bags or noncombustible containers with removable combustible liners) shall be designated as a Class I commodity.
(2) Where contained in plastic containers, ammonium nitrate shall be designated as a Class II commodity.
(3) Where contained in fiber packs or noncombustible containers in combustible packaging, ammonium nitrate shall be designated as a Class III commodity.

11.2.6.2 Extinguishing Devices.

11.2.6.2.1 Portable extinguishers shall be provided throughout the storage area and in the loading and unloading areas in accordance with the fire prevention code adopted by the jurisdiction and NFPA 10, *Standard for Portable Fire Extinguishers*.

11.2.6.2.2 When small hose systems are provided, they shall be in accordance with NFPA 14, *Standard for the Installation of Standpipe and Hose Systems*.

11.2.6.3 Fire Protection Water Supplies. Water supplies and fire hydrants shall be provided in accordance with the fire prevention code adopted by the jurisdiction and as required by the AHJ.

11.2.6.4 Remote Areas. The requirements for automatic sprinklers, water supplies, and fire hydrants set forth in 11.2.6.2 and 11.2.6.3 shall be permitted to be waived by the AHJ where storage facilities are located in remote areas.

11.2.7 Explosion Control. The requirements of 6.2.1.6 shall not apply.

11.2.8 Emergency and Standby Power. Standby power shall be provided when required by 6.2.1.8.

11.2.9 Limit Controls. Limit controls shall be provided when required by 6.2.1.7.

11.2.10* Alarms. (Reserved)

11.2.11 Monitoring/Supervision. Supervision shall be provided in accordance with 6.2.1.11.

11.2.12 Special Requirements.

11.2.12.1 Separation.

11.2.12.1.1 Ammonium nitrate shall be separated by fire barrier walls of not less than 1-hour fire resistance or located in a separate building from the storage of any of the following:

(1) Organic chemicals, acids, or other corrosive materials
(2) Compressed flammable gases
(3) Flammable and combustible materials, solids or liquids
(4) Other contaminating substances, including the following:
 (a) Wood chips
 (b) Organic materials
 (c) Chlorides
 (d) Phosphorus
 (e) Finely divided metals
 (f) Charcoals
 (g) Diesel fuels and oils

11.2.12.1.2 Walls referred to in 11.2.12.1.1 shall extend from the floor to the underside of the roof above.

11.2.12.1.3 In lieu of fire barrier walls, ammonium nitrate shall be permitted to be separated from the materials referred to in 11.2.12.1.1 by a space of at least 30 ft (9.1 m) or more, as required by the AHJ, and sills or curbs shall be provided to prevent mixing during fire conditions.

11.2.12.2 Incompatible Materials.

11.2.12.2.1 Flammable liquids, such as gasoline, kerosene, solvents, and light fuel oils, shall not be stored on the premises, unless the following criteria are met:

(1) The storage conforms to NFPA 30, *Flammable and Combustible Liquids Code*.
(2) Walls and sills or curbs are provided in accordance with 11.2.12.1.1 through 11.2.12.1.3.

11.2.12.2.2* LP-Gas shall not be stored on the premises, unless such storage conforms to NFPA 58, *Liquefied Petroleum Gas Code*.

11.2.12.3 Prohibited Articles.

11.2.12.3.1 Sulfur, materials that require blasting during processing or handling, and finely divided metals shall not be stored in the same building with ammonium nitrate, unless such storage conforms to NFPA 495, *Explosive Materials Code*.

11.2.12.3.2 Explosives and blasting agents shall not be stored in the same building with ammonium nitrate, unless otherwise permitted by NFPA 495, *Explosive Materials Code*.

11.2.12.3.3 Explosives and blasting agents shall be permitted to be stored in the same building with ammonium nitrate on the premises of makers, distributors, and user–compounders of explosives or blasting agents.

11.2.12.3.4 Where explosives or blasting agents are stored in separate buildings, other than on the premises of makers, distributors, and user–compounders of explosives or blasting agents, they shall be separated from the ammonium nitrate by the distances or barricades specified in NFPA 495, *Explosive Materials Code*.

11.2.12.3.5 Storage or operations on the premises of makers, distributors, and user–compounders of explosives or blasting agents shall conform to NFPA 495, *Explosive Materials Code*.

11.2.12.4* Lightning. In areas where lightning storms are prevalent, lightning protection shall be provided.

11.2.12.5 Control of Access. Provisions shall be made to prevent unauthorized personnel from entering the ammonium nitrate storage area.

11.3 Indoor Storage.

11.3.1* Detection Systems. (Reserved)

11.3.2 Storage Conditions/Arrangement. Storage arrangement shall be in accordance with 11.3.2.1 through 11.3.2.3.

11.3.2.1 Containers. Bags and containers used for ammonium nitrate shall comply with the specifications and standards established by the U.S. Department of Transportation (DOT).

11.3.2.2 Piles of Bags, Drums, or Other Containers.

11.3.2.2.1 Containers of solid ammonium nitrate shall not be placed into storage when the temperature of the ammonium nitrate exceeds 130°F (54.4°C).

11.3.2.2.2 Bags of ammonium nitrate shall not be stored within 30 in. (762 mm) of the walls and partitions of the storage building.

11.3.2.2.3 Piles shall comply with the following dimensions:

(1) The height of piles shall not exceed 20 ft (6.1 m).
(2) The width of piles shall not exceed 20 ft (6.1 m).
(3) The length of piles shall not exceed 50 ft (15.2 m), unless otherwise permitted by 11.3.2.2.3(4).
(4) Where the building is of noncombustible construction, or is protected by automatic sprinklers, the length of piles shall not be limited.

11.3.2.2.4 In no case shall the ammonium nitrate be stacked closer than 3 ft (0.9 m) below the roof or its supporting overhead structure.

11.3.2.2.5 Aisles shall be provided to separate piles by a clear space of not less than 3 ft (0.9 m) in width, with at least one service or main aisle in the storage area not less than 4 ft (1.2 m) in width.

11.3.2.2.6 Where storage facilities are located in remote areas, the requirements for pile sizes and aisles, as set forth in 11.3.2.2, shall be permitted to be waived by the AHJ.

11.3.2.3 Piles of Bulk Solid Storage.

11.3.2.3.1 Warehouses shall have ventilation, or be capable of ventilation in case of fire, that will, in the event of a fire, prevent the explosive decomposition of ammonium nitrate.

11.3.2.3.1.1* Buildings shall be ventilated so as to prevent confinement of decomposition gases.

11.3.2.3.2* Bulk storage structures shall not exceed a height of 40 ft (12.2 m).

11.3.2.3.2.1 Where bulk storage structures are constructed of noncombustible material and facilities for fighting a roof fire are provided, the height of the storage building shall only be limited by the building construction type as specified in the building code adopted by the jurisdiction.

11.3.2.3.3 Compartments.

11.3.2.3.3.1 Bins shall be clean and free of materials that can contaminate ammonium nitrate.

11.3.2.3.3.2* Due to the corrosive and reactive properties of ammonium nitrate, and to avoid contamination, galvanized iron, copper, lead, and zinc shall not be used in bin construction, except where such bins are protected against impregnation by ammonium nitrate.

11.3.2.3.3.3 Aluminum bins, and wooden bins protected against impregnation by ammonium nitrate, shall be permitted.

11.3.2.3.3.4 The warehouse shall be permitted to be subdivided into any desired number of ammonium nitrate storage compartments or bins.

11.3.2.3.3.5 The partitions dividing the ammonium nitrate storage from the storage of other products that would contaminate the ammonium nitrate shall be constructed to prevent the ammonium nitrate from becoming contaminated.

11.3.2.3.3.6 The ammonium nitrate storage bins or piles shall be clearly identified by signs reading AMMONIUM NITRATE with letters at least 2 in. (50.8 mm) high.

11.3.2.3.3.7 Piles or bins shall be sized and arranged so that all material in the pile is able to be moved out in order to minimize possible caking of the stored ammonium nitrate.

11.3.2.3.3.8* The height or depth of piles shall be limited by the pressure-setting tendency of the product; however, in no case shall the ammonium nitrate be piled higher at any point than 3 ft (0.9 m) below the roof or its supporting and overhead structure.

11.3.2.3.3.9 Ammonium nitrate shall not be placed into storage when the temperature of the product exceeds 130°F (54.4°C).

11.3.2.3.3.10 Dynamite, other explosives, and blasting agents shall not be used to break up or loosen caked ammonium nitrate.

11.3.3 Floors.

11.3.3.1 Floors shall be in accordance with 6.2.1.10.

11.3.3.2 All flooring in storage and handling areas shall be without open drains, traps, tunnels, pits, or pockets into which any molten ammonium nitrate is able to flow and be confined in the event of fire.

11.3.4 Detached Storage. The requirements of 6.2.3.4 shall apply.

11.3.5* Special Requirements. (Reserved)

11.4 Outdoor Storage.

11.4.1 Exposures. Outdoor storage of ammonium nitrate solids or liquids shall be separated from exposure hazards in accordance with 11.4.1.

11.4.1.1 Clearance from Combustibles. Clearance from combustible materials shall be in accordance with 6.2.7.1.

11.4.2 Weather Protection. When provided, weather protection shall be in accordance with 5.1.2 and 6.2.7.2.

11.4.3* Special Requirements — Outdoor Storage.

11.5 General Requirements for Use.

11.5.1 Spill Control. Spill control shall be provided for ammonium nitrate liquids in accordance with 6.3.1.4.

11.5.2 Drainage.

11.5.2.1 Drainage shall be provided for ammonium nitrate liquids in accordance with 6.3.1.4.2.10.

11.5.2.2 For ammonium nitrate solids, the requirements of 6.3.1.4.2.10 shall not apply.

11.5.3 Secondary Containment.

11.5.3.1 Secondary containment shall be provided for ammonium nitrate solids or liquids in accordance with 6.3.1.4.2.

11.5.3.2 For ammonium nitrate solids, the requirements of 6.3.1.4.2 shall not apply.

11.5.4 Ventilation. The requirements of 6.3.2.1.3 shall apply.

11.5.5* Treatment Systems. (Reserved)

11.5.6 Fire Protection System. An automatic fire sprinkler system shall be provided in accordance with 6.3.2.1.1.

11.5.7 Explosion Control. The requirements of 6.3.2.1.4 shall not apply.

11.5.8 Emergency and Standby Power. The requirements of 6.3.2.1.3.3 shall not apply.

11.5.9 Limit Controls. Limit controls shall be provided in accordance with 6.3.1.2.

11.5.10* Alarms. (Reserved)

11.5.11 Monitoring/Supervision. Supervision shall be provided in accordance with 6.3.1.8.

11.5.12 Clearance from Combustibles. (Reserved)

11.5.13 Floors. Floors where ammonium nitrate solids or liquids are dispensed or used in open systems shall be in accordance with 6.3.2.2.3.

11.5.14 System Design. System design shall be in accordance with 6.3.1.6.

11.5.15 Liquid Transfer. Liquid transfer shall be in accordance with 6.3.1.7.

11.5.16 Special Requirements. (Reserved)

11.6 Indoor Use.

11.6.1 Open Systems.

11.6.1.1 Ventilation. The requirements of 6.3.2.1.3 shall apply.

11.6.1.2 Explosion Control. The requirements of 6.3.2.1.4 shall not apply.

11.6.1.3 Spill Control, Drainage, and Containment. Secondary containment shall be provided for ammonium nitrate liquids in accordance with 6.3.2.2.4.

11.6.1.4* Special Requirements. (Reserved)

11.6.2 Closed Systems.

11.6.2.1 Ventilation. The requirements of 6.3.2.3.2 shall apply.

11.6.2.2 Explosion Control. The requirements of 6.3.2.1.4 shall not apply.

11.6.2.3 Spill Control, Drainage, and Containment. Spill control and secondary containment shall be provided for ammonium nitrate liquids in accordance with 6.3.2.3.3.

11.6.2.4* Special Requirements. (Reserved)

11.7 Outdoor Use.

11.7.1 Open Systems.

11.7.1.1 Location. Outdoor use and dispensing shall be located in accordance with 6.3.3.1.1.

11.7.1.2 Spill Control, Drainage, and Containment. Spill control and secondary containment shall be provided for ammonium nitrate liquids in accordance with 6.3.3.2.2.

11.7.1.3 Clearance from Combustibles. (Reserved)

11.7.1.4* Special Requirements. (Reserved)

11.7.2 Closed Systems.

11.7.2.1 Location. Outdoor use and dispensing shall be located in accordance with 6.3.3.1.1.

11.7.2.2 Spill Control, Drainage, and Containment. Spill control and secondary containment shall be provided for ammonium nitrate liquids in accordance with 6.3.3.3.2.

11.7.2.3* Clearance from Combustibles. (Reserved)

11.7.2.4* Special Requirements. (Reserved)

11.8 Handling.

11.8.1 Handling. Handling shall be in accordance with 6.3.4 and 11.8.1.

11.8.1.1 Vehicles and Lift Trucks.

11.8.1.1.1 Internal combustion motor vehicles, lift trucks, and cargo conveyors shall not be permitted to remain unattended in a building where ammonium nitrate is stored.

11.8.1.1.2* Fork trucks, tractors, platform lift trucks, and other specialized industrial trucks used within the warehouse shall be maintained so that fuels or hydraulic fluids do not contaminate the ammonium nitrate.

11.8.1.2* Handling Equipment. Hollow spaces in nitrate-handling equipment, where nitrate is able to collect and be confined under high pressure to become a source of explosion in the event of fire, shall be avoided.

11.8.2* Special Requirements. (Reserved)

Chapter 12   Corrosive Solids and Liquids

12.1 General. The requirements of this chapter shall apply to the storage, use, and handling of corrosive solids or liquids when the amount of corrosive solids or liquids exceeds the MAQs as set forth in Chapter 5. The storage, use, and handling of corrosive solids or liquids in any quantity shall also comply with the requirements of Chapters 1 through 4 and the applicable requirements of Chapters 5 through 10.

12.1.1 Construction Requirements. Buildings, or portions thereof, in which corrosive solids or liquids are stored, handled, or used shall be constructed in accordance with the building code.

12.2 General Requirements for Storage.

12.2.1 Spill Control. Spill control shall be provided for corrosive liquids in accordance with 6.2.1.9.2.

12.2.2 Drainage. When provided, drainage shall be in accordance with 6.2.1.9.3.11.

12.2.3 Secondary Containment. Secondary containment shall be provided for corrosive liquids in accordance with 6.2.1.9.3.

12.2.4 Ventilation. Ventilation shall be provided for open containers in accordance with 6.2.1.5.

12.2.5* Treatment Systems. (Reserved)

12.2.6 Fire Protection Systems. An automatic fire sprinkler system shall be provided in accordance with 6.2.1.1.

12.2.7 Explosion Control. The requirements of 6.2.1.6 shall not apply.

12.2.8 Emergency and Standby Power. Standby power shall be provided when required by 6.2.1.8.

12.2.9 Limit Controls. Limit controls shall be provided when required by 6.2.1.7.

12.2.10* Alarms. (Reserved)

12.2.11 Monitoring/Supervision. Supervision shall be provided in accordance with 6.2.1.11.

12.2.12* Special Requirements. (Reserved)

12.3 Indoor Storage.

12.3.1* Detection Systems. (Reserved)

12.3.2* Storage Conditions/Arrangement. (Reserved)

12.3.2.1* Reserved.

12.3.3 Floors. Floors shall be in accordance with 6.2.1.10.

12.3.4 Detached Storage. The requirements of 6.2.2.2, 6.2.3.4, 6.2.4.4, or 6.2.4.5 shall not apply.

12.3.5* Special Requirements. (Reserved)

12.4 Outdoor Storage.

12.4.1 Exposures. Outdoor storage of corrosive solids or liquids shall be separated from exposure hazards in accordance with 12.4.1.

12.4.1.1 Clearance from Combustibles. Clearance from combustible corrosives shall be in accordance with 6.2.7.1.

12.4.1.2 Location. Outdoors storage of corrosive solids or liquids shall not be within 20 ft (6.1 m) of property lines, streets, alleys, public ways, means of egress to a public way, or buildings not used exclusively for the storage, distribution, or manufacturing of such corrosive, except as provided in 12.4.1.3.

12.4.1.3 Distance Reduction. An unpierced 2-hour fire-resistive wall extending not less than 30 in. (762 mm) above and to the side of the storage area shall be permitted in lieu of the distance specified in 12.4.1.2.

12.4.2 Weather Protection. When provided, weather protection shall be in accordance with 5.1.2 and 6.2.7.2.

12.4.3* Special Requirements. (Reserved)

12.5 General Requirements for Use.

12.5.1 Spill Control. Spill control shall be provided for corrosive liquids in accordance with 6.3.1.4.

12.5.2 Drainage. When provided, drainage shall be in accordance with 6.3.1.4.2.10.

12.5.3 Secondary Containment. Secondary containment shall be provided for corrosive liquids in accordance with 6.3.1.4.2.

12.5.4 Ventilation. Ventilation shall be provided for open containers in accordance with 6.3.2.1.3 and 6.3.2.2.2.

12.5.5* Treatment Systems. (Reserved)

12.5.6 Fire Protection System. An automatic fire sprinkler system shall be provided in accordance with 6.3.2.1.1.

12.5.7 Explosion Control. The requirements of 6.3.2.1.4 shall not apply.

12.5.8 Emergency and Standby Power. Standby power shall be provided when required by 6.3.1.3.

12.5.9 Limit Controls. Limit controls shall be provided in accordance with 6.3.1.2.

12.5.10* Alarms. (Reserved)

12.5.11 Monitoring/Supervision. Supervision shall be provided in accordance with 6.3.1.8.

12.5.12 Clearance from Combustibles. Clearance from combustible corrosives shall be in accordance with 6.2.7.1.

12.5.13 Floors. Floors where corrosive solids or liquids are dispensed or used in open systems shall be in accordance with 6.3.2.2.3.

12.5.14 System Design. System design shall be in accordance with 6.3.1.6.

12.5.15 Liquid Transfer. Liquid transfer shall be in accordance with 6.3.1.7.

12.5.16* Special Requirements. (Reserved)

12.6 Indoor Use.

12.6.1 Open Systems.

12.6.1.1 Ventilation. Ventilation shall be provided in accordance with 6.3.2.2.2.

12.6.1.2 Explosion Control. The requirements of 6.3.2.1.4 shall not apply.

12.6.1.3 Spill Control, Drainage, and Containment. Secondary containment shall be provided for corrosive liquids in accordance with 6.3.2.2.4.

12.6.1.4* Special Requirements. (Reserved)

12.6.2 Closed Systems.

12.6.2.1 Ventilation. Ventilation shall be provided in accordance with 6.3.2.3.2.

12.6.2.2 Explosion Control. The requirements of 6.3.2.1.4 shall not apply.

12.6.2.3 Spill Control, Drainage, and Containment. Spill control and secondary containment shall be provided for corrosive liquids in accordance with 6.3.2.3.3.

12.6.2.4* Special Requirements. (Reserved)

12.7 Outdoor Use.

12.7.1 Open Systems.

12.7.1.1 Location. Outdoor use and dispensing shall be located in accordance with 6.3.3.1.1.

12.7.1.2 Spill Control, Drainage, and Containment. Spill control and secondary containment shall be provided for corrosive liquids in accordance with 6.3.3.2.2.

12.7.1.3 Clearance from Combustibles. Clearance from combustible materials shall be in accordance with 6.3.3.1.2.

12.7.1.4* Special Requirements. (Reserved)

12.7.2 Closed Systems.

12.7.2.1 Location. Outdoor use and dispensing shall be located in accordance with 6.3.3.1.1.

12.7.2.2 Spill Control, Drainage, and Containment. Spill control and secondary containment shall be provided for corrosive liquids in accordance with 6.3.3.3.2.

12.7.2.3 Clearance from Combustibles. Clearance from combustible materials shall be in accordance with 6.3.3.1.2.

12.7.2.4* Special Requirements. (Reserved)

12.8 Handling. Handling of corrosive solids or liquids in indoor and outdoor areas shall be in accordance with Section 12.8.

12.8.1 Handling. Handling shall be in accordance with 6.3.4.

12.8.2* Special Requirements. (Reserved)

Chapter 13 Flammable Solids

13.1 General. The requirements of this chapter shall apply to the storage, use, and handling of flammable solids when the amount of flammable solids exceeds the MAQ as set forth in Chapter 5. The storage, use, and handling of flammable solids in any quantity shall also comply with the requirements of Chapters 1 through 4 and the applicable requirements of Chapters 5 through 10.

13.1.1 Construction Requirements. Buildings, or portions thereof, in which flammable solids are stored, handled, or used shall be constructed in accordance with the building code.

13.2 General Requirements for Storage.

13.2.1 Spill Control. The requirements of 6.2.1.9.2 shall not apply.

13.2.2 Drainage. The requirements of 6.2.1.9.3.11 shall not apply.

13.2.3 Secondary Containment. The requirements of 6.2.1.9.3 shall not apply.

13.2.4 Ventilation. The requirements of 6.2.1.5 shall not apply.

13.2.5* Treatment Systems. (Reserved)

13.2.6 Fire Protection Systems. An automatic fire sprinkler system shall be provided in accordance with 6.2.1.1.

13.2.7 Explosion Control. The requirements of 6.2.1.6 shall not apply.

13.2.8 Emergency and Standby Power. Standby power shall be provided when required by 6.2.1.8.

13.2.9 Limit Controls. Limit controls shall be provided when required by 6.2.1.7.

13.2.10* Alarms. (Reserved)

13.2.11 Monitoring/Supervision. Supervision shall be provided in accordance with 6.2.1.11.

13.2.12* Special Requirements. (Reserved)

13.3 Indoor Storage.

13.3.1* Detection Systems. (Reserved)

13.3.2* Storage Conditions/Arrangement. (Reserved)

13.3.2.1* Reserved.

13.3.3 Floors. The requirements of 6.2.1.10 shall not apply.

13.3.4 Detached Storage. The requirements of 6.2.2.2, 6.2.3.4, 6.2.4.4, or 6.2.4.5 shall not apply.

13.3.5* Special Requirements. (Reserved)

13.4 Outdoor Storage.

13.4.1 Exposures. Outdoor storage of flammable solids shall be separated from exposure hazards in accordance with 13.4.1.

13.4.1.1 Clearance from Combustibles. Clearance from combustible materials shall be in accordance with 6.2.7.1.

13.4.1.2 Location. Outdoor storage of flammable solids shall not be within 20 ft (6.1 m) of property lines, streets, alleys, public ways, means of egress to a public way, or buildings not used exclusively for the storage, distribution, or manufacturing of such material, except as provided in 13.4.1.3.

13.4.1.3 Distance Reduction. An unpierced 2-hour fire–resistive wall extending not less than 30 in. (762 mm) above and to the side of the storage area shall be permitted in lieu of the distance specified in 13.4.1.2.

13.4.2 Weather Protection. When provided, weather protection shall be in accordance with 5.1.2 and 6.2.7.2.

13.4.3* Special Requirements. (Reserved)

13.4.3.1 Pile Size Limit. Flammable solids stored outdoors shall be separated into piles not larger than 5000 ft^3 (141 m^3).

13.4.3.2 Aisles. Aisle widths between piles shall not be less than one-half the height of the piles or 10 ft (3 m), whichever is greater.

13.5 General Requirements for Use.

13.5.1 Spill Control. The requirements of 6.3.1.4 shall not apply.

13.5.2 Drainage. The requirements of 6.3.1.4.2.10 shall not apply.

13.5.3 Secondary Containment. The requirements of 6.3.1.4.2 shall not apply.

13.5.4 Ventilation. Ventilation shall be provided for finely divided particles in open containers in accordance with 6.3.2.1.3 and 6.3.2.2.2.

13.5.5* Treatment Systems. (Reserved)

13.5.6 Fire Protection System. An automatic fire sprinkler system shall be provided in accordance with 6.3.2.1.1.

13.5.7 Explosion Control. The requirements of 6.3.2.1.4 shall not apply.

13.5.8 Emergency and Standby Power. Standby power shall be provided when required by 6.3.1.3.

13.5.9 Limit Controls. Limit controls shall be provided in accordance with 6.3.1.2.

13.5.10* Alarms. (Reserved)

13.5.11 Monitoring/Supervision. Supervision shall be provided in accordance with 6.3.1.8.

13.5.12 Clearance from Combustibles. Clearance from combustible materials shall be in accordance with 6.2.7.1.

13.5.13 Floors. Floors where flammable solids are dispensed or used in open systems shall be in accordance with 6.3.2.2.3.

13.5.14 System Design. System design shall be in accordance with 6.3.1.6.

13.5.15* Special Requirements. (Reserved)

13.6 Indoor Use.

13.6.1 Open Systems.

13.6.1.1 Ventilation. Ventilation shall be provided in accordance with 6.3.2.2.2.

13.6.1.2 Explosion Control. The requirements of 6.3.2.1.4 shall not apply.

13.6.1.3 Spill Control, Drainage, and Containment. The requirements of 6.3.2.2.4 shall not apply.

13.6.1.4* Special Requirements. (Reserved)

13.6.2 Closed Systems.

13.6.2.1 Ventilation. Ventilation shall be provided in accordance with 6.3.2.3.2.

13.6.2.2 Explosion Control. The requirements of 6.3.3.2.2 shall not apply.

13.6.2.3 Spill Control, Drainage, and Containment. The requirements of 6.3.2.3.3 shall not apply.

13.6.2.4* Special Requirements. (Reserved)

13.7 Outdoor Use.

13.7.1 Open Systems.

13.7.1.1 Location. Outdoor use and dispensing shall be located in accordance with 6.3.3.1.1.

13.7.1.2 Spill Control, Drainage, and Containment. The requirements of 6.3.3.2.2 shall not apply.

13.7.1.3 Clearance from Combustibles. Clearance from combustible materials shall be in accordance with 6.3.3.1.2.

13.7.1.4* Special Requirements. (Reserved)

13.7.2 Closed Systems.

13.7.2.1 Location. Outdoor use and dispensing shall be located in accordance with 6.3.3.1.1.

13.7.2.2 Spill Control, Drainage, and Containment. The requirements of 6.3.3.3.2 shall not apply.

13.7.2.3 Clearance from Combustibles. Clearance from combustible materials shall be provided in accordance with 6.3.3.1.2.

13.7.2.4* Special Requirements. (Reserved)

13.8 Handling. Handling of flammable solids in indoor and outdoor areas shall be in accordance with Section 13.8.

13.8.1 Handling. Handling shall be in accordance with 6.3.4.

13.8.2* Special Requirements. (Reserved)

Chapter 14 Organic Peroxide Formulations

14.1 General.

14.1.1* The requirements of this chapter shall apply to the storage, use, and handling of classified solid or liquid organic peroxide formulations when the amount of organic peroxide solids or liquids exceeds the MAQ as set forth in Chapter 5. The storage, use, and handling of solid or liquid organic peroxide formulations classified in classes I, II, III, and IV in any quantity shall also comply with the requirements of Chapters 1 through 4 and the applicable requirements of Chapters 5 through 10.

14.1.2* Construction Requirements. Buildings, or portions thereof, in which solid or liquid organic peroxide formulations are stored, handled, or used shall be constructed in accordance with the building code.

14.2 General Requirements for Storage.

14.2.1 Spill Control. Spill control shall be provided for organic peroxide liquid formulations in accordance with 6.2.1.9.2.

14.2.2 Drainage. When provided, drainage shall be in accordance with 6.2.1.9.3.11.

14.2.3 Secondary Containment. Secondary containment shall be provided for solid and liquid organic peroxide formulations in accordance with 6.2.1.9.3.

14.2.4* Ventilation. Ventilation shall be provided for open containers in accordance with 6.2.1.5.

14.2.5* Treatment Systems. (Reserved)

14.2.6 Fire Protection Systems. An automatic fire sprinkler system shall be provided in accordance with 14.2.6 and 6.2.1.1.

14.2.6.1* Where required by other provisions of this code, automatic sprinklers and water spray systems shall be designed and installed according to the requirements of NFPA 13, *Standard for the Installation of Sprinkler Systems*, and NFPA 15, *Standard for Water Spray Fixed Systems for Fire Protection*, and shall provide the following discharge densities:

(1) Class I — 0.50 gpm/ft^2 (20.4 L/min/m^2)
(2) Class II — 0.40 gpm/ft^2 (16.3 L/min/m^2)
(3) Class III — 0.30 gpm/ft^2 (12.2 L/min/m^2)
(4) Class IV — 0.25 gpm/ft^2 (10.2 L/min/m^2)

14.2.6.2 The system shall be designed as follows:

(1) It shall provide the required density over a 3000 ft^2 (280 m^2) area for areas protected by a wet pipe sprinkler system or 3900 ft^2 (360 m^2) for areas protected by a dry pipe sprinkler system.
(2) The entire area of any building of less than 3000 ft^2 (280 m^2) shall be used as the area of application.

14.2.6.3 Where required for detached storage buildings containing Class I organic peroxide formulations in quantities exceeding 2000 lb (907 kg), automatic sprinkler protection shall be open-head deluge-type, designed and installed in accordance with NFPA 13, *Standard for the Installation of Sprinkler Systems*.

14.2.7 Explosion Control. Explosion control shall be provided for liquid or solid organic peroxide formulations when required by 6.2.1.6.

14.2.8 Emergency and Standby Power. Standby power shall be provided when required by 6.2.1.8.

14.2.8.1 Standby power for temperature control shall be permitted to be replaced by alternative methods of temperature control.

14.2.9 Limit Controls. Limit controls shall be provided when required by 6.2.1.7.

14.2.10* Alarms. (Reserved)

14.2.11 Monitoring/Supervision. Supervision shall be provided in accordance with 6.2.1.11.

14.2.12 Special Requirements.

14.2.12.1 All areas containing organic peroxide formulations shall be conspicuously identified by means of a sign containing the words ORGANIC PEROXIDES and by the organic peroxide class and NFPA 704, *Standard System for the Identification of the Hazards of Materials for Emergency Response*, identification.

14.2.12.1.1 Different Classifications. When organic peroxide formulations having different classifications as defined by Section 4.1 are located in the same area, the NFPA 704, *Standard System for the Identification of the Hazards of Materials for Emergency Response* designations indicated for the area shall be appropriate for the most severe class present.

14.2.12.2 Packaging Marking. Original DOT shipping containers containing organic peroxide formulations shall be individually marked with the chemical name of the organic peroxide or with other pertinent information to indicate classification as required by this code.

14.2.12.3 Temperature Markings. Packages containing organic peroxide formulations that require temperature control shall be marked with the recommended temperature range.

14.2.12.4 Maintenance Operations. Maintenance operations in organic peroxide storage or use areas shall be subject to prior review by, and approval of, supervisory personnel.

14.2.12.5 Cutting and Welding.

14.2.12.5.1 Cutting and welding operations in organic peroxide storage or use areas shall not be conducted until all organic peroxide formulations have been removed from the area of storage or use.

14.2.12.5.1.1 Cutting and welding operations shall be conducted in accordance with the requirements of NFPA 51B, *Standard for Fire Prevention During Welding, Cutting, and Other Hot Work*.

14.2.12.6 Electrical. In addition to the requirements of 6.1.10, the following shall apply to the interior of any refrigerator or freezer cabinet used for the storage of Class I, Class II, or Class III organic peroxide formulations:

(1) The cabinet shall be considered a Class I, Group D, Division 1 location, as defined in Article 500 of *NFPA 70, National Electrical Code*.
(2) Any electrical equipment installed in the interior of such cabinets shall be approved for such use and shall be installed according to the requirements of Article 501 of *NFPA 70, National Electrical Code*.

14.2.12.6.1 Where the storage cabinet is ventilated, the following shall apply:

(1) The electrical equipment shall be considered a Class I, Division 2 location, as defined in Article 500 of *NFPA 70, National Electrical Code*
(2) Mechanical ventilation systems shall provide at least 1 ft^3/min/ft^2 (0.09 m^3/min/0.03 m^2) of floor area.

14.2.12.7 Combustible Waste. Accumulation of combustible waste in organic peroxide storage or use areas shall be prohibited.

14.2.12.8* Damaged Containers. Spilled material and leaking or damaged containers and packages shall immediately be removed for recovery or disposal away from the stored product or other combustibles.

14.2.12.9 Specific Disposal Procedures. Specific disposal procedures shall be established for all organic peroxide areas.

14.2.12.10 Heating and Cooling.

14.2.12.10.1 Temperature Range. Storage areas shall be maintained within the recommended storage temperature range for the materials requiring refrigerated storage.

14.2.12.10.2 Outside of Ambient Temperature. Where the required storage temperature range extends beyond normal ambient temperatures, the following criteria shall be met:

(1) High- or low-temperature limit switches, or both, as applicable, shall be installed and maintained in addition to the normal temperature controls.
(2) The limit switches shall actuate an alarm arranged to ensure prompt response.

14.2.12.10.3 Cooling Systems. Cooling systems shall not utilize direct expansion of a flammable gas.

14.2.12.10.4 Heating Systems. Heating systems shall use hot water, low pressure [a gauge pressure less than 15 psi (103 kPa)] steam, or indirectly heated warm air.

14.2.12.10.5 Container Contact. Heating coils, radiators, air diffusers, cooling coils, piping, and ducts shall be installed so as to prevent direct contact with containers and to prevent overheating or overcooling of the materials stored.

14.2.12.11 The following shall apply to any floors or open spaces located below the organic peroxide storage area:

(1) The floor of the storage area shall be made watertight and shall be provided with drainage that leads to a safe location.
(2) Every means shall be taken to ensure that spilled material cannot run down into areas below the organic peroxide storage area.

14.3 Indoor Storage.

14.3.1 Detection Systems. A detection system that detects smoke, temperature, or rate of temperature rise shall be provided in storage areas used for the storage of liquid and solid organic peroxide formulations.

14.3.2* Storage Conditions/Arrangement. Storage arrangement shall be in accordance with 14.3.2.

14.3.2.1 Storage Limitations. The MAQs of organic peroxide formulations that can be stored in a single area or building shall depend on the classification of the formulations, the classification of the storage facility, and sprinkler protection, as set forth in Table 14.3.2.1(a) and Table 14.3.2.1(b).

14.3.2.2 The quantity of Class III organic peroxide formulations as it appears in Table 14.3.2.1(a) in cutoff storage shall be permitted to be increased to 20,000 lb (9070 kg) if the walls or partitions providing the cutoff have a fire resistance rating of at least 4 hours.

14.3.2.3 Class I organic peroxide formulation cutoff storage as it appears in Table 14.3.2.1(b) shall have interior walls with a blast resistance of 432 psf (0.2 bar).

14.3.2.4* Class I organic peroxide formulation cutoff storage as it appears in Table 14.3.2.1(b) shall have deflagration venting provided for exterior walls.

Table 14.3.2.1(a) Maximum Quantity of Organic Formulations in Nonsprinklered Buildings

Class of Organic Peroxide Formulation	Segregated Storage		Cutoff Storage		Detached Storage Minimum Separation*					
					50 ft (15 m)		100 ft (30.5 m)		150 ft (46 m)	
	lb	kg	lb	kg	lb	kg	lb	kg	lb	kg
I	NA	NA	NA	NA	1,000	454	4,000	1,810	10,000	4,540
II	NA	NA	2,000	907	20,000	9,070	80,000	36,300	500,000	227,000
III	1,500	680	3,000	1,360	70,000	31,800	200,000	90,700	750,000	340,000
IV	100,000	45,400	200,000	90,700	300,000	136,000	500,000	227,000	1,000,000	454,000
V	UNL	UNL	UNL	UNL	UNL	UNL	UNL	UNL	UNL	UNL

*Minimum separation means the distance from the line of property that is or can be built upon, including the opposite side of a public way, or the distance from the nearest important building on the same property.
NA: Not applicable; UNL: Unlimited.

Table 14.3.2.1(b) Maximum Quantity of Organic Peroxide Formulations in Sprinklered Buildings

Class of Organic Peroxide Formulation	Segregated Storage		Cutoff Storage		Detached Storage Minimum Separation*					
					50 ft (15 m)		100 ft (30.5 m)		150 ft (46 m)	
	lb	kg	lb	kg	lb	kg	lb	kg	lb	kg
I	NA	NA	2,000	907	2,000	907	20,000	9,070	175,000	79,400
II	4,000	1,810	50,000	22,700	100,000	45,400	200,000	90,700	UNL	UNL
III	50,000	22,700	100,000	45,400	200,000	90,700	UNL	UNL	UNL	UNL
IV	UNL	UNL	UNL	UNL	UNL	UNL	UNL	UNL	UNL	UNL
V	UNL	UNL	UNL	UNL	UNL	UNL	UNL	UNL	UNL	UNL

*Minimum separation means the distance from the line of property that is or can be built upon, including the opposite side of a public way, or the distance from the nearest important building on the same property.
NA: Not applicable; UNL: Unlimited.

14.3.2.5* Where two or more different classes of organic peroxide formulations are stored in the same area, the following shall apply:

(1) The maximum quantity permitted shall be limited to the sum of the proportional amounts that each class bears to the maximum permitted for that class.
(2) The total of the proportional amounts shall not exceed 100 percent.

14.3.2.6 Where the storage area is protected by a specially engineered fire protection system acceptable to the AHJ, the quantity of organic peroxide formulations shall be permitted to be increased.

14.3.2.7 Organic peroxide formulations sensitive to shock shall not be stored where they can be exposed to the shock effects of explosive materials.

14.3.2.8 Storage Arrangements.

14.3.2.8.1 Storage shall be arranged to facilitate manual access and handling, to maintain pile stability, to minimize breakage and spillage, and to promote good housekeeping.

14.3.2.8.2 A clear space of at least 2 ft (0.6 m) shall be maintained between organic peroxide storage and uninsulated metal walls.

14.3.2.9 Separation Distance. The following shall apply to separation distances:

(1) Incompatible materials and flammable liquids shall not be stored within 25 ft (7.6 m) of organic peroxide formulations.
(2) The effective separation distance shall be maintained by floor slope, drains, or dikes to prevent liquid leakage from encroaching on the organic peroxide formulation storage area.
(3) Organic peroxide formulations that can also be classified as flammable liquids by their flash point shall be permitted to be stored with other organic peroxide formulations, and the more restrictive requirements of NFPA 30, *Flammable and Combustible Liquids Code*, or this code shall apply.

14.3.2.9.1 As an alternative to the 25 ft (7.6 m) separation distance of 14.3.2.9(1), a 1-hour liquidtight fire barrier shall be permitted.

14.3.2.9.2 Only closed containers and packages shall be permitted in storage areas.

14.3.2.9.3 Storage of bags, drums, and other containers and packages of organic peroxide formulations shall be in accordance with Table 14.3.2.9.3.

14.3.2.9.4 Storage of 55 gal (208 L) drums of Class I, Class II, or Class III organic peroxide formulations shall be stored only one drum high.

14.3.2.9.5* Storage of Class V organic peroxide formulations shall meet the requirements of NFPA 1, *Fire Code*, as applicable.

14.3.3 Floors. The requirements of 6.2.1.10 shall not apply.

14.3.4 Detached Storage.

14.3.4.1 General. The requirements of 6.2.2.2, 6.2.3.4, 6.2.4.4, or 6.2.4.5 shall not apply.

14.3.4.2 Building Location.

14.3.4.2.1 For Class I organic peroxide formulations, detached storage buildings shall be separated from each other in accordance with Table 14.3.4.2.1.

14.3.4.2.2 For Class II, III, and IV organic peroxide formulations, detached storage buildings separated by less than 50 ft (15.3 m) shall be considered to be a single area when applying the limits for Table 14.3.2.1(a) and Table 14.3.2.1(b).

14.3.4.3 Building Construction.

14.3.4.3.1* Detached storage buildings shall be single story, without a basement or crawl space.

14.3.4.3.2 Nonsprinklered buildings for storing more than 5000 lb (2270 kg) of Class I, Class II, or any refrigerated organic peroxide formulation that gives off flammable gases upon decomposition shall be built of noncombustible construction.

14.3.4.3.3* Buildings of combustible construction employing sun shields shall be permitted to be used for detached storage buildings storing less than 5000 lb (2270 kg) of organic peroxide formulations.

14.3.5* **Special Requirements. (Reserved)**

14.4 Outdoor Storage.

14.4.1 Exposures. Outdoor storage of solid or liquid organic peroxide formulations shall be separated from exposure hazards in accordance with 14.4.1.

14.4.1.1 Clearance from Combustibles. Clearance from combustible organic peroxide formulations shall be in accordance with 6.2.7.1.

14.4.1.2 Location. Outdoor storage of solid or liquid organic peroxide formulations shall not be within 20 ft (6.1 m) of property lines, streets, alleys, public ways, means of egress to a public way, or buildings not used exclusively for the storage, distribution, or manufacturing of such organic peroxide formulations, except as provided in 14.4.1.3.

14.4.1.3 Distance Reduction. An unpierced 2-hour fire-resistive wall extending not less than 30 in. (762 mm) above and to the side of the storage area shall be permitted in lieu of the distance specified in 14.4.1.2.

14.4.2 Weather Protection. Where provided, weather protection shall be in accordance with 5.1.2 and 6.2.7.2.

14.4.3* **Special Requirements. (Reserved)**

14.5 General Requirements for Use.

14.5.1 Spill Control. Spill control shall be provided for organic peroxide formulations liquids in accordance with 6.3.1.4.

14.5.2 Drainage. Where provided, drainage shall be in accordance with 6.3.1.4.2.10.

14.5.3 Secondary Containment. Secondary containment shall be provided for organic peroxide formulations solids or liquids in accordance with 6.3.1.4.2.

14.5.4 Ventilation. Ventilation shall be provided for open containers in accordance with 6.3.2.1.3 and 6.3.2.2.2.

Table 14.3.2.9.3 Provisions for Storage Arrangement by Class of Organic Peroxide Formulation

Class of Organic Peroxide Formulation	Maximum Pile Height ft	Maximum Pile Height m	Maximum Pile Width ft	Maximum Pile Width m	Minimum Main Aisle Width ft	Minimum Main Aisle Width m	Minimum Additional Aisle Width ft	Minimum Additional Aisle Width m
I*	6	1.8	4	1.2	8	2.4	4	1.2
II*	8	2.4	8	2.4	6	1.8	4	1.2
III*	8	2.4	8	2.4	6	1.8	4	1.2
IV	10	3.0	16	4.9	4	1.2	3	0.9
V	See 14.3.2.9.5							

*See 14.3.2.9.4.

Table 14.3.4.2.1 Separation of Individual Storage Buildings

Nonsprinklered Quantity lb	Nonsprinklered Quantity kg	Nonsprinklered Distance ft	Nonsprinklered Distance m	Automatic Sprinklered Quantity lb	Automatic Sprinklered Quantity kg	Automatic Sprinklered Distance ft	Automatic Sprinklered Distance m
1,000	454	20	6	2,000	907	20	6
4,000	1,810	75	23	20,000	9,070	75	23
10,000	4,540	100	30	175,000	79,400	100	30

14.5.5* Treatment Systems. (Reserved)

14.5.6 Fire Protection System. An automatic fire sprinkler system shall be provided in accordance with 6.3.2.1.1 and 14.2.6.

14.5.7 Explosion Control. Explosion control shall be provided for liquid and solid organic peroxide formulations when required by 6.3.2.1.4.

14.5.8* Emergency and Standby Power. Standby power shall be provided when required by 6.3.1.3.

14.5.9 Limit Controls. Limit controls shall be provided in accordance with 6.3.1.2.

14.5.10* Alarms. (Reserved)

14.5.11 Monitoring/Supervision. Supervision shall be provided in accordance with 6.3.1.8.

14.5.12 Clearance from Combustibles. Clearance from combustible organic peroxide formulations shall be in accordance with 6.2.7.1.

14.5.13 Floors. Floors where solid or liquid organic peroxide formulations are dispensed or used in open systems shall be in accordance with 6.3.2.2.3.

14.5.14 System Design. System design shall be in accordance with 6.3.1.6.

14.5.15 Liquid Transfer. Liquid transfer shall be in accordance with 6.3.1.7.

14.5.16 Special Requirements.

14.5.16.1 Storage directly related to the manufacturing formulation in process areas shall meet the requirements of 14.2.12 and be treated as a process area as addressed in this chapter.

14.5.16.2 Maintenance operations in organic peroxide process areas shall be subject to prior review by, and approval of, supervisory personnel.

14.5.16.3* Waste Disposal. Hazardous materials shall be disposed of in accordance with applicable federal, state, or local governing regulations.

14.6 Indoor Use.

14.6.1 Open Systems.

14.6.1.1 Ventilation. Ventilation shall be provided in accordance with 6.3.2.2.2.

14.6.1.2 Explosion Control. Explosion control shall be provided for liquid and solid organic peroxide formulations when required by 6.3.2.1.4.

14.6.1.3 Spill Control, Drainage, and Containment. Secondary containment shall be provided for organic peroxide formulations in accordance with 6.3.2.2.4.

14.6.1.4* Special Requirements. (Reserved)

14.6.2 Closed Systems.

14.6.2.1 Ventilation. Ventilation shall be provided in accordance with 6.3.2.3.2.

14.6.2.2 Explosion Control. Explosion control shall be provided for liquid and solid organic peroxide formulations when required by 6.3.2.1.4.

14.6.2.3 Spill Control, Drainage, and Containment. Spill control and secondary containment shall be provided for liquid organic peroxide formulations in accordance with 6.3.2.3.3.

14.6.2.4* Special Requirements. (Reserved)

14.7 Outdoor Use.

14.7.1 Open Systems.

14.7.1.1 Location. Outdoor use and dispensing shall be located in accordance with 6.3.3.1.1.

14.7.1.2 Spill Control, Drainage, and Containment. Spill control and secondary containment shall be provided for organic peroxide formulations liquids in accordance with 6.3.3.2.2.

14.7.1.3 Clearance from Combustibles. Clearance from combustible organic peroxide formulations shall be in accordance with 6.3.3.1.2.

14.7.1.4* Special Requirements. (Reserved)

14.7.2 Closed Systems.

14.7.2.1 Location. Outdoor use and dispensing shall be located in accordance with 6.3.3.1.1.

14.7.2.2 Spill Control, Drainage, and Containment. Spill control and secondary containment shall be provided for liquid organic peroxide formulations in accordance with 6.3.3.3.2.

14.7.2.3 Clearance from Combustibles. Clearance from combustible materials shall be provided in accordance with 6.3.3.1.2.

14.7.2.4* Special Requirements. (Reserved)

14.8 Handling. Handling of organic peroxide formulations in indoor and outdoor areas shall be in accordance with Section 14.8.

14.8.1 Handling. Handling shall be in accordance with 6.3.4.

14.8.2* Special Requirements. (Reserved)

Chapter 15   Oxidizer Solids and Liquids

15.1 General.

15.1.1 The requirements of this chapter shall apply to the storage, use, and handling of oxidizer solids or liquids when the amount of oxidizer solids or liquids exceeds the MAQ as set forth in Chapter 5 except as set forth in 15.1.1.1 and 15.1.1.2.

15.1.1.1 The requirements of 15.3.2.1 shall apply to storage of Class 1 oxidizers where stored in quantities in excess of 4000 lb (1814.4 kg), irrespective of whether the amount of oxidizer solids or liquids exceeds the MAQs permitted in control areas.

15.1.1.2 The requirements of 15.3.5 shall apply to the display and storage, of Class 1 through Class 3 oxidizers in mercantile, storage, or industrial occupancies where the general public has access to the material for sale and to the storage of oxidizing materials in such occupancies in areas that are not accessible to the public.

15.1.2 The storage, use, and handling of oxidizer solids or liquids in any quantity shall also comply with the requirements of Chapters 1 through 4 and the applicable requirements of Chapters 5 through 10.

15.1.3 Construction Requirements. Buildings, or portions thereof, in which oxidizing liquids and solids are stored, handled, or used shall be constructed in accordance with the building code.

15.1.4* The quantity and arrangement limits in this code shall not apply to the transient storage of oxidizers in process areas at plants where oxidizers are manufactured.

15.1.5 The construction requirements of this code shall not apply retroactively to the storage of solid and liquid oxidizers in existing buildings used for the storage of oxidizers at manufacturing plants.

15.1.6 Each class of oxidizer shall be considered independent of the others, and a facility shall be permitted to carry up to the maximum quantity for each class of material.

15.2 General Requirements for Storage.

15.2.1 Spill Control. Spill control shall be provided for oxidizer liquids in accordance with 6.2.1.9.2.

15.2.1.1* Where Class 2, Class 3, or Class 4 liquid oxidizers are stored, means shall be provided to prevent the liquid oxidizer from flowing out of a storage area into an area containing incompatible materials.

15.2.1.2* Spilled oxidizers, reacting oxidizers, and leaking or broken containers shall be removed immediately by a competent individual to a safe, secure, dry outside area or to a location designated by the competent individual to await disposal, in conformance with applicable regulations and manufacturer's and processor's instructions.

15.2.1.3 Spilled materials shall be placed in a clean, separate container and shall not be returned to the original container.

15.2.1.4 The disposal of spilled materials shall not be combined with that of ordinary trash.

15.2.2 Drainage. Where provided, drainage shall be in accordance with 6.2.1.9.3.11.

15.2.3 Secondary Containment. Secondary containment shall be provided for oxidizer solids and liquids in accordance with 6.2.1.9.3.

15.2.4 Ventilation. Ventilation shall be provided for Class 4 oxidizers in open containers in accordance with 6.2.1.5.

15.2.5* Treatment Systems. (Reserved)

15.2.6* Fire Protection Systems. An automatic fire sprinkler system shall be provided in accordance with 6.2.1.1, 15.3.2, and 15.3.5.

15.2.6.1* Dry Pipe and Preaction Sprinkler Systems.

15.2.6.1.1 Dry pipe and double-interlock preaction (DIPA) sprinkler systems shall not be permitted for protection of buildings or areas containing oxidizers except as provided for in 15.2.6.1.2 through 15.2.6.1.4.

15.2.6.1.2 Dry pipe and DIPA systems shall be permitted for protection of Class 1 oxidizers in Type I through Type IV building construction and Class 2 and Class 3 oxidizers in detached storage in Type I and Type II construction, as specified in the building code.

15.2.6.1.3 Dry pipe and DIPA sprinkler systems shall be permitted in mercantile occupancies when the oxidizers are stored in open-air environments, such as retail garden centers and buildings without exterior walls.

15.2.6.1.4 For Class 3 oxidizers, the location of dry pipe and DIPA sprinkler systems shall be approved by the AHJ.

15.2.6.2 Fire Protection Water Supplies.

15.2.6.2.1* Water supplies shall be adequate for the protection of the oxidizer storage by hose streams and automatic sprinklers.

15.2.6.2.2 The water system shall be capable of providing not less than 750 gpm (2840 L/min) where protection is by means of hose streams, or 500 gpm (1890 L/min) for hose streams in excess of the automatic sprinkler water demand.

15.2.6.2.3 The duration of the water supply shall be a minimum of 2 hours.

15.2.6.3 Portable Extinguishers.

15.2.6.3.1* Dry Chemical and CO$_2$ Extinguishers. The placement and use of carbon dioxide (CO$_2$) or dry chemical extinguishers containing ammonium compounds (Class A:B:C) shall be prohibited in areas where oxidizers that can release chlorine or bromine are stored.

15.2.6.3.2* Halon Extinguishers. Halon extinguishers shall not be used in areas where oxidizers are stored.

15.2.6.3.3* Halocarbon Clean Agent Extinguishers. Halocarbon clean agent extinguishers shall not be used in areas where oxidizers are stored, unless they have been tested to the satisfaction of the AHJ.

15.2.7 Explosion Control. The requirements of 6.2.1.6 shall not apply.

15.2.8 Emergency and Standby Power. Standby power shall be provided when required by 6.2.1.8.

15.2.9 Limit Controls. Limit controls shall be provided when required by 6.2.1.7.

15.2.9.1 Oxidizers shall be separated from sources of heat, such as heating units, piping, or ducts, so that they cannot be heated to within 25°F (14°C) of their decomposition temperature or to 125°F (52°C), whichever is lower and in accordance with the manufacturer's recommendations.

15.2.9.2 Oxidizers shall be stored so that the storage temperature cannot be within 25°F (14°C) of their decomposition temperature or 125°F (52°C), whichever is lower and in accordance with the manufacturer's recommendations.

15.2.10* Alarms. (Reserved)

15.2.11 Monitoring/Supervision. Supervision shall be provided in accordance with 6.2.1.11.

15.2.12* Special Requirements. This subsection contains specific requirements not found in Chapter 6.

15.2.12.1 Solid oxidizers shall not be stored directly beneath liquids.

15.2.12.2 Hydrogen peroxide (Class 2 through Class 4) stored in drums shall not be stored on wooden pallets.

15.2.12.3 At least one side of each pile of oxidizer shall be on an aisle.

15.2.12.4 Accumulation of combustible waste in oxidizer storage areas shall be prohibited.

15.2.12.5 Used, empty, combustible containers that previously contained oxidizers shall be stored in a detached or sprinklered area.

15.2.12.6 Storage shall be managed to prevent excessive dust accumulation.

15.2.12.7 Personnel Training and Procedures. Training and procedures shall be in accordance with 6.1.4.

15.2.12.8 Storage Containers, Tanks, and Bins.

15.2.12.8.1 Shipping Containers. Where a storage container for solid and liquid oxidizers also functions as the shipping container, the container shall meet the requirements of the U.S. Department of Transportation, 49 CFR 100 to end, or the *Canadian Ministry of Transport Regulations* (Transport Canada).

15.2.12.8.2 Tanks and Bins. Tanks for the storage of bulk liquid oxidizers and bins for the storage of bulk solid oxidizers shall meet the following requirements:

(1) Materials of construction shall be compatible with the oxidizer being stored.
(2) Tanks and bins shall be designed and constructed in accordance with federal, state, and local regulations or, as a minimum, in accordance with nationally recognized engineering practices [e.g., American Society of Mechanical Engineers (ASME), American Petroleum Institute (API)].
(3) Tanks and bins shall be equipped with a vent or other relief device to prevent overpressurization due to decomposition or fire exposure.

15.2.12.9 Materials Not Included. Incompatible materials shall not include approved packaging materials, pallets, or other dunnage.

15.2.12.10* Contact with Water. Oxidizers shall be stored to prevent contact with water, which can affect either container integrity or product stability.

15.2.12.11* Absorptive combustible packing materials used to contain water-soluble oxidizers that have become wet during either fire or nonfire conditions, and wooden pallets that are exposed to water solutions of an oxidizer, shall be relocated to a safe outside area and shall be disposed of properly.

15.2.12.12 Mercantile Signage for Different Classifications. Where oxidizers having different classifications are stored in the same area, the area shall be marked for the most severe hazard class present.

15.2.12.13 Clearance from Combustibles. Clearance from combustible materials shall be in accordance with 6.1.15.

15.2.12.13.1 The following shall apply where oxidizers are in segregated storage with flammable and combustible liquids:

(1) The oxidizer containers and flammable and combustible liquid containers shall be separated by at least 25 ft (7.6 m).
(2) The separation shall be maintained by dikes, drains, or floor slopes to prevent flammable liquid leakage from encroaching on the separation.

15.3 Indoor Storage.

15.3.1* Detection Systems. (Reserved)

15.3.2 Storage Conditions/Arrangement. Storage conditions and storage arrangements, when required, shall be in accordance with 15.3.2.

15.3.2.1 Bulk Storage of Class 1 Oxidizers.

15.3.2.1.1* Combustible Building Materials. Bulk storage in combustible buildings shall not come into contact with combustible building members, unless the members are protected by a compatible coating to prevent their impregnation by the oxidizer.

15.3.2.1.2 Bulk Storage Separation. Bulk storage, either in permanent bins or in piles, shall be separated from all other materials.

15.3.2.1.3 Bins. Bins shall be of noncombustible construction.

15.3.2.1.4 Wooden Bins. Wooden bins shall be permitted to be protected with a compatible coating to prevent impregnation of the combustible material by the oxidizer.

15.3.2.1.5 The MAQs of oxidizer shall not be limited when the building is protected by an approved fire sprinkler system in accordance with NFPA 1, *Fire Code*, Section 13.3.

15.3.2.2 Storage Arrangements of Class 1 Oxidizers.

15.3.2.2.1 Nonsprinklered Buildings. For Class 1 oxidizers stored in nonsprinklered buildings, the minimum aisle width shall be equal to the pile height.

15.3.2.2.2 Class 1 Oxidizers.

15.3.2.2.2.1 Application. Paragraph 15.3.2.2 shall apply to storage of Class 1 oxidizers where stored in quantities in excess of 4000 lb (1814 kg), irrespective of whether the amount of oxidizer solids or liquids exceeds the MAQ.

15.3.2.2.2.2 Storage Arrangements. Storage in quantities identified in Table 5.2.1.1.3, Table 5.2.1.2 through Table 5.2.1.8, Table 5.2.1.10.1, Table 5.2.1.13.3(a), and Table 15.3.2.2.2(A)(a) shall be permitted in nonsprinklered buildings.

(A) Storage of Class 1 Oxidizers. Storage of Class 1 oxidizers shall be in accordance with Table 15.3.2.2.2(A)(a) when stored in nonsprinklered or detached unprotected buildings or in accordance with Table 15.3.2.2.2(A)(b) when stored in sprinklered buildings.

Table 15.3.2.2.2(A)(a) Storage of Class 1 Oxidizers in a Nonsprinklered or Detached Unprotected Building

Storage Configurations and Allowable Distances	Detached Storage U.S. Units	Detached Storage Metric Units
Building limit	NL	NL
Pile limit	20 tons	18 met ton
Storage limit	8 ft	2.4 m
Pile width	16 ft	4.9 m
Maximum distance from any container to a working aisle	8 ft	2.4 m
Distance to next pile*		
Distance to wall[†]	4 ft	1.2 m
Distance to incompatible materials and combustible commodities	NP	NP

NL: Not limited. NP: Not permitted.
*See 15.3.2.2.2(C).
[†]See 15.3.2.2.2(D).

Table 15.3.2.2.2.2(A)(b) Storage of Class 1 Oxidizers in a Sprinklered Building

Storage Configurations and Allowable Distances	U.S. Units	Metric Units
Building limit	NL	NL
Pile limit	200 tons	181 met ton
Storage height	20 ft	6.1 m
Pile width	24 ft	7.3 m
Maximum distance from any container to a working aisle	12 ft	3.7 m
Distance to next pile*		
Distance to wall†	2 ft	0.6 m
Distance to incompatible materials and combustible commodities greater than NFPA 13 Class III	8 ft	2.4 m

NL: Not limited.
Note: If the storage is to be considered sprinklered, see Section 5.3.
*See 15.3.2.2.2.2(C).
†See 15.3.2.2.2.2(D).

(B) For Class 1 oxidizers stored in nonsprinklered buildings, the minimum aisle width shall be equal to the pile height.

(C) For Class 1 oxidizers stored in sprinklered buildings, the minimum aisle width shall be equal to the pile height, but the aisle width shall be not less than 4 ft (1.2 m) and not greater than 8 ft (2.4 m).

(D) There shall be no minimum distance from the pile to a wall for amounts less than 9000 lb (4082 kg).

(E) Class 1 oxidizers shall be permitted to be separated from ordinary combustible and incompatible materials by a solid noncombustible barrier or by a horizontal distance in accordance with Table 15.3.2.2.2.2(A)(a) or Table 15.3.2.2.2.2(A)(b).

15.3.2.2.3* Sprinkler Protection — Class 1. For applying the requirements of NFPA 13, *Standard for the Installation of Sprinkler Systems*, Class 1 oxidizers shall be designated as follows:

(1) Class 1 oxidizers in noncombustible or combustible containers (paper bags or noncombustible containers with removable combustible liners) shall be designated as a Class I commodity.
(2) Class 1 oxidizers contained in fiber drums, wooden or fiber boxes or barrels, or noncombustible containers in combustible packaging shall be designated as a Class II commodity.
(3) Class 1 oxidizers contained in plastic containers shall be designated as a Class III commodity.

15.3.2.2.4 Class 1 Detached Storage.

15.3.2.2.4.1 To be considered detached, a building for storage of Class 1 oxidizers shall be separated from the following:

(1) Flammable or combustible liquid storage
(2) Flammable gas storage
(3) Combustible material in the open
(4) Any building, passenger railroad, public highway, or other tanks

15.3.2.2.4.2 The minimum separation distance shall be 25 ft (7.6 m).

15.3.2.3 Class 2 Oxidizers.

15.3.2.3.1 Paragraph 15.3.2.3 shall apply to Class 2 oxidizers where stored in quantities in excess of the MAQ permitted in control areas.

15.3.2.3.2 Storage Arrangements of Class 2 Oxidizers. Class 2 oxidizers shall be permitted to be separated from ordinary combustible and incompatible materials by a solid noncombustible barrier or by a horizontal distance in accordance with Table 15.3.2.3.2.3(a) when stored in detached, unprotected buildings in accordance with the building code, or in accordance with Table 15.3.2.3.2.3(b).

15.3.2.3.2.1 The storage of Class 2 oxidizers shall be in a control area and at the appropriate protection level or shall be detached.

15.3.2.3.2.2 Walls shall have a fire resistance rating as required by the building code.

15.3.2.3.2.3 Storage of Class 2 Oxidizers. Storage of Class 2 oxidizers shall be in accordance with Table 15.3.2.3.2.3(a) when stored in nonsprinklered or detached, unprotected buildings or in accordance with Table 15.3.2.3.2.3(b) when stored in sprinklered buildings.

15.3.2.3.2.4 For Class 2 oxidizers stored in nonsprinklered buildings, the minimum aisle width shall be equal to the pile height.

15.3.2.3.2.5 For Class 2 oxidizers stored in sprinklered buildings, the minimum aisle width shall be equal to the pile height, but the aisle width shall be not less than 4 ft (1.2 m) and not greater than 8 ft (2.4 m).

15.3.2.3.2.6 For protection-level storage or detached storage under 4500 lb (2041 kg), there shall be no minimum separation distance between the pile and any wall.

15.3.2.3.2.7* The building limit shall be permitted to be four times the quantities shown in Table 15.3.2.3.2.3(b) for protection level storage if noncombustible containers are used and buildings are of Type I or Type II construction as specified in the building code.

15.3.2.3.2.8 Storage in glass carboys shall not be more than two carboys high.

15.3.2.3.2.9 Basement Storage.

(A) Storage in basements shall be prohibited.

(B) Where the oxidizer is stored in stationary tanks, storage in basements shall be permitted.

2013 Edition

Table 15.3.2.3.2.3(a) Storage of Class 2 Oxidizers in a Nonsprinklered or Detached Unprotected Building

Storage Configurations and Allowable Distances	Control Area Storage U.S. Units	Control Area Storage Metric Units	Protection Level Storage U.S. Units	Protection Level Storage Metric Units	Detached Storage U.S. Units	Detached Storage Metric Units
Building limit	2,250 lb	1,022 kg	9,000 lb	4,086 kg	100,000 lb	45,400 kg
Pile limit					20,000 lb	9,080 kg
Storage height	6 ft	1.8 m	8 ft	2.4 m	8 ft	2.4 m
Pile width	8 ft	2.4 m	12 ft	3.7 m	16 ft	4.9 m
Maximum distance from any container to a working aisle	4 ft	1.2 m	6 ft	1.8 m	8 ft	2.4 m
Distance to next pile*						
Distance to wall	4 ft	1.2 m	4 ft	1.2 m	4 ft	1.2 m
Distance to incompatible materials and combustible commodities	12 ft	3.7 m	NP	NP	NP	NP

NP: Not permitted.
*See 15.3.2.3.2.4.

Table 15.3.2.3.2.3(b) Storage of Class 2 Oxidizers in a Sprinklered Building

Storage Configurations and Allowable Distances	Control Area Storage U.S. Units	Control Area Storage Metric Units	Protection Level Storage U.S. Units	Protection Level Storage Metric Units	Detached Storage U.S. Units	Detached Storage Metric Units
Building limit	MAQ	MAQ	2000 tons	1814 met ton	NL	NL
Pile limit	NA	NA	100 tons	91 met ton	200 tons	181 met ton
Storage height[a]						
Pile width	16 ft	4.9 m	25 ft	7.6 m	25 ft	7.6 m
Maximum distance from any container to a working aisle	8 ft	2.4 m	12 ft	3.7 m	12 ft	3.7 m
Distance to next pile[b]						
Distance to wall[c]	2 ft	0.6 m	2 ft	0.6 m	2 ft	0.6 m
Distance to incompatible materials and combustible commodities	12 ft	3.7 m	NP	NP	NP	NP

MAQ: Maximum allowable quantity. NL: Not limited. NA: Not applicable. NP: Not permitted.
Note: If the storage is considered to be sprinklered, see 15.3.2.3.4.
[a]See 15.3.2.3.2.10(A) and Table 15.3.2.3.2.10(B).
[b]See 15.3.2.3.2.5.
[c]See 15.3.2.3.2.6.

15.3.2.3.2.10 Maximum Height of Storage.

(A) Maximum storage height for nonsprinklered buildings shall be in accordance with Table 15.3.2.3.2.3(a).

(B) Maximum storage height for sprinklered buildings shall be in accordance with Table 15.3.2.3.2.10(B).

15.3.2.3.3 Building Construction.

15.3.2.3.3.1 Construction materials that can come into contact with oxidizers shall be noncombustible.

15.3.2.3.3.2 All construction materials used in stories or basements below the storage of liquid oxidizers shall be noncombustible.

15.3.2.3.4 Sprinkler Protection.

15.3.2.3.4.1 Sprinkler protection for Class 2 oxidizers shall be designed in accordance with Table 15.3.2.3.2.10(B).

15.3.2.3.4.2 Ceiling sprinklers shall be high-temperature sprinklers.

15.3.2.3.4.3 Storage Protection with In-Rack Sprinklers.

(A) In-rack sprinklers shall be quick-response sprinklers with an ordinary-temperature rating and have a K-factor of not less than K = 8.0.

(B) In-rack sprinklers shall be designed to provide 25 psi (172 kPa) for the six most hydraulically remote sprinklers on each level.

(C) The in-rack sprinklers shall be 8 ft to 10 ft (2.4 m to 3.0 m) spacings in the longitudinal flue space at the intersection of the transverse flue spaces.

15.3.2.3.5 Detached Storage.

15.3.2.3.5.1 To be considered detached, a building for storage of Class 2 oxidizers shall be separated from the following:

Table 15.3.2.3.2.10(B) Ceiling Sprinkler Protection for Class 2 Oxidizers in Palletized or Bulk and Rack Storage Areas

Type of Storage	Ceiling Sprinklers Storage Height ft	Ceiling Sprinklers Storage Height m	Density gpm/ft^2	Density L/min/m^2	Area of Application ft^2	Area of Application m^2	In-Rack Sprinklers
Palletized or bulk	8	2.4	0.20	8	3750	348	—
Palletized or bulk	12	3.7	0.35	14	3750	348	—
Rack	12	3.7	0.20	8	3750	348	One line above each level of storage, except the top level
Rack	16	4.9	0.30	12	2000	186	One line above each level of storage, except the top level

(1) Flammable or combustible liquid storage
(2) Flammable gas storage
(3) Combustible material in the open
(4) Any building, passenger railroad, public highway, or other tanks

15.3.2.3.5.2 The minimum separation distance shall be in accordance with *NFPA 5000, Building Construction and Safety Code*.

15.3.2.4 Class 3 Oxidizers.

15.3.2.4.1 Paragraph 15.3.2.4 shall apply to Class 3 oxidizers where stored in quantities in excess of the MAQ permitted in control areas.

15.3.2.4.2 Type of Storage. The storage of Class 3 oxidizers shall be in a control area, at the appropriate protection level, or in detached storage.

15.3.2.4.3 Class 3 oxidizer storage shall be located on the ground floor only.

15.3.2.4.4 Protection level walls shall have a fire resistance rating as required by the building code.

15.3.2.4.5 Storage of Class 3 Oxidizers. Storage of Class 3 oxidizers shall be in accordance with Table 15.3.2.4.5(a) when stored in nonsprinklered or detached unprotected buildings or in accordance with Table 15.3.2.4.5(b) when stored in sprinklered buildings.

Table 15.3.2.4.5(a) Storage of Class 3 Oxidizers in a Nonsprinklered or Detached Unprotected Building

Storage Limit	U.S. Units	Metric Units
Building limit	40,000 lb	18,160 kg
Pile limit	10,000 lb	4,540 kg
Storage height	6 ft	1.8 m
Pile width	12 ft	3.7 m
Maximum distance from any container to a working aisle	8 ft	2.4 m
Distance to next pile*		
Distance to wall	4 ft	1.2 m
Distance to incompatible materials and combustible commodities	NP	NP

*See 15.3.2.4.5.

15.3.2.4.6 For Class 3 oxidizers stored in nonsprinklered buildings, the minimum aisle width shall be equal to the storage height, but the aisle width shall be not less than 4 ft (1.2 m) and need not be greater than 8 ft (2.4 m).

15.3.2.4.7 For protection-level storage or detached storage, no minimum separation distance shall be required between oxidizer storage of less than 2300 lb (1043 kg) (total weight in the storage area) and any wall.

15.3.2.4.8 Class 3 oxidizers shall be permitted to be separated from ordinary combustible and incompatible materials by a solid noncombustible barrier or by a horizontal distance in accordance with Table 15.3.2.4.5(a) or Table 15.3.2.4.5(b).

15.3.2.4.9 Storage in glass carboys shall be one carboy high.

15.3.2.4.10 Bulk storage in open bins or piles shall not be permitted.

15.3.2.4.11 Maximum Height of Storage.

15.3.2.4.11.1 Maximum storage height for nonsprinklered buildings shall be in accordance with Table 15.3.2.4.5(a).

15.3.2.4.11.2 Maximum storage height for sprinklered buildings shall be in accordance with Table 15.3.2.4.13.1(B).

15.3.2.4.12 Building Construction.

15.3.2.4.12.1 Buildings used for the storage of Class 3 liquid oxidizers shall not have basements.

15.3.2.4.12.2 Construction materials that can come into contact with oxidizers shall be noncombustible.

15.3.2.4.12.3 Storage of Class 3 oxidizers in excess of 30 tons (27.2 metric tons) shall be in buildings of Type I or Type II construction, as specified in the building code.

15.3.2.4.12.4 If Class 3 oxidizers are stored in accordance with rack storage requirements in Table 15.3.2.4.13.4(B), they shall be permitted to be in buildings of construction Type I through Type IV, as specified in the building code.

15.3.2.4.13 Sprinkler Criteria for Class 3 Oxidizers.

15.3.2.4.13.1 Class 3 Oxidizers Less than 2300 lb (1043 kg).

(A) Sprinkler design criteria for buildings that require sprinkler protection and contain total quantities of Class 3 oxidizers less than 2300 lb (1043 kg) shall be in accordance with the requirements of 15.3.2.4.13.1(B).

(B) Facilities that require sprinkler protection and contain total quantities of Class 3 oxidizers greater than 200 lb (91 kg), but less than 2300 lb (1043 kg), shall follow the sprinkler design criteria in Table 15.3.2.4.13.1(B).

15.3.2.4.13.2 Ceiling sprinklers shall be high-temperature sprinklers.

15.3.2.4.13.3 In-Rack Sprinkler Criteria.

(A) Where required by Table 15.3.2.4.13.1(B), in-rack sprinkler protection shall be as follows:

(1) In-rack sprinklers shall be installed above every level of oxidizer storage.
(2) In-rack sprinklers shall be spaced at maximum 4 ft (1.2 m) intervals to provide one sprinkler in each flue space.
(3) In-rack sprinklers shall be quick-response sprinklers with an ordinary-temperature rating and have a K-factor of not less than K = 8.0.
(4) In-rack sprinklers shall be designed to provide 25 psi (172 kPa) for the six most hydraulically remote sprinklers on each level.

(B) Class 3 oxidizers in racks meeting the requirements of 15.3.2.4.13.1(B) shall be permitted to be protected in accordance with 15.3.2.4.13.3.

15.3.2.4.13.4 Class 3 Oxidizers Greater than or Equal to 2300 lb (1043 kg).

(A) Facilities containing total quantities of Class 3 oxidizers equal to or greater than the threshold limits of 15.3.2.4.13 shall be protected in accordance with the requirements of 15.3.2.4.13.5(B).

(B) The sprinkler protection required by 15.3.2.4.13.4 shall be in accordance with Table 15.3.2.4.13.4(B).

15.3.2.4.13.5 Special In-Rack Sprinkler Protection for Class 3 Oxidizers.

(A) Where required by Table 15.3.2.4.13.4(B), special in-rack sprinkler protection, which is required by 15.3.2.4.13.5(B), 15.3.2.4.13.5(K), and 15.3.2.4.13.5(T), shall be as shown in Figure 15.3.2.4.13.5(A).

Table 15.3.2.4.5(b) Storage of Class 3 Oxidizers in a Sprinklered Building

Storage Limit	Control Area Storage U.S. Units	Control Area Storage Metric Units	Protection Level Storage U.S. Units	Protection Level Storage Metric Units	Detached Storage U.S. Units	Detached Storage Metric Units
Building limit	MAQ	MAQ	1200 tons	1090 met ton	NL	NL
Pile limit	NA	NA	30 tons	27 met ton	100 tons	91 met ton
Storage height[a]						
Pile width	12 ft	3.7 m	16 ft	4.9 m	20 ft	6.1 m
Maximum distance from any container to a working aisle	8 ft	2.4 m	10 ft	3 m	10 ft	3 m
Distance to next pile[b]						
Distance to wall[c]	2 ft	0.6 m	2 ft	0.6 m	2 ft	0.6 m
Distance to incompatible materials and combustible commodities	12 ft	3.7 m	NP	NP	NP	NP

MAQ: Maximum allowable quantity. NA: Not applicable. NP: Not permitted. NL: Not limited.
Note: If the storage is considered to be sprinklered, see the sprinkler system design requirements of 15.3.2.4.12.
[a]See 15.3.2.4.10, Table 15.3.2.4.12.1(B), and Table 15.3.2.4.12.3(B).
[b]See Table 15.3.2.4.12.1(b) and Table 15.3.2.4.12.3(b)
[c]See 15.3.2.4.6.

Table 15.3.2.4.13.1(B) Sprinkler Protection of Class 3 Oxidizers Stored in Total Quantities Greater than 200 lb (91 kg) but Less than 2300 lb (1043 kg)

Storage Parameters	Shelf	Bulk or Pile	Bulk or Pile	Rack
Maximum storage height	6 ft (1.8 m)	5 ft (1.5 m)	10 ft (3 m)	10 ft (3 m)
Maximum ceiling height	25 ft (7.6 m)	25 ft (7.6 m)	25 ft (7.6 m)	NA
Aisles — pile separation	4 ft (1.2 m) min. clear aisles	4 ft (1.2 m) min. clear aisles	8 ft (2.4 m) min. clear aisles	8 ft (2.4 m) min. clear aisles
Ceiling design criteria	0.45 gpm/ft^2/2000 ft^2	0.35 gpm/ft^2/or 5000 ft^2 or 0.6 gpm/2000 ft^2	0.65 gpm/ft^2/5000 ft^2	0.35 gpm/ft^2/or 5000 ft^2 or 0.6 gpm/ft^2/2000 ft^2
In-rack sprinklers	NP	NP	NA	See 15.3.2.4.12.2.
Hose stream demand	500 gpm	500 gpm	500 gpm	500 gpm
Duration	120 minutes	120 minutes	120 minutes	120 minutes

For SI units, 1 gal = 3.79 L. NA: Not applicable. NP: Not permitted.

Table 15.3.2.4.13.4(B) Sprinkler Protection of Class 3 Oxidizers Stored in Total Quantities of Greater than or Equal to 2300 lb (1043 kg)

Storage Parameters	Bulk or Pile	Rack
Maximum storage height	5 ft (1.5 m)	10 ft (3 m)
Maximum ceiling height	25 ft (7.6 m)	NP
Aisles — pile separation	8 ft (2.4 m) min. clear aisles	8 ft (2.4 m) min. clear aisles
Ceiling design criteria	0.35 gpm/ft^2/5000 ft^2 (1.32 L/min/m^2/464.5 m^2)	Predominant for other commodities but not less than ordinary hazard Group II
In-rack sprinklers	NP	See 15.3.2.4.12.4
Hose stream demand	500 gpm (1893 L/min)	500 gpm (1893 L/min)
Duration	120 minutes	120 minutes

NP: Not permitted.

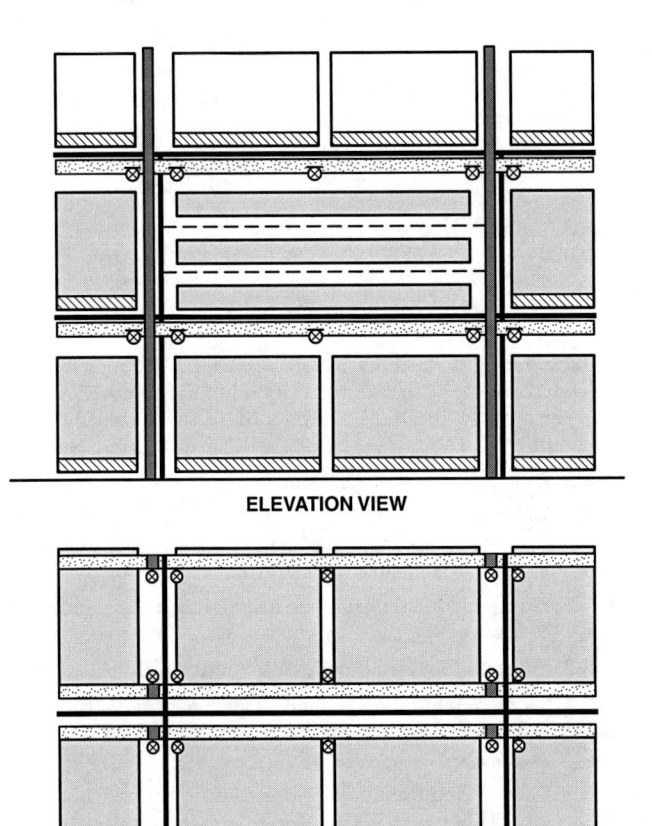

FIGURE 15.3.2.4.13.5(A) Arrangement of Barriers and In-Rack Sprinklers for Special Fire Protection Provisions.

(B) Racks shall be arranged in accordance with 15.3.2.4.13.5(C) through 15.3.2.4.13.5(J).

(C) Racks shall be of steel construction.

(D) Racks shall have vertical supports spaced no more than 10 ft (3.1 m) apart.

(E) Horizontal rack members shall be spaced not more than 6 ft (1.8 m) apart vertically.

(F) Display or storage shall be limited in height to two protected tiers.

(G) Horizontal barriers constructed of plywood at least ⅜ in. (9.5 mm) thick shall be provided above each level of oxidizing material storage, and the following criteria also shall be met:

(1) The barriers shall extend from rack face to rack face and shall be tight to the vertical barriers described in 15.3.2.4.13.5(H) and 15.3.2.4.13.5(I).
(2) The barriers shall be supported by horizontal rack members.

(H) Transverse vertical barriers constructed of plywood at least ⅜ in. (9.5 mm) thick shall be provided at the rack uprights extending from rack face to rack face.

(I) For double-row racks, longitudinal vertical barriers constructed of plywood at least ⅜ in. (9.5 mm) thick shall be provided at the rack uprights in the center of the rack.

(J) If intermediate shelves are used between the horizontal barriers, the shelves shall be constructed of open wire mesh or steel grating.

(K) In-rack automatic sprinklers shall be provided under each horizontal barrier and arranged in accordance with 15.3.2.4.13.5(L) through 15.3.2.4.13.5(S).

(L) For double-row racks, two lines of in-rack sprinklers shall be provided between the face of the rack and the longitudinal vertical barrier located in the center of the rack.

(M) For single-row racks, two lines of in-rack sprinklers shall be provided between each rack face.

(N) Three in-rack sprinklers shall be provided on each in-rack sprinkler line as follows:

(1) Two sprinklers on each line shall be spaced approximately 1½ in. (38.1 mm) from each transverse vertical barrier.
(2) One in-rack sprinkler on each in-rack sprinkler line shall be located approximately equidistant between the transverse vertical barriers.

(O) In-rack sprinklers shall be of the upright or pendent type, with the fusible element located no more than 6 in. (152.4 mm) from the horizontal barrier.

(P) The stock shall be maintained at least 6 in. (152.4 mm) below the sprinkler deflector.

(Q) In-rack sprinklers shall be K = 8.0, quick-response, ordinary-temperature-rated sprinklers.

(R) The in-rack sprinkler system shall be designed to supply 6 sprinklers on each line, with a total of 12 sprinklers operating at gauge pressure of 25 psi (172 kPa).

(S) The design of the in-rack sprinkler system shall be independent of, and shall not be required to be balanced with, ceiling sprinkler systems.

(T) Pallets, if used, shall be of the solid-deck type.

15.3.2.4.14 Detached Storage.

15.3.2.4.14.1 To be considered detached, a building for storage of Class 3 oxidizers shall be separated from the following:

(1) Flammable or combustible liquid storage
(2) Flammable gas storage
(3) Combustible material in the open
(4) Any building, passenger railroad, public highway, or other tanks

15.3.2.4.14.2 The minimum separation distance shall be in accordance with the building code.

15.3.2.5 Class 4 Oxidizers.

15.3.2.5.1 Paragraph 15.3.2.5 shall apply to Class 4 oxidizers where stored in quantities in excess of the MAQ permitted in control areas.

15.3.2.5.2 Outdoor container storage shall meet the requirements of nonsprinklered buildings.

15.3.2.5.3 Storage Arrangements.

15.3.2.5.3.1 The storage of Class 4 oxidizers shall be detached.

15.3.2.5.3.2 Storage in glass carboys shall be one carboy high.

15.3.2.5.3.3 Storage in drums, containers, or cases shall not exceed the limits outlined in Table 15.3.2.5.3.3.

Table 15.3.2.5.3.3 Storage of Class 4 Oxidizers in Drums, Containers, and Cases in a Sprinklered Building

Storage Configurations and Quantities	U.S. Units	Metric Units
Piles		
Length	10 ft	3.1 m
Width	4 ft	1.2 m
Height	8 ft	2.4 m
Distance to next pile	8 ft	2.4 m
Quantity limit per building	NL	NL

NL: Not limited.

15.3.2.5.3.4 Bulk storage in piles or fixed bins shall not be permitted.

15.3.2.5.4 Building Construction and Location.

15.3.2.5.4.1 Buildings shall be constructed as one story without basement.

15.3.2.5.4.2 Construction materials that could come into contact with oxidizers shall be noncombustible.

15.3.2.5.4.3 Storage areas shall be provided with means to vent fumes in an emergency.

15.3.2.5.4.4 A storage building or storage tank shall be located not less than the minimum distance provided in Table 15.3.2.5.4.4 from the following:

(1) Flammable liquid storage
(2) Combustible material in the open
(3) Any inhabited building, passenger railroad, public highway, property line, or tank other than oxidizer storage

Table 15.3.2.5.4.4 Separation of Buildings from Tanks Containing Class 4 Oxidizers

Weight of Class 4 Oxidizer		Distance	
lb	kg	ft	m
10–100	4.5–45.4	75	23
101–500	45.4–227	100	30
501–1,000	227–454	125	38
1,001–3,000	454–1,361	200	61
3,001–5,000	1,361–2,268	300	91
5,001–10,000	2,268–4,536	400	122
>10,000	>4,536	Subject to approval by the AHJ	

15.3.2.5.4.5* Where tanks are not separated from each other by 10 percent of the distance specified in Table 15.3.2.5.4.4 for the largest tank, the total contents of all tanks shall be used when applying Table 15.3.2.5.4.4.

15.3.2.5.4.6 Sprinkler Protection.

(A) Sprinkler protection for Class 4 oxidizers shall be installed on a deluge sprinkler system to provide water density of 0.35 gpm/ft^2 (14.4 L/min/m^2) over the entire storage area.

(B) Sprinkler protection shall be installed in accordance with NFPA 13, *Standard for the Installation of Sprinkler Systems.*

15.3.3 Floors. Floors shall be in accordance with 6.2.1.10.

15.3.4 Detached Storage. Detached storage shall be provided for oxidizer solids or liquids when required by 15.3.2 and 6.2.2.2, 6.2.3.4, 6.2.4.4, or 6.2.4.5.

15.3.5 Special Requirements. This subsection contains specific requirements not found in Chapter 6.

15.3.5.1 Application for Mercantile, Storage, or Industrial Occupancies. Paragraph 15.3.5 applies to the display and storage of Class 1 through Class 3 oxidizers in mercantile, storage, or industrial occupancies where the general public has access to the materials for sale and also applies to the storage of additional oxidizing materials in such occupancies in areas that are not accessible to the public.

15.3.5.2 General Requirements. Oxidizing materials that are displayed or stored in areas accessible to the general public shall meet the requirements of 15.3.5.2.1 through 15.3.5.2.13.2.

15.3.5.2.1* Oxidizing materials shall be separated from ordinary combustible and incompatible materials by a solid noncombustible barrier or by a horizontal distance of not less than 4 ft (1.2 m).

15.3.5.2.1.1 Ordinary combustibles shall not include approved packaging materials, pallets, or other dunnage used for the oxidizers.

15.3.5.2.1.2 Separation from ordinary combustible materials shall not be required for Class 1 oxidizers.

15.3.5.2.2 Solid oxidizing materials shall not be displayed directly beneath liquids.

15.3.5.2.3 For sprinklered mercantile occupancies and storage occupancies, storage heights and sprinkler protection criteria shall be in accordance with 15.3.2.2 through 15.3.3.

15.3.5.2.4 Storage and display of solids shall not exceed 200 lb/ft^2 (978 kg/m^2) of floor area actually occupied by solid merchandise.

15.3.5.2.5 Storage and display of liquids shall not exceed 20 gal/ft^2 (76 L/m^2) of floor area actually occupied by liquid merchandise.

15.3.5.2.6 Racks and shelves used for storage or display shall be of substantial construction and adequately braced and anchored.

15.3.5.2.7 Containers shall be approved for their intended use.

15.3.5.2.8 Individual containers in mercantile occupancies shall not exceed 100 lb (45.4 kg) capacity for solids or 10 gal (38 L) capacity for liquids.

15.3.5.2.9 Aisles 4 ft (1.2 m) in width shall be maintained on three sides of the storage or display area.

15.3.5.2.10 Hazard identification signs shall be provided in accordance with NFPA 1, *Fire Code*.

15.3.5.2.11 Storage Arrangements in Nonsprinklered Mercantile, Storage, or Industrial Occupancies.

15.3.5.2.11.1 Storage and display of Class 2 and Class 3 oxidizing materials shall extend not higher than 6 ft (1.8 m) from the floor to the top of the uppermost container.

15.3.5.2.11.2 The storage and display of Class 2 and Class 3 oxidizers shall not exceed 4 ft (1.2 m) in depth.

15.3.5.2.12 Containers. Individual containers less than 5 gal (19 L), or less than 25 lb (11 kg), shall be stored or displayed on pallets, racks, or shelves.

15.3.5.2.13 Quantity Limitations.

15.3.5.2.13.1 The quantity of oxidizing materials permitted in a mercantile, storage, or industrial occupancy shall not exceed the quantities given in Table 5.2.1.13.3(a) for either a nonsprinklered or sprinklered area, whichever is applicable.

15.3.5.2.13.2 Facilities that require sprinkler protection having total quantities of Class 3 oxidizers greater than 200 lb (91 kg), but less than 2300 lb (1043 kg), shall comply with 15.3.2.4.13.1(B).

15.4 Outdoor Storage.

15.4.1 Exposures. Outdoor storage of oxidizer solids or liquids shall be separated from exposure hazards in accordance with 15.4.1.

15.4.1.1 Clearance from Combustibles. Clearance from combustible materials shall be in accordance with 6.2.7.1.

15.4.1.2 Location. Outdoor storage of oxidizer solids or liquids shall not be within 20 ft (6.1 m) of property lines, streets, alleys, public ways, means of egress to a public way, or buildings not used exclusively for the storage, distribution, or manufacturing of such material, except as provided in 15.4.1.3.

15.4.1.3 Distance Reduction. An unpierced 2-hour fire-resistive wall extending not less than 30 in. (762 mm) above and to the side of the storage area shall be permitted in lieu of the distance specified in 15.4.1.2.

15.4.2 Weather Protection. When provided, weather protection shall be in accordance with 5.1.2 and 6.2.7.2.

15.4.3 Special Requirements. This subsection contains specific requirements not found in Chapter 6.

15.4.3.1 The size of outside storage tanks for Class 1, Class 2, and Class 3 oxidizers shall not be limited by this code.

15.4.3.2 The size of outside storage tanks for Class 4 oxidizers shall be limited in accordance with this code.

15.5 General Requirements for Use.

15.5.1 Spill Control. Spill control shall be provided for oxidizer liquids in accordance with 6.3.1.4.

15.5.2 Drainage. When provided, drainage shall be in accordance with 6.3.1.4.2.10.

15.5.3 Secondary Containment. Secondary containment shall be provided for oxidizer solids or liquids in accordance with 6.3.1.4.2.

15.5.4 Ventilation. Ventilation shall be provided for Class 4 oxidizers in open containers in accordance with 6.3.2.1.3 and 6.3.2.2.2.

15.5.5* Treatment Systems. (Reserved)

15.5.6 Fire Protection System. An automatic fire sprinkler system shall be provided in accordance with 6.3.2.1.1.

15.5.6.1 Portable Extinguishers.

15.5.6.1.1 Dry Chemical and CO$_2$ Extinguishers. The placement and use of carbon dioxide (CO$_2$) or dry chemical extinguishers containing ammonium compounds (Class A:B:C) shall be prohibited in areas where oxidizers that can release chlorine or bromine are stored.

15.5.6.1.2 Halon Extinguishers. Halon extinguishers shall not be used in areas where oxidizers are stored.

15.5.6.1.3 Halocarbon Clean Agent Extinguishers. Halocarbon clean agent extinguishers shall not be used in areas where oxidizers are stored, unless they have been tested to the satisfaction of the AHJ.

15.5.7 Explosion Control. The requirements of 6.3.2.1.4 shall not apply.

15.5.8 Emergency and Standby Power. Standby power shall be provided when required by 6.3.1.3.

15.5.9 Limit Controls. Limit controls shall be provided in accordance with 6.3.1.2.

15.5.10* Alarms. (Reserved)

15.5.11 Monitoring/Supervision. Supervision shall be provided in accordance with 6.3.1.8.

15.5.12 Clearance from Combustibles. Clearance from combustible materials shall be in accordance with 6.2.7.1.

15.5.13 Floors. Floors where oxidizer solids or liquids are dispensed or used in open systems shall be in accordance with 6.3.2.2.3.

15.5.14 System Design. System design shall be in accordance with 6.3.1.6.

15.5.15 Liquid Transfer. Liquid transfer shall be in accordance with 6.3.1.7.

15.5.16* Special Requirements. (Reserved)

15.6 Indoor Use.

15.6.1 Open Systems.

15.6.1.1 Ventilation. Ventilation shall be provided for Class 4 oxidizers in open containers in accordance with 6.3.2.2.2.

15.6.1.2 Explosion Control. The requirements of 6.3.2.1.4 shall not apply.

15.6.1.3 Spill Control, Drainage, and Containment. Secondary containment shall be provided for oxidizer liquids in accordance with 6.3.2.2.4.

15.6.1.4* Special Requirements. (Reserved)

15.6.2 Closed Systems.

15.6.2.1 Ventilation. The requirements of 6.3.2.3.2 shall not apply.

15.6.2.2 Explosion Control. The requirements of 6.3.2.1.4 shall not apply.

15.6.2.3 Spill Control, Drainage, and Containment. Spill control and secondary containment shall be provided for oxidizer liquids in accordance with 6.3.2.3.3.

15.6.2.4* Special Requirements. (Reserved)

15.7 Outdoor Use.

15.7.1 Open Systems.

15.7.1.1 Location. Outdoor use and dispensing shall be located in accordance with 6.3.3.1.1.

15.7.1.2 Spill Control, Drainage, and Containment. Spill control and secondary containment shall be provided for oxidizer liquids in accordance with 6.3.3.2.2.

15.7.1.3 Clearance from Combustibles. Clearance from combustible materials shall be in accordance with 6.3.3.1.2.

15.7.1.4* Special Requirements. (Reserved)

15.7.2 Closed Systems.

15.7.2.1 Location. Outdoor use and dispensing shall be located in accordance with 6.3.3.1.1.

15.7.2.2 Spill Control, Drainage, and Containment. Spill control and secondary containment shall be provided for liquids in accordance with 6.3.3.3.2.

15.7.2.3 Clearance from Combustibles. Clearance from combustible materials shall be provided in accordance with 6.3.3.1.2.

15.7.2.4* Special Requirements. (Reserved)

15.8 Handling. Handling of oxidizers in indoor and outdoor areas shall be in accordance with Section 15.8.

15.8.1 Handling. Handling shall be in accordance with 6.3.4.

15.8.2* Special Requirements. (Reserved)

Chapter 16 Reserved

Chapter 17 Pyrophoric Solids and Liquids

17.1 General. The requirements of this chapter shall apply to the storage, use, and handling of pyrophoric solids or liquids when the amount of pyrophoric solids or liquids exceeds the MAQ as set forth in Chapter 5. The storage, use, and handling of pyrophoric solids or liquids in any quantity shall also comply with the requirements of Chapters 1 through 4 and the applicable requirements of Chapters 5 through 10.

17.1.1 Construction Requirements. Buildings, or portions thereof, in which pyrophoric solids or liquids are stored, handled, or used shall be constructed in accordance with the building code.

17.2 General Requirements for Storage.

17.2.1 Spill Control. Spill control shall be provided for pyrophoric liquids in accordance with 6.2.1.9.2.

17.2.1.1* Liquid spills shall be directed away from tanks and containers.

17.2.2 Drainage. When provided, drainage shall be in accordance with 6.2.1.9.3.11.

17.2.3 Secondary Containment. Secondary containment shall be provided for pyrophoric liquids in accordance with 6.2.1.9.3.

17.2.3.1 Secondary containment shall be designed to prevent spilled liquids from accumulating under process vessels, storage tanks, and containers.

17.2.4 Ventilation. Ventilation shall be provided for open containers in accordance with 6.2.1.5.

17.2.5* Treatment Systems. (Reserved)

17.2.6* Fire Protection Systems. An approved fire protection system shall be provided in accordance with 6.2.1.1.

17.2.7 Explosion Control. The requirements of 6.2.1.6 shall not apply.

17.2.8 Emergency and Standby Power. Standby power shall be provided when required by 6.2.1.8.

17.2.9 Limit Controls. Limit controls shall be provided when required by 6.2.1.7.

17.2.10* Alarms. (Reserved)

17.2.11 Monitoring/Supervision. Supervision shall be provided in accordance with 6.2.1.11.

17.2.12* Special Requirements. (Reserved)

17.3 Indoor Storage.

17.3.1* Detection Systems. (Reserved)

17.3.2 Storage Conditions/Arrangement. Storage arrangement shall be in accordance with 17.3.2.

17.3.2.1* Storage Limitations. (Reserved)

17.3.3 Floors. Floors shall be in accordance with 6.2.1.10.

17.3.4 Detached Storage. The requirements of 6.2.2.2, 6.2.3.4, 6.2.4.4, or 6.2.4.5 shall not apply.

17.3.5* Special Requirements. (Reserved)

17.4 Outdoor Storage.

17.4.1 Exposures. Outdoor storage of pyrophoric solids or liquids shall be separated from exposure hazards in accordance with 17.4.1.

17.4.1.1 Clearance from Combustibles. Clearance from combustible materials shall be in accordance with 6.2.7.1.

17.4.1.2* Location. The separation of pyrophoric solids and liquids from buildings, property lines, streets, alleys, public ways, or means of egress to a public way shall be twice the separation required by NFPA 30, *Flammable and Combustible Liquids Code*, for an equivalent volume of Class I-B flammable liquid.

17.4.1.3 Distance Reduction. An unpierced 2-hour fire-resistive wall extending not less than 30 in. (762 mm) above and to the side of the storage area shall be permitted in lieu of the distance specified in 17.4.1.2.

17.4.2 Weather Protection. When provided, weather protection shall be in accordance with 5.1.2 and 6.2.7.2.

17.4.3* Special Requirements. (Reserved)

17.4.3.1* Storage Arrangement. The quantities, arrangement, and spacing for pyrophoric liquids and solids in tanks, portable tanks, and containers shall be in accordance with NFPA 30, *Flammable and Combustible Liquids Code*, as required for Class I-B flammable liquids.

17.5 General Requirements for Use.

17.5.1 Spill Control. Spill control shall be provided for pyrophoric liquids in accordance with 6.3.1.4. Spills shall be directed away from storage containers and equipment.

17.5.2 Drainage. When provided, drainage shall be in accordance with 6.3.1.4.2.10.

17.5.3 Secondary Containment. Secondary containment shall be provided for pyrophoric solids or liquids in accordance with 6.3.1.4.2.

17.5.4 Ventilation. The requirements of 6.3.2.1.3 and 6.3.2.2.2 shall not apply.

17.5.5* Treatment Systems. (Reserved)

17.5.6 Fire Protection System. An automatic fire sprinkler system shall be provided in accordance with 6.3.2.1.1.

17.5.7 Explosion Control. The requirements of 6.3.2.1.4 shall not apply.

17.5.8 Emergency and Standby Power. Standby power shall be provided when required by 6.3.1.3.

17.5.9 Limit Controls. Limit controls shall be provided in accordance with 6.3.1.2.

17.5.10* Alarms. (Reserved)

17.5.11 Monitoring/Supervision. Supervision shall be provided in accordance with 6.3.1.8.

17.5.12 Clearance from Combustibles. Clearance from combustible materials shall be in accordance with 6.2.7.1.

17.5.13 Floors. Floors where pyrophoric solids or liquids are dispensed or used in open systems shall be in accordance with 6.3.2.2.3.

17.5.14 System Design. System design shall be in accordance with 6.3.1.6.

17.5.15 Liquid Transfer. Liquid transfer shall be in accordance with 6.3.1.7.

17.5.16* Special Requirements. (Reserved)

17.6 Indoor Use.

17.6.1 Open Systems.

17.6.1.1 Ventilation. The requirements of 6.3.2.2.2 shall not apply.

17.6.1.2 Explosion Control. The requirements of 6.3.2.1.4 shall not apply.

17.6.1.3* Spill Control, Drainage, and Containment. Secondary containment for areas used to contain pyrophoric liquids shall be designed to separate or drain spilled liquids from the area containing tanks and containers.

17.6.1.4* Special Requirements. (Reserved)

17.6.2 Closed Systems.

17.6.2.1 Ventilation. The requirements of 6.3.2.2.2 shall not apply.

17.6.2.2 Explosion Control. The requirements of 6.3.3.2.2 shall not apply.

17.6.2.3 Spill Control, Drainage, and Containment. Spill control and secondary containment shall be provided for pyrophoric liquids in accordance with 6.3.2.3.3.

17.6.2.3.1* Secondary containment for areas used to contain pyrophoric liquids shall be designed to separate or drain spilled liquids from the area containing tanks and containers.

17.6.2.4* Special Requirements. (Reserved)

17.7 Outdoor Use.

17.7.1 Open Systems.

17.7.1.1 Location. Outdoor use and dispensing shall be located in accordance with 6.3.3.1.1.

17.7.1.2* Spill Control, Drainage, and Containment. Secondary containment for areas used to contain pyrophoric liquids shall be designed to separate or drain spilled liquids from the area containing tanks and containers.

17.7.1.3 Clearance from Combustibles. Clearance from combustible materials shall be in accordance with 6.3.3.1.2.

17.7.1.4* Special Requirements. (Reserved)

17.7.2 Closed Systems.

17.7.2.1 Location. Outdoor use and dispensing shall be located in accordance with 6.3.3.1.1.

17.7.2.2 Spill Control, Drainage, and Containment. Spill control and secondary containment shall be provided for pyrophoric liquids in accordance with 6.3.3.3.2.

17.7.2.2.1* Secondary containment for areas used to contain pyrophoric liquids shall be designed to separate or drain spilled liquids from the area containing tanks and containers.

17.7.2.3 Clearance from Combustibles. Clearance from combustible materials shall be provided in accordance with 6.3.3.1.2.

17.7.2.4* Special Requirements. (Reserved)

17.8 Handling. Handling of pyrophoric liquids in indoor and outdoor areas shall be in accordance with Section 17.8.

17.8.1 Handling. Handling shall be in accordance with 6.3.4.

17.8.2* Special Requirements. (Reserved)

Chapter 18 Toxic or Highly Toxic Solids and Liquids

18.1 General. The requirements of this chapter shall apply to the storage, use, and handling of toxic or highly toxic solids or liquids when the amount of toxic or highly toxic solids or liquids exceeds the MAQ as set forth in Chapter 5. The storage, use, and handling of toxic or highly toxic solids or liquids in any quantity shall also comply with the requirements of Chapters 1 through 4 and the applicable requirements of Chapters 5 through 10.

18.1.1 Construction Requirements. Buildings, or portions thereof, in which toxic or highly toxic solids or liquids are stored, handled, or used shall be constructed in accordance with the building code.

18.2 General Requirements for Storage.

18.2.1 Spill Control. Spill control shall be provided for toxic or highly toxic liquids in accordance with 6.2.1.9.2.

18.2.2 Drainage. When provided, drainage shall be in accordance with 6.2.1.9.3.11.

18.2.3 Secondary Containment. Secondary containment shall be provided for toxic or highly toxic solids or liquids in accordance with 6.2.1.9.3.

18.2.4 Ventilation. Ventilation shall be provided for open containers of highly toxic solids or liquids in accordance with 6.2.1.5.

18.2.5 Treatment Systems. The storage area for highly toxic liquids that liberate highly toxic vapors in the event of a spill or other accidental discharge shall not be located outside of a building unless effective collection and treatment systems are provided.

18.2.5.1 The treatment system shall comply with 21.3.9.3 for highly toxic gases.

18.2.6 Fire Protection Systems. An automatic fire sprinkler system shall be provided in accordance with 6.2.1.1.

18.2.7 Explosion Control. The requirements of 6.2.1.6 shall not apply.

18.2.8 Emergency and Standby Power. Standby power shall be provided when required by 6.2.1.8.

18.2.9 Limit Controls. Limit controls shall be provided when required by 6.2.1.7.

18.2.10* Alarms. (Reserved)

18.2.11 Monitoring/Supervision. Supervision shall be provided in accordance with 6.2.1.11.

18.2.12* Special Requirements. (Reserved)

18.3 Indoor Storage.

18.3.1* Detection Systems. (Reserved)

18.3.2* Storage Conditions/Arrangement. (Reserved)

18.3.2.1* Reserved.

18.3.3 Floors. Floors shall be in accordance with 6.2.1.10.

18.3.4 Detached Storage. The requirements of 6.2.2.2 shall not apply.

18.3.5* Special Requirements. (Reserved)

18.3.5.1 Highly toxic solids and liquids not stored in approved hazardous materials storage cabinets shall be isolated from other hazardous materials storage by a 1-hour-rated fire barrier.

18.4 Outdoor Storage.

18.4.1 Exposures. Outdoor storage of toxic or highly toxic solids or liquids shall be separated from exposure hazards in accordance with 18.4.1.

18.4.1.1 Clearance from Combustibles. Clearance from combustible materials shall be in accordance with 6.2.7.1.

18.4.1.2 Location. Outdoors storage of toxic or highly toxic solids or liquids shall not be within 20 ft (6.1 m) of property lines, streets, alleys, public ways, means of egress to a public way, or buildings not used exclusively for the storage, distribution, or manufacturing of such material, except as provided in 18.4.1.3.

18.4.1.3 Distance Reduction. An unpierced 2-hour fire–resistive wall extending not less than 30 in. (762 mm) above and to the side of the storage area shall be permitted in lieu of the distance specified in 18.4.1.2.

18.4.2 Weather Protection. Where provided, weather protection shall be in accordance with 5.1.2 and 6.2.7.2.

18.4.3* Special Requirements. (Reserved)

18.4.3.1 Fire-Extinguishing Systems. The outdoor storage area for highly toxic solids and liquids shall consist of fire-resistive containers or shall comply with one of the following:

(1) The storage area shall be protected by an automatic, open head, deluge fire sprinkler system in accordance with NFPA 13, *Standard for the Installation of Sprinkler Systems*.
(2) Storage shall be located under a noncombustible weather protection structure in accordance with 18.4.2, with the canopied area protected by an automatic fire sprinkler system in accordance with NFPA 13, *Standard for the Installation of Sprinkler Systems*.

18.4.3.2 Storage Arrangement.

18.4.3.2.1 Pile Size Limit. Highly toxic solids and liquids stored outdoors shall be separated into piles, each not larger than 2500 ft^3 (70.8 m^3).

18.4.3.2.2 Aisles. Aisle widths between piles shall not be less than one-half the height of the pile or 10 ft (3 m), whichever is greater.

18.4.3.3 Treatment System.

18.4.3.3.1 The storage area for highly toxic liquids that liberate highly toxic vapors in the event of a spill or other accidental discharge shall not be located outside of a building unless effective collection and treatment systems are provided.

18.4.3.3.2 The treatment system shall comply with the design requirements of Chapter 21 for highly toxic gases.

18.5 General Requirements for Use.

18.5.1 Spill Control. Spill control shall be provided for toxic or highly toxic liquids in accordance with 6.3.1.4.

18.5.2 Drainage. When provided, drainage shall be in accordance with 6.3.1.4.2.10.

18.5.3 Secondary Containment. Secondary containment shall be provided for toxic or highly toxic solids or liquids in accordance with 6.3.1.4.2.

18.5.4 Ventilation. Ventilation shall be provided for open containers of highly toxic solids or liquids in accordance with 6.3.2.1.3 and 6.3.2.2.2.

18.5.5 Treatment Systems. Exhaust scrubbers or other systems for processing vapors of highly toxic liquids shall be provided where a spill or accidental release of such liquids can be expected to release highly toxic vapors at normal temperature and pressure. Treatment systems and other processing systems shall be installed in accordance with the mechanical code adopted by the jurisdiction.

18.5.5.1 The treatment system shall comply with the design requirements of Chapter 21 for highly toxic gases.

18.5.6 Fire Protection System. An automatic fire sprinkler system shall be provided in accordance with 6.3.2.1.1.

18.5.7 Explosion Control. The requirements of 6.3.2.1.4 shall not apply.

18.5.8 Emergency and Standby Power. Standby power shall be provided when required by 6.3.1.3.

18.5.9 Limit Controls. Limit controls shall be provided in accordance with 6.3.1.2.

18.5.10* Alarms. (Reserved)

18.5.11 Monitoring/Supervision. Supervision shall be provided in accordance with 6.3.1.8.

18.5.12 Clearance from Combustibles. Clearance from combustible materials shall be in accordance with 6.2.7.1.

18.5.13 Floors. Floors where toxic or highly toxic solids or liquids are dispensed or used in open systems shall be in accordance with 6.3.2.2.3.

18.5.14 System Design. System design shall be in accordance with 6.3.1.6.

18.5.15 Liquid Transfer. Liquid transfer shall be in accordance with 6.3.1.7.

18.5.16* Special Requirements. (Reserved)

18.6 Indoor Use.

18.6.1 Open Systems.

18.6.1.1 Ventilation. Ventilation shall be provided in accordance with 6.3.2.3.2.

18.6.1.2 Explosion Control. The requirements of 6.3.2.1.4 shall not apply.

18.6.1.3 Spill Control, Drainage, and Containment. Secondary containment shall be provided for toxic or highly toxic liquids in accordance with 6.3.2.2.4.

18.6.1.4* Special Requirements. (Reserved)

18.6.2 Closed Systems.

18.6.2.1 Ventilation. Ventilation shall be provided in accordance with 6.3.2.3.2.

18.6.2.2 Explosion Control. The requirements of 6.3.2.1.4 shall not apply.

18.6.2.3 Spill Control, Drainage, and Containment. Spill control and secondary containment shall be provided for toxic or highly toxic liquids in accordance with 6.3.2.3.3.

18.6.2.4* Special Requirements. (Reserved)

18.7 Outdoor Use.

18.7.1 Open Systems.

18.7.1.1 Location. Outdoor use and dispensing shall be located in accordance with 6.3.3.1.1.

18.7.1.2 Spill Control, Drainage, and Containment. Spill control and secondary containment shall be provided for toxic or highly toxic liquids in accordance with 6.3.3.2.2.

18.7.1.3 Clearance from Combustibles. Clearance from combustible materials shall be in accordance with 6.3.3.1.2.

18.7.1.4* Special Requirements. (Reserved)

18.7.2 Closed Systems.

18.7.2.1 Location. Outdoor use and dispensing shall be located in accordance with 6.3.3.1.1.

18.7.2.2 Spill Control, Drainage, and Containment. Spill control and secondary containment shall be provided for toxic or highly toxic liquids in accordance with 6.3.3.3.2.

18.7.2.3 Clearance from Combustibles. Clearance from combustibles shall be provided in accordance with 6.3.3.1.2.

18.7.2.4* Special Requirements. (Reserved)

18.8 Handling. Handling of toxic or highly toxic solids or liquids in indoor and outdoor areas shall be in accordance with Section 18.8.

18.8.1 Handling. Handling shall be in accordance with 6.3.4.

18.8.2* Special Requirements. (Reserved)

Chapter 19   Unstable (Reactive) Solids and Liquids

19.1 General. The requirements of this chapter shall apply to the storage, use, and handling of unstable (reactive) solids or liquids when the amount of unstable (reactive) solids or liquids exceeds the MAQ as set forth in Chapter 5. The storage, use, and handling of unstable (reactive) solids or liquids in any quantity shall also comply with the requirements of Chapters 1 through 4 and the applicable requirements of Chapters 5 through 10.

19.1.1 Construction Requirements. Buildings, or portions thereof, in which unstable (reactive) solids or liquids are stored, handled, or used shall be constructed in accordance with the building code.

19.2 General Requirements for Storage.

19.2.1 Spill Control. Spill control shall be provided for unstable (reactive) liquids in accordance with 6.2.1.9.2.

19.2.2 Drainage. When provided, drainage shall be in accordance with 6.2.1.9.3.11.

19.2.3 Secondary Containment. Secondary containment shall be provided for unstable (reactive) solids or liquids in accordance with 6.2.1.9.3.

19.2.4 Ventilation. The requirements of 6.2.1.5 shall not apply.

19.2.5* Treatment Systems. (Reserved)

19.2.6 Fire Protection Systems. An automatic fire sprinkler system shall be provided in accordance with 6.2.1.1.

19.2.7 Explosion Control. Explosion control shall be provided for Class 3 or 4 unstable (reactive) solids or liquids when required by 6.2.1.6.

19.2.8 Emergency and Standby Power. Standby power shall be provided when required by 6.2.1.8.

19.2.9 Limit Controls. Limit controls shall be provided when required by 6.2.1.7.

19.2.10 Alarms. (Reserved)

19.2.11 Monitoring/Supervision. Supervision shall be provided in accordance with 6.2.1.11.

19.2.12 Special Requirements. Unstable (reactive) materials that are required to be stored under refrigeration to prevent a hazardous reaction shall be stored under refrigeration in accordance with the manufacturer's recommendations.

19.3 Indoor Storage.

19.3.1* Detection Systems. (Reserved)

19.3.2* Storage Conditions/Arrangement. (Reserved)

19.3.2.1* Reserved.

19.3.3 Floors. Floors shall be in accordance with 6.2.1.10.

19.3.4 Detached Storage. Detached storage shall be provided for Class 2, 3, or 4 unstable (reactive) solids or liquids when required by 6.2.2.2, 6.2.3.4, 6.2.4.4, or 6.2.4.5.

19.3.5 Special Requirements. Unstable (reactive) materials that are required to be stored under refrigeration to prevent a hazardous reaction shall be stored under refrigeration in accordance with the manufacturer's recommendations.

19.4 Outdoor Storage.

19.4.1 Exposures. Outdoor storage of unstable (reactive) solids or liquids shall be separated from exposure hazards in accordance with 19.4.1.

19.4.1.1 Clearance from Combustibles. Clearance from combustible materials shall be in accordance with 6.2.7.1.

19.4.1.2 Location.

19.4.1.2.1 Nondeflagrating Material. Outdoor storage of (Class 1 or 2) (nondeflagrating) unstable (reactive) solids or liquids shall not be within 20 ft (6.1 m) of property lines, streets, alleys, public ways, means of egress to a public way, or buildings not used exclusively for the storage, distribution, or manufacturing of such material, except as provided in 19.4.1.3.

19.4.1.2.2 Deflagrating Material. The outdoor storage area for (Class 3 nondetonable) unstable (reactive) solids and liquids (that can deflagrate) shall not be within 75 ft (23 m) of buildings, property lines, streets, alleys, public ways, or means of egress to a public way.

19.4.1.2.3 Detonable Material. Outdoor storage of Class 3 detonable or Class 4 unstable (reactive) solids and liquids shall be located in accordance with the requirements of NFPA 495, *Explosive Materials Code*, for Division 1.1 Explosive Materials.

19.4.1.3 Distance Reduction. An unpierced 2-hour fire-resistive wall extending not less than 30 in. (762 mm) above and to the side of the storage area shall be permitted in lieu of the distance specified in 19.4.1.2.1.

19.4.1.3.1 Nondeflagrating Materials. An unpierced 2-hour fire-resistive wall extending not less than 30 in. (762 mm) above and to the side of the storage area shall be permitted in lieu of the distance specified in 19.4.1.2.1 for (Class 1 and Class 2) (nondeflagrating) materials.

19.4.2 Weather Protection. When provided, weather protection shall be in accordance with 5.1.2 and 6.2.7.2.

19.4.3 Special Requirements. Unstable (reactive) materials that are required to be stored under refrigeration to prevent a hazardous reaction shall be stored under refrigeration in accordance with the manufacturer's recommendations.

19.4.3.1 Storage Arrangement.

19.4.3.1.1 Pile Size Limit. Unstable (reactive) solids and liquids stored outdoors shall be separated into piles, each not larger than 1000 ft^3 (28.3 m^3).

19.4.3.1.2 Aisles. Aisle widths between piles shall not be less than one-half the height of the pile or 10 ft (3 m), whichever is greater.

19.5 General Requirements for Use.

19.5.1 Spill Control. Spill control shall be provided for unstable (reactive) liquids in accordance with 6.3.1.4.

19.5.2 Drainage. When provided, drainage shall be in accordance with 6.3.1.4.2.10.

19.5.3 Secondary Containment. Secondary containment shall be provided for unstable (reactive) solids or liquids in accordance with 6.3.1.4.2.

19.5.4 Ventilation. The requirements of 6.3.2.1.3 and 6.3.2.2.2 shall not apply.

19.5.5* Treatment Systems. (Reserved)

19.5.6 Fire Protection System. An automatic fire sprinkler system shall be provided in accordance with 6.3.2.1.1.

19.5.7 Explosion Control. Explosion control shall be provided for Class 3 and Class 4 unstable (reactive) solids and liquids when required by 6.3.2.1.4.

19.5.8 Emergency and Standby Power. Standby power shall be provided when required by 6.3.1.3.

19.5.9 Limit Controls. Limit controls shall be provided in accordance with 6.3.1.2.

19.5.10* Alarms. (Reserved)

19.5.11 Monitoring/Supervision. Supervision shall be provided in accordance with 6.3.1.8.

19.5.12 Clearance from Combustibles. Clearance from combustible materials shall be in accordance with 6.2.7.1.

19.5.13 Floors. Floors where unstable (reactive) solids or liquids are dispensed or used in open systems shall be in accordance with 6.3.2.2.3.

19.5.14 System Design. System design shall be in accordance with 6.3.1.6.

19.5.15 Liquid Transfer. Liquid transfer shall be in accordance with 6.3.1.7.

19.5.16 Special Requirements. Unstable (reactive) materials that are required to be stored under refrigeration to prevent a hazardous reaction shall be stored under refrigeration in accordance with the manufacturer's recommendations.

19.6 Indoor Use.

19.6.1 Open Systems.

19.6.1.1 Ventilation. The requirements of 6.3.2.1.3 and 6.3.2.2.2 shall not apply.

19.6.1.2 Explosion Control. Explosion control shall be provided for Class 3 and Class 4 unstable (reactive) solids or liquids when required by 6.3.2.1.4.

19.6.1.3 Spill Control, Drainage, and Containment. Secondary containment shall be provided for unstable (reactive) liquids in accordance with 6.3.2.2.4.

19.6.1.4 Special Requirements. Unstable (reactive) materials that are required to be stored under refrigeration to prevent a hazardous reaction shall be stored under refrigeration in accordance with the manufacturer's recommendations.

19.6.2 Closed Systems.

19.6.2.1 Ventilation. The requirements of 6.3.2.1.3 and 6.3.2.2.2 shall not apply.

19.6.2.2 Explosion Control. Explosion control shall be provided for Class 3 and Class 4 unstable (reactive) solids or liquids when required by 6.3.2.1.4.

19.6.2.3 Spill Control, Drainage, and Containment. Spill control and secondary containment shall be provided for unstable (reactive) liquids in accordance with 6.3.2.3.3.

19.6.2.4 Special Requirements. Unstable (reactive) materials that are required to be stored under refrigeration to prevent a hazardous reaction shall be stored under refrigeration in accordance with the manufacturer's recommendations.

19.7 Outdoor Use.

19.7.1 Open Systems.

19.7.1.1 Location. Outdoor use and dispensing shall be located in accordance with 6.3.3.1.1.

19.7.1.2 Spill Control, Drainage, and Containment. Spill control and secondary containment shall be provided for unstable (reactive) liquids in accordance with 6.3.3.2.2.

19.7.1.3 Clearance from Combustibles. Clearance from combustible materials shall be in accordance with 6.3.3.1.2.

19.7.1.4 Special Requirements. Unstable (reactive) materials that are required to be stored under refrigeration to prevent a hazardous reaction shall be stored under refrigeration in accordance with the manufacturer's recommendations.

19.7.2 Closed Systems.

19.7.2.1 Location. Outdoor use and dispensing shall be located in accordance with 6.3.3.1.1.

19.7.2.2 Spill Control, Drainage, and Containment. Spill control and secondary containment shall be provided for unstable (reactive) liquids in accordance with 6.3.3.3.2.

19.7.2.3 Clearance from Combustibles. Clearance from combustibles shall be provided in accordance with 6.3.3.1.2.

19.7.2.4* Special Requirements. (Reserved)

19.8 Handling. Handling of unstable (reactive) solids or liquids in indoor and outdoor areas shall be in accordance with Section 19.8.

19.8.1 Handling. Handling shall be in accordance with 6.3.4.

19.8.2 Special Requirements. Unstable (reactive) materials that are required to be stored under refrigeration to prevent a hazardous reaction shall be stored under refrigeration in accordance with the manufacturer's recommendations.

Chapter 20   Water-Reactive Solids and Liquids

20.1 General. The requirements of this chapter shall apply to the storage, use, and handling of water-reactive solids or liquids when the amount of water-reactive solids or liquids exceeds the MAQ as set forth in Chapter 5. The storage, use, and handling of water-reactive solids or liquids in any quantity shall also comply with the requirements of Chapters 1 through 4 and the applicable requirements of Chapters 5 through 10.

20.1.1 Construction Requirements. Buildings, or portions thereof, in which water-reactive solids or liquids are stored, handled, or used shall be constructed in accordance with the building code.

20.2 General Requirements for Storage.

20.2.1 Spill Control. Spill control shall be provided for water-reactive liquids in accordance with 6.2.1.9.2.

20.2.2 Drainage. When provided, drainage shall be in accordance with 6.2.1.9.3.11.

20.2.3 Secondary Containment. Secondary containment shall be provided for water-reactive solids or liquids in accordance with 6.2.1.9.3.

20.2.4 Ventilation. Ventilation shall be provided for open containers in accordance with 6.2.1.5.

20.2.5* Treatment Systems. (Reserved)

20.2.6 Fire Protection Systems. An automatic fire sprinkler system shall be provided in accordance with 6.2.1.1.

20.2.7 Explosion Control. Explosion control shall be provided for Class 3 and Class 2, deflagrating water-reactives in accordance with 6.2.1.6.

20.2.8 Emergency and Standby Power. Standby power shall be provided when required by 6.2.1.8.

20.2.9 Limit Controls. Limit controls shall be provided when required by 6.2.1.7.

20.2.10* Alarms. (Reserved)

20.2.11 Monitoring/Supervision. Supervision shall be provided in accordance with 6.2.1.11.

20.2.12* Special Requirements. (Reserved)

20.3 Indoor Storage.

20.3.1* Detection Systems. (Reserved)

20.3.2* Storage Conditions/Arrangement. (Reserved)

20.3.2.1* Storage Limitations. (Reserved)

20.3.3 Floors. Floors shall be in accordance with 6.2.1.10.

20.3.4 Detached Storage. Detached storage shall be provided for Class 3 and Class 2, deflagrating water-reactive solids and liquids when required by 6.2.2.2, 6.2.3.4, 6.2.4.4, or 6.2.4.5.

20.3.5* Special Requirements. (Reserved)

20.4 Outdoor Storage.

20.4.1 Exposures. Outdoor storage of water-reactive solids or liquids shall be separated from exposure hazards in accordance with 20.4.1.

20.4.1.1 Clearance from Combustibles. Clearance from combustible materials shall be in accordance with 6.2.7.1.

20.4.1.2 Location. The outdoor storage area for Class 3 water-reactive solids and liquids shall not be within 75 ft (23 m) of buildings, property lines, streets, alleys, public ways, or means of egress to a public way.

20.4.1.2.1 Class 1 and 2 Materials. The outdoor storage area for Class 1 and Class 2 water-reactive solids and liquids shall not be within 20 ft (6.1 m) of buildings, property lines, streets, alleys, public ways, or means of egress to a public way, except as provided in 20.4.1.3.

20.4.1.3 Distance Reduction. An unpierced 2-hour fire-resistive wall extending not less than 30 in. (762 mm) above and to the side of the storage area shall be permitted in lieu of the distance specified in 20.4.1.2.

20.4.2 Weather Protection. When provided, weather protection shall be in accordance with 5.1.2 and 6.2.7.2.

20.4.3* Special Requirements. (Reserved)

20.4.3.1 Pile Size Limits. Pile sizes for water-reactive solids and liquids shall be limited as follows:

(1) Class 3 water-reactive solids and liquids shall be limited to piles not greater than 100 ft^3 (2.83 m^3).
(2) Class 1 or Class 2 water-reactive solids and liquids shall be limited to piles not greater than 1000 ft^3 (28.3 m^3).

20.4.3.2 Aisles. Aisle widths between piles shall not be less than one-half the height of the pile or 10 ft (3 m), whichever is greater.

20.5 General Requirements for Use.

20.5.1 Spill Control. Spill control shall be provided for water-reactive liquids in accordance with 6.3.1.4.

20.5.2 Drainage. When provided, drainage shall be in accordance with 6.3.1.4.2.10.

20.5.3 Secondary Containment. Secondary containment shall be provided for water-reactive solids or liquids in accordance with 6.3.1.4.2.

20.5.3.1 Secondary containment areas in outdoor areas subject to rainfall shall be designed with a means to prevent water from entering the area of containment or otherwise limited to prevent an uncontrolled reaction with water-reactive materials that might enter the area of containment.

20.5.4 Ventilation. Ventilation shall be provided for open containers in accordance with 6.3.2.1.3 and 6.3.2.2.2.

20.5.5* Treatment Systems. (Reserved)

20.5.6 Fire Protection System. An automatic fire sprinkler system shall be provided in accordance with 6.3.2.1.1.

20.5.7 Explosion Control. Explosion control shall be provided for Class 3 and Class 2, deflagrating water-reactives in accordance with 6.3.2.1.4.

20.5.8 Emergency and Standby Power. Standby power shall be provided when required by 6.3.1.3.

20.5.9 Limit Controls. Limit controls shall be provided in accordance with 6.3.1.2.

20.5.10* Alarms. (Reserved)

20.5.11 Monitoring/Supervision. Supervision shall be provided in accordance with 6.3.1.8.

20.5.12 Clearance from Combustibles. Clearance from combustible materials shall be in accordance with 6.2.7.1.

20.5.13 Floors. Floors where water-reactive solids or liquids are dispensed or used in open systems shall be in accordance with 6.3.2.2.3.

20.5.14 System Design. System design shall be in accordance with 6.3.1.6.

20.5.15 Liquid Transfer. Liquid transfer shall be in accordance with 6.3.1.7.

20.5.16* Special Requirements. (Reserved)

20.6 Indoor Use.

20.6.1 Open Systems.

20.6.1.1 Ventilation. Ventilation shall be provided in accordance with 6.3.2.2.2.

20.6.1.2 Explosion Control. Explosion control shall be provided for Class 3 and Class 2, deflagrating water-reactives in accordance with 6.3.2.1.4.

20.6.1.3 Spill Control, Drainage, and Containment. Secondary containment shall be provided for water-reactive liquids in accordance with 6.3.2.2.4.

20.6.1.3.1* Secondary containment used for Class 2 or Class 3 water-reactive solids and liquids in outdoor areas subject to rainfall shall be designed to prevent water from accumulating in the area of containment.

20.6.1.4* Special Requirements. (Reserved)

20.6.2 Closed Systems.

20.6.2.1 Ventilation. The requirements of 6.3.2.3.2 shall not apply.

20.6.2.2 Explosion Control. Explosion control shall be provided for Class 3 and Class 2, deflagrating water-reactives in accordance with 6.3.2.1.4.

20.6.2.3 Spill Control, Drainage, and Containment. Spill control and secondary containment shall be provided for water-reactive liquids in accordance with 6.3.2.2.4.

20.6.2.3.1* Secondary containment used for Class 2 or Class 3 water-reactive solids and liquids in outdoor areas subject to rainfall shall be designed to prevent water from accumulating in the area of containment.

20.6.2.4* Special Requirements. (Reserved)

20.7 Outdoor Use.

20.7.1 Open Systems.

20.7.1.1 Location. Outdoor use and dispensing shall be located in accordance with 6.3.3.1.1.

20.7.1.2 Spill Control, Drainage, and Containment. Spill control and secondary containment shall be provided for water-reactive liquids in accordance with 6.3.3.1.2.

20.7.1.2.1* Secondary containment used for Class 2 or Class 3 water-reactive solids and liquids in outdoor areas subject to rainfall shall be designed to prevent water from accumulating in the area of containment.

20.7.1.3 Clearance from Combustibles. Clearance from combustible materials shall be in accordance with 6.3.3.1.2.

20.7.1.4* Special Requirements. (Reserved)

20.7.2 Closed Systems.

20.7.2.1 Location. Outdoor use and dispensing shall be located in accordance with 6.3.3.1.1.

20.7.2.2 Spill Control, Drainage, and Containment. Spill control and secondary containment shall be provided for water-reactive liquids in accordance with 6.3.3.3.2.

20.7.2.3 Clearance from Combustibles. Clearance from combustible material shall be provided in accordance with 6.3.3.1.2.

20.7.2.4* Special Requirements. (Reserved)

20.8 Handling. Handling of water-reactive solids or liquids in indoor and outdoor areas shall be in accordance with Section 20.8.

20.8.1 Handling. Handling shall be in accordance with 6.3.4.

20.8.2* Special Requirements. (Reserved)

Chapter 21 Storage, Use, and Handling of Compressed Gases and Cryogenic Fluids in Portable and Stationary Containers, Cylinders, and Tanks

21.1 General Provisions.

21.1.1 Applicability. This chapter shall apply to the installation, storage, use, and handling of compressed gases and cryogenic fluids in portable and stationary containers, cylinders, equipment, and tanks in all occupancies. [55:1.1.1]

21.1.1.1 The requirements in this chapter shall apply to users, producers, distributors, and others who are involved with the storage, use, or handling of compressed gases or cryogenic fluids. [55:1.3]

21.1.1.2 Specific Applications.

21.1.1.2.1 This chapter shall not apply to the following:

(1)*Off-site transportation of compressed gases or cryogenic fluids
(2) Storage, use, and handling of radioactive gases in accordance with NFPA 801, *Standard for Fire Protection for Facilities Handling Radioactive Materials*
(3)*Use and handling of medical compressed gases at health care facilities in accordance with NFPA 99, *Health Care Facilities Code*
(4) Systems consisting of cylinders of oxygen and cylinders of fuel gas used for welding and cutting in accordance with NFPA 51, *Standard for the Design and Installation of Oxygen–Fuel Gas Systems for Welding, Cutting, and Allied Processes*
(5)*Flammable gases used as a vehicle fuel when stored on a vehicle
(6)*Storage, use, and handling of liquefied and nonliquefied compressed gases in laboratory work areas that are in accordance with NFPA 45, *Standard on Fire Protection for Laboratories Using Chemicals*
(7) Storage, use, and handling of liquefied petroleum gases in accordance with NFPA 58, *Liquefied Petroleum Gas Code*
(8) Storage, use, and handling of compressed gases within closed-cycle refrigeration systems complying with the mechanical code
(9) Liquefied natural gas (LNG) storage at utility plants under NFPA 59A, *Standard for the Production, Storage, and Handling of Liquefied Natural Gas (LNG)*
(10) Compressed natural gas (CNG) and liquefied natural gas (LNG) utilized as a vehicle fuel in accordance with NFPA 52, *Vehicular Gaseous Fuel Systems Code*
(11)*Compressed hydrogen gas (GH2), or liquefied hydrogen gas (LH2) generated, installed, stored, piped, used, or handled in accordance with NFPA 2, *Hydrogen Technologies Code*, when there are no specific or applicable requirements in NFPA 55
(12) Nonflammable mixtures of ethylene oxide with other chemicals
(13) Ethylene oxide in chambers 10 scf (0.283 Nm^3) or less in volume, or for containers holding 7.05 oz (200 g) of ethylene oxide or less

[55:1.1.2]

21.1.2 Hazardous Materials Classification.

21.1.2.1 Hazard Classification Pure Gases. Compressed gases and cryogenic fluids shall be classified according to hazard categories in accordance with Section 4.1.

21.1.2.2 Other Hazards. Although it is possible that there are other known hazards, the classification of such gases is not within the scope of this code and they shall be handled, stored, or used as an *other gas*. [55:5.1.2]

21.1.2.3 Mixtures. Mixtures shall be classified in accordance with the hazards of the mixture as a whole. [55:5.1.3]

21.1.2.4 Responsibility for Classification. Classification shall be performed by an approved organization, individual, or testing laboratory. [55:5.1.4]

21.1.2.5 Toxicity. The toxicity of gas mixtures shall be classified in accordance with CGA P-20, *Standard for the Classification of Toxic Gas Mixtures*, or by testing in accordance with 29 CFR 1910.1000 or DOT 49 CFR 173 or ISO 10298, *Determination of Toxicity of a Gas or Gas Mixture*. [55:5.1.4.1]

21.1.2.6 Flammability of Gas Mixtures. For gas mixtures other than those containing ammonia and nonflammable gases, flammability of gas mixtures shall be classified in accordance with CGA P-23, *Standard for Categorizing Gas Mixtures Containing Flammable and Nonflammable Components*; or by physical testing in accordance with ASTM E 681-01, *Standard Test Method for Concentration Limits of Flammability of Chemicals (Vapors and Gases)*; or ISO 10156, *Gases and Gas Mixtures — Determination of Fire Potential and Oxidizing Ability for the Selection of Cylinder Valve Outlets*. [55:5.1.4.2]

21.2 Building-Related Controls.

21.2.1 General.

21.2.1.1 Occupancy. Occupancies containing compressed gases and cryogenic fluids shall comply with this chapter in addition to other applicable requirements of this code. [55:6.1.1.1]

21.2.1.1.1 Occupancy Classification. The occupancy of a building or structure, or portion of a building or structure, shall be classified in accordance with 1.1.1.1. [**55**:6.1.1.2]

21.2.1.2 Flammable and Oxidizing Gases. [**55**:6.3.1.6]

21.2.1.2.1 Flammable and oxidizing gases shall not be stored or used in other than industrial and storage occupancies. [**55**:6.3.1.6.1]

21.2.1.2.2 Containers, cylinders, or tanks not exceeding 250 scf (7.1 Nm³) content at normal temperature and pressure (NTP) and used for maintenance purposes, patient care, or operation of equipment shall be permitted. [**55**:6.3.1.6.2]

21.2.1.3 Toxic and Highly Toxic Compressed Gases. Except for containers or cylinders not exceeding 20 scf (0.6 Nm³) content at NTP stored or used within gas cabinets or exhausted enclosures of educational occupancies, toxic or highly toxic compressed gases shall not be stored or used in other than industrial and storage occupancies. [**55**:6.3.1.7]

21.2.2 Control Areas.

21.2.2.1 Construction. Control areas shall be separated from each other by fire barriers in accordance with Table 5.2.2.1. [**55**:6.2.1]

21.2.2.2 Number. The number of control areas in buildings or portions of buildings shall be in accordance with 5.2.2.1.

21.2.2.3 Quantities Less than or Equal to the MAQ. Building-related controls in areas with compressed gases or cryogenic fluids stored or used within an indoor control area in quantities less than or equal to those shown in Table 5.2.1.4 through Table 5.2.1.10.1 shall be in accordance with 21.2.1.2, 21.2.1.3, 21.2.7, 21.2.8, 21.2.12, 21.2.15, and 21.2.16.

21.2.3 Occupancy Protection Levels.

21.2.3.1 Quantity Thresholds for Compressed Gases and Cryogenic Fluids Requiring Special Provisions. Where the quantities of compressed gases or cryogenic fluids stored or used within an indoor area exceed those shown in Table 5.2.1.4 through Table 5.2.1.10.1, the area shall meet the requirements for Protection Level 1 through 5 in accordance with the building code, based on 21.2.3.2. [**55**:6.3.1.1]

21.2.3.1.1 Quantities Greater than the MAQ. Building-related controls in areas with compressed gases or cryogenic fluids stored or used within an indoor area in quantities greater than those shown in Table 5.2.1.4 through Table 5.2.1.10.1 shall be in accordance with Section 21.2. [**55**:6.3.1.2]

21.2.3.1.2 Incompatible Materials. When the classification of materials in individual containers requires the area to be placed in more than one protection level, the separation of protection levels shall not be required providing the area is constructed to meet the requirements of the most restrictive protection level and that the incompatible materials are separated as required by 21.3.1.9.2. [**55**:6.3.1.4]

21.2.3.1.3 Multiple Hazards. Where a compressed gas or cryogenic fluid has multiple hazards, all hazards shall be addressed and controlled in accordance with the provisions for the protection level for which the threshold quantity is exceeded. [**55**:6.3.1.5]

21.2.3.2 Classification of Protection Levels. The protection level required shall be based on the hazard class of the material involved as indicated in 21.2.3.2.1 through 21.2.3.2.4. [**55**:6.3.2]

21.2.3.2.1 Protection Level 1. Occupancies used for the storage or use of unstable reactive Class 4 and unstable reactive Class 3 detonable compressed gases in quantities that exceed the quantity thresholds for gases requiring special provisions shall be classified Protection Level 1. [**55**:6.3.2.1]

21.2.3.2.2 Protection Level 2. Occupancies used for the storage or use of flammable, pyrophoric, and nondetonable, unstable reactive Class 3 compressed gases or cryogenic fluids in quantities that exceed the quantity thresholds for gases requiring special provisions shall be classified as Protection Level 2. [**55**:6.3.2.2]

21.2.3.2.3 Protection Level 3. Occupancies used for the storage or use of oxidizing, and unstable reactive Class 2 compressed gases or cryogenic fluids in quantities that exceed the quantity thresholds for gases requiring special provisions shall be classified as Protection Level 3. [**55**:6.3.2.3]

21.2.3.2.4 Protection Level 4. Occupancies used for the storage or use of toxic, highly toxic, and corrosive compressed gases in quantities that exceed the quantity thresholds for gases requiring special provisions shall be classified as Protection Level 4. [**55**:6.3.2.4]

21.2.4 Gas Rooms. [**55**:6.4]

21.2.4.1 Pressure Control. Gas rooms shall operate at a negative pressure in relationship to the surrounding area. [**55**:6.4.1]

21.2.4.2 Exhaust Ventilation. Gas rooms shall be provided with an exhaust ventilation system. [**55**:6.4.2]

21.2.4.3 Construction. Gas rooms shall be constructed in accordance with the building code. [**55**:6.4.3]

21.2.4.4 Separation. Gas rooms shall be separated from other occupancies by a minimum of 1-hour fire resistance. [**55**:6.4.4]

21.2.4.5 Limitation on Contents. The function of compressed gas rooms shall be limited to storage and use of compressed gases and associated equipment and supplies. [**55**:6.4.5]

21.2.5* Detached Buildings. Occupancies used for the storage or use of compressed gases, including individual bulk hydrogen compressed gas systems in quantities exceeding those specified in Table 21.2.5, shall be in detached buildings constructed in accordance with the provisions of the building code. [**55**:6.5]

21.2.6 Weather Protection. [**55**:6.6]

21.2.6.1 For other than explosive materials and hazardous materials presenting a detonation hazard, a weather protection structure shall be permitted to be used for sheltering outdoor storage or use areas, without requiring such areas to be classified as indoor storage or use. [**55**:6.6.1]

21.2.6.1.1 Weather protection shall be constructed in accordance with 6.2.7.2.

21.2.7 Electrical Equipment. Electrical wiring and equipment shall be in accordance with 21.2.7 and *NFPA 70, National Electrical Code.* [**55**:6.7]

Table 21.2.5 Detached Buildings Required Where Quantity of Material Exceeds Amount Shown

Gas Hazard	Class	Quantity of Material scf	Quantity of Material Nm³
Individual bulk hydrogen compressed gas systems	NA	15,000	425
Unstable reactive (detonable)	4 or 3	Quantity thresholds for gases requiring special provisions*	
Unstable reactive (nondetonable)	3	2,000	57
Unstable reactive (nondetonable)	2	10,000	283
Pyrophoric gas	NA	2,000	57

NA: Not applicable.
*See Table 6.3.1.1.
[**55:** Table 6.5]

21.2.7.1 Standby Power.

21.2.7.1.1 Where the following systems are required by this code for the storage or use of compressed gases or cryogenic fluids that exceed the quantity thresholds for gases requiring special provisions, such systems shall be connected to a standby power system in accordance with *NFPA 70, National Electrical Code*.

(1) Mechanical ventilation
(2) Treatment systems
(3) Temperature controls
(4) Alarms
(5) Detection systems
(6) Other electrically operated systems

[**55:**6.7.1, 6.7.1.1]

21.2.7.1.2 The requirements of 21.2.7.1 shall not apply where emergency power is provided in accordance with *NFPA 70, National Electrical Code*. [**55:**6.7.1.2]

21.2.7.2 Emergency Power. When emergency power is required, the system shall meet the requirements for a Protection Level 2 system in accordance with NFPA 110, *Standard for Emergency and Standby Power Systems*. [**55:**6.7.2]

21.2.8* Employee Alarm System. Where required by government regulations, an employee alarm system shall be provided to allow warning for necessary emergency action as called for in the emergency action plan required by 1.10.1, or for reaction time for safe egress of employees from the workplace or the immediate work area, or both. [**55:**6.8]

21.2.9* Explosion Control. Explosion control shall be provided as required by Table 21.2.9 in accordance with NFPA 69, *Standard on Explosion Prevention Systems*, where amounts of compressed gases in storage or use exceed the quantity thresholds requiring special provisions. [**55:**6.9]

21.2.10* Fire Protection Systems. Except as provided in 21.2.10.1, buildings or portions thereof required to comply with Protection Levels 1 through 5 shall be protected by an approved automatic fire sprinkler system complying with NFPA 13, *Standard for the Installation of Sprinkler Systems*. [**55:**6.10]

21.2.10.1 Rooms or areas that are of noncombustible construction with wholly noncombustible contents shall not be required to be protected by an automatic fire sprinkler system. [**55:**6.10.1]

21.2.10.2 Sprinkler System Design. When sprinkler protection is provided, the area in which compressed gases or cryogenic fluids are stored or used shall be protected with a sprinkler system designed to be not less than that required by NFPA 13, *Standard for the Installation of Sprinkler Systems*, for Ordinary Hazard Group 2. [**55:**6.10.2, 6.10.2.1]

21.2.10.2.1 When sprinkler protection is provided, the area in which the flammable or pyrophoric compressed gases or cryogenic fluids are stored or used shall be protected with a sprinkler system designed to be not less than that required by NFPA 13, *Standard for the Installation of Sprinkler Systems*, for Extra Hazard Group 1. [**55:**6.10.2.2]

21.2.11 Lighting. Approved lighting by natural or artificial means shall be provided for the storage areas. [**55:**6.11]

21.2.12 Hazard Identification Signs. [**55:**6.12]

21.2.12.1 Hazard identification signs shall be placed at all entrances to locations where compressed gases are produced, stored, used, or handled in accordance with NFPA 704, *Standard System for the Identification of the Hazards of Materials for Emergency Response*. [**55:**6.12.1]

21.2.12.1.1 Ratings shall be assigned in accordance with NFPA 704, *Standard System for the Identification of the Hazards of Materials for Emergency Response*. [**55:**6.11.1.1]

21.2.12.1.2 Identification of Gas Rooms and Cabinets. Rooms or cabinets containing compressed gases shall be conspicuously labeled as follows:

COMPRESSED GAS

[**55:**4.10.2.3]

21.2.12.1.3 The authority having jurisdiction shall be permitted to waive the signage requirements where consistent with safety. [**55:**6.12.1.2]

21.2.12.2 Signs. Signs shall not be obscured or removed. [**55:**6.12.2.1]

21.2.12.3 No Smoking. Signs prohibiting smoking or open flames within 25 ft (7.6 m) of area perimeters shall be provided in areas where toxic, highly toxic, corrosive, unstable reactive, flammable, oxidizing, or pyrophoric gases are produced, stored, or used. [**55:**6.12.2.2]

21.2.13 Spill Control, Drainage, and Secondary Containment. Spill control, drainage, and secondary containment shall not be required for compressed gases. [**55:**6.13]

21.2.14 Shelving. [**55:**6.14]

21.2.14.1 Shelves used for the storage of cylinders, containers, and tanks shall be of noncombustible construction and designed to support the weight of the materials stored. [**55:**6.14.1]

21.2.14.2 In seismically active areas, shelves and containers shall be secured from overturning. [**55:**6.14.2]

21.2.15 Vent Pipe Termination. The termination point for piped vent systems serving cylinders, containers, tanks, and gas systems used for the purpose of operational or emergency venting shall be located to prevent impingement exposure on the system served and to minimize the effects of high temperature thermal radiation or the effects of contact with the gas

Table 21.2.9 Explosion Control Requirements

Material	Class	Barricade Construction	Explosion Venting or Prevention Systems
Flammable cryogenic fluid	—	Not required	Required
Flammable gas	Nonliquefied	Not required	Required
	Liquefied	Not required	Required
Pyrophoric gas	—	Not required	Required
Unstable reactive gas	4	Required	Not required
	3 (detonable)	Required	Not required
	3 (nondetonable)	Not required	Required

[**55:** Table 6.9]

from the escaping plume to the supply system, personnel, adjacent structures, and ignition sources. [**55:**6.15]

21.2.16 Ventilation. Indoor storage and use areas and storage buildings for compressed gases and cryogenic fluids shall be provided with mechanical exhaust ventilation or natural ventilation, where natural ventilation is shown to be acceptable for the material as stored. [**55:**6.16]

21.2.16.1 Compressed Air. Subsection 21.2.16 shall not apply to cylinders, containers, and tanks containing compressed air. [**55:**6.16.2]

21.2.16.2 Mechanical Exhaust Ventilation. Where mechanical exhaust ventilation is provided, the system shall be operational during the time the building or space is occupied. [**55:**6.16.3]

21.2.16.2.1 Ventilation Rate. Mechanical exhaust or fixed natural ventilation shall be provided at a rate of not less than 1 scf/min/ft^2 (0.3048 Nm^3/min/m^2) of floor area over the area of storage or use. [**55:**6.16.3.2]

21.2.16.2.2 Continuous Operation. When operation of ventilation systems is required, systems shall operate continuously unless an alternative design is approved by the AHJ. [**55:**6.16.3.1]

21.2.16.2.3 Shutoff Controls. Where powered ventilation is provided, a manual shutoff switch shall be provided outside of the room in a position adjacent to the principal access door to the room or in an approved location. [**55:**6.16.3.3]

21.2.16.2.4 Manual Shutoff Switch. The switch shall be the break-glass or equivalent type and shall be labeled as follows:

WARNING: VENTILATION SYSTEM EMERGENCY SHUTOFF
[**55:**6.16.3.3.1]

21.2.16.3 Inlets to the Exhaust System. [**55:**6.16.4]

21.2.16.3.1 The exhaust ventilation system design shall take into account the density of the potential gases released. [**55:**6.16.4.1]

21.2.16.3.2 For gases that are heavier than air, exhaust shall be taken from a point within 12 in. (305 mm) of the floor. The use of supplemental inlets shall be allowed to be installed at points above the 12 in. (305 mm) threshold level. [**55:**6.16.4.2]

21.2.16.3.3 For gases that are lighter than air, exhaust shall be taken from a point within 12 in. (305 mm) of the ceiling. The use of supplemental inlets shall be allowed to be installed at points below the 12 in. (305 mm) threshold level. [**55:**6.16.4.3]

21.2.16.3.4 The location of both the exhaust and inlet air openings shall be designed to provide air movement across all portions of the floor or ceiling of the room or area to prevent the accumulation of vapors within the ventilated space. [**55:**6.16.4.4]

21.2.16.4 Recirculation of Exhaust. Exhaust ventilation shall not be recirculated within the room or building if the cylinders, containers, or tanks stored are capable of releasing hazardous gases. [**55:**6.16.5]

21.2.16.5 Ventilation Discharge. Ventilation systems shall terminate at a point not less than 50 ft (15 m) from intakes of air-handling systems, air-conditioning equipment, and air compressors. [**55:**6.16.6]

21.2.16.6 Air Intakes. Storage and use of compressed gases shall be located not less than 50 ft (15 m) from air intakes. For material-specific requirements, see 21.3.4 through 21.3.10. [**55:**6.16.7]

21.2.17 Gas Cabinets. Where a gas cabinet is required, is used to provide separation of gas hazards, or is used to increase the threshold quantity for a gas requiring special provisions, the gas cabinet shall be in accordance with 21.2.17.1 through 21.2.17.5. [**55:**6.17]

21.2.17.1 Construction. [**55:**6.17.1]

21.2.17.1.1 Materials of Construction. The gas cabinet shall be constructed of not less than 0.097 in. (2.46 mm) (12 gauge) steel. [**55:**6.17.1.1]

21.2.17.1.2 Access to Controls. The gas cabinet shall be provided with self-closing limited access ports or noncombustible windows to give access to equipment controls. [**55:**6.17.1.2]

21.2.17.1.3 Self-Closing Doors. The gas cabinet shall be provided with self-closing doors. [**55:**6.17.1.3]

21.2.17.2 Ventilation Requirements. [**55:**6.17.2]

21.2.17.2.1 The gas cabinet shall be provided with an exhaust ventilation system designed to operate at a negative pressure relative to the surrounding area. [**55:**6.17.2.1]

21.2.17.2.2 Where toxic; highly toxic; pyrophoric; unstable, reactive Class 3 or Class 4; or corrosive gases are contained, the velocity at the face of access ports or windows, with the access port or window open, shall not be less than 200 ft/min (61 m/min) average, with not less than 150 ft/min (46 m/min) at any single point. [**55:**6.17.2.2]

21.2.17.3 Fire Protection. Gas cabinets used to contain toxic, highly toxic, or pyrophoric gases shall be internally sprinklered. [**55:**6.17.3]

21.2.17.4 Quantity Limits. Gas cabinets shall contain not more than three containers, cylinders, or tanks. [**55:**6.17.4]

21.2.17.5 Separation of Incompatibles. Incompatible gases, as defined by Table 21.3.1.9.2, shall be stored or used within separate gas cabinets. [**55:**6.17.5]

21.2.18 Exhausted Enclosures. [**55:**6.18]

21.2.18.1 Ventilation Requirements. Where an exhausted enclosure is required or used to increase the threshold quantity for a gas requiring special provisions, the exhausted enclosure shall be provided with an exhaust ventilation system designed to operate at a negative pressure in relationship to the surrounding area. [**55:**6.18.1]

21.2.18.1.1 Control Velocity at Access Openings. Where toxic; highly toxic; pyrophoric; unstable, reactive Class 3 or Class 4; or corrosive gases are contained, the velocity at the face openings providing access shall be not less than 200 ft/min (61 m/min) average, with not less than 150 ft/min (46 m/min) at any single point. [**55:**6.18.1.1]

21.2.18.1.2 Separation of Incompatible Gases Within Enclosures. Cylinders, containers, and tanks within enclosures shall be separated in accordance with Table 21.3.1.9.2. [**55:**6.18.1.2]

21.2.18.1.3 Fire Protection. Exhausted enclosures shall be internally sprinklered. [**55:**6.18.1.3]

21.2.18.1.4 Separation. Incompatible gases, as defined by Table 21.3.1.9.2, shall be stored or used within separate exhausted enclosures. [**55:**6.18.2]

21.2.19 Source Valve. Bulk gas systems shall be provided with a source valve. [**55:**6.19]

21.2.19.1 The source valve shall be marked. [**55:**6.19.1]

21.2.19.2 The source valve shall be designated on the design drawings for the installation. [**55:**6.19.2]

21.3 Compressed Gases.

21.3.1 General. The storage, use, and handling of compressed gases in containers, cylinders, and tanks shall be in accordance with Sections 21.1, 21.3, and 21.6 as applicable.

21.3.1.1* Compressed Gas Systems. [**55:**7.1.1]

21.3.1.1.1 Design. Compressed gas systems shall be designed for the intended use and shall be designed by persons competent in such design. [**55:**7.1.1.1]

21.3.1.1.2 Installation. Installation of bulk compressed gas systems shall be supervised by personnel knowledgeable in the application of the standards for their construction and use. [**55:**7.1.1.2]

21.3.1.2 Listed and Approved Hydrogen Equipment. Listed and approved hydrogen generating and consuming equipment shall be in accordance with the listing requirements and manufacturers' instructions. [**55:**7.1.4, 7.1.4.1]

21.3.1.2.1 Such equipment shall not be required to meet the requirements of Section 21.3. [**55:**7.1.4.2]

21.3.1.3 Metal Hydride Storage Systems. [**55:**7.1.5]

21.3.1.3.1 General Requirements. [**55:**7.1.5.1]

21.3.1.3.1.1 Metal Hydride Storage System Requirements. The storage and use of metal hydride storage systems shall be in accordance with 21.3.1.3. [**55:**7.1.5.1.1]

21.3.1.3.1.2 Metal Hydride Systems Storing or Supplying Hydrogen. Those portions of the system that are used as a means to store or supply hydrogen shall also comply with Sections 21.3 and 21.6 as applicable. [**55:**7.1.5.1.2]

21.3.1.3.1.3 Classification. The hazard classification of the metal hydride storage system, as required by Section 4.1, shall be based on the hydrogen stored without regard to the metal hydride content. [**55:**7.1.5.1.3]

21.3.1.3.1.4 Listed or Approved Systems. Metal hydride storage systems shall be listed or approved for the application and designed in a manner that prevents the addition or removal of the metal hydride by other than the original equipment manufacturer. [**55:**7.1.5.1.4]

21.3.1.3.1.5 Containers, Design and Construction. Compressed gas cylinders, containers, and tanks shall be designed and constructed in accordance with 21.3.1.4.1. [**55:**7.1.5.1.5]

21.3.1.3.1.6 Service Life and Inspection of Containers. Metal hydride storage system cylinders, containers or tanks shall be inspected, tested, and requalified for service at not less than five year intervals. [**55:**7.1.5.1.6]

21.3.1.3.1.7 Marking and Labeling. Marking and labeling of cylinders, containers, tanks, and systems shall be in accordance with 21.3.1.3.1.7(A) through 21.3.1.3.1.7(D). [**55:**7.1.5.1.7]

(A) System Marking. Metal hydride storage systems shall be marked with the following:

(1) Manufacturer's name
(2) Service life indicating the last date the system can be used
(3) A unique code or serial number specific to the unit
(4) System name or product code that identifies the system by the type of chemistry used in the system
(5) Emergency contact name, telephone number, or other contact information
(6) Limitations on refilling of containers to include rated charging pressure and capacity.

[**55:**7.1.5.1.7.1]

(B) Valve Marking. Metal hydride storage system valves shall be marked with the following:

(1) Manufacturer's name
(2) Service life indicating the last date the valve can be used
(3) Metal hydride service in which the valve can be used, or a product code that is traceable to this information

[**55:**7.1.5.1.7.2]

(C) Pressure Relief Device Marking.

(1) Metal hydride storage system pressure relief devices shall be marked with the following:
 (a) Manufacturer's name
 (b) Metal hydride service in which the device can be used, or a product code that is traceable to this information
 (c) Activation parameters to include temperature, pressure, or both
(2) The required markings for pressure relief devices that are integral components of valves used on cylinders, containers and tanks shall be allowed to be placed on the valve. [**55:**7.1.5.1.7.3(A), 7.1.5.1.7.3(B)]

(D) Pressure Vessel Markings. Cylinders, containers, and tanks used in metal hydride storage systems shall be marked with the following:

(1) Manufacturer's name
(2) Design specification to which the vessel was manufactured
(3) Authorized body approving the design and initial inspection and test of the vessel
(4) Manufacturer's original test date
(5) Unique serial number for the vessel
(6) Service life identifying the last date the vessel can be used
(7) System name or product code that identifies the system by the type of chemistry used in the system

[**55:**7.1.5.1.7.4]

21.3.1.3.1.8 Temperature Extremes. Metal hydride storage systems, whether full or partially full, shall not be exposed to artificially created high temperatures exceeding 125°F (52°C) or subambient (low) temperatures unless designed for use under the exposed conditions. [**55:**7.1.5.1.8]

21.3.1.3.1.9 Falling Objects. Metal hydride storage systems shall not be placed in areas where they are capable of being damaged by falling objects. [**55:**7.1.5.1.9]

21.3.1.3.1.10 Piping Systems. Piping, including tubing, valves, fittings and pressure regulators, serving metal hydride storage systems shall be maintained gas tight to prevent leakage. [**55:**7.1.5.1.10]

(A) Leaking Systems. Leaking systems shall be removed from service. [**55:**7.1.5.1.10]

21.3.1.3.1.11 Refilling of Containers. The refilling of listed or approved metal hydride storage systems shall be in accordance with the listing requirements and manufacturers' instructions. [**55:**7.1.5.1.11]

(A) Industrial Trucks. The refilling of metal hydride storage systems shall be in accordance with NFPA 52, *Vehicular Gaseous Fuel Systems Code*. [**55:**7.1.5.1.11.1]

(B) Hydrogen Purity. The purity of hydrogen used for the purpose of refilling containers shall be in accordance with the listing and the manufacturer's instructions. [**55:**7.1.5.1.11.2]

21.3.1.3.1.12 Electrical. Electrical components for metal hydride storage systems shall be designed, constructed, and installed in accordance with *NFPA 70, National Electrical Code.* [**55:**7.1.5.1.12]

21.3.1.3.2 Portable Containers or Systems. [**55:**7.1.5.2]

21.3.1.3.2.1 Securing Containers. Containers, cylinders, and tanks shall be secured in accordance with 21.3.1.7.4. [**55:**7.1.5.2.1]

(A) Use on Mobile Equipment. Where a metal hydride storage system is used on mobile equipment, the equipment shall be designed to restrain containers, cylinders, or tanks from dislodgement, slipping, or rotating when the equipment is in motion. [**55:**7.1.5.2.1.1]

(B) Motorized Equipment. [**55:**7.1.5.2.1.2]

(1) Metal hydride storage systems used on motorized equipment shall be installed in a manner that protects valves, pressure regulators, fittings, and controls against accidental impact.
(2) Metal hydride storage systems including cylinders, containers, tanks, and fittings shall not extend beyond the platform of the mobile equipment.

21.3.1.3.2.2 Valves. Valves on containers, cylinders, and tanks shall remain closed except when containers are connected to closed systems and ready for use. [**55:**7.1.5.2.2]

21.3.1.4 Containers, Cylinders, and Tanks. [**55:**7.1.6]

21.3.1.4.1 Design and Construction. Containers, cylinders, and tanks shall be designed, fabricated, tested, and marked (stamped) in accordance with regulations of DOT, Transport Canada (TC) *Transportation of Dangerous Goods Regulations*, or the ASME *Boiler and Pressure Vessel Code*, "Rules for the Construction of Unfired Pressure Vessels," Section VIII. [**55:**7.1.6.1]

21.3.1.4.2 Defective Containers, Cylinders, and Tanks. [**55:**7.1.6.2]

21.3.1.4.2.1 Defective containers, cylinders, and tanks shall be returned to the supplier. [**55:**7.1.6.2.1]

21.3.1.4.2.2 Suppliers shall either repair the containers, cylinders, and tanks, remove them from service, or dispose of them in an approved manner. [**55:**7.1.6.2.2]

21.3.1.4.3 Supports. Stationary cylinders, containers, and tanks shall be provided with engineered supports of noncombustible material on noncombustible foundations. [**55:**7.1.6.3]

21.3.1.4.4 Cylinders, Containers, and Tanks Containing Residual Gas. Compressed gas cylinders, containers, and tanks containing residual product shall be treated as full except when being examined, serviced, or refilled by a gas manufacturer or distributor. [**55:**7.1.6.4]

21.3.1.4.5 Pressure Relief Devices. [**55:**7.1.6.5]

21.3.1.4.5.1 When required by 21.3.1.4.5.2, pressure relief devices shall be provided to protect containers and systems containing compressed gases from rupture in the event of overpressure from thermal exposure. [**55:**7.1.6.5.1]

21.3.1.4.5.2 Pressure relief devices to protect containers shall be designed and provided in accordance with CGA S-1.1, *Pressure Relief Device Standards – Part 1– Cylinders for Compressed Gases*, for cylinders; CGA S-1.2, *Pressure Relief Device Standards – Part 2 – Cargo and Portable Tanks for Compressed Gases*, for portable tanks; and CGA S-1.3, *Pressure Relief Device Standards – Part 3 – Stationary Storage Containers for Compressed Gases*, for stationary tanks or applicable equivalent requirements in the country of use. [**55:**7.1.6.5.2]

21.3.1.4.5.3 Pressure relief devices shall be sized in accordance with the specifications to which the container was fabricated. [**55:**7.1.6.5.3]

21.3.1.4.5.4 The pressure relief device shall have the capacity to prevent the maximum design pressure of the container or system from being exceeded. [**55:**7.1.6.5.4]

21.3.1.4.5.5 Pressure relief devices shall be arranged to discharge unobstructed to the open air in such a manner as to prevent any impingement of escaping gas upon the container, adjacent structures, or personnel. This requirement shall not apply to DOT specification containers having an internal volume of 2.0 ft^3 (0.057 m^3) or less. [**55:**7.1.6.5.5]

21.3.1.4.5.6 Pressure relief devices or vent piping shall be designed or located so that moisture cannot collect and freeze in a manner that would interfere with operation of the device. [**55:**7.1.6.5.6]

21.3.1.5 Cathodic Protection. When required, cathodic protection shall be in accordance with 21.3.1.5. [**55:**7.1.7]

21.3.1.5.1 Operation. When installed, cathodic protection systems shall be operated and maintained to continuously provide corrosion protection. [**55:**7.1.7.1]

21.3.1.5.2* Inspection. Container systems equipped with cathodic protection shall be inspected for the intended operation by a cathodic protection tester. [**55:**7.1.7.2]

21.3.1.5.2.1 The frequency of inspection shall be determined by the designer of the cathodic protection system. [**55:**7.1.7.2]

21.3.1.5.2.2 The cathodic protection tester shall be certified as being qualified by the National Association of Corrosion Engineers, International (NACE). [**55:**7.1.7.2.1]

21.3.1.5.3 Impressed Current Systems. Systems equipped with impressed current cathodic protection systems shall be inspected in accordance with the requirements of design and 21.3.1.3.1.12. [**55:**7.1.7.3]

21.3.1.5.3.1 The design limits of the cathodic protection system shall be available to the AHJ upon request. [**55:**7.1.7.3.1]

21.3.1.5.3.2 The system owner shall maintain the following records to demonstrate that the cathodic protection is in conformance with the requirements of the design:

(1) The results of inspections of the system
(2) The results of testing that has been completed

[**55:**7.1.7.3.2]

21.3.1.5.4 Corrosion Expert.

21.3.1.5.4.1 Repairs, maintenance, or replacement of a cathodic protection system shall be under the supervision of a NACE certified corrosion expert. [**55:**7.1.7.4]

21.3.1.5.4.2 The corrosion expert shall be certified by NACE as a senior corrosion technologist, a cathodic protection specialist, or a corrosion specialist or shall be a registered engineer with registration in a field that includes education and experience in corrosion control. [**55:**7.1.7.4.1]

21.3.1.6 Labeling Requirements. [**55:**7.1.8]

21.3.1.6.1 Containers. Individual compressed gas containers, cylinders, and tanks shall be marked or labeled in accordance with DOT requirements or those of the applicable regulatory agency. [**55:**7.1.8.1]

21.3.1.6.2 Label Maintenance. The labels applied by the gas manufacturer to identify the liquefied or nonliquefied compressed gas cylinder contents shall not be altered or removed by the user. [**55:**7.1.8.2]

21.3.1.6.3 Stationary Compressed Gas Cylinders, Containers, and Tanks. [**55:**7.1.8.3]

21.3.1.6.3.1 Stationary compressed gas cylinders, containers, and tanks shall be marked in accordance with NFPA 704, *Standard System for the Identification of the Hazards of Materials for Emergency Response*. [**55:**7.1.8.3.1]

21.3.1.6.3.2 Markings shall be visible from any direction of approach. [**55:**7.1.8.3.2]

21.3.1.6.4 Piping Systems. [**55:**7.1.8.4]

21.3.1.6.4.1 Except as provided in 21.3.1.6.4.2, piping systems shall be marked in accordance with ASME A13.1, *Scheme for the Identification of Piping Systems*, or other applicable approved standards as follows:

(1) Marking shall include the name of the gas and a direction-of-flow arrow.
(2) Piping that is used to convey more than one gas at various times shall be marked to provide clear identification and warning of the hazard.
(3) Markings for piping systems shall be provided at the following locations:
   (a) At each critical process control valve
   (b) At wall, floor, or ceiling penetrations
   (c) At each change of direction
   (d) At a minimum of every 20 ft (6.1 m) or fraction thereof throughout the piping run

[**55:**7.1.8.4.1]

21.3.1.6.4.2 Piping within gas manufacturing plants, gas processing plants, refineries, and similar occupancies shall be marked in an approved manner. [**55:**7.1.8.4.2]

21.3.1.7 Security. [**55:**7.1.9]

21.3.1.7.1 General. Compressed gas containers, cylinders, tanks, and systems shall be secured against accidental dislodgement and against access by unauthorized personnel. [**55:**7.1.9.1]

21.3.1.7.2 Security of Areas. Storage, use, and handling areas shall be secured against unauthorized entry. [**55:**7.1.9.2]

21.3.1.7.3 Physical Protection. [**55:**7.1.9.3]

21.3.1.7.3.1 Compressed gas cylinders, containers, tanks, and systems that could be exposed to physical damage shall be protected. [**55:**7.1.9.3.1]

21.3.1.7.3.2 Guard posts or other means shall be provided to protect compressed gas cylinders, containers, tanks, and systems indoors and outdoors from vehicular damage. *(See Section 4.11 of NFPA 55, Compressed Gases and Cryogenic Fluids Code.)* [**55:**7.1.9.3.2]

21.3.1.7.4 Securing Compressed Gas Cylinders, Containers, and Tanks. Compressed gas cylinders, containers, and tanks in use or in storage shall be secured to prevent them from falling or being knocked over by corralling them and securing them to a cart, framework, or fixed object by use of a restraint, unless otherwise permitted by 21.3.1.7.4.1 and 21.3.1.7.4.2. [**55:**7.1.9.4]

21.3.1.7.4.1 Compressed gas cylinders, containers, and tanks in the process of examination, servicing, and refilling shall not be required to be secured. [**55:**7.1.9.4.1]

21.3.1.7.4.2 At cylinder-filling plants, authorized cylinder requalifier's facilities, and distributors' warehouses, the nesting of cylinders shall be permitted as a means to secure cylinders. [**55:**7.1.9.4.2]

21.3.1.8 Valve Protection. [55:7.1.10]

21.3.1.8.1 General. Compressed gas cylinder, container, and tank valves shall be protected from physical damage by means of protective caps, collars, or similar devices. [55:7.1.10.1]

21.3.1.8.1.1 Valve protection of individual valves shall not be required to be installed on individual cylinders, containers, or tanks installed on tube trailers or similar transportable bulk gas systems equipped with manifolds that are provided with a means of physical protection that will protect the valves from physical damage when the equipment is in use. Protective systems required by DOT for over the road transport shall provide an acceptable means of protection. [55:7.1.10.1.1]

21.3.1.8.1.2 Valve protection of individual valves shall not be required on cylinders, containers, or tanks that comprise bulk or non-bulk gas systems where the containers are stationary, or portable equipped with manifolds, that are provided with physical protection in accordance with Section 4.11 and 7.1.9.3 of NFPA 55 or other approved means. Protective systems required by DOT for over the road transport shall provide an acceptable means of protection. [55:7.1.10.1.1.1]

21.3.1.8.2 Valve-Protective Caps. Where compressed gas cylinders, containers, and tanks are designed to accept valve-protective caps, the user shall keep such caps on the compressed gas cylinders, containers, and tanks at all times, except when empty, being processed, or connected for use. [55:7.1.10.2]

21.3.1.8.3 Valve Outlet Caps or Plugs. [55:7.1.10.3]

21.3.1.8.3.1 Gastight valve outlet caps or plugs shall be provided and in place for all full or partially full containers, cylinders, and tanks containing toxic, highly toxic, pyrophoric, or unstable reactive Class 3 or Class 4 gases that are in storage. [55:7.1.10.3.1]

21.3.1.8.3.2 Valve outlet caps and plugs shall be designed and rated for the container service pressure. [55:7.1.10.3.2]

21.3.1.9 Separation from Hazardous Conditions. [55:7.1.11]

21.3.1.9.1 General. [55:7.1.11.1]

21.3.1.9.1.1 Compressed gas cylinders, containers, tanks, and systems in storage or use shall be separated from materials and conditions that present exposure hazards to or from each other. [55:7.1.11.1.1]

21.3.1.9.2 Incompatible Materials. Gas cylinders, containers, and tanks shall be separated in accordance with Table 21.3.1.9.2. [55:7.1.11.2]

21.3.1.9.2.1 Subparagraph 21.3.1.9.2 shall not apply to gases contained within closed piping systems. [55:7.1.11.2.1]

21.3.1.9.2.2 The distances shown in Table 21.3.1.9.2 shall be permitted to be reduced without limit when compressed gas cylinders, tanks, and containers are separated by a barrier of noncombustible construction that has a fire resistance rating of at least 0.5 hour and interrupts the line of sight between the containers. [55:7.1.11.2.2]

21.3.1.9.2.3 The 20 ft (6.1 m) distance shall be permitted to be reduced to 5 ft (1.5 m) where one of the gases is enclosed in a gas cabinet or without limit where both gases are enclosed in gas cabinets. [55:7.1.11.2.3]

21.3.1.9.2.4 Cylinders without pressure relief devices shall not be stored without separation from flammable and pyrophoric gases with pressure relief devices. [55:7.1.11.2.4]

21.3.1.9.2.5 Spatial separation shall not be required between cylinders deemed to be incompatible in gas production facilities where cylinders are connected to manifolds for the purposes of filling and manufacturing procedures, assuming the prescribed controls for the manufacture of gas mixtures are in place. [55:7.1.11.2.5]

21.3.1.9.3* Clearance from Combustibles and Vegetation. Combustible waste, vegetation, and similar materials shall be kept a minimum of 10 ft (3 m) from compressed gas containers, cylinders, tanks, and systems. [55:7.1.11.3]

21.3.1.9.3.1 A noncombustible partition without openings or penetrations and extending sides not less than 18 in. (457 mm) above and to the sides of the storage area shall be permitted in lieu of the minimum distance. [55:7.1.11.3.1]

21.3.1.9.3.2 The noncombustible partition shall either be an independent structure or the exterior wall of the building adjacent to the storage area. [55:7.1.11.3.2]

21.3.1.9.4 Ledges, Platforms, and Elevators. Compressed gas cylinders, containers, and tanks shall not be placed near elevators, unprotected platform ledges, or other areas where compressed gas cylinders, containers, or tanks could fall for distances exceeding one-half the height of the cylinder, container, or tank. [55:7.1.11.4]

21.3.1.9.5 Temperature Extremes. Compressed gas cylinders, containers, and tanks, whether full or partially full, shall not be exposed to temperatures exceeding 125°F (52°C) or sub-ambient (low) temperatures unless designed for use under such exposure. [55:7.1.11.5]

21.3.1.9.6 Falling Objects. Compressed gas cylinders, containers, and tanks shall not be placed in areas where they are capable of being damaged by falling objects. [55:7.1.11.6]

21.3.1.9.7 Heating. Compressed gas cylinders, containers, and tanks, whether full or partially full, shall not be heated by devices that could raise the surface temperature of the cylinder, container, or tank to above 125°F (52°C). [55:7.1.11.7]

21.3.1.9.7.1 Electrically Powered Heating Devices. Electrical heating devices shall be in accordance with *NFPA 70, National Electrical Code*. [55:7.1.11.7.1]

21.3.1.9.7.2 Fail-Safe Design. Devices designed to maintain individual compressed gas cylinders, containers, or tanks at constant temperature shall be designed to be fail-safe. [55:7.1.11.7.2]

21.3.1.9.8 Sources of Ignition. Open flames and high-temperature devices shall not be used in a manner that creates a hazardous condition. [55:7.1.11.8]

21.3.1.9.9 Exposure to Chemicals. Compressed gas cylinders, containers, and tanks shall not be exposed to corrosive chemicals or fumes that could damage cylinders, containers, tanks, or valve-protective caps. [55:7.1.11.9]

21.3.1.9.10 Exposure to Electrical Circuits. Compressed gas cylinders, containers, and tanks shall not be placed where they could become a part of an electrical circuit. [55:7.1.11.10]

21.3.1.10 Service and Repair. Service, repair, modification, or removal of valves, pressure relief devices, or other compressed gas cylinder, container, or tank appurtenances shall be performed by trained personnel and with the permission of the container owner. [55:7.1.12]

Table 21.3.1.9.2 Separation of Gas Containers, Cylinders, and Tanks by Hazard Class

Gas Category	Other Gas	Unstable Reactive Class 2, Class 3, or Class 4 ft	m	Corrosive ft	m	Oxidizing ft	m	Flammable ft	m	Pyrophoric ft	m	Toxic or Highly Toxic ft	m
Toxic or highly toxic	NR	20	6.1	20	6.1	20	6.1	20	6.1	20	6.1	20	6.1
Pyrophoric	NR	20	6.1	20	6.1	20	6.1	20	6.1	20	6.1	20	6.1
Flammable	NR	20	6.1	20	6.1	20	6.1	20	6.1	20	6.1	20	6.1
Oxidizing	NR	20	6.1	20	6.1	—	—	—	—	—	—	—	—
Corrosive	NR	20	6.1	—	—	20	6.1	20	6.1	20	6.1	20	6.1
Unstable reactive Class 2, Class 3, or Class 4	NR	—	—	20	6.1	20	6.1	20	6.1	20	6.1	20	6.1
Other gas	—	NR		NR		NR		NR		NR		NR	

NR: No separation required.
[55: Table 7.1.11.2]

21.3.1.11 Unauthorized Use. Compressed gas cylinders, containers, and tanks shall not be used for any purpose other than to serve as a vessel for containing the product for which it was designed. [55:7.1.13]

21.3.1.12 Cylinders, Containers, and Tanks Exposed to Fire. Compressed gas cylinders, containers, and tanks exposed to fire shall not be used or shipped while full or partially full until they are requalified in accordance with the pressure vessel code under which they were manufactured. [55:7.1.14]

21.3.1.13 Leaks, Damage, or Corrosion. [55:7.1.15]

21.3.1.13.1 Removal from Service. Leaking, damaged, or corroded compressed gas cylinders, containers, and tanks shall be removed from service. [55:7.1.15.1]

21.3.1.13.2 Replacement and Repair. Leaking, damaged, or corroded compressed gas systems shall be replaced or repaired. [55:7.1.15.2]

21.3.1.13.3* Handling of Cylinders, Containers, and Tanks Removed from Service. Compressed gas cylinders, containers, and tanks that have been removed from service shall be handled in an approved manner. [55:7.1.15.3]

21.3.1.13.4 Leaking Systems. Compressed gas systems that are determined to be leaking, damaged, or corroded shall be repaired to a serviceable condition or shall be removed from service. [55:7.1.15.4]

21.3.1.14 Surfaces. [55:7.1.16]

21.3.1.14.1 To prevent bottom corrosion, cylinders, containers, and tanks shall be protected from direct contact with soil or surfaces where water might accumulate. [55:7.1.16.1]

21.3.1.14.2 Surfaces shall be graded to prevent accumulation of water. [55:7.1.16.2]

21.3.1.15 Storage Area Temperature. Storage area temperatures shall not exceed 52°C (125°F). [55:7.1.17.1]

21.3.1.16 Underground Piping. [55:7.1.18]

21.3.1.16.1 Underground piping shall be of welded construction without valves, unwelded mechanical joints, or connections installed underground. [55:7.1.18.1]

21.3.1.16.1.1 Valves or connections located in boxes or enclosures shall be permitted to be installed underground when such boxes or enclosures are accessible from above ground and where the valves or connections contained are isolated from direct contact with earth or fill. [55:7.1.18.1.1]

21.3.1.16.1.2 Valve boxes or enclosures installed in areas subject to vehicular traffic shall be constructed to resist uniformly distributed and concentrated live loads in accordance with the building code, for areas designated as vehicular driveways and yards, subject to trucking. [55:7.1.18.1.1.1]

21.3.1.16.1.3* Piping installed in trench systems located below grade where the trench is open to above shall not be considered to be underground. [55:7.1.18.1.2]

21.3.1.16.2 Contact with Earth.

21.3.1.16.2.1 Gas piping in contact with earth or other material that could corrode the piping shall be protected against corrosion in an approved manner. [55:7.1.18.2]

21.3.1.16.2.2 When cathodic protection is provided, it shall be in accordance with 21.3.1.5. [55:7.1.18.2.1]

21.3.1.16.3 Underground piping shall be installed on a bedding of at least 6 in. (150 mm) of well-compacted backfill material. [30:27.6.5.1; 55:7.1.18.3]

21.3.1.16.4 In areas subject to vehicle traffic, the pipe trench shall be of sufficient depth to permit a cover of at least 18 in. (450 mm) of well-compacted backfill material and pavement. In paved areas where a minimum 2 in. (50 mm) of asphalt is used, backfill between the pipe and the asphalt shall be permitted to be reduced to 8 in. (200 mm) minimum. In paved areas where a minimum 4 in. (100 mm) of reinforced concrete is used, backfill between the pipe and the asphalt shall be permitted to be reduced to 4 in. (100 mm) minimum. [**30:**5.5.5.2; **30:**27.6.5.2; **30:**27.6.5.3; **30:**27.6.5.4; **55:**7.1.18.4; **55:**7.1.18.5; **55:**7.1.18.6]

21.3.1.16.5 In areas not subject to vehicle traffic, the pipe trench shall be of sufficient depth to permit a cover of at least 12 in. (300 mm) of well-compacted backfill material. A greater burial depth shall be provided when required by the manufacturer's instructions or where frost conditions are present. [**30:**27.6.5.5; **30:**27.6.5.6; **55:**7.1.18.7; **55:**7.1.18.8]

21.3.1.16.6 Piping within the same trench shall be separated by two pipe diameters. Piping shall not need to be separated horizontally by more than 9 in. (230 mm). [**30:**27.6.5.7; **55:**7.1.18.9]

21.3.1.16.7 Two or more levels of pipes within the same trench shall be separated vertically by a minimum 6 in. (150 mm) of well-compacted backfill. [**30:**27.6.5.8; **55:**7.1.18.10]

21.3.2 Storage. [**55:**7.2]

21.3.2.1 General. [**55:**7.2.1]

21.3.2.1.1 Applicability. The storage of compressed gas containers, cylinders, and tanks shall be in accordance with 21.3.2.1. [**55:**7.2.1.1]

21.3.2.1.2 Upright Storage Flammable Gas in Solution and Liquefied Flammable Gas. Cylinders, containers, and tanks containing liquefied flammable gases and flammable gases in solution shall be positioned in the upright position. [**55:**7.2.1.2]

21.3.2.1.2.1 Cylinders and Containers of 1.3 Gal (5 L) or Less. Containers with a capacity of 1.3 gal (5 L) or less shall be permitted to be stored in a horizontal position. [**55:**7.2.1.2.1]

21.3.2.1.2.2 Cylinders, Containers, and Tanks Designed for Horizontal Use. Cylinders, containers, and tanks designed for use in a horizontal position shall be permitted to be stored in a horizontal position. [**55:**7.2.1.2.2]

21.3.2.1.2.3 Palletized Cylinders, Containers, and Tanks. Cylinders, containers, and tanks, with the exception of those containing flammable liquefied compressed gases, that are palletized for transportation purposes shall be permitted to be stored in a horizontal position. [**55:**7.2.1.2.3]

21.3.2.1.3 Classification of Weather Protection as an Indoor Versus Outdoor Area. For other than explosive materials and hazardous materials presenting a detonation hazard, a weather protection structure shall be permitted to be used for sheltering outdoor storage or use areas, without requiring such areas to be classified as indoor storage. [**55:**7.2.1.3]

21.3.2.2 Material-Specific Regulations. [**55:**7.2.2]

21.3.2.2.1 Indoor Storage. Indoor storage of compressed gases shall be in accordance with the material-specific provisions of 21.3.4 through 21.3.10. [**55:**7.2.2.1]

21.3.2.2.2 Exterior Storage. [**55:**7.2.2.2]

21.3.2.2.2.1 General. Exterior storage of compressed gases shall be in accordance with the material-specific provisions of 21.3.4 through 21.3.10. [**55:**7.2.2.2.1]

21.3.2.2.2.2 Separation. Distances from property lines, buildings, and exposures shall be in accordance with the material-specific provisions of 21.3.4 through 21.3.10. [**55:**7.2.2.2.2]

21.3.3 Use and Handling. [**55:**7.3]

21.3.3.1 General. [**55:**7.3.1]

21.3.3.1.1 Applicability. The use and handling of compressed gas containers, cylinders, tanks, and systems shall be in accordance with 21.3.3.1. [**55:**7.3.1.1]

21.3.3.1.2 Controls. [**55:**7.3.1.2]

21.3.3.1.2.1 Compressed gas system controls shall be designed to prevent materials from entering or leaving the process at an unintended time, rate, or path. [**55:**7.3.1.2.1]

21.3.3.1.2.2 Automatic controls shall be designed to be failsafe. [**55:**7.3.1.2.2]

21.3.3.1.3 Piping Systems. Piping, tubing, fittings, and related components shall be designed, fabricated, and tested in accordance with ANSI/ASME B31.3, *Process Piping*, or other approved standards. [**55:**7.3.1.3]

21.3.3.1.3.1 Integrity. Piping, tubing, pressure regulators, valves, and other apparatus shall be kept gastight to prevent leakage. [**55:**7.3.1.3.1]

21.3.3.1.3.2 Backflow Prevention. Backflow prevention or check valves shall be provided when the backflow of hazardous materials could create a hazardous condition or cause the unauthorized discharge of hazardous materials. [**55:**7.3.1.3.2]

21.3.3.1.4 Valves. [**55:**7.3.1.4]

21.3.3.1.4.1 Valves utilized on compressed gas systems shall be designed for the gas or gases and pressure intended and shall be accessible. [**55:**7.3.1.4.1]

21.3.3.1.4.2 Valve handles or operators for required shutoff valves shall not be removed or otherwise altered to prevent access. [**55:**7.3.1.4.2]

21.3.3.1.5 Vent Pipe Termination. [**55:**7.3.1.5]

21.3.3.1.5.1 Venting of gases shall be directed to an approved location. [**55:**7.3.1.5.1]

21.3.3.1.5.2 The termination point for piped vent systems serving cylinders, containers, tanks, and gas systems used for the purpose of operational or emergency venting shall be in accordance with 21.2.15. [**55:**7.3.1.5.2]

21.3.3.1.6 Upright Use. [**55:**7.3.1.6]

21.3.3.1.6.1 Compressed gas containers, cylinders, and tanks containing flammable liquefied gas, except those designed for use in a horizontal position and those compressed gas containers, cylinders, and tanks containing nonliquefied gases, shall be used in a "valve end up" upright position. [**55:**7.3.1.6.1]

21.3.3.1.6.2 An upright position shall include a position in which the container, cylinder, or tank axis is inclined as much as 45 degrees from the vertical and in which the relief device is always in direct communication with the gas phase. [**55:**7.3.1.6.2]

21.3.3.1.7 Inverted Use. Cylinders, containers, and tanks containing nonflammable liquefied gases shall be permitted to be used in the inverted position when the liquid phase is used. [**55:**7.3.1.7]

21.3.3.1.7.1 Flammable liquefied gases at processing plants shall be permitted to use this inverted position method while transfilling. [**55:**7.3.1.7.1]

21.3.3.1.7.2 The container, cylinder, or tank shall be secured, and the dispensing apparatus shall be designed for use with liquefied gas. [**55:**7.3.1.7.2]

21.3.3.1.8 Containers and Cylinders of 5 L (1.3 Gal) or Less. Containers or cylinders with a water volume of 1.3 gal (5 L) or less shall be permitted to be used in a horizontal position. [**55:**7.3.1.8]

21.3.3.1.9 Transfer. Transfer of gases between containers, cylinders, and tanks shall be performed by qualified personnel using equipment and operating procedures in accordance with CGA P-1, *Safe Handling of Compressed Gases in Containers.* [**55:**7.3.1.9]

21.3.3.1.10 Use of Compressed Gases for Inflation. Inflatable equipment, devices, or balloons shall only be pressurized or filled with compressed air or inert gases. [**55:**7.3.1.10]

21.3.3.1.11 Emergency Shutoff Valves. [**55:**7.3.1.11]

21.3.3.1.11.1 Accessible manual or automatic emergency shutoff valves shall be provided to shut off the flow of gas in case of emergency. [**55:**7.3.1.11.1]

(A)* Manual emergency shutoff valves or the device that activates an automatic emergency shutoff valve on a bulk source or piping system serving the bulk supply shall be identified by means of a sign. [**55:**7.3.1.11.1.1]

21.3.3.1.11.2 Emergency shutoffs shall be located at the point of use and at the tank, cylinder, or bulk source, and at the point where the system piping enters the building. [**55:**7.3.1.11.2]

21.3.3.1.12 Excess Flow Control. [**55:**7.3.1.12]

21.3.3.1.12.1 Where compressed gases having a hazard ranking in one or more of the following hazard classes in accordance with NFPA 704, *Standard System for the Identification of the Hazards of Materials for Emergency Response,* are carried in pressurized piping above a gauge pressure of 15 psi (103 kPa), an approved means of either leak detection with emergency shutoff or excess flow control shall be provided:

(1) Health hazard Class 3 or Class 4
(2) Flammability Class 4
(3) Reactivity Class 3 or Class 4
[**55:**7.3.1.12.1]

(A) Excess Flow Control Location with Hazardous Material Storage. Where the piping originates from within a hazardous material storage room or area, the excess flow control shall be located within the storage room or area. [**55:**7.3.1.12.1.1]

(B) Excess Flow Control Location with Bulk Storage. Where the piping originates from a bulk source, the excess flow control shall be located at the bulk source at a point immediately downstream of the source valve. [**55:**7.3.1.12.1.2]

21.3.3.1.12.2* The controls required by 21.3.3.1.12 shall not be required for the following:

(1) Piping for inlet connections designed to prevent backflow at the source
(2) Piping for pressure relief devices
(3) Where the source of the gas is not in excess of the quantity threshold indicated in Table 5.2.1.4 through Table 5.2.1.10.1
[**55:**7.3.1.12.2]

21.3.3.1.12.3 Location. The location of excess flow control shall be as specified in 21.3.3.1.12.1(A) and 21.3.3.1.12.1(B). [**55:**7.3.1.12.3]

(A) Where piping originates from a source located in a room or area, the excess flow control shall be located within the room or area. [**55:**7.3.1.12.3.1]

(B) Where piping originates from a bulk source, the excess flow control shall be as close to the bulk source as possible. [**55:**7.3.1.12.3.2]

21.3.3.1.12.4 Location Exemptions. The requirements of 21.3.3.1.12 shall not apply to the following:

(1) Piping for inlet connections designed to prevent backflow
(2) Piping for pressure-relief devices
(3) Systems containing 450 scf (12.7 m^3) or less of flammable gas
[**55:**7.3.1.12.4]

21.3.3.2 Material-Specific Regulations. [**55:**7.3.2]

21.3.3.2.1 Indoor Use. Indoor use of compressed gases shall be in accordance with 21.3.4 through 21.3.10. [**55:**7.3.2.1]

21.3.3.2.2 Exterior Use. [**55:**7.3.2.2]

21.3.3.2.2.1 General. Exterior use of compressed gases shall be in accordance with 21.3.4 through 21.3.10. [**55:**7.3.2.2.1]

21.3.3.2.2.2 Separation. Distances from property lines, buildings, and exposure hazards shall be in accordance with the material-specific provisions of 21.3.4 through 21.3.10. [**55:**7.3.2.2.2]

21.3.3.3 Handling. [**55:**7.3.3]

21.3.3.3.1 Applicability. The handling of compressed gas cylinders, containers, and tanks shall be in accordance with 21.3.3.3. [**55:**7.3.3.1]

21.3.3.3.2 Carts and Trucks. [**55:**7.3.3.2]

21.3.3.3.2.1 Cylinders, containers, and tanks shall be moved using an approved method. [**55:**7.3.3.2.1]

21.3.3.3.2.2 Where cylinders, containers, or tanks are moved by hand cart, hand truck, or other mobile device, such carts, trucks, or devices shall be designed for the secure movement of cylinders, containers, or tanks. [**55:**7.3.3.2.2]

21.3.3.3.3 Lifting Devices. Ropes, chains, or slings shall not be used to suspend compressed gas cylinders, containers, and tanks unless provisions at time of manufacture have been made on the cylinder, container, or tank for appropriate lifting attachments, such as lugs. [**55:**7.3.3.3]

21.3.4 Medical Gas Systems. Medical gas systems for health care shall be in accordance with NFPA 99, *Health Care Facilities Code.* [**55:**7.4]

21.3.5 Corrosive Gases. [**55:**7.5]

21.3.5.1 General. The storage or use of corrosive compressed gases exceeding the quantity thresholds for gases requiring special provisions as specified in Table 5.2.1.2 through Table 5.2.1.10.1 shall be in accordance with Sections 21.1 and 21.2 and 21.3.1 through 21.3.3 and 21.3.5. [**55:**7.5.1]

21.3.5.2 Distance to Exposures.

21.3.5.2.1 The outdoor storage or use of corrosive compressed gas shall not be within 20 ft (6.1 m) of buildings not associated with the manufacture or distribution of corrosive gases, lot lines, streets, alleys, public ways, or means of egress. [**55:**7.5.2]

21.3.5.2.2 A 2-hour fire barrier wall without openings or penetrations, and extending not less than 30 in. (762 mm) (above and to the sides of the storage or use area, shall be permitted in lieu of the 20 ft (6.1 m) distance. [55:7.5.2.1]

21.3.5.2.2.1* When a fire barrier is used to protect compressed gas systems, the system shall terminate downstream of the source valve. [55:7.5.2.1.1]

21.3.5.2.2.2 The fire barrier wall shall be either an independent structure or the exterior wall of the building adjacent to the storage or use area. [55:7.5.2.1.2]

21.3.5.2.2.3 The 2-hour fire barrier shall be located at least 5 ft (1.5 m) from any exposure. [55:7.5.2.1.3]

21.3.5.2.2.4 The 2-hour fire barrier shall not have more than two sides at approximately 90 degree (1.57 rad) directions, or not more than three sides with connecting angles of approximately 135 degrees (2.36 rad). [55:7.5.2.1.4]

21.3.5.3 Indoor Use. The indoor use of corrosive gases shall be provided with a gas cabinet, exhausted enclosure, or gas room. [55:7.5.3]

21.3.5.3.1 Gas Cabinets. Gas cabinets shall be in accordance with 21.2.17. [55:7.5.3.1]

21.3.5.3.2 Exhausted Enclosures. Exhausted enclosures shall be in accordance with 21.2.18. [55:7.5.3.2]

21.3.5.3.3 Gas Rooms. Gas rooms shall be in accordance with 21.2.4. [55:7.5.3.3]

21.3.5.3.4 Treatment Systems. Treatment systems, except as provided for in 21.3.5.3.4.1, gas cabinets, exhausted enclosures, and gas rooms containing corrosive gases in use shall be provided with exhaust ventilation, with all exhaust directed to a treatment system designed to process the accidental release of gas. [55:7.5.3.4]

21.3.5.3.4.1 Treatment systems shall not be required for corrosive gases in use where provided with the following:

(1) Gas detection in accordance with 21.3.9.3.2.1
(2) Fail-safe automatic closing valves in accordance with 21.3.9.3.2.2

[55:7.5.3.4.1]

21.3.5.3.4.2 Treatment systems shall be capable of diluting, adsorbing, absorbing, containing, neutralizing, burning, or otherwise processing the release of corrosive gas in accordance with 21.3.9.3.4.1. [55:7.5.3.4.2]

21.3.5.3.4.3 Treatment system sizing shall be in accordance with 21.3.9.3.4. [55:7.5.3.4.3]

21.3.6 Flammable Gases. [55:7.6]

21.3.6.1 Storage, Use, and Handling. [55:7.6.1]

21.3.6.1.1 The storage or use of flammable gases exceeding the quantity thresholds for gases requiring special provisions as specified in Table 5.2.1.2 through Table 5.2.1.10.1 shall be in accordance with Sections 21.1 and 21.2 and 21.3.1 through 21.3.3 and 21.3.6. [55:7.6.1.1]

21.3.6.1.2 Storage, use, and handling of gaseous hydrogen shall be in accordance with 21.3.6.1 and Section 21.6. [55:7.6.1.2]

21.3.6.2 Distance to Exposures. The outdoor storage or use of non-bulk flammable compressed gas shall be located from lot lines, public streets, public alleys, public ways, or buildings not associated with the manufacture or distribution of such gases in accordance with Table 21.3.6.2. [55:7.6.2]

21.3.6.2.1 Bulk hydrogen gas installations shall be in accordance with Section 21.6. [55:7.6.2.1]

21.3.6.2.1.1* Where a fire barrier is used to protect compressed gas systems, the system shall terminate downstream of the source valve. [55:7.6.2.1.1]

21.3.6.2.1.2 The fire barrier wall shall be either an independent structure or the exterior wall of the building adjacent to the storage or use area. [55:7.6.2.1.2]

21.3.6.2.2 Bulk gas systems for flammable gases other than hydrogen shall be in accordance with Section 21.6 where the quantity of flammable compressed gas exceeds 5000 scf (141.6 Nm^3). [55:7.6.2.2]

21.3.6.2.3 The configuration of the protective structure shall be designed to allow natural ventilation to prevent the accumulation of hazardous gas concentrations. [55:7.6.2.3]

21.3.6.2.4 Storage and use of flammable compressed gases shall not be located within 50 ft (15.2 m) of air intakes. [55:7.6.2.4]

21.3.6.2.5 Storage and use of flammable gases outside of buildings shall also be separated from building openings by 25 ft (7.6 m). Fire barriers shall be permitted to be used as a means to separate storage areas from openings or a means of egress used to access the public way. [55:7.6.2.5]

21.3.6.3 Ignition Source Control. Ignition sources in areas containing flammable gases shall be in accordance with 21.3.6.3. [55:7.6.4]

21.3.6.3.1 Static-Producing Equipment. Static-producing equipment located in flammable gas areas shall be grounded. [55:7.6.4.1]

21.3.6.3.2 No Smoking or Open Flame. Signs shall be posted in areas containing flammable gases communicating that smoking or the use of open flame, or both, is prohibited within 25 ft (7.6 m) of the storage or use area perimeter. [55:7.6.4.2]

21.3.6.3.3 Heating. Heating, where provided, shall be by indirect means. Equipment used for heating applications in rooms or areas where flammable gases are stored or used shall be listed and labeled for use in hazardous environments established by the gases present and shall be installed in accordance with the conditions of the listing and the manufacturer's installation instructions. [55:7.6.4.3]

21.3.6.4 Electrical. Areas in which the storage or use of compressed gases exceeds the quantity thresholds for gases requiring special provisions shall be in accordance with *NFPA 70, National Electrical Code*. [55:7.6.5]

21.3.6.5 Maintenance of Piping Systems. Maintenance of flammable gas system piping and components shall be performed annually by a qualified representative of the equipment owner. This shall include inspection for physical damage, leak tightness, ground system integrity, vent system operation, equipment identification, warning signs, operator information and training records, scheduled maintenance and retest records, alarm operation, and other safety related features. Scheduled maintenance and retest activities shall be formally documented and records shall be maintained a minimum of three years. [55:7.6.6.1; 55: 7.6.6.2; 55:7.6.6.3]

Table 21.3.6.2 Distance to Exposures for Non-Bulk Flammable Gases[a]

Maximum Amount per Storage Area (ft³)	Minimum Distance Between Storage Areas (ft)	Minimum Distance to Lot Lines of Property That Can Be Built Upon (ft)	Minimum Distance to Public Streets, Public Alleys, or Public Ways (ft)	Minimum Distance to Buildings on the Same Property — Less than 2-Hour Construction	2-Hour Construction	4-Hour Construction
0–4,225	5	5	5	5	0	0
4,226–21,125	10	10	10	10	5	0
21,126–50,700	10	15	15	20	5	0
50,701–84,500	10	20	20	20	5	0
84,501–200,000	20	25	25	20	5	0

For SI, 1 ft = 304.8 mm; 1 ft³ = 0.0283 m³.

[a]The minimum required distances shall not apply where fire barriers without openings or penetrations having a minimum fire resistive rating of 2 hours interrupt the line of sight between the storage and the exposure. The configuration of the fire barriers shall be designed to allow natural ventilation to prevent the accumulation of hazardous gas concentrations.
[55: Table 7.6.2]

21.3.7 Oxidizing Gases. [55:7.7]

21.3.7.1 General. The storage or use of oxidizing compressed gases exceeding the quantity thresholds for gases requiring special provisions as specified in Table 5.2.1.2 through Table 5.2.1.10.1 shall be in accordance with Sections 21.1 and 21.2 and 21.3.1 through 21.3.3 and 21.3.7. [55:7.7.1]

21.3.7.2 Distance to Exposures. The outdoor storage or use of oxidizing compressed gas shall be in accordance with Table 21.3.7.2. [55:7.7.2]

Table 21.3.7.2 Distance to Exposures for Oxidizing Gases Table

Quantity of Gas Stored (at NTP)		Distance to a Building Not Associated with the Manufacture or Distribution of Oxidizing Gases or to a Public Way or Property Line		Minimum Distance Between Storage Area	
ft³	m³	ft	m	ft	m
0–50,000	0–1416	5	1.5	5	1.5
50,001–100,000	1417–2832	10	3.0	10	3.0
≥ 100,001	≥ 2833	15	4.6	15	4.6

[55: Table 7.7.2]

21.3.7.2.1 The distances shall not apply where fire barriers having a minimum fire resistance of 2 hours interrupt the line of sight between the container and the exposure. [55:7.7.2.1]

21.3.7.2.1.1* Where a fire barrier is used to protect compressed gas systems, the system shall terminate downstream of the source valve. [55:7.7.2.1.1]

21.3.7.2.1.2 The fire barrier wall shall be either an independent structure or the exterior wall of the building adjacent to the storage or use area. [55:7.7.2.1.2]

21.3.7.2.2 The fire barrier shall be at least 5 ft (1.5 m) from the storage or use area perimeter. [55:7.7.2.2]

21.3.7.2.3 The configuration of the fire barrier shall allow natural ventilation to prevent the accumulation of hazardous gas concentrations. [55:7.7.2.3]

21.3.8 Pyrophoric Gases. [55:7.8]

21.3.8.1 General. Pyrophoric compressed gases exceeding the quantity thresholds for gases requiring special provisions as specified in Table 5.2.1.2 through Table 5.2.1.10.1 shall be stored and used in accordance with Sections 21.1 and 21.2 and 21.3.1 through 21.3.3 and 21.3.8. [55:7.8.1]

21.3.8.2 Silane and Silane Mixtures. Silane and silane mixtures shall be stored, used, and handled in accordance with the provisions of ANSI/CGA G13, *Storage and Handling of Silane and Silane Mixtures*. [55:7.8.2]

21.3.8.3 Distance to Exposures. The outdoor storage or use of pyrophoric compressed gas shall be in accordance with Table 21.3.8.3. [55:7.8.3]

21.3.8.3.1 The distances shall be allowed to be reduced to 5 ft (1.5 m) when fire barriers having a minimum fire resistance of 2 hours interrupt the line of sight between the container and the exposure. [55:7.8.3.1]

21.3.8.3.1.1* When a fire barrier is used to protect compressed gas systems, the system shall terminate downstream of the source valve. [55:7.8.3.1.1]

21.3.8.3.1.2 The fire barrier shall be either an independent structure or the exterior wall of the building adjacent to the storage or use area. [55:7.8.3.1.2]

21.3.8.3.2 The fire barrier shall be at least 5 ft (1.5 m) from the storage or use area perimeter. [55:7.8.3.2]

21.3.8.3.3 The configuration of the fire barrier shall allow natural ventilation to prevent the accumulation of hazardous gas concentrations. [55:7.8.3.3]

Table 21.3.8.3 Distance to Exposures for Pyrophoric Gases

Maximum Amount per Storage Area		Minimum Distance Between Storage Areas		Minimum Distance to Property Lines		Minimum Distance to Public Ways		Minimum Distance to Buildings on the Same Property					
								Nonrated or Openings Within 7.6 m (25 ft)		2 Hour and No Openings Within 7.6 m (25 ft)		4 Hour and No Openings Within 7.6 m (25 ft)	
ft^3	m^3	ft	m	ft	m	ft	m	ft	m	ft	m	ft	m
250	7.1	5	1.5	25	7.6	5	1.5	5	1.5	0	0	0	0
2500	71.0	10	3.0	50	15.2	10	3.0	10	3.0	5	1.5	0	0
7500	212.4	20	6.0	100	30.5	20	6.0	20	6.0	10	3.0	0	0

[**55:** Table 7.8.3]

21.3.9 Toxic and Highly Toxic Gases. [55:7.9]

21.3.9.1 General. The storage or use of toxic and highly toxic gases exceeding the quantity thresholds for gases requiring special provisions as specified in Table 5.2.1.2 through Table 5.2.1.10.1 shall be in accordance with Sections 21.1 and 21.2 and 21.3.1 through 21.3.3 and 21.3.9. [55:7.9.1]

21.3.9.2 Ventilation and Arrangement. [55:7.9.2]

21.3.9.2.1 Indoors. The indoor storage or use of highly toxic gases or toxic gases shall be provided with a gas cabinet, exhausted enclosure, or gas room. [55:7.9.2.1]

21.3.9.2.1.1 Gas cabinets shall be in accordance with 21.2.17. [55:7.9.2.1.1]

21.3.9.2.1.2 Exhausted enclosures shall be in accordance with 21.2.18. [55:7.9.2.1.2]

21.3.9.2.1.3 Gas rooms shall be in accordance with 21.2.4. [55:7.9.2.1.3]

21.3.9.2.2 Distance to Exposures. The outdoor storage or use of toxic or highly toxic compressed gases shall not be within 75 ft (23 m) of lot lines, streets, alleys, public ways or means of egress, or buildings not associated with such storage or use. [55:7.9.2.2]

21.3.9.2.2.1 A 2-hour fire barrier wall without openings or penetrations, and extending not less than 30 in. (762 mm) above and to the sides of the storage or use area, that interrupts the line of sight between the storage or use and the exposure, shall be permitted in lieu of the 75 ft (23 m) distance. [55:7.9.2.2.1]

(A) Where a fire barrier is used to protect compressed gas systems the system shall terminate downstream of the source valve. [55:7.9.2.2.1.1]

(B) The fire barrier wall shall be either an independent structure or the exterior wall of the building adjacent to the storage or use area. [55:7.9.2.2.1.2]

(C) The 2-hour fire barrier shall be located at least 1.5 m (5 ft) from any exposure. [55:7.9.2.2.1.3]

(D) The 2-hour fire barrier shall not have more than two sides at approximately 90 degree (1.5 rad) directions, or more than three sides with connecting angles of approximately 135 degrees (2.36 rad). [55:7.9.2.2.1.4]

21.3.9.2.2.2 Where the storage or use area is located closer than 23 m (75 ft) to a building not associated with the manufacture or distribution of toxic or highly toxic compressed gases, openings in the building other than for piping shall not be permitted above the height of the top of the 2-hour fire barrier wall or within 50 ft (15 m) horizontally from the storage area, regardless of whether the openings are shielded by a fire barrier. [55:7.9.2.2.2]

21.3.9.2.3 Air Intakes. Storage and use of toxic or highly toxic compressed gases shall not be located within 75 ft (23 m) of air intakes. [55:7.9.2.3]

21.3.9.3 Treatment Systems. Except as provided in 21.3.9.3.1 and 21.3.9.3.2, gas cabinets, exhausted enclosures, and gas rooms containing toxic or highly toxic gases shall be provided with exhaust ventilation, with all exhaust directed to a treatment system designed to process accidental release of gas. [55:7.9.3]

21.3.9.3.1 Storage of Toxic or Highly Toxic Gases. Treatment systems shall not be required for toxic or highly toxic gases in storage where cylinders, containers, and tanks are provided with the controls specified in 21.3.9.3.1.1 through 21.3.9.3.1.3. [55:7.9.3.1]

21.3.9.3.1.1 Valve Outlets Protected. Valve outlets shall be equipped with outlet plugs or caps, or both, rated for the container service pressure. [55:7.9.3.1.1]

21.3.9.3.1.2 Handwheels Secured. Where provided, handwheel-operated valves shall be secured to prevent movement. [55:7.9.3.1.2]

21.3.9.3.1.3 Containment Devices Provided. Approved cylinder containment vessels or cylinder containment systems shall be provided at an approved location. [55:7.9.3.1.3]

21.3.9.3.2 Use of Toxic Gases. Treatment systems shall not be required for toxic gases in use where containers, cylinders, and tanks are provided with the controls specified in 21.3.9.3.2.1 and 21.3.9.3.2.2. [55:7.9.3.2]

21.3.9.3.2.1 Gas Detection. [55:7.9.3.2.1]

(A) A gas detection system with a sensing interval not exceeding 5 minutes shall be provided. [55:7.9.3.2.1.1]

(B) The gas detection system shall monitor the exhaust system at the point of discharge from the gas cabinet, exhausted enclosure, or gas room. [55:7.9.3.2.1.2]

21.3.9.3.2.2 Fail-Safe Automatic Closing Valve. An approved automatic-closing fail-safe valve shall be located on or immediately adjacent to and downstream of active cylinder, container, or tank valves. [55:7.9.3.2.2]

(A) The fail-safe valve shall close when gas is detected at the permissible exposure limit, short-term exposure limit (STEL), or ceiling limit by the gas detection system. [55:7.9.3.2.2.1]

(B) For attended operations, a manual closing valve shall be permitted when in accordance 21.3.9.3.4.3. [55:7.9.3.2.2.2]

(C) For gases used at unattended operations for the protection of public health, such as chlorine at water or wastewater treatment sites, the automatic valve shall close if the concentration of gas detected by a gas detection system reaches one-half of the IDLH. [55:7.9.3.2.2.3]

(D) The gas detection system shall also alert persons on-site and a responsible person off-site when the gas concentration in the storage/use area reaches the OSHA PEL, OSHA ceiling limit, or STEL for the gas employed. [55:7.9.3.2.2.4]

21.3.9.3.3 Treatment System Design and Performance. Treatment systems shall be capable of diluting, adsorbing, absorbing, containing, neutralizing, burning, or otherwise processing stored or used toxic or highly toxic gas, or both. [55:7.9.3.3]

21.3.9.3.3.1 Where a total containment system is used, the system shall be designed to handle the maximum anticipated pressure of release to the system when it reaches equilibrium. [55:7.9.3.3.1]

21.3.9.3.3.2 Treatment systems shall be capable of reducing the allowable discharge concentrations to one-half the IDLH threshold at the point of discharge. [55:7.9.3.3.2]

21.3.9.3.4 Treatment System Sizing. [55:7.9.3.4]

21.3.9.3.4.1 Worst-Case Release of Gas. Treatment systems shall be sized to process the maximum worst-case release of gas based on the maximum flow rate of release from the largest vessel utilized in accordance with 21.3.9.3.4.2. [55:7.9.3.4.1]

21.3.9.3.4.2 Largest Compressed Gas Vessel. The entire contents of the single largest compressed gas vessel shall be considered. [55:7.9.3.4.2]

21.3.9.3.4.3 Attended Operations — Alternative Method of System Sizing. [55:7.9.3.4.3]

(A)* Where source cylinders, containers, and tanks are used in attended process operations, with an operator present at the enclosure where the activity occurs, the volume of the release shall be limited to the estimated amount released from the process piping system within a period not to exceed 5 minutes. [55:7.9.3.4.3.1]

(B) The process piping systems shall comply with 21.3.9.3.4.3(B)(1) through 21.3.9.3.4.3(B)(5).

(1) *Local Exhaust.* All gas transfer operations shall be conducted within a zone of local exhaust that is connected to a treatment system.
(2) *Gas Detection.* Gas detection shall be used to provide a warning to alert the operators to emission of gas into the zone of local exhaust, and the following requirements also shall apply:

(a) The system shall be capable of detecting gas at the permissible exposure limit or ceiling limit for the gas being processed.
(b) Activation of the gas detection system shall provide a local alarm.

(3) *Process Shutdown.* Operations involving the gas detected shall be shut down and leaks repaired.
(4) *Piping System Construction.* Piping systems used to convey gases shall be of all-welded construction throughout, with the exception of fittings used to connect containers, cylinders, or tanks, or any combination thereof, to the process system.
(5) *Piping System Accessibility.* Piping systems shall be designed to provide for readily accessible manual shutdown controls. [55:7.9.3.4.3.2]

21.3.9.3.5 Rate of Release. The time release shall be in accordance with Table 21.3.9.3.5 for the type of container indicated. [55:7.9.3.5]

Table 21.3.9.3.5 Rate of Release

Container Type	Nonliquefied Gases (min)	Liquefied Gases (min)
Cylinders without restrictive flow orifices	5	30
Portable tanks without restrictive flow orifices	40	240
All others	Based on peak flow from maximum valve orifice	Based on peak flow from maximum valve orifice

[55:7.9.3.5]

21.3.9.3.6* Maximum Flow Rate of Release. [55:7.9.3.6]

21.3.9.3.6.1 For portable containers, cylinders, and tanks, the maximum flow rate of release shall be calculated based on assuming the total release from the cylinder or tank within the time specified. [55:7.9.3.6.1]

21.3.9.3.6.2* When portable containers, cylinders, or tanks are equipped with reduced flow orifices, the worst-case rate of release shall be determined by the maximum achievable flow from the valve determined based on the following formula:

$$CFM = (767 \times A \times P)\left(\frac{28.96/MW}{60}\right)^{1/2}$$

where:
CFM = standard cubic feet per minute of gas of concern under flow conditions
A = area of orifice in square inches (*See Table A.21.3.9.3.6 for areas of typical restricted flow orifices.*)
P = supply pressure of gas at NTP in pounds per square inch absolute
MW = molecular weight

[55:7.9.3.6.2]

21.3.9.3.6.3 For mixtures, the average of molecular weights shall be used. [**55:**7.9.3.6.3]

21.3.9.4 Leaking Containers, Cylinders, and Tanks. When containers, cylinders, or tanks are used outdoors, in excess of the quantities specified in the column for unsprinklered areas (unprotected by gas cabinets or exhausted enclosures) in Table 5.2.1.2 through Table 5.2.1.10.1, a gas cabinet, exhausted enclosure, or containment vessel or system shall be provided to control leaks from leaking containers, cylinders, and tanks in accordance with 21.3.9.4.1 through 21.3.9.4.2.3. [**55:**7.9.4]

21.3.9.4.1 Gas Cabinets or Exhausted Enclosures. Where gas cabinets or exhausted enclosures are provided to handle leaks from containers, cylinders, or tanks, exhaust ventilation shall be provided that is directed to a treatment system in accordance with the provisions of 21.3.9.3. [**55:**7.9.4.1]

21.3.9.4.2 Containment Vessels or Systems. Where containment vessels or containment systems are provided, they shall comply with 21.3.9.4.2.1 through 21.3.9.4.2.3. [**55:**7.9.4.2]

21.3.9.4.2.1 Performance. Containment vessels or containment systems shall be capable of fully containing or terminating a release. [**55:**7.9.4.2.1]

21.3.9.4.2.2 Personnel. Trained personnel capable of operating the containment vessel or containment system shall be available at an approved location. [**55:**7.9.4.2.2]

21.3.9.4.2.3 Location. Containment vessels or systems shall be capable of being transported to the leaking cylinder, container, or tank. [**55:**7.9.4.2.3]

21.3.9.5 Emergency Power. [**55:**7.9.5]

21.3.9.5.1 General. Emergency power shall comply with 21.3.9.5 in accordance with *NFPA 70, National Electrical Code*. [**55:**7.9.5.1]

21.3.9.5.2 Alternative to Emergency Power. Emergency power shall not be required where fail-safe engineering is provided for mechanical exhaust ventilation, treatment systems, and temperature control, and standby power is provided to alternative systems that utilize electrical energy. [**55:**7.9.5.2]

21.3.9.5.3 Where Required. Emergency power shall be provided for the following systems:

(1) Exhaust ventilation
(2) Treatment system
(3) Gas detection system
(4) Temperature control system
(5) Required alarm systems
[**55:**7.9.5.3]

21.3.9.5.4 Level. Emergency power systems shall comply with the requirements for a Level 2 system in accordance with NFPA 110, *Standard for Emergency and Standby Power Systems*. [**55:**7.9.5.4]

21.3.9.6 Gas Detection. Except as provided in 21.3.9.6.1, a continuous gas detection system in accordance with 21.3.9.6.2 through 21.3.9.6.6 shall be provided for the indoor storage or use of toxic or highly toxic compressed gases. [**55:**7.9.6]

21.3.9.6.1 Where Gas Detection Is Not Required. A gas detection system shall not be required for toxic gases where the physiological warning properties for the gas are at a level below the accepted permissible exposure limit or ceiling limit for the gas. [**55:**7.9.6.1]

21.3.9.6.2 Local Alarm. The gas detection system shall initiate a local alarm that is both audible and visible. [**55:**7.9.6.2]

21.3.9.6.3 Alarm Monitored. The gas detection system shall transmit a signal to a constantly attended control station for quantities exceeding one toxic or highly toxic compressed gas cylinder. [**55:**7.9.6.3]

21.3.9.6.4 Automatic Shutdown. [**55:**7.9.6.4]

21.3.9.6.4.1 Activation of the gas detection system shall automatically shut off the flow of gas related to the system being monitored. [**55:**7.9.6.4.1]

21.3.9.6.4.2 An automatic shutdown shall not be required for reactors utilized for the production of toxic or highly toxic gases when such reactors are operated at pressures less than gauge pressure of 15 psi (103.4 kPa), constantly attended, and provided with readily accessible emergency shutoff valves. [**55:**7.9.6.4.2]

21.3.9.6.5 Detection Points. Detection shall be provided at the locations specified in 21.3.9.6.5.1 through 21.3.9.6.5.4. [**55:**7.9.6.5]

21.3.9.6.5.1 Treatment System Discharge. Detection shall be provided at the discharge from the treatment system. [**55:**7.9.6.5.1]

21.3.9.6.5.2 Point of Use. Detection shall be provided in the room or area in which the gas is used. [**55:**7.9.6.5.2]

21.3.9.6.5.3 Source. Detection shall be provided at the source container, cylinder, or tank used for delivery of the gas to the point of use. [**55:**7.9.6.5.3]

21.3.9.6.5.4 Storage. Detection shall be provided in the room or area in which the gas is stored. [**55:**7.9.6.5.4]

21.3.9.6.6 Level of Detection. The gas detection system shall detect the presence of gas at or below the permissible exposure limit or ceiling limit of the gas for those points identified in 21.3.9.6.5.2 and 21.3.9.6.5.3, and at not less than one-half the IDLH level for points identified in 21.3.9.6.5.1. [**55:**7.9.6.6]

21.3.9.7 Automatic Smoke Detection System. An automatic smoke detection system shall be provided for the indoor storage or use of highly toxic compressed gases in accordance with *NFPA 72, National Fire Alarm and Signaling Code*. [**55:**7.9.7]

21.3.10 Unstable Reactive Gases (Nondetonable). The storage or use of unstable reactive (nondetonable) gases exceeding the quantity thresholds for gases requiring special provisions as specified in Table 5.2.1.2 through Table 5.2.1.10.1 shall be in accordance with Sections 21.1 and 21.2 and 21.3.1 through 21.3.3 and 21.3.10. [**55:**7.10]

21.3.10.1 Distances to Exposures for Class 2. [**55:**7.10.1]

21.3.10.1.1 The outdoor storage or use of unstable reactive Class 2 compressed gas shall not be within 20 ft (6 m) of buildings, lot lines, streets, alleys, or public ways or means of egress. [**55:**7.10.1.1]

21.3.10.1.2 A 2-hour fire barrier wall without openings or penetrations shall be permitted in lieu of the 20 ft (6 m) distance required by 21.3.10.1.1. [**55:**7.10.1.2]

21.3.10.1.2.1* When a fire barrier is used to protect compressed gas systems, the system shall terminate downstream of the source valve. [**55:**7.10.1.2.1]

21.3.10.1.2.2 The fire barrier wall shall be either an independent structure or the exterior wall of the building. [**55:**7.10.1.2.2]

21.3.10.1.2.3 The 2-hour fire barrier shall be located at least 5 ft (1.5 m) from any exposure. [**55:**7.10.1.2.3]

21.3.10.1.2.4 The 2-hour fire barrier shall not have more than two sides at approximately 1.57 rad (90 degree) directions, or not more than three sides with connecting angles of approximately 135 degrees (2.36 rad). [**55:**7.10.1.2.4]

21.3.10.2 Distances to Exposures for Class 3. [**55:**7.10.2]

21.3.10.2.1 The outdoor storage or use of unstable reactive Class 3 (nondetonable) compressed gas shall not be within 75 ft (23 m) of buildings, lot lines, streets, alleys, or public ways or means of egress. [**55:**7.10.2.1]

21.3.10.2.2 A 2-hour fire barrier wall without openings or penetrations, and extending not less than 30 in. (762 mm) above and to the sides of the storage or use area, that interrupts the line of sight between the storage or use and the exposure shall be permitted in lieu of the 75 ft (23 m) distance specified in 21.3.10.2.1. [**55:**7.10.2.2]

21.3.10.2.2.1* When a fire barrier is used to protect compressed gas systems, the system shall terminate downstream of the source valve. [**55:**7.10.2.2.1]

21.3.10.2.2.2 The fire barrier wall shall be either an independent structure or the exterior wall of the building adjacent to the storage or use area. [**55:**7.10.2.2.2]

21.3.10.2.2.3 The 2-hour fire barrier shall be located at least 1.5 m (5 ft) from any exposure. [**55:**7.10.2.2.2]

21.3.10.2.2.4 The 2-hour fire barrier shall not have more than two sides at approximately 1.57 rad (90 degree) directions, or more than three sides with connecting angles of approximately 135 degrees (2.36 rad). [**55:**7.10.2.2.4]

21.3.10.3 Storage Configuration. [**55:**7.10.3]

21.3.10.3.1 Unstable reactive Class 3 compressed gases stored in cylinders, containers, or tanks shall be arranged to limit individual groups of cylinders, containers, or tanks to areas not exceeding 100 ft^2 (9.3 m^2). [**55:**7.10.3.1]

21.3.10.3.2 Multiple areas shall be separated by aisles. [**55:**7.10.3.2]

21.3.10.3.3 Aisle widths shall not be less than the height of the cylinders, containers, or tanks or 4 ft (1.2 m), whichever is greater. [**55:**7.10.3.3]

21.3.10.4 Basements. Unstable reactive compressed gases shall not be stored in basements. [**55:**7.10.4]

21.3.10.5 Unstable Reactive Gases (Detonable). [**55:**7.10.5]

21.3.10.5.1 Storage or Use. The storage or use of unstable reactive (detonable) gases exceeding the quantity thresholds for gases requiring special provisions as specified in Table 5.2.1.2 through Table 5.2.1.10.1 shall be in accordance with Sections 21.1 and 21.2, 21.3.1 through 21.3.3, and 21.3.10.5. [**55:**7.10.5.1]

21.3.10.5.2 Location. The location of storage areas shall be determined based on the requirements of the building code for explosive materials. [**55:**7.10.5.2]

21.4 Cryogenic Fluids.

21.4.1 General. This section shall apply to all cryogenic fluids, including those fluids regulated elsewhere in this code, except that when specific requirements are provided in Sections 21.5 or 21.7, those specific requirements shall apply as applicable. [**55:**8.1]

21.4.1.1 Storage, use, and handling of cryogenic fluids shall be in accordance with Sections 21.1, 21.2, and 21.4 as applicable. [**55:**8.1.1]

21.4.1.2 Storage, use and handling of inert cryogenic fluids shall be in accordance with CGA P-18, *Standard for Bulk Inert Gas Systems.* [**55:**8.1.2]

21.4.2* Containers — Design, Construction, and Maintenance. Containers employed for the storage or use of cryogenic fluids shall be designed, fabricated, tested, marked (stamped), and maintained in accordance with DOT regulations; Transport Canada (TC) *Transportation of Dangerous Goods Regulations*; the ASME *Boiler and Pressure Vessel Code*, "Rules for the Construction of Unfired Pressure Vessels"; or regulations of other administering agencies. [**55:**8.2]

21.4.2.1 Aboveground Tanks. Aboveground tanks for the storage of cryogenic fluids shall be in accordance with 21.4.2.1. [**55:**8.2.1]

21.4.2.1.1 Construction of the Inner Vessel. The inner vessel of storage tanks in cryogenic fluid service shall be designed and constructed in accordance with Section VIII, Division 1 of the ASME *Boiler and Pressure Vessel Code* and shall be vacuum jacketed in accordance with 21.4.2.1.2. [**55:**8.2.1.1]

21.4.2.1.2 Construction of the Vacuum Jacket (Outer Vessel). [**55:**8.2.1.2]

21.4.2.1.2.1 The vacuum jacket used as an outer vessel for storage tanks in cryogenic fluid service shall be of welded steel construction designed to withstand the maximum internal and external pressure to which it will be subjected under operating conditions to include conditions of emergency pressure relief of the annular space between the inner and outer vessel. [**55:**8.2.1.2.1]

21.4.2.1.2.2 The jacket shall be designed to withstand a minimum collapsing pressure differential of 30 psi (207 kPa). [**55:**8.2.1.2.2]

21.4.2.1.2.3 Vacuum Level Monitoring. [**55:**8.2.1.2.3]

(A) A connection shall be provided on the exterior of the vacuum jacket to allow measurement of the pressure within the annular space between the inner and outer vessel. [**55:**8.2.1.2.3.1]

(B) The connection shall be fitted with a bellows-sealed or diaphragm-type valve equipped with a vacuum gauge tube that is shielded to protect against damage from impact. [**55:**8.2.1.2.3.2]

21.4.2.2 Nonstandard Containers. [**55:**8.2.2]

21.4.2.2.1 Containers, equipment, and devices that are not in compliance with recognized standards for design and construction shall be permitted if approved by the authority having jurisdiction upon presentation of evidence that they are designed and constructed for safe operation. [**55:**8.2.2.1]

21.4.2.2.2 The following data shall be submitted to the authority having jurisdiction with reference to the deviation from the code with the application for approval:

(1) Type and use of container, equipment, or device
(2) Material to be stored, used, or transported
(3) Description showing dimensions and materials used in construction
(4) Design pressure, maximum operating pressure, and test pressure
(5) Type, size, and setting of pressure-relief devices

[55:8.2.2.2]

21.4.2.3 Foundations and Supports. Stationary tanks shall be provided with concrete or masonry foundations or structural steel supports on firm concrete or masonry foundations, and 21.4.2.3.1 through 21.4.2.3.5 also shall apply. [55:8.2.3]

21.4.2.3.1 Excessive Loads. Stationary tanks shall be supported to prevent the concentration of excessive loads on the supporting portion of the shell. [55:8.2.3.1]

21.4.2.3.2 Expansion and Contraction. Foundations for horizontal containers shall be constructed to accommodate expansion and contraction of the container. [55:8.2.3.2]

21.4.2.3.3 Support of Ancilliary Equipment. [55:8.2.3.3]

21.4.2.3.3.1* Foundations shall be provided to support the weight of vaporizers and/or heat exchangers. [55:8.2.3.3.1]

21.4.2.3.3.2 Foundations shall be designed to withstand soil and frost conditions as well as the anticipated seismic, snow, wind, and hydrostatic loading under operating conditions. [55:8.2.3.3.2]

21.4.2.3.4 Temperature Effects. Where drainage systems, terrain, or surfaces beneath stationary tanks are arranged in a manner that can subject stationary tank foundations or supports to temperatures below −130°F (−90°C), the foundations or supports shall be constructed of materials that are capable of withstanding the low-temperature effects of cryogenic fluid spillage. [55:8.2.3.4]

21.4.2.3.5 Corrosion Protection. Portions of stationary tanks in contact with foundations or saddles shall be painted to protect against corrosion. [55:8.2.3.5]

21.4.2.4 Pressure-Relief Devices. [55:8.2.4]

21.4.2.4.1 General. [55:8.2.4.1]

21.4.2.4.1.1 Pressure-relief devices shall be provided to protect containers and systems containing cryogenic fluids from rupture in the event of overpressure. [55:8.2.4.1.1]

21.4.2.4.1.2 Pressure-relief devices shall be designed in accordance with CGA S-1.1, *Pressure Relief Device Standards — Part 1 — Cylinders for Compressed Gases*, and CGA S-1.2, *Pressure Relief Device Standards — Part 2 — Cargo and Portable Tanks for Compressed Gases*, for portable tanks; and CGA S-1.3, *Pressure Relief Device Standards — Part 3 — Stationary Storage Containers for Compressed Gases*, for stationary tanks. [55:8.2.4.1.2]

21.4.2.4.2 Containers Open to the Atmosphere. Portable containers that are open to the atmosphere and are designed to contain cryogenic fluids at atmospheric pressure shall not be required to be equipped with pressure-relief devices. [55:8.2.4.2]

21.4.2.4.3 Equipment Other than Containers. Heat exchangers, vaporizers, insulation casings surrounding containers, vessels, and coaxial piping systems in which liquefied cryogenic fluids could be trapped due to leakage from the primary container shall be provided with a pressure-relief device. [55:8.2.4.3]

21.4.2.4.4 Sizing. [55:8.2.4.4]

21.4.2.4.4.1 Pressure relief devices shall be sized in accordance with the specifications to which the container was fabricated. [55:8.2.4.4.1]

21.4.2.4.4.2 The pressure relief device shall have the capacity to prevent the maximum design pressure of the container or system from being exceeded. [55:8.2.4.4.2]

21.4.2.4.5 Accessibility. Pressure relief devices shall be located such that they are accessible for inspection and repair. [55:8.2.4.5]

21.4.2.4.5.1* ASME pressure relief valves shall be sealed to prevent adjusting the set pressure by other than authorized personnel. [55:8.2.4.5.1]

21.4.2.4.5.2 Non-ASME pressure relief valves shall not be field adjusted. [55:8.2.4.5.2]

21.4.2.4.6 Arrangement. [55:8.2.4.6]

21.4.2.4.6.1 Pressure Relief Devices. Pressure relief devices shall be arranged to discharge unobstructed to the open air in such a manner as to prevent impingement of escaping gas on personnel, containers, equipment, and adjacent structures or its entrance into enclosed spaces. [55:8.2.4.6.1]

21.4.2.4.6.2 Portable Containers with Volume Less than 2 ft^3 (0.057 m^3). [55:8.2.4.6.2]

(A) The arrangement of the discharge from pressure relief devices from DOT-specified containers with an internal water volume of 2.0 ft^3 (0.057 m^3) or less shall be incorporated in the design of the container. [55:8.2.4.6.2.1]

(B) Additional safeguards regarding placement or arrangement shall not be required. [55:8.2.4.6.2.2]

21.4.2.4.7 Shutoffs Between Pressure Relief Devices and Containers. [55:8.2.5.7]

21.4.2.4.7.1 General. Shutoff valves installed between pressure relief devices and containers shall be in accordance with 21.4.2.4.7. [55:8.2.5.7.1]

21.4.2.4.7.2 Location. Shutoff valves shall not be installed between pressure relief devices and containers unless the valves or their use meet 21.4.2.4.7.2(A) or 21.4.2.4.7.2(B). [55:8.2.5.7.2]

(A) Security. Shutoff valves shall be locked in the open position, and their use shall be limited to service-related work performed by the supplier under the requirements of the ASME *Boiler and Pressure Vessel Code*. [55:8.2.4.7.2.1]

(B) Multiple Pressure Relief Devices. Shutoff valves controlling multiple pressure relief devices on a container shall be installed so that either the type of valve installed or the arrangement provides the full required flow through the minimum number of required relief devices at all times. [55:8.2.4.7.2.2]

21.4.2.4.8 Temperature Limits. Pressure relief devices shall not be subjected to cryogenic fluid temperatures except when operating. [55:8.2.4.8]

21.4.3 Pressure Relief Vent Piping. [55:8.3]

21.4.3.1 General. Pressure relief vent piping systems shall be constructed and arranged to direct the flow of gas to a safe location and in accordance with 21.4.3. [55:8.3.1]

21.4.3.2 Sizing. Pressure relief device vent piping shall have a cross-sectional area not less than that of the pressure relief device vent opening and shall be arranged so as not to restrict the flow of escaping gas. [**55:**8.3.2]

21.4.3.3 Arrangement. Pressure relief device vent piping and drains in vent lines shall be arranged so that escaping gas discharges unobstructed to the open air and does not impinge on personnel, containers, equipment, and adjacent structures or enter enclosed spaces. [**55:**8.3.3]

21.4.3.4 Installation. Pressure relief device vent lines shall be installed in a manner that excludes or removes moisture and condensation to prevent malfunction of the pressure-relief device due to freezing or ice accumulation. [**55:**8.3.4]

21.4.3.5 Overfilling. Controls shall be provided to prevent overfilling of stationary containers. [**55:**8.3.5]

21.4.4 Marking. [**55:**8.4]

21.4.4.1 General. Cryogenic containers and systems shall be marked in accordance with nationally recognized standards and in accordance with 21.4.4. [**55:**8.4.1]

21.4.4.1.1 Portable Containers. [**55:**8.4.1.1]

21.4.4.1.1.1 Portable cryogenic containers shall be marked in accordance with CGA C-7, *Guide to the Preparation of Precautionary Labeling and Marking of Compressed Gas Containers.* [**55:**8.4.1.1.1]

21.4.4.1.1.2* All DOT-4L/TC-4LM liquid cylinders shall have product identification visible from all directions with minimum 2 in. (51 mm) high letters. [**55:**8.4.1.1.2]

21.4.4.1.2 Stationary Tanks. Stationary tanks shall be marked in accordance with NFPA 704, *Standard System for the Identification of the Hazards of Materials for Emergency Response.* [**55:**8.4.1.2]

21.4.4.1.3 Identification Signs. Visible hazard identification signs shall be provided in accordance with NFPA 704, *Standard System for the Identification of the Hazards of Materials for Emergency Response,* at entrances to buildings or areas in which cryogenic fluids are stored, handled, or used. [**55:**8.4.1.3]

21.4.4.2 Identification of Contents. Stationary containers shall be placarded with the identity of their contents to indicate the name of the material contained. [**55:**8.4.2]

21.4.4.3 Container Specification. Stationary containers shall be marked with the manufacturing specification and maximum allowable working pressure on a permanent nameplate. [**55:**8.4.3]

21.4.4.3.1 The nameplate shall be installed on the container in an accessible location. [**55:**8.4.3.1]

21.4.4.3.2 The nameplate shall be marked in accordance with nationally recognized standards. [**55:**8.4.3.2]

21.4.4.4 Identification of Container Connections. [**55:**8.4.4]

21.4.4.4.1 Container inlet and outlet connections, liquid-level limit controls, valves, and pressure gauges shall be identified using one of the following methods:

(1) They shall be marked with a permanent tag or label identifying their function.
(2) They shall be identified by a schematic drawing that indicates their function and designates whether they are connected to the vapor or liquid space of the container.

[**55:**8.4.4.1; **55:**8.4.4.1.1; **55:**8.4.4.1.2]

21.4.4.4.2 When a schematic drawing is provided, it shall be attached to the container and maintained in a legible condition. [**55:**8.4.4.1.2.1]

21.4.4.5 Identification of Piping Systems. Piping systems shall be identified in accordance with ASME A13.1, *Scheme for the Identification of Piping Systems.* [**55:**8.4.5]

21.4.4.6 Identification of Emergency Shutoff Valves. Emergency shutoff valves on stationary containers shall be identified, visible, and indicated by means of a sign. [**55:**8.4.6]

21.4.5 Medical Cryogenic Systems. [**55:**8.5]

21.4.5.1 Bulk cryogenic fluid systems in medical gas applications at health care facilities shall be in accordance with Section 21.4, 21.1.1.2.1(3), and the material-specific requirements of Section 21.5, as applicable. [**55:**8.5.1]

21.4.5.1.1 Bulk cryogenic fluid systems shall be in accordance with the following provisions as applicable:

(1) Where located in a court, systems shall be in accordance with 21.4.13.2.7.
(2) Where located indoors, systems shall be in accordance with 21.4.13.1.
(3) Systems shall be installed by personnel qualified in accordance with CGA M-1, *Guide for Medical Gas Installations at Consumer Sites,* or ASSE 6015, *Professional Qualification Standard for Bulk Medical Gas Systems Installers.*
(4) Systems shall be installed in compliance with Food and Drug Administration Current Good Manufacturing Practices as found in 21 CFR 210 and 21 CFR 211

[**55:**8.5.1.1]

21.4.5.1.2 The following components of the bulk system shall be accessible and visible to delivery personnel during filling operations:

(1) Fill connection
(2) Top and bottom fill valves
(3) Hose purge valve
(4) Vent valve
(5) Full trycock valve
(6) Liquid level gauge
(7) Tank pressure gauge

[**55:**8.5.1.2]

21.4.5.1.3 Bulk cryogenic fluid system shall be anchored with foundations in accordance with the provisions of CGA M-1, *Guide for Medical Gas Installations at Consumer Sites.* [**55:**8.5.1.3]

21.4.5.1.4 Bulk cryogenic fluid systems shall consist of the following:

(1) One or more main supply vessel(s), whose capacity shall be determined after consideration of the customer usage requirements, delivery schedules, proximity of the facility to alternate supplies, and the emergency plan
(2) A contents gauge on each of the main vessel(s)
(3) A reserve supply sized for greater than an average day's supply, with the size of vessel or number of cylinders being determined after consideration of delivery schedules, proximity of the facility to alternate supplies, and the facility's emergency plan
(4) At least two main vessel relief valves and rupture discs installed downstream of a three-way (three-port) valve
(5) A check valve located in the primary supply piping upstream of the intersection with a secondary supply or reserve supply

[**55:**8.5.1.4]

21.4.5.1.5 Bulk cryogenic fluid reserve supply systems consisting of either a second cryogenic fluid source or a compressed gas source shall include the following:

(1) When the reserve source is a compressed gas source, the reserve shall be equipped with the following:
   (a) A cylinder manifold having not less than three gas cylinder connections or as otherwise required for an average of one day's gas supply
   (b) A pressure switch to monitor the pressure in the cylinder manifold
(2) When the reserve source is a second cryogenic fluid vessel, the reserve tank shall be equipped with the following:
   (a) An actuating switch or sensor to monitor the internal tank pressure
   (b) A contents gauge to monitor the liquid level
(3) When the reserve source is either a cryogenic fluid or compressed gas source, a check valve shall be provided to prevent backflow into the reserve system

[**55**:8.5.1.5]

21.4.5.1.6 Bulk cryogenic fluid systems shall include a fill mechanism consisting of the following components:

(1) A nonremovable product-specific fill connection in compliance with CGA V-6, *Standard Cryogenic Liquid Transfer Connection*
(2) A means to cap and secure the fill connection inlet
(3) A check valve to prevent product backflow from the fill inlet
(4) A fill hose purge valve
(5) Supports that hold the fill piping off the ground
(6) A secure connection between the bulk tank and the fill piping
(7) Supports as necessary to hold the fill line in position during all operations associated with the filling procedure

[**55**:8.5.1.6]

21.4.5.1.7 Where vaporizers are required to convert cryogenic liquid to the gaseous state, the vaporizer units shall conform to the following:

(1) Be permitted to operate by either ambient heat transfer or external thermal source (e.g., electric heater, hot water, steam)
(2) Be designed to provide capacity for the customer's peak and average flow rates under local conditions, seasonal conditions for weather and humidity, and structures that obstruct air circulation flow and sunlight
(3) If switching is required as part of the system design, have piping and manual/automatic valving configured in such a manner that operating vaporizer(s) or sections of the vaporizer can be switched to non-operating vaporizer or section of the vaporizer to de-ice through a valving configuration that assures continuous flow to the facility through either or both vaporizers and/or sections of the vaporizer if valving switchover fails

[**55**:8.5.1.7]

21.4.5.1.8 Where a vaporizer requires an external thermal source, the flow from the source of supply shall be unaffected by the loss of the external thermal source through either of the following:

(1) Reserve ambient heat transfer vaporizers capable of providing capacity for at least one day's average supply and piped so as to be unaffected by flow stoppage through the main vaporizer
(2) A reserve non-cryogenic source capable of providing at least one day's average supply

[**55**:8.5.1.8]

21.4.6 Security. [**55**:8.6]

21.4.6.1 General. Cryogenic containers and systems shall be secured against accidental dislodgement and against access by unauthorized personnel in accordance with 21.4.6. [**55**:8.6.1]

21.4.6.2 Security of Areas. Areas used for the storage of containers and systems shall be secured against unauthorized entry. [**55**:8.6.2]

21.4.6.3 Securing of Containers. Stationary containers shall be secured to foundations in accordance with the building code. [**55**:8.6.3]

21.4.6.3.1 Portable containers subject to shifting or upset shall be secured. [**55**:8.6.3.1]

21.4.6.3.2 Nesting shall be permitted as a means of securing portable containers. [**55**:8.6.3.2]

21.4.6.4 Securing of Vaporizers. Vaporizers, heat exchangers, and similar equipment shall be secured to foundations, and their connecting piping shall be designed and constructed to provide for the effects of expansion and contraction due to temperature changes. [**55**:8.6.4]

21.4.6.5 Physical Protection. Containers, piping, valves, pressure-relief devices, regulating equipment, and other appurtenances shall be protected against physical damage and tampering. [**55**:8.6.5]

21.4.7 Separation from Hazardous Conditions. [**55**:8.7]

21.4.7.1 General. Cryogenic containers and systems in storage or use shall be separated from materials and conditions that present exposure hazards to or from each other in accordance with 21.4.7. [**55**:8.7.1]

21.4.7.2* Stationary Cryogenic Containers. Stationary containers located outdoors shall be separated from exposure hazards in accordance with the minimum separation distances indicated in Table 21.4.7.2. [**55**:8.7.2]

21.4.7.2.1 Fire Barriers. A 2-hour fire barrier wall shall be permitted in lieu of the distances specified by Table 21.4.7.2, for items 1, 4, 7, 8, and 9, when in accordance with the provisions of 21.4.7.2.1.1 through 21.4.7.2.1.4. [**55**:8.7.2.1]

21.4.7.2.1.1 The fire barrier wall shall be without openings or penetrations with the exception of 21.4.7.2.1.2. [**55**:8.7.2.1.1]

21.4.7.2.1.2 Penetrations of the fire barrier wall by conduit or piping shall be permitted provided that the penetration is protected with a fire stop system in accordance with the building code. [**55**:8.7.2.1.1.1]

21.4.7.2.1.3 The fire barrier wall shall be either an independent structure or the exterior wall of the building adjacent to the storage system. [**55**:8.7.2.1.2]

21.4.7.2.1.4 The fire barrier wall shall be located not less than 5 ft (1.5 m) from any exposure. [**55**:8.7.2.1.3]

Table 21.4.7.2 Minimum Separation Distance Between Stationary Cryogenic Containers and Exposures

Exposure	Minimum Distance ft	Minimum Distance m
(1) Buildings, regardless of construction type	1	0.3
(2) Wall openings	1	0.3
(3) Air intakes	10	3.1
(4) Property lines	5	1.5
(5) Places of public assembly (assembly occupancies)	50	15
(6) Nonambulatory patient areas	50	15
(7) Combustible materials, such as paper, leaves, weeds, dry grass, or debris	15	4.5
(8) Incompatible hazardous materials	20	6.1
(9) Building exits	10	3.1

[**55:** Table 8.7.2]

Table 21.4.7.3 Minimum Separation Distance Between Portable Cryogenic Containers and Exposures

Exposure	Minimum Distance ft	Minimum Distance m
Building exits	10	3.1
Wall openings	1	0.3
Air intakes	10	3.1
Property lines	5	1.5
Room or area exits	3	0.9
Combustible materials, such as paper, leaves, weeds, dry grass, or debris	15	4.5
Incompatible hazardous materials	20	6.1

[**55:** Table 8.7.3]

21.4.7.2.1.5 The fire barrier wall shall not have more than two sides at 90 degree (1.57 rad) directions, or not more than three sides with connecting angles of 135 degrees (2.36 rad). [**55:**8.7.2.1.4]

(A) The connecting angles between fire barrier walls shall be permitted to be reduced to less than 135 degrees (2.36 rad) for installations consisting of three walls when in accordance with 8.13.2.7.2 of NFPA 55. [**55:**8.7.2.1.4.1]

21.4.7.2.1.6 Where the requirement of 21.4.7.2.1.5 is met, the bulk system shall be a minimum distance of 1 ft (0.3 m) from the fire barrier wall. [**55:**8.7.2.1.5]

21.4.7.2.2 Point-of-Fill Connections. Point-of-fill connections points serving stationary containers filled by mobile transport equipment shall not be positioned closer to exposures than the minimum distances in Table 21.4.7.2. [**55:**8.7.2.2]

21.4.7.2.3 Surfaces Beneath Containers. The surface of the area on which stationary containers are placed, including the surface of the area located below the point at which connections are made for the purpose of filling such containers, shall be compatible with the fluid in the container. [**55:**8.7.2.4]

21.4.7.3 Portable Cryogenic Containers. Portable containers used for cryogenic fluids located outdoors shall be separated from exposure hazards in accordance with Table 21.4.7.3. [**55:**8.7.3]

21.4.7.3.1 Non-bulk portable containers of liquefied hydrogen shall be separated from exposure hazards in accordance with Table 21.4.7.3.1. [**55:**8.7.3.1]

21.4.7.3.2 Fire Barriers. A 2-hour fire barrier wall shall be permitted in lieu of the distances specified by Table 21.4.7.3 when in accordance with the provisions of 21.4.7.3.2.1 through 21.4.7.3.2.4. [**55:**8.7.3.2]

21.4.7.3.2.1 The fire barrier wall shall be without openings or penetrations with the exception of 21.4.7.3.2.2. [**55:**8.7.3.2.1]

21.4.7.3.2.2 Penetrations of the fire barrier wall by conduit or piping shall be permitted provided that the penetration is protected with a firestop system in accordance with the building code. [**55:**8.7.3.2.1.1]

21.4.7.3.2.3 The fire barrier wall shall be either an independent structure or the exterior wall of the building adjacent to the storage system. [**55:**8.7.3.2.2]

21.4.7.3.2.4 The fire barrier wall shall be located not less than 5 ft (1.5 m) from any exposure. [**55:**8.7.3.2.3]

21.4.7.3.2.5 The fire barrier wall shall not have more than two sides at approximately 90 degree (1.57 rad) directions, or not more than three sides with connecting angles of approximately 135 degrees (2.36 rad). [**55:**8.7.3.2.4]

21.4.8 Electrical Wiring and Equipment. [**55:**8.8]

21.4.8.1 General. Electrical wiring and equipment shall be in accordance with *NFPA 70, National Electrical Code*, and 21.4.8. [**55:**8.8.1]

21.4.8.2 Location. Containers and systems shall not be located where they could become part of an electrical circuit. [**55:**8.8.2]

21.4.8.3 Electrical Ground and Bonding. Containers and systems shall not be used for electrical grounding. [**55:**8.8.3]

21.4.8.3.1 When electrical grounding and bonding is required, the system shall be in accordance with *NFPA 70, National Electrical Code*. [**55:**8.8.3.1]

21.4.8.3.2 The grounding system shall be protected against corrosion, including corrosion caused by stray electrical currents. [**55:**8.8.3.2]

21.4.9 Service and Repair. Service, repair, modification, or removal of valves, pressure relief devices, or other container appurtenances shall be in accordance with nationally recognized codes and standards. [**55:**8.9]

21.4.9.1 Containers. Containers that have been removed from service shall be handled in an approved manner. [**55:**8.9.1]

21.4.9.1.1 Testing. Containers, out of service in excess of 1 year, shall be inspected and tested as required in 21.4.9.1.2. [**55:**8.9.1.1]

21.4.9.1.2 Pressure Relief Device Testing. The pressure relief devices shall be tested for operability and to determine if they are set at the relief pressure required by the tank design. [**55:**8.9.1.2]

Table 21.4.7.3.1 Distance to Exposures for Non-Bulk Liquefied Hydrogen (LH$_2$)

Maximum Amount per Storage Area (gal)	Minimum Distance Between Storage Areas (ft)	Minimum Distance to Lot Lines of Property That Can Be Built Upon (ft)	Minimum Distance to Public Streets, Public Alleys or Public Ways (ft)	Minimum Distance to Buildings on the Same Property		
				Less than 2-Hour Construction	2-Hour Construction	4-Hour Construction
0–39.7	5	5	5	5	0	0
39.8–186.9	10	10	10	10	5	0
187–448.7	10	15	15	20	5	0
448.8–747.8	10	20	20	20	5	0
>747.8	20	25	25	20	5	0

For SI units: 1 ft = 305 mm.
Notes:
(1) For requirements on minimum distance to air intakes, see 7.6.2.4.
(2) For requirements on minimum distance to building openings including exits, see 7.6.2.5.
(3) When 8.7.3.2 is used as a means of distance reduction, the configuration of the fire barriers should be designed to allow natural ventilation to prevent the accumulation of hazardous gas concentrations.
[55: Table 8.7.3.1]

21.4.9.1.3 Containers that have previously been used for flammable cryogenic fluids and have been removed from service shall be purged with an inert gas to remove residual flammable gas and stored with all valves closed and the valve outlets plugged. [55:8.9.1.3]

21.4.9.2 Systems. Service and repair of containers or systems shall be performed by trained personnel in accordance with nationally recognized standards and with the permission of the container owner. [55:8.9.2]

21.4.10 Unauthorized Use. Containers shall not be used for any purpose other than to serve as a vessel for containing the product for which it is designated. [55:8.10]

21.4.11 Leaks, Damage, and Corrosion. [55:8.11]

21.4.11.1 Leaking, damaged, or corroded containers shall be removed from service. [55:8.11.1]

21.4.11.2 Leaking, damaged, or corroded systems shall be replaced, repaired, or removed from service. [55:8.11.2]

21.4.12 Lighting. Where required by the authority having jurisdiction, lighting, including emergency lighting, shall be provided for fire appliances and operating facilities such as walkways, control valves, and gates ancillary to stationary containers. [55:8.12]

21.4.13 Storage. [55:8.13]

21.4.13.1 Indoor Storage. [55:8.13.1]

21.4.13.1.1 Installation. Stationary containers indoors shall be installed in accordance with Sections 21.5 and 21.7 or ANSI/CGA P-18, *Standard for Bulk Inert Gas Systems*. [55:8.13.1.1]

21.4.13.1.2 Stationary Containers. Stationary containers shall be in accordance with 21.4.2. [55:8.13.1.2]

21.4.13.1.3 Cryogenic Fluids. Cryogenic fluids in stationary or portable containers stored indoors shall be stored in buildings, rooms, or areas constructed in accordance with the building code. [55:8.13.1.3]

21.4.13.1.4 Ventilation. Ventilation shall be in accordance with 21.2.16. [55:8.13.1.4]

21.4.13.2 Outdoor Storage. [55:8.13.2]

21.4.13.2.1 General. Cryogenic fluids in stationary or portable containers stored outdoors shall be in accordance with 21.4.13.2. [55:8.13.2.1]

21.4.13.2.2 Access. [55:8.13.2.2]

21.4.13.2.2.1 Stationary containers shall be located to provide access by mobile supply equipment and authorized personnel. [55:8.13.2.2]

21.4.13.2.2.2 Where exit access is provided to serve areas in which equipment is installed, the minimum width shall be not less than 28 in. (710 mm). [55:8.13.2.2.1]

21.4.13.2.3 Physical Protection. [55:8.13.2.3]

21.4.13.2.3.1 Cryogenic fluid cylinders, containers, tanks, and systems that could be exposed to physical damage shall be protected. [55:8.13.2.3]

21.4.13.2.3.2 Guard posts or other means shall be provided to protect cryogenic fluid cylinders, containers, tanks, and systems indoors and outdoors from vehicular damage. *(See 6.1.9.)* [55:8.13.2.3.1]

21.4.13.2.4 Diked Areas Containing Other Hazardous Materials. Containers of cryogenic fluids shall not be located within diked areas with other hazardous materials. [55:8.13.2.4]

21.4.13.2.5* Areas Subject to Flooding. Stationary containers located in flood hazard areas shall be anchored to prevent flotation during conditions of the design flood as designated by the building code. [55:8.13.2.5]

21.4.13.2.5.1 Elevated Tanks. Structures supporting elevated tanks to and tanks that are supported at a level above that designated in the design flood shall be anchored to resist lateral shifting due to flood and other hydrostatic effects. [55:8.13.2.5.1]

21.4.13.2.5.2 Underground Tanks. Underground tanks in flood hazard areas shall be anchored to prevent flotation, collapse, or lateral movement resulting from hydrostatic loads, including the effects of buoyancy, during conditions of the design flood. [**55:**8.13.2.5.2]

21.4.13.2.6 Drainage. [**55:**8.13.2.6]

21.4.13.2.6.1 The area surrounding stationary and portable containers shall be provided with a means to prevent accidental discharge of fluids from endangering personnel, containers, equipment, and adjacent structures and from entering enclosed spaces in accordance with NFPA 1, *Fire Code*. [**55:**8.13.2.6.1]

21.4.13.2.6.2 The stationary container shall not be placed where spilled or discharged fluids will be retained around the container. [**55:**8.13.2.6.2]

21.4.13.2.6.3 The provisions of 21.4.13.2.6.2 shall be permitted to be altered or waived where the authority having jurisdiction determines that the container does not constitute a hazard after consideration of special features such as the following:

(1) Crushed rock utilized as a heat sink
(2) Topographical conditions
(3) Nature of occupancy
(4) Proximity to structures on the same or adjacent property
(5) Capacity and construction of containers and character of fluids to be stored

[**55:**8.13.2.6.3]

21.4.13.2.6.4 Grade. [**55:**8.13.2.6.4]

(A) The grade for a distance of not less than 50 ft (15.2 m) from where cryogenic fluid storage or delivery systems are installed shall be higher than the grade on which flammable or combustible liquids are stored or used. [**55:**8.13.2.6.4]

(B)* Drainage Control.

(1) When the grade differential between the storage or delivery system and the flammable or combustible liquids storage or use area is not in accordance with 21.4.13.2.6.4(A), diversion curbs or other means of drainage control shall be used to divert the flow of flammable or combustible liquids away from the cryogenic system.
[**55:**8.13.2.6.4(A)]
(2) The means of drainage control shall prevent the flow of flammable or combustible liquid to a distance not less than 50 ft (15.2 m) from all parts of the delivery system.

[**55:**8.13.2.6.4(B)]

21.4.13.2.7 Outdoor Installations. [**55:**8.13.2.7]

21.4.13.2.7.1 Enclosed Courts. Stationary containers shall not be installed within enclosed courts. [**55:**8.13.2.7.1]

21.4.13.2.7.2* Courts. Stationary containers shall be sited so that they are open to the surrounding environment except that encroachment by building walls of unlimited height shall be permitted when in accordance with the distances specified by Table 21.4.7.2 or the material-specific tables in Sections 21.5 or 21.7. [**55:**8.13.2.7.2]

(A)* Where exterior building walls encroach on the system to form a court, the system shall be located at a distance not less than the height of the wall from at least two court walls. [**55:**8.13.2.7.2.1]

(B) The required distance between the exterior walls of the building forming the court and the container shall be determined independently without regard to fire barrier walls used to allow encroachment by fire exposure hazards. [**55:**8.13.2.7.2.2]

21.4.13.2.7.3 Fire Department Access. Fire department access roadways or other approved means shall be in accordance with NFPA 1, *Fire Code*. [**55:**8.13.2.7.3]

21.4.14 Use and Handling. [**55:**8.14]

21.4.14.1 General. Use and handling of containers and systems shall be in accordance with 21.4.14. [**55:**8.14.1]

21.4.14.1.1 Operating Instructions. Operating instructions shall be provided for installations that require the operation of equipment. [**55:**8.14.1.1]

21.4.14.1.2 Attended Delivery. A qualified person shall be in attendance at all times cryogenic fluid is transferred from mobile supply units to a storage system. [**55:**8.14.1.2]

21.4.14.1.3 Inspection. [**55:**8.14.1.3]

21.4.14.1.3.1 Cryogenic fluid storage systems shall be inspected and maintained by a qualified representative of the equipment owner as required by the material-specific requirements of Sections 21.5 and 21.7. [**55:**8.14.1.3.1]

(A)* The interval between inspections other than those specified by material-specific requirements shall be based on nationally recognized good practices or standards. [**55:**8.14.1.3.1.1]

21.4.14.1.3.2 A record of the inspection shall be prepared and provided to the user or the authority having jurisdiction upon request. [**55:**8.14.1.3.2]

21.4.14.1.4 Design. [**55:**8.14.1.4]

21.4.14.1.4.1 Nationally Recognized Good Practices. Where nationally recognized good practices or standards have been established for the process employed, such practices and standards shall be followed. [**55:**8.14.1.4.1]

21.4.14.1.4.2 Piping Systems. Piping, tubing, fittings, and related components shall be designed, fabricated, and tested in accordance with ASME B31.3, *Process Piping*, or other approved standards and shall be in accordance with 21.4.14.2. [**55:**8.14.1.4.2]

21.4.14.2 Piping and Appurtenances. [**55:**8.14.2]

21.4.14.2.1 Piping systems shall be designed for the use intended through the full range of pressure and temperature to which they will be subjected. [**55:**8.14.2.1]

21.4.14.2.2 Piping systems shall be designed and constructed to allow for expansion, contraction, vibration, settlement, and fire exposure. [**55:**8.14.2.2]

21.4.14.3 Joints. Joints in piping and tubing shall be in accordance with the requirements of ANSI/ASME B31.3, *Process Piping*, or other approved standards. [**55:**8.14.3]

21.4.14.4 Valves and Accessory Equipment. Valves and accessory equipment shall be acceptable for the intended use at the temperatures of the application and shall be designed and constructed to withstand the maximum pressure at the minimum temperature to which they will be subjected. [**55:**8.14.4]

21.4.14.5 Shutoff Valves on Containers. Shutoff valves shall be provided on all container connections, except for pressure-relief devices. [55:8.14.5]

21.4.14.5.1 Shutoff valves for containers with multiple pressure-relief devices shall be permitted in accordance with 21.4.2.4.7. [55:8.14.5.1]

21.4.14.5.2 Shutoff valves shall be accessible and located as close as practical to the container. [55:8.14.5.2]

21.4.14.6 Shutoff Valves on Piping. [55:8.14.6]

21.4.14.6.1 Shutoff valves shall be installed in piping containing cryogenic fluids where needed to limit the volume of liquid discharged in the event of piping or equipment failure. [55:8.14.6.1]

21.4.14.6.2 Pressure relief valves shall be installed where liquid or cold gas can be trapped between shutoff valves in the piping system. [55:8.14.6.2]

21.4.14.7 Physical Protection and Support. [55:8.14.7]

21.4.14.7.1 Aboveground piping systems shall be supported and protected from physical damage. [55:8.14.7.1]

21.4.14.7.2 Piping passing through walls shall be protected from mechanical damage. [55:8.14.7.2]

21.4.14.8 Corrosion Protection. [55:8.14.8]

21.4.14.8.1 Aboveground piping that is subject to corrosion shall be protected against corrosion. [55:8.14.8.1]

21.4.14.8.2 Belowground piping shall be protected against corrosion. [55:8.14.8.2]

21.4.14.9 Cathodic Protection. Where required, cathodic protection shall be in accordance with 21.4.14.9. [55:8.14.9]

21.4.14.9.1 Operation. Where installed, cathodic protection systems shall be operated and maintained to continuously provide corrosion protection. [55:8.14.9.1]

21.4.14.9.2 Inspection. [55:8.14.9.2]

21.4.14.9.2.1 Container systems equipped with cathodic protection shall be inspected for the intended operation by a cathodic protection tester. [55:8.14.9.2.1]

21.4.14.9.2.2 The cathodic protection tester shall be certified as being qualified by the National Association of Corrosion Engineers, International (NACE). [55:8.14.9.2.2]

21.4.14.9.3 Impressed Current Systems. [55:8.14.9.3]

21.4.14.9.3.1 Systems equipped with impressed current cathodic protection systems shall be inspected in accordance with the design and 21.4.14.9.2. [55:8.14.9.3.1]

21.4.14.9.3.2 The design limits shall be available to the AHJ upon request. [55:8.14.9.3.2]

21.4.14.9.3.3 The system owner shall maintain the following records to demonstrate that the cathodic protection is in conformance with the design:

(1) The results of inspections of the system
(2) The results of testing that has been completed
[55:8.14.9.3.3]

21.4.14.9.4 Corrosion Expert.

21.4.14.9.4.1 Repairs, maintenance, or replacement of a cathodic protection system shall be under the supervision of a corrosion expert certified by NACE. [55:8.14.9.4]

21.4.14.9.4.2 The corrosion expert shall be certified by NACE as a senior corrosion technologist, a cathodic protection specialist, or a corrosion specialist or shall be a registered engineer with registration in a field that includes education and experience in corrosion control. [55:8.14.9.4.1]

21.4.14.10 Testing. [55:8.14.10]

21.4.14.10.1 Piping systems shall be tested and proven free of leaks after installation as required by the codes and standards to which they are designed and constructed. [55:8.14.10.1]

21.4.14.10.2 Test pressures shall not be less than 150 percent of the maximum allowable working pressure when hydraulic testing is conducted or 110 percent when testing is conducted pneumatically. [55:8.14.10.2]

21.4.14.11 Material-Specific Requirements. [55:8.14.11]

21.4.14.11.1 Indoor Use. Indoor use of cryogenic fluids shall be in accordance with the material-specific provisions of Sections 21.5 and 21.7 or with ANSI/CGA P-18, *Standard for Bulk Inert Gas Systems*, and 21.4.14.2. [55:8.14.11.1]

21.4.14.11.2 Outdoor Use. [55:8.14.11.2]

21.4.14.11.2.1 General. Outdoor use of cryogenic fluids shall be in accordance with the material-specific provisions of Sections 21.5 and 21.7 or with ANSI/CGA P-18, *Standard for Bulk Inert Gas Systems*, and 21.4.14.2. [55:8.14.11.2.1]

21.4.14.11.2.2 Separation. Distances from property lines, buildings, and exposure hazards shall be in accordance with Table 21.4.7.2 and Table 21.4.7.3 and the material-specific provisions of Sections 21.5 and 21.7 or with ANSI/CGA P-18, *Standard for Bulk Inert Gas Systems*. [55:8.14.11.2.2]

21.4.14.11.2.3* Emergency Shutoff Valves. Accessible manual or automatic emergency shutoff valves shall be provided to shut off the cryogenic fluid supply in case of emergency. [55:8.14.11.2.3]

(A) Manual emergency shutoff valves or the device that activates an automatic emergency shutoff valve on a bulk source or piping systems serving the bulk supply shall be identified by means of a sign. [55:8.14.11.2.3.1(A)]

(B) Emergency shutoff valves shall be located at the point of use, at the source of supply, and at the point where the system piping enters the building. [55:8.14.11.2.3.2]

21.4.14.11.3 Filling and Dispensing. [55:8.14.11.3]

21.4.14.11.3.1 General. Filling and dispensing of cryogenic fluids shall be in accordance with 21.4.14.1.2. [55:8.14.11.3.1]

21.4.14.11.3.2 Dispensing Areas. Dispensing of cryogenic fluids associated with physical or health hazards shall be conducted in approved locations. [55:8.14.11.3.2]

(A) Indoor Dispensing Areas. Dispensing indoors shall be conducted in areas constructed in accordance with the building code. [55:8.14.11.3.2.1]

(B) Ventilation. Indoor areas in which cryogenic fluids are dispensed shall be ventilated in accordance with 21.2.16 and the IAPMO *Uniform Mechanical Code*. [55:8.14.11.3.2.2]

(C) Piping Systems. Piping systems utilized for filling or dispensing of cryogenic fluids shall be designed and constructed in accordance with 21.4.14.2. [55:8.14.11.3.2.3]

21.4.14.11.3.3 Vehicle Loading and Unloading Areas. Loading or unloading areas shall be constructed in accordance with Section 21.5 for liquid oxygen and Section 21.7 for liquid hydrogen or ANSI/CGA P-18, *Standard for Bulk Inert Gas Systems*, for inert cryogenic fluids, as applicable. [55:8.14.11.3.3]

21.4.14.11.3.4* A noncombustible, delivery vehicle spill pad shall be provided when required by the material-specific requirements of Chapter 9 of NFPA 55 for liquid oxygen, Chapter 11 of NFPA 55 for liquid hydrogen, or ANSI/CGA P-18, *Standard for Bulk Inert Gas Systems at Consumer Sites*. [55:8.14.11.3.4]

(A)* A noncombustible spill pad shall be provided for delivery areas where bulk liquid helium is transferred from delivery vehicles. [55:8.14.11.3.4.1]

21.4.14.11.3.5 Filling Controls. A pressure gauge and full trycock valve shall be provided and shall be visible from the delivery point to allow the delivery operator to monitor the internal pressure and liquid level of stationary containers during filling. [55:8.14.11.3.5]

(A) When the containers being filled are remote from the delivery point and pressure gauges or full trycock valves are not visible, redundant gauges and valves shall be installed at the filling connection. [55:8.14.11.3.5.1]

21.4.14.11.4 Handling. [55:8.14.11.4]

21.4.14.11.4.1 Applicability. Handling of cryogenic containers shall be in accordance with 21.4.14.11.4. [55:8.14.11.4.1]

21.4.14.11.4.2 Carts and Trucks. [55:8.14.11.4.2]

(A) Cryogenic containers shall be moved using an approved method. [55:8.14.11.4.2.1]

(B) Where cryogenic containers are moved by hand cart, hand truck, or other mobile device, that device shall be designed for the secure movement of the container. [55:8.14.11.4.2.2]

21.4.14.11.4.3 Design. Carts and trucks used to transport cryogenic containers shall be designed to provide a stable base for the commodities to be transported and shall have a means of restraining containers to prevent accidental dislodgement. [55:8.14.11.4.3]

21.4.14.11.4.4 Closed Containers. [55:8.14.11.4.4]

(A) Pressurized containers shall be closed while transported. [55:8.14.11.4.4.1]

(B) Containers designed for use at atmospheric conditions shall be transported with appropriate loose-fitting covers in place to prevent spillage. [55:8.14.11.4.4.2]

21.5 Bulk Oxygen Systems. Bulk oxygen systems shall comply with Chapter 9 of NFPA 55, *Compressed Gases and Cryogenic Fluids Code*.

21.6 Bulk Hydrogen Compressed Gas Systems. Bulk hydrogen compressed gas systems shall comply with Chapter 10 of NFPA 55, *Compressed Gases and Cryogenic Fluids Code*.

21.7 Bulk Liquefied Hydrogen Systems. Bulk hydrogen liquefied gas systems shall comply with Chapter 11 of NFPA 55, *Compressed Gases and Cryogenic Fluids Code*.

21.8 Gas Generation Systems. Gas generator systems shall comply with Chapter 12 of NFPA 55, *Compressed Gases and Cryogenic Fluids Code*.

21.9 Insulated Liquid Carbon Dioxide Systems. Insulated liquid carbon dioxide systems shall comply with Chapter 13 of NFPA 55, *Compressed Gases and Cryogenic Fluids Code*.

21.10 Storage, Handling, and Use of Ethylene Oxide for Sterilization and Fumigation. Storage, handling, and use of ethylene oxide for sterilization and fumigation shall comply with Chapter 14 of NFPA 55, *Compressed Gases and Cryogenic Fluids Code*.

21.11 Acetylene Cylinder Charging Plants. Acetylene cylinder charging plants engaged in the generation and compression of acetylene and in the charging of acetylene cylinders, either as their sole operation or in conjunction with facilities for charging other compressed gas cylinders shall comply with Chapter 15 of NFPA 55, *Compressed Gases and Cryogenic Fluids Code*.

Annex A Explanatory Material

Annex A is not a part of the requirements of this NFPA document but is included for informational purposes only. This annex contains explanatory material, numbered to correspond with the applicable text paragraphs.

A.1.1.1 Manufacturing operations are covered by this code when the manufacturing operation involves the storage or use of hazardous materials regulated by this code.

When quantities exceed Occupational Safety and Health Administration (OSHA) or Environmental Protection Agency (EPA) threshold quantities for hazardous materials (or classes of materials), additional federal requirements under the Process Safety Management (29 CFR 1910.119) and Risk Management Program (40 CFR Part 68) regulations may apply. These can be found at www.osha.gov and www.epa.gov.

A.1.1.1(10) It is not intended that NFPA 400 regulate compressed gases or cryogenic fluids outside of the scope of NFPA 55, *Compressed Gases and Cryogenic Fluids Code*, including LPG as regulated by NFPA 58, *Liquefied Petroleum Gas Code*, fuel gas as regulated by NFPA 54, *National Fuel Gas Code*, vehicular fuels as regulated by NFPA 52, *Vehicular Gaseous Fuel Systems Code*, or LNG as regulated by NFPA 59, *Utility LP-Gas Plant Code*. Refer to the specific exemptions referred to in 21.1.1.2.

A.1.2 The term *handling* includes onsite transportation.

A.1.8 Permit applications might require submittal of a hazardous materials management plan and a hazardous materials inventory statement in accordance with Sections 1.11 and 1.12.

A.1.11.1 See Annex C.3 for a model hazardous materials management Plan (HMMP).

A.1.12 See Annex C.2 for a model hazardous materials inventory statement (HMIS).

A.3.1 The use of parenthetical terms (solid, liquid, gas, and flammable and combustible liquid) following definitions extracted from other NFPA hazardous materials codes and standards is intended to aid the user in understanding the application of specific terms. The parenthetical terms apply only to extracted definitions.

A.3.2.1 Approved. The National Fire Protection Association does not approve, inspect, or certify any installations, procedures, equipment, or materials; nor does it approve or evaluate testing laboratories. In determining the acceptability of installations, procedures, equipment, or materials, the authority having jurisdiction may base acceptance on compliance with NFPA or other appropriate standards. In the absence of such standards, said authority may require evidence of proper installation, procedure, or use. The authority having jurisdiction may also refer to the listings or labeling practices of an organization that is concerned with product evaluations and is thus in a position to determine compliance with appropriate standards for the current production of listed items.

A.3.2.2 Authority Having Jurisdiction (AHJ). The phrase "authority having jurisdiction," or its acronym AHJ, is used in NFPA documents in a broad manner, since jurisdictions and approval agencies vary, as do their responsibilities. Where public safety is primary, the authority having jurisdiction may be a federal, state, local, or other regional department or individual such as a fire chief; fire marshal; chief of a fire prevention bureau, labor department, or health department; building official; electrical inspector; or others having statutory authority. For insurance purposes, an insurance inspection department, rating bureau, or other insurance company representative may be the authority having jurisdiction. In many circumstances, the property owner or his or her designated agent assumes the role of the authority having jurisdiction; at government installations, the commanding officer or departmental official may be the authority having jurisdiction.

A.3.2.3 Code. The decision to designate a standard as a "code" is based on such factors as the size and scope of the document, its intended use and form of adoption, and whether it contains substantial enforcement and administrative provisions.

A.3.2.5 Listed. The means for identifying listed equipment may vary for each organization concerned with product evaluation; some organizations do not recognize equipment as listed unless it is also labeled. The authority having jurisdiction should utilize the system employed by the listing organization to identify a listed product.

A.3.3.1 Absolute Pressure (Gas). Measured from this reference point, the standard atmospheric pressure at sea level is an absolute pressure of 101.3 kPa (14.7 psi). Absolute pressure in the inch-pound system is commonly denoted in terms of pounds per square inch absolute (psia). [55, 2013]

A.3.3.8 Bulk Hydrogen Compressed Gas System (Gas). The bulk system terminates at the source valve, which is the point where the gas supply, at service pressure, first enters the supply line, or at a piece of equipment that utilizes the hydrogen gas, such as a hydrogen dispenser. The containers are either stationary or movable, and the source gas for the system is stored as a compressed gas.

Bulk hydrogen compressed gas systems can include a bulk storage source, transfer piping and manifold system, compression system, and other components. The gaseous source can include a tube trailer, tube bank, or other high pressure storage vessels used to serve the piping system that transports hydrogen to the end user. Compressors can be installed downstream of the storage supply to boost the pressure of the source gas, and intermediate high pressure storage might be present. This is done where the end use requires hydrogen at a pressure higher than that of the bulk supply. In these instances, there may be intermediate storage vessels used to store the gas at elevated pressures. It is not uncommon for the bulk supply as delivered to be furnished at nominal gauge pressure of 3000 psi (20,684 kPa), and the intermediate high pressure storage to be stored at gauge pressures up to 15,000 psi (103,421 kPa). [55, 2013]

A.3.3.9 Bulk Inert Gas System (Gas). The bulk system terminates at the point where the gas supply, at service pressure, first enters the supply line. The containers are either stationary or movable, and the source gas is stored as a compressed gas or cryogenic fluid. [55, 2013]

A.3.3.10 Bulk Liquefied Hydrogen Gas System (Gas). The bulk system terminates at the source valve, which is commonly the point where the gas supply, at service pressure, first enters the supply line or a piece of equipment that utilizes the gas or the liquid, such as a hydrogen dispenser. The containers are either stationary or movable, and the source gas for the system is stored as a cryogenic fluid.

A bulk liquefied hydrogen gas system can include a liquid source where the liquid is vaporized and subsequently compressed and transferred to storage in the compressed gaseous form. It is common for liquid hydrogen systems to be equipped with vaporizers that are used to gasify the cryogen for ultimate use in the compressed state; however, there are also systems that can be used to transfer liquid in the cryogenic state. Bulk liquefied hydrogen gas systems can be either in an all-liquid state or in a hybrid system that can consist of storage containers for gas in the liquid state and other containers for gas in the compressed state. For the purposes of the application of the code, a hybrid system is viewed as a bulk liquefied hydrogen gas system. [55, 2013]

A.3.3.11 Bulk Oxygen System (Gas). The bulk oxygen system terminates at the point where oxygen at service pressure first enters the supply line. The oxygen containers are either stationary or movable, and the oxygen is stored as a compressed gas or cryogenic fluid. [55, 2013]

A.3.3.15 Combustible Dust. Dusts traditionally have been defined as a material 420 μm or smaller (capable of passing through a U.S. No. 40 standard sieve). Combustible particulates with an effective diameter of less than 420 μm should be deemed to fulfill the criterion of the definition. However, flat platelet-shaped particles, flakes, or particles of fibers with lengths that are large compared to their diameter usually do not pass through a 420 μm sieve yet still pose a deflagration hazard. Furthermore, many particulates accumulate electrostatic charge in handling, causing them to attract each other, forming agglomerates. Often agglomerates behave as if they were larger particles, yet when they are dispersed they present a significant hazard. Consequently, it can be inferred that any particle that has a surface area to volume ratio greater than that of a 420 μm diameter sphere should also be deemed can behave as a combustible dust. The determination of whether a sample of material is a combustible dust should be based on a screening test methodology such as the ASTM E 1226, *Standard Test Method for Explosibility of Combustible Dusts*, screening method. Alternatively, a standardized test method such as ASTM E 1515, *Standard Test Method for Minimum Explosible Concentration of Combustible Dusts*, or ASTM E 1226, *Standard Test Method for Explosibility of Combustible Dusts*, may be used for this determination.

Any time a combustible dust is processed or handled, a potential for deflagration exists. The degree of deflagration hazard varies, depending on the type of combustible dust and the processing methods used.

A dust explosion has the following four requirements:

(1) Combustible dust
(2) Dust dispersion in air or other oxidant at or exceeding the minimum explosible concentration (MEC)
(3) Ignition source such as an electrostatic discharge, an electric current arc, a glowing ember, a hot surface, welding slag, frictional heat, or a flame
(4) Confinement

Evaluation of the hazard of a combustible dust should be determined by the means of actual test data. Each situation should be evaluated and applicable tests selected. The following list represents the factors that are sometimes used in determining the deflagration hazard of a dust:

(1) Minimum explosible concentration (MEC)
(2) Minimum ignition energy (MIE)
(3) Particle size distribution
(4) Moisture content as received and as tested
(5) Maximum explosion pressure at optimum concentration
(6) Maximum rate of pressure rise at optimum concentration
(7) K_{St} (normalized rate of pressure rise) as defined in ASTM E 1226, *Test Method for Pressure and Rate of Pressure Rise for Combustible Dusts*
(8) Layer ignition temperature
(9) Dust cloud ignition temperature
(10) Limiting oxidant concentration (LOC) to prevent ignition
(11) Electrical volume resistivity
(12) Charge relaxation time
(13) Chargeability

[654, 2013]

A.3.3.17 Compressed Gas System. A compressed gas system can consist of a compressed gas container or containers, reactors, and appurtenances, including pumps, compressors, and connecting piping and tubing. [55, 2013]

A.3.3.19.1 Container (Flammable and Combustible Liquid). The U.S. DOT defines *non-bulk packaging* as having up to 119 gal (450 L) capacity in 49 CFR 171.8. [30, 2012]

A.3.3.19.6 Nonmetallic Container (Solid, Flammable and Combustible Liquid). Permissible nonmetallic containers for shipping Class I, Class II, and Class IIIA liquids are governed by the hazardous materials transportation regulations promulgated by the United Nations publication *Recommendations on the Transport of Dangerous Goods* and the U.S. Department of Transportation's *Hazardous Materials Regulations*. Small tanks for Class IIIB liquids are not governed by these regulations. Fiber portable tanks for Class IIIB liquids include composite designs consisting of a multi-ply cardboard box with a rigid or flexible plastic bladder. [30, 2012]

A.3.3.19.9 Nonmetallic Intermediate Bulk Container (Flammable and Combustible Liquid). Permissible nonmetallic containers for shipping Class I, Class II, and Class IIIA liquids are governed by the hazardous materials transportation regulations promulgated by the United Nations Publication *Recommendations on the Transport of Dangerous Goods* and the U.S. Department of Transportation's *Hazardous Materials Regulations*. Intermediate bulk containers for Class IIIB liquids are not governed by these regulations. Fiber portable tanks for Class IIIB liquids include composite designs consisting of a multi-ply cardboard box with a rigid or flexible plastic bladder. [30, 2012]

A.3.3.19.12.1 Stationary Tank (Gas). A stationary tank does not include a cylinder having less than 1000 lb (453.5 kg) water capacity.

A.3.3.19.13.1 Atmospheric Tank (Flammable and Combustible Liquid). Older-style flat roof tanks were designed to operate at pressures of atmospheric through a gauge pressure of 0.5 psi measured at the top of the tank. This limitation was established to avoid continuous stress on the roof plates of the tank. [30, 2012]

A.3.3.19.14 Portable Tank (Flammable and Combustible Liquid). The term *portable tank* does not include an intermediate bulk container (IBC). The standards of construction for portable tanks are different from those used for the construction of containers and IBCs.

A.3.3.19.14.1 Portable Tank (Gas). A portable tank (gas) does not include any cylinder having less than 1000 lb (453.5 kg) water capacity, cargo tank, tank car tank, or trailer carrying cylinders of over 1000 lb (453.5 kg) water capacity.

A.3.3.19.14.2 Nonmetallic Portable Tank (Flammable and Combustible Liquid). Permissible nonmetallic portable tanks for shipping Class I, Class II, and Class IIIA liquids are governed by the hazardous materials transportation regulations promulgated by the United Nations publication *Recommendations on the Transport of Dangerous Goods* and the U.S. Department of Transportation's *Hazardous Materials Regulations*. Small tanks for Class IIIB liquids are governed by either UN or DOT hazardous materials regulations. Fiber portable tanks for Class IIIB liquids include composite designs consisting of a multi-ply cardboard box with a rigid or flexible plastic bladder [30, 2012]

A.3.3.19.15 Pressure Vessel. Pressure vessels of any type can be subject to additional regulations imposed by various states or other legal jurisdictions. Users should be aware that compliance with DOT or ASME requirements might not satisfy all of the required regulations for the location in which the vessel is to be installed or used. Pressure vessels may be constructed to meet requirements of other regulatory agencies, including regulations for Transport, Canada (TC) or various ANSI standards that may be applicable for specific uses. [55, 2013]

A.3.3.19.16 Cylinder (Gas). The term *cylinder (gas)* does not include a portable tank, tank car, multi-unit tank car tank, or cargo tank.

A.3.3.19.16.1 Cylinder Pack (Gas) The frame system is allowed to be on skids or wheels to permit movement. [55, 2013]

A.3.3.19.17.1 Tube Trailer (Gas). The characteristic internal water volume of individual tubular cylinders ranges from 43 ft^3 (1218 L) to 93 ft^3 (2632 L) or a water capacity of 2686 lb (1218 kg) to 5803 lb (2632 kg).

A.3.3.19.18 ISO Module. The frame of an ISO container module and its corner casings are specifically designed and dimensioned to be used in multimodal transportation service on container ships, special highway chassis, and container on flatcar railroad equipment.

A.3.3.19.19 Safety Can (Liquid). Safety cans listed to ANSI/UL 30, *Standard for Metal Safety Cans*, are limited to 5 U.S. gal (19 L). ANSI/UL 1313, *Standard for Non-Metallic Safety Cans or Petroleum Products*, allows or capacities up to 5 Imperial gal (23 L). [30, 2012]

A.3.3.23 Cylinder (Gas). The term *cylinder (gas)* does not include a portable tank, multiunit tank car tank, cargo tank, or tank car.

A.3.3.26 Cylinder Pack (Gas). *Six-packs* and *twelve-packs* are terms used to further define cylinder packs with a specific number of cylinders involved. The characteristic internal water volume of individual cylinders in a cylinder pack ranges from 1.52 ft^3 to 1.76 ft^3 (43 L to 50 L) or a water capacity of from 95 lb to 110 lb (43 kg to 50 kg). [55, 2013]

A.3.3.36 Exhausted Enclosure (Gas). Such enclosures include laboratory hoods, exhaust fume hoods, and similar appliances and equipment used to retain and exhaust locally the gases, fumes, vapors, and mists that could be released. Rooms or areas provided with general ventilation, in and of themselves, are not exhausted enclosures. [55, 2013]

A.3.3.37 Explosion Control (Gas). NFPA 68, *Standard on Explosion Protection by Deflagration Venting*, provides guidance on the use of deflagration venting systems for use in buildings and other enclosures. The primary purpose of a venting system is to relieve the overpressure produced in an explosion to limit the potential damage to the building where the explosion occurs. Although some structural damage can be anticipated, the use of relief venting is expected to prevent massive building failure and collapse. In cases where detonation is probable, venting is often used in conjunction with barricade construction where the pressure-resistant portions of the building have been constructed to resist the pressures anticipated should an explosive event occur. Design of barricade systems is highly specialized, and the subject of military standards applicable to the subject. NFPA 69, *Standard on Explosion Prevention Systems*, provides guidance on the use of suppression, ventilation systems, and the limiting of oxidants as a means to prevent the occurrence of an explosion. When relief vents are to be used as a means to provide explosion relief, the fundamental requirements of *NFPA 5000, Building Construction and Safety Code*, for structural elements including snow, wind, and seismic events should be considered. In some instances, the requirements for wind resistance can impose more rigorous requirements on the relief vents than required by the engineering analysis used to determine the relief pressure. In such cases, users must demonstrate that the relief vents will not become airborne or release in such a manner as to create secondary hazards within or external to the building in which they are installed. Specific designs may require approval by the AHJ. [55, 2013]

A.3.3.39 Explosive. Explosives in Class 1 are divided into six divisions as follows:

(1) Division 1.1 consists of explosives that have a mass explosion hazard. A mass explosion is one that affects almost the entire load instantaneously.
(2) Division 1.2 consists of explosives that have a projection hazard but not a mass explosion hazard.
(3) Division 1.3 consists of explosives that have a fire hazard and either a minor blast hazard or a minor projection hazard, or both, but not a mass explosion hazard.
(4) Division 1.4 consists of explosives that present a minor explosion hazard. The explosive effects are largely confined to the package, and no projection of fragments of appreciable size or range is to be expected. An external fire must not cause virtually instantaneous explosion of almost the entire contents of the package.
(5) Division 1.5 consists of very insensitive explosives. (The probability of transition from burning to detonation is greater when large quantities are transported in a vessel.) This division is comprised of substances that have a mass explosion hazard but are so insensitive that there is very little probability of initiation or of transition from burning to detonation under normal conditions of transport.

(6) Division 1.6 consists of extremely insensitive articles that do not have a mass explosion hazard. (The risk from articles of Division 1.6 is limited to the explosion of a single device.) This division is comprised of articles that contain only extremely insensitive detonating substances and that demonstrate a negligible probability of accidental initiation or propagation.

A list of explosives determined to be within the scope of Title 18, United States Code, Chapter 40, is published at least annually by the Bureau of Alcohol, Tobacco, Firearms and Explosives (ATF), U.S. Department of Justice. The classification of explosives described in the *Hazardous Materials Regulations* of the U.S. DOT is provided in Annex E. These regulations were revised in 1991. The term includes, but is not limited to, dynamite, black powder, pellet powder, initiating explosives, detonators, safety fuses, squibs, detonating cord, igniter cord, and igniters. The term includes any material determined to be within the scope of Title 18, United States Code, Chapter 40, and also includes any material classified as an explosive by the U.S. DOT in 49 CFR, 100–199.

A.3.3.40 Explosive Decomposition. The term includes both deflagration and detonation.

A.3.3.41 Explosive Reaction. For further information on venting explosive reactions, see NFPA 68, *Standard on Explosion Protection by Deflagration Venting*.

A.3.3.44 Flammable Liquid (Class I). Flammable liquids do not include compressed gases or cryogenic fluids. Flammable liquids are further categorized into a group known as Class I liquids. The Class I category is subdivided as follows:

(1) Class I-A liquids are those having a flash point below 73°F (22.8°C) and a boiling point below 100°F (37.8°C).
(2) Class I-B liquids are those having a flash point below 73°F (22.8°C) and a boiling point at or above 100°F (37.8°C).
(3) Class I-C liquids are those having a flash point at or above 73°F (22.8°C) and below 100°F (37.8°C).

A.3.3.45 Flammable Solid. Flammable solids include finely divided solid materials that, when dispersed in air as a cloud, could be ignited and cause an explosion.

A.3.3.47.1 Compressed Gas (Gas). The states of a compressed gas are categorized as follows:

(1) Nonliquefied compressed gases are gases, other than those in solution, that are in a packaging under the charged pressure and are entirely gaseous at a temperature of 20°C (68°F).
(2) Liquefied compressed gases are gases that, in a packaging under the charged pressure, are partially liquid at a temperature of 20°C (68°F). Cryogenic fluids represent a transient state of a gas that is created through the use of refrigeration. Cryogenic fluids cannot exist in the liquid form or partial liquid form at temperatures of 20°C (68°F), hence, they are not "compressed gases" as defined.
(3) Compressed gases in solution are nonliquefied gases that are dissolved in a solvent.
(4) Compressed gas mixtures consist of a mixture of two or more compressed gases contained in a packaging, the hazard properties of which are represented by the properties of the mixture as a whole.

[55, 2013]

A.3.3.47.7 Irritant Gas (Gas). A chemical is a skin irritant if, when tested on the intact skin of albino rabbits by the methods of 16 CFR 1500.41, for an exposure of 4 or more hours or by other appropriate techniques, it results in an empirical score of 5 or more. A chemical is classified as an eye irritant if so determined under the procedure listed in 16 CFR 1500.42, or other appropriate techniques. [**55,** 2013]

A.3.3.47.9 Other Gas (Gas). A gas classified as an "Other Gas" might be a nonflammable gas or an inert gas. [**55,** 2013]

A.3.3.47.13 Unstable Reactive Gas (Gas). Unstable reactive materials are subdivided into five classifications. Class 4 materials are materials that in themselves are readily capable of detonation or explosive decomposition or explosive reaction at normal temperatures and pressures. They include the following:

(1) Materials that are sensitive to localized thermal or mechanical shock at normal temperatures and pressures
(2) Materials that have an instantaneous power density (product of heat of reaction and reaction rate) at 482°F (250°C) of 1000 W/mL or greater

Class 3 materials are materials that in themselves are capable of detonation or explosive decomposition or explosive reaction but require a strong initiating source or heat under confinement before initiation.

Class 3 materials include the following:

(1) Materials that have an instantaneous power density (product of heat of reaction and reaction rate) at 482°F (250°C) at or above 100 W/mL and below 1000 W/mL
(2) Materials that are sensitive to thermal or mechanical shock at elevated temperatures and pressures
(3) Materials that react explosively with water without requiring heat or confinement

Class 2 materials are materials that readily undergo violent chemical change at elevated temperatures and pressures, including the following:

(1) Materials that have an instantaneous power density (product of heat of reaction and reaction rate) at 482°F (250°C) at or above 10 W/mL and below 100 W/mL
(2) Materials that react violently with water or form potentially explosive mixtures with water

Class 1 materials are materials that in themselves are normally stable but that can become unstable at elevated temperatures and pressures, including the following:

(1) Materials that have an instantaneous power density (product of heat of reaction and reaction rate) at 482°F (250°C) at or above 0.01 W/mL and below 10 W/mL
(2) Materials that react vigorously with water, but not violently
(3) Materials that change or decompose on exposure to air, light, or moisture

Class 0 materials are materials that in themselves are normally stable, even under fire conditions, including the following:

(1) Materials that have an instantaneous power density (product of heat of reaction and reaction rate) at 482°F (250°C) below 0.01 W/mL
(2) Materials that do not react with water
(3) Materials that do not exhibit an exotherm at temperatures less than or equal to 932°F (500°C) when tested by differential scanning calorimetry
[**55,** 2013]

A.3.3.48 Gas Cabinet (Gas). Doors and access ports for exchanging cylinders and accessing pressure-regulating controls are permitted to be included as part of a gas cabinet. [**55,** 2013]

A.3.3.50 Gas Room (Gas). Gas rooms must be constructed and utilized in accordance with 21.2.4. [**55,** 2013]

A.3.3.51 Gaseous Hydrogen System (Gas). The system includes stationary or portable containers, pressure regulators, pressure-relief devices, manifolds, interconnecting piping, and controls as required.

The gaseous hydrogen system terminates at the point where hydrogen at service pressure first enters the distribution piping. [**55,** 2013]

A.3.3.53 Hazard Rating (Gas). The criteria for hazard rating are as defined in NFPA 704, *Standard System for the Identification of the Hazards of Materials for Emergency Response.* [**55,** 2013]

A.3.3.56 Immediately Dangerous to Life and Health (IDLH) (Gas). This level is established by the National Institute for Occupational Safety and Health (NIOSH). If adequate data do not exist for precise establishment of IDLH data, an independent certified industrial hygienist, industrial toxicologist, or appropriate regulatory agency should make such determination. [**55,** 2013]

A.3.3.57 ISO Module (Gas). The characteristic internal water volume of individual tubular cylinders is 43 ft^3 (1218 L) or a water capacity of 2686 lb (1218 kg). The frame of an ISO container module and its corner castings are specially designed and dimensioned to be used in multi-modal transportation service on container ships, special highway chassis, and container-on-flatcar railroad equipment. [**55,** 2013]

A.3.3.58.2 Permissible Exposure Limit (PEL) (Gas). The maximum permitted time-weighted average exposures to be utilized are those published in 29 CFR 1910.1000. [**55,** 2013]

A.3.3.58.3 Short-Term Exposure Limit (STEL) (Gas). STEL limits are published in 29 CFR 1910.1000. [**55,** 2013]

A.3.3.59 Liquefied Hydrogen System (Gas). The system includes stationary or portable containers, including unconnected reserves, pressure regulators, pressure relief devices, manifolds, interconnecting piping, and controls as required.

The system originates at the storage container fill connection and terminates at the point where hydrogen at service pressure first enters the supply line. [**55,** 2013]

A.3.3.61.2 Corrosive Material. A chemical is considered to be corrosive if it destroys or irreversibly changes the structure of the tissue at the site of contact within a specified period of time using one of the *in vivo* or *in vitro* OECD test methods authorized in 49 CFR Part 173.137. For purposes of this code, this term does not refer to action on inanimate surfaces (e.g., steel or aluminum). Available testing data produced prior to September 30, 1995 from the test method in Appendix A to 49 CFR Part 173 in effect on October 1, 1994 can also be used to determine the corrosivity of a material.

A.3.3.61.4 Hazardous Material. Hazardous wastes might or might not be classified as hazardous materials. Management and disposal of hazardous waste is regulated by the EPA under the Resource Conservation and Recovery Act (RCRA). EPA requires wastes identified as hazardous to be handled, stored, treated, and disposed of according to the stipulations of the RCRA hazardous waste program in 40 CFR 260 to 265 and 40 CFR 266 to 299.

A.3.3.61.5 Incompatible Material. Information on incompatible materials can be found in material safety data sheets (MSDS) or manufacturers' product bulletins.

A.3.3.61.6 Limited-Combustible (Material). Material subject to increase in combustibility or flame spread index beyond the limits herein established through the effects of age, moisture, or other atmospheric condition is considered combustible. See NFPA 259, *Standard Test Method for Potential Heat of Building Materials*, and NFPA 220, *Standard on Types of Building Construction*.

A.3.3.61.7 Noncombustible Material. See NFPA 220, *Standard on Types of Building Construction*.

Materials that are reported as having passed ASTM E 136-96a, *Standard Test Method for Behavior of Materials in a Vertical Tube Furnace at 750 Degrees C*, are considered noncombustible materials. For the purposes of this code, noncombustible construction and limited-combustible construction are both considered to be noncombustible.

A.3.3.61.9 Toxic Material. While categorization is basically simple in application, the degree of hazard depends on many variables that should be carefully considered individually and in combination. Some examples include the following:

(1) Materials wherein the toxic component or mixtures thereof are inextricably bound and cannot be released so there is little or no potential for exposure
(2) Nonfriable solid hazardous materials existing in product forms and in the demonstrated absence of inhalable particles that might not present the same inhalation hazard as the chemical components existing in a friable state
(3) Mixtures of toxic materials with ordinary materials, such as water, that might not warrant classification as toxic

Any hazard evaluation that is required for the precise categorization of toxic material is required to be performed by experienced, technically competent persons.

A.3.3.61.9.1 Highly Toxic Material. While categorization is basically simple in application, the degree of hazard depends on many variables that should be carefully considered individually and in combination. Some examples include the following:

(1) Materials wherein the highly toxic component or mixtures thereof are inextricably bound and cannot be released so there is little or no potential for exposure
(2) Nonfriable solid hazardous materials existing in product forms and in the demonstrated absence of inhalable particles that might not present the same inhalation hazard as the chemical components existing in a friable state
(3) Mixtures of highly toxic materials with ordinary materials, such as water, that might not warrant classification as highly toxic

Any hazard evaluation that is required for the precise categorization of highly toxic material is required to be performed by experienced, technically competent persons.

A.3.3.61.10 Unstable (Reactive) Material. Unstable (reactive) material is classified as follows:

(1) Class 4 unstable (reactive) materials are those that, in themselves, are readily capable of detonation, explosive decomposition, or explosive reaction at normal temperatures and pressures and include, among others, materials that are sensitive to localized thermal or mechanical shock at normal temperatures and pressures.
(2) Class 3 unstable (reactive) materials are those that, in themselves, are capable of detonation, explosive decomposition, or explosive reaction, but that require a strong initiating source or that must be heated under confinement before initiation, and include, among others, materials that are sensitive to thermal or mechanical shock at elevated temperatures and pressures.
(3) Class 2 unstable (reactive) materials are those that readily undergo violent chemical change at elevated temperatures and pressures and include, among others, materials that exhibit an exotherm at temperatures less than or equal to 30°F (−1°C) when tested by differential scanning calorimetry.
(4) Class 1 unstable (reactive) materials are those that, in themselves, are normally stable, but that can become unstable at elevated temperatures and pressures and include among others, materials that change or decompose on exposure to air, light, or moisture and that exhibit an exotherm at temperatures greater than 30°F (−1°C), but less than or equal to 57°F (14°C), when tested by differential scanning calorimetry.

A.3.3.61.10.1 Class 1 Unstable (Reactive). Materials that have an instantaneous power density (product of heat of reaction and reaction rate) at 482°F (250°C) at or above 0.01 W/mL and below 10 W/mL. [**704:** Table 7.2]

A.3.3.61.10.2 Class 2 Unstable (Reactive). Materials that have an instantaneous power density (product of heat of reaction and reaction rate) at 482°F (250°C) at or above 10 W/mL and below 100 w/mL. [**704:** Table 7.2]

A.3.3.61.10.3 Class 3 Unstable (Reactive). Materials that are sensitive to thermal and mechanical shock elevated temperatures and pressures. Materials that have an instantaneous power density (product of heat of reaction and reaction rate) at 482°F (250°C) at or above 100 W/mL and below 1000 W/mL. [**704:** Table 7.2]

A.3.3.61.10.4 Class 4 Unstable (Reactive). Materials that are sensitive to localized thermal or mechanical shock at normal temperatures and pressures. Materials that have an instantaneous power density (product of heat of reaction and reaction rate) at 482°F (250°C) of 1000 W/mL or greater.

A.3.3.61.11 Water-Reactive Material. *Class 1 Water-Reactive Materials.* Materials whose heat of mixing is at or above 30 cal/g and less than 100 cal/g. *Class 2 Water-Reactive Materials.* Materials whose heat of mixing is at or above 100 cal /g and less than 600 cal/g. *Class 3 Water-Reactive Materials.* Materials whose heat of mixing is greater or equal to 600 cal/g. [**704:** Table F.2]

A.3.3.63 Maximum Allowable Quantity Per Control Area (MAQ). See A.5.1.

A.3.3.65 Mobile Supply Unit (Gas). Examples include ISO modules, tube trailers, and cylinder packs. [55, 2013]

A.3.3.66 Nesting (Gas). A wall or a railing could be used to provide a means of solid support.

A.3.3.67 Normal Temperature and Pressure (NTP) (Gas). There are different definitions of normal conditions. The normal conditions defined here are the ones most commonly used in the compressed gas and cryogenic fluid industry. [55, 2013]

A.3.3.68.1 Assembly Occupancy. Assembly occupancies might include the following:

(1) Armories
(2) Assembly halls

(3) Auditoriums
(4) Bowling lanes
(5) Club rooms
(6) College and university classrooms, 50 persons and over
(7) Conference rooms
(8) Courtrooms
(9) Dance halls
(10) Drinking establishments
(11) Exhibition halls
(12) Gymnasiums
(13) Libraries
(14) Mortuary chapels
(15) Motion picture theaters
(16) Museums
(17) Passenger stations and terminals of air, surface, underground, and marine public transportation facilities
(18) Places of religious worship
(19) Pool rooms
(20) Recreation piers
(21) Restaurants
(22) Skating rinks
(23) Special amusement buildings, regardless of occupant load
(24) Theaters

Assembly occupancies are characterized by the presence or potential presence of crowds with attendant panic hazard in case of fire or other emergency. They are generally open or occasionally open to the public, and the occupants, who are present voluntarily, are not ordinarily subject to discipline or control. Such buildings are ordinarily occupied by able-bodied persons and are not used for sleeping purposes. Special conference rooms, snack areas, and other areas incidental to, and under the control of, the management of other occupancies, such as offices, fall under the 50-person limitation.

Restaurants and drinking establishments with an occupant load of fewer than 50 persons should be classified as mercantile occupancies.

A.3.3.68.2 Business Occupancy. Business occupancies include the following:

(1) Air traffic control towers (ATCTs)
(2) City halls
(3) College and university instructional buildings, classrooms under 50 persons, and instructional laboratories
(4) Courthouses
(5) Dentists' offices
(6) Doctors' offices
(7) General offices
(8) Outpatient clinics (ambulatory)
(9) Town halls

Doctors' and dentists' offices are included, unless of such character as to be classified as ambulatory health care occupancies. (See 3.3.68.6.1.)

Birth centers should be classified as business occupancies if they are occupied by fewer than four patients, not including infants, at any one time; do not provide sleeping facilities for four or more occupants; and do not provide treatment procedures that render four or more patients, not including infants, incapable of self-preservation at any one time. For birth centers occupied by patients not meeting these parameters, see A.3.3.68.6 or A.3.3.68.6.1, as appropriate.

Service facilities common to city office buildings, such as newsstands, lunch counters serving fewer than 50 persons, barber shops, and beauty parlors are included in the business occupancy group.

City halls, town halls, and courthouses are included in this occupancy group, insofar as their principal function is the transaction of public business and the keeping of books and records. Insofar as they are used for assembly purposes, they are classified as assembly occupancies.

A.3.3.68.3 Day-Care Occupancy. Day-care occupancies include the following:

(1) Adult day-care occupancies, except where part of a health care occupancy
(2) Child day-care occupancies
(3) Day-care homes
(4) Kindergarten classes that are incidental to a child day-care occupancy
(5) Nursery schools

In areas where public schools offer only half-day kindergarten programs, many child day-care occupancies offer state-approved kindergarten classes for children who need full-day care. Because these classes are normally incidental to the day-care occupancy, the requirements of the day-care occupancy should be followed.

A.3.3.68.4 Detention and Correctional Occupancy. Detention and correctional occupancies include the following:

(1) Adult and juvenile substance abuse centers
(2) Adult and juvenile work camps
(3) Adult community residential centers
(4) Adult correctional institutions
(5) Adult local detention facilities
(6) Juvenile community residential centers
(7) Juvenile detention facilities
(8) Juvenile training schools

A.3.3.68.5 Educational Occupancy. Educational occupancies include the following:

(1) Academies
(2) Kindergartens
(3) Schools

An educational occupancy is distinguished from an assembly occupancy in that the same occupants are regularly present.

A.3.3.68.6 Health Care Occupancy. Health care occupancies include the following:

(1) Hospitals
(2) Limited care facilities
(3) Nursing homes

Occupants of health care occupancies typically have physical or mental illness, disease, or infirmity. They also include infants, convalescents, or infirm aged persons.

A.3.3.68.6.1 Ambulatory Health Care Occupancy. It is not the intent that occupants be considered to be incapable of self-preservation just because they are in a wheelchair or use assistive walking devices, such as a cane, a walker, or crutches. Rather it is the intent to address emergency care centers that receive patients who have been rendered incapable of self-preservation due to the emergency, such as being rendered unconscious as a result of an accident or being unable to move due to sudden illness.

A.3.3.68.7 Industrial Occupancy. Industrial occupancies include the following:

(1) Drycleaning plants
(2) Factories of all kinds
(3) Food processing plants
(4) Gas plants
(5) Hangars (for servicing/maintenance)
(6) Laundries
(7) Power plants
(8) Pumping stations
(9) Refineries
(10) Sawmills
(11) Telephone exchanges

In evaluating the appropriate classification of laboratories, the AHJ should treat each case individually, based on the extent and nature of the associated hazards. Some laboratories are classified as occupancies other than industrial; for example, a physical therapy laboratory or a computer laboratory.

A.3.3.68.7.1 General Industrial Occupancy. General industrial occupancies include multistory buildings where floors are occupied by different tenants or buildings suitable for such occupancy and, therefore, are subject to possible use for types of industrial processes with a high density of employee population.

A.3.3.68.8 Mercantile Occupancy. Mercantile occupancies include the following:

(1) Auction rooms
(2) Department stores
(3) Drugstores
(4) Restaurants with fewer than 50 persons
(5) Shopping centers
(6) Supermarkets

Office, storage, and service facilities incidental to the sale of merchandise and located in the same building should be considered part of the mercantile occupancy classification.

A.3.3.68.10 Multiple Occupancy. *Multiple occupancy* describes a situation where more than one occupancy classification exists in a building. The terms *mixed occupancy* and *separated occupancy* refer to subdivisions of multiple occupancies, and include their own unique protection requirements.

A.3.3.68.11 Residential Board and Care Occupancy. The following are examples of facilities that are classified as residential board and care occupancies:

(1) Group housing arrangement for physically or mentally handicapped persons who normally attend school in the community, attend worship in the community, or otherwise use community facilities
(2) Group housing arrangement for physically or mentally handicapped persons who are undergoing training in preparation for independent living, for paid employment, or for other normal community activities
(3) Group housing arrangement for the elderly that provides personal care services but that does not provide nursing care
(4) Facilities for social rehabilitation, alcoholism, drug abuse, or mental health problems that contain a group housing arrangement and that provide personal care services but do not provide acute care
(5) Assisted living facilities
(6) Other group housing arrangements that provide personal care services but not nursing care

A.3.3.68.12 Residential Occupancy. Residential occupancies are treated as separate occupancies in this code as follows:

(1) One- and two-family dwellings
(2) Lodging or rooming houses
(3) Hotels, motels, and dormitories
(4) Apartment buildings

A.3.3.68.14 Storage Occupancy. Storage occupancies include the following:

(1) Barns
(2) Bulk oil storage
(3) Cold storage
(4) Freight terminals
(5) Grain elevators
(6) Hangars (for storage only)
(7) Parking structures
(8) Stables
(9) Truck and marine terminals
(10) Warehouses

Storage occupancies are characterized by the presence of relatively small numbers of persons in proportion to the area.

A.3.3.70 Organic Peroxide Formulation. Terms such as *accelerator, catalyst, initiator, curing agent,* and so forth, are sometimes used to describe organic peroxide formulations. These terms are misleading because they can also refer to materials that are not or do not contain organic peroxides, some of which might present increased hazard when mixed with organic peroxides.

A.3.3.72 Oxidizer. Examples of other oxidizing gases include bromine, chlorine, and fluorine.

The classification of oxidizers is based on the technical committee's evaluation of available scientific and technical data, actual experience, and its considered opinion. Classification refers to the pure oxidizer. Gross contamination can cause oxidizers of all classes to undergo exothermic or explosive reaction, particularly if they also are subjected to confinement and heating. *(See G.3.2 through G.3.4 for oxidizer classifications.)*

The classification of oxidizers is based on the degree to which an oxidizing chemical increases, if at all, the burning rate of available combustible fuels. Factors that can influence the burning rate of oxidizers are concentration, particle size, product form, product packaging, and packaging configuration. Examples of Class 1, 2, 3, and 4 chemical oxidizers are listed in Annex G.3. The definition of the current classes and the oxidizers listed as typical of each Class in Annex G.3 are based on the technical committee's evaluation of available data, experience, and results of tests done by the Bureau of Mines and GE Research in the 1970s.

The definition of Class 1, 2, 3, and 4 oxidizers is subjective. Currently, there is no bench scale test method that adequately measures the burning rate of oxidizers for large-scale storage. The UN's *Recommendations on the Transport of Dangerous Goods* includes a bench scale test method (Test O.1) to assign packing groups to solid oxidizers. Thirty grams (1.06 oz) of a mixture of the test substance and cellulose powder is ignited with a Nichrome wire. The time from ignition to the end of visible burning of the mixture is compared with the burning time of several different mixtures of potassium bromate (Class 3) and cellulose powder. The test does not characterize chemical reactivity or thermal stability. The test is not representative of packaged oxidizers. The determination of burning time is strongly dependent on test conditions, particle size, and the test operator's perception of the end of active burning.

The Fire Protection Research Foundation (FPRF) published *National Oxidizing Pool Chemicals Storage Fire Test Project* in August 1998. The technical report includes literature abstracts, large-scale calorimetry test data, and intermediate scale rack storage tests. The peak rate of heat release of packaging and packaged oxidizers trichloroisocyanuric acid (Trichlor, Class 1) and calcium hypochlorite (available chlorine >68%, Class 3) are summarized in Table A.3.3.72.

Table A.3.3.72 Results of Large-Scale Calorimetry Tests with Packaging and Packaged Oxidizers on Wood Pallets

Oxidizer and Packaging	Total Weight with Pallets (lb)	Peak Convective HRR (kW)
40 cartons of empty HDPE 2 lb capacity containers	300	1736
40 cartons of pea gravel filled HDPE 2 lb capacity containers	1631	464
40 cartons of granular Trichlor in HDPE 2 lb capacity containers	1891	649
40 cartons of tablet form Trichlor in HDPE 2 lb capacity containers	1882	877
48 cartons of granular calcium hypochlorite in 1 lb capacity Surlin (plastic) bags	1468	6696
36 cartons of granular calcium hypochlorite in HDPE 1 lb capacity containers	1452	>16184

For SI units, 1 lb = 0.45 kg.

Source: FPRF, *National Oxidizing Pool Chemicals Storage Fire Test Project*, Aug. 1998.

The Class 1 Trichlor did not increase the burning rate of the combustible packaging. Class 3 calcium hypochlorite (available chlorine >68%) caused a severe increase in the burning rate of the combustible packaging.

In 2006, the FPRF published a report on the *Development of an Enhanced Hazard Classification System for Oxidizers*. The report includes a review of fire losses, historical test data, and current test methods for oxidizing materials used by transportation and environmental regulatory agencies. Two classification schemes with multiple test methods and performance-based criteria were proposed to distinguish between Class 1, 2, 3, and 4 oxidizers in a storage situation.

Future FPRF effort is proposed to define an appropriate bench scale test, validated by medium scale free burn testing, for oxidizers. The goal of the enhanced classification system would be to prescribe tests and use performance based criteria to define the different classes of oxidizers based on the degree of burning rate enhancement, chemical reactivity, and thermal stability.

The FPRF completed a project that resulted in the development of a bench-scale test, validated by intermediate scale testing, for solid oxidizers. An enhanced classification system with prescribed tests and performance-based criteria to define the different classes of oxidizers based on the degree of burning rate enhancement was developed. [Buc, Elizabeth C., *Oxidizer Classification Research Project: Tests and Criteria*, Fire Protection Research Foundation, November 2009]

A.3.3.75 Protection Level. NFPA uses the concept of protection levels in a manner that is analogous to Group H occupancies in other model codes. Although NFPA 1, *Fire Code*, and *NFPA 5000, Building Construction and Safety Code*, do not have unique occupancy classifications for occupancies containing hazardous materials, Protection Levels 1 to 5 in NFPA codes and standards reflect increased building safety requirements that are applicable to occupancies containing hazardous materials, which generally correlate to the Group H, Division 1 to 5 occupancy classifications in other codes.

A.3.3.77 Secondary Containment. Examples of secondary containment include dikes, curbing, remote impoundment, and double-walled tanks.

A.3.3.81 Storage (Hazardous Material). Storage can include transient storage, which is intended to describe those materials being staged for transport. They are called transient while they are in the manufacturing area because they are not in their storage location. In the manufacturing location, finished goods can be found in a packaged state where they can be further palletized or otherwise arranged or collected awaiting transportation.

A.3.3.83 Tank. Pipes and piping systems are not considered to be tanks.

A.3.3.83.2 Portable Tank. A portable tank does not include any cylinder having less than 453.5 kg (1000 lb) water capacity, cargo tank, tank car tank, or trailers carrying cylinders of over 453.5 kg (1000 lb) water capacity. [55, 2013]

A.3.3.83.3 Stationary Tank. A stationary tank does not include a cylinder having less than 453.5 kg (1000 lb) water capacity. [55, 2013]

A.3.3.86 Tube Trailer (Gas). The characteristic internal water volume of individual tubular cylinders ranges from 43 ft^3 (1218 L) to 93 ft^3 (2632 L) or a water capacity of 2686 lb (1218 kg) to 5803 lb (2632 kg). [55, 2013]

A.3.3.87 Use. Examples of use include, but are not limited to, blending, mixing, reacting, distillation, heating or cooling, pumping, compressing, drying, screening, filling, loading and unloading, repackaging, scrubbing, absorbing, neutralizing, and incineration.

A.3.3.87.1 Closed System Use. Examples of closed systems for solids and liquids include reaction process operations and product conveyed through a piping system into a closed vessel, system, or piece of equipment.

A.3.3.87.2 Open System Use. Examples of open systems for solids and liquids include dispensing from or into open beakers or containers, and dip tank and plating tank operations.

A.3.4.7 Exposure Fire. An exposure fire usually refers to a fire that starts outside a building, such as a wildlands fire or vehicle fire, and that, consequently, exposes the building to a fire. [*101:* A.3.3.75]

A.3.4.8 Fire Model. Due to the complex nature of the principles involved, models are often packaged as computer software. Any relevant input data, assumptions, and limitations needed to properly implement the model will be attached to the fire models. [*101:* A.3.3.86]

A.3.4.9 Fire Scenario. A fire scenario defines the conditions under which a proposed design is expected to meet the fire safety goals. Factors typically include fuel characteristics, ignition sources, ventilation, building characteristics, and occupant locations and characteristics. The term *fire scenario* includes more than the characteristics of the fire itself but excludes design specifications and any characteristics that do not vary from one fire to another; the latter are called assumptions. The term is used here to mean only those specifications required to calculate the fire's development and effects, but, in other contexts, the term might be used to mean both the initial specifications and the subsequent development and effects (that is, a complete description of fire from conditions prior to ignition to conditions following extinguishment). [*101:*A.3.3.90]

A.3.4.10 Fuel Load. Fuel load includes interior finish and trim.

A.3.4.13 Performance Criteria. Performance criteria are stated in engineering terms. Engineering terms include temperatures, radiant heat flux, and levels of exposure to fire products. Performance criteria provide threshold values used to evaluate a proposed design.

A.3.4.14 Proposed Design. The design team might develop a number of trial designs that will be evaluated to determine whether they meet the performance criteria. One of the trial designs will be selected from those that meet the performance criteria for submission to the AHJ as the proposed design.

The proposed design is not necessarily limited to fire protection systems and building features. It also includes any component of the proposed design that is installed, established, or maintained for the purpose of life safety, without which the proposed design could fail to achieve specified performance criteria. Therefore, the proposed design often includes emergency procedures and organizational structures that are needed to meet the performance criteria specified for the proposed design.

A.4.1 The categorization and classification of hazardous materials enables the code user to determine the applicability of requirements based on hazard category and class related to the physical and health hazards of materials. The current definitions found in Chapter 3 have been developed using a compilation of criteria found in NFPA codes and standards, requirements of the U.S. Department of Transportation, and in some cases definitions established by OSHA in 29 CFR.

A system known as Globally Harmonized System of Classification and Labeling of Chemicals (GHS) has been developed based on standards for classification published by the United Nations (UN) Subcommittee of Experts on the GHS. The United States continues its efforts to incorporate the GHS in its federal regulatory scheme. OSHA plans to issue a final rule to harmonize its Hazard Communication Standard (29 CFR 1910.1200) with the GHS in August 2011.

It is anticipated by the Committee that over time, the GHS will be reviewed for applicability and possible integration into the regulatory scheme developed in NFPA 400 for hazardous materials storage, handling, and use. The evolution of this system of classification will be facilitated by the changes associated with classification, labeling, and Safety Data Sheets. It is not anticipated that the GHS will be fully implemented immediately within NFPA 400, recognizing the historical basis that exists for some of the classifications of materials, such as flammable and combustible liquids.

A.4.4 Where a conflict exists between applicable requirements, an analysis should be made and the proper applicable requirement should be implemented or conformed to subject to the approval of the AHJ.

A.4.5 The safe handling, collection, and disposal of hazardous waste can be accomplished only if the physical, chemical, and hazardous properties of its components are known and that information is properly applied. The categorization of a material as waste is normally under the purview of the user. In some cases the waste might be contaminated or "off spec" material, or material where the concentration of the hazardous components has been diluted. In other cases the waste might consist of cleaning materials that have become contaminated with a hazardous material.

The classifiers of waste are cautioned that the classification of hazardous waste under the requirements of the Environmental Protection Agency (EPA) or Department of Transportation (DOT) for labeling required for shipping purposes might not correspond to the system of classification incorporated into Section 4.1. In addition, some judgment is needed to apply the code in circumstances where the waste material is not in a form that is normally encountered when the hazardous material employed is in its virgin state. For example, a material that might not have been hazardous in its pure form might become hazardous when it becomes contaminated as use occurs. A tank of water used for rinsing parts on a plating line will eventually become contaminated by the materials that are being rinsed from parts as they travel through the line. If the concentration of the material being rinsed from parts becomes high enough, the content of hazardous materials in the rinse tank might be present in a concentration sufficient enough to cause the waste rinse water to be classified as hazardous. See Section B.5 for examples on the classification of dilute solutions of common corrosive materials.

In many cases the waste material could be a mixture of materials that must be classified in accordance with the requirements of Section 4.3.

A.4.5.1 Just because a decision has been made that a material no longer has a useful life does not exempt the material from compliance with the applicable provisions of the code. Materials that have been classified as hazardous based on the system of classification used in Section 4.1 are required to comply with applicable sections of the code in the same manner as may be required for nonwaste material.

A.5.1 This chapter introduces the concepts of control areas and MAQ. The purpose is to permit limited amounts of hazardous contents in occupancies having minimum controls without triggering the more restrictive Protection Level 1 through Protection Level 4 building requirements. The MAQ in Table 5.2.1.1.3, Table 5.2.1.2 through Table 5.2.1.8, and Table 5.2.1.10.1 is based on demonstrated need and historical safe storage and use of hazardous contents. Section 5.3, however, establishes additional controls for occupancies exceeding the hazardous contents limits prescribed for control areas.

All of the hazardous materials within the scope of 1.1.1 are high hazard contents; see 4.2.1.1. However, not all of the hazardous materials categories are placed into High Hazard Levels 1–4 requiring Protection Levels 1–4 are considered to be high hazard contents, and some of these materials have been recognized as being of low or ordinary hazards, depending on their nature in a fire. In some cases, Class 1 unstable (reactive) materials, Class 1 water-reactive materials, and Class IV and Class V organic peroxides do not have a MAQ and, therefore, are not required to comply with the requirements for Protection Level 1 through Protection Level 4. Figure A.5.1 helps to illustrate the conditions under which the protection level requirements are applicable.

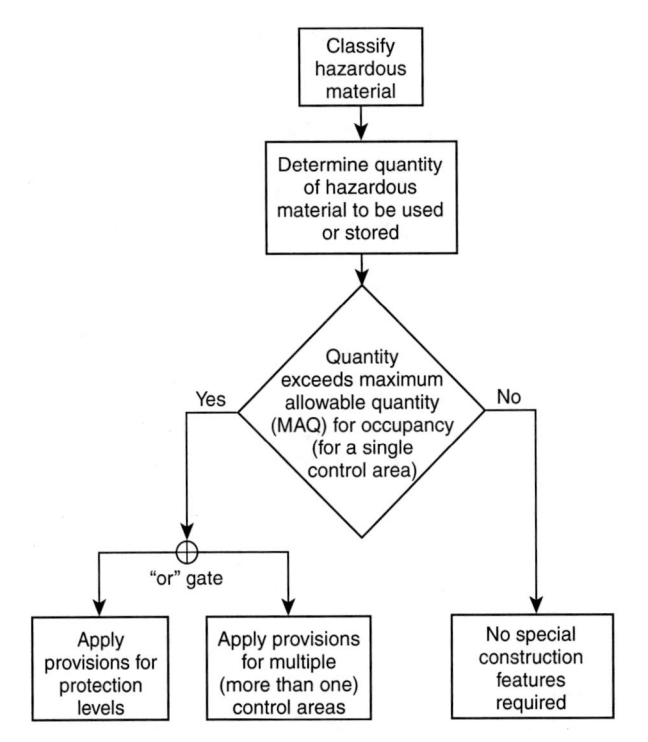

FIGURE A.5.1 Application of Chapter 5 and Chapter 6 Requirements for Hazardous Materials. [5000:Figure A.34.1.1]

A.6.1.1.1 Outdoor control areas are not classified with protection levels.

A.6.1.1.2 Outdoor control areas are not classified with protection levels.

A.6.1.2 *Readily available* can mean access to the product manufacturer's or user's paper or electronic copies of MSDSs.

A.6.1.3.4 There might be additional regulations that must be complied with to notify other agencies.

A.6.1.4 The hazard potential of a facility is not dependent on any single factor. Physical size, number of employees, and the quantity and the nature of the hazardous materials are important considerations. The level of training can vary with the complexity of the facility under consideration.

A.6.1.4.4 Emergency responders can include on-site personnel that have been designated and trained to respond to emergencies, persons from the public sector such as fire department personnel, or persons from the private sector that can be contracted or otherwise engaged to perform emergency response duties. *(See Annex I.)*

A.6.1.4.4.1 OSHA describes an Incident Command System as a standardized on-scene incident management concept designed specifically to allow responders to adopt an integrated organizational structure equal to the complexity and demands of any single incident or multiple incidents without being hindered by jurisdictional boundaries.

A.6.1.4.4.2 Responses to releases of hazardous materials where there is no potential safety or health hazard such as fire, explosion, or chemical exposure are not considered emergency responses as defined within the context of this code.

A.6.1.4.4.3 Emergency response training will vary depending on the level of emergency response required and by the requirements of the governmental agency.

A.6.1.5.3.1 The approved powered industrial trucks addressed in NFPA 505, *Fire Safety Standard for Powered Industrial Trucks Including Type Designations, Areas of Use, Conversions, Maintenance, and Operations*, are trucks that are listed by a testing laboratory for the use intended and should be tested and labeled in accordance with ANSI/UL 558, *Standard for Safety Industrial Trucks, Internal Combustion Engine-Powered*, or ANSI/UL 583, *Standard for Safety Electric Battery-Powered Industrial Trucks*. [**505:**1.3.3]

A.6.1.14 For seismic requirements and the seismic zone in which the material is located, see the building code.

A.6.1.16.1 Maintenance procedures are an important part of any mechanical integrity program. They should contain information on which equipment is covered; what tests and inspections are to be performed; how to perform the tests and inspections in accordance with recognized industry standards and manufacturer's recommendations; what constitutes acceptance of the measured parameters; corrective actions to be taken if the equipment does not meet requirements; and the frequency of the testing and inspection. For examples of additional guidance, refer to *Guidelines for Mechanical Integrity Systems* (AIChE/CCPS); *Guidelines for Safe and Reliable Instrumented Protective Systems* (AIChE/CCPS); and *Guidelines for Writing Effective Operating and Maintenance Procedures* (AIChE/CCPS).

A.6.1.16.2.3 Testing can include visual inspection, x-ray, spark testing, pressure testing, leak testing, or other nondestructive methods.

A.6.2.1.6 The following items should be considered in the design:

(1) Deflagration vents designed to release from the exterior walls or roofs of the building should discharge directly to the exterior of the building where an unoccupied space of not less than 50 ft (15 m) in width is provided between the exterior walls of the building and the property line, unless the vents comply with A.6.2.1.6(2).
(2) Deflagration vents designed to remain attached to the building when venting a deflagration should be located so that the discharge opening is not less than 10 ft (3050 mm) vertically from window openings and exit discharge doors in the building and not less than 20 ft (6100 mm) horizontally from exit discharge doors in the building, window openings and exit discharge doors in adjacent buildings on the same property, and property lines.
(3) Deflagration vents should not discharge into the interior of the building.
(4) Additional guidance for deflagration venting can be found in NFPA 68, *Standard on Explosion Protection by Deflagration Venting*.
(5) An authoritative standard used for the design of barricades is TM5-13000 (NAVFAC P-397, AFR 88-22), "Structures to Resist the Effects of Accidental Explosions."

A.6.2.2.2.1 The use of multistoried detached buildings that may be needed to house special processes in occupancies requiring Protection Level 1 controls may be able to be approved through the use of alternative materials and methods. As detonation of Protection Level 1 materials is contemplated, the analysis of the proposed design must consider activities, occupancy, and means of egress from each level of the building. In some instances the "floors" in the process area may be of open grated construction. The restrictions regarding use for other purposes are intended to exclude other uses not directly related to the process or storage being conducted. Control rooms, restrooms, and ancillary electrical and mechanical rooms directly associated with the process are allowed. An engineering office, conference room, cafeteria, or similar use, although related to the process, would not be allowed, as these uses have occupancy that is outside of that intended to be addressed by Protection Level 1 controls.

It is to be expected that materials with multiple hazards may be present, and not intended that such materials be excluded providing those that are incompatible are separated by distance or barrier as required. Also see 6.2.2.2.3.

A.6.2.3.4.1 The use of multistoried detached buildings that may be needed to house special processes in occupancies requiring Protection Level 1 controls may be able to be approved through the use of alternative materials and methods. As detonation of Protection Level 1 materials is contemplated, the analysis of the proposed design must consider activities, occupancy, and means of egress from each level of the building. In some instances the "floors" in the process area may be of open grated construction. The restrictions regarding use for other purposes are intended to exclude other uses not directly related to the process or storage being conducted. Control rooms, restrooms, and ancillary electrical and mechanical rooms directly associated with the process are allowed. An engineering office, conference room, cafeteria, or similar use, although related to the process, would not be allowed, as these uses have occupancy that is outside of that intended to be addressed by Protection Level 1 controls.

It is to be expected that materials with multiple hazards may be present, and not intended that such materials be excluded providing those that are incompatible are separated by distance or barrier as required. Also see 6.2.2.2.3.

A.6.2.4.4.1 The use of multistoried detached buildings that may be needed to house special processes in occupancies requiring Protection Level 1 controls may be able to be approved through the use of alternative materials and methods. As detonation of Protection Level 1 materials is contemplated, the analysis of the proposed design must consider activities, occupancy, and means of egress from each level of the building. In some instances the "floors" in the process area may be of open grated construction. The restrictions regarding use for other purposes are intended to exclude other uses not directly related to the process or storage being conducted. Control rooms, restrooms, and ancillary electrical and mechanical rooms directly associated with the process are allowed. An engineering office, conference room, cafeteria, or similar use, although related to the process, would not be allowed, as these uses have occupancy that is outside of that intended to be addressed by Protection Level 1 controls.

It is to be expected that materials with multiple hazards may be present, and not intended that such materials be excluded providing those that are incompatible are separated by distance or barrier as required. Also see 6.2.2.2.3.

A.6.3.1 For storage, see Section 6.3.

A.7.1 Laboratory operations defined in NFPA 45, *Standard on Fire Protection for Laboratories Using Chemicals*, are not considered to be industrial processes.

A.7.1.2.1(3) One example is a maximum airborne concentration that does exceed an Emergency Response Planning Guide (ERPG-2) concentration at 65.6 ft (20 m) for 1 hour.

A.7.2.1 Understanding the hazards associated with chemicals and applying a means to control those hazards will vary depending on the nature of the chemicals used and the processing conditions. The level of understanding needed may consist of reviewing the basic hazard information contained within material safety data sheets for chemicals being used, or to more detailed analytical techniques, including, but not limited to, a formal process hazards analysis described in other publications.

A.7.3.1.2 Operating procedures help control the hazards in a process and provide guidance and direction on how to operate the process. Operating procedures also provide information about the hazards of the process and how those hazards are controlled and are also essential for training the operators. Operating procedures contain, but are not limited to, the following:

(1) Clear instructions for all phases of operation, including startup, normal operation, emergency shutdown, emergency operations, and startup after an unscheduled shutdown or maintenance
(2) The safe limits of operation for each process variable, the consequences of deviations, and the corrective actions that should be taken
(3) A discussion of the safety systems that are used to control the hazards of the process, including but not limited to instrumentation, alarms, interlocks, pressure relief and effluent handling systems, water sprays, deluge systems, and containment systems
(4) Safe work practices for preparing equipment for maintenance, including but not limited to lockout/tagout, opening process equipment, confined space entry, hot work and admission of visitors, contractor, maintenance and other support personnel into the process area

For guidance on preparing operating procedures, refer to the latest editions of *Guidelines for Technical Management of Chemical Process Safety* (AIChE/CCPS); *Guidelines for Safe Process Operations and Maintenance* (AIChE/CCPS); and *Guidelines for Writing Effective Operating and Maintenance Procedures* (AIChE/CCPS).

A.7.3.2.2 The inspection and testing of alarms, interlocks, and controls are to ensure the safe operation of process equipment as designed. These systems include, but are not limited to, emergency alarms, shutdown systems, and isolation systems.

A.7.4 Conditions that might require repeating a review include, but are not limited to, the following:

(1) When changes occur in the materials in process
(2) When changes occur in process equipment
(3) When changes occur in process control
(4) When changes occur in operating procedures

A.7.5.1 The investigation should begin as soon as possible to avoid loss of critical information, but should be initiated not later than 48 hours after the incident. The contributing and root causes of the incident should be determined. A procedure should be in place to promptly address and resolve incident findings. All actions to correct the causes and the dates completed should be documented. The incident report should be communicated to all affected personal. Measures should be taken to prevent a recurrence.

A.9.1.2 See Annex D.

A.10.1 The performance option of this code establishes acceptable levels of risk for facilities (i.e., buildings and other structures and the operations therewith associated) as addressed in Section 1.3. (Note that *facility* and *building* can be used interchangeably; *facility* is the more general term.) While the performance option of this code does contain goals, objectives, and performance criteria necessary to provide for an acceptable level of risk, it does not describe how to meet these goals, objectives, and performance criteria. Design and engineering are needed to meet the provisions of Chapter 5. For fire protection designs, the *SFPE Engineering Guide to Performance-Based Fire Protection Analysis and Design of Buildings* provides a framework for these assessments.

Preconstruction design requirements address those issues, which have to be considered before the certificate of occupancy is issued for a facility.

A.10.1.1 Performance code approaches written for other model codes can be used by the AHJ.

A.10.1.2 Performance code approaches written for other model codes can be used by the AHJ.

A.10.1.3 Qualifications should include experience, education, and credentials that demonstrate knowledge and responsible use of applicable models and methods.

A.10.1.4 The *SFPE Engineering Guide to Performance-Based Fire Protection Analysis and Design of Buildings* outlines a process for using a performance-based approach in the design and assessment of building fire safety design and identifies parameters that should be considered in the analysis of a performance-based design. As can be seen, this process requires the involvement of all stakeholders who have a share or interest in the successful completion of the project. The steps that are recommended by the *SFPE Engineering Guide to Performance-Based Fire Protection Analysis and Design of Buildings* for this process are shown in Figure A.10.1.4.

The guide specifically addresses building fire safety performance-based design. It might not be directly applicable to performance-based designs involving other systems and operations covered within this code, such as hot work operations or hazardous materials storage. However, the various steps for defining, developing, evaluating, and documenting the performance-based design should still provide a useful framework for the overall design process.

The steps in the performance-based design process are as follows:

(1) *Step 1: Defining Project Scope.* The first step in a performance-based design is to define the scope of the project. Defining the scope consists of identifying and documenting the following:
   (a) Constraints on the design and project schedule
   (b) The stakeholders associated with project
   (c) The proposed building construction and features desired by the owner or tenant
   (d) Occupant and building characteristics
   (e) The intended use and occupancy of the building
   (f) Applicable codes and regulations
   An understanding of these items is needed to ensure that a performance-based design meets the stakeholders' needs.

(2) *Step 2: Identifying Goals.* Once the scope of the project is defined, the next step in the performance-based design process is to identify and document the fire safety goals of various stakeholders. Fire safety goals could include levels of protection for people and property, or they could provide for continuity of operations, historical preservation, and environmental protection. Goals could be unique for different projects, based on the stakeholders' needs and desires. The stakeholders should discuss which goals are the most important for the project. In order to avoid problems later in the design process, all stakeholders should be aware of and agree to the goals prior to proceeding with the performance-based design process (*see Step 7*).

(3) *Step 3: Defining Stakeholder and Design Objectives.* The third step in the design process is to develop objectives. The objectives are essentially the design goals that are further refined into tangible values that can be quantified in engineering terms. Objectives could include mitigating the consequences of a fire expressed in terms of dollar values, loss of life, or other impact on property operations, or maximum allowable conditions, such as extent of fire spread, temperature, spread of combustion products, and so forth.

(4) *Step 4: Developing Performance Criteria.* The fourth step in the design process is the development of performance criteria to be met by the design. These criteria are a further refinement of the design objectives and are numerical values to which the expected performance of the trial designs can be compared. Performance criteria could include threshold values for temperatures of materials, gas temperatures, carboxyhemoglobin (COHb) levels, smoke obscuration, and thermal exposure levels.

(5) *Step 5: Developing Design Scenarios.* Once the performance criteria have been established, the engineer will develop and analyze design alternatives to meet performance criteria. The first part of this process is the identification of possible scenarios and design scenarios. Fire scenarios are descriptions of possible fire events, and consist of fire characteristics, building characteristics (including facility operations), and occupant characteristics. The fire scenarios identified will subsequently be filtered (i.e., combined or eliminated) into a subset of design fire scenarios against which trial designs will be evaluated. Hazardous materials scenarios can be treated similarly.

(6) *Step 6: Developing Trial Design(s).* Once the project scope, performance criteria, and design scenarios are established, the engineer develops preliminary designs, referred to as trial designs, intended to meet the project requirements. The trial design(s) include proposed fire protection systems, construction features, and operation that are provided in order for a design to meet the performance criteria when evaluated using the design fire scenarios. The evaluation method should also be determined at this point. The evaluation methods used should be appropriate for the situation and agreeable to the stakeholders.

(7) *Step 7: Developing a Fire Protection Engineering Design Brief.* At this point in the process a fire protection engineering design brief should be prepared and provided to all stakeholders for their review and concurrence. This

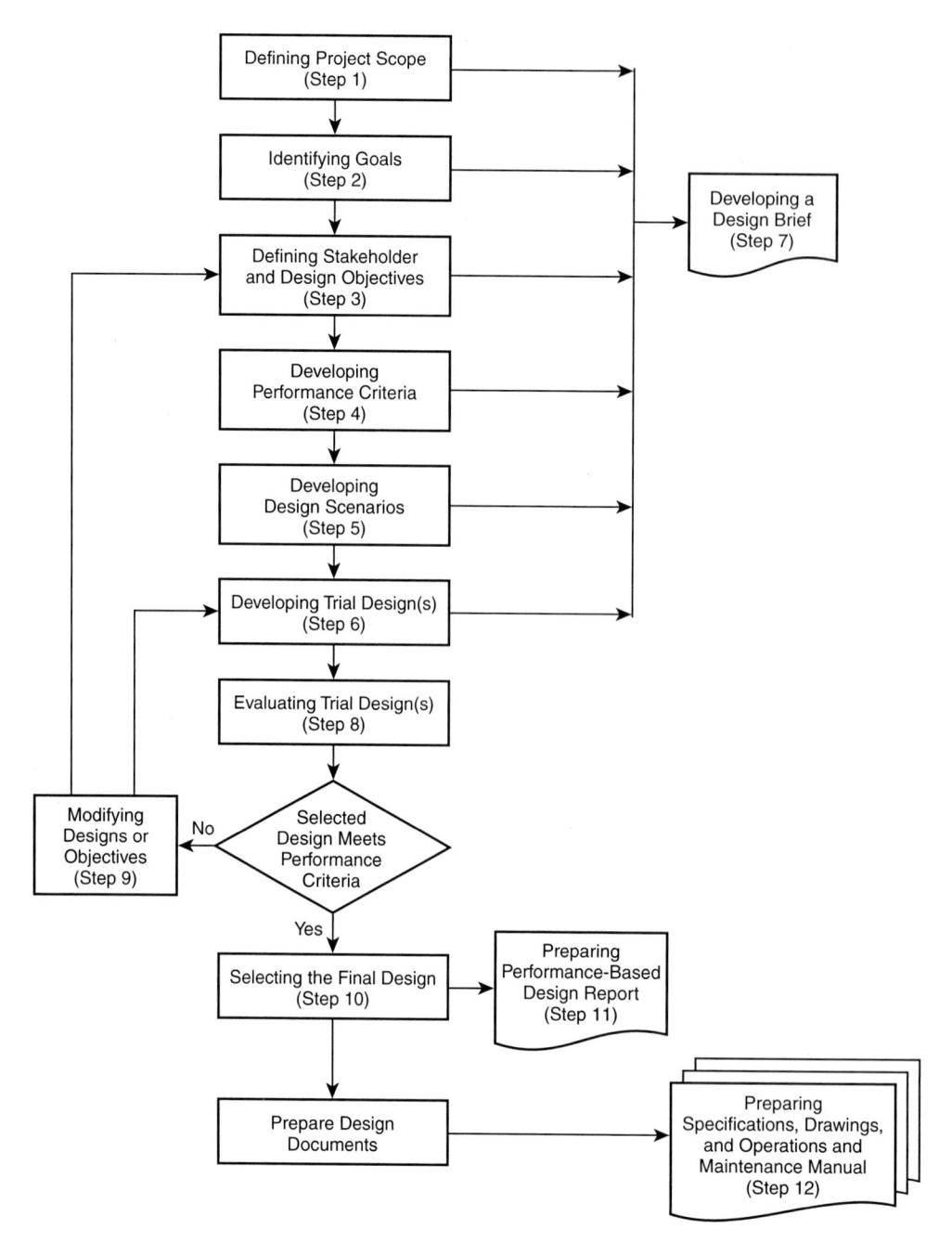

FIGURE A.10.1.4 Steps in the Performance-Based Analysis and the Conceptual Design Procedure for Fire Protection Design.

brief should document the project scope, goals, objectives, trial designs, performance criteria, design fire scenarios, and analysis methods. Documenting and agreeing upon these factors at this point in the design process will help avoid possible misunderstandings later.

(8) *Step 8: Evaluating Trial Designs.* Each trial design is then evaluated using each design scenario. The evaluation results will indicate whether the trial design will meet the performance criteria. Only trial design(s) that meet the performance criteria can be considered as final design proposals. Yet, the performance criteria can be revised with the stakeholders' approval. The criteria cannot be arbitrarily changed to ensure that a trial design meets a criterion, but can be changed based on additional analysis and the consideration of additional data.

(9) *Step 9: Modifying Designs or Objectives.* If none of the trial designs evaluated comply with the previously agreed upon performance criteria, it could be necessary to either develop and evaluate new trial designs, or revisit the objectives and performance criteria previously agreed upon by the stakeholders to determine if stakeholder objectives and performance criteria should be modified.

(10) *Step 10: Selecting the Final Design.* Once an acceptable trial design is identified using the evaluation, it can be considered for the final project design. If multiple trial designs are evaluated, further analysis will be needed to

select a final design. The selection of an acceptable trial design for the final design could be based on a variety of factors, such as financial considerations, timeliness of installation, system and material availability, ease of installation, maintenance and use, and other factors.

(11) *Step 11: Preparing Performance-Based Design Report.* Once the final design is identified, design documents need to be prepared. Proper documentation will ensure that all stakeholders understand what is necessary for the design implementation, maintenance, and continuity of the fire protection design. The documentation should include the fire protection engineering design brief, a performance design report, detailed specifications and drawings, and a facility operations and maintenance manual.

(12) *Step 12: Preparing Specifications, Drawings, and Operations and Maintenance Manual.* The specifications and drawings portion of the performance-based design report convey to building and system designers and installing contractors how to implement the performance design. Specifications and drawings could include required sprinkler densities; hydraulic characteristics and spacing requirements; the fire detection and alarm system components and programming; special construction requirements, including means of egress and location of fire-resistive walls; compartmentation; and the coordination of interactive systems. The detailed specifications are the implementation document of the performance-based design report. The detailed drawings will graphically represent the results of the performance design. The operations and maintenance (O&M) manual clearly states the requirement of the facility operator to ensure that the components of the performance design are in place and operating properly. The O&M manual describes the commissioning requirements and the interaction of the different systems' interfaces. All subsystems are identified, and inspection and testing regimes and schedules are created.

The O&M manual also gives instruction to the facility operator on restrictions placed on facility operations. These limitations are based on the engineering assumptions made during the design and analysis. These limiting factors could include critical fire load, sprinkler design requirements, building use and occupancy, and reliability and maintenance of systems. The O&M manual can be used to communicate to tenants and occupants these limits and their responsibilities as a tenant. It could also be used as a guide for renovations and changes. It also can be used to document agreements between stakeholders.

A.10.1.5 A third-party reviewer is a person or group of persons chosen by the AHJ to review proposed performance-based designs. Qualifications of the third-party reviewer should include experience, education, and credentials that demonstrate knowledge and responsible use of applicable models and methods.

A.10.1.8 See Step 12 of A.10.1.4 for a description of these documents.

A.10.1.9 Information that could be needed by the fire service arriving at the scene of a fire in a performance-based designed facility includes, but is not limited to, the following:

(1) Safe shutdown procedures of equipment and processes
(2) Facility personnel responsible for assisting the fire service
(3) Operating procedures required to maintain the effectiveness of the performance-based designed fire protection system (i.e., when it is and is not appropriate to alter, shut down, or turn off a design feature; assumptions that have to be maintained if a fire occurs; suggested fire-fighting tactics that relate to the specific nature of the performance-based design)

The design specifications and O&M manual documentation described in 10.1.8 should provide a guide for the facility owner and tenants to follow in order to maintain the required level of safety anticipated by the original design. It should also provide a guide for the AHJ to use in conducting ongoing inspections of the facility.

A.10.1.10 Continued compliance with the goals and objectives of the code involves many factors. The building construction, including openings, interior finish, and fire- and smoke-resistive construction, and the building and fire protection systems need to retain at least the same level of performance as is provided for by the original design parameters. The use and occupancy should not change to the degree that assumptions made about the occupant characteristics, combustibility of furnishings, and existence of trained personnel are no longer valid. In addition, actions provided by other personnel, such as emergency responders, should not be diminished below the documented assumed levels. Also, actions needed to maintain reliability of systems at the anticipated level need to meet the initial design criteria.

Subsection 10.1.10 deals with issues that arise after the facility has been constructed and a certificate of occupancy has been issued. Therefore, any changes to the facility or the operations conducted therein, up to and including the demolition of the facility, that affect the assumptions of the original design are considered part of the management of change.

The following is a process for evaluating performance-based facilities:

(1) Review of original design analysis and documentation as follows:
   (a) Assumptions
   (b) Input parameter values
   (c) Predictions and/or results of other calculations
(2) Review of design analysis and documentation for any subsequent renovations, additions, modifications, and so forth, as in Step 1 of A.10.1.4
(3) Review of the facility's operations and maintenance manual, including any and all revisions to it
(4) On-site inspection, involving the following:
   (a) Consideration of "prescriptive" issues (e.g., blocked egress paths, poor maintenance of systems)
   (b) Comparison of assumptions to specific, pertinent on-site conditions
   (c) Comparison of input parameter values to pertinent on-site conditions
   (d) Review of maintenance and testing documentation to ensure adherence to the schedules detailed in the facility's O&M manual
(5) Reconciliation of discrepancies as follows:
   (a) A listing of discrepancies
   (b) Consultation with the facility owner and/or their representative
   (c) Preparation of a schedule that reconciles the discrepancies

A.10.1.11 Private fire inspection services can be used to meet this provision provided that they are qualified to assess the impact of changes on the performance-based design and assumptions.

A.10.2.2 The performance criteria in Section 10.2 define an acceptable level of performance that should be agreed upon by the stakeholders, including the owner and the AHJ. The acceptable level of performance can vary widely between facilities based on a number of factors, including the existence of potential ignition sources, potential fuel loads present, reactivity and quantity of hazardous materials present, the nature of the operations conducted at the facility, and the characteristics and number of personnel likely to be present at the facility.

A.10.2.2.1 Many of the performance criteria related to safety from fire can also be found in the annex of NFPA *101, Life Safety Code*.

A.10.2.2.2 It is anticipated that the design provides protection for occupants who are not intimate with the initial unintentional detonation or deflagration of explosive materials, and individuals immediately adjacent to the property. It is recognized that employees should be trained and knowledgeable in the hazards of the materials present in the workplace. It is recognized that some of these individuals could experience psychological and physical injuries, such as hearing problems, on either a short or long term basis. However, the intent is that they do not experience thermal burns or loss of life or limb as a direct result of the explosion.

It is not the intent of the code to provide protection against explosions caused by acts of terrorism. This would involve the introduction of an unknown quantity of explosives in an unknown location within or adjacent to a building. Where protection is needed against such acts of terrorism, the appropriate military and law enforcement agencies should be consulted.

A.10.2.2.3 Given the nature and variety of hazardous materials, more than one performance criterion for a specific facility could need to be developed. Criteria have to be developed for each hazardous material and possibly for different personnel; for example, higher levels of exposure can be tolerated by personnel that are in some way protected than those personnel having no protection. Development of performance criteria for hazardous materials should be developed by the facility owner and the facility's safety personnel in conjunction with the AHJ and the emergency response personnel expected to respond to an incident.

It is anticipated that the design provides protection for occupants inside or immediately adjacent to the facility who are not intimate with the initial unauthorized release of hazardous materials, or the initial unintentional reaction of hazardous materials. However, it is assumed that these individuals depart from the area of the incident in a time frame reasonable for their circumstances, based on their observation of the event, or some other form of notification.

It is also anticipated that employees and emergency response personnel are trained and aware of the hazardous materials present in the facility, and the potential consequences of their involvement in the incident, and take appropriate measures to ensure their own safety during search and rescue operations.

It is not the intent of the code to provide protection against acts of terrorism involving the introduction of hazardous materials into a facility. This involves the introduction of an unknown quantity of materials in an unknown location within or adjacent to a building. Where protection is needed against such acts of terrorism, the appropriate military and law enforcement agencies should be consulted.

A.10.2.2.4 Each facility designed using a performance-based approach most likely has different levels of acceptable and unacceptable property damage. This reflects the unique aspects of the performance-based designed facility and the reasons for pursuing a performance-based design. Therefore, the definition of an acceptable and an unacceptable level of property damage results from discussions between the facility's owner, manager and engineer, the designer, (possibly) the insurance underwriter and field engineer, and the AHJ. There could be cases where a property damage criterion is not needed.

Note that the structural integrity performance criteria for property damage most likely differ from the structural integrity performance criteria for life safety. This reflects the difference in the associated objectives: A life safety criterion probably is more restrictive than one for property damage.

A.10.2.2.5 Each facility designed using a performance-based approach most likely has a different level of acceptable and unacceptable interruption of the facility's mission. This reflects the unique aspects of the performance-based designed facility and the reasons for pursuing a performance-based design. Therefore, the definition of an acceptable and an unacceptable interruption of the facility's mission results from discussions between the facility's owner, manager and engineer, the designer, (possibly) the insurance underwriter and field engineer, and the AHJ. There could be cases where a mission continuity criterion is not needed.

A.10.3.2 In jurisdictions where NFPA electrical standards are not adopted, the provisions of the electrical standards adopted by the AHJ should be used.

A.10.3.4 In jurisdictions where NFPA *101, Life Safety Code*, is not adopted, the provisions of the building code adopted by the AHJ should be used.

A.10.4 Many events can occur during the life of a facility; some have a higher probability of occurrence than others. Some events, though not typical, could have a devastating effect on the facility. A reasonable design should be able to achieve the goals, objectives, and performance criteria of this code for any typical or common design scenario and for some of the nontypical, potentially devastating scenarios, up to some level commensurate with society's expectations as reflected in this code.

The challenge in selecting design scenarios is finding a manageable number that are sufficiently diverse and representative so that, if the design is reasonably safe for those scenarios, it should then be reasonably safe for all scenarios, except for those specifically excluded as being unrealistically severe or sufficiently infrequent to be fair tests of the design.

A.10.4.1.2 The *SFPE Engineering Guide to Performance-Based Fire Protection Analysis and Design of Buildings* identifies methods for evaluating fire scenarios.

A.10.4.1.3 It is desirable to consider a wide variety of different design scenarios to evaluate the complete capabilities of the building or structure. Design scenarios should not be limited to one or two worst-case events.

A.10.4.2.1 An example of such a scenario for a health care occupancy is a patient room with two occupied beds with a fire initially involving one bed and the room door open. This is a cursory example in that much of the explicitly required information indicated in 10.4.2.1 can be determined from the information provided in the example. Note that it is usually necessary to consider more than one scenario to capture the features and conditions typical of an occupancy.

A.10.4.2.2 Examples of such scenarios are a fire involving ignition of gasoline as an accelerant in a means of egress, clothing racks in corridors, renovation materials, and other fuel configurations that can cause an ultrafast fire. The means of egress chosen is the doorway with the largest egress capacity among doorways normally used in the ordinary operation of the building. The baseline occupant characteristics for the property are assumed. At ignition, doors are assumed to be open throughout the building.

A.10.4.2.3 An example of such a scenario is a fire in a storage room adjacent to the largest occupiable room in the building. The contents of the room of fire origin are specified to provide the largest fuel load and the most rapid growth in fire severity consistent with the normal use of the room. The adjacent occupiable room is assumed to be filled to capacity with occupants. Occupants are assumed to be somewhat impaired in whatever form is most consistent with the intended use of the building. At ignition, doors from both rooms are assumed to be open. Depending on the design, doorways connect the two rooms or they connect via a common hallway or corridor.

For purposes of this scenario, an occupiable room is a room that could contain people (i.e., a location within a building where people are typically found).

A.10.4.2.4 An example of such a scenario is a fire originating in a concealed wall- or ceiling-space adjacent to a large, occupied function room. Ignition involves concealed combustibles, including wire or cable insulation and thermal or acoustical insulation. The adjacent function room is assumed to be occupied to capacity. The baseline occupant characteristics for the property are assumed. At ignition, doors are assumed to be open throughout the building.

A.10.4.2.5 An example of such a scenario is a cigarette fire in a trash can. The trash can is close enough to room contents to ignite more substantial fuel sources but is not close enough to any occupant to create an intimate-with-ignition situation. If the intended use of the property involves the potential for some occupants to be incapable of movement at any time, then the room of origin is chosen as the type of room likely to have such occupants, filled to capacity with occupants in that condition. If the intended use of the property does not involve the potential for some occupants to be incapable of movement, then the room of origin is chosen to be an assembly or function area characteristic of the use of the property, and the trash can is placed so that it is shielded by furniture from suppression systems. At ignition, doors are assumed to be open throughout the building.

A.10.4.2.6 An example of such a scenario is a fire originating in the largest fuel load of combustibles possible in normal operation in a function or assembly room or in a process/manufacturing area, characteristic of the normal operation of the property. The configuration, type, and geometry of the combustibles are chosen so as to produce the most rapid and severe fire growth or smoke generation consistent with the normal operation of the property. The baseline occupant characteristics for the property are assumed. At ignition, doors are assumed to be closed throughout the building.

This scenario includes everything from a big couch fire in a small dwelling to a rack storage fire in combustible liquids stock in a big box retail store.

A.10.4.2.7 An example of such a scenario is an exposure fire. The initiating fire is the closest and most severe fire possible consistent with the placement and type of adjacent properties and the placement of plants and combustible adornments on the property. The baseline occupant characteristics of the property are assumed.

This category includes wildland/urban interface fires and exterior wood shingle problems, where applicable.

A.10.4.2.8 This scenario addresses a set of conditions with a typical fire originating in the building with any one passive or active fire protection system or feature being ineffective. Examples include unprotected openings between floors or between fire walls or fire barrier walls, rated fire doors that fail to close automatically or are blocked open, sprinkler system water supply that is shut off, a fire alarm system that is nonoperative, a smoke management system that is not operational, or automatic smoke dampers that are blocked open. This scenario should represent a reasonable challenge to the other building features provided by the design and presumed to be available.

The exemption from Fire Design Scenario 8 is applied to each active or passive fire protection system individually and requires two different types of information to be developed by analysis and approved by the AHJ. System reliability is to be analyzed and accepted. Design performance in the absence of the system is also to be analyzed and accepted, but acceptable performance does not require fully meeting the stated goals and objectives. It might not be possible to meet fully the goals and objectives if a key system is unavailable, and yet no system is totally reliable. The AHJ determines which level of performance, possibly short of the stated goals and objectives, is acceptable, given the very low probability (that is, the system's unreliability probability) that the system will not be available.

A.10.4.3.1 This scenario is intended to address facilities where explosives and products containing explosives are manufactured, stored, sold, or handled. From an overall safety standpoint, the operations being performed at these facilities should include stringent safety procedures that significantly reduce the likelihood of an explosion from occurring. However, if an explosion does occur, protection methods such as storage magazines, property set backs, deflagration, and explosion venting and containment need to be in place, as appropriate, to minimize potential injury and loss of life and property.

Where products containing explosives, such as pyrotechnic displays or fireworks, are stored, handled, or used in buildings, such as arenas, an explosion scenario should not result in significant injuries to occupants not intimate with the materials.

A.10.4.4 Design hazardous materials scenarios should explicitly account for the following:

(1) Occupant activities, training, and knowledge
(2) Number and location of occupants
(3) Discharge location and surroundings
(4) Hazardous materials' properties
(5) Ventilation, inerting, and dilution systems and conditions
(6) Normal and emergency operating procedures

(7) Safe shutdown and other hazard mitigating systems and procedures
(8) Weather conditions affecting the hazard
(9) Potential exposure to off-site personnel

Design hazardous materials scenarios should be evaluated as many times as necessary by varying the factors previously indicated. Design hazardous materials scenarios could need to be established for each different type of hazardous material stored or used at the facility.

A.10.4.4.4.2 This provision should be applied to each protection system individually and requires two different types of information to be developed by analysis and approved by the AHJ. System reliability is to be analyzed and accepted. Design performance in the absence of the system is also to be analyzed and accepted, but acceptable performance does not require fully meeting the stated goals and objectives. It might not be possible to meet fully the goals and objectives if a key system is unavailable, and yet no system is totally reliable. The AHJ determines which level of performance, possibly short of stated goals and objectives, is acceptable, given the very low probability (that is, the systems' unreliability probability) that the system will be unavailable.

A.10.4.5.1 An example of such a scenario would involve a fire or earthquake effectively blocking the principal entrance/exit but not immediately endangering the occupants. The full occupant load of the assembly space has to exit using secondary means.

A.10.6 The assessment of precision required in 10.7.7 requires a sensitivity and uncertainty analysis, which can be translated into safety factors.

Sensitivity Analysis. The first run a model user makes should be labeled as the base case, using the nominal values of the various input parameters. However, the model user should not rely on a single run as the basis for any performance-based fire safety system design. Ideally, each variable or parameter that the model user made to develop the nominal input data should have multiple runs associated with it, as should combinations of key variables and parameters. Thus, a sensitivity analysis should be conducted that provides the model user with data that indicates how the effects of a real fire could vary and how the response of the proposed fire safety design could also vary.

The interpretation of a model's predictions can be a difficult exercise if the model user does not have knowledge of fire dynamics or human behavior.

Reasonableness Check. The model user should first try to determine whether the predictions actually make sense; that is, they don't upset intuition or preconceived expectations. Most likely, if the results don't pass this test, an input error has been committed.

Sometimes the predictions appear to be reasonable but are, in fact, incorrect. For example, a model can predict higher temperatures farther from the fire than close to it. The values themselves could be reasonable; for example, they are not hotter than the fire, but they don't "flow" down the energy as expected.

A margin of safety can be developed using the results of the sensitivity analysis in conjunction with the performance criteria to provide the possible range of time during which a condition is estimated to occur.

Safety factors and margin of safety are two concepts used to quantify the amount of uncertainty in engineering analyses. Safety factors are used to provide a margin of safety and represent, or address, the gap in knowledge between the theoretically perfect model; that is, reality and the engineering models that can only partially represent reality.

Safety factors can be applied to either the predicted level of a physical condition or to the time at which the condition is predicted to occur. Thus, a physical or a temporal safety factor, or both, can be applied to any predicted condition. A predicted condition (that is, a parameter's value) and the time at which it occurs are best represented as distributions. Ideally, a computer fire model predicts the expected or nominal value of the distribution. Safety factors are intended to represent the spread of these distributions.

Given the uncertainty associated with data acquisition and reduction, and the limitations of computer modeling, any condition predicted by a computer model can be thought of as an expected or nominal value within a broader range. For example, an upper layer temperature of 1110°F (600°C) is predicted at a given time. If the modeled scenario is then tested (that is, full-scale experiment based on the computer model's input data), the actual temperature at that given time could be 1185°F (640°C) or 1085°F (585°C). Therefore, the temperature should be reported either as 1110°F, +75°F or −25°F (600°C, +40°C or −15°C) or as a range of 1085°F to 1184°F (585°C to 640°C).

Ideally, predictions are reported as a nominal value, a percentage, or an absolute value. As an example, an upper layer temperature prediction could be reported as 1112°F (600°C), 86°F (30°C), or 1112°F (600°C), 5 percent. In this case, the physical safety factor is 0.05 (i.e., the amount by which the nominal value should be degraded and enhanced). Given the state-of-the-art of computer fire modeling, this is a very low safety factor. Physical safety factors tend to be on the order of tens of percent. A safety factor of 50 percent is not unheard of.

Part of the problem in establishing safety factors is that it is difficult to state the percentage or range that is appropriate. These values can be obtained when the computer model predictions are compared to test data. However, using computer fire models in a design mode does not facilitate this since (1) the room being analyzed has not been built yet and (2) test scenarios do not necessarily depict the intended design.

A sensitivity analysis should be performed based on the assumptions that affect the condition of interest. A base case that uses all nominal values for input parameters should be developed. The input parameters should be varied over reasonable ranges, and the variation in predicted output should be noted. This output variation can then become the basis for physical safety factors.

The temporal safety factor addresses the issue of when a condition is predicted and is a function of the rate at which processes are expected to occur. If a condition is predicted to occur 2 minutes after the start of the fire, then this can be used as a nominal value. A process similar to that described for physical safety factors can also be employed to develop temporal safety factors. In this case, however, the rates (e.g., of heat release and toxic product generation) will be varied instead of absolute values (e.g., material properties).

The margin of safety can be thought of as a reflection of societal values and can be imposed by the AHJ for that purpose. Since the time for which a condition is predicted is most likely the focus of the AHJ (e.g., the model predicts occupants have 5 minutes to safely evacuate), the margin of safety is characterized by temporal aspects and tacitly applied to the physical margin of safety.

Escaping the harmful effects of fire (or mitigating them) is, effectively, a race against time. When assessing fire safety system designs based on computer model predictions, the choice of an acceptable time is important. When an AHJ is faced with the predicted time of untenability, a decision needs to be made regarding whether sufficient time is available to ensure the safety of facility occupants. The AHJ is assessing the margin of safety. Is there sufficient time to get everyone out safely? If the AHJ feels that the predicted egress time is too close to the time of untenability, then the AHJ can impose an additional time that the designer has to incorporate into the system design. In other words, the AHJ can impose a greater margin of safety than that originally proposed by the designer.

A.10.7.1 The *SFPE Engineering Guide to Performance-Based Fire Protection Analysis and Design of Buildings* describes the documentation that should be provided for a performance-based design.

Proper documentation of a performance design is critical to the design acceptance and construction. Proper documentation also ensures that all parties involved understand what is necessary for the design implementation, maintenance, and continuity of the fire protection design. If attention to details is maintained in the documentation, then there should be little dispute during approval, construction, startup, and use.

Poor documentation could result in rejection of an otherwise good design, poor implementation of the design, inadequate system maintenance and reliability, and an incomplete record for future changes or for testing the design forensically.

A.10.7.2 The sources, methodologies, and data used in performance-based designs should be based on technical references that are widely accepted and used by the appropriate professions and professional groups. This acceptance is often based on documents that are developed, reviewed, and validated under one of the following processes:

(1) Standards developed under an open consensus process conducted by recognized professional societies, codes or standards organizations, or governmental bodies
(2) Technical references that are subject to a peer review process and published in widely recognized peer-reviewed journals, conference reports, or other publications
(3) Resource publications such as the *SFPE Handbook of Fire Protection Engineering*, which are widely recognized technical sources of information

The following factors are helpful in determining the acceptability of the individual method or source:

(1) Extent of general acceptance in the relevant professional community. Indications of this acceptance include peer-reviewed publication, widespread citation in the technical literature, and adoption by or within a consensus document.
(2) Extent of documentation of the method, including the analytical method itself, assumptions, scope, limitations, data sources, and data reduction methods.
(3) Extent of validation and analysis of uncertainties. This includes comparison of the overall method with experimental data to estimate error rates as well as analysis of the uncertainties of input data, uncertainties and limitations in the analytical method, and uncertainties in the associated performance criteria.
(4) Extent to which the method is based on sound scientific principles.
(5) Extent to which the proposed application is within the stated scope and limitations of the supporting information, including the range of applicability for which there is documented validation. Factors such as spatial dimensions, occupant characteristics, and ambient conditions can limit valid applications.

In many cases, a method is built from and includes numerous component analyses. These component analyses should be evaluated using the same factors that are applied to the overall method as outlined in items (1) through (5).

A method to address a specific fire safety issue, within documented limitations or validation regimes, might not exist. In such a case, sources and calculation methods can be used outside of their limitations, provided that the design team recognizes the limitations and addresses the resulting implications.

The technical references and methodologies to be used in a performance-based design should be closely evaluated by the design team and the AHJ, and possibly by a third-party reviewer. The strength of the technical justification should be judged using criteria in items (1) through (5). This justification can be strengthened by the presence of data obtained from fire testing.

A.10.7.11 Documentation for modeling should conform to ASTM E 1472, *Standard Guide for Documenting Computer Software for Fire Models*, although most, if not all, models were originally developed before this standard was promulgated.

A.11.1.1 Determine the classification of ammonium nitrate in accordance with Chapter 4 and then apply the appropriate MAQs in Chapter 5 tables. Chapter 11 will then take precedence to address the specific requirements for solid and liquid ammonium nitrate, if the MAQ is exceeded. The classification of ammonium nitrate is dependent on the properties of the specific material or mixture of materials as a whole. When used as a fertilizer, it is common for ammonium nitrate to exist as a component of a chemical mixture. It is not uncommon for the user to describe the mixture as ammonium nitrate when in reality the mixture can contain components that contribute to altering the end classification of the material. The manufacturer's material safety data sheet (MSDS) must be used to assess the overall hazards of these materials within the context of the classification scheme integral to Chapter 4. The user is cautioned that the DOT shipping classification for transportation purposes alone is not a sufficient means by which to determine the hazards of these materials. Ammonium nitrate in the undiluted or pure form has a higher degree of overall hazard than does ammonium nitrate when mixed or blended with materials that can reduce the concentration. However, the materials with which it is blended cannot be inert materials, and the effects of the added components can only be determined by careful review of the MSDS. The tables in Chapter 5 are hazard-specific; they are not "chemical-specific." Ammonium nitrate as such is not included in the tables, because the actual hazard classification varies with the material under consideration. The question must be answered as to whether the material is an oxidizer, and if so what Class; whether it is an unstable reactive, and if so what Class; or whether there are other physical or health hazards attendant to the mixture under evaluation.

A.11.1.1.1 Ammonium nitrate and ammonium nitrate–based materials that are DOT Hazard Class 1 sensitive should be stored in accordance with the requirements of NFPA 495, *Explosive Materials Code*. Sensitivity is determined by the application of the UN Test Series 1 test, which includes testing to determine impact sensitivity, friction sensitivity, sensitivity to electrostatic discharge, and thermal stability.

A.11.1.4 Ammonium nitrate is capable of detonating with the blast effect of about half the quantity of explosives if heated under confinement that permits high-pressure buildup or if subjected to strong shocks, such as those from an explosive. The sensitivity of ammonium nitrate to detonation is increased by elevated temperatures or by contamination. *(See Chapter 7.)*

A.11.2.5 The "reserved sections" evolved during the development of the document to accommodate a templated approach to chapter content and to allow the committee and the public to establish needed requirements that might otherwise have been overlooked during the development stage. The committee seeks to maintain each of these sections to validate the fact that either no requirements are needed or to allow the generation of provisions suitable to the materials involved.

A.11.2.6.1.1.1 When determining whether greater quantities should be permitted without sprinkler protection, the AHJ should take into consideration proximity of the storage building to congested areas and the potential for presence of contaminants in the storage building.

A.11.2.10 See A.11.2.5.

A.11.2.12.2.2 It is recommended that electric or LP-Gas–powered trucks be employed, rather than gasoline- or diesel-powered trucks, to reduce the potential for contamination to ammonium nitrate.

A.11.2.12.4 See NFPA 780, *Standard for the Installation of Lightning Protection Systems*.

A.11.3.1 See A.11.2.5.

A.11.3.2.3.1.1 Buildings should be sufficiently ventilated to prevent the confinement of gases generated from the decomposition of ammonium nitrate. As stated in the *Summary Report* from the European Commission, Joint Research Center workshop on ammonium nitrate:

"Pure ammonium nitrate can undergo thermal decomposition if it receives enough energy. Gases are then emitted, especially nitrogen oxides and ammonia. With adequate ventilation, the decomposition stops as soon as the energy flow stops. The decomposition rate is not dangerously high at moderate temperatures, and the overall thermal effect is not significant since the exothermic reactions are accompanied by endothermic disassociation, which can in turn give rise to a steady state reaction provided the gases produced can escape freely and the system is adiabatic. The decomposition is catalyzed by a number of substances such as chlorides, which can affect the above balance."

A.11.3.2.3.2 *Bulk material* refers to material that is in the unpackaged state.

A.11.3.2.3.3.2 Steel or wood can be protected by special coatings such as sodium silicate, epoxy coatings, or polyvinyl chloride coatings.

A.11.3.2.3.3.8 Bulk and bagged ammonium nitrate can become caked and degrade in storage. This is a factor affected by humidity and temperature in the storage space and by pellet quality. Temperature cycles through 90°F (32°C) and high atmospheric humidity are undesirable for storage in depth.

A.11.3.5 See A.11.2.5.

A.11.4.3 Many of the general principles for the storage of ammonium nitrate–based fertilizers apply equally to fertilizers stored in the open and those stored in a building. It is generally recommended that bagged ammonium nitrate fertilizers should not be stored in large piles outdoors.

It should be noted that repeated temperature cycles can cause physical deterioration of some products. Physical deterioration can result in the breakdown of the fertilizer particles and damage to packages. The product should be protected from direct sunlight. Due note should be taken of ground conditions when storing outdoors to avoid damage to the product. Outdoor storage areas should be protected against unauthorized access, for example, by means of a fence. Warnings against unauthorized entry should be posted.

A.11.5.5 See A.11.2.5.

A.11.5.10 See A.11.2.5.

A.11.6.1.4 See A.11.2.5.

A.11.6.2.4 See A.11.2.5.

A.11.7.1.4 See A.11.2.5.

A.11.7.2.3 See A.11.2.5.

A.11.7.2.4 See A.11.2.5.

A.11.8.1.1.2 It is recommended that electric or LP-Gas–powered trucks be employed rather than gasoline- or diesel-powered trucks to reduce the potential for contamination to ammonium nitrate.

A.11.8.1.2 Examples of hollow spaces include hollow conveyor rollers and hollow screw conveyor shafts.

A.11.8.2 See A.11.2.5.

A.12.2.5 See A.11.2.5.

A.12.2.10 See A.11.2.5.

A.12.2.12 See A.11.2.5.

A.12.3.1 See A.11.2.5.

A.12.3.2 See A.11.2.5.

A.12.3.2.1 See A.11.2.5.

A.12.3.5 See A.11.2.5.

A.12.4.3 See A.11.2.5.

A.12.5.5 See A.11.2.5.

A.12.5.10 See A.11.2.5.

A.12.5.16 See A.11.2.5.

A.12.6.1.4 See A.11.2.5.

A.12.6.2.4 See A.11.2.5.

A.12.7.1.4 See A.11.2.5.

A.12.7.2.4 See A.11.2.5.

A.12.8.2 See A.11.2.5.

A.13.2.5 See A.11.2.5.

A.13.2.10 See A.11.2.5.

A.13.2.12 See A.11.2.5.

A.13.3.1 See A.11.2.5.

A.13.3.2 See A.11.2.5.

A.13.3.2.1 See A.11.2.5.

A.13.3.5 See A.11.2.5.

A.13.4.3 See A.11.2.5.

A.13.5.5 See A.11.2.5.

A.13.5.10 See A.11.2.5.

A.13.5.15 See A.11.2.5.

A.13.6.1.4 See A.11.2.5.

A.13.6.2.4 See A.11.2.5.

A.13.7.1.4 See A.11.2.5.

A.13.7.2.4 See A.11.2.5.

A.13.8.2 See A.11.2.5.

A.14.1.1 The classification system for organic peroxides is package dependent. To address the scope of NFPA 400 for storage, use and handling each organic peroxide formulation is to be classified with respect to quantity and type of container. Classification should be done by professionals familiar with the properties of the organic peroxide formulation. Property information used for classification of organic peroxide formulations for UN Transportation of Dangerous Goods can be useful for the NFPA 400 classification. Other useful information includes density, small fire test data and fire data for response to sprinkler conditions. For further guidance, see Annex F.

A.14.1.2 For information on combustible or limited-combustible construction, see NFPA 220, *Standard on Types of Building Construction*.

A.14.2.4 In the venting equation, use the fuel characteristic constant for "gases with fundamental burning velocity less than 1.3 times that of propane." See NFPA 68, *Standard on Explosion Protection by Deflagration Venting*, for information on vent design. Refer to manufacturers' technical data for information on organic peroxide formulations that give off flammable gases upon decomposition.

A.14.2.5 See A.11.2.5.

A.14.2.6.1 Fire protection systems for material in containers other than original DOT packaging, including bulk tanks, and materials in the unpackaged state should be designed by design professionals familiar with the nature of the product under fire conditions.

A.14.2.10 See A.11.2.5.

A.14.2.12.8 The method of disposal can vary depending on the specific formulation and materials with which they might have been contaminated. Refer to the manufacturer or the supplier of the specific formulation for advice.

A.14.3.2 The classification system described in Section 4.1 is used only to determine the storage requirements established by this code. It is not meant to be a substitute for the hazard identification system established by NFPA 704, *Standard System for the Identification of the Hazards of Materials for Emergency Response*. Since the hazard characteristics of organic peroxide formulations vary widely depending on the type of organic peroxide, the diluent, and their relative concentrations, each specific formulation will have to be rated individually according to the criteria established in NFPA 704, *Standard System for the Identification of the Hazards of Materials for Emergency Response*.

For the purpose of this document, an important building is one that is occupied or that contains facilities vital to the operation of the plant.

A.14.3.2.4 In the venting equation, use the fuel characteristic constant for "gases with fundamental burning velocity less than 1.3 times that of propane." See NFPA 68, *Standard on Explosion Protection by Deflagration Venting*, for information on vent design. Refer to manufacturers' technical data for information on organic peroxide formulations that give off flammable gases upon decomposition.

A.14.3.2.5 For example, a sprinklered building, detached by 50 ft (15.3 m), can contain up to 500 lb (227 kg) of Class I, 50,000 lb (22,700 kg) of Class II, and 50,000 lb (22,700 kg) of Class III formulations, according to the following ratios:

(1) Class I:

$$\frac{500 \text{ lb}}{2000 \text{ lb (max)}} \times 100 = 25\% \quad \frac{227 \text{ kg}}{907 \text{ kg (max)}} \times 100 = 25\%$$

(2) Class II:

$$\frac{50,000 \text{ lb}}{100,000 \text{ lb (max)}} \times 100 = 50\% \quad \frac{22,700 \text{ kg}}{45,400 \text{ kg (max)}} \times 100 = 50\%$$

(3) Class III:

$$\frac{50,000 \text{ lb}}{200,000 \text{ lb (max)}} \times 100 = 25\% \quad \frac{22,700 \text{ lb}}{90,700 \text{ lb (max)}} \times 100 = 25\%$$

In no case does the quantity in storage exceed the maximum for its class, nor does the sum of the percentages exceed 100 percent.

A.14.3.2.9.5 Since no commercially available Class I organic peroxide formulations are supplied in 55 gal (208 L) drums, there is no requirement for such storage.

A.14.3.4.3.1 A detached, mechanically refrigerated building for storing organic peroxide formulations that require temperature control is illustrated in Figure A.14.3.4.3.1.

A.14.3.4.3.3 Figure A.14.3.4.3.3 is an example of a nonrefrigerated building for storing less than 5000 lb (2270 kg) of organic peroxide formulations for detached storage as allowed by 14.3.4.3.3.

A.14.3.5 See A.11.2.5.

A.14.4.3 See A.11.2.5.

A.14.5.5 See A.11.2.5.

A.14.5.8 Considerations should be given for maintaining proper refrigeration capability in the event of a loss of power. Some materials, when frozen, could cause separation of a carrier from the organic peroxide.

A.14.5.10 See A.11.2.5.

A.14.5.16.3 The method of disposal can vary depending on the specific formulation and materials.

A.14.6.1.4 See A.11.2.5.

A.14.6.2.4 See A.11.2.5.

A.14.7.1.4 See A.11.2.5.

A.14.7.2.4 See A.11.2.5.

A.14.8.2 See A.11.2.5.

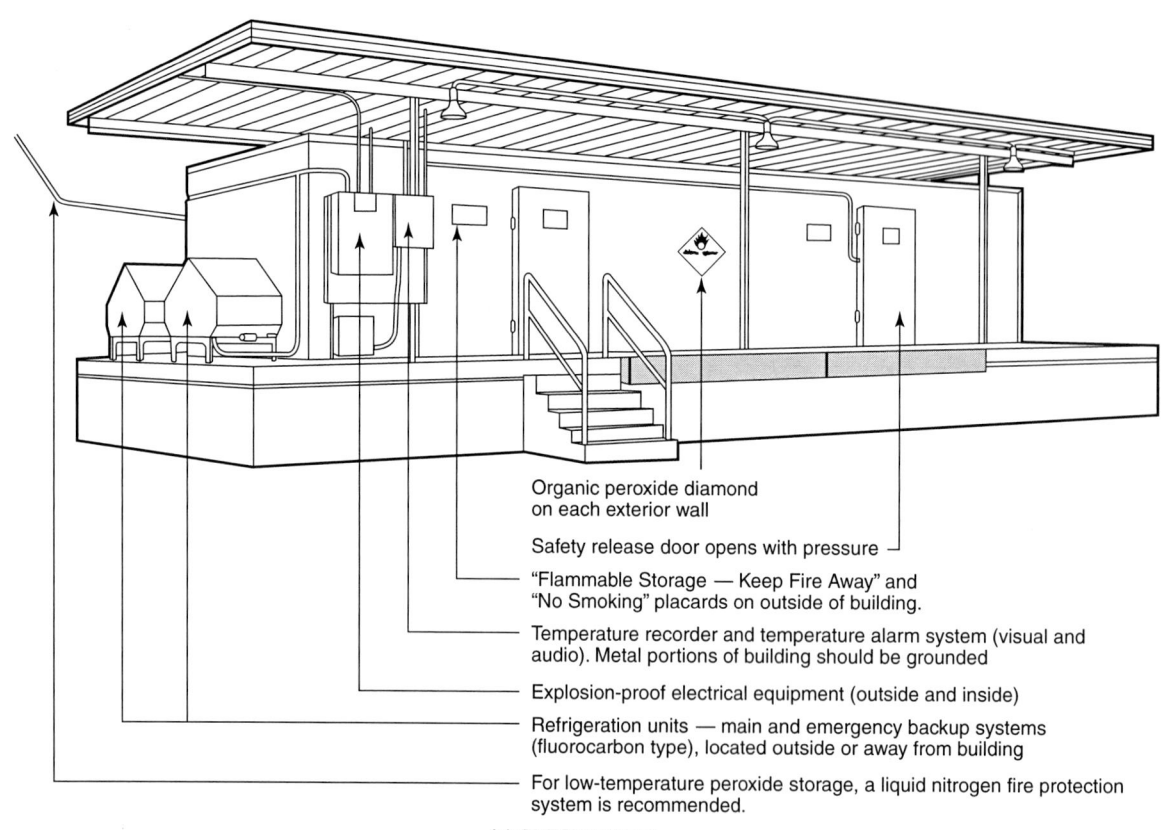

Organic peroxide diamond on each exterior wall

Safety release door opens with pressure

"Flammable Storage — Keep Fire Away" and "No Smoking" placards on outside of building.

Temperature recorder and temperature alarm system (visual and audio). Metal portions of building should be grounded

Explosion-proof electrical equipment (outside and inside)

Refrigeration units — main and emergency backup systems (fluorocarbon type), located outside or away from building

For low-temperature peroxide storage, a liquid nitrogen fire protection system is recommended.

(a) OUTSIDE VIEW

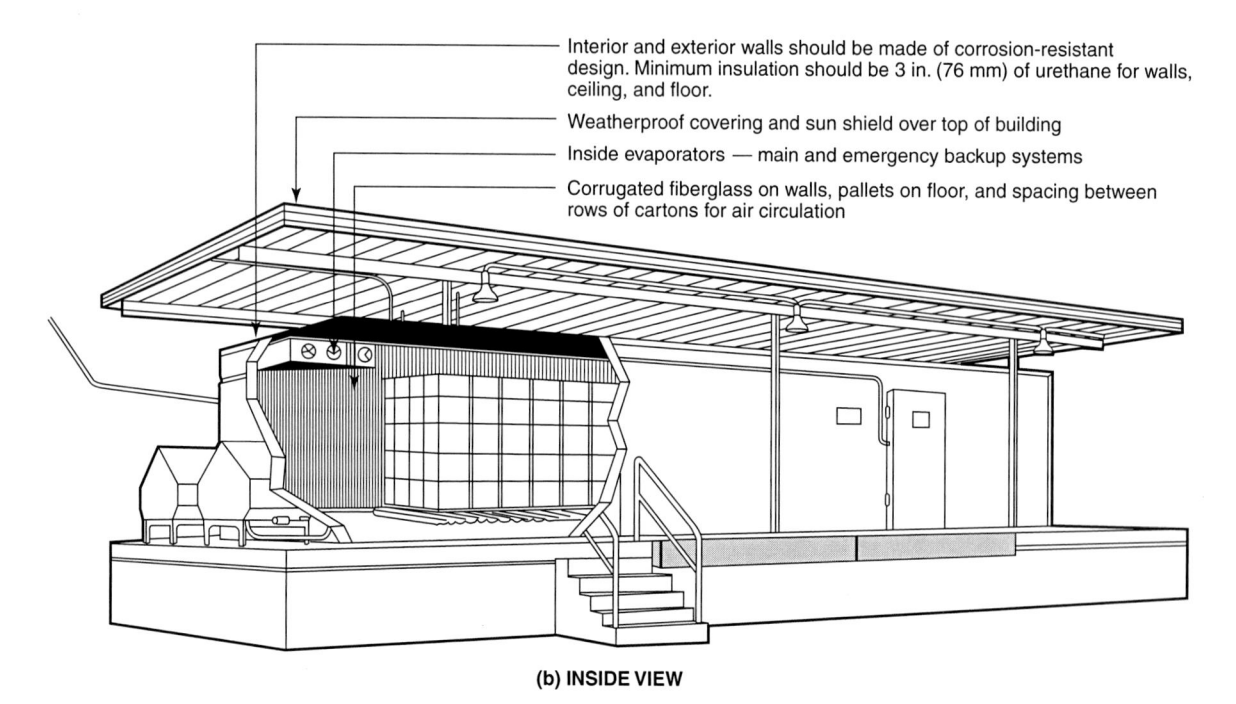

Interior and exterior walls should be made of corrosion-resistant design. Minimum insulation should be 3 in. (76 mm) of urethane for walls, ceiling, and floor.

Weatherproof covering and sun shield over top of building

Inside evaporators — main and emergency backup systems

Corrugated fiberglass on walls, pallets on floor, and spacing between rows of cartons for air circulation

(b) INSIDE VIEW

FIGURE A.14.3.4.3.1 Refrigerated Storage Building and Key Recommendations.

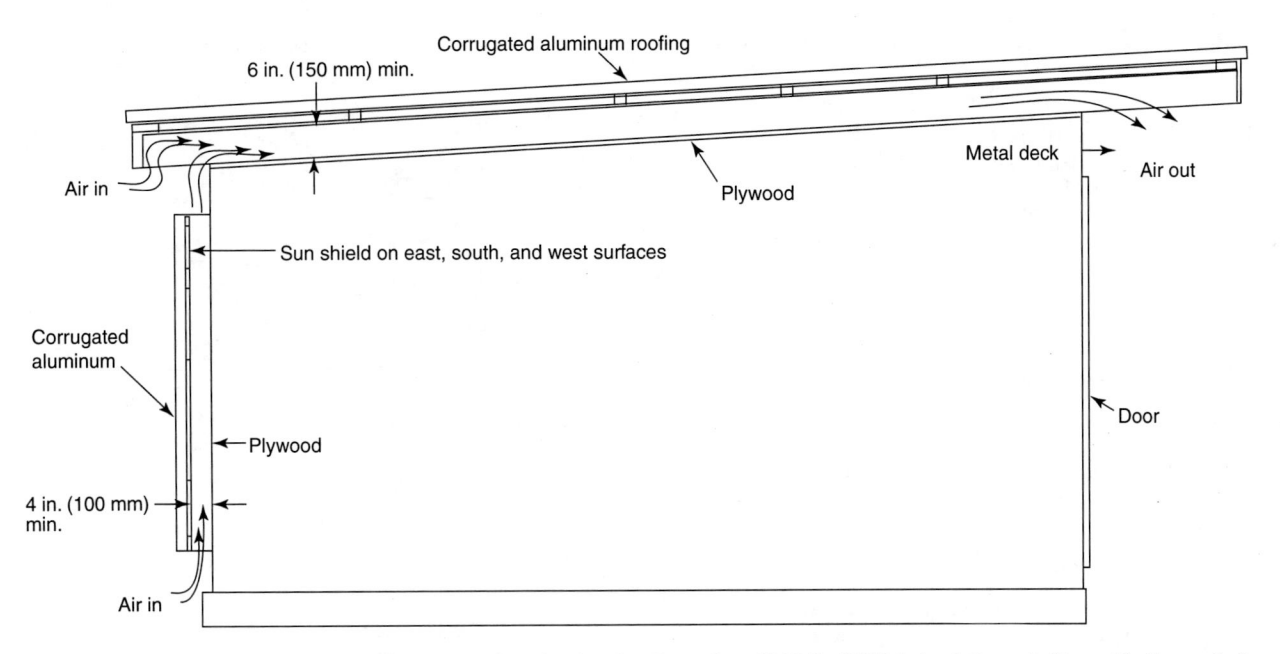

FIGURE A.14.3.4.3.3 Detached Storage Building for Storing Less than 5000 lb (2270 kg) of Organic Peroxide Formulations.

A.15.1.4 In the manufacturing process, materials are collected and staged for transportation from manufacturing areas to a storage or warehouse location. Transient storage is intended to describe those materials being staged for transport. They are called transient while they are in the manufacturing area because they are not in their storage location. In the manufacturing location, finished goods can be found in a packaged state where they can be further palletized or otherwise arranged or collected awaiting transportation.

A.15.2.1.1 The NFPA *Fire Protection Guide to Hazardous Materials* should be used for guidance on compatibility.

A.15.2.1.2 Spill control, drainage, and containment are typically required under environmental regulations. Check the building code to determine whether it contains spill control requirements.

The decomposition of stored commercially available strengths of liquid and solid oxidizers can emit toxic gases. Additionally, the runoff from spills of stored oxidizers or from oxidizers mixed with fire-extinguishing agents can contain materials hazardous to the environment.

The hazards of stored oxidizers can manifest themselves in one or more of five distinct hazardous situations as follows:

(1) They can increase the burning rate of combustible materials.
(2) They can cause spontaneous ignition of combustible materials.
(3) They can decompose rapidly.
(4) They can liberate hazardous gases.
(5) They can undergo self-sustained decomposition, which can result in an explosion.
(6) They can react explosively if mixed with incompatibles or in fire conditions.

A.15.2.5 See A.11.2.5.

A.15.2.6 Automatic sprinklers are an effective method to control fires involving oxidizers in conjunction with the other fire prevention requirements in the document.

A.15.2.6.1 Dry pipe and double-interlock preaction (DIPA) sprinkler systems are generally prohibited by 15.2.6.1.1 for use with oxidizers. In mercantile occupancies with open-air environments that are already protected by these types of systems as prescribed by other codes, it is considered acceptable to store quantities defined by this code, with the recognition that these commodities may not be adequately protected. Outside storage in this manner is preferred to inside storage.

A.15.2.6.2.1 Conditions that affect the need for hydrant protection include nearness of the exposures, size and construction of the building, amount and class of the oxidizer stored, and availability of public fire protection.

A.15.2.6.3.1 A dry-chemical fire-extinguishing agent containing ammonium compounds (such as some A:B:C agents) should not be used on oxidizers that contain chlorine and bromine. The reaction between the oxidizer and the ammonium salts in the fire-extinguishing agent can produce the explosive compound nitrogen trichloride (NCl_3). Carbon dioxide or other extinguishing agents that function by a smothering action for effective use are of no value in extinguishing fires involving oxidizers.

A.15.2.6.3.2 Halon extinguishers should not be used on fires involving oxidizers because they can react with the oxidizer.

A.15.2.6.3.3 Halocarbon clean agent extinguishers as identified in NFPA 2001, *Standard on Clean Agent Fire Extinguishing Systems*, are chemically similar to Halon and unless proved different should be assumed to react with the oxidizer.

A.15.2.10 See A.11.2.5.

A.15.2.12 Care should be exercised because some oxidizers are mutually incompatible. Chlorinated isocyanurates and hypochlorites are examples of oxidizers that are incompatible. The NFPA *Fire Protection Guide to Hazardous Materials* lists many oxidizers and other materials that result in hazardous interactions.

A.15.2.12.10 This requirement to restrict exposure to water is not intended to apply to the application of fire protection water.

A.15.2.12.11 Where absorptive combustible packing materials used to contain water-soluble oxidizers have become wet during either fire or nonfire conditions, the oxidizer can impregnate the packing material. This creates a serious fire hazard when the packing material dries. Wooden pallets that are exposed to water solutions of an oxidizer also can exhibit this behavior.

A.15.3.1 See A.11.2.5.

A.15.3.2.1.1 Impregnation of wood for fire retardancy or to prevent decay does not protect the wood from impregnation by the oxidizer.

A.15.3.2.2.3 The term *commodity* is used as defined in NFPA 13, *Standard for the Installation of Sprinkler Systems*.

A.15.3.2.3.2.7 Only the building limit, not the pile limit, height, or width, can be increased by this provision.

A.15.3.2.5.4.5 For example, two tanks containing 4000 lb (1814 kg) and 3000 lb (1360 kg) of Class 4 oxidizer are separated by 25 ft (7.6 m). Because they are separated by less than 10 percent of 300 ft (92 m), the total quantity of 7000 lb (3175 kg) requires a minimum separation of 400 ft (122 m) to the nearest important structure in accordance with 15.3.2.5.3.4.

A.15.3.5.2.1 Recommended mercantile store arrangements for mutually incompatible oxidizers are shown in Figure A.15.3.5.2.1(a) and Figure A.15.3.5.2.1(b). These two diagrams illustrate arrangements that minimize the chance of exposure to incompatible materials. Wherever possible, vertical separation should be maintained between incompatible materials.

A.15.5.5 See A.11.2.5.

Shelf 1: Oxidizer A   Shelf 4: Oxidizer B   Shelf 7: Oxidizer C
Shelf 2: Oxidizer A   Shelf 5: Oxidizer B   Shelf 8: Oxidizer C
Shelf 3: Oxidizer A   Shelf 6: Oxidizer B   Shelf 9: Oxidizer C

Oxidizers A, B, and C are mutually incompatible.

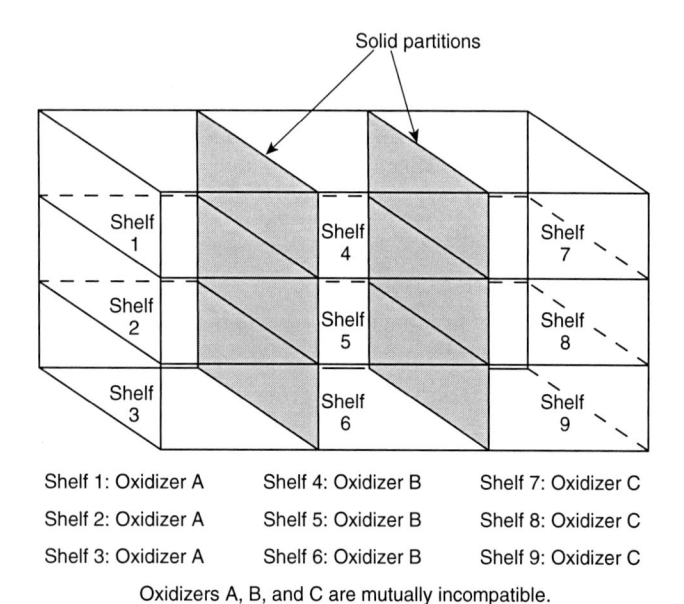

FIGURE A.15.3.5.2.1(a) Recommended Mercantile Store Arrangement for Mutually Incompatible Oxidizers.

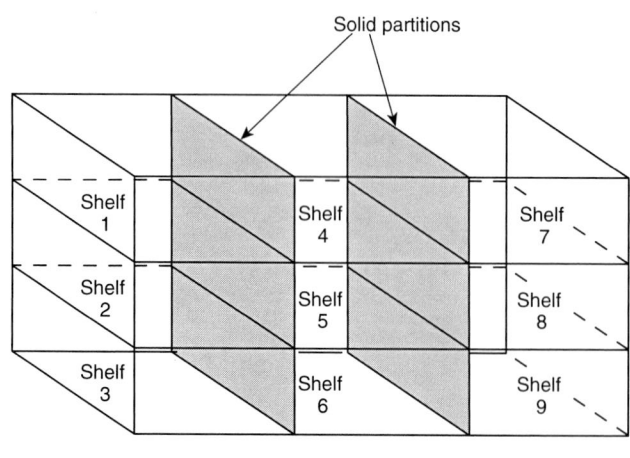

Shelf 1: Oxidizer A   Shelf 4: Oxidizer C   Shelf 7: Oxidizer D
Shelf 2: Inert   Shelf 5: Inert   Shelf 8: Inert
Shelf 3: Oxidizer B   Shelf 6: Incompatible liquid   Shelf 9: Incompatible liquid

Oxidizers A, B, C, and D are mutually incompatible with each other and with the incompatible liquids.

FIGURE A.15.3.5.2.1(b) Recommended Mercantile Store Arrangement for Mutually Incompatible Oxidizers and Other Incompatible Materials.

A.15.5.10 See A.11.2.5.

A.15.5.16 See A.11.2.5.

A.15.6.1.4 See A.11.2.5.

A.15.6.2.4 See A.11.2.5.

A.15.7.1.4 See A.11.2.5.

A.15.7.2.4 See A.11.2.5.

A.15.8.2 See A.11.2.5.

A.17.2.1.1 The retention of spilled pyrophoric liquids around process tanks, storage tanks, or vessels and other containers should be avoided to prevent a catastrophic failure of the vessels or containers in the event of fire.

A.17.2.5 See A.11.2.5.

A.17.2.6 Pyrophoric liquids catch fire easily and are often water reactive. The amount of water needed to put out a fire may depend on the volume of material burning. Adding insufficient amounts of water could result in an uncontrolled reaction.

A.17.2.10 See A.11.2.5.

A.17.2.12 See A.11.2.5.

A.17.3.1 See A.11.2.5.

A.17.3.2.1 See A.11.2.5.

A.17.3.5 See A.11.2.5.

A.17.4.1.2 When solids are involved, an approximation of the liquid volume of the containers used is to be determined. For example, if the solids were packaged in a 55-gallon drum, a volume of 55 gal would be used. If the solids were packaged in 1-gallon containers, the volume would be determined accordingly.

A.17.4.3 See A.11.2.5.

A.17.4.3.1 In no event should the distance between exposures indicated in 17.4.1.2 be less than twice the distance required by NFPA 30, *Flammable and Combustible Liquids Code*, for an equivalent volume of Class IB flammable liquid.

A.17.5.5 See A.11.2.5.

A.17.5.10 See A.11.2.5.

A.17.5.16 See A.11.2.5.

A.17.6.1.3 Secondary containment areas can be designed to be remote from process or storage areas. Drainage can be used as a means to remove the spilled liquid and transport it to a remote location. Buried tanks can be used as a means to contain spilled liquids. Sloped floors or floors designed to drain spilled liquids away from storage tanks and container storage all serve to minimize a fire event created by a spill.

A.17.6.1.4 See A.11.2.5.

A.17.6.2.3.1 See A.17.6.1.3.

A.17.6.2.4 See A.11.2.5.

A.17.7.1.2 See A.17.6.1.3.

A.17.7.1.4 See A.11.2.5.

A.17.7.2.2.1 See A.17.6.1.3.

A.17.7.2.4 See A.11.2.5.

A.17.8.2 See A.11.2.5.

A.18.2.10 See A.11.2.5.

A.18.2.12 See A.11.2.5.

A.18.3.1 See A.11.2.5.

A.18.3.2 See A.11.2.5.

A.18.3.2.1 See A.11.2.5.

A.18.3.5 See A.11.2.5.

A.18.4.3 See A.11.2.5.

A.18.5.10 See A.11.2.5.

A.18.5.16 See A.11.2.5.

A.18.6.1.4 See A.11.2.5.

A.18.6.2.4 See A.11.2.5.

A.18.7.1.4 See A.11.2.5.

A.18.7.2.4 See A.11.2.5.

A.18.8.2 See A.11.2.5.

A.19.2.5 See A.11.2.5.

A.19.3.1 See A.11.2.5.

A.19.3.2 See A.11.2.5.

A.19.3.2.1 See A.11.2.5.

A.19.5.5 See A.11.2.5.

A.19.5.10 See A.11.2.5.

A.19.7.2.4 See A.11.2.5.

A.20.2.5 See A.11.2.5.

A.20.2.10 See A.11.2.5.

A.20.2.12 See A.11.2.5.

A.20.3.1 See A.11.2.5.

A.20.3.2 See A.11.2.5.

A.20.3.2.1 See A.11.2.5.

A.20.3.5 See A.11.2.5.

A.20.4.3 See A.11.2.5.

A.20.5.5 See A.11.2.5.

A.20.5.10 See A.11.2.5.

A.20.5.16 See A.11.2.5.

A.20.6.1.3.1 Secondary containment areas can be designed to be remote from process or storage areas. Drainage can be used as a means to remove spilled liquids and transport them to a remote location.

A.20.6.1.4 See A.11.2.5.

A.20.6.2.3.1 See A.20.6.1.3.1.

A.20.6.2.4 See A.11.2.5.

A.20.7.1.2.1 See A.20.6.1.3.1.

A.20.7.1.4 See A.11.2.5.

A.20.7.2.4 See A.11.2.5.

A.20.8.2 See A.11.2.5.

A.21.1.1.2.1(1) For regulations on the transportation of gases, see 49 CFR 100 to 179 (Transportation) and *Transportation of Dangerous Goods Regulations*. [**55:** A.1.1.2(1)]

A.21.1.1.2.1(3) It is intended that installations of bulk oxygen systems regulated by NFPA 99, *Health Care Facilities Code*, also comply with the requirements of Chapter 9 of NFPA 55, *Compressed Gases and Cryogenic Fluids Code*. The bulk oxygen system terminates at the point where oxygen at service pressure first enters the supply line. [**55:** A.1.1.2(3)]

A.21.1.1.2.1(5) For information, see NFPA 55, *Compressed Gases and Cryogenic Fluids Code*, or NFPA 58, *Liquefied Petroleum Gas Code*. [**55:** A.1.1.2(6)]

A.21.1.1.2.1(6) The storage of gases outside of laboratory work areas is covered by this standard. [**55:** A.1.1.2(7)]

A.21.1.1.2.1(11) NFPA 55 is used as the source document for the fundamental requirements for compressed hydrogen gas (GH2), or liquefied hydrogen gas (LH2) system installations. Correlation between NFPA 55 and NFPA 2, *Hydrogen Technologies Code*, is the responsibility of the two technical committees involved. The installation requirements for bulk GH2 or LH2 are viewed as fundamental provisions. On the other hand, use-specific requirements for designated applications such as vehicular fueling are not resident in NFPA 55 and are under the purview of the NFPA 2 Technical Committee. Where there are specific provisions or controls included in NFPA 55, the specific controls of NFPA 55 will govern except that modifications made to provisions that have been extracted can be followed when the modifications have been made within NFPA's extract procedure as indicated in the *Manual of Style for NFPA Technical Committee Documents*. [**55:** A.1.1.2(1)]

A.21.2.5 Bulk hydrogen compressed gas systems terminate at the source valve. In cylinder filling or packaging operations, cylinders located on filling manifolds located downstream of the source valve are not considered to be part of the bulk gas system. For definitions of source valve and bulk hydrogen compressed gas system, see 3.3.88 and 3.3.93.2 of NFPA 55. Additional requirements for source valves can be found in Section 6.19 of NFPA 55. [55: A.6.5]

A.21.2.8 Under the requirements of 29 CFR 1910.38 established by OSHA regulations, employers must establish an employee alarm system that complies with 29 CFR 1910.165. The requirements of 29 CFR 1910.165 for the employee alarm system include, but are not limited to, systems that are capable of being perceived above ambient noise or light levels by all employees in the affected portions of the workplace. Tactile devices may be used to alert those employees who would not otherwise be able to recognize the audible or visual alarm. The alarm system may be electrically powered or powered by pneumatic or other means. State, local, or other governmental regulations may also establish requirements for employee alarm systems. [55: A.6.7]

A.21.2.9 NFPA 55, *Compressed Gases and Cryogenic Fluids Code*, provides more information on this subject. [55: A.6.8]

A.21.2.10 The intent of this section is to require a water-based fire extinguishing system to keep vessels containing compressed gases cool in the event of an exposure fire, thereby minimizing the likelihood of a release and associated consequences. Accordingly, alternative fire extinguishing systems, such as dry-chemical or gaseous agent systems, should not be substituted. [55: A.6.9]

A.21.3.1.1 The equipment referenced is intended to include fuel cell applications, generation of hydrogen from portable or transportable hydrogen generation equipment, batteries, and similar devices and equipment that utilize hydrogen for the purpose of power generation. It does not include hydrogen production facilities intended to produce hydrogen used for distribution or repackaging operations operated by gas producers, distributors, and repackagers. [55: A.7.1.1]

A.21.3.1.5.2 Figure A.21.3.1.5.2 is a schematic showing the separation distances required under 21.3.1.5.2. [55: A.7.1.6.2]

A.21.3.1.9.3 Clearance is required from combustible materials to minimize the effects of exposure fires to the materials stored or used. The requirement to separate the materials from vegetation should not be interpreted to mean that the area is maintained free of all vegetation. In some settings, gas systems are located on grounds that are maintained with formal landscaping. Some judgment must be exercised to determine whether the vegetation poses what might be viewed as an exposure hazard to the materials stored. Cut lawns, formal landscaping, and similar vegetation do not ordinarily present a hazard and should be allowed. On the other hand, tall, dry grass or weeds and vegetation that fringes on the border of an urban–wildland interface might be viewed as a hazard. [55:7.1.10.3]

A.21.3.1.13.3 The gas supplier should be consulted for advice under these circumstances. [55: A.7.1.15.3]

A.21.3.1.16.1.3 Underground piping systems are those systems that are buried and in contact with earth fill or similar materials. Piping located in open-top or grated-top trenches is not considered to be underground although it may be below grade. [55:7.1.18.1.2]

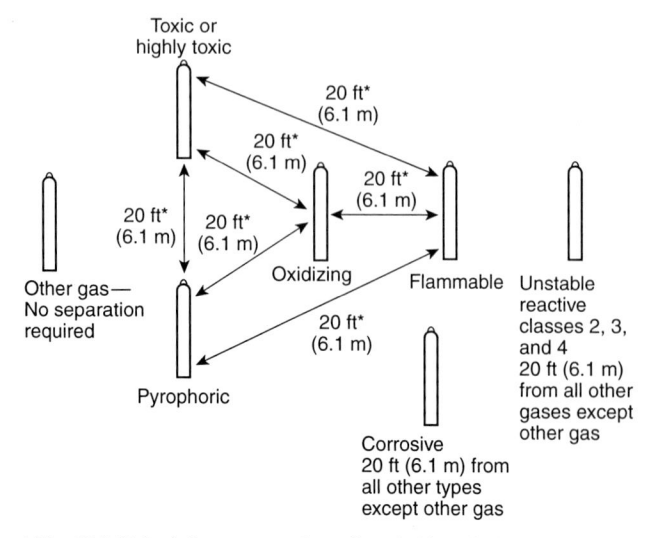

* The 20 ft (6.1 m) distance may be reduced without limit when separated by a barrier of noncombustible materials at least 1.5 m (5 ft) high that has a fire-resistant rating of at least ½ hour.

FIGURE A.21.3.1.5.2 Separation of Gas Cylinders by Hazard.

A.21.3.3.1.11.1(A) In operations where an automatic emergency shutoff valve is activated by a control system that is operated from a remote station or by remote station software, the software system should be designed to provide a visual indication of the emergency shutdown control system. The visual emergency shutdown function should be able to be identified by trained operators and recognizable to emergency response personnel. [55: A.7.3.1.11.1.1]

A.21.3.3.1.12.2 An approved means of leak detection and emergency shutoff is one way of meeting the requirements for excess flow control. [55:7.3.1.12.2]

A.21.3.5.2.2.1 Portions of the system upstream of the source valve include the containers or bulk supply as well as control equipment designed to control the flow of gas into a piping system. The piping system downstream of the source valve is protected by excess flow control should failure occur in the piping system and is not required to be protected by the fire barrier. The fire barrier serves to protect those portions of the system that are the most vulnerable, along with the necessary controls used to operate the system. [55:7.5.2.1.1]

A.21.3.6.2.1.1 See A.21.3.5.2.2.1. [55: A.7.6.2.1.1]

A.21.3.7.2.1.1 See A.21.3.5.2.2.1. [55: A.7.7.2.1.1]

A.21.3.8.3.1.1 See A.21.3.5.2.2.1. [55: A.7.8.3.1.1]

A.21.3.9.3.4.3(A) See A.21.3.5.2.2.1. [55: A.7.9.2.2.1.1]

A.21.3.9.3.6 The areas for typical restricted flow orifices are shown in Table A.21.3.9.3.6. [55: A.7.9.3.6]

A.21.3.9.3.6.2 The formula has been taken from industry publications, including the Scott Specialty Gases, *Design and Safety Handbook*. It is based on estimated flow rates for air at 70°F (21°C) discharging to normal atmospheric pressure through an average shape and quality orifice. It can be assumed to be ±15 percent accurate. Correction factors have been built into the formula as presented in 21.3.9.3.6.2 to accommodate the use of gases other than air (e.g., use of specific gravity data). [55: A.7.9.3.6.2]

Table A.21.3.9.3.6 Typical Orifice Areas

Orifice Diameter		Area	
in.	cm	in.^{2}	cm^2
0.006	0.015	2.83×10^{-5}	1.83×10^{-4}
0.010	0.025	7.85×10^{-5}	5.06×10^{-4}
0.014	0.036	1.54×10^{-4}	9.93×10^{-4}

A.21.3.10.1.2.1 See A.21.3.5.2.2.1. [55: A.7.10.1.2.1]

A.21.3.10.2.2.1 See A.21.3.5.2.2.1. [55: A.7.10.2.2.1]

A.21.4.2 Pressure vessels of any type may be subject to additional regulations imposed by various states or other legal jurisdictions. Users should be aware that compliance with DOT or ASME requirements might not satisfy all of the required regulations for the location in which the vessel is to be installed or used. Liquid oxygen containers should be fabricated from materials meeting the impact test requirements of paragraph UG-84 of the ASME *Boiler and Pressure Vessel Code*, Section VIII. [55: A.8.2]

A.21.4.2.3.3.1 Vaporizers or heat exchangers used to vaporize cryogenic fluids can accumulate a large load of ice during operation. Additional requirements to be considered in the design include snow load for the area where the installation is located as well as the requirements for seismic conditions. The operating conditions of systems vary, and the designer has a responsibility to consider all the loads that might be imposed. Foundations that could be used to support delivery vehicles as well might require special consideration relevant to live loads as well as for the dead loads imposed by the equipment itself. [55: A.8.2.3.3]

A.21.4.2.4.5.1 Pressure relief valves typically are spring-loaded valves where the relief pressure is set by adjustment of a spring. Valves should be sealed to prevent adjustment by other than authorized personnel typically found at a retest facility. An ASME pressure relief valve is designed to comply with the requirements of the ASME *Boiler and Pressure Vessel Code* and typically is equipped with a wire seal to prevent tampering. [55: A.8.2.5.5.1]

A.21.4.4.1.1.2 An example of this identification is 360 degree wrap-around tape. [55: 8.1.1.2]

A.21.4.7.2 It is not uncommon to have inert cryogenic fluids used to provide stage effects for theatrical performances that are conducted within assembly occupancies. The fluids are sometimes placed within these occupancies with special controls, including ventilation systems, fire detection systems, monitors for oxygen deficiency, warning signs, and remote fill indicating devices that indicate tank volume when a remote filling point is provided and stationary tanks are involved.

Such installations are normally permitted on a case-by-case basis under the requirements of Section 1.5.

Clearance is required from combustible materials to minimize the effects of exposure fires to the materials stored or used. The requirement to separate the materials from vegetation should not be interpreted to mean that the area is maintained free of all vegetation. In some settings, gas systems are located on grounds that are maintained with formal landscaping. Some judgment must be exercised to determine whether the vegetation poses what might be viewed as an exposure hazard to the materials stored. Cut lawns, formal landscaping, and similar vegetation do not ordinarily present a hazard, and should be allowed. On the other hand, tall, dry grass or weeds and vegetation that fringes on the border of an urban–wildland interface might be viewed as a hazard. [55: A.8.7.2]

A.21.4.13.2.5 Flood hazard areas typically are identified on either (1) the special flood hazard area shown on the flood insurance rate map or (2) the area subject to flooding during the design flood and shown on a jurisdiction's flood hazard map or otherwise legally designated. [55: A.8.13.2.5]

A.21.4.13.2.6.4(B) The intent of these provisions is to make certain that the cryogenic installation is not exposed to the potential of a pool fire from the release of flammable or combustible liquids. Cryogenic fluids are not diked in order that they are allowed to dissipate should leakage occur. Studies conducted by NASA (NSS 1740.16, *Safety Standard for Hydrogen and Hydrogen Systems*) show that the use of dikes around liquid hydrogen storage facilities serves to prolong ground-level flammable cloud travel and that the dispersion mechanism is enhanced by vaporization-induced turbulence. The travel of spilled or leaked cryogenic fluid to distances greater than a few feet (meters) from the source given the nature of the typical leak is considered to be implausible due to the character of cryogenic fluids and their ability to quickly absorb heat from the surrounding environment.

A.21.4.13.2.7.2 The placement of stationary containers is limited with respect to exposure hazards. Table 21.4.7.2 establishes the minimum separation distance between a building and any stationary tank at 1 ft (0.3 m). Additional limitations are placed on wall openings, air intakes, and other exposures. The material-specific tables for liquid hydrogen and liquid oxygen specify increased distances according to the type of construction adjacent to the tank. A problem arises when courtyards are configured so as to interrupt the free movement of air around a tank where an asphyxiation hazard, a flammable hazard, or an oxygen-enriched environment can be created. [55: A.8.13.2.7.2]

Placement of stationary containers proximate to the wall of the building served is allowable provided the minimum separation distances for exposure hazards are met. When additional walls encroach on the installation to form a court, the focus of concern shifts away from the exposure hazards associated with the building itself to the hazards associated with personnel due to hazardous atmospheres that can be created due to the lack of free air movement and ventilation.

By specifying the minimum distance between the tank and the encroaching walls that form the court, the circulation of adequate air is ensured. Placing the tank at not less than the height of two of the three encroaching walls results in creating an opening such that the angular dimension between the top of two of the three encroaching walls and the point over which the tank is placed is not greater than 45 degrees, thereby allowing the circulation of air through the space in which the tank is installed.

A.21.4.13.2.7.2(A) See Figure A.21.4.13.2.7.2(A).

A.21.4.14.1.3.1(A) CGA P-18, *Standard for Bulk Inert Gas Systems at Consumer Sites*, recommends periodic inspection intervals for inert gas systems. [55: A.8.14.1.3.1.1]

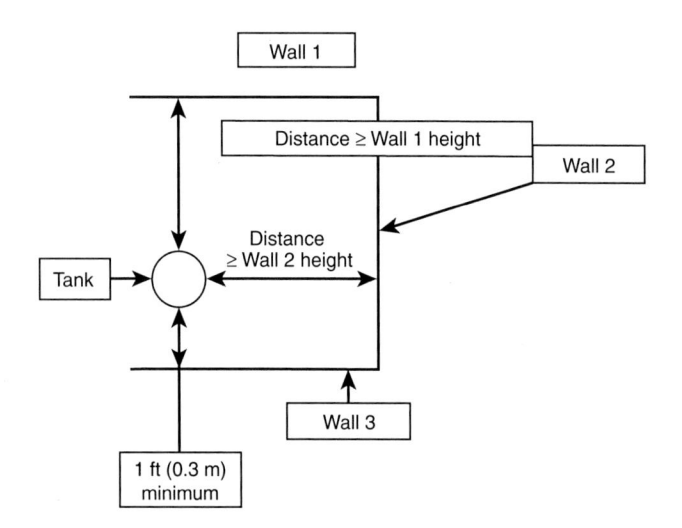

FIGURE A.21.4.13.2.7.2(A) Illustration of Minimum Separation Distance to Exposure from Stationary Tank.

A.21.4.14.11.2.3 In operations where an automatic emergency shutoff valve is activated by a control system that is operated from a remote station or by remote station software, the software system should be designed to provide a visual indication of the emergency shutdown control system. The visual emergency shutdown function should be able to be identified by trained operators and recognizable to emergency response personnel. [55: A.8.14.11.2.3.1]

A.21.4.14.11.3.4 The inert cryogens, nitrogen and argon, do not require the installation of a noncombustible spill pad, because they do not typically condense oxygen from the air in sufficient quantities to pose a hazard during transfer. [55: A.8.14.11.3.4]

A.21.4.14.11.3.4(A) The noncombustible spill pad is provided for liquid helium transfer operations, because the cryogen is at a temperature that is sufficiently low enough to liquefy oxygen, presenting a hazard when in contact with combustible surfaces. [55: A.8.14.11.3.4.1]

Annex B Chemical Data

This annex is not a part of the requirements of this NFPA document but is included for informational purposes only.

B.1 General. The information provided in Annex B is not a part of the requirements of this document but is included for informational purposes.

B.2 Hazard Recognition. Chapter 5 introduces the concepts of control areas and MAQs. The purpose is to permit limited amounts of hazardous materials in occupancies having minimum controls without triggering the more restrictive Protection Level 1 through Protection Level 5 building requirements. The allowable quantities in Table 5.2.1.1.3, Table 5.2.1.2 through Table 5.2.1.8, and Table 5.2.1.10.1 are based on demonstrated need and historical safe storage and use of hazardous contents. The preponderance of provisions contained in Chapter 6 and those of Chapters 11 through 21 establish additional controls for occupancies exceeding the hazardous materials limits (MAQs) prescribed for control areas.

Not all of the hazardous materials categories are placed into the high hazard category, and some of these materials (contents) have been recognized as being of low or ordinary hazard, depending on their nature in a fire. For example, Class IIIB combustible liquids, Class 1 unstable (reactive) materials, Class 1 water-reactive materials, Class 1 oxidizing solids and liquids, and Class IV and Class V organic peroxides are hazardous materials, which, in some cases, do not have a MAQ and, therefore, are not required to comply with the requirements for Protection Level 1 through Protection Level 5. Some materials, though classified as high hazard, such as aerosols, are exempt from the requirements of NFPA 400, as they are regulated elsewhere within the regulatory scheme developed by NFPA. For additional exceptions, see 1.1.2. [5000: A.34.1.1]

Figure B.2 helps to illustrate the conditions under which the protection level requirements are applicable. [5000: A.34.1.1]

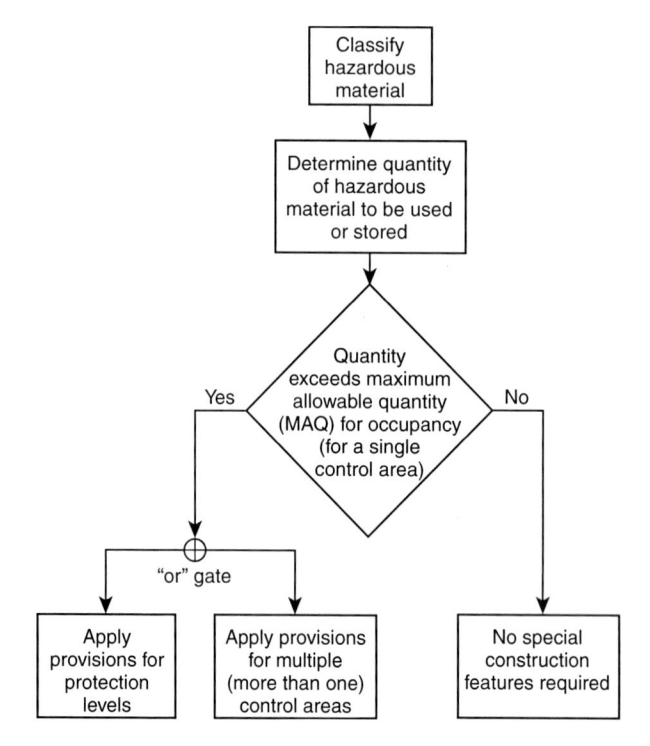

FIGURE B.2 Flow Chart Illustrating Protection Level Applicability.

Material safety data sheets (MSDS) are used as a primary means to assess the hazards of a specific material. In the U.S., the OSHA Hazard Communication Rule (29 CFR 1900.1200) prescribes what information is to be provided by MSDS. Over the years there have been a number of guidelines prepared that describe the information that is to be included. ANSI Z400.1, *Hazardous Industrial Chemicals—Material Safety Data Sheets—Preparation*, specifies the general layout of MSDS, 16 headings with standardized wording, the numbering and order of these headings, and the information required to complete an MSDS. The major headings of this standard include:

Section 1: Product and Company Identification
Section 2: Hazards Identification
Section 3: Composition/Information on Ingredients
Section 4: First Aid Measures
Section 5: Fire Fighting Measures
Section 6: Accidental Release Measures
Section 7: Handling and Storage
Section 8: Exposure Controls/Personal Protection
Section 9: Physical and Chemical Properties
Section 10: Stability and Reactivity
Section 11: Toxicological Information
Section 12: Ecological Information
Section 13: Disposal Considerations
Section 14: Transport Information
Section 15: Regulatory Information
Section 16: Other Information

The American Chemical Society publishes chemical abstracts as pointers to the chemical literature. Since 1907, their Chemical Abstracts Service (CAS) has indexed and summarized chemistry-related articles from more than 40,000 scientific journals, in addition to patents, conference proceedings, and other documents pertinent to chemistry, life sciences, and many other fields. In total, abstracts for more than 25 million documents are accessible online through CAS.

Substance identification is a special strength of CAS. It is widely known as the CAS Registry, the largest substance identification system in existence. When CAS processes a chemical substance newly encountered in the literature, its molecular structure diagram, systematic chemical name, molecular formula, and other identifying information are added to the Registry, and it is assigned a unique CAS Registry Number. The Registry now contains records for more than 30 million organic and inorganic substances and more than 58 million sequences.

Individual chemicals are identified through the use of a CAS registry number, commonly referred to as the CAS number or CASRN. The number, which has no chemical significance, is used to link the material through its molecular structure into an index system where the Chemical Abstracts name is provided.

The CAS number is unique for each given material; however, with few exceptions, mixtures of chemicals are not assigned a CAS number per se, since each individual component of the mixture has its own unique CAS number. For the purposes of hazard classification and the application of NFPA 400, there are three primary identifiers for each chemical that must be known:

(1) CAS number (unless it is a chemical mixture)
(2) Concentration (typically expressed in weight percent for solids or liquids and volume percent for gases)
(3) Physical state (solid, liquid, or gas)

For example, consider the material hydrochloric acid, also called hydrogen chloride. It can exist in the anhydrous form (as a gas) or in a water solution as the aqueous liquid material of varying concentrations. The hazard properties of the material vary with the form.

The regulatory approach used by NFPA 400 is based on hazard classification of the materials to be regulated. The materials under consideration must be evaluated to classify their hazards within the context of the code. The starting point begins with the MSDS, where the material can be identified by name, and other information, such as CAS registry number and physical state, is provided. Although there are 16 different main headings in an MSDS, the primary need for classification of materials rests with determining the physical and health hazards of the material or mixture in question.

Within the context of NFPA 400, the user must determine whether the physical and/or health hazards of the material place it into one or more of the following hazard categories:

(1) Corrosive solids and liquids
(2) Flammable solids
(3) Organic peroxide formulations
(4) Oxidizer solids and liquids
(5) Pyrophoric solids and liquids
(6) Toxic and highly toxic solids and liquids
(7) Unstable (reactive) solids and liquids
(8) Water-reactive solids and liquids

Each of the hazard categories can be further subdivided into subcategories, each with its attendant hazard properties. For example, oxidizer solids and liquids are subdivided into Class 4, Class 3, Class 2, and Class 1 subcategories commonly referred to as the hazard class.

Although it might be expected that the above nomenclature would appear on an MSDS, this is not always the case. Therefore, the user must review the physical and chemical properties, as well as the health hazard information provided, in order to make a determination as to the appropriate hazard category and class for the material to be regulated.

B.3 *Chemical Family* — **A Pointer to Hazard Classification.**

B.3.1 General. It is quite common that preparers of MSDS indicate the *chemical family* to which a material belongs, that is, the group of chemical substances that have a similar molecular structure. For example, materials such as acetone, methyl ethyl ketone, and amyl ethyl ketone are members of the *ketone* family. While the properties of various hazardous materials within a chemical family may vary, the chemical family becomes a pointer to the more likely hazard categories of the material under consideration.

While hundreds of thousands of chemicals are in use, this annex categorizes the more commonly used industrial chemicals into chemical families or unique groupings that have similar properties. Materials and/or chemicals exhibit a wide range of properties, some of which are hazardous. This code provides guidance for known physical and health hazards of materials within its scope.

B.3.2 Chemical Families Related to Hazard Category. Table B.3.2 provides a summary of chemical families with associated physical and health hazard properties, which are subdivided into specific categories. This table is for informational purposes only. The physical and health hazards indicated are broad representations for the various chemical families. These classifications are not intended to cover all the hazards of a material. A more detailed description of the chemical families, subfamilies, and chemical structure of specific hazards are contained in the explanatory material following the table. For specific information, the chemical-specific MSDS must be consulted. Additional information can be obtained from the manufacturer.

Table B.3.2 NFPA 400 Chemical Data

			PHYSICAL HAZARDS (2,3)							HEALTH HAZARDS (2,3)			
CHEMICAL FAMILY[1]	CHEMICAL STRUCTURE	Unstable Reactive	Water Reactive	Oxidizer	Pyrophoric	Flammable Solid	Organic Peroxide[6]	Flammable/ Combustible[5]	Corrosive	Toxic	Highly Toxic	
		(S, L, G)*	(S, L, G)	(S, L, G)	(S, G)	(S)	(S, L)	(S, L, G)	(S, L, G)	(S, L, G)	(S, L, G)	EXAMPLES (CAS No.) The following examples and their classifications represent neat, undiluted, commercially available products[4]
Acids — Carboxylic	R-COOH, Ar-COOH	-	-	-	-	-	-	✓	✓✓	✓	-	Formic acid (64-18-6), acetic acid (64-19-7), benzoic acid (65-85-0), acrylic acid (79-10-7), oxalic acid (144-62-7), propanoic acid (79-09-4), 4-amino-3,5,6-trichloropicolinic acid (1918-02-1), 2-hydroxybenzoic acid (69-72-7), citric acid (77-92-9), benzoic acid (65-85-0)
Peroxy	R-OOH, Ar-OOH	✓✓✓	-	✓✓✓	-	✓	✓✓✓	✓	✓✓	✓✓	-	Peroxyacetic acid (79-21-0), m-chloro perbenzoic acid (937-14-4), peroxymonosulfuric acid (7722-86-3)
Mineral		-	✓	-	-	-	-	-	✓✓✓	✓	-	Hydrochloric acid (7647-01-0), sulfuric acid (7664-93-9), phosphoric acid (7664-38-2)
Gaseous		-	✓	-	-	-	-	-	✓✓✓	✓✓✓	-	Hydrogen chloride (7647-01-0), hydrogen bromide (10035-10-6), hydrogen fluoride (7664-39-3), boron trichloride (10294-34-5), boron trifluoride (7637-07-2)
Oxidizing		-	-	✓✓✓	-	-	-	-	✓✓✓	✓✓	✓	Nitric acid (7697-37-2), chloric acid (7790-93-4), chlorosulfonic acid (7790-94-5)
Alcohols — Aliphatic	R-OH	-	-	-	-	-	-	✓✓✓	-	✓	-	Methanol (67-56-1), ethanol (64-17-5), isopropanol (67-63-0), t-butanol (75-65-0), glycerol (56-81-5), 1-hexanol (111-27-3), 2-octanol (123-96-6)
Aromatic	Ar-OH	-	-	-	-	✓	-	-	✓✓	✓✓	-	Phenol (108-95-2), 1,2-dihydroxybenzene (catechol) (120-80-9), 2-naphthol (135-19-3), 2,4-dichloro-phenol (120-83-2), 4-methylphenol (p-cresol) (106-44-5)

Table B.3.2 Continued

CHEMICAL FAMILY[1]	CHEMICAL STRUCTURE	PHYSICAL HAZARDS [2,3]							HEALTH HAZARDS [2,3]			EXAMPLES (CAS No.) The following examples and their classifications represent neat, undiluted, commercially available products[4]
		Unstable Reactive	Water Reactive	Oxidizer	Pyrophoric	Flammable Solid	Organic Peroxide[6]	Flammable/ Combustible[5]	Corrosive	Toxic	Highly Toxic	
		(S, L, G)*	(S, L, G)	(S, L, G)	(S, G)	(S)	(S, L)	(S, L, G)	(S, L, G)	(S, L, G)	(S, L, G)	
Alkyl halides	R-X	-	-	-	-	-	-	✓	-	✓✓	-	Bromoform (75-25-2), chloroform (67-66-3), 1,2-dichloroethane (ethylene dichloride) (107-06-2), 1,2-dichlorotetrafluoro-ethane (76-14-2), 1,2-dibromoethane (ethylene dibromide) (106-93-4), methyl bromide (74-83-9), 1,2-dichloropropane (propylene dichloride) (78-87-5)
Amines	Aliphatic, organic	R-NH$_2$, R$_2$NH, R$_3$N	-	-	-	-	-	-	✓✓✓	✓✓	✓	-	Ethylamine (75-04-7), ethylenediamine (107-15-3), pyrrolidine (123-75-1), trimethylamine (75-50-3), hexylamine (111-26-2), isopropylamine (75-31-0), triethylamine (121-44-8), morpholine (110-91-8), butylamine (109-73-9)
	Aromatic	Ar-NH$_2$, Ar(N)	-	-	-	-	-	-	✓	✓	✓✓✓	-	Diethyltoluenediamine (68479-98-1), aniline (62-53-3), pyridine (110-86-1), N,N-diethyl aniline (91-66-7), 3-methylpyridine (3-picoline) (108-99-6), p-phenylenediamine (4-aminoaniline) (106-50-3), 4-aminotoluene (p-toluidine) (106-49-0), 2,4-diamino-toluene (TDA) (95-80-7)
Bases	Alkalis		-	✓	-	-	-	-	-	✓✓✓	✓	-	Sodium hydroxide (1310-73-2), potassium hydroxide (1310-58-3), sodium carbonate (497-19-8)
	Gaseous		-	-	-	-	-	-	✓✓✓	✓✓✓	-	-	Ammonia (7664-41-7), methylamine (74-89-5), trimethylamine (75-50-3)
Carbides / Nitrides		M-C$_2$, M-N	-	✓	-	-	✓	-	-	-	-	-	Calcium carbide (75-20-7), lithium nitride (26134-62-3), gallium nitride (25617-97-4), boron nitride (10643-11-5)

(continues)

Table B.3.2 Continued

CHEMICAL FAMILY[1]		CHEMICAL STRUCTURE	PHYSICAL HAZARDS [2,3]							HEALTH HAZARDS [2,3]			
			Unstable Reactive	Water Reactive	Oxidizer	Pyrophoric	Flammable Solid	Organic Peroxide[6]	Flammable/ Combustible[5]	Corrosive	Toxic	Highly Toxic	EXAMPLES (CAS No.) The following examples and their classifications represent neat, undiluted, commercially available products[4]
			(S, L, G)*	(S, L, G)	(S, L, G)	(S, G)	(S)	(S, L)	(S, L, G)	(S, L, G)	(S, L, G)	(S, L, G)	
Carbonyl compounds	Acid anhydrides	R₁-C(O)OC(O)-R₂	–	✓	–	–	–	–	✓	✓✓✓	✓	–	n-Butyric anhydride (106-31-0), maleic anhydride (108-31-6), propionic anhydride (123-62-6), isobutyric anhydride (97-72-3), phthalic anhydride (85-44-9), acetic anhydride (108-24-7), trifluoroacetic anhydride (407-25-0)
	Acyl halides	R, Ar-C(O)X, R,Ar-SO₂-X	–	✓✓✓	–	–	–	–	✓	✓✓✓	✓✓	–	Acetyl chloride (75-36-5), sulfonyl chloride (7791-25-5), benzoyl chloride (98-88-4), methanesulfonyl chloride (124-63-0), p-toluene sulfonyl chloride (98-59-9), trichloroacetyl chloride (76-02-8), pivaloyl chloride (3268-49-3)
	Aldehydes	RCH=O, Ar-CH=O	–	–	–	–	–	–	✓✓✓	–	–	–	Formaldehyde (50-00-0), acetaldehyde (75-07-0), butyraldehyde (123-72-8), benzaldehyde (100-52-7), 2-butenal (crotonaldehyde) (4170-30-3), n-valeraldehyde (110-62-3), p-methoxybenzaldehyde (4-anisaldehyde) (123-11-5), 2-propenal (acrolein) (107-02-8)
	Esters	R₁(C=O)OR₂	–	–	–	–	–	–	✓	–	–	–	Methyl formate (107-31-3), methyl acrylate (2-propenoic acid methyl ester), (96-33-3), benzenedicarboxylic acid dioctyl ester (117-84-0), ethyl ethanoate (ethyl acetate) (141-78-6), butanedioic acid dimethyl ester (dimethyl fumarate) (106-65-0), oleic acid methyl ester (112-62-9), n-butyl acetate (123-86-4)
	Halides	C(O)X₂, C(S)X₂	✓	✓✓✓	–	–	–	–	✓	✓✓✓	–	✓✓✓	Phosgene (75-44-5), carbonyl fluoride (353-50-4), thiophosgene (463-71-8), oxalyl chloride (79-37-8), trichloromethyl chloroformate (diphosgene) (503-38-8), methyl chloroformate (79-22-1)

Table B.3.2 Continued

CHEMICAL FAMILY[1]	CHEMICAL STRUCTURE	PHYSICAL HAZARDS [2,3]							HEALTH HAZARDS [2,3]			EXAMPLES (CAS No.) The following examples and their classifications represent neat, undiluted, commercially available products[4]
		Unstable Reactive	Water Reactive	Oxidizer	Pyrophoric	Flammable Solid	Organic Peroxide[6]	Flammable/ Combustible[5]	Corrosive	Toxic	Highly Toxic	
		(S, L, G)*	(S, L, G)	(S, L, G)	(S, G)	(S)	(S, L)	(S, L, G)	(S, L, G)	(S, L, G)	(S, L, G)	
Ketones	R₁R₂C=O	-	-	-	-	-	-	✓✓✓	-	✓	-	Methyl propyl ketone (107-87-9), methyl isoamyl ketone (110-12-3), acetone (67-64-1), cyclohexanone (108-94-1), 1-chloro-2-propanone (chloroacetone) (78-95-5), 2-butanone (methyl ethyl ketone) (78-93-3), cyclopentanone (120-92-3), acetophenone (98-86-2), methyl isobutyl ketone (108-10-1), limonene (138-86-3), 1,3-dichloroacetone (534-07-6)
Cyanides	Gaseous	-	-	-	-	-	-	✓	✓	-	✓✓✓	Hydrogen cyanide (74-90-8), cyanogen chloride (506-77-4), cyanogen (460-19-5)
	Inorganic	M-CN	-	✓	-	-	-	-	-	-	-	✓✓✓	Sodium cyanide (143-33-9), trimethylsilyl cyanide (7677-24-9), potassium cyanide (151-50-8)
	Organic (nitriles)	R, Ar-CN	-	-	-	-	-	-	✓✓	-	✓	-	Acetonitrile (75-05-8), benzonitrile (100-47-0), chloroacetonitrile (107-14-2), 2-propenenitrile (acrylonitrile) (107-13-1), butyronitrile (109-74-0)
Epoxides		✓	-	-	-	-	-	✓✓✓	✓	✓	✓	Ethylene oxide (75-21-8), propylene oxide (75-56-9), 1,2-epoxybutane (106-88-7), 1-chloro-2,3-epoxypropane (epichlorohydrin) (106-89-8)

(continues)

Table B.3.2 *Continued*

CHEMICAL FAMILY[1]	CHEMICAL STRUCTURE	PHYSICAL HAZARDS [2,3]							HEALTH HAZARDS [2,3]			
		Unstable Reactive (S, L, G)*	Water Reactive (S, L, G)	Oxidizer (S, L, G)	Pyrophoric (S, G)	Flammable Solid (S)	Organic Peroxide[6] (S, L)	Flammable/ Combustible[5] (S, L, G)	Corrosive (S, L, G)	Toxic (S, L, G)	Highly Toxic (S, L, G)	EXAMPLES (CAS No.) The following examples and their classifications represent neat, undiluted, commercially available products[4]
Ethers/ glycols	R-O-R	-	-	-	-	-	-	✓✓	-	✓	-	1,2-Dimethoxyethane (glyme) (110-71-4), diethyl ether (60-29-7), furan (110-00-9), tetrahydrofuran (THF) (109-99-9), polyethylene glycol (25322-68-3), 1,4-dioxane (123-91-1), 1,3-butylene glycol (107-88-0), methyl vinyl ether (107-25-5), ethylene glycol monomethyl ether (EGME, 2-methoxyethanol) (109-86-4), dipropylene glycol monomethyl ether (DPM, 1-(2-methoxy-2-methylethoxy)-2-propanol) (34590-94-8)
Gases	Flammable	-	-	-	-	-	-	✓✓✓	-	-	-	Acetylene (74-86-2), hydrogen (1333-74-0), methane (74-82-8), propane (74-98-6)
	Halogens	X-X	-	✓	✓	-	-	-	-	✓✓✓	✓✓	-	Chlorine (7782-50-5), fluorine (7782-41-4), bromine trifluoride (7787-71-5), chlorine trifluoride (7790-91-2), bromine pentafluoride (7789-30-2)
	Nonflammable	-	-	-	-	-	-	-	-	-	-	Carbon dioxide (124-38-9), helium (7440-59-7), argon (7440-37-1)
	Oxidizing	-	-	✓✓✓	-	-	-	-	-	-	-	Oxygen (7782-44-7)
	Pyrophoric	-	-	-	✓✓✓	-	-	-	-	-	-	Silane (7803-62-5), methyl silane (992-94-9), disilane (1590-87-0)
	Sulfur Gases	R-SH	-	-	-	-	-	-	✓✓	✓	✓✓	-	Hydrogen sulfide (7783-06-4), methyl mercaptan (74-93-1), sulfur dioxide (7446-09-5)
Hydro-carbons	Aliphatic	R	-	-	-	-	-	-	✓✓✓	-	-	-	Cyclopentane (287-92-3), hexane (110-54-3), dodecane (112-40-3), butane (106-97-8)

2013 Edition

Table B.3.2 *Continued*

CHEMICAL FAMILY[1]	CHEMICAL STRUCTURE	PHYSICAL HAZARDS [2,3]							HEALTH HAZARDS [2,3]			
		Unstable Reactive	Water Reactive	Oxidizer	Pyrophoric	Flammable Solid	Organic Peroxide[6]	Flammable/ Combustible[5]	Corrosive	Toxic	Highly Toxic	EXAMPLES (CAS No.) The following examples and their classifications represent neat, undiluted, commercially available products[4]
		(S, L, G)*	(S, L, G)	(S, L, G)	(S, G)	(S)	(S, L)	(S, L, G)	(S, L, G)	(S, L, G)	(S, L, G)	
Alkenes	$R_1CH=CHR_2$	✓	-	-	-	-	-	✓✓✓	-	✓	-	Vinyl acetate (108-05-4), vinyl benzene (styrene) (100-42-5), vinyl chloride (75-01-4), ketene (463-51-4), 1-butene (106-98-9), 2-methyl-butene (513-35-9), 1,4-dichloro-2-butene (764-41-0), 3-chloro-1-propene (allyl chloride) (107-05-1), butadiene (106-99-0)
Alkynes	$R_1C\equiv CR_2$, $R-C\equiv C-H$	✓✓	-	-	-	-	-	✓	-	✓	-	1,1,1,4,4,4-hexafluoro-2-butyne (692-50-2), 2-butyne-1,4-diol (110-65-6), 1-propyne (74-99-7), 2-propyn-1-ol (107-19-7)
Aromatic	Ar	-	-	-	-	✓	-	✓✓✓	-	✓✓	✓	Benzene (71-43-2), toluene (108-88-3), cumene (98-82-8), naphthalene (91-20-3), chlorobenzene (108-90-7), 1,2,3-trichlorobenzene (87-61-6), 3,4-dichloro-trifluoro toluene (328-84-7), 1,2-dimethyl benzene (o-xylene) (95-47-6), 1,4-dichlorobenzene (p-dichlorobenzene) (106-46-7), ethylbenzene (100-41-4)
Isocyanates	R-N=C=O, Ar-N=C=O	✓✓✓	✓✓	-	-	-	-	✓	✓	✓✓	✓	Toluene diisocyanate (TDI) (584-84-9), methylene bisphenyl isocyanate (MDI) (101-68-8), hexamethylene diisocyanate (HDI) (822-06-0), p-toluenesulfonyl isocyanate (4083-64-1), methyl isocyanate (624-83-9)
Metals / Metal Alkyls	M-R	-	✓✓✓	-	✓✓✓	-	-	-	✓✓✓	✓	-	Butyllithium (109-72-8), triethylaluminum (97-93-8), triethylborane (97-94-9), n-butylethylmagnesium (62202-86-2), diethyl zinc (557-20-0)

(continues)

Table B.3.2 *Continued*

CHEMICAL FAMILY[1]		CHEMICAL STRUCTURE	PHYSICAL HAZARDS [2,3]							HEALTH HAZARDS [2,3]			
			Unstable Reactive	Water Reactive	Oxidizer	Pyrophoric	Flammable Solid	Organic Peroxide[6]	Flammable/ Combustible[5]	Corrosive	Toxic	Highly Toxic	
			(S, L, G)*	(S, L, G)	(S, L, G)	(S, G)	(S)	(S, L)	(S, L, G)	(S, L, G)	(S, L, G)	(S, L, G)	EXAMPLES (CAS No.) The following examples and their classifications represent neat, undiluted, commercially available products[4]
	Metal Halides	M-X	-	-	-	-	-	-	-	✓	✓✓	✓	Aluminum chloride (7446-70-0), chromium (III) chloride (10025-73-7), copper(I) chloride (7758-89-6), silver bromide (7785-23-1), ruthenium (II) chloride (10049-08-8), titanium tetrachloride (7550-45-0), tin chloride (7772-99-8), tungsten hexafluoride (7783-82-6)
	Metal Hydrides (solids)	M-H	-	✓✓✓	-	-	✓✓✓	-	-	✓✓✓	✓	-	Lithium aluminum hydride (16853-85-3), sodium borohydride (16940-66-2), sodium hydride (7646-69-7), lithium hydride (7580-67-8)
	Metal Hydrides (gases)	M-H	-	-	-	-	-	-	✓✓✓	-	-	✓✓✓	Diborane (19287-45-7), hydrogen selenide (7783-07-5), phosphine (7803-51-2)
	Metals (alkali)	M	-	✓✓✓	-	-	✓✓✓	-	-	✓✓✓	✓✓	-	Sodium (7440-23-5), lithium (7439-93-2), potassium (7440-09-7)
	Metals (powdered)	M	-	✓✓✓	-	-	✓✓✓	-	-	-	-	-	Aluminum (7429-90-5), magnesium (7439-95-4), titanium (7440-32-6), zirconium (7440-67-7)
Nitrated compounds	Nitro	R, Ar-NO$_2$	✓✓	-	-	-	-	-	✓✓	✓	✓✓	✓	Nitromethane (75-52-5), o-nitroaniline (88-74-4), dinitrotoluene (25321-14-6), p-dinitrobenzene (100-25-4), m-nitrotoluene (99-08-1), 1-chloro-4-nitro-benzene (100-00-5), p-nitrophenol (100-02-7), nitro-p-nitroaniline (100-01-6), 1,4-diamino-2-nitrobenzene (5307-14-2), 1-nitropropane (108-03-2)
	Azo (aliphatic)	R-N=N-R	✓✓✓	-	-	-	✓✓	-	-	-	✓✓	✓	Diethyl azodicarboxylate (1972-28-7), 1,1'-azobis (cyanocyclohexane) (2094-98-6), 2,2'-azobis (2-methylbutyronitrile) (13472-08-7), azoisobutyronitrile (AIBN) (78-67-1), 2,2'-azobis (2,4-dimethylvaleronitrile) (4419-11-8)

Table B.3.2 Continued

CHEMICAL FAMILY[1]	CHEMICAL STRUCTURE	PHYSICAL HAZARDS [2,3]							HEALTH HAZARDS [2,3]			EXAMPLES (CAS No.) The following examples and their classifications represent neat, undiluted, commercially available products[4]
		Unstable Reactive	Water Reactive	Oxidizer	Pyrophoric	Flammable Solid	Organic Peroxide[6]	Flammable/ Combustible[5]	Corrosive	Toxic	Highly Toxic	
		(S, L, G)*	(S, L, G)	(S, L, G)	(S, G)	(S)	(S, L)	(S, L, G)	(S, L, G)	(S, L, G)	(S, L, G)	
Azo (aromatic)	Ar-N=N-Ar	-	-	-	-	-	-	-	-	✓	✓	Azobenzene (103-33-3), p-aminoazobenzene (Aniline Yellow) (60-09-3), p-dimethylaminoazo-benzene-sulfonic acid (Methyl Orange) (547-58-0), 1-(2-methoxy-phenylazo)-2-naphthol (Sudan Red G) (1229-55-6), 4-acetamido-2'-hydroxy-5'-methylazobenzene (Disperse Yellow 3) (2832-40-8), 4-[N-(2-cyanoethyl)-N-ethylamino]-4'-nitroazobenzene (Disperse Orange 25) (31482-56-1)
Azides	R, Ar-N$_3$	✓✓✓	-	-	-	-	-	-	-	-	✓✓✓	Sodium azide (26628-22-8)
Inorganic Nitrites	M-NO$_2$	-	-	✓✓✓	-	-	-	-	✓	✓	-	Sodium nitrite (7632-00-0), potassium nitrite (7758-09-0)
Inorganic Nitrates	M-NO$_3$	✓	-	✓✓✓	-	-	-	✓	✓	✓	✓	Sodium nitrate (7631-99-4), silver nitrate (7761-88-8), zinc nitrate (7779-88-6), lithium nitrate (7790-69-4), lead nitrate (10099-74-8), potassium nitrate (7757-79-1)
Nitrogen-Halogen compounds	R-N-X	✓	✓	✓✓✓	-	-	-	-	✓✓	✓✓	✓	Trichloroisocyanuric acid (87-90-1), sodium dichloroisocyanurate (2893-78-9), N-bromosuccinimide (128-08-5), 1-bromo-3-chloro-5,5-dimethylhydantoin (BCDMH) (126-06-7)
Oxyanion	M-ClO$_3$, M-ClO$_2$, M-ClO$_4$, M-OCl	✓	✓	✓✓✓	-	-	-	-	✓	✓✓	✓	Sodium chlorite (7758-19-2), sodium chlorate (7775-09-9), sodium perchlorate (7601-89-0), ammonium perchlorate (7790-98-9), calcium hypochlorite (7778-54-3), potassium bromate (7758-01-2), lithium hypochlorite (13840-33-0)

(continues)

Table B.3.2 *Continued*

CHEMICAL FAMILY[1]	CHEMICAL STRUCTURE	PHYSICAL HAZARDS [2,3]							HEALTH HAZARDS [2,3]			
		Unstable Reactive	Water Reactive	Oxidizer	Pyrophoric	Flammable Solid	Organic Peroxide[6]	Flammable/ Combustible[5]	Corrosive	Toxic	Highly Toxic	EXAMPLES (CAS No.) The following examples and their classifications represent neat, undiluted, commercially available products[4]
		(S, L, G)*	(S, L, G)	(S, L, G)	(S, G)	(S)	(S, L)	(S, L, G)	(S, L, G)	(S, L, G)	(S, L, G)	
Peroxides Organic	R-O-O-R	✓✓✓	-	✓	-	-	✓✓✓	✓✓	✓	✓✓	✓	Benzoyl peroxide (94-36-0), diacetyl peroxide (>70%) (110-22-5), dibenzoyl peroxide (94-36-0), methyl ethyl ketone peroxide (>60%) (97-02-9), di-t-butyl peroxide (110-05-4), t-amyl hydroperoxide (3425-61-4), cumene hydroperoxide (80-15-9), t-butyl peroxyacetate (107-71-1)
Metal / Inorganic	M-O-O	-	✓	✓✓✓	-	-	-	-	✓	-	-	Sodium perborate (10486-00-7), sodium percarbonate (15630-89-4), magnesium peroxide (1335-26-8), sodium peroxide (1313-60-6)
Phosphorous-Halogen Compounds	O=P-X$_3$, P-X	-	✓✓✓	-	-	-	-	-	✓✓✓	✓	-	Phosphorus pentachloride (10026-13-8), phosphorus trichloride (7719-12-2), phosphorus oxychloride (10025-87-3), phosphorus pentafluoride (7647-19-0)

*(S, L, G) refers to whether hazards apply to "Solid," "Liquid," and/or "Gaseous" physical forms.
✓✓✓ Indicates that most or all of the chemicals within the family or sub-family have the indicated physical and health hazards.
✓✓ Indicates that *some* of the chemicals in the family *may* have this additional physical and health hazards.
✓ Indicates that only a select few chemicals within a specific family display the relevant physical and health hazards.
"-" = Not applicable for the specific chemical category.
Ar = phenyl ring; X = halogen (i.e., fluorine, chlorine, bromine, iodine); R = organic; M = metal.
Additional Source Material:
http://www.epa.gov/oppt/chemrtk/
http://www.epa.gov/oppt/chemrtk/pubs/update/hpvchmlt.htm
http://www.osha.gov/pls/oshaweb/owadisp.show_document?p_table=STANDARDS&p_id=9761
http://www.osha.gov/SLTC/emergencypreparedness/guides/chemical.html

Footnotes to Table B.3.2:
1. Source material for the chemical families includes *Bretherick's Handbook of Reactive Chemical Hazards* (Elsevier Science & Technology Books), 7th ed.; *Comprehensive Guide to Hazardous Properties of Chemical Substances* (Wiley Interscience); *Guidelines for Chemical Reactivity Evaluation and Application to Process Design* (Tables 2.4 and 2.5) (Center for Chemical Process Safety (CCPS)/AIChE).
2. The physical and health hazards are BROAD representations for the various classes of chemicals. These classifications are NOT intended to cover all hazards of a material. For specific information, the chemical-specific MSDS MUST be consulted. Additional information can be obtained from the manufacturer.
3. For additional concentration dependent hazard categories, see B.5.
4. Source material for the examples listed includes *US EPA High Production Volume (HPV) Challenge Program List*; the *OECD (Organization for Economic Co-operation and Development) Integrated HPV Database*; *Bretherick's Handbook of Reactive Chemical Hazards* (Elsevier Science & Technology Books), 7th ed.; *The Handbook of Compressed Gases* (Compressed Gas Association) 4th Ed.; U.S. Dept of Labor 29 CFR 1910.119 *Appendix A — List of Highly Hazardous Chemicals, Toxics and Reactives*.
5. The "flammable or combustible" hazard categories are NOT regulated under NFPA 400. However, many chemicals exhibit the hazard properties of flammability or combustibility.
6. "Peroxide" is not a hazard characteristic but a unique chemical family with a range of properties listed as a specific physical hazard under NFPA 400.

B.3.2.1 Table Descriptions. Nineteen general chemical families are listed in the first column of Table B.3.2. The chemical families include organic chemicals, inorganic chemicals, gases, and metals. Some of the general chemical families are further divided into subfamilies if one or more hazard category or categories further depend on chemical structure. The second column, Chemical Structure, shows the basic chemical formula or structure representing the chemical family and/or subfamilies.

The next several columns list the seven physical hazard categories and three health hazard categories. The specific hazard categories are defined in Chapter 3. The physical hazard categories include the following:

(1) Unstable Reactive
(2) Water Reactive
(3) Oxidizer
(4) Pyrophoric
(5) Flammable Solid
(6) Organic Peroxide
(7) Flammable/Combustible

The health hazards include the following:

(1) Corrosive
(2) Toxic
(3) Highly Toxic

Hazard categories are defined by the following symbols. A triple check mark (✓✓✓) is used to indicate that most or all of the chemicals within the family or subfamily have the indicated physical or health hazard. A double check mark (✓✓) is used to identify that *some* of the chemicals in the family *might* have this additional hazard. A single check mark (✓) indicates that only a select few chemicals within a specific family display the relevant physical and health hazard(s). The check marks are provided to inform the user as to the likely property of materials in each of the hazard categories listed. However, it must be recognized that the ultimate classification of a material is dependent on the application of the definitions found in Chapter 3 and the interpretation of the information provided relative to tests conducted by authoritative entities within the framework established by the definitions.

The last column provides examples of chemicals with the indicated hazards. The examples illustrate materials in the concentrated or undiluted state. Concentration-specific hazards for common materials are provided in the explanatory material following the table (see Section B.5).

B.3.2.2 Multiple Hazard Materials. A specific chemical can exhibit multiple hazard categories. In other words, there could be materials with more than one physical hazard property that also have one or more health hazard properties. The regulatory controls integral to NFPA 400 require that all hazards be addressed. It is incumbent on the code user to identify each applicable hazard property in order to properly classify the hazards of the material. It should also be recognized that each of the hazards considered could be concentration dependent.

B.3.2.2.1 Illustration of Table B.3.2. To illustrate the utility of Table B.3.2, consider the chemical family of mineral acids, listed in column 1 of Table B.3.2. Specific examples of mineral acids are listed in the last column of Table B.3.2. Well-known mineral acids are hydrochloric acid and sulfuric acid. The row entries with dashes (—) under the physical hazard categories indicate that, in general, mineral acids are not considered to have the physical hazards of being unstable/reactive, oxidizer, pyrophoric, flammable solids, organic peroxides, or flammable/combustible. Specific mineral acids are water reactive (✓) based on concentration and the specific mineral acid itself. The row entries show the principal hazard properties of mineral acids are Health Hazards, especially Corrosive (✓✓✓). The one checkmark under Toxic (✓) indicates that a select few of the chemicals in the mineral acid family have this additional health hazard. See B.4.1.1 for additional information on mineral acids. MSDS for the specific mineral acid should be consulted for more detailed information relating to physical and health hazards.

B.3.3 ADDITIONAL SOURCE MATERIAL:

http://www.epa.gov/oppt/chemrtk/

http://www.epa.gov/oppt/chemrtk/pubs/update/hpvchmlt.htm

http://www.osha.gov/pls/oshaweb/owadisp.show_document?p_table=STANDARDS&p_id=9761

http://www.osha.gov/SLTC/emergencypreparedness/guides/chemical.html

B.4 Description of Chemical Families.

B.4.1 General. Dilution can cause the hazard characteristics of an individual chemical to diminish until the property is no longer pertinent. Each chemical must be individually reviewed by the manufacturer to provide the data to assess the physical and health hazards. For compressed gases, there are accepted standards that can be used to estimate both the flammability and toxicity without actual test data.

B.4.1.1 Acids.

B.4.1.1.1 Acids (Carboxylic) (R-COOH, Ar-COOH). Carboxylic acids are weak acids, unlike mineral acids, such as hydrochloric acid. Most are readily soluble in water. Physical and health properties vary significantly based on molecular weight and the number of carboxylic acid groups. Smaller molecular weight aliphatic carboxylic acids (such as formic and acetic acid) are liquids and are flammable and corrosive. Larger chain, higher molecular weight carboxylic acids are often solids with minimal hazards (such as citric acid). Aromatic acids are sometimes corrosive.

B.4.1.1.2 Acids (Peroxy) (R-OOH, Ar-OOH). All peroxy acids are classified as organic peroxides and are classified as oxidizers and corrosive. Aromatic peroxy acids (such as perbenzoic acid) are solids and are unstable reactive and toxic. Most are pastes or liquids and require refrigeration. Some forms of this acid family are often found as their sodium, potassium, or ammonium salts.

B.4.1.1.3 Acids (Mineral). These are all strong acids, are liquids, and are corrosive, even in dilute solutions. These include hydrofluoric acid (HF), hydrochloric acid (HCl), hydrobromic acid (HBr), phosphoric acid (H_3PO_4), and sulfuric acid (H_2SO_4). In some cases they are toxic and water reactive depending on acid and concentration.

B.4.1.1.4 Acid (Gaseous). The common acid gases, which include hydrogen bromide (HBr), hydrogen chloride (HCl), hydrogen fluoride (HF), and hydrogen iodide (HI), are corrosive and in some cases toxic. They are highly soluble in water, forming the corresponding aqueous acid and are packaged as liquefied compressed gases. Other acid gases include boron trichloride (BCl_3), boron trifluoride (BF_3) and silicon tetrafluoride (SiF_4).

B.4.1.1.5 Acid (Oxidizing). Some strong acids are also oxidizing acids, most commonly nitric acid (HNO_3). As oxidizers, they are also corrosive and toxic. These physical and health properties are exhibited even in dilute solutions.

B.4.1.2 Alcohols.

B.4.1.2.1 Aliphatic Alcohols (R-OH). The category includes primary (1°), secondary (2°), and tertiary (3°) branched and cyclic alcohols. Most common alcohols include methanol, ethanol, isopropanol, t-butanol (2-methylpropan-2-ol), n-butanol (butan-1-ol) and cyclohexanol. Many alcohols, especially smaller chain alcohols, are highly flammable even in dilute solutions. This generally does not hold true for the small-chain glycols (or polyhydroxylated compounds), such as propylene glycol which have significantly higher boiling points. Most smaller chain aliphatic alcohols are readily soluble in water. Longer chain alcohols "fatty alcohols" (e.g., dodecanol, hexadecanol and octadecanol) are solids, are not flammable, and are not miscible with water.

B.4.1.2.2 Aromatic Alcohols (Ar-OH). The most common aromatic alcohol is phenol (hydroxybenzene). Others include the dihydroxybenzenes (e.g., catechol) and hydroxytoluenes (e.g., o-cresol). Most phenols are usually solids or high boiling point liquids and readily soluble in water. Phenol and p-cresol are highly corrosive and toxic. Functionalized phenol derivatives (e.g., 2,4-dichlorophenol), while also soluble in water, are not flammable and can be toxic. Higher molecular weight phenols such as hydroxynaphthalene (e.g., naphthol) can also be toxic but are not corrosive. The chemical and physical properties of aliphatic and aromatic alcohols vary significantly depending on the structure of the alcohol and other functional groups.

B.4.1.3 Alkyl Halides (R-X). This chemical family includes halogenated alkyl analogues, such as methylene chloride, chloroform, carbon tetrachloride, bromoform, dichloroethane, perchloroethylene, methyl bromide and methyl iodide, fluoroethane, and Freon® derivatives. Often these chemicals are nonflammable gases and liquids, used as fire extinguishers, refrigerants, and solvents. The most widely known category is the chlorofluorocarbons (CFCs). Nonflammable gases include bromochlorodifluoromethane (Halon 1211) and dichlorodifluoromethane (Freon-12). Some chemicals in this family are flammable. Highly substituted alkyl halides (i.e., those chemicals with many halogen atoms present in a molecule) such as 1,2-dichloroethane and 1,1,2,2-tetrachloroethane are liquids and toxic.

B.4.1.4 Amines.

B.4.1.4.1 Amines (Aliphatic) ($R-NH_2$, R_2NH, R_3N). The aliphatic amines consist of primary (1°), secondary (2°), and tertiary (3°) branched compounds. Lower molecular weight amines such as ethylamine, propylamine, butylamine and triethylamine are highly flammable liquids, corrosive and readily soluble in water. Some are toxic. Many amines, such as methylamine, are sold in diluted aqueous solutions, and are typically flammable. (For ammonia, see B.4.1.5.2.)

B.4.1.4.2 Amines (Aromatic) ($Ar-NH_2$, $Ar(N)$). This family includes substituted aromatic amines, such as benzene derivatives (e.g., aniline, and o-aminoaniline) and hetroaromatics (e.g., pyridine and picoline). Most of these chemicals are solids or liquids and may be readily soluble in water and are toxic. Some are flammable. Health hazards associated with these chemicals depend heavily on the ring structure, degree of substitution, and location of the nitrogen(s) within the heteroaromatic ring.

B.4.1.5 Bases.

B.4.1.5.1 Alkalis. Bases are found either as solids or as concentrated aqueous solutions. Most bases are highly corrosive with all tissues with which they come in contact. Bases, such as sodium carbonate (Na_2CO_3), sodium hydroxide (NaOH), and potassium hydroxide (KOH), readily absorb moisture from the air. When dissolved in water, these chemicals often liberate substantial heat and form corrosive solutions in concentrated form. The corrosiveness and toxicity of these chemicals decreases with dilution.

B.4.1.5.2 Gaseous. The common basic gases, ammonia (NH_3) and the lower molecular weight amines (methylamine, dimethylamine, trimethylamine) are all are corrosive but not toxic. They are highly soluble in water and are liquefied compressed gases. The common bases are flammable gases with a narrow flammability range. They are often sold commercially as aqueous solutions, which are also flammable.

B.4.1.6 Carbides/Nitrides. Carbides have varying degrees of physical hazards. Carbides, such as calcium carbide (CaC_2) and sodium carbide (Na_2C_2), react violently with water, are flammable in the presence of moisture, and could be corrosive. Other carbides, such as zirconium carbide (ZrC), tungsten carbide (WC), and silicon carbide (SiC), have little reactivity. Nitrides, such as boron nitride (BN), are usually stable.

B.4.1.7 Carbonyl Compounds.

B.4.1.7.1 Carbonyl Compounds (Acid Anhydrides) (R_1-C(O)OC(O)-R_2). These chemicals, often referred to as simply "anhydrides," are more reactive than their corresponding carboxylic acids. Anhydrides react with water to form the corresponding acid or base, and are often good dehydrating agents. Lower molecular weight anhydrides, such as acetic anhydride, propionic anhydride, and isobutyric anhydride, are most often corrosive, flammable, and could react violently with water. Functionalized anhydrides such as trifluoroacetic anhydride are highly corrosive and highly water reactive. Aromatic anhydrides, such as phthalic anhydride, are also corrosive but not water reactive.

B.4.1.7.2 Carbonyl Compounds (Acyl Halides) (R, Ar-C(O)X; R, Ar-SO_2-X). These chemicals include the most common acid halides and sulfonyl halides and are considerably more reactive than the corresponding anhydrides. Acyl halides are most often corrosive, water reactive, and volatile. Higher molecular weight aromatic acid halides, such as benzoyl chloride, are toxic and corrosive and have limited water solubility and lower water reactivity. Lower molecular weight acid halides such as acetyl chloride are flammable, highly corrosive, and react violently with water.

B.4.1.7.3 Carbonyl Compounds (Aldehydes) (R-CH=O, Ar-CH=O). Most aldehydes are volatile organic compounds. Simple, lower molecular weight alkyl aldehydes, such as acetaldehyde, propionaldehyde (methylacetaldehyde), butyraldehyde, and 2-butenaldehyde (crotonaldehyde), for example, exist as liquids, and are most often highly flammable. Formaldehyde is known to be toxic. Many aromatic aldehydes, such as benzaldehyde, have limited flammability.

B.4.1.7.4 Carbonyl Compounds (Esters) ($R_1O(C=O)R_2$). In general, the category possesses few physical or health hazards. Aliphatic and aromatic esters are significantly more stable than the acid anhydrides and are not water reactive. Lower molecular weight alkyl esters, such as methyl formate, ethyl acetate, and n-butyl acetate, are flammable liquids.

B.4.1.7.5 Carbonyl Compounds (Halides) (C(O)X₂, C(S)X₂). These compounds are very reactive chemicals and are considered highly toxic, highly water reactive, and corrosive. Phosgene is a nonflammable gas, while thiophosgene and oxalyl chloride are liquids. Trichloromethyl chloroformate (diphosgene) and methyl chloroformate are liquids and less reactive but still water reactive.

B.4.1.7.6 Carbonyl Compounds (Ketones) (R₁R₂C=O). Similar to aldehydes, most ketones are volatile organic compounds. Many ketones are also flammable liquids. Simple, low molecular weight ketones, such as acetone, cyclohexanone, methyl ethyl ketone (MEK), and methyl isobutyl ketone (MIBK), for example, are liquids and highly flammable. Common functionalized ketones, such as chloroacetone, 1,3-dichloro-2-propanone, and chloroacetophenone (chloromethyl phenyl ketone), while not flammable, are toxic. Many aromatic ketones have limited flammability.

B.4.1.8 Cyanides.

B.4.1.8.1 Cyanides (Gaseous). The common cyanide gases, hydrogen cyanide (HCN), cyanogen chloride (ClCN), and cyanogen (C₂N₂), are highly toxic. Hydrogen cyanide is a liquid, but is treated and packaged as a gas. Cyanogen and hydrogen cyanide are flammable, while cyanogen chloride is corrosive.

B.4.1.8.2 Cyanides (Inorganic) (M-CN). Common inorganic cyanides include sodium cyanide (NaCN) and trimethylsilyl cyanide (TMSCN). This family is characterized as highly toxic. Cyanide salts are readily soluble in water and highly toxic.

Trimethylsilyl cyanide is water reactive. The family does not include the many organic compounds that contain the CN group (called nitriles). Nitriles do not display the toxicity of the inorganic cyanides such as sodium and potassium cyanide.

B.4.1.8.3 Nitriles (Organic). Common, lower molecular weight nitriles, including acetonitrile and 2-propenenitrile (acrylonitrile), are highly flammable liquids and toxic. Many aromatic nitriles (benzonitriles) are solids and often toxic, depending on substituents. Benzonitriles have limited flammability.

B.4.1.9 Epoxides. Epoxides are very reactive chemicals. Common epoxides include ethylene oxide, which is a gas, and propylene oxide and 1-chloro-2,3-epoxypropane (epichlorohydrin), which are liquids. These chemicals most often have flammable, toxic, water-reactive, and unstable reactive hazard characteristics.

B.4.1.10 Ethers/Glycols (R-O-R). This broad category includes both simple alcohol ethers and polyhydroxylated glycol ethers. Simple, low molecular weight ethers such as diethyl ether or vinyl ether are low boiling liquids or compressed gases and highly flammable. Cyclic ethers, such as tetrahydrofuran (THF) and 1,4-dioxane, are highly flammable liquids while slightly toxic. Common higher molecular weight glycol ethers, such as 1,2-dimethoxyethane (glyme), ethylene glycol monomethyl ether (EGME, 2-methoxyethanol), dipropylene glycol monomethyl ether (DPM, 1-(2-methoxy-2-methylethoxy)-2-propanol), propylene glycol monomethyl ether (PGME, 1-methoxy-2-propanol), diethylene glycol monomethyl ether (DEGME), and dipropylene glycol monomethyl ether (DPGME), are often water soluble liquids and combustible. Lower molecular weight glycol ethers are flammable liquids. Many are high boiling point liquids.

B.4.1.11 Gases. Within the context of the model codes, gases are regulated as either compressed gases or as cryogenic fluids. Compressed gases can be found either in the nonliquefied or liquefied state. Any gas can be liquefied at a sufficiently low temperature by increasing its pressure through the use of compression. Gases that cannot be liquefied at normal ambient temperatures are called "permanent" gases. A permanent gas is able to be liquefied by reducing the temperature below ambient temperatures and increasing its pressure. However, at normal ambient temperatures of 68°F (20°C) these gases remain in a nonliquefied state.

The scientific explanation for this phenomenon is generally explained in the following discussion. There is a temperature for each gas at or below which it can be liquefied by pressure, but above which it is impossible to liquefy at any pressure. This temperature is called the critical temperature of the gas. At temperatures above the critical temperature, the substance can exist only in the gaseous state regardless of the pressure applied. The pressure that will just liquefy a gas at its critical temperature is called the critical pressure. In other words, the critical pressure of a gas is equal to the vapor pressure exerted by the liquefied gas at its critical temperature. All that is necessary to liquefy a gas is to cool it to its critical temperature and subject it to a pressure equal to or greater than its critical pressure. The farther below the critical temperature it is cooled, the less the pressure required for liquefaction. At the critical conditions of temperature and pressure the gaseous and liquid forms of the substance have the same density.

Atmospheric air is a mixture of permanent gases and principally composed of argon, oxygen, and nitrogen. Under normal ambient conditions it remains in the gaseous state. The critical temperature of air is −221.1°F (−140.6°C). The critical pressure is an absolute pressure of 547 psi (3771 kPa, absolute). To liquefy compressed air, the temperature must be reduced to −221.1°F or less with a commensurate increase in pressure above 547 psia. By comparison, liquefied petroleum gas (LP-Gas), is a mixture of hydrocarbon gases, principally propane and butane, which is found in the liquid form under ambient conditions. These gases have a critical temperature well in excess of 68°F (20°C), and as a result, they are found as liquefied compressed gases under ambient temperatures.

Cryogenic fluids are refrigerated liquefied gases with a boiling point lower than −130°F (−90°C) at an atmospheric pressure of an absolute pressure of 14.7 psi (101.3 kPa, absolute). They are maintained in the cryogenic (super-cooled) state by artificial means.

B.4.1.11.1 Gases (Flammable). Common nonliquefied flammable compressed gases include carbon monoxide and hydrogen. Other flammable gases are hydrocarbon gases. The alkanes include methane (CH₄), ethane (C₂H₆), and propane (C₃H₈). Ethane and propane are liquefied compressed gases at ambient temperature. The alkenes include ethylene (C₂H₄) and propylene (C₃H₆), both liquefied compressed gases, and the alkynes include acetylene (C₂H₂). Acetylene is an unstable reactive gas; it is found in cylinders, packaged as a compressed gas dissolved in a solution of acetone or dimethyl formamide. While acetylene can be liquefied at ambient temperatures, for safety reasons it is shipped as a nonliquefied compressed gas.

B.4.1.11.2 Gases (Halogens) (X-X). The pure halogen gases, fluorine (F₂), chlorine (Cl₂), bromine trifluoride (BrF₃), and chlorine trifluoride (ClF₃), are extremely powerful oxidizers, and are corrosive and toxic. Fluorine and chlorine are only slightly soluble in water, while bromine trifluoride and chlorine trifluoride are extremely water reactive. Bromine trifluoride is explosive on contact with water. Fluorine is a compressed gas while chlorine, bromine trifluoride, and chlorine trifluoride are liquefied compressed gases.

Gases that are fully halogenated, such as hexafluoroethane (C_2F_6), carbon tetrafluoride (CF_4), and sulfur hexafluoride (SF_6), are inert and nonreactive.

B.4.1.11.3 Gases (Non-Flammable). The atmospheric gases, with the exception of oxygen, have limited chemical reactivity, and are not corrosive, flammable, or toxic. These gases include nitrogen, argon, and carbon dioxide. Their greatest hazard is asphyxiation. The rare gases, such as helium, neon, krypton, xenon, and argon, were once thought to be inert (having no chemical activity at all); however, within the last 20 years compounds have been made through the use of strong oxidizer gases, such as fluorine, to form nitrogen trifluoride.

B.4.1.11.4 Gases (Oxidizing). The more common oxidizing gases are oxygen, nitrous oxide, and nitrogen trifluoride. Oxygen and nitrogen trifluoride are compressed gases, while nitrous oxide is a liquefied compressed gas.

B.4.1.11.5 Gases (Pyrophoric). Gases with an autoignition temperature below 130°F (54°C) are classified as pyrophoric. Silane (SiH_4) is probably one of the most common pyrophoric gases found in use today. Other pyrophoric gases include methylsilane (CH_3SiH_3) and disilane (Si_2H_6). Silane and methylsilane are compressed gases, while disilane is a liquefied compressed gas. Some pyrophoric gases, such as phosphine (PH_3) and diborane (B_2H_6), are also highly toxic. Although all pyrophoric gases are flammable by nature, they are regulated as pyrophoric gases within the context of the model codes.

B.4.1.11.6 Gases (Sulfur Gases) (R-SH). The common sulfur gases are hydrogen sulfide (H_2S), methyl mercaptan (CH_3SH), and carbonyl sulfide (COS) and are toxic and flammable. They are all liquefied compressed gases

B.4.1.12 Hydrocarbons.

B.4.1.12.1 Hydrocarbons (Aliphatic) (R). Commonly referred to as saturated hydrocarbons, alkanes as a whole are unreactive chemicals. The aliphatic hydrocarbons pentane, decane, and cyclohexane are flammable liquids. Lower molecular weight hydrocarbons such as methane, ethane, propane, and butane are flammable compressed gases.

B.4.1.12.2 Hydrocarbons (Alkenes) ($R_1CH=CHR_2$). Alkenes are a very broad category of hydrocarbons and are commonly referred to as unsaturated hydrocarbons, olefins, or vinyl compounds. Alkenes are relatively stable compounds, but are more reactive than alkanes. Smaller chain alkenes, such as ethylene, propylene, and butene, are all flammable gases and readily form explosive mixtures with air. Common derivatized alkenes, such as styrene (vinyl benzene), vinyl chloride (monochloroethylene), vinyl acetate, and 1,4-dichloro-2-butene, are toxic. Some are flammable liquids. They also readily polymerize (without inhibitors), which leads to unstable reactive characteristics.

B.4.1.12.3 Hydrocarbons (Alkynes) ($R_1C\equiv CR_2$, $R-C\equiv CH$). Of all the aliphatic hydrocarbons, alkynes are the most reactive. Many alkynes are highly reactive and considered unstable reactive, especially as molecular weights increase. Many halogenated alkynes and metal derivatives can be explosive. The most common alkynes are gases, including acetylene (ethyne — see Flammable Gases) and methyl acetylene (1-propyne), can form explosive mixtures with air. The most common derivitized alkyne is propargyl alcohol (2-propyn-1-ol), which is flammable, corrosive, and toxic.

B.4.1.12.4 Hydrocarbons (Aromatic) (Ar). This family is very broad and derived from such compounds as benzene and toluene and have limited alkyl (methyl, ethyl, etc.) substitution on the ring. Smaller aromatic hydrocarbons (benzene, toluene (methyl benzene), ethyl benzene, and xylene) are flammable liquids and are sometimes toxic. High molecular weight compounds with many aromatic rings (such as naphthalene and anthracene) are solids and are often toxic. Substituted analogues, such as dichlorobenzene, have varying degrees of toxicity based on the degree of substitution and arrangement on its ring structure. Many are also flammable solids.

B.4.1.13 Isocyanates (R-N=C=O, Ar-N=C=O). This family includes compounds such as toluene diisocyanate (TDI), p-toluenesulfonyl isocyanate, and methylene bisphenyl isocyanate (MDI). The chemicals are liquids and are typically unstable reactive, water-reactive, corrosive, and toxic. Some are highly toxic. Some are violently water reactive.

B.4.1.14 Metals.

B.4.1.14.1 Metal Alkyls (M-R). All metal alkyls are pyrophoric, corrosive, and highly reactive. The simple metal alkyls trimethylaluminum (TMAl), trimethylgallium (TMG), and trimethylindium (TMI) are pyrophoric liquids. They are also violently water reactive. Dimethylzinc and trimethylaluminum are also unstable reactive. Tetramethyltin is a flammable liquid.

B.4.1.14.2 Metal Halides (M-X). Physical and health hazards of this chemical family vary significantly based on the corresponding metal. Most metal halides are typically inert (such as sodium chloride [table salt], calcium chloride, magnesium fluoride, aluminum chloride, and palladium (II) chloride), while some have a much higher reactivity (such as silver bromide and chromium (III) chloride) and are strong oxidizers. The chemical and physical properties vary significantly depending on the metal. If a metal halide contains a heavy metal, such as lead, chromium, thallium, and mercury, it is assumed to be highly toxic. Fluoride and bromide salts are more toxic than the corresponding chloride salts.

B.4.1.14.3 Metal Hydrides (Solids). Compounds such as lithium aluminum hydride ($LiAlH_4$), sodium borohydride ($NaBH_4$), and sodium hydride (NaH) are flammable solids, water-reactive, and corrosive. Metal hydrides react violently with water.

B.4.1.14.4 Metal Hydrides (Gaseous). The more common metal hydride gases are arsine (arsenic hydride, AsH_3), diborane (boron hydride, B_2H_6), hydrogen selenide (selenium hydride, H_2Se), and phosphine (phosphorous hydride, PH_3). In general, these chemicals are toxic, liquefied compressed gases, with many being highly toxic. They are flammable and some have autoignition temperatures low enough to make them pyrophoric, such as diborane and phosphine. The key exception is silane (SiH_4), which is not toxic. Silane is a compressed gas rather than a liquefied compressed gas.

B.4.1.14.5 Metals (Alkali). This category includes sodium, potassium, and lithium. All are highly corrosive and can often explode if they are exposed to water. They are all flammable solids as well.

B.4.1.14.6 Metals (Powdered). Metals, especially those in a finely divided state, are usually categorized as flammable solids, such as aluminum, magnesium, sodium, and potassium. Some, but not all, react violently and are water-reactive. Some are also toxic.

B.4.1.15 Nitrated Organic Compounds.

B.4.1.15.1 Organic Nitro Compounds (R, Ar-NO$_2$). Most often, smaller alkyl nitro compounds, such as nitromethane, are flammable, unstable reactive, and often toxic. Aromatic nitro analogues are toxic or highly toxic and unstable reactive, the latter being dependent on the amount of ring substitution.

B.4.1.15.2 Azo (Aliphatic) (R-N=N-R). Aliphatic azo derivatives are inherently unstable and readily decompose, often violently, upon the application of heat. Aliphatic azo compounds are characterized as unstable reactive, flammable solids and are often toxic.

B.4.1.15.3 Azo (Aromatic) (Ar-N=N-Ar). Aromatic azo derivatives have superior thermal stability properties compared to aliphatic azo derivatives. Many aromatic azo derivatives are quite stable and often used as dyes. They have a wide array of chemical and physical properties depending on the substituents on the aromatic ring and the number of azo groups present in the molecule (mono-, dis-, tris-, tetrakis-, etc.). Most exhibit low to moderate toxicity.

B.4.1.15.4 Azides (R, Ar-N$_3$). The most common chemicals of this family are the metal azides, including sodium and lithium azide. All the compounds in this family are unstable reactive and highly toxic.

B.4.1.15.5 Nitrites (Inorganic) (M-NO$_2$). The most common nitrites are sodium and potassium nitrite. All are strong oxidizers and toxic.

B.4.1.15.6 Nitrates (Inorganic) (M-NO$_3$). Examples of inorganic nitrates include sodium nitrate, silver nitrate, zinc nitrate, lithium nitrate, and lead nitrate. While all inorganic nitrates are strong oxidizers, the physical and health properties vary significantly depending on the metal. Many of these compounds are corrosive and may have unstable reactive properties. Toxicity varies with the associated metal.

B.4.1.16 Nitrogen-Halogen compounds (R-N-X). This chemical family includes chlorinated isocyanurates (trichloroisocyanuric acid, sodium dichloroisocyanurate), halogenated succinimides (N-bromosuccinimide), and halogenated hydantoins (e.g. 1-bromo-3-chloro-5,5-dimethylhydantoin). Some are strong oxidizers and corrosive in their pure states, with varying properties of unstable reactive, water-reactive, and toxicity hazards. Specially formulated chlorinated isocyanurate products have been shown to reduce oxidizer properties.

B.4.1.17 Oxyanion (M-ClO$_2$, M-ClO$_3$, M-ClO$_4$, M-OCl). This chemical family includes chlorites, chlorates, perchlorates, bromates, and hypochlorites. The most common chemicals are sodium chlorite (NaClO$_2$), sodium chlorate (NaClO$_3$), ammonium perchlorate (NH$_4$ClO$_4$), potassium bromate (KBrO$_3$), and calcium hypochlorite (Ca(OCl)$_2$). Most are strong oxidizers and corrosive in their pure states with varying properties of unstable reactive, water reactive, and toxicity hazards. Chlorites and chlorates are most commonly found as diluted solutions that reduce toxicity and oxidizing properties. Specially formulated calcium hypochlorite products have been shown to reduce their oxidizing properties. Sodium hypochlorite (liquid bleach) is too unstable in solid form and is found only in dilute solutions that are corrosive.

B.4.1.18 Peroxides.

B.4.1.18.1 Peroxide (Organic) (R-O-O-R). The common organic peroxides include such chemicals as t-amyl hydroperoxide, dibenzoyl peroxide, di-t-butyl peroxide, diacetyl peroxide, methyl ethyl ketone peroxide, diisopropyl peroxydicarbonate, and cumyl hydroperoxide. Organic peroxides possess a wide range of properties based on the many physical forms and concentrations and have a large range of safety-related properties, including physical as well as health hazards. Organic peroxides are either used as the technically pure compound or as formulations where the peroxide might be found in a diluted form, such as solutions, pastes, or solid granules.

Organic peroxide formulations vary in reactivity hazard from self-extinguishing to the potential for a violent deflagration or detonation. Decomposition can be initiated by heat, friction, mechanical shock, or contamination, though sensitivity to these stimuli varies greatly. Dilution with water or other solvents is used as a means to reduce the level of sensitivity to outside stimuli and the potential for decomposition. Refrigeration is also used as a means to reduce the potential for decomposition. The health hazards of these materials as provided in commerce vary greatly depending on concentration and formulation itself.

B.4.1.18.2 Metal Peroxides (Inorganic) (M-O-O). Metal peroxides, such as sodium peroxide and calcium peroxide, are all oxidizers. Some are corrosive and water reactive. Reaction with water can be explosive in some instances.

B.4.1.19 Phosphorus-Halogen Compounds (O=P-X$_3$, P-X). These phosphorus analogues are corrosive and often react violently with water and include such chemicals as phosphorus oxychloride (POCl$_3$), phosphorus trichloride (PCl$_3$), and phosphorus pentachloride (PCl$_5$). They are water reactive, corrosive, and toxic.

B.5 Hazard Category Based on Concentration.

B.5.1 General. Some chemicals exhibit different physical and/or health hazards based on the concentration. Some pertinent examples of concentration-dependent hazards of specific chemicals are provided in the following list. Additional information on concentration-dependent hazards should be contained in the MSDS.

(1) *Acetic Acid (64-19-7).* Concentration: 100 percent — corrosive, flammable/combustible; 36 percent aqueous — corrosive; <5 percent aqueous — not corrosive.
(2) *Ammonia (7664-41-7).* Concentration: anhydrous — corrosive, flammable gas; <50 percent aqueous — not corrosive.
(3) *Formaldehyde (50-00-0).* Concentration: anhydrous — flammable, corrosive, highly toxic; 37 percent aqueous — combustible, highly toxic 10 percent aqueous — combustible.
(4) *Hydrogen Fluoride (7664-39-3).* Concentration: anhydrous — corrosive, water reactive, toxic; 10–48 percent — corrosive, toxic; 2–10 percent aqueous — corrosive.
(5) *Nitric Acid (7697-37-2).* Concentration: 7–40 percent aqueous — oxidizer, corrosive; 1–6 percent aqueous — not oxidizer, not corrosive.
(6) *Phosphine (CAS numbers based on concentration).* Concentration: 5 percent phosphine, 95 percent nitrogen — pyrophoric, toxic; phosphine: 2 percent phosphine, 98 percent nitrogen — toxic.
(7) *Phosphoric Acid (7664-38-2).* Concentration: 85–86 percent aqueous — corrosive; <80 percent aqueous — not corrosive.

(8) *Potassium Hydroxide (1310-58-3)*. Concentration: 100 percent — corrosive, water reactive, toxic; 45 percent aqueous — corrosive, water reactive; 5 percent aqueous — corrosive.

(9) *2-Propanol (Isopropanol) (67-63-0)*. Concentration:> 91 percent aqueous — flammable; 25–50 percent aqueous — combustible.

(10) *Sodium chlorate (7775-09-9)*. Concentration: 100 percent — corrosive, oxidizer, unstable reactive; 40–50 percent aqueous — corrosive, oxidizer.

(11) *Sodium hydroxide (1310-73-2)*. Concentration: 100 percent — corrosive, water reactive, toxic; 1–50 percent aqueous — corrosive.

(12) *Sulfuric Acid (7664-93-9)*. Concentration: 92–98 percent aqueous — corrosive, water reactive, toxic; 12.7–50 percent aqueous — corrosive, water reactive, toxic; 4–12.6 percent aqueous — corrosive.

(13) *Sodium Hypochlorite (7681-52-9)*. Concentration: 12–15 percent aqueous — corrosive; 3–5 percent aqueous — not corrosive.

B.6 Material Safety Data Sheets (MSDS) — A Starting Point for Hazards Identification.

B.6.1 Material safety data sheets (MSDS) have been established as a primary means of hazard identification under OSHA's Hazard Communication program. MSDS are provided by manufacturers or importers as a means to communicate hazards within a set of standardized terms and elements or bodies of information.

B.6.2 The use of the ANSI format in the preparation of MSDS is not mandatory; however, most manufacturers include information that relates to the sixteen sections referenced in B.2. In order to classify the hazards of a given material, users should refer to key sections of the MSDS that contain the following information:

(1) Product identification
(2) Hazards identification
(3) Physical and chemical properties
(4) Stability and reactivity
(5) Toxicological information
(6) Transportation information

Each section should contain relevant information that can be used in the hazard classification process. The following paragraphs provide useful information to help the user with these MSDS sections.

B.6.2.1 Product Identification. Product identification will typically include the chemical name, common name, and synonyms. Pure materials, sometimes referred to as "neat" to indicate that they are in an undiluted form, are typically referred to by their chemical name. However, it is not uncommon to find that the manufacturer has identified the material under a trade name chosen by that particular manufacturer. Chemical synonyms will frequently be shown; however, it should be expected that the list of synonyms may be an abbreviated listing and that there may be other synonyms that are not listed.

For chemical mixtures the material will typically be identified by its trade name. Some confusion can be created when a material in its "neat" form is further identified in the Hazard Identification section as containing other constituents. Commercially available materials even in the pure or neat form contain impurities from the manufacturing process. Although there is no hard-and-fast rule, materials in concentrations of 95 percent or greater are generally considered to be in the pure form and are referred to by the CASRN for the major component. The impurities from manufacturing are generally not considered for the purposes of material identification and such materials are not considered to be "mixtures" of chemicals per se.

The product identification section provides additional information, including the identification of the manufacturer of the material and nomenclature intended to link the MSDS to the label provided on the material in the container(s) as furnished by the manufacturer.

The composition of the material or information on ingredients is either incorporated into or follows the material and company identification. The composition section typically lists the hazardous components as identified by OSHA, and not those categories used by NFPA 400. Although the OSHA hazard categories have been incorporated into the regulatory scheme used by NFPA 400, there are differences and the converse is not true. For example, OSHA does not incorporate the traditional NFPA hazard class.

The primary differences center on the use of subclasses of hazards that are not identified in the OSHA approach. For example, within the hazard category of oxidizer, there are four subcategories or Classes of hazards recognized under the NFPA system, e.g., Class 4, Class 3, Class 2, and Class 1 materials. Hazard classes are used to describe a range of hazards within a given hazard category, and the class system is used for materials that are oxidizers other than oxidizing gases, organic peroxides, unstable reactives, and water reactives. Although not the subject of regulation by NFPA 400, flammable liquids are further subdivided into Class I, Class II, and Class III, and combustible liquids are further subdivided into Class II, IIIA, and IIIB liquids.

The composition section is required to list components of a material that are present in concentrations of 1 percent or more. For materials that are identified as carcinogens under the OSHA definitions, the material must be listed if its concentration exceeds 0.1 percent. The MSDS may also list components that are nonhazardous. The CASRN for each component is typically listed in this section of the MSDS.

B.6.2.2 Hazards Identification. The hazard identification section of MSDS is used to provide an emergency overview of the material to include a description of its physical properties, including its physical state (solid, liquid, gas). The overview typically provides general information on significant physical hazards (e.g., fire, explosion, and instability), as well as information on potential health effects that can result from exposure to the material. While the information is useful in terms of a gross assessment of hazards, additional information found elsewhere in the MSDS is needed in order to properly classify the material.

B.6.2.3 Physical and Chemical Properties. The physical and chemical properties of the materials are included in this section of the MSDS. It is typical to find a wide array of physical and chemical properties listed. Examples of some of the physical and chemical properties of interest include, but are not limited to the following:

(1) Appearance (color, physical form, shape)
(2) Odor
(3) Odor threshold
(4) Physical state
(5) pH
(6) Melting/freezing point (specify which)

(7) Initial boiling point and boiling range
(8) Flash point
(9) Evaporation rate
(10) Flammability (solid, gas)
(11) Upper/lower flammability or explosive limits
(12) Vapor pressure
(13) Vapor density
(14) Specific gravity or relative density
(15) Solubility(ies) (specify solvent, e.g., water)

B.6.2.4 Stability and Reactivity. The section on stability and reactivity of materials typically describes conditions which affect the intrinsic stability of a material. An intrinsic property is a property that is inherent in the material in and of itself, as compared to its properties under conditions that are brought about by the environment in which it is located. Environmental conditions can be described as extrinsic conditions, such as when the material is exposed to heat, fire, shock, or other effects.

This section of the MSDS is used as a means to assess its nature within the context of the unstable reactive hazard category. While many materials have an intrinsic stability, they can become unstable when exposed to high temperatures or mechanical or physical shock. Therefore, the information found on an MSDS might have to be supplemented by referring to other authoritative sources regarding the reactivity of the material.

B.6.2.5 Toxicological Properties. The section on toxicological information contains information on the health effects of the material or its components. It typically supports the detail provided in the section on hazards identification in the MSDS. The information provided is written for use by healthcare professionals and those that have the technical training and experience in the safety and toxicology aspects of interface with materials from a toxicological perspective.

However, this section of the MSDS contains information that is used to establish the approach to control integral to NFPA 400 with respect to toxicity and corrosivity. Data including the effects of acute exposure to mammals and other life forms or information regarding the irreversible destruction of tissue at the site of contact will be found in this section of the MSDS.

There may be other information regarding the toxicological effects resulting in but not limited to irritation, sensitization, carcinogenicity, reproductive effects, and genetic and target organ effects, none of which fall under the scope of NFPA 400.

B.6.2.6 Transportation. The system of classification used by the Department of Transportation to classify materials for shipment purposes is not compatible with the system used to classify materials within the context of NFPA 400. It must be recognized that although the OSHA system of hazard communication has some similarity to the system used by the Department of Transportation, it is not wholly compatible. The OSHA hazard communication system embodied in the MSDS does not correlate with the system used in 49 CFR as developed for transportation purposes. The OSHA system contemplates that users and producers of hazardous materials will encounter these materials in their unpackaged state where the materials are reasonably foreseen to have a potential for bodily contact or use within the work environment on a regular basis. On the other hand, the DOT system of control views the materials in their final packaging as required for transportation where the materials are not subject to exposure to personnel except under upset conditions. However, with the effort to implement the United Nations Globally Harmonized System of Classification and Labeling of Chemicals, this may change.

These differences aside, users may find additional information in the section for transportation on the MSDS, which may or may not be further explained in preceding sections. It is important to recognize that the classification for the purposes of transportation will not suffice as a means to assign the material to a given hazard category under the requirements of NFPA 400, and the user must carefully apply the material specific definitions found in Chapter 3 along with the criteria obtained from the MSDS and other resources in order to determine the appropriate classification of a given material.

Annex C Hazardous Materials Management Plans and Hazardous Materials Inventory Statements

This annex is not a part of the requirements of this NFPA document unless specifically adopted by the authority having jurisdiction.

C.1 Scope. Hazardous materials inventory statements (HMIS) and hazardous materials management plans (HMMP), which are required by the AHJ pursuant to Chapter 1, must be provided for hazardous materials in accordance with Annex C.

Exception No. 1: Materials that have been satisfactorily demonstrated not to present a potential danger to public health, safety, or welfare, based upon the quantity or condition of storage, when approved.

Exception No. 2: Chromium, copper, lead, nickel, and silver need not be considered hazardous materials for the purposes of this annex unless they are stored in a friable, powdered, or finely divided state. Proprietary and trade secret information must be protected under the laws of the state or AHJ.

C.2 Hazardous Materials Inventory Statements (HMIS).

C.2.1 Where Required. A separate HMIS must be provided for each building, including its appurtenant structures, and each exterior facility in which hazardous materials are stored. The hazardous materials inventory statement must list by hazard class all hazardous materials stored. The hazardous materials inventory statement must include the following information for each hazardous material listed:

(1) Hazard class
(2) Common or trade name
(3) Chemical name, major constituents, and concentrations if a mixture; if a waste, the waste category
(4) Chemical Abstracts Service Registry number (CAS number), which can be found in the MSDS
(5) Whether the material is pure or a mixture, and whether the material is a solid, liquid, or gas
(6) Maximum aggregate quantity stored at any one time
(7) Storage conditions related to the storage type, temperature, and pressure

C.2.2 Changes to HMIS. An amended HMIS must be provided within 30 days of the storage of any hazardous materials that changes or adds a hazard class or that is sufficient in quantity to cause an increase in the quantity which exceeds 5 percent for any hazard class.

C.3 Hazardous Materials Management Plan (HMMP).

C.3.1 General. Applications for a permit to store hazardous materials must include an HMMP standard form or short form in accordance with C.3.3 and must provide a narrative description of the operations and processes taking place at the facility. *(See Figure C.3.1.)*

2013 Edition

SAMPLE FORMAT OF
HAZARDOUS MATERIALS MANAGEMENT PLAN (HMMP) INSTRUCTIONS

SECTION I — FACILITY DESCRIPTION

1.1 Part A

1. Fill out Items 1 through 11 and sign the declaration.
2. Only Part A of this section is required to be updated and submitted annually, or within 30 days of a change.

1.2 Part B — General Facility Description (Site Plan)

1. Provide a site plan on 8½ in. by 11 in. (215 mm by 279 mm) paper, using letters on the top and bottom margins and numbers on the right and left side margins, showing the location of all buildings, structures, chemical loading areas, parking lots, internal roads, storm and sanitary sewers, wells, and adjacent property uses.
2. Indicate the approximate scale, northern direction, and date the drawing was completed.
3. List all special land uses within 1 mi (1.609 km).

1.3 Part C — Facility Storage Map (Confidential Information)

1. Provide a floor plan of each building on 8½ in. by 11 in. (215 mm by 279 mm) paper, using letters on the top and bottom margins and numbers on the right and left side margins, with approximate scale and northern direction, showing the location of each storage area. Mark map clearly "Confidential — Do Not Disclose" for trade-secret information as specified by federal, state, and local laws.
2. Identify each storage area with an identification number, letter, name, or symbol.
3. Show the following:
   (a) Accesses to each storage area.
   (b) Location of emergency equipment.
   (c) The general purpose of other areas within the facility.
   (d) Location of all aboveground and underground tanks to include sumps, vaults, below-grade treatment systems, piping, etc.
4. Provide the following on the map or in a map key or legend for each storage area:
   (a) A list of hazardous materials, including wastes
   (b) Hazard class of each hazardous waste
   (c) The maximum quantity for hazardous materials
   (d) The contents and capacity limit of all tanks at each area and indicate whether they are above or below ground
5. List separately any radioactives, cryogens, and compressed gases for each facility.
6. Trade-secret information shall be listed as specified by federal, state, and local laws.

© 2012 National Fire Protection Association

SECTION II — HAZARDOUS MATERIALS INVENTORY STATEMENT (HMIS)

2.1 Part A — Declaration

Fill out all appropriate information.

2.2 Part B — Inventory Statement

1. You must complete a separate inventory statement for all waste and nonwaste hazardous materials. List all hazardous materials in alphabetical order by hazard class.
2. Inventory Statement Instructions.

Column	Information Required
1	Provide hazard class for each material.
2	**Nonwaste.** Provide the common or trade name of the regulated material. **Waste.** In lieu of trade names, you may provide the waste category.
3	Provide the chemical name and major constituents and concentrations, if a mixture.
4	Enter the chemical abstracts service registry number (CAS number) found in the MSDS. For mixtures, enter the CAS number of the mixture as a whole if it has been assigned a number distinct from its constituents. For a mixture that has no CAS number, leave this item blank.
5	Enter the following descriptive codes as they apply to each material. You may list more than one code, if applicable. P = Pure M = Mixture S = Solid L = Liquid G = Gas
6	Provide the maximum aggregate quantity of each material handled at any one time by the business. For underground tanks, list the maximum volume [in gallons (liters)] of the tank. Enter the estimated average daily amount on site during the past year.
7	Enter the units used in Column 6 as: lb = Pounds gal = Gallons cf = Cubic Feet
8	Enter the number of days that the material was present on site (during the last year).

NFPA 400 (p. 1 of 8)

FIGURE C.3.1 Sample Format of Hazardous Materials Management Plan (HMMP) Instructions.

Column	Information Required
9	Enter the storage codes below for type, temperature, and pressure:

Type

- A = Aboveground Tank
- B = Belowground Tank
- C = Tank Inside Building
- D = Steel Drum
- E = Plastic or Nonmetallic Drum
- F = Can
- G = Carboy
- H = Silo
- I = Fiber Drum
- J = Bag
- K = Box
- L = Cylinder
- M = Glass Bottle or Jug
- N = Plastic Bottles or Jugs
- O = Tote Bin
- P = Tank Wagon
- Q = Rail Car
- R = Other

Temperature

- 4 = Ambient
- 5 = Greater than Ambient
- 6 = Less than Ambient, but not Cryogenic [less than −150°F (−101.1°C)]
- 7 = Cryogenic conditions [less than −150°F (−101.1°C)]

Pressure

- 1 = Ambient (Atmospheric)
- 2 = Greater than Ambient (Atmospheric)
- 3 = Less than Ambient (Atmospheric)

10   For each material listed, provide the SARA Title III hazard class as listed below. You may list more than one class. These categories are defined in 40 CFR 370.66.

Physical Hazard

- F = Fire
- P = Sudden Release of Pressure
- R = Reactivity

Health Hazard

- I = Immediate (Acute)
- D = Delayed (Chronic)

11   **Waste Only.** For each waste, provide the total estimated amount of hazardous waste handled throughout the course of the year.

SECTION III — SEPARATION AND MONITORING

3.1 Part A — Aboveground

Fill out Items 1 through 6, or provide similar information for each storage area shown on the facility map. Use additional sheets as necessary.

3.2 Part B — Underground

1. Complete a separate page for each underground tank, sump, vault, belowgrade treatment system, etc.
2. Check the type of tank and method(s) that applies to your tank(s) and piping, and answer the appropriate questions. Provide any additional information in the space provided or on a separate sheet.

SECTION IV — WASTE DISPOSAL

Check all that apply and list the associated wastes for each method checked.

SECTION V — RECORD KEEPING

Include a brief description of your inspection procedures. You are also required to keep an inspection log and recordable discharge log, which are designed to be used in conjunction with routine inspections for all storage facilities or areas. Place a check in each box that describes your forms. If you do not use the sample forms, provide copies of your forms for review and approval.

SECTION VI — EMERGENCY RESPONSE PLAN

1. This plan should describe the personnel, procedures, and equipment available for responding to a release or threatened release of hazardous materials that are stored, handled, or used on site.
2. A check or a response under each item indicates that a specific procedure is followed at the facility, or that the equipment specified is maintained on site.
3. If the facility maintains a more detailed emergency response plan on site, indicate this in Item 5. This plan shall be made available for review by the inspecting jurisdiction.

SECTION VII — EMERGENCY RESPONSE TRAINING PLAN

1. This plan should describe the basic training plan used at the facility.
2. A check in the appropriate box indicates the training is provided or the records are maintained.
3. If the facility maintains a more detailed emergency response training plan, indicate this in Item 4. This plan shall be made available for review by the inspecting jurisdiction.

© 2012 National Fire Protection Association

FIGURE C.3.1 *Continued*

HAZARDOUS MATERIALS MANAGEMENT PLAN
SECTION I: FACILITY DESCRIPTION

Part A — General Information

1. Business Name: _____ Phone: _____
   Address: _____

2. Person Responsible for the Business:

Name	Title	Phone
_____	_____	_____

3. Emergency Contacts:

Name	Title	Home Number	Work Number
_____	_____	_____	_____
_____	_____	_____	_____

4. Person Responsible for the Application/Principal Contact:

Name	Title	Phone
_____	_____	_____

5. Property Owner:

Name	Address	Phone
_____	_____	_____

6. Principal Business Activity: _____
7. Number of Employees: _____
8. Number of Shifts: _____
9. Hours of Operation: _____
10. SIC Code: _____
11. Dunn and Bradstreet Number: _____
12. Declaration:
    I certify that the information above and on the following parts is true and correct to the best of my knowledge.

    Signature: _____ Date: _____
    Print Name: _____ Title: _____
    (Must be signed by owner/operator or designated representative)

Part B — General Facility Description/Site Plan

(Use grid format in Part C)

Special land uses within 1 mi (1.609 km): _____
_____
_____
_____

© 2012 National Fire Protection Association   NFPA 400 (p. 3 of 8)

FIGURE C.3.1 *Continued*

SECTION I: FACILITY DESCRIPTION *(Continued)*
Part C—Facility Map
(Use grid format below)

	A	B	C	D	E	F	G	H	I	J	K	L	M	N	
1															1
2															2
3															3
4															4
5															5
6															6
7															7
8															8
9															9
10															10
11															11
12															12
13															13
14															14
15															15
16															16
17															17
	A	B	C	D	E	F	G	H	I	J	K	L	M	N	

BUSINESS NAME

DATE

ADDRESS CITY

PAGE _____ OF _____

SECTION II: HAZARDOUS MATERIALS INVENTORY STATEMENT

Part A—Declaration

1. Business Name: _____
2. Address: _____
3. Declaration:
   Under penalty of perjury, I declare the above and subsequent information, provided as part of the hazardous materials inventory statement, is true and correct.

Signature: _____ Date: _____

Print Name: _____ Title: _____

(Must be signed by owner/operator or designated representative)

© 2012 National Fire Protection Association NFPA 400 (p. 4 of 8)

FIGURE C.3.1 *Continued*

SECTION II: HAZARDOUS MATERIALS INVENTORY STATEMENT *(Continued)*

Part B—Hazardous Materials Inventory Statement

(1) Hazard Class	(2) Common/Trade Name	(3) Chemical Name, Components and Concentration	(4) Chemical Abstract Service No.	(5) Physical State

(6) Maximum Quantity on Hand at Any Time	(7) Units	(8) Days on Site	(9) Storage Code (Type, Pressure, Temperature)	(10) SARA Class	(11) Annual Waste Throughput

SECTION III: SEPARATION, SECONDARY CONTAINMENT, AND MONITORING

Part A—Aboveground Storage Areas

Storage Area Identification (as shown on facility map): _____

1. Storage Type:
   - ____ Original containers
   - ____ Inside machinery
   - ____ 55 gal (208.2 L) drums or storage shed
   - ____ Pressurized vessel
   - ____ Safety cans
   - ____ Bulk tanks
   - ____ Outside barrels
   - ____ Other: _____

2. Storage Location:
   - ____ Inside building
   - ____ Secured
   - ____ Outside building

3. Separation:
   - ____ All materials
   - ____ Compatible
   - ____ Separation by 20 ft (6.1 m)
   - ____ One-hour separation wall/partition
   - ____ Approved cabinets
   - ____ Other: _____

© 2012 National Fire Protection Association

NFPA 400 (p. 5 of 8)

FIGURE C.3.1 *Continued*

SECTION III: SEPARATION, SECONDARY CONTAINMENT, AND MONITORING (Continued)

4. Secondary Containment:
   - _____ Approved cabinet
   - _____ Tray
   - _____ Vaulted tank
   - _____ Double-wall tank
   - _____ Secondary drums
   - _____ Bermed, coated floor
   - _____ Other: _____
   _____

5. Monitoring:
   - _____ Visual
   - _____ Continuous
   - _____ Other: _____

   Attach specifications if necessary

6. Monitoring Frequency:
   - _____ Daily
   - _____ Weekly
   - _____ Other: _____

   Attach additional sheets as necessary

Part B—Underground

Single-Wall Tanks and Piping

Tank Area Identification (as shown on facility map): _____

1. _____ Backfill vapor wells
   Model and manufacturer: _____
   Continuous or monthly testing: _____
2. _____ Groundwater monitoring wells
3. _____ Monthly precision tank test
4. _____ Piping
   Monitoring method: _____
   Frequency: _____
5. _____ Other: _____

Double-Wall Tanks and Piping

Tank Area Identification (as shown on facility map): _____

1. Method of monitoring the annular space: _____
2. Frequency: ❑ Continuous ❑ Daily ❑ Weekly ❑ Other: _____
3. List the type of secondary containment for piping: _____
4. List method of monitoring the secondary containment for piping: _____
5. Are there incompatible materials within the same vault? ❑ Yes ❑ No
   If yes, how is separate secondary containment provided? _____

Note: If you have continuous monitoring equipment, you shall maintain copies of all service and maintenance work. Such reports shall be made available for review on site, and shall be submitted to the fire prevention bureau upon request.

Attach additional sheets as necessary

SECTION IV: WASTE DISPOSAL

- _____ Discharge to the Sanitary Sewer—
  Wastes: _____
  _____

- _____ Licensed Waste Hauler—
  Wastes: _____
  _____

- _____ Pretreatment—
  Wastes: _____
  _____

- _____ Recycle—
  Wastes: _____
  _____

© 2012 National Fire Protection Association

NFPA 400 (p. 6 of 8)

FIGURE C.3.1 *Continued*

SECTION IV: WASTE DISPOSAL *(Continued)*

_____ Other—
    Describe method: _____
    Wastes: _____

_____ No Waste

SECTION V: RECORD KEEPING

Description of our inspection program: _____
_____
_____

_____ We will use the attached sample forms in our inspection program.

_____ We will not use the sample forms. We have attached a copy of our own forms.

SECTION VI: EMERGENCY RESPONSE PLAN

1. In the event of an emergency, the following shall be notified:
    A. On-Site Responders:

Name	Title	Phone
_____	_____	_____
_____	_____	_____

    B. Method of Notification to Responder:
        _____ Automatic alarm   _____ Verbal
        _____ Manual alarm   _____ Other: _____
        _____ Phone

    C. Agency and Phone Number: _____
        Fire Department: _____
        State Office of Emergency: _____
        Services: _____
        Other: _____

2. Designated Local Emergency Medical Facility:

Name	Address	Phone (24 hours)
_____	_____	_____

3. Mitigation Equipment:
    A. Monitoring Devices:
        _____ Toxic or flammable gas detection
        _____ Fluid detection
        _____ Other: _____

    B. Spill Containment:
        _____ Absorbents   _____ Other: _____

    C. Spill Control and Treatment
        _____ Vapor scrubber   _____ Mechanical ventilation
        _____ Pumps/vacuums   _____ Secondary containment
        _____ Neutralizer   _____ Other: _____

© 2012 National Fire Protection Association   NFPA 400 (p. 7 of 8)

FIGURE C.3.1 *Continued*

SECTION VI: EMERGENCY RESPONSE PLAN (Continued)

4. Evacuation:
   - _____ Immediate area evacuation routes posted
   - _____ Entire building evacuation procedures developed
   - _____ Assembly areas preplanned
   - _____ Evacuation maps posted
   - _____ Other: _____

5. Supplemental hazardous materials emergency response plan on site
   Location: _____
   Responsible person: _____
   Phone: _____

SECTION VII: EMERGENCY RESPONSE TRAINING PLAN

1. Person responsible for the emergency response training plan:

Name	Title	Phone

2. Training Requirements:
   A. All employees trained in the following as indicated:
      - _____ Procedures for internal alarm/notification
      - _____ Procedures for notification of external emergency response organizations
      - _____ Location and content of the emergency response plan
   B. Chemical handlers are trained in the following as indicated:
      - _____ Safe methods for handling and storage of hazardous materials
      - _____ Proper use of personal protective equipment
      - _____ Locations and proper use of fire- and spill-control equipment
      - _____ Specific hazards of each chemical to which they may be exposed
   C. Emergency response team members are trained in the following:
      - _____ Procedures for shutdown of operations
      - _____ Procedures for using, maintaining, and replacing facility emergency and monitoring equipment

3. The following records are maintained for all employees:
   - _____ Verification that training was completed by the employee
   - _____ Description of the type and amount of introductory and continuing training
   - _____ Documentation on and description of emergency response drills conducted at the facility

4. A more comprehensive and detailed emergency response training plan is maintained on site.
   Location: _____
   Responsible person: _____
   Phone: _____

© 2012 National Fire Protection Association

FIGURE C.3.1 *Continued*

C.3.2 Information Required. The HMMP standard form must include the following information.

C.3.2.1 General Information. General information, including business name and address, emergency contacts, business activity, business owner or operator, SIC code, number of employees and hours, Dunn and Bradstreet number, and signature of owner, operator, or designated representative must be included.

C.3.2.2 General Site Plan. A general site plan drawn at a legible scale which must include, but not be limited to, the location of buildings, exterior storage facilities, permanent access ways, evacuation routes, parking lots, internal roads, chemical loading areas, equipment cleaning areas, storm and sanitary sewer accesses, emergency equipment, and adjacent property uses must be included. The exterior storage areas must be identified with the hazard class and the maximum quantities per hazard class of hazardous materials stored. When required by the AHJ, information regarding the location of wells, flood plains, earthquake faults, surface water bodies, and general land uses within 1 mi (1.6 km) of the facility boundaries must be included.

C.3.2.3 Building Floor Plan. A building floor plan drawn to a legible scale, which must include, but not be limited to, hazardous materials storage areas within the building and must indicate rooms, doorways, corridors, means of egress and evacuation routes must be included. Each hazardous materials storage facility must be identified by a map key that lists the individual hazardous materials, their hazard class, and quantity present for each area.

C.3.2.4 Hazardous Materials Handling. Information showing that activities involving the handling of hazardous materials between the storage areas and manufacturing processes on site are conducted in a manner to prevent the accidental release of such materials must be included.

C.3.2.5 Chemical Compatibility and Separation. Information showing procedures, controls, signs, or other methods used to ensure separation and protection of stored materials from factors that could cause accidental ignition or reaction of ignitable, reactive, or incompatible materials in each area must be included.

C.3.2.6 Monitoring Program. Information including, but not limited to, the location, type, manufacturer's specifications, if applicable, and suitability of monitoring methods for each storage facility when required must be included.

C.3.2.7 Inspection and Record Keeping. Schedules and procedures for inspecting safety and monitoring and emergency equipment must be included. The permittee must develop and follow a written inspection procedure acceptable to the AHJ for inspecting the facility for events or practices that could lead to unauthorized discharges of hazardous materials. Inspections must be conducted at a frequency appropriate to detect problems prior to a discharge. An inspection check sheet must be developed to be used in conjunction with routine inspections. The check sheet must provide for the date, time, and location of inspection; note problems and dates and times of corrective actions taken; and include the name of the inspector and the countersignature of the designated safety manager for the facility.

C.3.2.8 Employee Training. A training program appropriate to the types and quantities of materials stored or used must be conducted to prepare employees to safely handle hazardous materials on a daily basis and during emergencies. The training program must include the following:

(1) Instruction in safe storage and handling of hazardous materials, including maintenance of monitoring records
(2) Instruction in emergency procedures for leaks, spills, fires or explosions, including shutdown of operations and evacuation procedures
(3) Record-keeping procedures for documenting training given to employees

C.3.2.9 Emergency Response. A description of facility emergency procedures must be provided.

C.3.3 HMMP Short Form — (Minimal Storage Site). A facility must qualify as a minimal storage site if the quantity of each hazardous material stored in one or more facilities in an aggregate quantity for the facility is 500 lb (227 kg) or less for solids, 55 gal (208.2 L) or less for liquids, or 200 ft^3 (5.7 m^3) or less at NTP for compressed gases and does not exceed the threshold planning quantity as listed in 40 CFR, Part 355, Sections 302 and 304. The applicant for a permit for a facility that qualifies as a minimal storage site must be permitted to file the short form HMMP. Such plan must include the following components:

(1) General facility information
(2) A simple line drawing of the facility showing the location of storage facilities and indicating the hazard class or classes and physical state of the hazardous materials being stored
(3) Information describing that the hazardous materials will be stored and handled in a safe manner and will be appropriately contained, separated, and monitored
(4) Assurance that security precautions have been taken, employees have been appropriately trained to handle the hazardous materials and react to emergency situations, adequate labeling and warning signs are posted, adequate emergency equipment is maintained, and the disposal of hazardous materials will be in an appropriate manner

C.4 Maintenance of Records. Hazardous materials inventory statements and hazardous materials management plans must be maintained by the permittee for a period of not less than three (3) years after submittal of updated or revised versions. Such records must be made available to the AHJ upon request.

Annex D   Security Information

This annex is not a part of the requirements of this NFPA document but is included for informational purposes only.

D.1 Security Plans.

D.2 Informational References Relevant to Security. The following documents or portions thereof are listed here as informational resources only. They are not a part of the requirements of this document.

D.2.1 American Chemistry Council. *Responsible Care Management System® and Responsible Care® Security Code of Management Practices,* American Chemistry Council, 700 Second Street, NE, Washington, DC 20002, Phone: 202-249-700, www.americanchemistry.com

This code is designed to help companies achieve continuous improvement in security performance using a risk-based approach to identify, assess, and address vulnerabilities, prevent or mitigate incidents, enhance training and response capabilities, and maintain and improve relationships with key stakeholders.

D.2.2 American Institute of Chemical Engineers. *Guidelines for Analyzing and Managing the Security Vulnerabilities of Fixed Chemical Sites,* June 2003, Center for Chemical Process Safety, American Institute of Chemical Engineers, 3 Park Avenue, New York, NY, 10016-5991, Phone: 1-800-242-4363, www.aiche.org

This publication demonstrates a process and tools for managing the security vulnerability of sites that produce and handle chemicals, petroleum products, pharmaceuticals, and related materials such as fertilizers and water treatment chemicals. The publication includes enterprise screening, site screening, protection analysis, security vulnerability assessment, and action planning and tracking.

D.2.3 American Petroleum Institute.

D.2.3.1 API Recommended Practice 70, *Security for Offshore Oil and Natural Gas Operations,* American Petroleum Institute, 1220 L Street, NW, Washington, DC, 20005-4070. Phone: 1-800-854-7179; 303-397-7956 (local and international); www.api.org

This document is intended to assist the offshore oil and natural gas drilling and producing operators and contractors in assessing security needs during the performance of oil and natural gas operations. It includes information on security awareness, conducting security vulnerability assessments when warranted, and developing security plans for offshore facilities.

D.2.3.2 API Bulletin, October 2004, *Security Vulnerability Assessment for the Petroleum and Petrochemical Industries,* American Petroleum Institute, 1220 L Street, NW, Washington, DC, 20005-4070. Phone: 1-800-854-7179; 303-397-7956 (local and international); www.api.org

The publication describes an approach for assessing security vulnerabilities that is widely applicable to the types of facilities operated by the industry and the security issues they face. The objective of conducting a security vulnerability assessment (SVA) is to identify security hazards, threats, and vulnerabilities facing a facility, and to evaluate the countermeasures to provide for the protection of the public, workers, national interests, the environment, and the company. With this information security risks can be assessed and strategies can be formed to reduce vulnerabilities as required. SVA is a tool to assist management in making decisions on the need for countermeasures to address the threats and vulnerabilities.

D.2.3.3 API Bulletin, April 2005, *Security Guidance for the Petroleum and Petrochemical Industries,* American Petroleum Institute, 1220 L Street, NW, Washington, DC, 20005-4070. Phone: 1-800-854-7179; 303-397-7956 (local and international); www.api.org

This document provides general security guidance and other reference data on applicable regulatory requirements, which can be tailored to meet the differing security needs of the petroleum industry. This security guidance is by necessity general in nature. It is intended to provide an overview of security issues in the petroleum industry and provide general guidance on effective policies and practices.

D.2.4 Chlorine Institute. Chlorine Institute, *The Security Management Plan for the Transportation and On-site Storage and Use of Chlorine Cylinders, Ton Containers and Cargo Tanks,* The Chlorine Institute, 1300 Wilson Boulevard, Arlington, VA 22209, Phone: 703-741-5760, www.chlorineinstitute.org

The Security Management Plan for the Transportation and On-Site Storage and Use of Chlorine Cylinders, Ton Containers and Cargo Tanks (the CI Cylinder, Ton and Cargo Tank Plan) contains mandatory actions on the part of the chlor-alkali industry to achieve greater chlorine security. Two critical elements of the CI Cylinder, Ton and Cargo Tank Plan include the implementation of baseline countermeasures and actions at higher threat levels. The implementation examples given are intended solely to stimulate thinking and offer helpful ideas on implementing the CI Cylinder, Ton and Cargo Tank Plan. They are in no way intended to establish a standard, legal obligation, or preferred option for any practice. Other approaches not described here may be just as effective, or even more effective, for a particular company. If a company so chooses, it may adopt any of these examples or may modify them to fit the company's unique situation.

D.2.5 Compressed Gas Association.

D.2.5.1 CGA P-50—2005, *Site Security Guidelines,* 4221 Walney Road, 5th Floor, Chantilly, VA 20151, Phone: 703-788-2700, www.cganet.com

This publication provides guidance to the compressed gas industry for assessing security risks and identifying and implementing preventive security measures at fixed sites. It is intended as a resource to help managers at individual facilities make security decisions based on risk. The guide does not attempt to provide an all-inclusive list of security considerations for compressed gas companies nor does it address transportation security and security at customer sites.

CGA P-51—2004, *Transportation Security Guideline for the Compressed Gas Industry,* 4221 Walney Road, 5th Floor, Chantilly, VA 20151, Phone: 703-788-2700, www.cganet.com

This publication is intended for management personnel, transportation specialists, and all other personnel that are responsible for the safe and secure transportation of raw materials and products. It applies to both for-hire and private motor carriers. It contains tools and resources that are useful when assessing security issues related to the transportation of hazardous materials. It also provides guidance for compliance with the U.S. Department of Transportation (DOT) regulation HM-232, Security Requirements for Offerors and Transporters of Hazardous Materials.

The implementation of the information in this publication will vary according to the compressed gas being distributed and the mode and route of transportation.

D.2.5.2 CGA P-52—2005, *Security Guidelines for Qualifying Customers Purchasing Compressed Gases,* 4221 Walney Road, 5th Floor, Chantilly, VA 20151, Phone: 703-788-2700, www.cganet.com

This document provides guidelines to the compressed gas industry for qualifying customers who purchase products considered at risk for illegal use.

D.2.6 Federal Motor Carrier Association. Federal Motor Carrier Safety Administration (FMCSA), *Guide to Developing an Effective Security Plan for the Highway Transportation of Hazardous Materials,* Federal Motor Carrier Safety Administration, United States Department of Transportation, 400 7th Street SW, Washington, DC 20590, Phone: 1-800-832-5660, www.fmcsa.dot.gov

The guide is designed to provide the hazardous materials industry with information to understand the nature of the threats against hazardous materials transportation, identify the vulnerabilities to those threats that exist in a facility, and address actions to reduce the vulnerabilities identified at a facility.

D.2.7 Institute of Makers of Explosives. Safety Library Publication No. 27 (SLP-27), *Security in Manufacturing, Transportation, Storage and Use of Commercial Explosives*, January 2005. Institute of Makers of Explosives, 1120 Nineteenth Street, NW, Suite 310, Washington, DC 20036, Phone: 202-429-9280, www.ime.org

SLP-27 presents security recommendations for commercial explosives operations in a regulation-style format. Appendices include a sample site security plan, vulnerability assessment, employee identification system, and recommendations for enhanced security when security risks have temporarily increased. Although occasional reference may be made to federal regulations, a deliberate effort was made to provide recommendations that do not simply repeat the regulations. Other IME publications should also be consulted for additional, detailed information that might be appropriate.

D.2.8 National Association of Chemical Distributors. *Responsible Distribution Process*, National Association of Chemical Distributors, 1560 Wilson Boulevard, Arlington, VA 22209, Phone: 703-527-6223, www.nacd.com

Responsible Distribution Process (RDP) is designed to help companies achieve continuous improvement in security as well as in environmental, health, and safety performance using a risk-based approach to develop site and transportation security programs, select carriers based on security criteria, pre-qualify customers for certain security-sensitive chemicals, conduct a security vulnerability assessment, and undergo independent, third-party verification of management system.

D.2.9 National Fire Protection Association.

D.2.9.1 NFPA 601, *Standard for Security Services in Fire Loss Prevention*, National Fire Protection Association, 1 Batterymarch Park, Quincy, MA 02169-7471, Phone: 617-770-3000, www.nfpa.org

The requirements of this standard are intended to aid management in defining the requirements, duties, and training for individuals to perform security services to protect a property against fire loss.

D.2.9.2 NFPA 730, *Guide for Premises Security*, National Fire Protection Association, 1 Batterymarch Park, Quincy, MA 02169-7471, Phone: 617-770-3000, www.nfpa.org

This guide describes construction, protection, and occupancy features and practices, intended to reduce security vulnerabilities to life and of property.

D.2.9.3 NFPA 731, *Standard for the Installation of Electronic Premises Security Systems*, National Fire Protection Association, 1 Batterymarch Park, Quincy, MA 02169-7471, Phone: 617-770-3000, www.nfpa.org

This standard covers the application, location, installation, performance, testing, and maintenance of physical security systems and their components.

D.2.10 *Organic Peroxide Safety Division Society of the Plastics Industry*, 202-974-5217, www.OPPSD.org

This organization provides the following information relative to organic peroxides:

(1) Identification of the hazards of organic peroxides
(2) Disposal information
(3) Regulations
(4) Safety and health information
(5) Storage and handling information
(6) Transportation information

Annex E Properties and Uses of Ammonium Nitrate and Fire-Fighting Procedures

This annex is not a part of the requirements of this NFPA document but is included for informational purposes only.

E.1 Ammonium nitrate is a compound containing nitrogen, hydrogen, and oxygen (NH_4NO_3). It is commercially produced by reacting nitric acid with ammonia and evaporating the resultant solution of ammonium nitrate to make a concentrated ammonium nitrate melt, which is then spray granulated in a prilling tower or pelletized or flaked by some other means. References that discuss the production of ammonium nitrate include *Nitric Acid and Fertilizer Nitrates* and *The Fertilizer Manual*.

For interstate shipments, the U.S. Department of Transportation classifies *ammonium nitrate* with not more than 0.2 percent total combustible material, including any organic substance, calculated as carbon to the exclusion of any other added substance as an oxidizer Division 5.1. *Ammonium nitrate* with more than 0.2 percent combustible substances, including any organic substance calculated as carbon to the exclusion of any other added substance as a Division 1.1D material. *Ammonium nitrate based fertilizers* may be classified as an oxidizer Division 5.1, or in some cases as a Division 9 material (Miscellaneous Hazardous Material). See U.S. DOT Transportation Regulations 49 CFR 172.101.

The requirements for classification of ammonium nitrate as a Division 5.1 oxidizer by the Department of Transportation are described in the United Nations publication, *Recommendations on the Transport of Dangerous Goods, Model Regulations*, 14th revised edition, 2005. Such oxidizing materials can yield oxygen upon decomposition under fire conditions and will, therefore, under proper conditions of mixing, vigorously support combustion if involved in a fire with combustible materials.

Ammonium nitrate in higher concentrations is capable of undergoing detonation with about half the blast effect of explosives, if heated under confinement that permits high pressure buildup, or if subjected to strong shocks, such as those from an explosive. The sensitivity of ammonium nitrate to detonation increases at elevated temperatures. Additional information on the explosive nature of ammonium nitrate, including the degree of confinement along with the effect of certain inert diluents, such as chalk, limestone, dolomite, etc., can be found in U.S. Bureau of Mines Report of Investigations 4994, *Investigations on the Explosibility of Ammonium Nitrate*, August 1953.

Industrial use of ammonium nitrate extends to use as an ingredient in blasting agents. When a carbonaceous or organic substance such as fuel (or diesel) oil, nut hulls, or carbon black is added and mixed in with ammonium nitrate, the mixture could become a blasting agent. A blasting agent as defined by NFPA 495, *Explosive Materials Code*, is a material or mixture that meets the requirements of the DOT "Hazardous Material Regulations," as set forth in 49 CFR Parts 173.56, 173.57, and 173.58, Explosive 1.5D.

Test data on ammonium nitrate are included in the U.S. Bureau of Mines Report of Investigations 6746, *Sympathetic Detonation of Ammonium Nitrate and Ammonium Nitrate Fuel Oil*; Report of Investigations 6903, *Further Studies on Sympathetic Detonation;* and Report of Investigations 6773, *Explosion Hazards of Ammonium Nitrate Under Fire Exposure*. On the basis of these reports, a Table of Recommended Separation Distances of Ammonium Nitrate and Blasting Agents from Explosives or Blasting Agents has been developed *(See Table 9.4.2.2(b) of NFPA 495)*. However, the table is only valid for ammonium nitrate and ammonium-nitrate-based materials that are NOT DOT Hazard Class 1 sensitive. The table is only applicable to materials that show positive results in the UN Test Series 1 sensitivity and thermal stability tests and negative results in the UN Test Series 2 Gap Tests. Products that show positive results when tested in the UN Test Series 1 and 2 tests could potentially be classified as having a mass explosion hazard. NFPA 495 requires that Hazard Class 1 materials be stored in accordance with the requirements for high explosives (Division 1.1) under the quantity-distance requirements of the American Table of Distances (ATD) developed by the Institute of Makers of Explosives (IME) and published in NFPA 495.

The maximum quantities of material indicated by the ATD are limited to quantities less than what may be found on sites where large amounts of ammonium nitrate or ammonium nitrate mixtures may be found. The Department of Defense Explosives Safety Board (DODESB) currently uses software called SAFER along with table of distance methods to assess DOD potential explosives sites. The IME, in collaboration with the DODESB, APT Research, Canadian and U.S. regulatory agencies has developed a software called IMESAFR. The software incorporates risk based methodology to address the impact of siting for explosives and explosive operations. Provisions for ammonium nitrate are included using an approach and distances based on TNT equivalency.

While blasting agents should not be confused with fertilizer products, extreme care should be taken to ensure that stored ammonium nitrate does not become sensitized by intimate mixing with carbonaceous, organic, or combustible material.

It is a common agricultural practice to blend or mix ammonium nitrate with other fertilizer materials such as diammonium phosphate, sulfate, and potash materials. Such mixed fertilizers containing less than 60 percent ammonium nitrate are not covered by this code. Fertilizer materials that contain ammonium nitrate are commonly described, not by their chemical composition, but by their plant nutrient value (N-P-K-S) values. For example, agricultural grade ammonium nitrate will appear in the market place with a guaranteed nitrogen content of 34-0-0. This means there is a guaranteed analysis of 34 percent total nitrogen, with 0 percent phosphate and 0 percent potassium guaranteed. The theoretical maximum nitrogen content of pure or 100 percent ammonium nitrate is 35 percent by weight. The typical nitrogen content of ammonium nitrate fertilizer offered in the market place is usually between 28 and 34 percent. Other nutrients such as sulfates or phosphates, added hardening agents, coating agents, and residual water make up the balance.

If the total available nitrogen in an ammonium nitrate–based fertilizer comes from ammonium nitrate, the percentage of ammonium nitrate can be determined through the use of the following formula:

% ammonium nitrate = (% total nitrogen listed in the fertilizer/ 0.35) [Eq. 1]

For example a fertilizer is indicated as being 30-0-0, then:

(30/0.35) = 85.7% ammonium nitrate

However, when some, but not all of the nitrogen could come from other nitrogen compounds in the mixture, the percentage of nitrogen for each component containing nitrogen in the fertilizer mixture must first be determined.

For example, a fertilizer product described as 28-0-0-5(S) has a guaranteed analysis of 28 percent total nitrogen, 0 percent phosphate, 0 percent potassium and 5 percent sulfur. Whether the nitrogen is derived from ammonium nitrate or another nitrogen fertilizer source must be disclosed by the manufacturer in order to determine the hazard classification of the material. This type of information is usually found on the MSDS provided by the manufacturer where the names of the material included in the mixture along with the concentration of each material is expressed. It is not unusual for a range of concentrations to be given on an MSDS, and users are cautioned to assume the ammonium nitrate concentration to be at the top of the range.

By use of Equation 1, it can be seen that ammonium nitrate fertilizers with a nitrogen content of less than 21 percent by weight derived from ammonium nitrate (60 percent ammonium nitrate) are not regulated by Chapter 11.

(21/0.35) = 60% ammonium nitrate

With proper precautions against fire and explosion, ammonium nitrate can be stored safely at a plant, in distributors' warehouses, or on a farm.

E.2 Suggested Fire-Fighting Procedure

E.2.1 Should a fire break out in an area where ammonium nitrate is stored, or in a vehicle transporting ammonium nitrate, it is important that the mass be kept cool and the burning be promptly extinguished. Large volumes of water should be applied as quickly as possible.

If fires reach massive and uncontrollable proportions, firefighting personnel should evacuate the area and withdraw to a safe location. Where possible, fire fighters should withdraw and allow structure or vehicle to burn if it can be done safely.

E.2.2 As much ventilation as possible should be provided to the fire area. Rapid dissipation of both the products of decomposition and the heat of reaction is very important.

E.2.3 The fire from should be approached from upwind, as the vapors from burning ammonium nitrate are very toxic. Self-contained breathing apparatus of types approved by OSHA should be used to protect personnel against gases.

E.2.4 After extinguishment of the fire, the loose and contaminated unsalvageable ammonium nitrate should be disposed of according to federal, state, and local environmental agencies' acceptable practices or regulations. Any residue that cannot be removed by sweeping should be washed away with hose (contaminated water from flushing must be disposed of as discussed above). Flushing and scrubbing of all areas should be very thorough to ensure the dissolving of all residue. Wet empty bags should be removed, and disposed of as discussed previously.

Annex F Typical Organic Peroxide Formulations

This annex is not a part of the requirements of this NFPA document but is included for informational purposes only.

F.1 General. The assignment of the organic peroxide formulation classifications shown in the tables in this annex are based on the container sizes shown. A change in the container size could affect the classification.

For an alphabetical listing of typical organic peroxide formulations, see Table F.1.

Table F.1 Typical Organic Peroxide Formulations

Organic Peroxide	Concentration	Diluent	Control °F	Control °C	Emergency °F	Emergency °C	Health	Flammability	Reactivity	Class	Container
t-Amyl hydroperoxide	88	Water					3	3	2	III	55 gal (208 L)
t-Amyl peroxyacetate	60	OMS					2	3	2	III	5 gal (19 L)
t-Amyl peroxybenzoate	96	—					2	3	2	II	5 gal (19 L)
t-Amyl peroxy-2-ethylhexanoate	96	—	68	20	77	25	0	3	2	III	55 gal (208 L)
t-Amyl peroxyneodecanoate	75	OMS	32	0	50	10	1	3	2	III	5 gal (19 L)
t-Amyl peroxypivalate	75	OMS	50	10	59	15	1	3	2	III	5 gal (19 L)
t-Butyl cumyl peroxide	95	—					2	2	2	IV	55 gal (208 L)
n-Butyl-4,4-di(t-butyl peroxy) valerate	98	—					2	3	2	II	5 gal (19 L)
t-Butyl hydroperoxide	90	Water and t-BuOH					3	3	3	I	5 gal (19 L)
t-Butyl hydroperoxide[3]	70	DTBP and t-BuOH					3	3	3	II	55 gal (208 L)
t-Butyl hydroperoxide[3]	70	Water					3	2	2	IV	55 gal (208 L)
t-Butyl monoperoxymaleate	98	—					2	3	3	I	50 @ 1 lb (50 @ 0.5 kg)
t-Butyl peroxyacetate	75	OMS					1	3	3	I	5 gal (19 L)
t-Butyl peroxyacetate	60	OMS					1	3	3	I	5 gal (19 L)
t-Butyl peroxybenzoate	98	—					1	3	3	II	5 gal (19 L)
t-Butyl peroxy-2-ethylhexanoate	97	—	68	20	77	25	1	3	3	III	5 gal (19 L)
t-Butyl peroxy-2-ethylhexanoate	97	—	68	20	77	25	1	3	3	II	55 gal (208 L)
t-Butyl peroxy-2-ethylhexanoate	50	DOP or OMS	86	30	95	35	1	2	2	IV	5 gal (19 L)
t-Butyl peroxy-2-ethylhexanoate	50	DOP or OMS	86	30	95	35	1	2	2	III	55 gal (208 L)
t-Butylperoxy 2-ethylhexyl carbonate	95	—					1	3	2	III	5 gal (19 L)
t-Butyl peroxyisobutyrate	75	OMS	59	15	68	20	2	3	3	II	5 gal (19 L)
t-Butylperoxy isopropyl carbonate	92	OMS					1	3	3	I	5 gal (19 L)
t-Butylperoxy isopropyl carbonate	75	OMS					1	3	3	II	5 gal (19 L)
t-Butyl peroxyneodecanoate	75	OMS	32	0	50	10	2	3	2	III	5 gal (19 L)
t-Butyl peroxypivalate	75	OMS	32	0	50	10	2	3	3	II	5 gal (19 L)
t-Butyl peroxypivalate	45	OMS	32	0	50	10	2	2	2	IV	5 gal (19 L)
Cumyl hydroperoxide	88	Cumene					3	2	2	III	55 gal (208 L)
Cumyl peroxyneodecanoate	75	OMS	14	−10	32	0	1	3	2	III	5 gal (19 L)
Cumyl peroxyneoheptanoate	75	OMS	32	0	50	10	2	3	2	III	5 gal (19 L)
Diacetyl peroxide	25	DMP	68	20	77	25	2	3	3	II	5 gal (19 L)
1,1-Di(t-amylperoxy) cyclohexane	80	OMS or BBP					2	3	2	III	5 gal (19 L)
Dibenzoyl peroxide	98	—					1	3	4	I	1 lb (0.5 kg)
Dibenzoyl peroxide	78	Water					1	2	3	II	25 lb (11 kg)
Dibenzoyl peroxide	75	Water					1	2	2	III	25 lb (11 kg)
Dibenzoyl peroxide	70	Water					1	2	2	IV	25 lb (11 kg)
Dibenzoyl peroxide (paste)	55	Plasticizer	T[4]				1	2	2	III	350 lb (160 kg)
Dibenzoyl peroxide (paste)	55	Plasticizer and water	T				1	2	2	IV	350 lb (160 kg)
Dibenzoyl peroxide (paste)	50	Plasticizer	T				1	2	2	III	380 lb (170 kg)
Dibenzoyl peroxide (paste)	50	Plasticizer and water	T				1	2	2	IV	380 lb (170 kg)
Dibenzoyl peroxide (slurry)	40	Water and plasticizer	T				1	2	2	IV	380 lb (170 kg)
Dibenzoyl peroxide (slurry)	40	Water					1	2	2	IV	5 gal (19 L)

Table F.1 *Continued*

Organic Peroxide	Concentration	Diluent	Control °F	Control °C	Emergency °F	Emergency °C	Health	Flammability	Reactivity	Class	Container
Dibenzoyl peroxide (powder)	35	Dicalcium phosphate dihydrate or calcium sulfate dihydrate					1	0	0	V	100 lb (45 kg)
Dibenzoyl peroxide (powder)	35	Starch					1	2	2	IV	100 lb (45 kg)
Di(4-*t*-butylcyclohexyl) peroxydicarbonate	98	—	86	30	95	35	1	3	2	III	88 lb (40 kg)
Di-*t*-butyl peroxide[3]	99	—					1	3	2	III	55 gal (208 L)
2,2-Di(*t*-butylperoxy) butane	50	Toluene					1	3	3	I	1 gal (4 L)
1,1-Di(*t*-butylperoxy) cyclohexane	80	OMS or BBP					1	3	3	II	5 gal (19 L)
Di-*sec*-butyl peroxydicarbonate	98	—	−4	−20	14	−10	1	3	3	II	1 gal (4 L)
Di-*sec*-butyl peroxydicarbonate	75	OMS	−4	−20	14	−10	1	3	3	II	5 gal (19 L)
Di(2-*t*-butylperoxy-isopropyl) benzene	96	—					1	2	2	III	100 lb (45 kg)
Di(2-*t*-butylperoxyisopropyl) benzene	40	Clay					1	1	0	V	100 lb (45 kg)
Di(butylperoxy) phthalate	40	DBP					2	2	2	IV	30 gal (110 L)
1,1-Di(*t*-butylperoxy)-3,3,5-trimethyl-cyclohexane	75–95	—					2	3	3	II	5 gal (19 L)
1,1-Di(*t*-butylperoxy)-3,3,5-trimethyl-cyclohexane	40	Calcium carbonate					1	1	1	V	100 lb (45 kg)
Dicetyl peroxydicarbonate	85	—	86	30	95	35	1	2	2	IV	44 lb (20 kg)
Dicumyl peroxide	98	—					2	2	2	IV	55 gal (208 L)
Dicumyl peroxide	40	Clay or calcium carbonate					1	1	1	V	100 lb (45 kg)
Didecanoyl peroxide	98	—	86	30	95	35	1	3	2	III	50 lb (23 kg)
Di-2,4-dichlorobenzoyl peroxide	50	DBP and silicone		T			1	2	2	III	5 gal (19 L)
Di(2-ethylhexyl) peroxydicarbonate	97	—	−4	−20	14	−10	1	3	3	II	1 gal (4 L)
Di(2-ethylhexyl) peroxydicarbonate	40	OMS	5	−15	23	−5	1	2	2	IV	5 gal (19 L)
Diisopropyl peroxydicarbonate	99	—	5	−15	23	−5	2	3	4	I	10 lb (4.5 kg)
Diisopropyl peroxydicarbonate	30	Toluene	14	−10	32	0	2	3	2	III	5 gal (2.3 kg)
Di-*n*-propyl peroxydicarbonate	98	—	−13	−25	5	−15	2	3	4	I	1 gal (4 L)
Di-*n*-propyl peroxydicarbonate	85	OMS	−13	−25	5	−15	2	3	4	I	1 gal (4 L)
Dilauroyl peroxide	98	—					1	2	2	IV	110 lb (50 kg)
2,5-Dimethyl-2,5-di(benzoylperoxy)hexane	95	—					2	3	3	II	4 @ 5 lb (4 @ 2.3 kg)
2,5-Dimethyl-2,5-di(*t*-butylperoxy)hexane	92	—					2	3	2	III	30 gal (110 L)
2,5-Dimethyl-2,5-di(*t*-butylperoxy)hexane	47	Calcium carbonate or silica					1	1	1	V	100 lb (45 kg)
2,5-Dimethyl-2,5-di(2-ethylhexanoylperoxy)hexane	90	—	68	20	77	25	0	3	2	III	5 gal (19 L)
2,5-Dimethyl-2,5-dihydro-peroxyhexane	70	Water					2	3	3	II	100 lb (45 kg)
Ethyl-3,3-di(*t*-amylperoxy) butyrate	75	OMS					1	3	2	III	5 gal (19 L)
Ethyl-3,3-di(*t*-butylperoxy) butyrate	75	OMS					2	2	2	III	5 gal (19 L)
Ethyl-3,3-di(*t*-butylperoxy) butyrate	40	Clay or calcium silicate					1	3	2	V	100 lb (45 kg)

(continues)

Table F.1 *Continued*

Organic Peroxide	Concentration	Diluent	Control °F	Control °C	Emergency °F	Emergency °C	Health	Flammability	Reactivity	Class	Container
p-Menthyl hydroperoxide	54	Alcohols and ketones					3	2	2	IV	55 gal (208 L)
Methyl ethyl ketone peroxide	9.0% AO	DMP					3	2	2	III	5 gal (19 L)
Methyl ethyl ketone peroxide	5.5% AO	DMP					3	2	2	IV	5 gal (19 L)
Methyl ethyl ketone peroxide	9.0% AO	Water and glycols					3	2	2	IV	5 gal (19 L)
Methyl ethyl ketone peroxide and Cyclohexanone peroxide mixture	9.0% AO	DMP					3	2	2	III	5 gal (19 L)
2,4-Pentanedione peroxide	4.0% AO	Water and solvent					2	1	1	IV	5 gal (19 L)
Peroxyacetic acid, Type E, stabilized	43	Water, HOAc, and H$_2$O$_2$					3	2	3	II	30 gal (110 L)

Recommended Maximum Temperatures[1]; Hazard Identification[2]

[1]These columns refer to temperatures in the Department of Transportation (DOT) Organic Peroxides Table. Refer to document 49 CFR 173.225 for details.
[2]The column refers to NFPA 704, *Standard System for the Identification of the Hazards of Materials for Emergency Response*, hazard ratings for health, flammability, and reactivity. See NFPA 704 for details.
[3]See NFPA 30, *Flammable and Combustible Liquids Code*, for additional storage requirements.
[4]T — Temperature control should be considered to reduce fire hazard depending on packaging size and recommendations in manufacturers' literature.
Note: Diluents: AO — Active oxygen; BBP — Butyl benzyl phthalate; DBP — Dibutyl phthalate; DMP — Dimethyl phthalate; DOP — Dioctyl phthalate; DTBP — Di-tertiary-butyl peroxide; HOAc — Acetic acid; H$_2$O$_2$ — Hydrogen peroxide; OMS — Odorless mineral spirits; *t*-BuOH — Tertiary butanol.

F.2 Class I Formulations.

F.2.1 Fire Hazard Characteristics. Class I formulations present a deflagration hazard through easily initiated, rapid explosive decomposition. Class I includes some formulations that are relatively safe only under closely controlled temperatures. Either excessively high or low temperatures can increase the potential for severe explosive decomposition.

F.2.2 Fire-Fighting Information. The immediate area should be evacuated and the fire should be fought from a remote location. Some damage to structures from overpressure can be expected should a deflagration occur.

F.2.3 Typical Class I Formulations. See Table F.2.3.

F.3 Class II Formulations.

F.3.1 Fire-Hazard Characteristics. Class II formulations present a severe fire hazard similar to Class I flammable liquids. The decomposition is not as rapid, violent, or complete as that produced by Class I formulations. As with Class I formulations, this class includes some formulations that are relatively safe when under controlled temperatures or when diluted.

F.3.2 Fire-Fighting Information. Fires should be fought from a safe distance because a hazard exists from rupturing containers.

F.3.3 Typical Class II Formulations. See Table F.3.3.

F.4 Class III Formulations.

F.4.1 Fire Hazard Characteristics. Class III formulations present a fire hazard similar to Class II combustible liquids. They are characterized by rapid burning and high heat liberation due to decomposition.

F.4.2 Fire-Fighting Information. Caution should be observed due to possible unexpected increases in fire intensity.

F.4.3 Typical Class III Formulations. See Table F.4.3.

F.5 Class IV Formulations.

F.5.1 Fire Hazard Characteristics. Class IV formulations present fire hazards that are easily controlled. Reactivity has little effect on fire intensity.

F.5.2 Fire-Fighting Information. Normal fire-fighting procedures can be used.

F.5.3 Typical Class IV Formulations. See Table F.5.3.

F.6 Class V Formulations.

F.6.1 Fire Hazard Characteristics. Class V formulations do not present severe fire hazards. Those that do burn do so with less intensity than ordinary combustibles.

F.6.2 Fire-Fighting Information. Fire-fighting procedures need primarily consider the combustibility of containers.

F.6.3 Typical Class V Formulations. See Table F.6.3.

Table F.2.3 Typical Class I Formulations

Organic Peroxide	Concentration	Diluent	Control °F	Control °C	Emergency °F	Emergency °C	Health	Flammability	Reactivity	Container
t-Butyl hydroperoxide	90	Water & t-BuOH					3	3	3	5 gal (19 L)
t-Butyl monoperoxymaleate	98	—					2	3	3	50 @ 1 lb (50 @ 0.5 kg)
t-Butyl peroxyacetate	75	OMS					1	3	3	5 gal (19 L)
t-Butyl peroxyacetate	60	OMS					1	3	3	5 gal (19 L)
t-Butylperoxy isopropyl carbonate	92	OMS					1	3	3	5 gal (19 L)
Dibenzoyl peroxide	98	—					1	3	4	1 lb (0.5 kg)
2,2-Di(t-butylperoxy) butane	50	Toluene					1	3	3	1 gal (4 L)
Diisopropyl peroxydicarbonate	99	—	5	−15	23	−5	2	3	4	10 lb (4.5 kg)
Di-n-propyl peroxydicarbonate	98	—	−13	−25	5	−15	2	3	4	1 gal (4 L)
Di-n-propyl peroxydicarbonate	85	OMS	−13	−25	5	−15	2	3	4	1 gal (4 L)

Recommended Maximum Temperatures[1]; Hazard Identification[2]

[1]These columns refer to temperatures in the Department of Transportation (DOT) Organic Peroxides Table. Refer to document 49 CFR 173.225 for details.
[2]The column refers to NFPA 704, *Standard System for the Identification of the Hazards of Materials for Emergency Response*, hazard ratings for health, flammability, and reactivity. See NFPA 704 for details.
Note: Diluents: OMS — Odorless mineral spirits; t-BuOH —Tertiary butanol.

Table F.3.3 Typical Class II Formulations

Organic Peroxide	Concentration	Diluent	Control °F	Control °C	Emergency °F	Emergency °C	Health	Flammability	Reactivity	Container
t-Amyl peroxybenzoate	96	—					2	3	2	5 gal (19 L)
n-Butyl-4,4-di(t-butylperoxy) valerate	98	—					2	3	2	5 gal (19 L)
t-Butyl hydroperoxide[3]	70	DTBP and t-BuOH					3	3	3	55 gal (208 L)
t-Butyl peroxybenzoate	98	—					1	3	3	5 gal (19 L)
t-Butyl peroxy-2-ethyl-hexanoate	97	—	68	20	77	25	1	3	3	55 gal (208 L)
t-Butyl peroxyisobutyrate	75	OMS	59	15	68	20	2	3	3	5 gal (19 L)
t-Butylperoxy isopropyl carbonate	75	OMS					1	3	3	5 gal (19 L)
t-Butyl peroxypivalate	75	OMS	32	0	50	10	2	3	3	5 gal (19 L)
Diacetyl peroxide	25	DMP	68	20	77	25	2	3	3	5 gal (19 L)
Dibenzoyl peroxide	78	Water					1	2	3	25 lb (11 kg)
1,1-Di(t-butylperoxy) cyclohexane	80	OMS or BBP					1	3	3	5 gal (19 L)
Di-sec-butyl peroxydicarbonate	98	—	−4	−20	14	−10	1	3	3	1 gal (4 L)
Di-sec-butyl peroxydicarbonate	75	OMS	−4	−20	14	−10	1	3	3	5 gal (19 L)
1,1-Di(t-butylperoxy)-3,3,5-trimethyl-cyclohexane	75–95	—					2	3	3	5 gal (19 L)
Di(2-ethylhexyl) peroxydicarbonate	97	—	−4	−20	14	−10	1	3	3	1 gal (4 L)
2,5-Dimethyl-2,5-di(benzoylperoxy) hexane	95	—					2	3	3	4 @ 5 lb (4 @ 2.3 kg)
2,5-Dimethyl-2,5-dihydroperoxy hexane	70	Water					2	3	3	100 lb (45 kg)

Recommended Maximum Temperatures[1]; Hazard Identification[2]

[1]These columns refer to temperatures in the Department of Transportation (DOT) Organic Peroxides Table. Refer to document 49 CFR 173.225 for details.
[2]The column refers to NFPA 704, *Standard System for the Identification of the Hazards of Materials for Emergency Response*, hazard ratings for health, flammability, and reactivity. See NFPA 704 for details.
Note: Diluents: BBP — Butyl benzyl phthalate; DMP — Dimethyl phthalate; DTBP — Di-tertiary-butyl peroxide; OMS — Odorless mineral spirits; t-BuOH —Tertiary butanol.

Table F.4.3 Typical Class III Formulations

Organic Peroxide	Concentration	Diluent	Control °F	Control °C	Emergency °F	Emergency °C	Health	Flammability	Reactivity	Container
t-Amyl hydroperoxide	88	Water					3	3	2	55 gal (208 L)
t-Amyl peroxyacetate	60	OMS					2	3	2	5 gal (19 L)
t-Amyl peroxy-2-ethylhexanoate	96	—	68	20	77	25	0	3	2	55 gal (208 L)
t-Amyl peroxyneodecanoate	75	OMS	32	0	50	10	1	3	2	5 gal (19 L)
t-Amyl peroxypivalate	75	OMS	50	10	59	15	1	3	2	5 gal (19 L)
t-Butyl peroxy-2-ethylhexanoate	97	—	68	20	77	25	1	3	3	5 gal (19 L)
t-Butyl peroxy-2-ethylhexanoate	50	DOP or OMS	86	30	95	35	1	2	2	55 gal (208 L)
t-Butyl peroxy-2-ethylhexyl carbonate	95	—					1	3	2	5 gal (19 L)
t-Butyl peroxyneodecanoate	75	OMS	32	0	50	10	2	3	2	5 gal (19 L)
Cumyl hydroperoxide	88	Cumene					3	2	2	55 gal (208 L)
Cumyl peroxyneodecanoate	75	OMS	14	−10	32	0	1	3	2	5 gal (19 L)
Cumyl peroxyneoheptanoate	75	OMS	32	0	50	10	2	3	2	5 gal (19 L)
1,1-Di(t-amylperoxy) cyclohexane	80	OMS or BBP					2	3	2	5 gal (19 L)
Dibenzoyl peroxide	75	Water					1	2	2	25 lb (11 kg)
Dibenzoyl peroxide (paste)	55	Plasticizer	T[4]				1	2	2	350 lb (160 kg)
Dibenzoyl peroxide (paste)	50	Plasticizer	T				1	2	2	380 lb (170 kg)
Di(4-t-butylcyclohexyl) peroxydicarbonate	98	—	86	30	95	35	1	3	2	88 lb (40 kg)
Di-t-butyl peroxide[3]	99	—					1	3	2	55 gal (208 L)
Di(2-t-butylperoxy-isopropyl) benzene	96	—					1	2	2	100 lb (45 kg)
Didecanoyl peroxide	98	—	86	30	95	35	1	3	2	50 lb (23 kg)
Di-2,4-dichlorobenzoyl peroxide	50	DBP and silicone	T				1	2	2	5 gal (19 L)
Diisopropyl peroxydicarbonate	30	Toluene	14	−10	32	0	2	3	2	5 lb (2.3 kg)
2,5-Dimethyl-2,5-di (t-butylperoxy) hexane	92	—					2	3	2	30 gal (110 L)
2,5-Dimethyl-2,5-di-(2-ethyl hexanoylperoxy) hexane	90	—		20		25	0	3	2	5 gal (19 L)
Ethyl-3,3-di (t-amylperoxy) butyrate	75	OMS					1	3	2	5 gal (19 L)
Ethyl-3,3-di (t-butylperoxy) butyrate	75	OMS					2	2	2	5 gal (19 L)
Methyl ethyl ketone peroxide	9.0% AO	DMP					3	2	2	5 gal (19 L)
Methyl ethyl ketone peroxide and Cyclohexanone peroxide mixture	9.0% AO	DMP					3	2	2	5 gal (19 L)

[1]These columns refer to temperatures in the Department of Transportation (DOT) Organic Peroxides Table. Refer to document 49 CFR 173.225 for details.
[2]The column refers to NFPA 704, *Standard System for the Identification of the Hazards of Materials for Emergency Response*, hazard ratings for health, flammability, and reactivity. See NFPA 704 for details.
[3]Also a flammable liquid; see NFPA 30, *Flammable and Combustible Liquids Code*, for storage requirements.
[4]T — Temperature control should be considered to reduce fire hazard depending on packaging size and recommendations in manufacturers' literature.
Note: Diluents: AO — Active oxygen; BBP — Butyl benzyl phthalate; DBP — Dibutyl phthalate; DMP — Dimethyl phthalate; DOP — Dioctyl phthalate; OMS — Odorless mineral spirits.

Table F.5.3 Typical Class IV Formulations

Organic Peroxide	Concentration	Diluent	Control °F	Control °C	Emergency °F	Emergency °C	Health	Flammability	Reactivity	Container
t-Butyl cumyl peroxide	95	—					2	2	2	55 gal (208 L)
t-Butyl hydroperoxide	70	Water					3	2	2	55 gal (208 L)
t-Butyl peroxy-2-ethylhexanoate	50	DOP or OMS	86	30	95	35	1	2	2	5 gal (19 L)
t-Butyl peroxypivalate	45	OMS	32	0	50	10	2	2	2	5 gal (19 L)
Dibenzoyl peroxide	70	Water					1	2	2	25 lb (11 kg)
Dibenzoyl peroxide (paste)	55	Plasticizer and water		T			1	2	2	350 lb (160 kg)
Dibenzoyl peroxide (paste)	50	Plasticizer and water		T			1	2	2	380 lb (170 kg)
Dibenzoyl peroxide (slurry)	40	Water and plasticizer		T			1	2	2	380 lb (170 kg)
Dibenzoyl peroxide (slurry)	40	Water					1	2	2	5 gal (19 L)
Dibenzoyl peroxide (powder)	35	Starch					1	2	2	100 lb (45 kg)
Di(t-butylperoxy) phthalate	40	DBP					2	2	2	30 gal (110 L)
Dicetyl peroxydicarbonate	85	—	86	30	95	35	1	2	2	44 lb (20 kg)
Dicumyl peroxide	98	—					2	2	2	55 gal (208 L)
Di(2-ethylhexyl) peroxydicarbonate	40	OMS	5	−15	23	−5	1	2	2	5 gal (19 L)
Dilauroyl peroxide	98						1	2	2	110 lb (50 kg)
p-Menthyl hydroperoxide	54	Alcohols and ketones		T			3	2	2	55 gal (208 L)
Methyl ethyl ketone peroxide	55% AO	DMP					3	2	2	5 gal (19 L)
Methyl ethyl ketone peroxide	9.0% AO	Water and glycols					3	2	2	5 gal (19 L)
2,4-Pentanedione peroxide	4.0% AO	Water and solvent					2	1	1	5 gal (19 L)

[1]These columns refer to temperatures in the Department of Transportation (DOT) Organic Peroxides Table. Refer to document 49 CFR 173.225 for details.
[2]The column refers to NFPA 704, *Standard System for the Identification of the Hazards of Materials for Emergency Response*, hazard ratings for health, flammability, and reactivity. See NFPA 704 for details.
T — Temperature control should be considered to reduce fire hazard depending on packaging size and recommendations in manufacturers' literature.
Note: Diluents: DBP— Dibutyl phthalate; DMP— Dimethyl phthalate; DOP— Dioctyl phthalate; OMS — Odorless mineral spirits; AO — Active oxygen.

Table F.6.3 Typical Class V Formulations

Organic Peroxide	Concentration	Diluent	Control °F	Control °C	Emergency °F	Emergency °C	Health	Flammability	Reactivity	Container
Dibenzoyl peroxide (powder)	35	Dicalcium phosphate dehydrate or calcium sulfate dihydrate					1	0	0	100 lb (45 kg)
Di(2-t-butylperoxyisopropyl) benzene	40	clay					1	1	0	100 lb (45 kg)
1,1-Di(t-butylperoxy)-3,3,5-trimethylcyclohexane	40	Calcium carbonate					1	1	1	100 lb (45 kg)
Dicumyl peroxide	40	Clay or calcium carbonate					1	1	1	100 lb (45 kg)
2,5-Dimethyl-2,5-di(t-butylperoxy) hexane	47	Calcium carbonate or silica					1	1	1	100 lb (45 kg)
Ethyl-3,3-di(t-butylperoxy)butyrate	40	Clay or calcium silicate					1	3	2	100 lb (45 kg)

[1]These columns refer to temperatures in the Department of Transportation (DOT) Organic Peroxides Table. Refer to document 49 CFR 173.225 for details.
[2]The column refers to NFPA 704, *Standard System for the Identification of the Hazards of Materials for Emergency Response*, hazard ratings for health, flammability, and reactivity. See NFPA 704 for details.
AO — Active oxygen.

Annex G Oxidizers

This annex is not a part of the requirements of this NFPA document but is included for informational purposes only.

G.1 General.

G.1.1 Solid Oxidizers. Oxidizers can have both physical and health hazards. The tests and criteria are based on burning rate only and do not address other physical hazards of oxidizers, such as thermal instability and chemical reactivity, or health hazards of gaseous products generated during combustion or decomposition. If confined, gaseous products generated from oxidizer decomposition can result in overpressure events and explosions. Cumulative research test data indicate the burning rate of solid oxidizers is principally a function of the oxidizer and its concentration, and to a lesser degree, its physical form (e.g., powder, granular or tablets). Inclusive in the influence of the oxidizer and its concentration are the amount and type of additives (if any) as well as the degree of moisture content of the oxidizer or hydrated salt additives. The tests and criteria apply to oxidizers or formulations containing oxidizers that are found in high volume commerce, use, and storage and do not apply to the evaluation of ammonia nitrate, oxidizer-containing explosive mixtures, pyrotechnic mixtures, and oxidizers stored in noncombustible vessels or in noncombustible packaging. Because some oxidizers are packaged in noncombustible packaging the tests and criteria involve combustible test packaging consisting of HDPE plastic screw-top containers or bottles inside a corrugated board carton, which may not be representative of oxidizers in their normal packaging. Lastly, the tests and criteria assign an oxidizer to a NFPA Class for storage and are not applicable to and should not be confused with Department of Transportation (DOT) and United Nations (UN) Packing Group (III, II, I) assignments and vice versa. The UN and DOT Division 5.1 solid oxidizer packing groups are different from, and not synonymous with, the NFPA Class (1, 2, 3, 4) assignments for storage, handling and use.

The oxidizer classification method consists of two reaction-to-fire tests: (1) a bench-scale screening test with 30 g mixtures of oxidizer and dried cellulose powder exposed to a glowing wire and (2) an intermediate-scale test with 24 lb of oxidizer in combustible test packaging exposed to a constant external fire source. The key physical indicators of burning rate from the intermediate-scale testing of typical commercial oxidizers and formulated products in test packaging exposed to an external flaming ignition source are peak convective heat release rate and the burning time calculated from the radiant heat flux profile. The key physical indicators of burning rate from the screening test of oxidizer-cellulose powder mixtures are mass loss rate and burning time calculated from the mass data. Temperature and flame height data from the bench-scale screening test are secondary indicators used to distinguish between weak oxidizers, strong oxidizers, and oxidizers that principally decompose. These values show a range consistent with the range in observed burning behavior. From a fire protection standpoint, oxidizers that principally decompose are not considered a high hazard.

G.1.2 Tests and Criteria. Oxidizers and formulated products containing an oxidizer shall be assigned to Class 1, Class 2, Class 3, or Class 4 according to the tests and criteria specified in Table G.1.2(a) and Table G.1.2(b).

Table G.1.2(a) NFPA Oxidizer Class Tests and Criteria (Metric Units)

Class	Maximum Mass Loss Rate * (g/s)	Active Burning Time ** (s)	Peak Convective Heat Release Rate (kW)	Active Burning Time Based on Radiant Heat Flux Profile*** (s)
	Bench-Scale Screening Test [0.06 lb (30 g) mixtures with cellulose powder]		Intermediate-Scale Fire Exposure Test [24-lb (10.8 kg) in test packaging]	
Class 1	≤0.3	≥30	≤100	≥120
Class 2	0.3<MLR<3	6< t_{active} <30	100–200	60< t_{active} <120
Class 3	≥3	≤6	≥200	≤60
Class 4	Generally meets the Class 3 criteria plus evidence to support explosive reaction due to contamination or exposure to thermal or physical shock including UN and/or GHS designations.			

MLR: Mass loss rate.
t_{active}: active burning time calculated from test data.
* Maximum mass loss rate from 20 to 80% the final measured mass (mf) of 1:1, 4:1, and 9:1 oxidizer:cellulose (by weight) mixtures.
** Calculated from the mass loss profiles.
***Calculated from the width of the curve at ½ the peak radiant heat flux.

Table G.1.2(b) NFPA Oxidizer Class Tests and Criteria (U.S. Units)

Class	Maximum Mass Loss Rate * [g/s]	Active Burning Time ** [s]	Peak Convective Heat Release Rate [kW]	Active Burning Time Based on Radiant Heat Flux Profile*** [s]
	Bench-Scale Screening Test [0.06 lb (30 g) mixtures with cellulose powder]		Intermediate-Scale Fire Exposure Test [24 lb (10.8 kg) in test packaging]	
Class 1	≤0.04	≥0.5	≤100	≥2
Class 2	0.04<MLR<0.4	0.1< t_{active} <0.5	100–200	1< t_{active} <2
Class 3	≥0.4	≤0.1	≥200	≤1
Class 4	Generally meets the Class 3 criteria plus evidence to support explosive reaction due to contamination or exposure to thermal or physical shock including UN and/or GHS designations.			

MLR: Mass loss rate.
t_{active}: active burning time calculated from test data.
*Maximum mass loss rate from 20 to 80% the final measured mass (mf) of 1:1, 4:1, and 9:1 oxidizer:cellulose (by weight) mixtures.
**Calculated from the mass loss profiles.
***Calculated from the width of the curve at ½ the peak radiant heat flux.

G.1.3 Definitions.

G.1.3.1 Active Burning Time. Duration of burning with flaming combustion, or decomposition with minor flaming combustion, calculated from test data. From bench-scale screening of oxidizer-cellulose powder mixture test data, the active burning time is calculated as the time from first measurable mass loss to the time at which 80 percent of the mixture is consumed and/or decomposed. From intermediate-scale of oxidizers in combustible test packaging radiant heat flux test data, the active burning time is the width of the curve at one-half the peak radiant heat flux.

G.1.3.2 Burning Behavior. The complete characterization of a material or mixture's reaction to fire including both visual descriptors and test data.

G.1.3.3 Burning Rate. The principal physical hazard of oxidizer fires described by the intensity or quantity of energy release, in the form of heat and light or accelerated fire, and time duration over which the energy is released.

G.1.3.4 Fire-test-response Characteristic. A response characteristic of a material, product, or assembly to a prescribed source of heat or flame, under controlled fire conditions; such response characteristics may include, but are not limited to, ease of ignition, flame spread, heat release, mass loss, smoke generation, fire resistance, and toxic potency of smoke [**ASTM E 176-10,** *Standard Terminology of Fire Standards*].

G.1.3.5 Formulated Product. A product that contains an oxidizer solid or liquid as one of its constituents, including admixtures. Some oxidizers are not sold in pure form (e.g., lithium hypochlorite, calcium hypochlorite). Formulations include chemical by-products and unreacted raw materials inevitably present in the product and intentionally added diluents and exotherm control agents, such as hydrated salt crystals coarsely blended with the manufactured oxidizer. The MSDS and stereoscopic examination are used to distinguish between a homogeneous material and an admixture of two or more granular solids.

G.1.3.6 Heat Release Rate (HRR). Measure of fire intensity based on quantity of heat evolved, produced, or released during combustion, usually expressed per unit time (J/s) or per unit quantity of material (J/g). [**ASTM E 176-10,** *Standard Terminology of Fire Standards*].

G.1.3.7 Mass Loss. The change in mass of a solid material to gaseous products during combustion or decomposition expressed per unit quantity of material (g/g, %).

G.1.3.8 Mass Burning Rate. Mass loss per unit time (g/s, kg/min) by materials burning under specified conditions [**ASTM E 176-10,** *Standard Terminology of Fire Standards*].

G.1.3.9 Screening Test. A fire-response test performed to determine whether a material, product, or assembly (a) exhibits any unusual fire-related characteristics, (b) has certain expected fire-related characteristics, or (c) is capable of being preliminary categorized according to the fire characteristic in question [**ASTM E 176**].

G.1.3.10 Test Packaging. Packaging for solid (granular, tablet, or powder) oxidizers during the intermediate-scale fire exposure test consisting of six, high-density polyethylene (HDPE) containers in a double-wall corrugated board carton.

G.1.3.11 Visual Burning Duration. Duration (s, min) of visible flaming combustion, as measured with a stopwatch.

G.1.4 Bench-Scale Screening Test. The solid oxidizer (granular, powder, crystalline) is evaluated in the particle size and distribution intended for storage, handling, and use. For tablets, the pre-tablet or raw material is tested. Thirty gram (30 g) mixtures (1:1, 4:1, and 9:1 by mass) of the oxidizer or formulated product and dry cellulose powder, with moisture content less than 0.5 percent w/w, are exposed to a glowing Nichrome wire energized to 150 W on a datalogging laboratory balance in a laboratory hood. The mass loss rate of each mixture is calculated from test data. The mixture with the highest or maximum mass loss rate is compared to the mass loss rate and burning rate duration criteria in Table G.1.2. The bench-scale screening test is a screening test capable of distinguishing weak oxidizers (Class 1), strong oxidizers (Class 3), and oxidizers that principally decompose.

G.1.4.1 Test Materials.

Cellulose Powder. Whatman cellulose powder is spread in a pan so the depth of powder is less than or equal to 0.25 in. and dried in a laboratory oven at 221°F (105°C) for 4 hours. After drying, the powder is transferred to a desiccator cabinet with desiccant. When cool, the moisture content is measured using an analytical moisture analyzer or by gravimetric analysis.

Oxidizer. The chemical composition and physical properties of the oxidizer or formulated product containing an oxidizer being evaluated are recorded. The physical form is characterized as granular, crystalline, powder, or tablet; the particle size and distribution are measured with calibrated sieves and recorded as mass percent of each particle size fraction. The test material is not ground or subject to any mechanical attrition or sieving to reduce the particle size.

Common Salt. A series of tests are performed with common salt-cellulose powder mixtures. Common salt does not contribute to burning rate of cellulose powder. Fine, coarse, pellet, and solid common salt is commercially available at feed stores.

G.1.4.2 Instrumentation and Test Set-Up.

Laboratory Balance. A laboratory balance is positioned and leveled inside a clean laboratory hood. A metal frame, constructed of welded steel and having two pins at the diagonal of the weigh pan, is used to center scale protection materials. The metal frame does not contact the laboratory balance. The laboratory balance programmable response-time settings are optimized to establish the data output interval. Data collection at 0.5 or 1 second intervals are typical. Data-logging parameters are similarly set at the computer interface and software to collect and record time-stamped mass data. Any autocalibration functions of the balance are disabled during tests.

Protection Materials. The laboratory balance weighing pan is protected with three layers of high-temperature ceramic fiberboard. For example, a balance weighing surface with dimensions 6 in. × 6 in. would be protected with a bottom or base layer of Kaowool HT board (12 in. × 12 in. × ½ in.). The base layer extends beyond the balance to capture material ejected from the test platform. Two openings in the base layer correspond to the location of the centering pins of the metal frame. The middle layer is Kaowool HT board (7 in. × 7 in. × ½ in.), and the top layer, or test platform, is Kaowool PM board (4½ in. × 4½ in. × ¼ in.). The base layer of protection remains on the balance after each trial. Due to heat retained from the glowing wire and/or test materials, the two top layers of ceramic board on the base layer are removed after each test. The middle layer of HT board can be reused after cooling to room temperature. A suitable barrier is constructed around the laboratory balance and protection materials to prevent air currents from the operating hood from influencing the balance stability. For example, a barrier may consist of two, ½-in. thick fiber boards — one on each side of the balance extending from the back of the hood to the front of the hood.

Thermocouples (Optional). Three, K-type air thermocouples (TC) are secured to a ring stand to one side of the protected lab balance. The tips of the thermocouples are centered above the test platform. The distance from the surface of the test platform recommended to capture the range in plume temperatures are 3 in. (7.6 cm), 6 in. (15.2 cm), and 9 in. (22.8 cm). A fourth K-type thermocouple monitors the ambient temperature. The TCs are attached to the data acquisition system programmed to record the plume temperatures over the same time interval as the lab balance (e.g., 0.5 and 1 second intervals). The fixed-height thermocouples are also used to estimate peak flame height during a test.

Ignition source. A Nichrome wire is formed as specified in the UN Test O.1 method. The length of the wire is 30±1 cm; the wire diameter is 0.6±0.05 mm. A variable laboratory power supply is used to regulate the voltage and current to the wire to achieve 150±7 W when energized. Conductors from the power supply output are secured to one or more ceramic terminal blocks. For example, the first terminal block, secured with a clamp at the rear of the lab balance, has conductors to a second ceramic terminal block near the test platform, and the looped Nichrome wire is inserted in the second terminal block to complete the circuit. The looped portion of the wire is centered over the test platform.

G.1.4.3 Test Methodology.

Test Mixtures. Three concentrations of oxidizer-cellulose powder mixtures evaluated are (1) 1:1 by mass mixtures containing 0.03 lb (15 g) oxidizer and 0.03 lb (15 g) dried cellulose powder; (2) 4:1 by mass mixtures containing 0.05 lb (24 g) oxidizer and 0.01 lb (6 g) dried cellulose powder; and (3) 9:1 by mass mixtures containing 0.06 lb (27 g) oxidizer and 0.006 lb (3 g) dried cellulose powder. Five trials of each concentration are tested.

Single Test Procedure. Each mixture of oxidizer and dried cellulose powder is prepared immediately prior to each trial in a test series. A second laboratory balance is used to weigh the required amounts of cellulose powder and oxidizer. The materials are transferred to and combined in a clean, labeled polyethylene container (500 mL) with a screw top lid. Mixing of the contents is done by inverting (not shaking) the container no less than 25 times. After mixing, the contents of the container are transferred into a clean funnel (70 mm dia, 102 mL volume) positioned stem-down in an Erlenmeyer flask. The stem opening at the base of the funnel is sealed with tape. The funnel with the mixture is tamped lightly. Using cardstock paper, the funnel with the mixture is inverted over the looped Nichrome wire ignition source on the test platform. When the cardstock is removed, gently twisting the funnel over the wire allows for uniform settling of the mixture around the ignition wire on the test platform.

The balance is tared to zero. The sash of the hood is lowered and the hood blower is energized. The laboratory temperature and relative humidity are recorded. Balance stability is confirmed, data acquisition is initiated, baseline data is collected, and then the Nichrome wire is energized at the power supply. A stopwatch is activated when the wire is energized. Mass loss and the temperature data are collected until spreading discoloration and/or visible flaming combustion cease. In the event of little or no flaming combustion, mass and temperature data are collected for 5 minutes.

After each trial, the Nichrome wire is released from the terminal block, and the top two layers of balance protection materials with the test residue are removed and set aside in the hood to cool to room temperature. After cooling, the mass of the post-test residue is measured and recorded. The post-test material is transferred to a labeled glass jar for waste disposal or further characterization by chemical analysis, if desired.

In preparation for the next trial, a new test platform is positioned on the laboratory balance, a new Nichrome wire is inserted into the terminal block, and a new data acquisition file is created. After each series of tests, the hood, test area, and funnel are thoroughly cleaned.

A video-recorded demonstration of the single test procedure is available at www.nfpa.org/foundation.

G.1.4.4 Test Sequence.
The oxidizer:cellulose powder mixtures are tested in the following sequence: 1:1 (5 trials), 4:1 (5 trials), then 9:1 (5 trials). If either the 1:1 or 4:1 mixture results in vigorous burning with stopwatch burning durations less than 6 seconds and/or the calculated peak mass loss rate is greater than 3 g/s, the 9:1 mixture does not need to be tested. For comparison, a salt-cellulose powder mixture (5 trials) corresponding to the oxidizer-cellulose powder mixtures that exhibits the more intense burning behavior are tested using the same procedure.

G.1.4.5 Test Data.

Visual. Photographs and/or video recordings are used to document, at a minimum, one representative trial in a test series. Visual observations to record and report include the peak flame height above the test platform; whether the pile ignited readily or was slow to ignite; whether flames readily spread over the pile or were slow to spread; the flame color; the relative volume and color of gaseous products generated; material displaced from the test platform, if any; unusual burning behavior such as swelling or "boiling"; observable or clear dependence of burning rate on the duration of the energized wire; irregular or intermittent burning; and presence of unburned or uninvolved material remaining at the end of a test.

Calculated. The percent material consumed is calculated from the final measured mass (mf) over the initial mass (mi) of the mixture times 100 (e.g., mf/mi × 100). The final measured mass is the mass remaining on the test platform after combustion, which, if the material does not continue to decompose or smolder, is easily determined because the mass data plateaus or the mass remains constant. If the material continues to decompose after flaming combustion, the final measured mass is the mass after five minutes from energizing the wire. The final recorded mass, or amount of mixture consumed, is used to calculate the mass of the test mixture at 20 percent and 80 percent consumed (i.e., 0.20 mf and 0.80 mf). The active burning time is the time from first measurable mass loss to the time at 80 percent consumed (0.80 mf). First measurable mass loss is defined as, upon energizing the wire, the first time-stamped mass data that leads a continuous series of decreasing mass at the pile as ignition, combustion, or decomposition occurs. The mass loss rate and active burning-time data, reduced from each trial mixture, are then used to calculate the average and sample standard deviation.

G.1.4.6 Test Criteria. The bench-scale screening test criteria, based on maximum mass loss rate (MLR), shown in Table G.1.2(a). The maximum mass loss rate of the oxidizer-fuel mixture is determined from the reduced 1:1, 4:1, and 9:1 mixture test data. If the burning behavior is found to depend on the duration of wire continuity, the highest mass loss rate is used instead of the average; or a sufficient number of trials are conducted to average tests with similar wire continuity durations. If the maximum mass loss rate is less than or equal to 0.3 g/s and the active burning time is greater than or equal to 30 seconds, the oxidizer is assigned to Class 1. If the maximum mass loss rate is greater than or equal to 3 g/s and the active burning time is 6 seconds or less, the oxidizer is assigned to Class 3. If the mass loss rate and active burning time do not meet the criteria for Class 1 or Class 3, the oxidizer is assigned to candidate Class 2. The candidate Class 2 materials should be subjected to intermediate-scale fire exposure testing in order to confirm the Class as Class 1, Class 2, or Class 3. If confirmatory intermediate-scale fire exposure testing is not done, the material is Class 2. A Class 4 oxidizer generally meets the Class 3 burning rate criteria plus evidence to support explosive reaction due to contamination or exposure the thermal or physical shock.

G.1.5 Intermediate-Scale Fire Exposure Test. The solid oxidizer (granular, powder, crystalline, tablet) is evaluated in the form and concentration intended for storage, handling, and use. 24 lb (10.8 kg) of the oxidizer in combustible test packaging is centered on a drywall-lined table and inside the opening of a U-shaped propane-fueled burner and ignited under a calibrated 2 MW hood instrumented in accordance with ASTM E 2067. The peak convective heat release rate, less the burner contribution, is calculated from gas temperature rise calorimetry equations. The duration of active burning is calculated from radiant heat flux transducers, less the burner contribution, at a fixed distance from the packaged test material. The peak convective heat release rate of the oxidizer in test packaging is compared to the peak convective heat release rate and burning rate duration criteria in Table G.1.2(a).

G.1.5.1 Test Materials.

Oxidizer. The chemical composition and physical properties of the oxidizer or formulated product containing an oxidizer being evaluated are recorded. The oxidizer or formulated physical form is characterized as granular, crystalline, powder, or tablet. The test material is not ground or subject to any mechanical attrition or sieving to reduce the particle size. The original packaging of the oxidizer is recorded.

Common Salt. Tests are performed with common salt in the identical test packaging as the oxidizer. If the oxidizer is in tablet form, then sodium chloride tablets of similar shape are machined from blocks of salt. Fine, coarse, pellet, and solid salt are commercially available at feed stores.

Combustible Test Packaging. High-density polyethylene (HDPE) wide mouth containers with screw top lids or 1 lb bags in corrugated board cartons and HDPE pails are used as combustible test packaging. The 60 oz (1774 cm^3) HDPE container with lid accommodates most oxidizer solids based on density; 85 oz (2514 cm^3) containers can be used for low density (i.e., powder form) oxidizers. Each HDPE container holds 4 lb (1.8 kg) of oxidizer. The HDPE containers or 1 lb bags are arranged in corrugated board cartons with doubled-wall construction. The dimensions of the corrugated board carton that enclose six 60 oz DPE containers (or twenty-four 1 lb bags) are 16 in. × 10 in. × 8 in. (40.6 cm × 25.4 cm × 20.3 cm). The dimensions of the corrugated board carton to enclose six 85 oz HDPE containers are 16 in. × 10 in. × 10 in. (40.6 cm × 20.3 cm × 20.3 cm). If the material is sold or stored in plastic bottles, the test is performed with the doubled-wall carton containing six HDPE bottles each with 4 lb of material. If the material is sold or stored in 1 lb bags, the test is performed with twenty-four 1 lb bags of material arranged in the 16 in. × 10 in. × 8 in. doubled-wall carton. If the material is sold or stored in HDPE pails, the test is performed with 24 lb of material in a HDPE pail.

G.1.5.2 Instrumentation and Test Set-Up.

Laboratory Balance. A laboratory balance inside a laboratory hood is used to measure the oxidizer in the as-received packaging for transfer into the test packaging. The mass of oxidizer in each container and/or bag is recorded.

Hood. A minimum 2 MW capacity hood designed and equipped with instrumentation described ASTM E 2067, *Standard Practice for Full-Scale Oxygen Consumption Calorimetry Fire Tests*, is required to capture and measure the temperature of the gaseous products of combustion or decomposition. Gas temperature rise and not oxygen consumption calorimetry is used to calculate the heat release rate.

Burn Table. A welded metal table, with a removable top and tray, is centered and leveled under the hood. The bottom of the tray is lined with ¼ in. thick drywall (3 ft × 3 ft). Four short walls made using strips of drywall and taped to the tray bottom contain and prevent the flow of material from the tray during a test.

Ignition Source. A U-shaped burner is constructed from threaded black gas pipe (1 in. NPS) and cast iron threaded fittings. The distance between the two legs of the U-shaped burner is 17¼ in. (43.8 cm); the length of each leg is 20¼ in. (50.8 cm). Each leg of the burner has 38 openings each with a diameter 0.0135 in. (0.34 mm); the pipe joining the two legs has 26 drilled openings. When centered, the distance from the burner to the sides of the carton (16 in. × 10 in. × 8 in.) is 4 in. (10.2 cm) on three sides; the third side is open. The burner does not contact the protected load cell, table, or tray. LP gas is supplied to the burner from a 100 lb (23.6 gal) cylinder. The flow rate to the burner is adjusted using a regulator at the cylinder outlet. Using the effective heat of combustion of propane (46.4 kJ/g), for a 38 kW fire the mass flow rate of propane gas to the burner is 0.82 g/s.

Radiant Heat Flux Transducers. Two calibrated, water-cooled, Schmidt-Boelter incident radiant heat flux (0-50 kW/m^2) transducers are affixed to a rigid stand and positioned next to the table with the sensors center with the carton between the legs of the U-shaped burner. The distance from the floor to the lower target is 4 ft 2 in. (1.2 m); the distance between the lower and upper target is 18 in. (0.45 m). The distance from the heat flux sensors to the center of the table where the carton is positioned is 3 ft 2 in. (0.95 m). With respect to the test packaging, the lower heat flux transducer is located at the height of the top section of the carton (or pail). The second heat flux transducer is located at 16 in. (0.4 m) above the top of the carton.

Thermocouples (Optional). Four, K-type fiberglass insulated thermocouples (TC) are attached to each carton or pail. One TC is taped to the exterior bottom center of the carton or pail; a second TC is taped to the exterior top center of the carton or pail. When the test packaging is a carton, a hole is punched through one side of the carton, through which two TCs are inserted. If the carton contains HDPE containers, a hole is drilled through the lid of one container and a TC is inserted into the material inside. The hole in the lid is sealed with tape.

The second TC is secured to the side exterior center of one HDPE container with the bead positioned between the container and the carton wall. The bead of the TC is exposed (e.g., not taped). If packaged in 1 lb bags, the orientation of the bags is mixed vertically and horizontally inside the carton. A slit is made in one of the horizontal bags in the center of the carton through which a TC is inserted into the material. The TC is secured and the opening in the bag is sealed with tape. A second TC is taped to the exterior of one bag. If the test packaging is a pail, a hole is drilled in the top of the pail, through which two TCs are inserted. One TC is positioned inside the test material; the second TC is taped to the top inside of the lid. The opening in the lid of the pail is taped after securing the TCs. The temperature at the thermocouples are recorded using a data acquisition system.

G.1.5.3 Test Methodology. Before each test, the temperature and relative humidity inside the burn facility are recorded. At the start of a test, a 2-minute baseline of data is collected. The gas burner is ignited at 2 minutes and a timer is activated. The gaseous products of combustion and/or decomposition are entrained in the hood and exhaust collection duct. The burner remains on for the duration of a test and for sufficient time after enhanced burning of the packaged test material to return to burner baseline values. For inert materials and weaker oxidizers, the burner remains on for up to 20 minutes. For stronger oxidizers, the burner remains on for 10 minutes. At the conclusion of a test, the regulator at the propane cylinder supplying fuel to the burner is closed. The test material is observed for residual fire or decomposition. The posttest residue is photographed and examined — specifically noting evidence of a phase change (i.e., molten) and the presence of unburned combustible packaging material(s). After cooling, the posttest residue is transferred to hazardous waste drums for disposal.

G.1.5.4 Test Sequence. The test materials are specific to each oxidizer subject to Class assignment. It is recommended that bench-scale screening tests are performed prior to intermediate-scale testing to understand the potential burning behavior. Neat or technical grade oxidizer and the formulated product(s), neat or technical grade oxidizer and formulated product stored, handled our used in different physical forms and by-products of formulating and use or waste streams are assigned to a Class using the same methodology. A typical test series includes hood calibration, empty test packaging, test packaging with common salt, formulated oxidizer in test packaging, neat oxidizer in test packaging, formulated product in test packaging, and hood calibration. Twenty-four pound quantity common salt and oxidizer are tested.

G.1.5.5 Test Data.

Visual. Photographs and video recordings document the intermediate-scale fire exposure test of the oxidizer in test packaging, specifically the visual increase in burning behavior when the test packaging is compromised and the oxidizer is involved. Other notable observations include the generation, relative quantity, and color of gaseous products, flame color, and the presence or absence of residual flaming or decomposition after the burner is extinguished.

Calculated. The convective heat release rate is calculated from the mass flow rate and temperature of combustion gases in the exhaust duct (Equation 1). The width of the curve at one-half the peak radiant heat flux profile is used to calculate the duration of active burning. The propane burner convective heat release rate is subtracted from the peak convective heat release rate to arrive at the heat release rate from the packaged oxidizer (Equation 2).

$$\dot{q}_{conv} = \dot{m} c_p (T_g - T_a)$$

where:
$\dot{q}_{conv}$ = convective heat release rate (kW)
$\dot{m}$ = mass flow in exhaust duct (kg/s)
c_p = specific heat of combustion gas (kJ/kg-K)
T_g = gas temperature (K)
T_a = ambient temperature (K)

$$\dot{q}_{oxidizer} = \dot{q}_{conv} - \dot{q}_{conv,burner} \quad (\text{kW})$$

G.1.5.6 Test Criteria. The intermediate-scale fire exposure test criteria, based on the peak convective heat release rate, is summarized in Table G.1.2(a). If the peak convective heat release rate is less than or equal to 100 kW and the active burning time is greater than or equal to 120 seconds, the oxidizer is assigned to Class 1. If the peak convective heat release rate is greater than or equal to 200 kW and the active burning time is 60 seconds or less, the oxidizer is assigned to Class 3. If the peak convective heat release rate is between 100 and 200 kW, the oxidizer is assigned to candidate Class 2. Peak convective heat release rate takes precedence over duration of active burning. A Class 4 oxidizer meets the Class 3 burning rate criteria plus there is evidence to support explosive reaction due to contamination or exposure to the thermal or physical shock.

G.2 Typical Oxidizers.

G.2.1 General. Unless concentration is specified, undiluted material is referenced. The lists of oxidizers in G.2.2 through G.2.4 are provided to clarify how the committee has classified typical oxidizers. The oxidizers marked with ** are classed based on the results of tests and criteria in Table G.1.2(a). The lists are not all-inclusive and are amended to reflect how typical oxidizers are used, handled and stored.

G.2.2 Class 1 Oxidizer.

(16) Potassium monopersulfate (45 percent $KHSO_5$ or 90 percent triple salt)**

G.2.3 Class 2 Oxidizer.

Calcium hypochlorite (48 percent or less by weight unless covered by other formulations in G.1.2)

    Calcium peroxide (75 percent)**
    Sodium persulfate (99 percent)**

G.2.4 Class 3 Oxidizer.

Calcium hypochlorite (over 48 percent by weight unless covered by other formulations in G.1.2)

    Potassium perchlorate (99 percent)**
    Potassium permanganate (>97.5 percent)**

G.3 Typical Oxidizers.

G.3.1 General. Unless concentration is specified, undiluted material is referenced. The lists of oxidizers in G.3.2 through G.3.5 are provided to clarify how the committee has classified typical oxidizers. The lists are not all-inclusive and are amended to reflect typical oxidizers used.

G.3.2 Class 1 Oxidizers. The following are typical Class 1 oxidizers:

(1) All inorganic nitrates (unless otherwise classified)
(2) All inorganic nitrites (unless otherwise classified)
(3) Ammonium persulfate
(4) Barium peroxide

(5) Calcium hypochlorite (nominal 80 percent, maximum 81 percent) blended with magnesium sulfate heptahydrate (nominal 20 percent, minimum 19 percent) having an available chlorine of less than or equal to 66 percent and a total water content of at least 17 percent.
(6) Calcium peroxide
(7) Hydrogen peroxide solutions (greater than 8 percent up to 27.5 percent)
(8) Lead dioxide
(9) Lithium hypochlorite (39 percent or less available chlorine)
(10) Lithium peroxide
(11) Magnesium peroxide
(12) Manganese dioxide
(13) Nitric acid (40 percent concentration or less)
(14) Perchloric acid solutions (less than 50 percent by weight)
(15) Potassium dichromate
(16) Potassium percarbonate
(17) Potassium persulfate
(18) Sodium carbonate peroxide
(19) Sodium dichloro-s-triazinetrione dihydrate (sodium dichloroisocyanurate dihydrate)
(20) Sodium dichromate
(21) Sodium perborate (anhydrous)
(22) Sodium perborate monohydrate
(23) Sodium perborate tetrahydrate
(24) Sodium percarbonate
(25) Sodium persulfate
(26) Strontium peroxide
(27) Trichloro-s-triazinetrione [trichloroisocyanuric acid (TCCA; trichlor), all physical forms]
(28) Zinc peroxide

G.3.3 Class 2 Oxidizers. The following are typical Class 2 oxidizers:

(1) Barium bromate
(2) Barium chlorate
(3) Barium hypochlorite
(4) Barium perchlorate
(5) Barium permanganate
(6) 1-Bromo-3-chloro-5,5-dimethylhydantoin (BCDMH)
(7) Calcium chlorate
(8) Calcium chlorite
(9) Calcium hypochlorite (50 percent or less by weight unless covered by other formulations in Section G.3).
(10) Calcium perchlorate
(11) Calcium permanganate
(12) Chromium trioxide (chromic acid)
(13) Copper chlorate
(14) Halane (1,3-dichloro-5,5-dimethylhydantoin)
(15) Hydrogen peroxide (greater than 27.5 percent up to 52 percent)
(16) Lead perchlorate
(17) Lithium chlorate
(18) Lithium hypochlorite (more than 39 percent available chlorine)
(19) Lithium perchlorate
(20) Magnesium bromate
(21) Magnesium chlorate
(22) Magnesium perchlorate
(23) Mercurous chlorate
(24) Nitric acid (more than 40 percent but less than 86 percent)
(25) Nitrogen tetroxide
(26) Perchloric acid solutions (more than 50 percent but less than 60 percent)
(27) Potassium perchlorate
(28) Potassium permanganate
(29) Potassium peroxide
(30) Potassium superoxide
(31) Silver peroxide
(32) Sodium chlorite (40 percent or less by weight)
(33) Sodium perchlorate
(34) Sodium perchlorate monohydrate
(35) Sodium permanganate
(36) Sodium peroxide
(37) Strontium chlorate
(38) Strontium perchlorate
(39) Thallium chlorate
(40) Urea hydrogen peroxide
(41) Zinc bromate
(42) Zinc chlorate
(43) Zinc permanganate

G.3.4 Class 3 Oxidizers. The following are typical Class 3 oxidizers:

(1) Ammonium dichromate
(2) Calcium hypochlorite (over 50 percent by weight unless covered in other formulations in Section G.3)
(3) Calcium hypochlorite (over 50 percent by weight)
(4) Chloric acid (10 percent maximum concentration)
(5) Hydrogen peroxide solutions (greater than 52 percent up to 91 percent)
(6) Mono-(trichloro)-tetra-(monopotassium dichloro)-penta-s-triazinetrione
(7) Nitric acid, fuming (more than 86 percent concentration)
(8) Perchloric acid solutions (60 percent to 72 percent by weight)
(9) Potassium bromate
(10) Potassium chlorate
(11) Potassium dichloro-s-triazinetrione (potassium dichloroisocyanurate)
(12) Sodium bromate
(13) Sodium chlorate
(14) Sodium chlorite (over 40 percent by weight)
(15) Sodium dichloro-s-triazinetrione anhydrous (sodium dichloroisocyanurate anhydrous)

G.3.5 Class 4 Oxidizers. The following are typical Class 4 oxidizers:

(1) Ammonium perchlorate (particle size greater than 15 microns)
(2) Ammonium permanganate
(3) Guanidine nitrate
(4) Hydrogen peroxide solutions (greater than 91 percent)
(5) Tetranitromethane

Ammonium perchlorate less than 15 microns is classified as an explosive and, as such, is not covered by this code. (See NFPA 495, *Explosive Materials Code*.)

G.4 Safety Information on Oxidizers Used in Detergents.

G.4.1 Handling Swimming Pool Chemicals. Oxidizers and sanitizers for swimming pools are some of the most widely used, manufactured, and distributed oxidizers. Anyone handling or using swimming pool chemicals should be fully aware of proper storage and handling requirements, as well as emergency and first-aid procedures in case of an accident. Chlorinated pool chemicals are incompatible with many chemicals associated with pool care, including algaecides, pool conditioners (stabilizers), clarifiers, and other types of chlorine. It is essential to follow all storage and handling procedures in order to prevent conditions that might cause emergencies, such as a fire or explosion. This section includes specific information on pool oxidizers.

Calcium hypochlorite (cal hypo), lithium hypochlorite, and chlorinated isocyanurates (dichlor and trichlor) are not combustibles. They are oxidizers. Some oxidizers can cause the spontaneous ignition and increase the burning rate of combustible materials, including the majority of their packaging material. Some oxidizers decompose rapidly and undergo self-sustained decomposition, which can result in an intense fire or explosion. The decomposition of dry chlorinated pool chemicals can also produce toxic and corrosive gases.

Because of the composition and properties of calcium hypochlorite, lithium hypochlorite, and chlorinated isocyanurates, special precautions are required to prevent contact and reaction with each other and other chemicals. Reactions will occur if they are physically mixed together.

Emergency responders should be aware of oxidizers being stored in their area of response, visit the facilities, and obtain copies of the MSDS associated with the chemicals being stored. Knowledge of the facility and the chemicals being stored makes any response more efficient and effective.

Containers should be stored away from combustible or flammable products, and product packaging should be kept clean and free of all contamination, including other pool treatment products, acids, organic materials, nitrogen-containing compounds, dry powder fire extinguishers (containing mono-ammonium phosphate), oxidizers, all corrosive liquids, flammable or combustible materials, and so forth.

G.4.1.1 Calcium Hypochlorite. Calcium hypochlorite, commonly known as cal hypo, decomposes above 350°F (177°C). The decomposition will generate oxygen and heat, possibly resulting in a fire of great intensity if combustible materials are present. Direct-exposure fire could cause the materials to decompose, the container to erupt, and the fire to reach vastly higher levels of intensity. Decomposition leaves an inert residue consisting mainly of calcium chloride. Cal hypo (over 50 percent by weight) is classified as a Class 3 oxidizer. Cal hypo (50 percent or less by weight) is classified as a Class 2 oxidizer.

G.4.1.2 Lithium Hypochlorite. Lithium hypochlorite decomposes at 275°F (135°C), producing oxygen, lithium hydroxide, lithium chlorates, and hazardous gases. Contamination with moisture, organic matter, or other chemicals may start a chemical reaction that generates heat, hazardous gases, fire, and explosion. Lithium hypochlorite (available chlorine of 39 percent or less) is classified as a Class 1 oxidizer. Lithium hypochlorite (more than 39 percent available chlorine) is classified as a Class 2 oxidizer.

G.4.1.3 Sodium Dichloroisocyanurate. Sodium dichloroisocyanurate is commonly known as dichlor. It decomposes in the range of 428°F to 482°F (220°C to 250°C) and can generate enough heat to ignite items such as paper and wood. Dichlors will sustain thermal decomposition above 428°F (220°C), even in the absence of oxygen. Decomposition results in a yellow or brown porous inert residue. Anhydrous dichlor is classified as a Class 3 oxidizer. Dichlor dihydrate is classified by NFPA as a Class 1 oxidizer.

G.4.1.4 Trichloroisocyanuric Acid. Trichloroisocyanuric acid is commonly known as trichlor. It decomposes in the range of 428°F to 482°F (220°C to 250°C). Decomposition of trichlor requires a continuous source of heat. Once the heat source is removed, trichlor will not continue to decompose. Partial decomposition leaves a yellow or brown residue. Complete decomposition leaves only traces of residue. Trichlor is classified by NFPA as a Class 1 oxidizer.

G.4.1.5 Sodium Hypochlorite. Sodium hypochlorite (7681-52-9) solutions are not classified as oxidizers by NFPA. Sodium hypochlorite is manufactured by reacting chlorine with dilute sodium hydroxide solution. Solutions are generally formulated in the range of 3–20 percent sodium hypochlorite by weight. The balance of the solution consists of water, sodium chloride, and sodium hydroxide. Depending upon the residual quantity of sodium hydroxide in the finished product, it is classified as an irritant material or a corrosive material as those terms are defined in OSHA's Hazard Communication Standard, 29 CFR 1910.1200. Generally speaking, solutions with less than 1 percent residual caustic are irritants, while solutions containing more than 1 percent residual caustic are classified as corrosives. Total evaporation of sodium hypochlorite solutions yields water and sodium chloride. Unlike calcium hypochlorite, sodium hypochlorite does not exist outside of solution. Sodium hypochlorite solutions do not readily yield oxygen or other oxidizing gases and do not initiate or promote combustion of combustible materials. The major decomposition pathway of hypochlorite ion evolves chlorite ion which combines with additional hypochlorite ion to form chlorates, which in turn form chlorides. The formation of oxygen from decomposing hypochlorite ion is a very slow side reaction, although the rate may increase with exposure to transition metals. Other oxidizing gases, for example, chlorine, are not evolved in the decomposition.

G.4.2 Specific Response Information for Chlorinated Isocyanurates (Dichlor, Trichlor). It is necessary for emergency responders to be aware of the properties of chlorinated isocyanurates (dichlor, trichlor) that can create hazardous conditions. The reaction of these chemicals or mixtures containing these chemicals with other materials can lead to the generation of hazardous gases and fire.

When stored correctly and not exposed to other materials, these chemicals are safe to transport, store, handle, and use. However, in emergencies, conditions can occur that will cause containers to rupture and material to spill or become contaminated. It is important that correct actions be taken quickly in response to these conditions.

The best approach to dealing with the reactivity of these chemicals is to assume that they will react with anything they contact. Some of the reactions, particularly those with fuels (kerosene, diesel oil, etc.) and some other organic materials, are very fast and violent. Others take some time to happen. An example of this is when spilled material is placed in a dumpster with no apparent reaction. Hours later, a fire occurs because of a slow reaction with other material.

Other oxidizers, particularly cal hypo, also react with chlorinated isocyanurates. Wet mixtures of chlorinated isocyanurates and calcium hypochlorite react vigorously, releasing large volumes of chlorine (Cl_2) gas.

The following suggested actions and precautions should be taken during an emergency where chlorinated isocyanurates are present:

(1) Emergency responders need to know their capabilities and limitations. If you are not completely sure that you can deal effectively with an emergency, get help from other responders or the manufacturer of the chemical. Contact chemical manufacturers directly or through Chemtrec® at 800-424-9300.
(2) During an emergency, only allow necessary personnel in the affected area.
(3) Because hazardous gases might be present, be sure to have self-contained breathing apparatus (SCBA) available and wear when necessary. Other personal protective equipment might also be necessary to use.
(4) Do not flush these chemicals or otherwise allow them to go into waterways or sewers without clearance from the appropriate officials.
(5) If there is any sign of a reaction taking place, cordon off and do not approach the area until a complete assessment has taken place.
(6) Breached containers of chlorinated isocyanurate products that become wet can generate nitrogen trichloride (NCl$_3$), a potential explosion hazard in confined environments. Contact the manufacturer for detailed instructions when handling wet chlorinated isocyanurate products. Do not repackage a wet product.
(7) Do not put spilled material back into its original container or any trash receptacle.
(8) Read the MSDS and product label for additional safety information.

Chlorinated isocyanurate products should be stored in sealed original containers in a cool, dry well-ventilated area. If the product has been contaminated, decomposition can occur. Signs of decomposition are heat product discoloration, gas formation, or package degradation. See Section G.5 for additional information.

G.4.3 Specific Response Information for Calcium Hypochlorite. It is necessary for emergency responders to be aware of the properties of calcium hypochlorite that can create hazardous conditions. The reactions of calcium hypochlorite or mixtures containing calcium hypochlorite with other materials can lead to fire and hazardous gases. When stored correctly and not exposed to other materials, these chemicals are safe to transport, store, handle, and use. However, in emergencies, conditions can occur that will cause containers to rupture and material to spill or become contaminated. It is important that correct actions be taken quickly in response to these conditions.

In its initial stage, the decomposition of calcium hypochlorite [Ca(OCl)$_2$] proceeds to calcium chloride and oxygen and calcium chlorate. This reaction is an exothermic reaction, which can produce sufficient heat to decompose the product and ignite surrounding materials. Thermal runaway reaction does not occur as long as material is at equilibrium, where the heat generated is equal to the heat lost to the surroundings. A secondary reaction can give off chlorine gas.

Other oxidizers, particularly chlorinated isocyanurates, also react with calcium hypochlorite. Wet mixtures of calcium hypochlorite and chlorinated isocyanurates react vigorously, releasing large volumes of chlorine (Cl$_2$) gas.

The following suggested actions and precautions should be taken during an emergency where calcium hypochlorite is present:

(1) Emergency responders need to know their capabilities and limitations. If you are not completely sure that you can deal effectively with an emergency, get help from other responders or the manufacturer of the chemical. Contact chemical manufacturers directly or through Chemtrec® at 800-424-9300.
(2) During an emergency, allow only necessary personnel in the affected area.
(3) Because hazardous gases might be present, be sure to have self-contained breathing apparatus (SCBA) available and wear when necessary. Other personal protective equipment might also be necessary to use.
(4) Do not flush these chemicals or otherwise allow them to go into waterways or sewers without clearance from the appropriate officials.
(5) If there is any sign of a reaction taking place, cordon off and do not approach the area until a complete assessment has taken place.
(6) Do not put spilled material back into its original container or any trash receptacle.
(7) Read the MSDS and product label for additional safety information.

Calcium hypochlorite products should be stored in sealed original containers in a cool, dry, well-ventilated area. These products must not be stored at temperatures above 125°F (52°C). Storage above this temperature for an extended period of time (5 days or more) can result in decomposition, evolution of chlorine gas, and heat sufficient to ignite combustible products.

If calcium hypochlorite has been contaminated or stored at elevated temperatures above 125°F (52°C) for an extended period of time, decomposition can occur. Signs of decomposition are heat; calcium chloride (CaCl$_2$) release, which can be seen as moisture on the surrounding walls from the CaCl$_2$ absorbing moisture from the air; Cl$_2$ gas plus container discoloration; or degradation of the packaging.

Extra caution should be taken when handling calcium hypochlorite or any other oxidizer that might be decomposing.

If the material shows signs of decomposition, it should be moved to a safe, protected, and well-ventilated area away from other hazardous materials. This movement would prevent a fire spreading in the event of rapid decomposition.

Special care should be taken when overpacking material that could be slowly decomposing to be sure that the heat can be dissipated and that a runaway reaction does not occur.

If the decomposing material cannot be moved, move other hazardous or combustible material out of the area.

A fire water protection source should be available during the disposal and cleanup operation in case the product starts an accelerated decomposition. Water can be used to mitigate decomposing calcium hypochlorite; once the material is thoroughly wet, the risk of a runaway reaction has been greatly reduced. Lime can be added to reduce the fuming or off gassing of wet calcium hypochlorite.

G.5 Methods and Procedures for Emergency Response Involving Solid Oxidizers.

G.5.1 Sodium Percarbonate. Sodium percarbonate (CAS 15630-89-4) or sodium carbonate perhydrate is a solid adduct of hydrogen peroxide (Na$_2$CO$_3$·3/2H$_2$O$_2$) used in detergent formulations. The active oxygen content of granular solid sodium percarbonate ranges from 12 to 14.5 percent. Granular particles are typically coated. Sodium percarbonate (99 percent) is a Class 1 oxidizer. Sodium percarbonate and sodium percarbonate–rich mixtures (>70 wt percent) are sensitive to gross contamination, to heat, and to reducing agents and are potentially explosive if mixed with organics. Sodium percarbonate and its formulated products have the propensity to undergo exothermic decomposition with the rapid release of oxygen, water as steam, and heat sufficient to ignite nearby combustible materials. The kinetics and decomposition reactions are complex. The self-accelerating decomposition temperature (SADT), the lowest ambient temperature at which self-accelerating decomposition may occur in a material in the packaging used for transportation, is reported to be 168°F (76°C) for 25 kg packages and 122°F (50°C) for 1 ton bags. If improperly discarded or mixed with combustible trash, a fire can result.

G.5.2 Oxidizer Hazards. Incidents that involve oxidizers must be handled in a timely manner and with an understanding of the hazards and properties of the materials involved. This section identifies the key elements that must be understood when dealing with oxidizers that are under distress either from a spill, contamination, decomposition, or fire from a source other than the oxidizers.

The hazards of stored oxidizers can manifest themselves in one or more of six distinct hazardous situations as follows:

(1) They increase the burning rate of combustible materials.
(2) They can cause spontaneous ignition of combustible materials.
(3) They can decompose rapidly.
(4) They can liberate hazardous gases.
(5) They can undergo self-sustained decomposition, which can result in an explosion.
(6) They can react explosively if mixed with incompatibles or in fire conditions.

G.5.3 Handling Incidents Involving Oxidizers. Anyone handling or using oxidizers should be fully aware of proper storage and handling requirements as well as emergency and first-aid procedures in case of an accident. Oxidizers are incompatible with many chemicals or other materials. It is essential to follow all storage and handling procedures in order to prevent conditions that might cause emergencies, such as a fire or explosion.

Before attempting to clean any oxidizer spill, be certain that the spilled material is dry and has not been contaminated. If there are any signs that a reaction has begun (hissing, bubbling, smoking, gassing, burning, or bulging or hot containers), evacuate the area immediately and contact your local fire department for assistance. If the product is not reacting but has mixed with chemicals or other materials, contact your local fire department. If you have any concerns regarding emergency procedures, immediately contact Chemtrec® at 800-424-9300 or the manufacturer for emergency instructions.

G.5.3.1 General considerations when responding to an oxidizer incident are as follows:

(1) Use trained personnel who understand the specific hazards of the oxidizers involved.
(2) Consult the manufacturer for technical assistance.
(3) Understand the reaction characteristic of the hazards of the specific oxidizer involved.
(4) Use a specific protocol on how to clean up the oxidizers involved.
(5) Prevent oxidizer and incompatibles from contacting each other.
(6) Control temperature below the maximum recommended storage temperature.
(7) If there are signs of decomposition, allow for heat dissipation.
(8) Control the cleanup site, including moving overpack containers to a safe and secure location, preferably outside the storage building.
(9) Move container to a safe, secure, dry, open outside area, or to a location designated by the competent individual, to await disposal in conformance with applicable regulations and manufacturer's or processor's instructions.
(10) Monitor overpacks to ensure that a slow decomposition reaction cannot lead to a self-accelerated decomposition reaction or fire.
(11) Manage the size and location of the cleanup pile so that a decomposition reaction cannot spread to other areas.
(12) Have water available for early intervention if a reaction starts.
(13) Do not use any material or equipment that could contaminate the spilled material.
(14) Do not dispose of the material with incompatible chemicals or materials.
(15) Keep material dry during cleanup and, if material becomes damp, see G.5.4.
(16) Do not allow unnecessary or untrained personnel in the area during the cleanup.
(17) Wear appropriate protective gear and refer to Emergency Response Plan or material safety data sheet (MSDS).
(18) Store cleanup supplies in a cabinet or marked off area where they can be accessed quickly when needed.
(19) Train employees in the cleanup procedures of the facility.

G.5.3.1.1 Water is the most important element in controlling an oxidizer incident or fire. The proper use of water is the most important element in controlling a fire involving oxidizers. Do not use dry chemical extinguishing agent on oxidizer fires.

G.5.3.1.2 The following are guidelines for the use of water in fire control:

(1) Water in sufficient quantities stops or prevents an oxidizer fire from spreading.
(2) Water in sufficient quantities greatly reduces the reactivity of most oxidizers. Refer to the MSDS to determine the characteristics of the specific oxidizers that you are handling.
(3) Adding water normally slows the decomposition, reduces liberation of hazardous gas, and eliminates self-sustained decomposition.
(4) Some oxidizers, primarily trichlor, can react with small amounts of water over a period of time and form NCl_3, a potentially explosive compound. Even though NCl_3 is formed, water should continue to be added. Water in sufficient quantities is still the best method to control an oxidizer in a fire. Consult the manufacturer on how to handle and dispose of damp oxidizers.
(5) Some oxidizers can dry out after wetting and, if contaminated, can react, causing a possible fire.
(6) The water runoff from an oxidizer fire should be contained to protect the environment.

G.5.3.2 Spill Responses. If you have expertise addressing chemical spills, be sure to evaluate whether the material you are handling and the containers you are using are dry and uncontaminated. Follow applicable regulations when disposing of any material. Whether or not there is a fire, call the supplier for instructions on how best to clean up and remove spilled material and for other useful information. (Use the emergency telephone number on the container, the MSDS, or other information supplied by the manufacturer. Additional emergency information can be obtained through Chemtrec® and Canutec.)

G.5.3.3 Procedure for Cleaning Uncontaminated Dry Spills. If the spill is dry and uncontaminated and there are no signs of decomposition or fire, the following approach should be used. Alternate or additional procedures might be advisable, depending upon site-specific circumstances. Users must tailor the cleanup to their own particular circumstances. Contact the manufacturer for further instructions.

The following procedure should be used:

(1) Evaluate and respond as follows:
   (a) If reacting, call the fire department.
   (b) If product is contaminated with any other chemical or material, call the fire department.
   (c) In the event of a large spill [100 lb (45.4 kg) or more], call the fire department.
   (d) In the event of a small spill [under 100 lb (45.4 kg)], proceed only if trained, or refer to manufacturer's instructions.
   (e) Contact the manufacturer.
(2) Isolate and ventilate the area as follows:
   (a) Mark off area.
   (b) Keep people away.
   (c) Do not breathe dust.
   (d) Open doors and windows.
(3) Wear protective clothing as follows:
   (a) Rubber or neoprene gloves, boots, and aprons
   (b) Protective goggles or safety glasses
   (c) NIOSH/MSHA-approved respirator or breathing apparatus
(4) Get two clean, dry, plastic containers (or suitable containers) large enough to hold the spilled material and proceed as follows:
   (a) Line clean, suitable container with two clear-plastic bags.
   (b) Place damaged container into one of the suitable containers.
   (c) Label the container(s) properly and identify contents.
   (d) Loosely place lid and leave unsealed.
   (e) Do not place spilled chemical into original container.
(5) Get clean broom and shovel and proceed as follows:
   (a) Carefully sweep up spilled chemical.
   (b) Place spilled material in clean clear-plastic bag.
   (c) Place plastic bag into second container.
   (d) Label container(s) accordingly to identify contents.
(6) Remove containers to isolated area as follows:
   (a) Move waste material to a safe and protected location in case there is a decomposition reaction.
   (b) Keep away from children and high traffic areas.
   (c) Avoid getting process duct wet.
(7) Thoroughly wash area with water to remove residue.
(8) Wash and dry the following equipment:
   (a) Broom and shovel
   (b) Protective clothing
(9) Contact manufacturer for proper disposal of chemicals.

G.5.4 Specific Hazards of Oxidizer Fires, Reacting Oxidizers, and Large Oxidizer Incidents.

G.5.4.1 Emergency Response Plans and Actions. It is the responsibility of each facility to have an emergency plan and train their employees in the requirements of the plan.

It is the primary responsibility of each facility employee to follow the pre-established guidelines set forth in an emergency plan.

G.5.4.2 Specific Emergencies.

G.5.4.2.1 Fire and Fume Hazards. Oxidizers are not combustible per se. However, if oxidizers are heated and/or contaminated to their decomposition range by an outside source, they can decompose, resulting in the generation of heat. The intensity of the decomposition can be sufficient to ignite paper and wood and a fire can result. Upon thermal decomposition, some oxidizers can give off dense clouds of gases that can be toxic, noxious, and very difficult to see through. Check the MSDS or contact the manufacturer for the possible types of hazardous decomposition products during a thermal decomposition.

In case of fire or decomposition, immediately implement your emergency plan to minimize loss of life or property. An emergency plan commonly includes the following steps:

(1) In the event of an emergency, contact your local fire department, ambulatory service, or police department immediately.
(2) State your full name, company name, address, and telephone number.
(3) State nature of emergency (i.e., fire, gas leak).
(4) State type of assistance required (i.e., ambulance, fire).
(5) If possible, stay on the line until the emergency operator understands the information.

Emergency numbers should be pre-set on all store phones to assist calling. Numbers should be in bold or colored print.

The following are issues regarding the use of personal protective equipment that should be considered:

(1) Be prepared to use the appropriate personal protective equipment, which can include SCBA, in an emergency.
(2) For small, controllable fires, use appropriate safety equipment. Only trained personnel should attempt to extinguish fires. Do not fight any fire alone.
(3) If swimming pool chemicals are involved in a fire or reaction, use large quantities of water. Do not use dry chemical extinguishers because they can contain ammonium compounds, which could react and release toxic or explosive gases. Provisions should be made for the containment of runoff water (i.e., diking with sandbags, dirt, or other suitable material). If there is a fire or if the pool chemical product is contaminated with another chemical, the area should be evacuated and the fire department called immediately, even if the building has a sprinkler system.
(4) Direct unnecessary personnel away from the area.

Do not allow oxidizers or fire water to enter sewers, waterways, or trash containers, and keep unneutralized and chlorinated chemicals out of sewers, watersheds, or water systems.

G.5.4.2.2 Reacting Oxidizers. Oxidizers are stable when stored in a cool, dry, well-ventilated area and not contaminated by other materials, such as acids, bases, or easily oxidizable materials. Oxidizers can become dangerous if mishandled, improperly stored, or contaminated. They could become unstable or undergo a decomposition reaction, which could produce intense heat, hazardous gases, fire, or explosion.

Oxidizers are also incompatible with many of the other chemicals used in commerce, such as organic solvents, algaecides, other oxidizers, and pH adjusting materials. Some of the materials that are incompatible with oxidizers are listed as follows:

(1) Acids
(2) Alcohols (methyl, ethyl, propyl, and higher alcohols)
(3) Aliphatic and aromatic unsaturated compounds
(4) Amines
(5) Ammonia and ammonium salts
(6) Bases
(7) Carbonated beverages
(8) Ethers
(9) Floor sweeping compounds
(10) Glycerin
(11) Paint, oils, and greases
(12) Peroxides (hydrogen, sodium, calcium, etc.)
(13) Petroleum products (gasoline, kerosene, etc.)
(14) Phenols
(15) Other oxidizers
(16) Quaternary ammonium compounds ("quats"), such as algaecides
(17) Reducing agents (sulfides, sulfites, bisulfites, thiosulfates)
(18) Solvents (toluene, xylene, etc.)

It should be noted that this list is not comprehensive. For more information on the incompatibilities between pool chemicals and other materials, the appropriate pool chemical supplier or manufacturer should be contacted.

Some oxidizers, such as trichloroisocyanuric acid (TCCA; trichlor) can give off toxic gases and form NCl_3 if small amounts of water are added. Special precautions should be used when handling these oxidizers. If containers of one of these oxidizers become wet, they could contain NCl_3, which is a potential explosive. Before handling wet oxidizers, the manufacturer should be contacted for instructions.

A response to a reacting oxidizer incident is as follows:

(1) Contact appropriate emergency personnel. Responder should assess the nature and magnitude of the emergency.
(2) If there are any signs that a reaction has begun (hissing, bubbling, smoking, gassing, burning, or bulging or hot containers), evacuate the area immediately and contact the local fire department for assistance. If the product is not reacting but has mixed with other chemicals or other materials, contact your local fire department.
(3) Additional information can be obtained by using the emergency telephone number on the container or other information supplied by the manufacturer or by calling Chemtrec®.
(4) Water in sufficient quantities greatly reduces the reactivity of most oxidizers and can stop or prevent a fire. Water slows the decomposition reaction, reduces liberation of hazardous gas, and eliminates self-sustained decomposition.
(5) When overpacking product, continuously monitor to be sure that the product is not decomposing, because if the heat of decomposition cannot be dissipated, then the increased temperature can result in a self-sustained decomposition and possible fire.
(6) On-site neutralization might be the only acceptable solution for reacting and contaminated material.
(7) Have a sufficient water source available to stop an oxidizer reaction in case a decomposition reaction starts.
(8) Contamination and high temperatures are the major reasons an oxidizer reaction starts. During a cleanup, packaging materials should be handled so that the product is not contaminated and the temperatures of all packages are maintained below the recommended storage temperature for the specific oxidizers involved.
(9) Contaminated oxidizers should never be mixed with packaging material. Only original noncontaminated packaging material can be in overpack.
(10) Do not place spilled chemicals into the trash. Contact with incompatible materials could cause a reaction.
(11) Keep spilled material dry. If allowed to stand in damp or wet areas, tear-producing vapors can result. Dampening the product with water during the cleanup process can cause a decomposition reaction.
(12) Keep unneutralized and chlorinated chemicals out of sewers, watersheds, or water systems.

G.5.4.2.3 Personal Protective Equipment. When handling chemicals or cleaning up a spill, the manufacturer's MSDS for personal protective equipment recommendations should be consulted. Recommended personal protective equipment includes the following:

(1) Chemical-resistant gloves
(2) Chemical-resistant boots
(3) Chemical-resistant coveralls/aprons
(4) Face shields
(5) NIOSH-approved respiratory protection for the conditions

A NIOSH-approved, positive-pressure, self-contained breathing apparatus (SCBA) plus any other necessary personal protective equipment should be worn if toxic fumes are present. Chlorine and other toxic gases can be released during a fire or decomposing reaction.

Annex H Compressed Gases and Cryogenic Fluids

This annex is not a part of the requirements of this NFPA document but is included for informational purposes only.

H.1 Attended Operations.

H.1.1 Introduction. Section 112(r) of the Clean Air Act (CAA) mandates that the U.S. Environmental Protection Agency (EPA) promulgate a regulatory program to prevent accidental releases of regulated toxic and flammable substances and reduce the severity of releases that do occur. The rule, published on June 20, 1996, formally appears in the Code of Federal Regulations as 40 CFR 68 and is officially titled "Accidental Release Prevention Requirements: Risk Management Programs Under Clean Air Act Section 112(r)(7)."

H.1.1.1 In addition to qualified judgment and expertise, the following three resources must be considered in the selection of alternative release scenarios in evaluating the hazards of any system:

(1) The five scenarios listed in Section 68.28 of 40 CFR 68
(2) The 5-year accident history of all accidental releases from covered processes that resulted in deaths, injuries, or significant property damage on-site or all known off-site deaths, injuries, evacuations, sheltering-in-place, or property or environmental damage
(3) The hazard review or process hazards analysis completed as part of the required prevention program

H.1.1.2 The five scenarios encompassed in Section 68.28 of 40 CFR 68 of the regulation include the following:

(1) Transfer hose releases due to splits or sudden hose uncoupling (typical of delivery operations)
(2) Process piping releases from failures at flanges, joints, welds, valves and valve seals, and drains or bleeds
(3) Process vessel or pump releases due to cracks, seal failure, or drain, bleed, or plug failure
(4) Vessel overfilling and spill or overpressurization and venting through relief valves or rupture disks
(5) Shipping container mishandling and breakage or puncturing leading to a spill

H.1.1.3 Based on comparable analysis, it was determined that the most likely alternative release scenario having an off-site impact from compressed gas systems would be a process piping failure that either is outdoors or is indoors and entrained into an unspecified exhaust system. In either case, discharge results in a continuous emission resulting in a plume on-site or off-site. An accidental release of this type might occur due to mechanical failure, corrosion, failure of a piping component such as a joint or valve, or another cause.

H.1.1.4 The flow rate through a pipe during a release is computed based on the pressure of the container, cylinder, or tank; the liquid head (if a liquid is involved); the fluid density; the line's resistance to flow (based primarily on diameter, length, and number of bends); and the open area available to flow at the exit.

H.1.2 Parameters. Each parameter, whether selected by the user or preselected, as is typical, is explained in H.1.2.1 through H.1.2.5.

H.1.2.1 Container, Cylinder, or Tank Pressure. The highest normal operating pressure should be used for the tank pressure.

H.1.2.2 Liquid Head. The liquid head is the amount of pressure exerted by the weight of the liquid column. For most small containers and cylinders, the liquid head is normally small and can usually be ignored.

H.1.2.3 Fluid Density. Fluid density is the density of the fluid under consideration.

H.1.2.4 Line Length and Configuration. Line configuration is specific to the configuration under consideration.

H.1.2.5 Pipe Break Flow Area. Most piping breaks result in less than the full pipe diameter being open to flow. For example, a full-guillotine break is not nearly as likely as a reduced-flow area break or a small leak. It is unlikely that small leaks will have an off-site impact. Therefore, it is appropriate to select as an alternative release case a piping failure characterized by a fraction of the full-open area that is typical of the majority of piping failures while significantly greater than that of a small leak.

For the purposes of calculation, a 20 percent flow rate versus a full bore line break should be used. Statistics indicate that piping failures of this magnitude would be expected to occur between 2 and 10 times as often as a full-guillotine break.

H.1.3 Calculations to demonstrate the "maximum credible worst-case leak" must be engineered, and factors to include the nature of flow must be considered, including whether the gas or vapor flowing is gaseous, liquid, or a two-phase-type flow. Detailed air dispersion models and methods of calculation are available. The choice of the model or methodology, or both, must be established by engineering principles and applied by those versed in such matters.

H.2 Physical Properties of Hydrogen.

H.2.1 Physical Properties. Hydrogen is a flammable gas. It is colorless, odorless, tasteless, and nontoxic. It is the lightest gas known, having a specific gravity of 0.0695 (air = 1.0). Hydrogen diffuses rapidly in air and through materials not normally considered porous.

H.2.1.1 Hydrogen burns in air with a pale blue, almost invisible flame. At atmospheric pressure, the ignition temperature of hydrogen–air mixtures has been reported by the U.S. Bureau of Mines to be as low as 932°F (500°C). The flammable limits of hydrogen–air mixtures depend on pressure, temperature, and water vapor content. At atmospheric pressure, the flammable range is approximately 4 percent to 75 percent by volume of hydrogen in air.

H.2.1.2 Hydrogen remains a gas even at high pressures. It is liquefied when cooled to its boiling point of –423°F (–253°C).

H.2.1.3 Hydrogen is nontoxic, but it can cause anoxia (asphyxiation) when it displaces the normal 21 percent oxygen in a confined area without ventilation that will maintain an oxygen content exceeding 19.5 percent. Because hydrogen is colorless, odorless, and tasteless, its presence cannot be detected by the human senses.

H.2.2 Physical Properties of Liquefied Hydrogen. Liquefied hydrogen is transparent, odorless, and not corrosive or noticeably reactive. The boiling point at atmospheric pressure is –423°F (–253°C). It is only as heavy as water. Liquefied hydrogen converted to gaseous hydrogen at standard conditions it expands approximately 850 times.

Annex I   Emergency Response Guideline

This annex is not a part of the requirements of this NFPA document but is included for informational purposes only.

I.1 Emergency Response. A Company Emergency Responder is a person who responds to an emergency who is trained and certified under the requirements of 29 CFR 1910.120(q). The Emergency Response (ER) Team Leader is a leader of a Hazardous Material Team that responds to an emergency.

The emergency response training requirements for handling hazardous materials emergencies are found in 29 CFR 1910.120 (OSHA); and although these requirements are focused on hazardous waste they are appropriate for use with nonwaste materials. Once the material is released in an incident it is viewed as waste from the OSHA perspective.

Congress and OSHA require facilities that handle hazardous waste to comply with the OSHA 29 CFR 1910.120 hazardous waste operations and emergency response standard (known as HAZWOPER) when responding to an emergency. This rule, issued on March 6, 1989, is intended to protect the health and safety of workers, from exposure to toxic and hazardous materials releases. An important criterion to consider is that the emergency response training should be tailored to meet product-specific requirements.

The training requirements on how to respond to an emergency are included in these recommendations. The OSHA regulations define "what an emergency response is" and outline the different training requirements for various responder levels. In addition, the methodology of emergency response is outlined, and the requirements of an emergency response plan are identified and listed. The information below is a summary of the training recommendations and the health and safety program for individuals who might have to identify an emergency or respond to an emergency or non-emergency response.

Training should be based on the duties and functions to be performed by each responder for their specific facility. The skill and knowledge levels required for responders should be conveyed through training before the responders are permitted to take part in an actual emergency operations incident.

I.2 What Is An Emergency Response According to OSHA? OSHA defines an emergency response as a response effort by employees from outside the immediate release area or by other designated responders to an occurrence which results, or is likely to result, in an uncontrolled release of hazardous substances.

I.3 What Is Not an Emergency Response? Responses to incidental releases of hazardous substance where the substance can be absorbed, neutralized, or otherwise controlled at the time of release by employees in the immediate release area or by maintenance personnel are not considered to be emergency responses within the scope of this standard.

Responses to releases of hazardous substances where there is no significant potential safety or health hazard (i.e., fire, explosion, or chemical exposure) are not considered to be emergency responses.

Spills of this nature are small and can be cleaned up as a normal job function. Typically, they include the small drips and leaks that often occur around pipe junctions or valves, or spills of small quantities of chemicals.

I.4 Training Curriculum for Emergency Response. Training should be based on the duties and function to be performed by each responder. The skill and knowledge levels required for responders should be conveyed to them through training before they are permitted to take part in actual incident emergency operations. Employees who participate, or are expected to participate, in emergency or non-emergency responses, should be given training as follows depending on the specific hazards of the material and the duties and function that are required of the responder:

I.4.1 First Responder Awareness Level. First responders at the awareness level are individuals who are likely to witness or discover a hazardous substance release and who have been trained to initiate an emergency response sequence by notifying the proper authorities of the release. They would take no further action beyond notifying the authorities of the release. First responders at the awareness level should have sufficient training or have had sufficient experience to objectively demonstrate the following competencies:

(1) Understand what hazardous substances are and the risks associated with them in an incident for their facility
(2) Understand the types of hazards at their facility
(3) Know the hazardous materials present at their facility
(4) Understand the potential outcomes associated with an emergency created when hazardous substances are present
(5) Understand the role of the first responder awareness individual in the employer's emergency response plan, including site security and control and the U.S. Department of Transportation's *Emergency Response Guidebook*

(6) Able to realize the need for additional resources, and to make appropriate notifications to the communication center
(7) Understand the site safety and health plan, including confined space entry, decontamination procedures, and spill containment program

I.4.2 First Responder Operations Level. First responders at the operations level are individuals who respond to releases or potential releases of hazardous substances as part of the initial response to the site for the purpose of protecting nearby persons, property, or the environment from the effects of the release. They are trained to respond in a defensive fashion without actually trying to stop the release. Their function is to contain the release from a safe distance, keep it from spreading, and prevent exposures. The employer should certify that first responders at the operational level have received at least 8 hours of training or have sufficient experience to objectively demonstrate competency in the following areas in addition to those listed for the awareness level:

(1) Understand the hazards and risks associated with the hazardous materials they work with and risk assessment techniques
(2) Understand the types of hazards at their facility
(3) Know the hazardous materials present at their facility
(4) Understand the potential outcomes associated with an emergency created when the hazardous materials they work with are present
(5) Able to identify hazardous materials
(6) Understand their role in their company's emergency response plan (including facility security plan) and how to use the NAERG Book *(North America Emergency Response Guide)*
(7) Able to realize the need for additional resources and make appropriate notification to the communication center
(8) Understand the site safety and health plan, including confined space entry, decontamination procedures, and spill containment program
(9) Know how to select and use proper personal protective equipment
(10) Understand hazardous materials terms
(11) Know how to perform basic control, containment and/or confinement within the capabilities of the resources and personal protective equipment available with their unit
(12) Know how to implement basic decontamination procedures
(13) Understand the relevant standard response operation procedures and termination procedures

I.4.3 Hazardous Materials Technician. Hazardous materials technicians are individuals who respond to releases or potential releases for the purpose of stopping the release. They assume a more aggressive role than a first responder at the operations level in that they are responsible for approaching the point of release in order to plug, patch, or otherwise stop the release of a hazardous substance. The employer should certify that hazardous materials technicians have received at least 24 hours of training equal to the first responder operations level and in addition have competency in the following areas:

(1) Training that meets the requirements for first responder operations and awareness level
(2) Know how to implement the employer's emergency response plan

(3) Know the classification, identification, and verification of known and unknown materials by using field survey instruments and equipment
(4) Able to function within an assigned role in the Incident Command System
(5) Know how to select and use proper specialized chemical personal protective equipment provided to the hazardous materials technician
(6) Understand hazard and risk assessment techniques
(7) Able to perform advance control, containment, and/or confinement operations within the capabilities of the resources and personal protective equipment available with the unit
(8) Understand and implement decontamination procedures
(9) Understand termination procedures
(10) Understand basic chemical and toxicological terminology and behavior

I.4.4 Hazardous Materials Specialist. Hazardous materials specialists are individuals who respond with and provide support to hazardous materials technicians. Their duties parallel those of the hazardous materials technician; however, their duties require a more directed or specific knowledge of the various substances they could be called upon to contain. The hazardous materials specialist would also act as the site liaison with federal, state, local and other government authorities in regards to emergency incidents. The employer should certify that hazardous materials specialists have received at least 24 hours of training equal to the technician level and in addition have competency in the following areas:

(1) Know how to implement the local emergency response plan
(2) Understand classification, identification, and verification of known and unknown materials by using advanced survey instruments and equipment
(3) Know the state emergency response plan
(4) Able to select and use proper specialized chemical personal protective equipment provided to the hazardous materials specialist
(5) Understand in-depth hazard and risk techniques
(6) Able to perform specialized control, containment, and/or confinement operations within the capabilities of the resources and personal protective equipment available
(7) Able to determine and implement decontamination procedures
(8) Able to develop a site safety and control plan
(9) Understand chemical, radiological, and toxicological terminology and behavior

I.4.5 On-Scene Incident Commander. Incident commanders, who will assume control of the incident scene beyond the first responder awareness level, should receive at least 24 hours of training equal to the first responder operations level. In addition, the employer should certify that the incident commanders have competency in the following areas:

(1) Know and be able to implement the employer's incident command system
(2) Know how to implement the employer's emergency response plan
(3) Know and understand the hazards and risks associated with employees working in chemical protective clothing
(4) Know how to implement the local emergency response plan
(5) Know of the state emergency response plan and of the Federal Regional Response Team

(6) Know and understand the importance of decontamination procedures
(7) Understand the requirements and responsibilities for all levels of emergency response personnel

I.4.6 Hazardous Materials (HAZMAT) Response Team. A hazardous materials (HAZMAT) response team is an organized group of employees, designated by the employer, who are expected to perform work to handle and control actual or potential leaks or spills of hazardous substances requiring possible close approach to the substance. The team members perform responses to releases or potential releases of hazardous substances for the purpose of control or stabilization of the incident. The training requirements of various team members are listed above.

I.5 Example Training Curriculum. Training required should be based on the hazards of the materials present and the potential exposures to the emergency response team and the community as a result of an incident. The details of the training should be based on the duties and the functions the responder is required to perform. Locations with an emergency response plan based on public fire department or a contract response team response to emergencies and non-emergencies can train their employees only to a first responder awareness level.

The following example illustrates the curriculum for hazardous materials technicians for emergency and non-emergency responses in a chlorine and caustic manufacturing complex. The requirements for other facilities may be significantly different. Other training curriculums may be available from other resources including trade associations.

This list of qualifications was taken from the 2000 edition of NFPA 472, *Standard on Professional Competence of Responders to Hazardous Materials Incidents,* and changed to meet the requirements to respond to incidents involving chlorine and caustic.

Individuals that respond to know hazardous materials and unknown hazardous material to mitigate or control a release should have the most in-depth training. These individuals should know how to assess the situations to determine the hazards and potential exposure so the risk can be determined. The ability to predict potential outcomes associated with an emergency or non-emergency and to realize the need for additional resources. These individuals need to be able to understand and prepare an emergency response plan. The facilities management should understand the training requirement of the HAZMAT team members to ensure their ability to respond to emergency situations. The facilities management should determine the potential emergencies that could occur at the facilities and develop pre-emergency plans. An emergency response plan for a potential facility emergency should be written and include the following information:

(1) Pre-emergency planning and coordination with outside parties
(2) Personnel roles, lines of authority, training, and communication
(3) Emergency recognition and prevention
(4) Safe distances and places of refuge
(5) Site security and control
(6) Evacuation routes and procedures
(7) Decontamination
(8) Emergency medical treatment and first aid
(9) Emergency alerting and response procedures
(10) Critique of response and follow-up
(11) Personnel protective equipment and emergency equipment

Emergency exercises should be conducted to determine potential problem areas that need to be correct. Preplanning for emergencies is accomplished by determining communication requirements, conducting facility tours with internal and external responders, coordinating resources, and sharing information. These activities will improve the ability for a hazardous materials team to respond.

The following information from NFPA 472 lists the training recommendation for hazardous materials technicians. A hazardous materials technician is one who responds to releases or potential releases for the purpose of stopping the release. A hazardous material technician should be trained to the first responder awareness and operational levels listed in NFPA 472 and the competencies listed below. Hazardous materials technicians also shall receive any additional training to meet applicable United States Department of Transportation (DOT), United States Environmental Protection Agency (EPA), Occupational Safety and Health Administration (OSHA), and other appropriate state, local, or provincial occupational health and safety regulatory requirements that might apply.

Hazardous materials technicians are those persons who respond to releases or potential releases of hazardous materials for the purpose of controlling the release. Hazardous materials technicians are expected to use specialized chemical protective clothing and specialized control equipment.

The required competencies listed below are what a hazardous materials technician needs to know. Therefore, in addition to being competent at both the first responder awareness and operational levels, the hazardous materials technician should be able to do the following:

(1) Analyze a hazardous materials incident to determine the magnitude of the problem in terms of outcomes by completing the following tasks:
  (a) Survey the hazardous materials incident to identify special containers involved, to identify or classify unknown materials, and to verify the presence and concentrations of hazardous materials through the use of monitoring equipment
  (b) Collect and interpret hazard and response information from printed resources, technical resources, computer databases, and monitoring equipment
  (c) Determine the extent of damage to containers
  (d) Predict the likely behavior of released materials and their containers when multiple materials are involved
  (e) Estimate the size of an endangered area using computer modeling, monitoring equipment, or specialists in this field
(2) Plan a response within the capabilities of available personnel, personal protective equipment, and control equipment by completing the following tasks:
  (a) Identify the response objectives for hazardous materials incidents
  (b) Identify the potential action options available by response objective
  (c) Select the personal protective equipment required for a given action option
  (d) Select the appropriate decontamination procedures
  (e) Develop a plan of action, including safety considerations, consistent with the local emergency response plan and the organization's standard operating procedures, and within the capability of the available personnel, personal protective equipment, and control equipment

(3) Implement the planned response consistent with the organization's standard operating procedures and safety considerations by completing the following tasks:
  (a) Perform the duties of an assigned hazardous materials branch position within the local incident management system (IMS)
  (b) Don, work in, and doff appropriate personal protective clothing, including, but not limited to, both liquid splash- and vapor-protective clothing with appropriate respiratory protection
  (c) Perform the control functions identified in the plan of action
(4) Evaluate the progress of the planned response by evaluating the effectiveness of the control functions.
(5) Terminate the incident by completing the following tasks:
  (a) Assist in the incident debriefing
  (b) Assist in the incident critique
  (c) Provide reports and documentation of the incident

I.6 Competencies — Analyzing the Incident.

I.6.1 Surveying the Hazardous Materials Incident. The hazardous materials technician should be able to understand the workings and identify chlorine and caustic containers if involved in an incident and, given the appropriate equipment, identify or classify unknown materials, verify the identity of the hazardous materials, and determine the concentration of hazardous materials. The hazardous materials technician should be able to do the following:

(1) Given examples of various specialized containers, identify each container by name and identify the material, and its hazard class, that is typically found in the container
(2) Given examples of the following railroad cars, identify each car by type and identify at least one material, and its hazard class, that is typically found in each car:
  (a) Cryogenic liquid tank cars
  (b) High-pressure tube cars
  (c) Nonpressure tank cars
  (d) Pneumatically unloaded hopper car
  (e) Pressure tank cars
  (f) Cars and truck designed to handle chlorine and caustic materials
(3) Be able to identify unknown materials, one of which is a solid, one a liquid, and one a gas, identify or classify by hazard each unknown material.
(4) Identify the steps in an analysis process for identifying chlorine and caustic containers as well as unknown solid and liquid materials.
(5) Identify the steps in an analysis process for chlorine and caustic and unknown atmosphere.
(6) Identify the type(s) of monitoring equipment, test strips, and reagents used to determine identifying the following hazards:
  (a) Chlorine
  (b) Caustic
  (c) Corrosivity (pH)
  (d) Flammability
  (e) Oxidation potential
  (f) Oxygen deficiency
  (g) Radioactivity
  (h) Toxic levels
(7) Identify the capabilities and limiting factors associated with the selection and use of the following monitoring equipment, test strips, and reagents:

(a) Chlorine
(b) Caustic
(c) Carbon monoxide meter
(d) Colorimetric tubes
(e) Combustible gas indicator
(f) Oxygen meter
(g) Passive dosimeter
(h) Photo ionization detectors
(i) pH indicators and/or pH meters
(j) Radiation detection instruments
(k) Reagents
(l) Test strips

(8) Have the ability to identify hazardous materials using the monitoring equipment, test strips, and reagents; select the appropriate equipment; and demonstrate the proper techniques to identify and quantify the materials listed above.

(9) Demonstrate the field maintenance and testing procedures for the monitoring equipment, test strips, and reagents provided by the authority having jurisdiction.

I.6.2 Collecting and Interpreting Hazard and Response Information. Given access to printed resources, technical resources, computer databases, and monitoring equipment, the hazardous materials technician should collect and interpret hazard and response information not available from the current edition of the *North American Emergency Response Guidebook* or a material safety data sheet (MSDS). The hazardous materials technician should be able to do the following:

(1) Identify and interpret the types of hazard and response information available from each of the following resources and explain the advantages and disadvantages of each resource:
   (a) Hazardous materials databases
   (b) Maps and diagrams
   (c) Monitoring equipment
   (d) Reference manuals
   (e) Technical information centers (i.e., CHEMTREC/CANUTEC/SETIQ)
   (f) Technical information specialists

(2) Describe the following terms and explain their significance in the risk assessment process:
   (a) Acid, caustic
   (b) Air reactivity
   (c) Boiling point
   (d) Catalyst
   (e) Chemical interactions
   (f) Chemical reactivity
   (g) Compound, mixture
   (h) Concentration
   (i) Corrosivity (pH)
   (j) Critical temperatures and pressure
   (k) Expansion ratio
   (l) Flammable (explosive) range (LEL and UEL)
   (m) Fire point
   (n) Flash point
   (o) Halogenated hydrocarbon
   (p) Ignition (autoignition) temperature
   (q) Inhibitor
   (r) Instability
   (s) Ionic and covalent compounds
   (t) Maximum safe storage temperature (MSST)
   (u) Melting point/freezing point
   (v) Miscibility
   (w) Organic and inorganic
   (x) Oxidation potential
   (y) pH
   (z) Physical state (solid, liquid, gas)
   (aa) Polymerization
   (bb) Radioactivity
   (cc) Saturated, unsaturated, and aromatic hydrocarbons
   (dd) Self-accelerating decomposition temperature (SADT)
   (ee) Solution, slurry
   (ff) Specific gravity
   (gg) Strength
   (hh) Sublimation
   (ii) Temperature of product
   (jj) Toxic products of combustion
   (kk) Vapor density
   (ll) Vapor pressure
   (mm) Viscosity
   (nn) Volatility
   (oo) Water reactivity
   (pp) Water solubility

(3) Describe the heat transfer processes that occur as a result of a cryogenic liquid spill specifically for chlorine.

(4) Given a hazardous material scenarios and the appropriate reference materials, identify the signs and symptoms of exposure to each material and the target organ effects of exposure to that material.

(5) Given the scenario of a chlorine line break determine the area of evacuation.

(6) Identify two methods for determining the pressure in bulk packaging or facility containers.

(7) Identify one method for determining the amount of lading remaining in damaged bulk packaging or facility containers.

(8) Describe the condition of the container involved in the incident.

(9) Given simulated facility and transportation container damage, the hazardous materials technician should describe the damage.

(10) Given examples of containers, DOT specification markings for nonbulk and bulk packaging, and the appropriate reference guide, identify the basic design and construction features of each container.

(11) Identify the basic design and construction features, including closures, of the following bulk containers:
   (a) Cargo tanks:
      i. Dry bulk cargo tanks
      ii. MC-306/DOT-406 cargo tanks
      iii. MC-307/DOT-407 cargo tanks
      iv. MC-312/DOT-412 cargo tanks
      v. MC-331 cargo tanks
      vi. MC-338 cargo tanks
   (b) Railroad cars:
      i. Chlorine
      ii. Caustic
      iii. Cryogenic liquid tank cars
      iv. High-pressure tube cars
      v. Nonpressure tank cars
      vi. Pneumatically unloaded hopper cars
      vii. Pressure tank cars

(12) Identify the basic design and construction features including closures of the following non-bulk containers for chlorine and caustic.

(13) Identify the types of damage that a pressure container could incur.
(14) Given examples of tank car damage, identify the type of damage in each example by name.

I.6.3 Predicting Likely Behavior of Materials and Their Containers When Multiple Materials Are Involved. Given examples of both facility and transportation incidents involving multiple hazardous materials, the hazardous materials technician shall predict the likely behavior of the material in each case. The hazardous materials technician should be able to do the following:

(1) Identify resources available that indicate the effects of mixing various hazardous materials.
(2) Identify the impact of the following fire and safety features on the behavior of the products during an incident at a bulk storage facility and explain their significance in the risk assessment process:
  (a) Fire protection systems
  (b) Monitoring and detection systems
  (c) Product spillage and control (impoundment and diking)
  (d) Tank spacing
  (e) Tank venting and flaring systems
  (f) Transfer operations

I.6.4 Estimating the Likely Size of an Endangered Area for Chlorine and Caustic. Given various containers and transportation hazardous materials incidents, the hazardous materials technician should estimate the likely size, shape, and concentrations associated with the release of materials involved in the incident by using computer modeling, monitoring equipment, or specialists in this field. The hazardous materials technician should be able to do the following:

(1) Identify local resources for dispersion pattern prediction and modeling including computers, monitoring equipment, or specialists in the field
(2) Given the concentrations of the released material, identify the steps for determining the extent of the hazards (e.g., physical, safety, and health) within the endangered area of a hazardous materials incident
(3) Describe the following toxicological terms and exposure values and explain their significance in the risk assessment process:
  (a) Parts per million (ppm)
  (b) Parts per billion (ppb)
  (c) Lethal dose (LD50)
  (d) Lethal concentrations (LC50)
  (e) Permissible exposure limit (PEL)
  (f) Threshold limit value time-weighted average (TLV-TWA)
  (g) Threshold limit value short-term exposure limit (TLV-STEL)
  (h) Threshold limit value ceiling (TLV-C)
  (i) Immediately dangerous to life and health value (IDLH)

I.6.5 Identifying Response Objectives. Given simulated chlorine and caustic containers and transportation problems, the hazardous materials technician should describe the response objectives for each problem. The hazardous materials technician should be able to describe the steps for determining response objectives (defensive, offensive, nonintervention) given an analysis of a hazardous materials incident.

I.6.6 Identifying the Potential Action Options. Given simulated facility and transportation hazardous materials incidents, the hazardous materials technician should identify the possible action options (defensive, offensive, and nonintervention) by response objective for each problem. The hazardous materials technician should be able to identify the possible action options to accomplish a given response objective.

I.6.7 Selecting Personal Protective Equipment. Given situations with chlorine, caustic and unknown hazardous materials, the hazardous materials technician should determine the appropriate personal protective equipment for the action options specified in the plan of action in each situation. The hazardous materials technician should be able to do the following:

(1) Identify the four levels of personal protective equipment (EPA/NIOSH or NFPA 472) and describe the equipment for each level and the condition under which each level is used
(2) Identify the factors to be considered in selecting the proper respiratory protection for a specified action option
(3) Describe the advantages, limitations, and proper use of the following types of respiratory protection at hazardous materials incidents:
  (a) Positive pressure self-contained breathing apparatus
  (b) Positive pressure air line respirators with required escape unit
  (c) Air-purifying respirators
(4) Identify the process for selecting the proper respiratory protection at hazardous materials incidents
(5) Identify the operational components of air purifying respirators and airline respirators by name and describe their functions
(6) Identify the factors to be considered in selecting the proper chemical-protective clothing for a specified action option
(7) Describe the following terms and explain their impact and significance on the selection of chemical-protective clothing:
  (a) Degradation
  (b) Penetration
  (c) Permeation
(8) Identify at least three indications of material degradation of chemical-protective clothing
(9) Identify the three types of vapor-protective and splash-protective clothing and describe the advantages and disadvantages of each type
(10) Identify the relative advantages and disadvantages of the following heat exchange units used for the cooling of personnel in chemical-protective clothing:
  (a) Air-cooled
  (b) Ice-cooled
  (c) Water-cooled
(11) Identify the process for selecting the proper protective clothing at hazardous materials incidents
(12) For chlorine and caustic determine the appropriate protective clothing construction materials for a given action option using chemical compatibility charts
(13) Identify the physical and psychological stresses that can affect users of specialized protective clothing

I.6.8 Developing Appropriate Decontamination Procedures. For chlorine and caustic incidents, the hazardous materials technician should select an appropriate decontamination procedure and determine the equipment required to implement that procedure. The hazardous materials technician should be able to identify the advantages and limitations and describe an

be invalid or unconstitutional, such decision shall not affect the validity or constitutionality of the remaining portions of this ordinance. The *[governing body]* hereby declares that it would have passed this ordinance, and each section, subsection, clause, or phrase hereof, irrespective of the fact that any one or more sections, subsections, sentences, clauses, and phrases be declared unconstitutional.

SECTION 6 That the *[jurisdiction's keeper of records]* is hereby ordered and directed to cause this ordinance to be published.

[NOTE: An additional provision may be required to direct the number of times the ordinance is to be published and to specify that it is to be in a newspaper in general circulation. Posting may also be required.]

SECTION 7 That this ordinance and the rules, regulations, provisions, requirements, orders, and matters established and adopted hereby shall take effect and be in full force and effect *[time period]* from and after the date of its final passage and adoption.

Annex K   Informational References

K.1 Referenced Publications. The documents or portions thereof listed in this annex are referenced within the informational sections of this code and are not part of the requirements of this document unless also listed in Chapter 2 for other reasons.

K.1.1 NFPA Publications. National Fire Protection Association, 1 Batterymarch Park, Quincy, MA 02169-7471.

NFPA 1, *Fire Code*, 2012 edition.

NFPA 13, *Standard for the Installation of Sprinkler Systems*, 2013 edition.

NFPA 30, *Flammable and Combustible Liquids Code*, 2012 edition.

NFPA 45, *Standard on Fire Protection for Laboratories Using Chemicals*, 2011 edition.

NFPA 52, *Vehicular Gaseous Fuel Systems Code*, 2010 edition.

NFPA 54, *National Fuel Gas Code*, 2012 edition.

NFPA 55, *Compressed Gases and Cryogenic Fluids Code*, 2013 edition.

NFPA 58, *Liquefied Petroleum Gas Code*, 2011 edition.

NFPA 59, *Utility LP-Gas Plant Code*, 2012 edition.

NFPA 68, *Standard on Explosion Protection by Deflagration Venting*, 2007 edition.

NFPA 69, *Standard on Explosion Prevention Systems*, 2008 edition.

NFPA 99, *Health Care Facilities Code*, 2012 edition.

NFPA 101®, *Life Safety Code®*, 2012 edition.

NFPA 220, *Standard on Types of Building Construction*, 2012 edition.

NFPA 259, *Standard Test Method for Potential Heat of Building Materials*, 2008 edition.

NFPA 472, *Standard for Competence of Responders to Hazardous Materials/Weapons of Mass Destruction Incidents*, 2013 edition.

NFPA 495, *Explosive Materials Code*, 2010 edition.

NFPA 505, *Fire Safety Standard for Powered Industrial Trucks Including Type Designations, Areas of Use, Conversions, Maintenance, and Operations*, 2011 edition.

NFPA 601, *Standard for Security Services in Fire Loss Prevention*, 2010 edition.

NFPA 704, *Standard System for the Identification of the Hazards of Materials for Emergency Response*, 2012 edition.

NFPA 730, *Guide for Premises Security*, 2011 edition.

NFPA 731, *Standard for the Installation of Electronic Premises Security Systems*, 2011 edition.

NFPA 780, *Standard for the Installation of Lightning Protection Systems*, 2011 edition.

NFPA 2001, *Standard on Clean Agent Fire Extinguishing Systems*, 2012 edition.

NFPA 5000®, *Building Construction and Safety Code®*, 2012 edition.

FPRF, *Development of an Enhanced Hazard Classification System for Oxidizers*, 2006.

FPRF, *National Oxiding Pool Chemicals Storage Fire Test Project*, 1998.

FPRF, *Oxidizer Classification Research Project: Tests and Criteria*, 2009.

FPRF, *The Transition of the Hazardous Materials Codes and the Emergence of the Threshold Quantity System to NFPA 1 UFC*, Fluer, Inc., 2008.

NFPA *Fire Protection Guide to Hazardous Materials*, 2002 edition.

SFPE, *Engineering Guide to Performance-Based Fire Protection Analysis and Design of Buildings*, 2005.

SFPE, *Handbook of Fire Protection Engineering*, 2008.

K.1.2 Other Publications.

K.1.2.1 AIChE Publications. American Institute of Chemical Engineers, Three Park Avenue, New York, NY 10016-5991, www.aiche.org.

Guidelines for Analyzing and Managing the Security Vulnerabilities of Fixed Chemical Sites, Center for Chemical Process Safety, June 2003.

Guidelines of Chemical Reactivity Evaluation and Application to Process Design, 1995.

Guidelines for Mechanical Integrity Systems, 2006.

Guidelines for Safe and Reliable Instrumented Protective Systems, 2007.

Guidelines for Safe Process Operation and Maintenance, 1995.

Guidelines for Technical Management of Chemical Process Safety, 1993.

K.1.2.2 ANSI Publications. American National Standards Institute, Inc., 25 West 43rd Street, 4th Floor, New York, NY 10036.

ANSI Z400.1, *Hazardous Industrial Chemicals—Material Safety Data Sheets—Preparation*, 2004.

K.1.2.3 API Publications. American Petroleum Institute, 1220 L Street, NW, Washington, DC, 20005-4070, www.api.org.

API Bulletin, *Security Vulnerability Assessment for the Petroleum and Petrochemical Industries*, October 2004.

API Bulletin, *Security Guidance for the Petroleum and Petrochemical Industries*, April 2005.

API Recommended Practice 70, *Security for Offshore Oil and Natural Gas Operations*.

K.1.2.4 ASME Publications. American Society of Mechanical Engineers, Three Park Avenue, New York, NY 10016-5990.

ASME *Boiler and Pressure Vessel Code*, "Rules for the Construction of Unfired Pressure Vessels," Section VIII, 2001.

K.1.2.5 ASTM Publications. ASTM International, 100 Barr Harbor Drive, P.O. Box C700, West Conshohocken, PA 19428-2959.

ASTM E 136-96a, *Standard Test Method for Behavior of Materials in a Vertical Tube Furnace at 750 Degrees C*, 1998.

ASTM E 176, *Standard Terminology of Fire Standards*, 2010.

ASTM E 1515, *Standard Test Method for Minimum Explosible Concentration of Combustible Dusts*, 2007.

ASTM E 1226, *Standard Test Method for Explosibility of Combustible Dusts*, 2010.

ASTM E 1472, *Standard Guide for Documenting Computer Software for Fire Models*, 2007.

ASTM E 2067, *Standard Practice for Full-Scale Oxygen Consumption Calorimetry Fire Tests*, 2008.

K.1.2.6 CGA Publications. Compressed Gas Association, 4221 Walney Road, Fifth Floor, Chantilly, VA 20151-2923, www.cganet.com.

CGA P-50, *Site Security Guidelines*, 2005.

CGA P-51, *Transportation Security Guideline for the Compressed Gas Industry*, 2004.

CGA P-52, *Security Guidelines for Qualifying Customers Purchasing Compressed Gases*, 2005.

Handbook of Compressed Gases, 1999.

K.1.2.7 CTC Publications. Canadian Transport Commission, Queen's Printer, Ottawa, Ontario, Canada. (Available from the Canadian Communications Group Publication Centre, Ordering Department, Ottawa, Ontario, Canada K1A 0S9.)

Transportation of Dangerous Goods Regulations.

K.1.2.8 UL Publications. Underwriters Laboratories Inc., 333 Pfingsten Road, Northbrook, IL 60062-2096.

ANSI/UL 30, *Standard for Metal Safety Cans*, 1995, Revised 2009.

ANSI/UL 558, *Standard for Safety Industrial Trucks, Internal Combustion Engine-Powered*, 1996, Revised 2010.

ANSI/UL 583, *Standard for Safety Electric-Battery-Powered Industrial Trucks*, 1996, Revised 2010.

ANSI/UL 1313, *Standard for Non-Metallic Safety Cans for Petroleum Products*, 2003, Revised 2007.

K.1.2.9 UN Publications. United Nations Publications, Sales Section, DC2-853, Dept. I004, New York, NY 10017.

Recommendations on the Transport of Dangerous Goods, Model Regulations, 14th revised edition, 2005.

Recommendation on Transportation of Dangerous Goods, Tests and Criteria, fourth edition, 2004.

K.1.2.10 U.S. Government Publications. U.S. Government Printing Office, Washington, DC 20402.

Title 16, Code of Federal Regulations, Part 1500.41.

Title 16, Code of Federal Regulations, Part 1500.42.

Title 16, Code of Federal Regulations, Part 40.

Title 29, Code of Federal Regulations, Part 1910.38.

Title 29, Code of Federal Regulations, Parts 1910.119 and 1910.120.

Title 29, Code of Federal Regulations, Part 1910.165.

Title 29, Code of Federal Regulations, Part 1910.1000.

Title 29, Code of Federal Regulations, Part 1910.1200.

Title 40, Code of Federal Regulations, Part 68.

Title 40, Code of Federal Regulations, Parts 260–299, and Parts 355 and 370.3.

Title 49, Code of Federal Regulations, Parts 100–199.

NSS 1740.16, *Safety for Hydrogen and Hydrogen Systems*, 1997.

TM5-13000 (NAVFAC P-397, AFR 88-22), "Structures to Resist the Effects of Accidental Explosions." November 1990.

U.S. Department of Transportation, *Emergency Response Guide Book*, 2008.

U.S. Department of Transportation, *Hazardous Materials Regulations*.

U.S. Department of Transportation, *Transportation of Dangerous Goods Regulations*.

U.S. EPA *High Production Volume (HPV) Challenge Program List*.

U.S. Bureau of Mines, Pittsburgh Mining and Safety Research Center, 4800 Forbes Avenue, Pittsburgh, PA 15213.

Report of Investigations 4994, *Investigations of the Explosibility of Ammonium Nitrate*, 1953.

Report of Investigations 6746, *Sympathetic Detonation of Ammonium Nitrate and Ammonium Nitrate Fuel Oil*, 1966.

Report of Investigations 6773, *Explosion Hazards of Ammonium Nitrate Under Fire Exposure*, 1966.

Report of Investigations 6903, *Further Studies on Sympathetic Detonation*, 1966.

K.1.2.11 Other Publications.

Bretherick's Handbook of Reactive Chemical Hazards, Elsevier Science and Technology Books, 7th ed., 2007.

Chlorine Institute, *The Security Management Plan for the Transportation and On-site Storage and Use of Chlorine Cylinders, Ton Containers and Cargo Tanks*, The Chlorine Institute, 1300 Wilson Boulevard, Arlington, VA 22209, www.chlorineinstitute.org.

Comprehensive Guide to Hazardous Properties of Chemical Substances, 3rd ed., Wiley Interscience, Hoboken, NJ, 2007.

Federal Motor Carrier Safety Administration (FMCSA), *Guide to Developing an Effective Security Plan for the Highway Transportation of Hazardous Materials*, Federal Motor Carrier Safety Administration, United States Department of Transportation, 400 7th Street SW, Washington, DC 20590, www.fmcsa.dot.gov.

Guidelines for Writing Effective Operating and Maintenance Procedures,

NAERG, *North America Emergency Response Guide*, USDOT, Transport Canada, and Secretariat of Communications and Transportation of Mexico (SCT), 2008.

Nitric Acid and Fertilizer Nitrates, edited by Cornelius Keleti, published by Marcel Dekker, Inc., 1985.

OECD (*Organization for Economic Co-operation and Development*) *Integrated HPV Database*, OECD, Paris, France.

Organic Peroxide Safety Division Society of the Plastics Industry, www.OPPSD.org.

Responsible Care Management System® and Responsible Care® Security Code of Management Practices, American Chemistry Council, 700 Second Street, NE, Washington, DC 20002, www.americanchemistry.com.

Responsible Distribution Process, National Association of Chemical Distributors, 1560 Wilson Boulevard, Arlington, VA 22209, www.nacd.com.

Safety Library Publication No. 27 (SLP-27), *Security in Manufacturing, Transportation, Storage and Use of Commercial Explosives*, January 2005. Institute of Makers of Explosives, 1120 Nineteenth Street, NW, Suite 310, Washington, DC 20036, www.ime.org.

Scott Specialty Gases, *Design and Safety Handbook*, 4th ed., Pennsylvania, 2006.

Summary Report, Workshop on Ammonium Nitrate, 30 January–1 February 2002, Major Accident Hazard Bureau, European Commission's Joint Research Center, Ispra, Italy, p. 5.

The Fertilizer Manual, 1998, Kluwer Academic Publishers, The United Nations Industrial Development Organization and the International Fertilizer Development Center.

K.2 Informational References. The following documents or portions thereof are listed here as informational resources only. They are not a part of the requirements of this document.

K.2.1 NFPA Publications. National Fire Protection Association, 1 Batterymarch Park, Quincy, MA 02169-7471.

NFPA 10, *Standard for Portable Fire Extinguishers*, 2010 edition.

NFPA 14, *Standard for the Installation of Standpipe and Hose Systems*, 2010 edition.

NFPA 24, *Standard for the Installation of Private Fire Service Mains and Their Appurtenances*, 2013 edition.

NFPA 25, *Standard for the Inspection, Testing, and Maintenance of Water-Based Fire Protection Systems*, 2011 edition.

NFPA 51, *Standard for the Design and Installation of Oxygen–Fuel Gas Systems for Welding, Cutting, and Allied Processes*, 2013 edition.

NFPA 53, *Recommended Practice on Materials, Equipment, and Systems Used in Oxygen-Enriched Atmospheres*, 2011 edition.

NFPA 59A, *Standard for the Production, Storage, and Handling of Liquefied Natural Gas (LNG)*, 2013 edition.

NFPA 70®, *National Electrical Code®*, 2011 edition.

NFPA 77, *Recommended Practice on Static Electricity*, 2007 edition.

NFPA 86, *Standard for Ovens and Furnaces*, 2011 edition.

NFPA 221, *Standard for High Challenge Fire Walls, Fire Walls, and Fire Barrier Walls*, 2012 edition.

NFPA 251, *Standard Methods of Tests of Fire Resistance of Building Construction and Materials*, 2006 edition.

NFPA 496, *Standard for Purged and Pressurized Enclosures for Electrical Equipment*, 2008 edition.

NFPA 560, *Standard for the Storage and Handling, and Use of Ethylene Oxide for Sterilization and Fumigation*, 2007 edition.

NFPA 654, *Standard for the Prevention of Fire and Dust Explosions from the Manufacturing, Processing, and Handling of Combustible Particulate Solids*, 2013 edition.

K.2.2 Other Publications.

OPPSD/SPI. *Organic Peroxide Producers Safety Division*, The Society of the Plastics Industry, Inc., 1667 K Street, NW, Suite 1000, Washington, DC 20006-1620, www.OPPSD.org.

K.3 References for Extracts in Informational Sections.

ASTM E 176-10, *Standard Terminology of Fire Standards*, 2010.

NFPA 30, *Flammable and Combustible Liquids Code*, 2012 edition.

NFPA 55, *Compressed Gases and Cryogenic Fluids Code*, 2013 edition.

NFPA 101®, *Life Safety Code®*, 2012 edition.

NFPA 505, *Fire Safety Standard for Powered Industrial Trucks Including Type Designations, Areas of Use, Conversions, Maintenance, and Operations*, 2011 edition.

NFPA 654, *Standard for the Prevention of Fire and Dust Explosions from the Manufacturing, Processing, and Handling of Combustible Particulate Solids*, 2013 edition.

NFPA 704, *Standard System for the Identification of the Hazards of Materials for Emergency Response*, 2012 edition.

NFPA 5000®, *Building Construction and Safety Code®*, 2012 edition.

Index

Copyright © 2012 National Fire Protection Association. All Rights Reserved.

The copyright in this index is separate and distinct from the copyright in the document that it indexes. The licensing provisions set forth for the document are not applicable to this index. This index may not be reproduced in whole or in part by any means without the express written permission of NFPA.

-A-

Absolute Pressure (Gas)
   Definition 3.3.1, A.3.3.1
Administration .... Chap. 1
   Application 1.3
      Buildings 1.3.4
      Conflicts 1.3.1
      Multiple Occupancies 1.3.2
      Severability 1.3.5
      Vehicles and Marine Vessels 1.3.3
   Emergency Planning 1.10
      Activation 1.10.2
      Emergency Action Plan 1.10.1
   Enforcement 1.7
   Equivalency 1.5
      Alternatives 1.5.3
      Approval 1.5.8
      Modifications 1.5.4
      Tests 1.5.9
   Facility Closure 1.9
      Closure Plan 1.9.4
      Facilities Out of Service 1.9.3
         Facilities Permanently Out of Service ... 1.9.3.2
         Facilities Temporarily Out of Service 1.9.3.1
   Hazardous Materials Inventory Statement (HMIS) 1.12, A.1.12
   Hazardous Materials Management Plan (HMMP) 1.11
   Permits 1.8, A.1.8
      Plans and Specifications 1.8.1
      Stop Work or Evacuation 1.8.2
   Plan Review 1.13
   Purpose 1.2, A.1.2
   Retroactivity 1.4
   Scope 1.1
      Applicability 1.1.1, A.1.1.1
         Multiple Hazards 1.1.1.2
         Occupancies 1.1.1.1
      Exemptions 1.1.2
   Technical Assistance 1.14
   Units and Formulas 1.6
Alternative Calculation Procedure
   Definition 3.4.1
      Ambulatory Health Care Occupancies 5.2.1.6
Ammonium Nitrate Solids and Liquids .... Chap. 11
   General 11.1
      Construction Requirements 11.1.5
   General Requirements for Storage 11.2
      Alarms (Reserved) 11.2.10, A.11.2.10
      Drainage 11.2.2
      Emergency and Standby Power 11.2.8
      Explosion Control 11.2.7
      Fire Protection Systems 11.2.6
         Automatic Sprinklers 11.2.6.1
            Packaged in Bags 11.2.6.1.1
         Extinguishing Devices 11.2.6.2
         Fire Protection Water Supplies 11.2.6.3
         Remote Areas 11.2.6.4
      Limit Controls 11.2.9
      Monitoring/Supervision 11.2.11
      Secondary Containment 11.2.3
      Special Requirements 11.2.12
         Control of Access 11.2.12.5
         Incompatible Materials 11.2.12.2

         Lightning 11.2.12.4, A.11.2.12.4
         Prohibited Articles 11.2.12.3
         Separation 11.2.12.1
      Spill Control 11.2.1
      Treatment Systems (Reserved) 11.2.5, A.11.2.5
      Ventilation 11.2.4
   General Requirements for Use 11.5
      Alarms 11.5.10, A.11.5.10
      Clearance from Combustibles (Reserved) 11.5.12
      Drainage 11.5.2
      Emergency and Standby Power 11.5.8
      Explosion Control 11.5.7
      Fire Protection System 11.5.6
      Floors 11.5.13
      Limit Controls 11.5.9
      Liquid Transfer 11.5.15
      Monitoring/Supervision 11.5.11
      Secondary Containment 11.5.3
      Special Requirements (Reserved) 11.5.16
      Spill Control 11.5.1
      System Design 11.5.14
      Treatment Systems (Reserved) 11.5.5, A.11.5.5
      Ventilation 11.5.4
   Handling 11.8
      Handling 11.8.1
         Handling Equipment 11.8.1.2, A.11.8.1.2
         Vehicles and Lift Trucks 11.8.1.1
      Special Requirements (Reserved) 11.8.2, A.11.8.2
   Indoor Storage 11.3
      Detached Storage 11.3.4
      Detection Systems (Reserved) 11.3.1, A.11.3.1
      Floors 11.3.3
      Special Requirements (Reserved) 11.3.5, A.11.3.5
      Storage Conditions/Arrangement 11.3.2
         Containers 11.3.2.1
         Piles of Bags, Drums, or Other Containers 11.3.2.2
         Piles of Bulk Solid Storage 11.3.2.3
            Compartments 11.3.2.3.3
   Indoor Use 11.6
      Closed Systems 11.6.2
         Explosion Control 11.6.2.2
         Special Requirements (Reserved) 11.6.2.4, A.11.6.2.4
         Spill Control, Drainage, and Containment 11.6.2.3
         Ventilation 11.6.2.1
      Open Systems 11.6.1
         Explosion Control 11.6.1.2
         Special Requirements (Reserved) 11.6.1.4, A.11.6.1.4
         Spill Control, Drainage, and Containment 11.6.1.3
         Ventilation 11.6.1.1
   Outdoor Storage 11.4
      Exposures 11.4.1
         Clearance from Combustibles 11.4.1.1
      Special Requirements — Outdoor Storage 11.4.3, A.11.4.3
      Weather Protection 11.4.2
   Outdoor Use 11.7
      Closed Systems 11.7.2
         Clearance from Combustibles (Reserved) 11.7.2.3, A.11.7.2.3
         Location 11.7.2.1
         Special Requirements (Reserved) 11.7.2.4, A.11.7.2.4
         Spill Control, Drainage, and Containment 11.7.2.2

INDEX

Open Systems 11.7.1
    Clearance from Combustibles 11.7.1.3
    Location 11.7.1.1
    Special Requirements (Reserved) 11.7.1.4, A.11.7.1.4
    Spill Control, Drainage, and Containment 11.7.1.2

Analysis
Definition 3.4.2
Sensitivity Analysis
    Definition 3.4.2.1
Uncertainty Analysis
    Definition 3.4.2.2

Approved
Definition 3.2.1, A.3.2.1

Area
Control Area
    Definition 3.3.2.1
Definition 3.3.2
Indoor Area (Gas)
    Definition 3.3.2.2
Organic Peroxide Storage Area
    Definition 3.3.2.3
Outdoor Area (Gas)
    Definition 3.3.2.4
Outdoor Control Area
    Definition 3.3.2.5

ASME
Definition 3.3.3
    Assembly Occupancies 5.2.1.2

ASTM (Gas)
Definition 3.3.4

Authority Having Jurisdiction (AHJ)
Definition 3.2.2, A.3.2.2

-B-

Basement
Definition 3.3.5

Building
Definition 3.3.6

Building Code
Definition 3.3.7

Bulk Hydrogen Compressed Gas System (Gas)
Definition 3.3.8, A.3.3.8

Bulk Inert Gas System (Gas)
Definition 3.3.9, A.3.3.9

Bulk Liquefied Hydrogen Gas System (Gas)
Definition 3.3.10, A.3.3.10

Bulk Oxygen System (Gas)
Definition 3.3.11, A.3.3.11
    Business Occupancies 5.2.1.10

-C-

CFR
Definition 3.3.12

CGA (Gas)
Definition 3.3.13

Chemical Data .... Annex B

Classification of Materials, Wastes, and Hazard of Contents .... Chap. 4
Classification of High Hazard Contents 4.2
    General 4.2.1
Classification of Waste 4.5, A.4.5
Hazardous Material Classification 4.1, A.4.1
Mixtures 4.3
Multiple Hazards 4.4, A.4.4

Code
Definition 3.2.3, A.3.2.3

Combustible
Definition 3.3.14

Combustible Dust
Definition 3.3.15, A.3.3.15

Combustible Liquid
Definition 3.3.16

Compressed Gas System
Definition 3.3.17, A.3.3.17

Compressed Gases and Cryogenic Fluids .... Annex H

Consumer Fireworks
Definition 3.3.18

Container
Aboveground Tank (Flammable and Combustible Liquid)
    Definition 3.3.19.13
Aerosol Container (Liquid)
    Definition 3.3.19.20
ASME Container
    Definition 3.3.19.3
Closed Container (Flammable and Combustible Liquid)
    Definition 3.3.19.2
Combustible Containers
    Definition 3.3.19.4
Compressed Gas Container (Gas)
    Definition 3.3.19.17
Container (Flammable and Combustible Liquid)
    Definition 3.3.19.1, A.3.3.19.1
Cylinder (Gas)
    Definition 3.3.19.16, A.3.3.19.16
Cylinder Containment Vessel (Gas)
    Definition 3.3.19.11
Definition 3.3.19
Ethylene Oxide Drum
    Definition 3.3.19.7
Intermediate Bulk Container (IBC) —
    (Flammable and Combustible Liquid)
    Definition 3.3.19.8
ISO Module
    Definition 3.3.19.18, A.3.3.19.18
Noncombustible Containers
    Definition 3.3.19.5
Nonmetallic Container
    (Solid, Flammable and Combustible Liquid)
    Definition 3.3.19.6, A.3.3.19.6
Nonmetallic Intermediate Bulk Container
    (Flammable and Combustible Liquid)
    Definition 3.3.19.9, A.3.3.19.9
Overpack Container
    Definition 3.3.19.10
Portable Tank (Flammable and Combustible Liquid)
    Definition 3.3.19.14, A.3.3.19.14
Pressure Vessel
    Definition 3.3.19.15, A.3.3.19.15
Safety Can (Liquid)
    Definition 3.3.19.19, A.3.3.19.19
Storage Tank (Flammable and Combustible Liquid)
    Definition 3.3.19.12

Continuous Gas Detection System (Gas)
Definition 3.3.20

Corrosive Solids and Liquids .... Chap. 12
General 12.1
    Construction Requirements 12.1.1
General Requirements for Storage 12.2
    Alarms (Reserved) 12.2.10, A.12.2.10
    Drainage 12.2.2
    Emergency and Standby Power 12.2.8
    Explosion Control 12.2.7
    Fire Protection Systems 12.2.6
    Limit Controls 12.2.9
    Monitoring/Supervision 12.2.11
    Secondary Containment 12.2.3
    Special Requirements (Reserved) 12.2.12, A.12.2.12
    Spill Control 12.2.1
    Treatment Systems 12.2.5, A.12.2.5
    Ventilation 12.2.4
General Requirements for Use 12.5
    Alarms (Reserved) 12.5.10, A.12.5.10
    Clearance from Combustibles 12.5.12
    Drainage 12.5.2

2013 Edition

HAZARDOUS MATERIALS CODE

Emergency and Standby Power 12.5.8
Explosion Control 12.5.7
Fire Protection System 12.5.6
Floors 12.5.13
Limit Controls 12.5.9
Liquid Transfer 12.5.15
Monitoring/Supervision 12.5.11
Secondary Containment 12.5.3
Special Requirements (Reserved) 12.5.16, A.12.5.16
Spill Control 12.5.1
System Design 12.5.14
Treatment Systems (Reserved) 12.5.5, A.12.5.5
Ventilation 12.5.4
Handling 12.8
Handling 12.8.1
Special Requirements (Reserved) 12.8.2, A.12.8.2
Indoor Storage 12.3
Detached Storage 12.3.4
Detection Systems (Reserved) 12.3.1, A.12.3.1
Floors 12.3.3
Special Requirements (Reserved) 12.3.5, A.12.3.5
Storage Conditions/Arrangement (Reserved) 12.3.2, A.12.3.2
Reserved 12.3.2.1, A.12.3.2.1
Indoor Use 12.6
Closed Systems 12.6.2
Explosion Control 12.6.2.2
Special Requirements (Reserved) 12.6.2.4, A.12.6.2.4
Spill Control, Drainage, and Containment 12.6.2.3
Ventilation 12.6.2.1
Open Systems 12.6.1
Explosion Control 12.6.1.2
Special Requirements (Reserved) 12.6.1.4, A.12.6.1.4
Spill Control, Drainage, and Containment 12.6.1.3
Ventilation 12.6.1.1
Outdoor Storage 12.4
Exposures 12.4.1
Clearance from Combustibles 12.4.1.1
Distance Reduction 12.4.1.3
Location 12.4.1.2
Special Requirements (Reserved) 12.4.3, A.12.4.3
Weather Protection 12.4.2
Outdoor Use 12.7
Closed Systems 12.7.2
Clearance from Combustibles 12.7.2.3
Location 12.7.2.1
Special Requirements (Reserved) 12.7.2.4, A.12.7.2.4
Spill Control, Drainage, and Containment 12.7.2.2
Open Systems 12.7.1
Clearance from Combustibles 12.7.1.3
Location 12.7.1.1
Special Requirements (Reserved) 12.7.1.4, A.12.7.1.4
Spill Control, Drainage, and Containment 12.7.1.2
Court
Definition 3.3.21
Enclosed Court
Definition 3.3.21.1
Cryogenic Fluid (Gas)
Definition 3.3.22
Cylinder (Gas)
Definition 3.3.23, A.3.3.23
Cylinder Containment System (Gas)
Definition 3.3.24
Cylinder Containment Vessel (Gas)
Definition 3.3.25
Cylinder Pack (Gas)
Definition 3.3.26, A.3.3.26

-D-

Data Conversion
Definition 3.4.3
Day-Care Occupancies 5.2.1.4

Definitions .... Chap. 3
Deflagration
Definition 3.3.27
Design Fire Scenario
Definition 3.4.4
Design Specification
Definition 3.4.5
Design Team
Definition 3.4.6
Detached Building
Definition 3.3.28
Detention and Correctional Occupancies 5.2.1.7
Detonation
Definition 3.3.29
Different Classifications 14.2.12.1.1
Distributor (Gas)
Definition 3.3.30
DOT
Definition 3.3.31

-E-

Educational Occupancies 5.2.1.3
Emergency Planning, Fire Risk Control, and Chemical Hazard Requirements for Industrial Processes .... Chap. 7
Document Retention 7.6
General 7.1, A.7.1
Analysis of Upset Conditions 7.1.2
Applicability 7.1.1
Substantiating Documentation 7.1.3
Incident Investigation Plan 7.5
Documentation 7.5.2
General 7.5.1, A.7.5.1
Operating and Maintenance Procedures 7.3
Maintenance Procedures 7.3.2
Contents 7.3.2.2, A.7.3.2.2
General 7.3.2.1
Operating Procedures 7.3.1
Contents 7.3.1.2, A.7.3.1.2
General 7.3.1.1
Review 7.3.1.3
Process Review and Plan Preparation 7.2
Emergency Action Planning 7.2.3
Plan Access 7.2.3.3
Plan Review 7.2.3.4
Plan Updating 7.2.3.5
Provisions Within the Emergency Action Plan 7.2.3.2
Written Emergency Action Plan 7.2.3.1
Fire Risk Controls 7.2.2
General 7.2.1, A.7.2.1
Safety Reviews 7.4, A.7.4
Emergency Response
Definition 3.3.32
Emergency Response Guideline .... Annex I
Emergency Response Liaison
Definition 3.3.33
Emergency Shutoff Valve (Gas)
Automatic Emergency Shutoff Valve (Gas)
Definition 3.3.34.1
Definition 3.3.34
Manual Emergency Shutoff Valve (Gas)
Definition 3.3.34.2
Equipment, Devices, and Systems Requiring Testing 6.1.17.2.1
Excess Flow Control (Gas)
Definition 3.3.35
Exhausted Enclosure (Gas)
Definition 3.3.36, A.3.3.36
Explanatory Material .... Annex A
Explosion Control (Gas)
Definition 3.3.37, A.3.3.37

Explosion Vent
   Definition 3.3.38
Explosive
   Definition 3.3.39, A.3.3.39
Explosive Decomposition
   Definition 3.3.40, A.3.3.40
Explosive Reaction
   Definition 3.3.41, A.3.3.41
Exposure Fire
   Definition 3.4.7, A.3.4.7

-F-

Fire Model
   Definition 3.4.8, A.3.4.8
Fire Prevention Code
   Definition 3.3.42
Fire Protection System
   Definition 3.3.43
Fire Scenario
   Definition 3.4.9, A.3.4.9
   Design Fire Scenario
      Definition 3.4.9.1
Flammable Liquid (Class I)
   Definition 3.3.44, A.3.3.44
Flammable Solid
   Definition 3.3.45, A.3.3.45
Flammable Solids .... Chap. 13
   General 13.1
      Construction Requirements 13.1.1
   General Requirements for Storage 13.2
      Alarms (Reserved) 13.2.10, A.13.2.10
      Drainage 13.2.2
      Emergency and Standby Power 13.2.8
      Explosion Control 13.2.7
      Fire Protection Systems 13.2.6
      Limit Controls 13.2.9
      Monitoring/Supervision 13.2.11
      Secondary Containment 13.2.3
      Special Requirements (Reserved) 13.2.12, A.13.2.12
      Spill Control 13.2.1
      Treatment Systems (Reserved) 13.2.5, A.13.2.5
      Ventilation 13.2.4
   General Requirements for Use 13.5
      Alarms (Reserved) 13.5.10, A.13.5.10
      Clearance from Combustibles 13.5.12
      Drainage 13.5.2
      Emergency and Standby Power 13.5.8
      Explosion Control 13.5.7
      Fire Protection System 13.5.6
      Floors 13.5.13
      Limit Controls 13.5.9
      Monitoring/Supervision 13.5.11
      Secondary Containment 13.5.3
      Special Requirements (Reserved) 13.5.15, A.13.5.15
      Spill Control 13.5.1
      System Design 13.5.14
      Treatment Systems (Reserved) 13.5.5, A.13.5.5
      Ventilation 13.5.4
   Handling 13.8
      Handling 13.8.1
      Special Requirements (Reserved) 13.8.2, A.13.8.2
   Indoor Storage 13.3
      Detached Storage 13.3.4
      Detection Systems (Reserved) 13.3.1, A.13.3.1
      Floors 13.3.3
      Special Requirements (Reserved) 13.3.5, A.13.3.5
      Storage Conditions/Arrangement (Reserved) 13.3.2, A.13.3.2
         Reserved 13.3.2.1, A.13.3.2.1
   Indoor Use 13.6
      Closed Systems 13.6.2
         Explosion Control 13.6.2.2

         Special Requirements (Reserved) 13.6.2.4, A.13.6.2.4
         Spill Control, Drainage, and Containment 13.6.2.3
         Ventilation 13.6.2.1
      Open Systems 13.6.1
         Explosion Control 13.6.1.2
         Special Requirements (Reserved) 13.6.1.4, A.13.6.1.4
         Spill Control, Drainage, and Containment 13.6.1.3
         Ventilation 13.6.1.1
   Outdoor Storage 13.4
      Exposures 13.4.1
         Clearance from Combustibles 13.4.1.1
         Distance Reduction 13.4.1.3
         Location 13.4.1.2
      Special Requirements (Reserved) 13.4.3, A.13.4.3
         Aisles 13.4.3.2
         Pile Size Limit 13.4.3.1
      Weather Protection 13.4.2
   Outdoor Use 13.7
      Closed Systems 13.7.2
         Clearance from Combustibles 13.7.2.3
         Location 13.7.2.1
         Special Requirements (Reserved) 13.7.2.4, A.13.7.2.4
         Spill Control, Drainage, and Containment 13.7.2.2
      Open Systems 13.7.1
         Clearance from Combustibles 13.7.1.3
         Location 13.7.1.1
         Special Requirements (Reserved) 13.7.1.4, A.13.7.1.4
         Spill Control, Drainage, and Containment 13.7.1.2
Fuel Load
   Definition 3.4.10, A.3.4.10
Fundamental Requirements .... Chap. 6
   General Requirements 6.1
      Applicability 6.1.1
      Electrical Wiring and Equipment 6.1.10
         General 6.1.10.1
         Static Accumulation 6.1.10.2
      Empty Containers and Tanks 6.1.7
      General Storage 6.1.13
         Shelf Storage 6.1.13.2
            Shelf Construction 6.1.13.2.1
         Storage 6.1.13.1
      Hazardous Materials Storage Cabinets 6.1.18
      Ignition Source Controls 6.1.5
         Energy-Consuming Equipment 6.1.5.3
            Powered Industrial Trucks 6.1.5.3.1, A.6.1.5.3.1
         Open Flames and High-Temperature Devices 6.1.5.2
         Smoking 6.1.5.1
      Installation of Tanks 6.1.19
         Aboveground Tanks 6.1.19.2
            Marking 6.1.19.2.3
         Underground Tanks 6.1.19.1
      Maintenance Required 6.1.16
      Material Safety Data Sheets (MSDS) 6.1.2, A.6.1.2
      Outdoor Storage and Use Areas 6.1.15
      Personnel Training 6.1.4, A.6.1.4
         Awareness 6.1.4.1
            Completion 6.1.4.1.1
            Emergency Plan 6.1.4.1.3
            Hazard Communications 6.1.4.1.2
         Documentation 6.1.4.6
         Emergency Responders 6.1.4.4, A.6.1.4.4
            Emergency Response Team Leader ... 6.1.4.4.1, A.6.1.4.4.1
            On-Site Emergency Response Team ... 6.1.4.4.3, A.6.1.4.4.3
            Response to Incipient Events 6.1.4.4.2, A.6.1.4.4.2
         Emergency Response Liaison 6.1.4.3
         Operations Personnel 6.1.4.2
            Actions in an Emergency 6.1.4.2.5
            Changes 6.1.4.2.6
            Dispensing, Using, and Processing 6.1.4.2.2
            Physical and Health Hazard Properties 6.1.4.2.1

Storage... 6.1.4.2.3
Transport (Handling)... 6.1.4.2.4
Training Mandated by Other Agencies... 6.1.4.5
Protection from Light... 6.1.11
Protection from Vehicles... 6.1.9
Release of Hazardous Materials... 6.1.3
Container Failure... 6.1.3.5
Control and Mitigation of Unauthorized Releases... 6.1.3.2
Notification of Unauthorized Releases... 6.1.3.4, A.6.1.3.4
Overpack Containers... 6.1.3.6
Prohibited Releases... 6.1.3.1
Records of Unauthorized Releases... 6.1.3.3
Responsibility for Cleanup of Unauthorized Releases... 6.1.3.7
Seismic Protection... 6.1.14, A.6.1.14
Shock Padding... 6.1.14.1
Separation of Incompatible Materials... 6.1.12
Signs... 6.1.8
General... 6.1.8.1
Design and Construction... 6.1.8.1.1
Language... 6.1.8.1.2
Maintenance... 6.1.8.1.3
Hazardous Materials Identification... 6.1.8.2
Identification of Containers, Cartons, and Packages... 6.1.8.2.2
NFPA 704 Placard... 6.1.8.2.1
No Smoking Signs... 6.1.8.3
Systems, Equipment, and Processes... 6.1.6
Additional Regulations for Supply Piping for Health Hazard Materials... 6.1.6.3
Design and Construction of Containers and Tanks... 6.1.6.1
Equipment, Machinery, and Alarms... 6.1.6.4
Piping, Tubing, Valves, and Fittings... 6.1.6.2
Testing... 6.1.17
Requirements for Occupancies Storing Quantities of Hazardous Materials Exceeding the Maximum Allowable Quantities per Control Area for High Hazard Contents... 6.2
Indoor Storage General Requirements... 6.2.1
Building Height Exception... 6.2.1.2
Egress... 6.2.1.4
Capacity of Means of Egress... 6.2.1.4.2
Dead Ends... 6.2.1.4.4
Doors... 6.2.1.4.5
Number of Means of Egress... 6.2.1.4.3
Travel Distance Limit... 6.2.1.4.1
Explosion Control... 6.2.1.6, A.6.2.1.6
Fire Protection Systems... 6.2.1.1
Floors in Storage Rooms... 6.2.1.10
Limit Controls... 6.2.1.7
Pressure Control... 6.2.1.7.2
Temperature Control... 6.2.1.7.1
Separation of Occupancies Having High Hazards... 6.2.1.3
Spill Control and Secondary Containment for Hazardous Materials Liquids and Solids... 6.2.1.9
General... 6.2.1.9.1
Secondary Containment... 6.2.1.9.3
Spill Control... 6.2.1.9.2
Standby and Emergency Power... 6.2.1.8
Supervision of Alarm, Detection, and Automatic Fire-Extinguishing Systems... 6.2.1.11
Ventilation... 6.2.1.5
Outdoor Storage... 6.2.7
Clearance from Combustibles... 6.2.7.1
Secondary Containment... 6.2.7.3
Containment Pallets... 6.2.7.3.3
General... 6.2.7.3.1
Where Required... 6.2.7.3.2
Weather Protection... 6.2.7.2
Protection Level 1... 6.2.2
Detached Building Required... 6.2.2.2
Frangible Building... 6.2.2.4
General... 6.2.2.1
Minimum Distance to Property Lines or Horizontal Separation... 6.2.2.3
Protection Level 2... 6.2.3
Detached Building Required... 6.2.3.4
Exterior Wall Required... 6.2.3.2
General... 6.2.3.1
Minimum Distance to Property Lines or Horizontal Separation... 6.2.3.3
Water-Reactive Materials... 6.2.3.5
Protection Level 3... 6.2.4
Detached Building Required... 6.2.4.4
Detached Unprotected Building... 6.2.4.5
Exterior Wall Required... 6.2.4.2
General... 6.2.4.1
Minimum Distance to Property Lines or Horizontal Separation... 6.2.4.3
Roofs... 6.2.4.6
Water-Reactive Materials... 6.2.4.7
Protection Level 4... 6.2.5
Highly Toxic Solids and Liquids... 6.2.5.2
Protection Level 5... 6.2.6
Requirements for Use, Dispensing, and Handling of Hazardous Materials in Amounts Exceeding Maximum Allowable Quantities... 6.3
General... 6.3.1, A.6.3.1
Lighting... 6.3.1.5
Limit Controls... 6.3.1.2
General... 6.3.1.2.1
Liquid Level... 6.3.1.2.4
Pressure Control... 6.3.1.2.3
Temperature Control... 6.3.1.2.2
Liquid Transfer... 6.3.1.7
Spill Control and Secondary Containment for Hazardous Materials Liquids... 6.3.1.4
Secondary Containment... 6.3.1.4.2
Spill Control... 6.3.1.4.1
Standby and Emergency Power... 6.3.1.3
Supervision of Alarm, Detection, and Automatic Fire-Extinguishing Systems... 6.3.1.8
System Design... 6.3.1.6
Uses Not Required to Comply... 6.3.1.1
Handling... 6.3.4
Carts and Trucks... 6.3.4.3
Attendance... 6.3.4.3.5
Construction... 6.3.4.3.3
Design... 6.3.4.3.1
Incompatible Materials... 6.3.4.3.6
Speed-Control Devices... 6.3.4.3.2
Spill Control... 6.3.4.3.4
Carts and Trucks Required... 6.3.4.2
Emergency Alarm for Transportation of Hazardous Materials in Corridors or Exit Enclosures... 6.3.4.4
General... 6.3.4.1
Indoor Dispensing and Use... 6.3.2
General Indoor Requirements... 6.3.2.1
Explosion Control... 6.3.2.1.4
Fire Protection Systems... 6.3.2.1.1
Protection Level 1 through Protection Level 4... 6.3.2.1.2
Ventilation... 6.3.2.1.3
Indoor — Closed Systems... 6.3.2.3
General... 6.3.2.3.1
Spill Control and Secondary Containment for Hazardous Materials Liquids... 6.3.2.3.3
Ventilation... 6.3.2.3.2
Indoor — Open Systems... 6.3.2.2
Floor Construction... 6.3.2.2.3
General... 6.3.2.2.1
Spill Control and Secondary Containment for Hazardous Materials Liquids... 6.3.2.2.4
Ventilation... 6.3.2.2.2

INDEX

Outdoor Dispensing and Use 6.3.3
   General 6.3.3.1
      Clearance from Combustibles 6.3.3.1.2
      Location 6.3.3.1.1
      Weather Protection 6.3.3.1.3
   Outdoor — Open Systems 6.3.3.2
      General 6.3.3.2.1
      Spill Control and Secondary Containment for Hazardous Materials Liquids 6.3.3.2.2
   Outdoor — Closed Systems 6.3.3.3
      General 6.3.3.3.1
      Spill Control and Secondary Containment for Hazardous Materials Liquids 6.3.3.3.2

-G-

Gallon (Gas)
   Definition 3.3.46
Gas
   Compressed Gas (Gas)
      Definition 3.3.47.1, A.3.3.47.1
   Corrosive Gas (Gas)
      Definition 3.3.47.2
   Definition 3.3.47
   Flammable Gas (Gas)
      Definition 3.3.47.3
   Flammable Liquefied Gas (Gas)
      Definition 3.3.47.4
   Highly Toxic Gas (Gas)
      Definition 3.3.47.5
   Inert Gas (Gas)
      Definition 3.3.47.6
   Irritant Gas (Gas)
      Definition 3.3.47.7, A.3.3.47.7
   Nonflammable Gas (Gas)
      Definition 3.3.47.8
   Other Gas (Gas)
      Definition 3.3.47.9, A.3.3.47.9
   Oxidizing Gas (Gas)
      Definition 3.3.47.10
   Pyrophoric Gas (Gas)
      Definition 3.3.47.11
   Toxic Gas (Gas)
      Definition 3.3.47.12
   Unstable Reactive Gas (Gas)
      Definition 3.3.47.13, A.3.3.47.13
Gas Cabinet (Gas)
   Definition 3.3.48, A.3.3.48
Gas Manufacturer/Producer (Gas)
   Definition 3.3.49
Gas Room (Gas)
   Definition 3.3.50, A.3.3.50
Gaseous Hydrogen System (Gas)
   Definition 3.3.51, A.3.3.51
   General 5.2.1.1

-H-

Handling
   Definition 3.3.52
Hazard Rating (Gas)
   Definition 3.3.53, A.3.3.53
Hazardous Materials Management Plans and Hazardous Materials Inventory Statements .... Annex C
Hazardous Materials Storage Cabinet
   Definition 3.3.54
      Health Care Occupancies 5.2.1.5
      High Hazard Level 1 Contents 4.2.1.2.1
      High Hazard Level 2 Contents 4.2.1.2.2
      High Hazard Level 3 Contents 4.2.1.2.3
      High Hazard Level 4 Contents 4.2.1.2.4
High Hazard Level Contents
   Definition 3.3.55

High Hazard Level 1 Contents
   Definition 3.3.55.1
High Hazard Level 2 Contents
   Definition 3.3.55.2
High Hazard Level 3 Contents
   Definition 3.3.55.3
High Hazard Level 4 Contents
   Definition 3.3.55.4

-I-

Identification of Gas Rooms and Cabinets 21.2.12.1.2
Immediately Dangerous to Life and Health (IDLH) (Gas)
   Definition 3.3.56, A.3.3.56
      Industrial Occupancies 5.2.1.11
Informational References .... Annex K
Input Data Specification
   Definition 3.4.11
ISO Module (Gas)
   Definition 3.3.57, A.3.3.57

-L-

Labeled
   Definition 3.2.4
Limit
   Ceiling Limit
      Definition 3.3.58.1
   Definition 3.3.58
   Permissible Exposure Limit (PEL) (Gas)
      Definition 3.3.58.2, A.3.3.58.2
   Short-Term Exposure Limit (STEL) (Gas)
      Definition 3.3.58.3, A.3.3.58.3
Liquefied Hydrogen System (Gas)
   Definition 3.3.59, A.3.3.59
Listed
   Definition 3.2.5, A.3.2.5

-M-

Manufacturing Plants
   Definition 3.3.60
Material
   Combustible (Material)
      Definition 3.3.61.1
   Corrosive Material
      Definition 3.3.61.2, A.3.3.61.2
   Definition 3.3.61
   Hazard Material
      Definition 3.3.61.3
   Hazardous Material
      Definition 3.3.61.4, A.3.3.61.4
   Incompatible Material
      Definition 3.3.61.5, A.3.3.61.5
   Limited-Combustible (Material)
      Definition 3.3.61.6, A.3.3.61.6
   Noncombustible Material
      Definition 3.3.61.7, A.3.3.61.7
   Pyrophoric Material
      Definition 3.3.61.8
   Toxic Material
      Definition 3.3.61.9, A.3.3.61.9
   Unstable (Reactive) Material
      Definition 3.3.61.10, A.3.3.61.10
   Water-Reactive Material
      Definition 3.3.61.11, A.3.3.61.11
Material Safety Data Sheet (MSDS)
   Definition 3.3.62
Maximum Allowable Quantity Per Control Area (MAQ)
   Definition 3.3.63, A.3.3.63

2013 Edition

Mechanical Code (Gas)
   Definition 3.3.64
       Mercantile Occupancies 5.2.1.9
Mobile Supply Unit (Gas)
   Definition... 3.3.65, A.3.3.65

-N-

Nesting (Gas)
   Definition... 3.3.66, A.3.3.66
Normal Temperature and Pressure (NTP) (Gas)
   Definition... 3.3.67, A.3.3.67

-O-

Occupancy
   Assembly Occupancy
      Definition 3.3.68.1, A.3.3.68.1
   Business Occupancy
      Definition 3.3.68.2, A.3.3.68.2
   Day-Care Occupancy
      Definition 3.3.68.3, A.3.3.68.3
      Definition 3.3.68
   Detention and Correctional Occupancy
      Definition 3.3.68.4, A.3.3.68.4
   Educational Occupancy
      Definition 3.3.68.5, A.3.3.68.5
   Health Care Occupancy
      Definition 3.3.68.6, A.3.3.68.6
   Industrial Occupancy
      Definition 3.3.68.7, A.3.3.68.7
   Mercantile Occupancy
      Definition 3.3.68.8, A.3.3.68.8
   Mixed Occupancy
      Definition 3.3.68.9
   Multiple Occupancy
      Definition.................................... 3.3.68.10, A.3.3.68.10
   Residential Board and Care Occupancy
      Definition.................................... 3.3.68.11, A.3.3.68.11
   Residential Occupancy
      Definition.................................... 3.3.68.12, A.3.3.68.12
   Separated Occupancy
      Definition... 3.3.68.13
   Storage Occupancy
      Definition.................................... 3.3.68.14, A.3.3.68.14
Occupant Characteristics
   Definition 3.4.12
Organic Peroxide
   Definition 3.3.69
Organic Peroxide Formulation
   Class I
      Definition 3.3.70.1
   Class II
      Definition 3.3.70.2
   Class III
      Definition 3.3.70.3
   Class IV
      Definition 3.3.70.4
   Class V
      Definition 3.3.70.5
   Definition... 3.3.70, A.3.3.70
Organic Peroxide Formulations .... Chap. 14
   General 14.1
   Construction Requirements 14.1.2, A.14.1.2
   General Requirements for Storage 14.2
      Alarms (Reserved) 14.2.10, A.14.2.10
      Drainage... 14.2.2
      Emergency and Standby Power 14.2.8
      Explosion Control 14.2.7
      Fire Protection Systems 14.2.6
      Limit Controls 14.2.9
      Monitoring/Supervision 14.2.11

      Secondary Containment 14.2.3
      Special Requirements...................................... 14.2.12
         Combustible Waste................................... 14.2.12.7
         Cutting and Welding................................. 14.2.12.5
         Damaged Containers 14.2.12.8, A.14.2.12.8
         Electrical.. 14.2.12.6
         Heating and Cooling................................ 14.2.12.10
            Container Contact.............................. 14.2.12.10.5
            Cooling Systems 14.2.12.10.3
            Heating Systems 14.2.12.10.4
            Outside of Ambient Temperature............... 14.2.12.10.2
            Temperature Range 14.2.12.10.1
         Maintenance Operations............................. 14.2.12.4
         Packaging Marking 14.2.12.2
         Specific Disposal Procedures 14.2.12.9
         Temperature Markings............................... 14.2.12.3
      Spill Control 14.2.1
      Treatment Systems (Reserved) 14.2.5, A.14.2.5
      Ventilation................................... 14.2.4, A.14.2.4
   General Requirements for Use 14.5
      Alarms (Reserved) 14.5.10, A.14.5.10
      Clearance from Combustibles 14.5.12
      Drainage... 14.5.2
      Emergency and Standby Power.................... 14.5.8, A.14.5.8
      Explosion Control 14.5.7
      Fire Protection System 14.5.6
      Floors... 14.5.13
      Limit Controls 14.5.9
      Liquid Transfer.. 14.5.15
      Monitoring/Supervision 14.5.11
      Secondary Containment 14.5.3
      Special Requirements..................................... 14.5.16
         Waste Disposal............................ 14.5.16.3, A.14.5.16.3
      Spill Control 14.5.1
      System Design 14.5.14
      Treatment Systems (Reserved) 14.5.5, A.14.5.5
      Ventilation... 14.5.4
   Handling 14.8
      Handling 14.8.1
      Special Requirements (Reserved) 14.8.2, A.14.8.2
   Indoor Storage 14.3
      Detached Storage.. 14.3.4
         Building Construction 14.3.4.3
         Building Location 14.3.4.2
         General... 14.3.4.1
      Detection Systems 14.3.1
      Floors... 14.3.3
      Special Requirements (Reserved) 14.3.5, A.14.3.5
      Storage Conditions/Arrangement 14.3.2, A.14.3.2
         Separation Distance 14.3.2.9
         Storage Arrangements 14.3.2.8
         Storage Limitations 14.3.2.1
   Indoor Use 14.6
      Closed Systems.. 14.6.2
         Explosion Control 14.6.2.2
         Special Requirements (Reserved) 14.6.2.4, A.14.6.2.4
         Spill Control, Drainage, and Containment 14.6.2.3
         Ventilation 14.6.2.1
      Open Systems... 14.6.1
         Explosion Control 14.6.1.2
         Special Requirements (Reserved) 14.6.1.4, A.14.6.1.4
         Spill Control, Drainage, and Containment 14.6.1.3
         Ventilation 14.6.1.1
   Outdoor Storage.. 14.4
      Exposures 14.4.1
         Clearance from Combustibles........................ 14.4.1.1
         Distance Reduction 14.4.1.3
         Location.. 14.4.1.2
      Special Requirements (Reserved) 14.4.3, A.14.4.3
      Weather Protection.. 14.4.2
   Outdoor Use 14.7

INDEX

Closed Systems.. 14.7.2
    Clearance from Combustibles........................ 14.7.2.3
    Location.. 14.7.2.1
    Special Requirements (Reserved)......... 14.7.2.4, A.14.7.2.4
    Spill Control, Drainage, and Containment 14.7.2.2
Open Systems.. 14.7.1
    Clearance from Combustibles........................ 14.7.1.3
    Location.. 14.7.1.1
    Special Requirements (Reserved)......... 14.7.1.4, A.14.7.1.4
    Spill Control, Drainage, and Containment 14.7.1.2

OSHA (Gas)
Definition 3.3.71

Oxidizer
Class 1
    Definition 3.3.72.1
Class 2
    Definition 3.3.72.2
Class 3
    Definition 3.3.72.3
Class 4
    Definition 3.3.72.4
Definition.. 3.3.72, A.3.3.72

Oxidizer Solids and Liquids .... Chap. 15
General.. 15.1
    Construction Requirements................................ 15.1.3
General Requirements for Storage 15.2
    Alarms (Reserved) 15.2.10, A.15.2.10
    Drainage.. 15.2.2
    Emergency and Standby Power 15.2.8
    Explosion Control.. 15.2.7
    Fire Protection Systems 15.2.6, A.15.2.6
        Dry Pipe and Preaction Sprinkler Systems 15.2.6.1, A.15.2.6.1
        Fire Protection Water Supplies......................... 15.2.6.2
        Portable Extinguishers................................. 15.2.6.3
            Dry Chemical and CO_2 Extinguishers 15.2.6.3.1, A.15.2.6.3.1
            Halocarbon Clean Agent Extinguishers 15.2.6.3.3, A.15.2.6.3.3
            Halon Extinguishers 15.2.6.3.2, A.15.2.6.3.2
    Limit Controls 15.2.9
    Monitoring/Supervision 15.2.11
    Secondary Containment................................. 15.2.3
    Special Requirements........................ 15.2.12, A.15.2.12
        Clearance from Combustibles...................... 15.2.12.13
        Contact with Water................... 15.2.12.10, A.15.2.12.10
        Materials Not Included.............................. 15.2.12.9
        Mercantile Signage for Different Classifications.... 15.2.12.12
        Personnel Training and Procedures 15.2.12.7
        Storage Containers, Tanks, and Bins................. 15.2.12.8
            Shipping Containers............................... 15.2.12.8.1
            Tanks and Bins.................................... 15.2.12.8.2
    Spill Control 15.2.1
    Treatment Systems (Reserved) 15.2.5, A.15.2.5
    Ventilation.. 15.2.4
General Requirements for Use................................ 15.5
    Alarms (Reserved) 15.5.10, A.15.5.10
    Clearance from Combustibles 15.5.12
    Drainage.. 15.5.2
    Emergency and Standby Power 15.5.8
    Explosion Control.. 15.5.7
    Fire Protection System 15.5.6
        Portable Extinguishers................................. 15.5.6.1
            Dry Chemical and CO2 Extinguishers 15.5.6.1.1
            Halocarbon Clean Agent Extinguishers........... 15.5.6.1.3
            Halon Extinguishers 15.5.6.1.2
    Floors.. 15.5.13
    Limit Controls 15.5.9
    Liquid Transfer... 15.5.15
    Monitoring/Supervision 15.5.11
    Secondary Containment................................. 15.5.3
    Special Requirements (Reserved) 15.5.16, A.15.5.16

Spill Control 15.5.1
System Design 15.5.14
Treatment Systems (Reserved) 15.5.5, A.15.5.5
Ventilation.. 15.5.4
Handling 15.8
    Handling 15.8.1
    Special Requirements (Reserved) 15.8.2, A.15.8.2
Indoor Storage.. 15.3
    Detached Storage.. 15.3.4
    Detection Systems (Reserved) 15.3.1, A.15.3.1
    Floors.. 15.3.3
    Special Requirements.................................... 15.3.5
        Application for Mercantile, Storage, or Industrial Occupancies 15.3.5.1
        General Requirements............................... 15.3.5.2
            Containers.. 15.3.5.2.12
            Quantity Limitations............................. 15.3.5.2.13
        Storage Arrangements in Nonsprinklered Mercantile, Storage, or Industrial Occupancies 15.3.5.2.11
    Storage Conditions/Arrangement........................ 15.3.2
    Bulk Storage of Class 1 Oxidizers....................... 15.3.2.1
        Bins 15.3.2.1.3
        Bulk Storage Separation 15.3.2.1.2
        Combustible Building Materials 15.3.2.1.1, A.15.3.2.1.1
        Wooden Bins....................................... 15.3.2.1.4
    Class 2 Oxidizers 15.3.2.3
        Building Construction 15.3.2.3.3
        Detached Storage 15.3.2.3.5
        Sprinkler Protection 15.3.2.3.4
        Storage Arrangements of Class 2 Oxidizers........ 15.3.2.3.2
    Class 3 Oxidizers 15.3.2.4
        Building Construction 15.3.2.4.12
        Detached Storage 15.3.2.4.14
        Maximum Height of Storage..................... 15.3.2.4.11
        Sprinkler Criteria for Class 3 Oxidizers........... 15.3.2.4.13
        Storage of Class 3 Oxidizers........................ 15.3.2.4.5
        Type of Storage 15.3.2.4.2
    Class 4 Oxidizers 15.3.2.5
        Building Construction and Location 15.3.2.5.4
        Storage Arrangements 15.3.2.5.3
    Storage Arrangements of Class 1 Oxidizers............ 15.3.2.2
        Class 1 Detached Storage 15.3.2.2.4
        Class 1 Oxidizers 15.3.2.2.2
        Nonsprinklered Buildings 15.3.2.2.1
        Sprinkler Protection — Class 1...... 15.3.2.2.3, A.15.3.2.2.3
Indoor Use 15.6
    Closed Systems... 15.6.2
        Explosion Control.................................... 15.6.2.2
        Special Requirements (Reserved) 15.6.2.4, A.15.6.2.4
        Spill Control, Drainage, and Containment 15.6.2.3
        Ventilation.. 15.6.2.1
    Open Systems... 15.6.1
        Explosion Control.................................... 15.6.1.2
        Special Requirements (Reserved) 15.6.1.4, A.15.6.1.4
        Spill Control, Drainage, and Containment 15.6.1.3
        Ventilation 15.6.1.1
Outdoor Storage.. 15.4
    Exposures 15.4.1
        Clearance from Combustibles....................... 15.4.1.1
        Distance Reduction 15.4.1.3
        Location.. 15.4.1.2
    Special Requirements.................................... 15.4.3
    Weather Protection....................................... 15.4.2
Outdoor Use 15.7
    Closed Systems... 15.7.2
        Clearance from Combustibles....................... 15.7.2.3
        Location.. 15.7.2.1
        Special Requirements (Reserved) 15.7.2.4, A.15.7.2.4
        Spill Control, Drainage, and Containment 15.7.2.2

2013 Edition

Open Systems	15.7.1
Clearance from Combustibles	15.7.1.3
Location	15.7.1.1
Special Requirements (Reserved)	15.7.1.4, A.15.7.1.4
Spill Control, Drainage, and Containment	15.7.1.2
Oxidizers	Annex G

-P-

Performance Criteria
Definition	3.4.13, A.3.4.13

Performance-Based Option ... Chap. 10
Design Scenarios	10.4, A.10.4
General	10.4.1
Required Design Scenarios — Explosion	10.4.3
Explosion Design Scenario 1	10.4.3.1, A.10.4.3.1
Required Design Scenarios — Fire	10.4.2
Fire Design Scenario 1	10.4.2.1, A.10.4.2.1
Fire Design Scenario 2	10.4.2.2, A.10.4.2.2
Fire Design Scenario 3	10.4.2.3, A.10.4.2.3
Fire Design Scenario 4	10.4.2.4, A.10.4.2.4
Fire Design Scenario 5	10.4.2.5, A.10.4.2.5
Fire Design Scenario 6	10.4.2.6, A.10.4.2.6
Fire Design Scenario 7	10.4.2.7, A.10.4.2.7
Fire Design Scenario 8	10.4.2.8, A.10.4.2.8
Required Design Scenarios — Hazardous Materials	10.4.4, A.10.4.4
Hazardous Materials Design Scenario 1	10.4.4.1
Hazardous Materials Design Scenario 2	10.4.4.2
Hazardous Materials Design Scenario 3	10.4.4.3
Hazardous Materials Design Scenario 4	10.4.4.4
Required Design Scenarios — Safety During Building Use	10.4.5
Building Use Design Scenario 1	10.4.5.1, A.10.4.5.1
Building Use Design Scenario 2	10.4.5.2
Documentation Requirements	10.7
Design Scenarios	10.7.6
Evidence of Modeler Capability	10.7.12
Facility Design Specifications	10.7.3
General	10.7.1, A.10.7.1
Input Data	10.7.7
Modeling Features	10.7.11, A.10.7.11
Occupant Characteristics	10.7.5
Output Data	10.7.8
Performance Criteria	10.7.4
Performance Evaluation	10.7.13
Prescriptive Requirements	10.7.10
Safety Factors	10.7.9
Technical References and Resources	10.7.2, A.10.7.2
Use of Performance-Based Design Option	10.7.14
Evaluation of Proposed Designs	10.5
General	10.5.1
Input Data	10.5.3
Data	10.5.3.1
Data Requirements	10.5.3.2
Uncertainty and Conservatism of Data	10.5.3.3
Output Data	10.5.4
Use	10.5.2
Validity	10.5.5
General	10.1, A.10.1
Annual Certification	10.1.11, A.10.1.11
Application	10.1.1, A.10.1.1
Approved Qualifications	10.1.3, A.10.1.3
Design Feature Maintenance	10.1.10, A.10.1.10
Final Determination	10.1.7
Goals and Objectives	10.1.2, A.10.1.2
Hazardous Materials	10.1.12
Independent Review	10.1.5, A.10.1.5
Information Transfer to the Fire Service	10.1.9, A.10.1.9
Operations and Maintenance (O&M) Manual	10.1.8, A.10.1.8
Plan Submittal Documentation	10.1.4, A.10.1.4
Sources of Data	10.1.6
Special Definitions	10.1.13
Performance Criteria	10.2
General	10.2.1
Specific Performance Criteria	10.2.2, A.10.2.2
Emergency Responder Protection	10.2.2.7
Explosion Conditions	10.2.2.2, A.10.2.2.2
Fire Conditions	10.2.2.1, A.10.2.2.1
Hazardous Materials Exposure	10.2.2.3, A.10.2.2.3
Occupant Protection from Structural Failure	10.2.2.8
Occupant Protection from Untenable Conditions	10.2.2.6
Property Protection	10.2.2.4, A.10.2.2.4
Public Welfare	10.2.2.5, A.10.2.2.5
Retained Prescriptive Requirements	10.3
Electrical Systems	10.3.2, A.10.3.2
Equivalency	10.3.5
General	10.3.3
Means of Egress	10.3.4, A.10.3.4
Systems and Features	10.3.1
Safety Factors	10.6, A.10.6

Permissible Storage and Use Locations ... Chap. 5
Control Areas	5.2
Construction Requirements for Control Areas	5.2.2
Number of Control Areas	5.2.2.1
General	5.1, A.5.1
Control Areas or Special Protection Required	5.1.1
High Hazard Contents	5.1.3
Weather Protection Structures	5.1.2
Outdoor Areas	5.4
Outdoor Control Areas	5.4.1
General	5.4.1.1
Maximum Allowable Quantity per Outdoor Control Area	5.4.1.2
Number of Outdoor Control Areas	5.4.1.3
Outdoor Storage and Use Areas	5.4.2
Protection Levels	5.3
Detached Building Required for High Hazard Level 2 and High Hazard Level 3 Materials	5.3.7
Protection Level 1	5.3.3
Protection Level 2	5.3.4
Protection Level 3	5.3.5
Protection Level 4	5.3.6

Person
Definition	3.3.73

Pile
Definition	3.3.74

Properties and Uses of Ammonium Nitrate and Fire-Fighting Procedures ... Annex E

Proposed Design
Definition	3.4.14, A.3.4.14

Protection Level
Definition	3.3.75, A.3.3.75

Pyrophoric Solids and Liquids ... Chap. 17
General	17.1
Construction Requirements	17.1.1
General Requirements for Storage	17.2
Alarms (Reserved)	17.2.10, A.17.2.10
Drainage	17.2.2
Emergency and Standby Power	17.2.8
Explosion Control	17.2.7
Fire Protection Systems	17.2.6, A.17.2.6
Limit Controls	17.2.9
Monitoring/Supervision	17.2.11
Secondary Containment	17.2.3
Special Requirements (Reserved)	17.2.12, A.17.2.12
Spill Control	17.2.1
Treatment Systems (Reserved)	17.2.5, A.17.2.5
Ventilation	17.2.4
General Requirements for Use	17.5
Alarms (Reserved)	17.5.10, A.17.5.10
Clearance from Combustibles	17.5.12
Drainage	17.5.2
Emergency and Standby Power	17.5.8

Explosion Control	17.5.7
Fire Protection System	17.5.6
Floors	17.5.13
Limit Controls	17.5.9
Liquid Transfer	17.5.15
Monitoring/Supervision	17.5.11
Secondary Containment	17.5.3
Special Requirements (Reserved)	17.5.16, A.17.5.16
Spill Control	17.5.1
System Design	17.5.14
Treatment Systems (Reserved)	17.5.5, A.17.5.5
Ventilation	17.5.4
Handling	17.8
Handling	17.8.1
Special Requirements (Reserved)	17.8.2, A.17.8.2
Indoor Storage	17.3
Detached Storage	17.3.4
Detection Systems (Reserved)	17.3.1, A.17.3.1
Floors	17.3.3
Special Requirements (Reserved)	17.3.5, A.17.3.5
Storage Conditions/Arrangement	17.3.2
Storage Limitations (Reserved)	17.3.2.1, A.17.3.2.1
Indoor Use	17.6
Closed Systems	17.6.2
Explosion Control	17.6.2.2
Special Requirements (Reserved)	17.6.2.4, A.17.6.2.4
Spill Control, Drainage, and Containment	17.6.2.3
Ventilation	17.6.2.1
Open Systems	17.6.1
Explosion Control	17.6.1.2
Special Requirements (Reserved)	17.6.1.4, A.17.6.1.4
Spill Control, Drainage, and Containment	17.6.1.3, A.17.6.1.3
Ventilation	17.6.1.1
Outdoor Storage	17.4
Exposures	17.4.1
Clearance from Combustibles	17.4.1.1
Distance Reduction	17.4.1.3
Location	17.4.1.2, A.17.4.1.2
Special Requirements (Reserved)	17.4.3, A.17.4.3
Storage Arrangement	17.4.3.1, A.17.4.3.1
Weather Protection	17.4.2
Outdoor Use	17.7
Closed Systems	17.7.2
Clearance from Combustibles	17.7.2.3
Location	17.7.2.1
Special Requirements (Reserved)	17.7.2.4, A.17.7.2.4
Spill Control, Drainage, and Containment	17.7.2.2
Open Systems	17.7.1
Clearance from Combustibles	17.7.1.3
Location	17.7.1.1
Special Requirements (Reserved)	17.7.1.4, A.17.7.1.4
Spill Control, Drainage, and Containment	17.7.1.2, A.17.7.1.2

-R-

Referenced Publications	Chap. 2
General	2.1
NFPA Publications	2.2
Other Publications	2.3
References for Extracts in Mandatory Sections	2.4
Remotely Located, Manually Activated Shutdown Control (Gas)	
Definition	3.3.76
Residential Occupancies	5.2.1.8

-S-

Safe Location	
Definition	3.4.15
Safety Factor	
Definition	3.4.16
Safety Margin	
Definition	3.4.17
Sample Ordinance for Adopting NFPA 400	Annex J
Secondary Containment	
Definition	3.3.77, A.3.3.77
Security for Hazardous Materials	Chap. 9
General	9.1
Applicability	9.1.1
Security Plan	9.1.2, A.9.1.2
Security Information	Annex D
Sensitivity Analysis	
Definition	3.4.18
Shall	
Definition	3.2.6
Should	
Definition	3.2.7
Special Quantity Limits for Mercantile, Industrial, and Storage Occupancies	5.2.1.13
General	5.2.1.13.1
Special Controls Required for Increased Quantities	5.2.1.13.2
Special Maximum Allowable Quantity Increases for Storage in Mercantile, Storage, and Industrial Occupancies	5.2.1.13.3
Specification	
Definition	3.4.19
Design Specification	
Definition	3.4.19.1
Input Data Specification	
Definition	3.4.19.2
Spill Control	
Definition	3.3.78
Stakeholder	
Definition	3.4.20
Standard Cubic Foot of Gas (Gas)	
Definition	3.3.79
Storage (Hazardous Material)	
Definition	3.3.81, A.3.3.81
Storage Height	
Definition	3.3.82
Storage Occupancies	5.2.1.12
Storage, Compressed Gases or Cryogenic Fluids (Gas)	
Bulk Solid Storage	
Definition	3.3.80.1
Definition	3.3.80
Detached Storage	
Definition	3.3.80.2
Segregated Storage	
Definition	3.3.80.3
Storage, Use, and Handling of Compressed Gases and Cryogenic Fluids in Portable and Stationary Containers, Cylinders, and Tanks	Chap. 21
Acetylene Cylinder Charging Plants	21.11
Building-Related Controls	21.2
Control Areas	21.2.2
Construction	21.2.2.1
Number	21.2.2.2
Quantities Less than or Equal to the MAQ	21.2.2.3
Detached Buildings	21.2.5, A.21.2.5
Electrical Equipment	21.2.7
Emergency Power	21.2.7.2
Standby Power	21.2.7.1
Employee Alarm System	21.2.8, A.21.2.8
Exhausted Enclosures	21.2.18
Ventilation Requirements	21.2.18.1
Control Velocity at Access Openings	21.2.18.1.1
Fire Protection	21.2.18.1.3
Separation	21.2.18.1.4
Separation of Incompatible Gases Within Enclosures	21.2.18.1.2

2013 Edition

Explosion Control	21.2.9, A.21.2.9
Fire Protection Systems	21.2.10, A.21.2.10
Sprinkler System Design	21.2.10.2
Gas Cabinets	21.2.17
Construction	21.2.17.1
Access to Controls	21.2.17.1.2
Materials of Construction	21.2.17.1.1
Self-Closing Doors	21.2.17.1.3
Fire Protection	21.2.17.3
Quantity Limits	21.2.17.4
Separation of Incompatibles	21.2.17.5
Ventilation Requirements	21.2.17.2
Gas Rooms	21.2.4
Construction	21.2.4.3
Exhaust Ventilation	21.2.4.2
Limitation on Contents	21.2.4.5
Pressure Control	21.2.4.1
Separation	21.2.4.4
General	21.2.1
Flammable and Oxidizing Gases	21.2.1.2
Occupancy	21.2.1.1
Occupancy Classification	21.2.1.1.1
Toxic and Highly Toxic Compressed Gases	21.2.1.3
Hazard Identification Signs	21.2.12
No Smoking	21.2.12.3
Signs	21.2.12.2
Lighting	21.2.11
Occupancy Protection Levels	21.2.3
Classification of Protection Levels	21.2.3.2
Protection Level 1	21.2.3.2.1
Protection Level 2	21.2.3.2.2
Protection Level 3	21.2.3.2.3
Protection Level 4	21.2.3.2.4
Quantity Thresholds for Compressed Gases and Cryogenic Fluids Requiring Special Provisions	21.2.3.1
Incompatible Materials	21.2.3.1.2
Multiple Hazards	21.2.3.1.3
Quantities Greater than the MAQ	21.2.3.1.1
Shelving	21.2.14
Source Valve	21.2.19
Spill Control, Drainage, and Secondary Containment	21.2.13
Vent Pipe Termination	21.2.15
Ventilation	21.2.16
Air Intakes	21.2.16.6
Compressed Air	21.2.16.1
Inlets to the Exhaust System	21.2.16.3
Mechanical Exhaust Ventilation	21.2.16.2
Continuous Operation	21.2.16.2.2
Manual Shutoff Switch	21.2.16.2.4
Shutoff Controls	21.2.16.2.3
Ventilation Rate	21.2.16.2.1
Recirculation of Exhaust	21.2.16.4
Ventilation Discharge	21.2.16.5
Weather Protection	21.2.6
Bulk Hydrogen Compressed Gas Systems	21.6
Bulk Liquefied Hydrogen Systems	21.7
Bulk Oxygen Systems	21.5
Compressed Gases	21.3
Corrosive Gases	21.3.5
Distance to Exposures	21.3.5.2
General	21.3.5.1
Indoor Use	21.3.5.3
Exhausted Enclosures	21.3.5.3.2
Gas Cabinets	21.3.5.3.1
Gas Rooms	21.3.5.3.3
Treatment Systems	21.3.5.3.4
Flammable Gases	21.3.6
Distance to Exposures	21.3.6.2
Electrical	21.3.6.4
Ignition Source Control	21.3.6.3
Heating	21.3.6.3.3
No Smoking or Open Flame	21.3.6.3.2

Static-Producing Equipment	21.3.6.3.1
Maintenance of Piping Systems	21.3.6.5
Storage, Use, and Handling	21.3.6.1
General	21.3.1
Cathodic Protection	21.3.1.5
Corrosion Expert	21.3.1.5.4
Impressed Current Systems	21.3.1.5.3
Inspection	21.3.1.5.2, A.21.3.1.5.2
Operation	21.3.1.5.1
Compressed Gas Systems	21.3.1.1, A.21.3.1.1
Design	21.3.1.1.1
Installation	21.3.1.1.2
Containers, Cylinders, and Tanks	21.3.1.4
Cylinders, Containers, and Tanks Containing Residual Gas	21.3.1.4.4
Defective Containers, Cylinders, and Tanks	21.3.1.4.2
Design and Construction	21.3.1.4.1
Pressure Relief Devices	21.3.1.4.5
Supports	21.3.1.4.3
Cylinders, Containers, and Tanks Exposed to Fire	21.3.1.12
Labeling Requirements	21.3.1.6
Containers	21.3.1.6.1
Label Maintenance	21.3.1.6.2
Piping Systems	21.3.1.6.4
Stationary Compressed Gas Cylinders, Containers, and Tanks	21.3.1.6.3
Leaks, Damage, or Corrosion	21.3.1.13
Handling of Cylinders, Containers, and Tanks Removed from Service	21.3.1.13.3, A.21.3.1.13.3
Leaking Systems	21.3.1.13.4
Removal from Service	21.3.1.13.1
Replacement and Repair	21.3.1.13.2
Listed and Approved Hydrogen Equipment	21.3.1.2
Metal Hydride Storage Systems	21.3.1.3
General Requirements	21.3.1.3.1
Portable Containers or Systems	21.3.1.3.2
Security	21.3.1.7
General	21.3.1.7.1
Physical Protection	21.3.1.7.3
Securing Compressed Gas Cylinders, Containers, and Tanks	21.3.1.7.4
Security of Areas	21.3.1.7.2
Separation from Hazardous Conditions	21.3.1.9
Clearance from Combustibles and Vegetation	21.3.1.9.3, A.21.3.1.9.3
Exposure to Chemicals	21.3.1.9.9
Exposure to Electrical Circuits	21.3.1.9.10
Falling Objects	21.3.1.9.6
General	21.3.1.9.1
Heating	21.3.1.9.7
Incompatible Materials	21.3.1.9.2
Ledges, Platforms, and Elevators	21.3.1.9.4
Sources of Ignition	21.3.1.9.8
Temperature Extremes	21.3.1.9.5
Service and Repair	21.3.1.10
Storage Area Temperature	21.3.1.15
Surfaces	21.3.1.14
Unauthorized Use	21.3.1.11
Underground Piping	21.3.1.16
Contact with Earth	21.3.1.16.2
Valve Protection	21.3.1.8
General	21.3.1.8.1
Valve Outlet Caps or Plugs	21.3.1.8.3
Valve-Protective Caps	21.3.1.8.2
Medical Gas Systems	21.3.4
Oxidizing Gases	21.3.7
Distance to Exposures	21.3.7.2
General	21.3.7.1
Pyrophoric Gases	21.3.8
Distance to Exposures	21.3.8.3
General	21.3.8.1
Silane and Silane Mixtures	21.3.8.2

Storage	21.3.2
General	21.3.2.1
Applicability	21.3.2.1.1
Classification of Weather Protection as an Indoor Versus Outdoor Area	21.3.2.1.3
Upright Storage Flammable Gas in Solution and Liquefied Flammable Gas	21.3.2.1.2
Material-Specific Regulations	21.3.2.2
Exterior Storage	21.3.2.2.2
Indoor Storage	21.3.2.2.1
Toxic and Highly Toxic Gases	21.3.9
Automatic Smoke Detection System	21.3.9.7
Emergency Power	21.3.9.5
Alternative to Emergency Power	21.3.9.5.2
General	21.3.9.5.1
Level	21.3.9.5.4
Where Required	21.3.9.5.3
Gas Detection	21.3.9.6
Alarm Monitored	21.3.9.6.3
Automatic Shutdown	21.3.9.6.4
Detection Points	21.3.9.6.5
Level of Detection	21.3.9.6.6
Local Alarm	21.3.9.6.2
Where Gas Detection Is Not Required	21.3.9.6.1
General	21.3.9.1
Leaking Containers, Cylinders, and Tanks	21.3.9.4
Containment Vessels or Systems	21.3.9.4.2
Gas Cabinets or Exhausted Enclosures	21.3.9.4.1
Treatment Systems	21.3.9.3
Maximum Flow Rate of Release	21.3.9.3.6, A.21.3.9.3.6
Rate of Release	21.3.9.3.5
Storage of Toxic or Highly Toxic Gases	21.3.9.3.1
Treatment System Design and Performance	21.3.9.3.3
Treatment System Sizing	21.3.9.3.4
Use of Toxic Gases	21.3.9.3.2
Ventilation and Arrangement	21.3.9.2
Air Intakes	21.3.9.2.3
Distance to Exposures	21.3.9.2.2
Indoors	21.3.9.2.1
Unstable Reactive Gases (Nondetonable)	21.3.10
Basements	21.3.10.4
Distances to Exposures for Class 2	21.3.10.1
Distances to Exposures for Class 3	21.3.10.2
Storage Configuration	21.3.10.3
Unstable Reactive Gases (Detonable)	21.3.10.5
Location	21.3.10.5.2
Storage or Use	21.3.10.5.1
Use and Handling	21.3.3
General	21.3.3.1
Applicability	21.3.3.1.1
Containers and Cylinders of 5 L (1.3 Gal) or Less	21.3.3.1.8
Controls	21.3.3.1.2
Emergency Shutoff Valves	21.3.3.1.11
Excess Flow Control	21.3.3.1.12
Inverted Use	21.3.3.1.7
Piping Systems	21.3.3.1.3
Transfer	21.3.3.1.9
Upright Use	21.3.3.1.6
Use of Compressed Gases for Inflation	21.3.3.1.10
Valves	21.3.3.1.4
Vent Pipe Termination	21.3.3.1.5
Handling	21.3.3.3
Applicability	21.3.3.3.1
Carts and Trucks	21.3.3.3.2
Lifting Devices	21.3.3.3.3
Material-Specific Regulations	21.3.3.2
Exterior Use	21.3.3.2.2
Indoor Use	21.3.3.2.1
Cryogenic Fluids	21.4
Containers — Design, Construction, and Maintenance	21.4.2, A.21.4.2

Aboveground Tanks	21.4.2.1
Construction of the Inner Vessel	21.4.2.1.1
Construction of the Vacuum Jacket (Outer Vessel)	21.4.2.1.2
Foundations and Supports	21.4.2.3
Corrosion Protection	21.4.2.3.5
Excessive Loads	21.4.2.3.1
Expansion and Contraction	21.4.2.3.2
Support of Ancilliary Equipment	21.4.2.3.3
Temperature Effects	21.4.2.3.4
Nonstandard Containers	21.4.2.2
Pressure-Relief Devices	21.4.2.4
Accessibility	21.4.2.4.5
Arrangement	21.4.2.4.6
Containers Open to the Atmosphere	21.4.2.4.2
Equipment Other than Containers	21.4.2.4.3
General	21.4.2.4.1
Shutoffs Between Pressure Relief Devices and Containers	21.4.2.4.7
Sizing	21.4.2.4.4
Temperature Limits	21.4.2.4.8
Electrical Wiring and Equipment	21.4.8
Electrical Ground and Bonding	21.4.8.3
General	21.4.8.1
Location	21.4.8.2
General	21.4.1
Leaks, Damage, and Corrosion	21.4.11
Lighting	21.4.12
Marking	21.4.4
Container Specification	21.4.4.3
General	21.4.4.1
Identification Signs	21.4.4.1.3
Portable Containers	21.4.4.1.1
Stationary Tanks	21.4.4.1.2
Identification of Container Connections	21.4.4.4
Identification of Contents	21.4.4.2
Identification of Emergency Shutoff Valves	21.4.4.6
Identification of Piping Systems	21.4.4.5
Medical Cryogenic Systems	21.4.5
Pressure Relief Vent Piping	21.4.3
Arrangement	21.4.3.3
General	21.4.3.1
Installation	21.4.3.4
Overfilling	21.4.3.5
Sizing	21.4.3.2
Security	21.4.6
General	21.4.6.1
Physical Protection	21.4.6.5
Securing of Containers	21.4.6.3
Securing of Vaporizers	21.4.6.4
Security of Areas	21.4.6.2
Separation from Hazardous Conditions	21.4.7
General	21.4.7.1
Portable Cryogenic Containers	21.4.7.3
Fire Barriers	21.4.7.3.2
Stationary Cryogenic Containers	21.4.7.2, A.21.4.7.2
Fire Barriers	21.4.7.2.1
Point-of-Fill Connections	21.4.7.2.2
Surfaces Beneath Containers	21.4.7.2.3
Service and Repair	21.4.9
Containers	21.4.9.1
Pressure Relief Device Testing	21.4.9.1.2
Testing	21.4.9.1.1
Systems	21.4.9.2
Storage	21.4.13
Indoor Storage	21.4.13.1
Cryogenic Fluids	21.4.13.1.3
Installation	21.4.13.1.1
Stationary Containers	21.4.13.1.2
Ventilation	21.4.13.1.4

Outdoor Storage	21.4.13.2
Access	21.4.13.2.2
Areas Subject to Flooding	21.4.13.2.5, A.21.4.13.2.5
Diked Areas Containing Other Hazardous Materials	21.4.13.2.4
Drainage	21.4.13.2.6
General	21.4.13.2.1
Outdoor Installations	21.4.13.2.7
Physical Protection	21.4.13.2.3
Unauthorized Use	21.4.10
Use and Handling	21.4.14
Cathodic Protection	21.4.14.9
Corrosion Expert	21.4.14.9.4
Impressed Current Systems	21.4.14.9.3
Inspection	21.4.14.9.2
Operation	21.4.14.9.1
Corrosion Protection	21.4.14.8
General	21.4.14.1
Attended Delivery	21.4.14.1.2
Design	21.4.14.1.4
Inspection	21.4.14.1.3
Operating Instructions	21.4.14.1.1
Joints	21.4.14.3
Material-Specific Requirements	21.4.14.11
Filling and Dispensing	21.4.14.11.3
Handling	21.4.14.11.4
Indoor Use	21.4.14.11.1
Outdoor Use	21.4.14.11.2
Physical Protection and Support	21.4.14.7
Piping and Appurtenances	21.4.14.2
Shutoff Valves on Containers	21.4.14.5
Shutoff Valves on Piping	21.4.14.6
Testing	21.4.14.10
Valves and Accessory Equipment	21.4.14.4
Gas Generation Systems	21.8
General Provisions	21.1
Applicability	21.1.1
Specific Applications	21.1.1.2
Hazardous Materials Classification	21.1.2
Flammability of Gas Mixtures	21.1.2.6
Hazard Classification Pure Gases	21.1.2.1
Mixtures	21.1.2.3
Other Hazards	21.1.2.2
Responsibility for Classification	21.1.2.4
Toxicity	21.1.2.5
Insulated Liquid Carbon Dioxide Systems	21.9
Storage, Handling, and Use of Ethylene Oxide for Sterilization and Fumigation	21.10

-T-

Tank

Container Tank	
Definition	3.3.83.1
Definition	3.3.83, A.3.3.83
Portable Tank	
Definition	3.3.83.2, A.3.3.83.2
Stationary Tank	
Definition	3.3.83.3, A.3.3.83.3

TC (Gas)

Definition	3.3.85
Testing Frequency	6.1.17.2.2

Toxic or Highly Toxic Solids and Liquids ... Chap. 18

General	18.1
Construction Requirements	18.1.1
General Requirements for Storage	18.2
Alarms (Reserved)	18.2.10, A.18.2.10
Drainage	18.2.2
Emergency and Standby Power	18.2.8
Explosion Control	18.2.7
Fire Protection Systems	18.2.6
Limit Controls	18.2.9
Monitoring/Supervision	18.2.11
Secondary Containment	18.2.3
Special Requirements (Reserved)	18.2.12, A.18.2.12
Spill Control	18.2.1
Treatment Systems	18.2.5
Ventilation	18.2.4
General Requirements for Use	18.5
Alarms (Reserved)	18.5.10, A.18.5.10
Clearance from Combustibles	18.5.12
Drainage	18.5.2
Emergency and Standby Power	18.5.8
Explosion Control	18.5.7
Fire Protection System	18.5.6
Floors	18.5.13
Limit Controls	18.5.9
Liquid Transfer	18.5.15
Monitoring/Supervision	18.5.11
Secondary Containment	18.5.3
Special Requirements (Reserved)	18.5.16, A.18.5.16
Spill Control	18.5.1
System Design	18.5.14
Treatment Systems	18.5.5
Ventilation	18.5.4
Handling	18.8
Handling	18.8.1
Special Requirements (Reserved)	18.8.2, A.18.8.2
Indoor Storage	18.3
Detached Storage	18.3.4
Detection Systems (Reserved)	18.3.1, A.18.3.1
Floors	18.3.3
Special Requirements (Reserved)	18.3.5, A.18.3.5
Storage Conditions/Arrangement (Reserved)	18.3.2, A.18.3.2
Reserved	18.3.2.1, A.18.3.2.1
Indoor Use	18.6
Closed Systems	18.6.2
Explosion Control	18.6.2.2
Special Requirements (Reserved)	18.6.2.4, A.18.6.2.4
Spill Control, Drainage, and Containment	18.6.2.3
Ventilation	18.6.2.1
Open Systems	18.6.1
Explosion Control	18.6.1.2
Special Requirements (Reserved)	18.6.1.4, A.18.6.1.4
Spill Control, Drainage, and Containment	18.6.1.3
Ventilation	18.6.1.1
Outdoor Storage	18.4
Exposures	18.4.1
Clearance from Combustibles	18.4.1.1
Distance Reduction	18.4.1.3
Location	18.4.1.2
Special Requirements (Reserved)	18.4.3, A.18.4.3
Fire-Extinguishing Systems	18.4.3.1
Storage Arrangement	18.4.3.2
Aisles	18.4.3.2.2
Pile Size Limit	18.4.3.2.1
Treatment System	18.4.3.3
Weather Protection	18.4.2
Outdoor Use	18.7
Closed Systems	18.7.2
Clearance from Combustibles	18.7.2.3
Location	18.7.2.1
Special Requirements (Reserved)	18.7.2.4, A.18.7.2.4
Spill Control, Drainage, and Containment	18.7.2.2
Open Systems	18.7.1
Clearance from Combustibles	18.7.1.3
Location	18.7.1.1
Special Requirements (Reserved)	18.7.1.4, A.18.7.1.4
Spill Control, Drainage, and Containment	18.7.1.2

Treatment System (Gas)

Definition	3.3.84

Tube Trailer (Gas)

Definition	3.3.86, A.3.3.86

Typical Organic Peroxide Formulations ... Annex F

-U-

Uncertainty Analysis
   Definition 3.4.21
Unstable (Reactive) Solids and Liquids .... Chap. 19
   General 19.1
     Construction Requirements 19.1.1
   General Requirements for Storage 19.2
     Alarms (Reserved) 19.2.10
     Drainage 19.2.2
     Emergency and Standby Power 19.2.8
     Explosion Control 19.2.7
     Fire Protection Systems 19.2.6
     Limit Controls 19.2.9
     Monitoring/Supervision 19.2.11
     Secondary Containment 19.2.3
     Special Requirements 19.2.12
     Spill Control 19.2.1
     Treatment Systems (Reserved) 19.2.5, A.19.2.5
     Ventilation 19.2.4
   General Requirements for Use 19.5
     Alarms (Reserved) 19.5.10, A.19.5.10
     Clearance from Combustibles 19.5.12
     Drainage 19.5.2
     Emergency and Standby Power 19.5.8
     Explosion Control 19.5.7
     Fire Protection System 19.5.6
     Floors 19.5.13
     Limit Controls 19.5.9
     Liquid Transfer 19.5.15
     Monitoring/Supervision 19.5.11
     Secondary Containment 19.5.3
     Special Requirements 19.5.16
     Spill Control 19.5.1
     System Design 19.5.14
     Treatment Systems (Reserved) 19.5.5, A.19.5.5
     Ventilation 19.5.4
   Handling 19.8
     Handling 19.8.1
     Special Requirements 19.8.2
   Indoor Storage 19.3
     Detached Storage 19.3.4
     Detection Systems (Reserved) 19.3.1, A.19.3.1
     Floors 19.3.3
     Special Requirements 19.3.5
     Storage Conditions/Arrangement (Reserved) 19.3.2, A.19.3.2
       Reserved 19.3.2.1, A.19.3.2.1
   Indoor Use 19.6
     Closed Systems 19.6.2
       Explosion Control 19.6.2.2
       Special Requirements 19.6.2.4
       Spill Control, Drainage, and Containment 19.6.2.3
       Ventilation 19.6.2.1
     Open Systems 19.6.1
       Explosion Control 19.6.1.2
       Special Requirements 19.6.1.4
       Spill Control, Drainage, and Containment 19.6.1.3
       Ventilation 19.6.1.1
   Outdoor Storage 19.4
     Exposures 19.4.1
       Clearance from Combustibles 19.4.1.1
       Distance Reduction 19.4.1.3
         Nondeflagrating Materials 19.4.1.3.1
       Location 19.4.1.2
         Deflagrating Material 19.4.1.2.2
         Detonable Material 19.4.1.2.3
         Nondeflagrating Material 19.4.1.2.1
     Special Requirements 19.4.3
       Storage Arrangement 19.4.3.1
         Aisles 19.4.3.1.2
         Pile Size Limit 19.4.3.1.1
     Weather Protection 19.4.2

   Outdoor Use 19.7
     Closed Systems 19.7.2
       Clearance from Combustibles 19.7.2.3
       Location 19.7.2.1
       Special Requirements (Reserved) 19.7.2.4, A.19.7.2.4
       Spill Control, Drainage, and Containment 19.7.2.2
     Open Systems 19.7.1
       Clearance from Combustibles 19.7.1.3
       Location 19.7.1.1
       Special Requirements 19.7.1.4
       Spill Control, Drainage, and Containment 19.7.1.2
Use
   Closed System Use
     Definition 3.3.87.1, A.3.3.87.1
   Definition 3.3.87, A.3.3.87
   Open System Use
     Definition 3.3.87.2, A.3.3.87.2

-V-

Valve Outlet Cap or Plug (Gas)
   Definition 3.3.88
Valve Protection Cap (Gas)
   Definition 3.3.89
Valve Protection Device (Gas)
   Definition 3.3.90
Verification Method
   Definition 3.4.22

-W-

Waste
   Definition 3.3.91
Water-Reactive Solids and Liquids .... Chap. 20
   General 20.1
     Construction Requirements 20.1.1
   General Requirements for Storage 20.2
     Alarms (Reserved) 20.2.10, A.20.2.10
     Drainage 20.2.2
     Emergency and Standby Power 20.2.8
     Explosion Control 20.2.7
     Fire Protection Systems 20.2.6
     Limit Controls 20.2.9
     Monitoring/Supervision 20.2.11
     Secondary Containment 20.2.3
     Special Requirements (Reserved) 20.2.12, A.20.2.12
     Spill Control 20.2.1
     Treatment Systems (Reserved) 20.2.5, A.20.2.5
     Ventilation 20.2.4
   General Requirements for Use 20.5
     Alarms (Reserved) 20.5.10, A.20.5.10
     Clearance from Combustibles 20.5.12
     Drainage 20.5.2
     Emergency and Standby Power 20.5.8
     Explosion Control 20.5.7
     Fire Protection System 20.5.6
     Floors 20.5.13
     Limit Controls 20.5.9
     Liquid Transfer 20.5.15
     Monitoring/Supervision 20.5.11
     Secondary Containment 20.5.3
     Special Requirements (Reserved) 20.5.16, A.20.5.16
     Spill Control 20.5.1
     System Design 20.5.14
     Treatment Systems (Reserved) 20.5.5, A.20.5.5
     Ventilation 20.5.4
   Handling 20.8
     Handling 20.8.1
     Special Requirements (Reserved) 20.8.2, A.20.8.2
   Indoor Storage 20.3
     Detached Storage 20.3.4
     Detection Systems (Reserved) 20.3.1, A.20.3.1

2013 Edition

Floors 20.3.3
Special Requirements (Reserved) 20.3.5, A.20.3.5
Storage Conditions/Arrangement (Reserved) 20.3.2, A.20.3.2
Storage Limitations (Reserved) 20.3.2.1, A.20.3.2.1
Indoor Use 20.6
Closed Systems... 20.6.2
Explosion Control... 20.6.2.2
Special Requirements (Reserved) 20.6.2.4, A.20.6.2.4
Spill Control, Drainage, and Containment 20.6.2.3
Ventilation 20.6.2.1
Open Systems 20.6.1
Explosion Control... 20.6.1.2
Special Requirements (Reserved) 20.6.1.4, A.20.6.1.4
Spill Control, Drainage, and Containment 20.6.1.3
Ventilation 20.6.1.1
Outdoor Storage 20.4
Exposures 20.4.1
Clearance from Combustibles........................... 20.4.1.1

Distance Reduction 20.4.1.3
Location... 20.4.1.2
Class 1 and 2 Materials............................ 20.4.1.2.1
Special Requirements (Reserved) 20.4.3, A.20.4.3
Aisles.. 20.4.3.2
Pile Size Limits.. 20.4.3.1
Weather Protection.. 20.4.2
Outdoor Use 20.7
Closed Systems... 20.7.2
Clearance from Combustibles........................... 20.7.2.3
Location... 20.7.2.1
Special Requirements (Reserved) 20.7.2.4, A.20.7.2.4
Spill Control, Drainage, and Containment 20.7.2.2
Open Systems 20.7.1
Clearance from Combustibles........................... 20.7.1.3
Location... 20.7.1.1
Special Requirements (Reserved) 20.7.1.4, A.20.7.1.4
Spill Control, Drainage, and Containment 20.7.1.2

Sequence of Events Leading to Issuance of this NFPA Committee Document

Step 1: Call for Proposals

- Proposed new Document or new edition of an existing Document is entered into one of two yearly revision cycles, and a Call for Proposals is published.

Step 2: Report on Proposals (ROP)

- Committee meets to act on Proposals, to develop its own Proposals, and to prepare its Report.
- Committee votes by written ballot on Proposals. If two-thirds approve, Report goes forward. Lacking two-thirds approval, Report returns to Committee.
- Report on Proposals (ROP) is published for public review and comment.

Step 3: Report on Comments (ROC)

- Committee meets to act on Public Comments to develop its own Comments, and to prepare its report.
- Committee votes by written ballot on Comments. If two-thirds approve, Report goes forward. Lacking two-thirds approval, Report returns to Committee.
- Report on Comments (ROC) is published for public review.

Step 4: Technical Report Session

- *"Notices of intent to make a motion"* are filed, are reviewed, and valid motions are certified for presentation at the Technical Report Session. ("Consent Documents" that have no certified motions bypass the Technical Report Session and proceed to the Standards Council for issuance.)
- NFPA membership meets each June at the Annual Meeting Technical Report Session and acts on Technical Committee Reports (ROP and ROC) for Documents with "certified amending motions."
- Committee(s) vote on any amendments to Report approved at NFPA Annual Membership Meeting.

Step 5: Standards Council Issuance

- Notification of intent to file an appeal to the Standards Council on Association action must be filed within 20 days of the NFPA Annual Membership Meeting.
- Standards Council decides, based on all evidence, whether or not to issue Document or to take other action, including hearing any appeals.

Committee Membership Classifications

The following classifications apply to Technical Committee members and represent their principal interest in the activity of the committee.

M   *Manufacturer:* A representative of a maker or marketer of a product, assembly, or system, or portion thereof, that is affected by the standard.

U   *User:* A representative of an entity that is subject to the provisions of the standard or that voluntarily uses the standard.

I/M   *Installer/Maintainer:* A representative of an entity that is in the business of installing or maintaining a product, assembly, or system affected by the standard.

L   *Labor:* A labor representative or employee concerned with safety in the workplace.

R/T   *Applied Research/Testing Laboratory:* A representative of an independent testing laboratory or independent applied research organization that promulgates and/or enforces standards.

E   *Enforcing Authority:* A representative of an agency or an organization that promulgates and/or enforces standards.

I   *Insurance:* A representative of an insurance company, broker, agent, bureau, or inspection agency.

C   *Consumer:* A person who is, or represents, the ultimate purchaser of a product, system, or service affected by the standard, but who is not included in the *User* classification.

SE   *Special Expert:* A person not representing any of the previous classifications, but who has a special expertise in the scope of the standard or portion thereof.

NOTES:
1. "Standard" connotes code, standard, recommended practice, or guide.
2. A representative includes an employee.
3. While these classifications will be used by the Standards Council to achieve a balance for Technical Committees, the Standards Council may determine that new classifications of members or unique interests need representation in order to foster the best possible committee deliberations on any project. In this connection, the Standards Council may make appointments as it deems appropriate in the public interest, such as the classification of "Utilities" in the National Electrical Code Committee.
4. Representatives of subsidiaries of any group are generally considered to have the same classification as the parent organization.

STAY UP-TO-DATE. JOIN NFPA® TODAY!

☑ **YES** Please enroll me as a member of NFPA for the term checked below. Activate all benefits, and ship my *Member Kit* including the *Benefits Guide* and other resources to help me make the most of my NPFA membership. *Please allow three to four weeks for the kit to arrive.*

BILLING INFORMATION:

Name _____ Title _____
Organization _____
Address _____
City _____ State _____ Zip/Postal Code _____
Country _____
Phone _____ E-mail _____

Priority Code: 8J-MIS-

PLEASE ANSWER THE FOLLOWING QUESTIONS:

Job Title *(check one)*
- ❏ Architect, Engineer, Consultant, Contractor (C17)
- ❏ Facilities Safety Officer (F14)
- ❏ Fire Chief, Other Fire Service (A11)
- ❏ Loss Control, Risk Manager (L11)
- ❏ Inspector, Building Official, Fire Marshal (F03)
- ❏ Owner, President, Manager, Administrator (C10)
- ❏ Other (please specify): (G11) _____

Type of Organization *(check one)*
- ❏ Architecture, Engineering, Contracting (A14)
- ❏ Commercial Firm (Office, Retail, Lodging, Restaurant) (G13)
- ❏ Electrical Services, Installation (J11)
- ❏ Fire Service, Public and Private (AA1)
- ❏ Government (C12)
- ❏ Industrial Firm (Factory, Warehouse) (C11)
- ❏ Institutional (Health Care, Education, Detention, Museums) (B11)
- ❏ Insurance, Risk Management (B12)
- ❏ Utilities (G12)
- ❏ Other (please specify): (G11) _____

4 EASY WAYS TO JOIN

Fax: 1-800-593-6372, Outside the U.S. +1-508-895-8301
Mail: NFPA Membership Services Center,
11 Tracy Drive, Avon, MA 02322-9908
Online: nfpa.org
Call: 1-800-344-3555
Outside the U.S. call +1-617-770-3000

6/12-D

TERMS AND PAYMENT:
- ❏ 1 year ($165)
- ❏ 2 years ($300) **SAVE $30**
- ❏ 3 years ($430) **SAVE $65**

Annual membership dues include a $45 subscription to *NFPA Journal®*. Regular membership in NFPA is individual and non-transferable. NFPA Journal is a registered trademark of the National Fire Protection Association, Quincy, MA 0216 Voting privileges begin after 180 days of individual membership. Prices subject to change.

PAYMENT METHOD:

Check One:
- ❏ **Payment Enclosed** *(Make check payable to NFPA.)*
- ❏ **Purchase Order** *(Please attach this form to your P.O.)*
- ❏ **Bill Me Later** *(Not available on International memberships.)*

Charge My: ❏ VISA ❏ MasterCard ❏ AmEx ❏ Discover

Card # _____

Expiration Date _____

Name on Card _____

Signature _____

International members: Please note prepayment is required on all International orders. Be sure to enclose a check or select your preferred credit card option.

100% MONEY-BACK GUARANTEE
If anytime during your first year you decide membership is not for you, let us know and you'll receive a 100% refund of your dues.